PowerScore LSAT

Logical Reasoning Question Type Training

Volume 1: LSAT PrepTests 1 through 20

The complete text of every LSAT Logical Reasoning question from PrepTest 1 through 20 sorted according to PowerScore's famous Logical Reasoning question categorization system.

Published by
PowerScore Publishing, a division of PowerScore Incorporated
57 Hasell Street
Charleston, SC 29401

Author: David M. Killoran
Steven G. Stein

Manufactured in Canada

08 18 20 16

ISBN: 978-0-9826618-3-3

CONTENTS

Chapter Nine: Method of Reasoning and Method—AP Questions

Chapter Ten: Flaw in the Reasoning Questions

Chapter Eleven: Parallel Reasoning and Parallel Flaw Questions

Chapter Twelve: Evaluate the Argument Questions

Chapter Thirteen: Cannot Be True Questions

Chapter Fourteen: Point at Issue/Point of Agreement Questions

Chapter Fifteen: Principle Questions

Reasoning Type Chapters

Chapter Sixteen: Conditional Reasoning Questions

Chapter Seventeen: Cause and Effect Reasoning

Chapter Eighteen: Numbers and Percentages Questions

Chapter Nineteen: Formal Logic Questions

Answer Key

About PowerScore

PowerScore is one of the nation's fastest growing test preparation companies. Founded in 1997, PowerScore offers LSAT, GMAT, GRE, SAT, and ACT preparation classes in over 150 locations in the U.S. and abroad. Preparation options include Full-Length courses, Weekend courses, Live Online courses, and private tutoring. For more information, please visit our website at www.powerscore.com or call us at (800) 545-1750.

For supplemental information about this book, please visit the *Logical Reasoning: Question Type Training* website at www.powerscore.com/lsatbibles. The website contains additions to the text and answers to questions submitted by students.

Chapter One: Introduction

1

Welcome to *LSAT Logical Reasoning Question Type Training, Volume 1* by PowerScore. In this book you will find every Logical Reasoning question from LSAT PrepTests 1 through 20, arranged in groups according to the classification system used in the renowned *PowerScore LSAT Logical Reasoning Bible*.

Grouping each question by type provides a number of practical benefits:

- The 997 questions in this book are an excellent practice resource, and an ideal supplement to the *LSAT Logical Reasoning Bible* and *LSAT Logical Reasoning Bible Workbook*.

- Grouping the questions by classification provides practice with specific types of questions, allowing particular focus on the question types you find most challenging.

- By examining questions with certain basic similarities, you can analyze the features of each question type in order to better understand how problems are constructed, how they can be most easily recognized, and how they can best be solved. This is especially the case if you have already read the *PowerScore LSAT Logical Reasoning Bible*.

- Even if you have not yet read the *LSAT Logical Reasoning Bible*, this book provides an excellent practice resource, allowing you to develop your familiarity with various question types and with the Logical Reasoning section in general.

At the end of this book a complete answer key is provided; however, no explanations are provided.

If you are looking to further improve your LSAT score, we also recommend that you pick up copies of the PowerScore LSAT Logic Games Bible and PowerScore LSAT Reading Comprehension Bible.

In our LSAT courses, in our admissions consulting programs, and in our publications, we always strive to present the most accurate and up-to-date information available. Consequently, we have devoted a section of our website to *LSAT Logical Reasoning: Question Type Training* students. This free online resource area offers supplements to the book material, answers questions posed by students, offers study plans, and provides updates as needed. There is also an official book evaluation form that we hope you will use. The exclusive *LSAT Logical Reasoning: Question Type Training* online area can be accessed at:

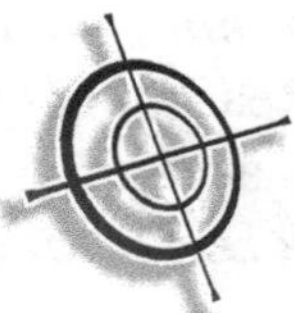

powerscore.com/lsatbibles

If you wish to ask questions about items in this book, please visit our free LSAT discussion forum at:

forum.powerscore.com/lsat

The forum offers hundreds of answers to student questions, including many lengthy answers and conceptual discussions from the authors of this book.

If you have an issue that you prefer not to discuss on the public forum, please do not hesitate to email us at:

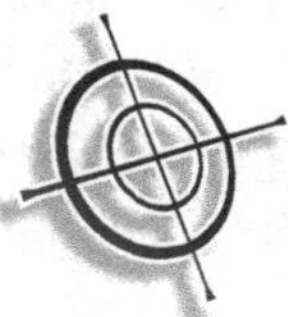

lsatbibles@powerscore.com

We are happy to assist you in your LSAT preparation in any way, and we look forward to hearing from you!

A Brief Overview of the LSAT

The Law School Admission Test is administered four times a year: in February, June, September/October, and December. This standardized test is required for admission to any American Bar Association-approved law school. According to LSAC, the producers of the test, the LSAT is designed "to measure skills that are considered essential for success in law school: the reading and comprehension of complex texts with accuracy and insight; the organization and management of information and the ability to draw reasonable inferences from it; the ability to think critically; and the analysis and evaluation of the reasoning and arguments of others." The LSAT consists of the following five sections:

- 2 Sections of Logical Reasoning (short arguments, 24-26 questions each)
- 1 Section of Reading Comprehension (3 long reading passages, 2 short comparative reading passages, 26-28 total questions)
- 1 Section of Analytical Reasoning (4 logic games, 22-24 total questions)
- 1 Experimental Section of one of the above three section types.

You are given 35 minutes to complete each section. The experimental section is unscored and is not returned to the test taker. A break of 10 to 15 minutes is given between the 3rd and 4th sections.

The five-section test is followed by a 35-minute writing sample.

The Logical Reasoning Section

Each Logical Reasoning Section is composed of approximately 24 to 26 short arguments. Every short argument is followed by a question such as: "Which one of the following weakens the argument?", "Which one of the following parallels the argument?", or "Which one of the following must be true according to the argument?" The key to this section is time management and an understanding of the reasoning types and question types that frequently appear.

Since there are two scored sections of Logical Reasoning on every LSAT, this section accounts for approximately 50% of your score.

At the conclusion of the LSAT, and for five business days afterwards, you have the option of cancelling your score. Unfortunately, there is no way to determine exactly what your score would be before cancelling.

The Analytical Reasoning Section

This section, also known as Logic Games, is often the most difficult for students taking the LSAT for the first time. The section consists of four games or puzzles, each followed by a series of five to eight questions. The questions are designed to test your ability to evaluate a set of relationships and to make inferences about those relationships. To perform well on this section you must understand the types of games that frequently appear and develop the ability to properly diagram the rules and make inferences.

The Reading Comprehension Section

This section is composed of three long reading passages, each approximately 450 words in length, and two shorter comparative reading passages. The passage topics are drawn from a variety of subjects, and each passage is followed by a series of five to eight questions that ask you to determine viewpoints in the passage, analyze organizational traits, evaluate specific sections of the passage, or compare facets of two different passages.

The Experimental Section

Each LSAT contains one undesignated experimental section, and it does not count towards your score. The experimental can be any of the three section types previously discussed, and the purpose of the section is to test and evaluate questions that will be used on *future* LSATs. By pretesting questions before their use in a scored section, the experimental helps the makers of the test determine the test scale.

The Writing Sample

For many years the Writing Sample was administered before the LSAT.

A 35-minute Writing Sample is given at the conclusion of the LSAT. The Writing Sample is not scored, but a copy is sent to each of the law schools to which you apply. In the Writing Sample you are asked to write a short essay that defends one of two possible courses of action.

You must attempt the Writing Sample! If you do not, LSAC reserves the right not to score your test.

Do not agonize over the Writing Sample; in law school admissions, the Writing Sample is not a major determining element for three reasons: the admissions committee is aware that the essay is given after a grueling three hour test and is about a subject you have no personal interest in; they already have a better sample of your writing ability in the personal statement; and the committee has a limited amount of time to evaluate each application.

The LSAT Scoring Scale

Each administered LSAT contains approximately 101 questions, and each LSAT score is based on the total number of questions a test taker correctly answers, a total known as the raw score. After the raw score is determined, a unique Score Conversion Chart is used for each LSAT to convert the raw score into a scaled LSAT score. Since June 1991, the LSAT has used a 120 to 180 scoring scale, with 120 being the lowest possible score and 180 being the highest possible score. Notably, this 120 to 180 scale is just a renumbered version of the 200 to 800 scale most test takers are familiar with from the SAT and GMAT. Just drop the "1" and add a "0" to the 120 and 180.

Although the number of questions per test has remained relatively constant over the last eight years, the overall logical difficulty of each test has varied. This is not surprising since the test is made by humans and there is no precise way to completely predetermine logical difficulty. To account for these variances in test "toughness," the test makers adjust the Scoring Conversion Chart for each LSAT in order to make similar LSAT scores from different tests mean the same thing. For example, the LSAT given in June may be logically more difficult than the LSAT given in December, but by making the June LSAT scale "looser" than the December scale, a 160 on each test would represent the same level of performance. This scale adjustment, known as equating, is extremely important to law school admissions offices around the country. Imagine the difficulties that would be posed by unequated tests: admissions officers would have to not only examine individual LSAT scores, but also take into account which LSAT each score came from. This would present an information nightmare.

The LSAT Percentile Table

It is important not to lose sight of what LSAT scaled scores actually represent. The 120 to 180 test scale contains 61 different possible scores. Each score places a student in a certain relative position compared to other test takers. These relative positions are represented through a percentile that correlates to each score. The percentile indicates where the test taker ranks in the overall pool of test takers. For example, a score of 165 represents the 93rd percentile, meaning a student with a score of 165 scored better than 93 percent of the people who have taken the test in the last three years. The percentile is critical since it is a true indicator of your positioning relative to other test takers, and thus law school applicants.

Since the LSAT has 61 possible scores, why didn't the test makers change the scale to 0 to 60? Probably for merciful reasons. How would you tell your friends that you scored a 3 on the LSAT? 123 sounds so much better.

Charting out the entire percentage table yields a rough "bell curve." The number of test takers in the 120s and 170s is very low (only 1.6% of all test takers receive a score in the 170s), and most test takers are bunched in the middle, comprising the "top" of the bell. In fact, approximately 40% of all test takers score between 145 and 155 inclusive, and about 70% of all test takers score between 140 and 160 inclusive.

There is no penalty for answering incorrectly on the LSAT. Therefore, you should guess on any questions you cannot complete.

The median score on the LSAT scale is approximately 151. The median, or middle, score is the score at which approximately 50% of test takers have a lower score and 50% of test takers have a higher score. Typically, to achieve a score of 151, you must answer between 56 and 61 questions correctly from a total of 101 questions. In other words, to achieve a score that is perfectly average, you can miss between 40 and 45 questions. Thus, it is important to remember that you don't have to answer every question correctly in order to receive an excellent LSAT score. There is room for error, and accordingly you should never let any single question occupy an inordinate amount of your time.

The Use of the LSAT

The use of the LSAT in law school admissions is not without controversy. It is largely taken for granted that your LSAT score is one of the most important determinants of the type of school you can attend. At many law schools a multiplier made up of your LSAT score and your undergraduate grade point average is used to help determine the relative standing of applicants, and at some schools a sufficiently high multiplier guarantees your admission.

For all the importance of the LSAT, it is not without flaws. As a standardized test currently given in the paper-and-pencil format, there are a number of skills that the LSAT cannot measure, such as listening skills, note-taking ability, perseverance, etc. LSAC is aware of these limitations and as a matter of course they warn all law schools about overemphasizing LSAT results. Still, since the test ultimately returns a number for each student, it is hard to escape the tendency to rank applicants accordingly. Fortunately, once you get to law school the LSAT is forgotten. Consider the test a temporary hurdle you must leap in order to reach your ultimate goal.

For more information on the LSAT, or to register for the test, contact LSAC at (215) 968-1001 or at their website at www.lsac.org.

The Logical Reasoning Section

The focus of this book is on the Logical Reasoning section of the LSAT, and each Logical Reasoning section contains a total of 24 to 26 questions. Since you have thirty-five minutes to complete the section, you have an average of approximately one minute and twenty-five seconds to complete each question. Of course, the amount of time you spend on each question will vary with the difficulty of each question and the total number of questions per section. For virtually all students the time constraint is a major obstacle, and as we progress through this book we will discuss time management techniques as well as time-saving techniques that you can employ within the section.

On average, you have 1 minute and 25 seconds to complete each question.

The Section Directions

Each Logical Reasoning section is prefaced by the following directions:

> "The questions in this section are based on the reasoning contained in brief statements or passages. For some questions, more than one of the choices could conceivably answer the question. However, you are to choose the best answer; that is, the response that most accurately and completely answers the question. You should not make assumptions that are by commonsense standards implausible, superfluous, or incompatible with the passage. After you have chosen the best answer, blacken the corresponding space on your answer sheet."

Because these directions precede every Logical Reasoning section, you should familiarize yourself with them now. Once the LSAT begins, *never* waste time reading the directions for any section.

Let's examine these directions more closely. Consider the following sentences: "For some questions, more than one of the choices could conceivably answer the question. However, you are to choose the best answer; that is, the response that most accurately and completely answers the question." By stating up front that more than one answer choice could suffice to answer the question, the makers of the test compel you to read every single answer choice before making a selection. If you read only one or two answer choices and then decide you have the correct one, you could end up choosing an answer that has some merit but is not as good as a later answer. One of the test makers' favorite tricks is to place a highly attractive wrong answer choice immediately before the correct answer choice in the hopes that you will pick the wrong answer choice and then move to the next question without having considered the other answers.

Always read each of the five answer choices before deciding which answer one is correct.

The other part of the directions that is interesting is the sentence that states, "You should not make assumptions that are by commonsense standards implausible, superfluous, or incompatible with the passage." The implication here is that you can make some assumptions when working with questions, but not other assumptions. Of course, LSAC does not hand out a list of what constitutes a commonsense assumption! Even outside of the LSAT, the test makers do not clearly state what assumptions are acceptable or unacceptable for you to make, mainly because such a list would be almost infinite. For LSAT purposes, approaching each question you can take as true any statement or idea that the average American would be expected to believe on the basis of generally known and accepted facts. For example, in a question you can assume that the sky sometimes becomes cloudy, but you cannot assume that the sky is always cloudy (unless stated explicitly by the question). LSAT questions will *not* require you to make assumptions based on extreme ideas (such as that it always rains in Seattle) or ideas not in the general domain of knowledge (such as the per capita income of residents of France). Please note that this does not mean that the LSAT cannot set up scenarios where they discuss ideas that are extreme or outside the bounds of common knowledge. Within a Logical Reasoning question, the test makers can and do discuss complex or extreme ideas; in these cases, they will give you context for the situation by providing additional information. However, be careful about assuming something to be true (unless you believe it is a widely accepted fact or the test makers indicate you should believe it to be true).

Here's an example of what the test makers might expect you to be aware of: when "television" is introduced in a stimulus, you are expected to know, among other things, what a TV show is, that TV can portray the make-believe or real, and what actors do.

Approaching the Questions

When examining the three parts, students sometimes wonder about the best strategy for attacking a question: should I read the question stem first? Should I preview the five answer choices? The answer is *Read the parts in the order given*. That is, first read the stimulus, then read the question stem, and finally read each of the five answer choices. Although this may seem like a reasonable, even obvious, approach we mention it here because some LSAT texts advocate reading the question stem before reading the stimulus. We are certain that these texts are seriously mistaken, and here are a few reasons why:

1. Understanding the stimulus is the key to answering any question, and reading the question stem first tends to undermine the ability of students to fully comprehend the information in the stimulus. On easy questions this distraction tends not to have a significant negative impact, but on more difficult questions the student often is forced to read the stimulus twice in order to get full comprehension, thus wasting valuable time. Literally, by reading the question stem first, students are forced to juggle two things at once: the question stem and the information in the stimulus. That can be a difficult task when under time pressure. The bottom line is that any viable strategy must be effective for questions at all difficulty levels, but when you read the question stem first you

cannot perform optimally. True, the approach works with the easy questions, but those questions could have been answered correctly regardless of the approach used.

2. Reading the question stem first often wastes valuable time since the typical student will read the stem, then read the stimulus, and then read the stem again. Unfortunately, there simply is not enough time to read every question stem twice.

3. Some question stems refer to information given in the stimulus, or add new conditions to the stimulus information. Thus, reading the stem first is of little value and often confuses or distracts the student when he or she goes to read the stimulus.

4. On stimuli with two questions, reading one stem biases the reader to look for that specific information, possibly causing problems while doing the second question, and reading both stems before reading the stimulus wastes entirely too much time and leads to confusion.

5. For truly knowledgeable test takers there are situations that arise where the question stem is fairly predictable. One example—and there are others—is with a question type called Resolve the Paradox. Usually, when you read the stimulus that accompanies these questions, an obvious paradox or discrepancy is presented. Reading the question stem beforehand does not add anything to what you would have known just from reading the stimulus. In later chapters we will discuss this situation and others where you can predict the question stem with some success.

6. Finally, we believe that one of the main principles underlying the read-the-question-stem-first approach is flawed. Many advocates of the approach claim that it helps the test taker avoid the "harder" questions, such as Parallel Reasoning or Method of Reasoning. However, test data show that questions of any type can be hard or easy. Some Method of Reasoning questions are phenomenally easy whereas some Method of Reasoning questions are extremely difficult. In short, the question stem is a poor indicator of difficulty because question difficulty is more directly related to the complexity of the stimulus and the corresponding answer choices.

Understandably, reading the question stem before the stimulus might sound like a good idea at first, but for the majority of students (especially those trying to score in the 160s and above), the approach tends to be a hindrance, not a help. Solid test performance depends on your ability to quickly comprehend complex argumentation; do not make your task harder by reading the question stem first.

In our experience, the vast majority of high-scoring LSAT takers read the stimulus first.

Analyzing the Stimulus

As you read the stimulus, initially focus on making a quick analysis of the topic under discussion. What area has the author chosen to write about? You will be more familiar with some topics than with others, but do not assume that everything you know "outside" of the stimulus regarding the topic is true and applies to the stimulus. For example, say you work in a real estate office and you come across an LSAT question about property sales. You can use your work experience and knowledge of real estate to help you better understand what the author is discussing, but do not assume that things will operate in the stimulus exactly as they do at your workplace. Perhaps property transactions in your state are different from those in other states, or perhaps protocols followed in your office differ from those elsewhere. In an LSAT question, look carefully at what the author says about the topic at hand; statements presented as facts on the LSAT can and do vary from what occurs in the "real world." This discrepancy between the "LSAT world" and the "real world" is one you must always be aware of: although the two worlds overlap, things in the LSAT world are often very different from what you expect. From our earlier discussion of commonsense assumptions we know that you can assume that basic, widely-held facts will hold true in the LSAT world, but by the same token, you cannot assume that specialized information that you have learned in the real world will hold true on the LSAT. We will discuss "outside information" in more detail when we discuss LSAT question types.

Reading closely is a critical LSAT skill.

Next, make sure to read the entire stimulus very carefully. The makers of the LSAT have extraordinarily high expectations about the level of detail you should retain when you read a stimulus. Many questions will test your knowledge of small, seemingly nitpicky variations in phrasing, and reading carelessly is LSAT suicide. In many respects, the requirement forced upon you to read carefully is what makes the time constraint so difficult to handle. Every test taker is placed at the nexus of two competing elements: the need for speed (caused by the timed element) and the need for patience (caused by the detailed reading requirement). How well you manage these two elements strongly determines how well you perform. Later in this chapter we will discuss how to practice using time elements, and near the end of the book we will discuss section management techniques.

Finally, analyze the structure of the stimulus: what pieces are present and how do those pieces relate to each other? In short, you are tasked with knowing as much as possible about the statements made by the author, and in order to do so, you must understand how the test makers create LSAT arguments. We will discuss argumentation in more detail in a moment.

The Question Stem

The question stem follows the stimulus and poses a question directed at the stimulus. In some ways the question stem is the most important part of each problem because it specifies the task you must perform in order to get credit for the problem.

LSAT question stems cover a wide range of tasks, and will variously ask you to:

- identify details of the stimulus
- describe the structure of the argument
- strengthen or weaken the argument
- identify inferences, main points, and assumptions
- recognize errors of reasoning
- reconcile conflicts
- find arguments that are identical in structure

Analyzing the Question Stem

When examining a typical Logical Reasoning section, you may come to the conclusion that there are dozens of different types of question stems. The test makers create this impression by varying the words used in each question stem. As we will see shortly, even though they use different words, many of these question stems are identical in terms of what they ask you to do.

In order to easily handle the different questions, we categorize the question stems that appear on the LSAT. Fortunately, every question stem can be defined as a certain type, and the more familiar you are with the question types, the faster you can respond when faced with individual questions. Thus, one of your tasks is to learn each question type and become familiar with the characteristics that define each type.

Prephrasing Answers

Most students tend to simply read the question stem and then move on to the answer choices without further thought. This is disadvantageous because these students run a greater risk of being tempted by the expertly constructed incorrect answer choices. One of the most effective techniques for quickly finding correct answer choices and avoiding incorrect answer choices is prephrasing. Prephrasing an answer involves quickly speculating on what you expect the correct answer will be based on the information in the stimulus.

Although every answer you prephrase may not be correct, there is great value in considering for a moment what elements could appear in the correct answer choice. Students who regularly prephrase find that they are more readily able to eliminate incorrect answer choices, and of course, many times their prephrased answer is correct. And, as we will see in later chapters, there are certain stimulus and question stem combinations on the LSAT that yield predictable answers, making prephrasing even more valuable. In part, prephrasing puts you in an attacking mindset: if you look ahead and consider a possible answer choice, you are forced to involve yourself in the problem. This process helps keep you alert and in touch with the elements of the problem.

The Answer Choices

All LSAT questions have five lettered answer choices and each question has only one correct, or "credited," response. As with other sections, the correct answer in a Logical Reasoning question must meet the Uniqueness Rule of Answer Choices™, which states that "Every correct answer has a unique logical quality that meets the criteria in the question stem. Every incorrect answer has the opposite logical quality." The correctness of the answer choices themselves conforms to this rule: there is one correct answer choice; the other four answer choices are the opposite of correct, or incorrect.

The Primary Objectives™

Please take a moment to review the Primary Objectives™ below as these recommendations form a cohesive strategy for attacking any Logical Reasoning question.

Primary Objective #1: Determine whether the stimulus contains an argument or if it is only a set of factual statements.

Primary Objective #2: If the stimulus contains an argument, identify the conclusion of the argument. If the stimulus contains a fact set, examine each fact.

Primary Objective #3: If the stimulus contains an argument, determine if the argument is strong or weak.

Primary Objective #4: Read closely and know precisely what the author said. Do not generalize!

Primary Objective #5: Carefully read and identify the question stem. Do not assume that certain words are automatically associated with certain question types.

Primary Objective #6: Prephrase: after reading the question stem, take a moment to mentally formulate your answer to the question stem.

Primary Objective #7: Always read each of the five answer choices.

Primary Objective #8: Separate the answer choices into Contenders and Losers. After you complete this process, review the Contenders and decide which answer is the correct one.

Primary Objective #9: If all five answer choices appear to be Losers, return to the stimulus and re-evaluate the argument.

Logical Reasoning Classifications Explained

In the following chapters, the Logical Reasoning questions from PrepTests 1 through 20 are presented in groups by classification type. The classification system we use is comprehensive, and is explained in detail in the *PowerScore LSAT Logical Reasoning Bible*. The following is a brief description of each classification type.

Question Type Chapters

Chapters Two through Fifteen are sets of questions categorized by question type.

Chapter Two—Must Be True/Most Supported

This category is simply known as "Must Be True." Must Be True questions ask you to identify the answer choice that is best proven by the information in the stimulus. Question stem examples:

> "If the statements above are true, which one of the following must also be true?"
>
> "Which one of the following can be properly inferred from the passage?"

Most Supported questions ask you to find the answers most strongly supported by the information in the stimulus.

Chapter Three—Main Point

Main Point questions are a variant of Must Be True questions. As you might expect, a Main Point question asks you to find the primary conclusion made by the author. Question stem example:

> "The main point of the argument is that"

Chapter Four—Weaken

Weaken questions ask you to attack or undermine the author's argument. Question stem example:

> "Which one of the following, if true, most seriously weakens the argument?"

Chapter Five—Strengthen/Support

These questions ask you to select the answer choice that provides support for the author's argument or strengthens it in some way. Question stem examples:

> "Which one of the following, if true, most strengthens the argument?"

> "Which one of the following, if true, most strongly supports the statement above?"

Chapter Six—Justify the Conclusion

Justify the Conclusion questions ask you to supply a piece of information that, when added to the premises, proves the conclusion. Question stem example:

> "Which one of the following, if assumed, allows the conclusion above to be properly drawn?"

Chapter Seven—Assumption

These questions ask you to identify an assumption of the author's argument. Question stem example:

> "Which one of the following is an assumption required by the argument above?"

Chapter Eight—Resolve the Paradox

Every Resolve the Paradox stimulus contains a discrepancy or seeming contradiction. You must find the answer choice that best resolves the situation. Question stem example:

> "Which one of the following, if true, would most effectively resolve the apparent paradox above?"

Chapter Nine—Method of Reasoning and Method—AP

Method of Reasoning questions ask you to describe, in abstract terms, the way in which the author made his or her argument. Question stem example:

> "Which one of the following describes the technique of reasoning used above?"

A Method—AP asks you to identify the role of a specific part of the argument. Question stem example:

> "Which one of the following most accurately describes the role played in the argument by the statement that photosynthesis requires carbon dioxide?"

Method—AP questions appear at the start of the chapter, and are then followed by the general Method of Reasoning questions.

Chapter Ten—Flaw in the Reasoning

Flaw in the Reasoning questions ask you to describe, in abstract terms, the error of reasoning committed by the author. Question stem example:

> "The reasoning in the astronomer's argument is flawed because this argument"

Chapter Eleven—Parallel Reasoning and Parallel Flaw

Parallel Reasoning questions ask you to identify the answer choice that contains reasoning most similar in structure to the reasoning presented in the stimulus. Question stem example:

> "Which one of the following arguments is most similar in its pattern of reasoning to the argument above?"

The stimulus for a Parallel Reasoning question can contain either valid or invalid reasoning. When a Parallel Reasoning stimulus contains flawed reasoning, we identify it as a Parallel Flaw question.

Note that this chapter mixes Parallel Reasoning and Parallel Flaw questions, and any question with a stimulus that contains flawed reasoning is classified as Parallel Flaw question. If there is no flaw in the stimulus, the question is classified as a Parallel Reasoning question.

Chapter Twelve—Evaluate the Argument

With Evaluate the Argument questions you must decide which answer choice will allow you to determine the logical validity of the argument. Question stem example:

> "The answer to which one of the following questions would contribute most to an evaluation of the argument?"

Chapter Thirteen—Cannot Be True

Cannot Be True questions ask you to identify the answer choice that cannot be true or is most weakened based on the information in the stimulus. Question stem example:

> "If the statements above are true, which one of the following CANNOT be true?"

Chapter Fourteen—Point at Issue/Point of Agreement

Point at Issue questions require you to identify a point of contention between two speakers, and thus these questions appear almost exclusively with two-speaker stimuli. Question stem example:

> "Watkins and Garciaa disagree about whether"

This chapter also contains the only Point of Agreement question to appear in the first 20 PrepTests.

Chapter Fifteen—Principle

Principle questions (PR) are not a separate question type but are instead an "overlay" that appears in a variety of question types. For example, there are Strengthen Principle questions (Strengthen—PR), Justify Principle questions (Justify—PR), and Cannot Be True Principle questions (Cannot—PR), among others. In a question stem, the key indicator that the Principle concept is present is the word "principle." Here are several examples of Principle question stems:

> "Which one of the following judgments most closely conforms to the principle above?" (Must—PR)

> "Which one of the following principles most helps to justify the reasoning above?" (Strengthen—PR)

Reasoning Type Chapters

Chapters Sixteen through Nineteen are sets of questions categorized by reasoning type. As such, each chapter contains a variety of question types.

Chapter Sixteen—Conditional Reasoning

Conditional reasoning is the broad name given to logical relationships composed of sufficient and necessary conditions. Any conditional statement consists of at least one sufficient condition and at least one necessary condition.

Conditional reasoning is a fundamental component of both the Logical Reasoning and Logic Games sections of the LSAT, and is probably the most frequently tested concept on the LSAT.

Chapter Seventeen—Causal Reasoning

Cause and effect reasoning asserts or denies that one thing causes another, or that one thing is caused by another. On the LSAT, cause and effect reasoning appears in many Logical Reasoning problems, often in the conclusion where the author mistakenly claims that one event causes another.

Chapter Eighteen—Numbers and Percentages

Similar to Cause and Effect Reasoning, Conditional Reasoning, and Formal Logic, the concept of Numbers and Percentages is featured in many LSAT stimuli. Because many test takers are prone to making false assumptions when working with these questions, examining the way in which the test makers present and test these concepts is extremely beneficial.

Chapter Nineteen—Formal Logic

Formal Logic problems revolve around conditional relationships and the use of terms such as "some" and "most." Formal Logic is simply a standard way of translating relationships into symbols and then making inferences from those symbolized relationships. And, because certain combinations always yield the same inference regardless of the underlying topic, a close study of the combinations that appear frequently on the test allows you to move quickly and confidently when attacking Formal Logic problems.

2

Chapter Two: Must Be True Questions

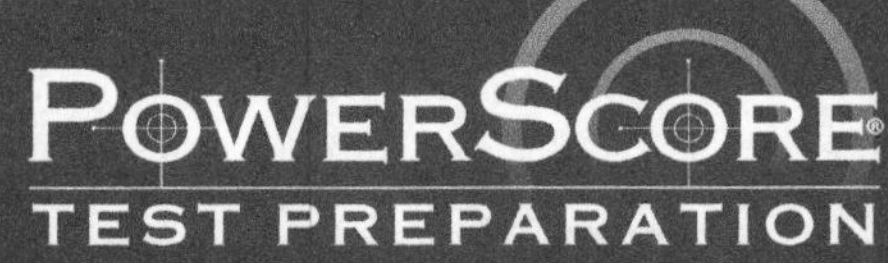

1. Early in this century Alfred Wegener developed the concept of continental drift. His ideas were rejected vehemently because he postulated no identifiable force strong enough to make the continents move. We have come to accept Wegener's theory, not because we have pinpointed such a force, but because new instruments have finally allowed continental movement to be confirmed by observation.

The passage best illustrates which one of the following statements about science?

(A) The aim of science is to define the manifold of nature within the terms of a single harmonious theory.
(B) In accepting a mathematical description of nature, science has become far more accurate at identifying underlying forces.
(C) The paradox of science is that every improvement in its measuring instruments seems to make adequate theories harder to work out.
(D) Science, employing statistics and the laws of probability, is concerned not with the single event but with mass behavior.
(E) When the events a theory postulates are detected, the theory is accepted even without an explanation of how those events are brought about.

2. The theory of military deterrence was based on a simple psychological truth, that fear of retaliation makes a would-be aggressor nation hesitate before attacking and is often sufficient to deter it altogether from attacking. Clearly, then, to maintain military deterrence, a nation would have to be believed to have retaliatory power so great that a potential aggressor nation would have reason to think that it could not defend itself against such retaliation.

If the statements above are true, which one of the following can be properly inferred?

(A) A would-be aggressor nation can be deterred from attacking only if it has certain knowledge that it would be destroyed in retaliation by the country it attacks.
(B) A nation will not attack another nation if it believes that its own retaliatory power surpasses that of the other nation.
(C) One nation's failing to attack another establishes that the nation that fails to attack believes that it could not withstand a retaliatory attack from the other nation.
(D) It is in the interests of a nation that seeks deterrence and has unsurpassed military power to let potential aggressors against it become aware of its power of retaliatory attack.
(E) Maintaining maximum deterrence from aggression by other nations requires that a nation maintain a retaliatory force greater than that of any other nation.

3. A population of game ducks at a western lake contains 55 males to every 45 females, while a population of game ducks at an eastern lake contains 65 males for every 35 females. Among those ducks that have not yet bred there are only slightly more males than females, but among older ducks the number of males greatly exceeds the number of females. Because there are appreciably more males among adult ducks than among young ducks, we can infer that the greater the disparity in overall sex ratios, the greater the percentage of older male ducks in the population.

   Which one of the following can be inferred from the passage?

   (A) The population of game ducks at the western lake contains a lower percentage of adult males than the population at the eastern lake contains.
   (B) The population of game ducks at the eastern lake contains a higher percentage of nonadult game ducks than the population at the western lake contains.
   (C) The total number of male game ducks is higher in the eastern lake's population than in the western lake's population.
   (D) The number of nonadult ducks hatched in a breeding season is higher in the eastern lake's population than in the western lake's population.
   (E) Adult female game ducks outnumber nonadult female game ducks in the eastern lake's population.

4. Computer operating system software has become increasingly standardized. But when a large business with multiple, linked computer systems uses identical operating system software on all of its computers, a computer vandal who gains access to one computer automatically has access to the data on all the computers. Using a program known as a "virus," the vandal can then destroy much of the data on all the computers. If such a business introduced minor variations into its operating system software, unauthorized access to all the computers at the same time could be virtually eliminated. Furthermore, variations in operating system software can be created without any loss of computer compatibility to the business. Therefore, it is advisable for businesses to implement such variations.

   Which one of the following can be inferred from the passage?

   (A) If a business does not introduce variety into its computer operating systems, it will lose data on its computers because of damage from virus programs.
   (B) If a computer virus program is introduced into a business' computer, all of the data on that computer will be destroyed.
   (C) If a business introduces variety into its linked computer operating systems, it will have increased overall protection for its systems, but will not have protected every computer from viral invasion.
   (D) If a business does not have multiple, linked computer systems, its computers cannot be protected from computer viruses.
   (E) If minor variations are created in computer operating system software, it will be easier to access the data on the computers that use that software.

5. Most people in the United States view neither big nor small business as particularly efficient or dynamic and regard both as providing consumers with fairly priced goods and services. However, most people consistently perceive small business as a force for good in society, whereas big business is perceived as socially responsible only in times of prosperity.

The statements above, if true, would provide the strongest support for which one of the following hypotheses?

(A) Most people in the United States give little thought to the value of business to society.
(B) If big business were more efficient, it would be perceived more favorably by the public generally.
(C) If small business were regarded as being more dynamic, it, too, would receive strongly favorable ratings only in times of general prosperity.
(D) Even if people did not regard big business as providing consumers with value for their money, they would still regard it as socially responsible in times of general prosperity.
(E) Many people in the United States regard the social responsibility of big business as extending beyond providing consumers with fairly priced goods and services.

6. Only 1,000 to 2,000 species of fruit flies exist worldwide. Nowhere in the world are fruit flies more taxonomically diverse than in the Hawaiian islands, which host some 500 species. A subset of fruit flies called the picture-winged drosophilids is represented in Hawaii by 106 species. All of the fruit fly species now present in the Hawaiian archipelago are thought to be the descendants of the same one or two ancestral females.

Which one of the following can be inferred from the passage?

(A) All of the picture-winged drosophilids in Hawaii are believed to be the descendants of the same one or two ancestral female fruit flies.
(B) Picture-winged drosophilids are found only in the Hawaiian islands.
(C) All of the 1,000 to 2,000 species of fruit flies worldwide are believed to be the descendants of one or two females.
(D) If 500 new species of fruit flies were discovered, then Hawaiian fruit flies would no longer be the most taxonomically diverse population.
(E) Some fruit flies originated in Hawaii and spread from there to other parts of the world.

7. The most successful economies have been, and will continue to be, those that train as many people as possible in the human skills required to research, to develop, and to apply new technology. Japan is a model for this sort of training effort. Europe as a whole is in a weaker position: there is a shortage of skilled labor trained to use the new technologies, and there are not enough scientists able to develop and apply the technology. However, even in Japan there is a shortage of technically qualified people, and, like most European countries, Japan has far too many workers qualified to perform only menial tasks.

Which one of the following can be properly inferred from the passage?

(A) There is a greater worldwide shortage of research scientists than there is of engineers.
(B) Japan is not the best country against which to measure a country's economic success.
(C) Japan's successful economy depends upon an uncommonly narrow base of highly skilled labor.
(D) To be economically more successful, Europe needs to train more people in the new technologies.
(E) European countries have economies that are more successful than those of most other countries.

8. The Baysville Chamber of Commerce recently met to discuss a proposal to beautify the Baysville area's freeways by relocating power lines, adding landscaping, and removing billboards. At the meeting, Mary Simms, who was representing an outdoor advertising company, declared, "Billboards are the basis of our business. If they are torn down, our ability to earn a living will be severely damaged." "I don't agree," said Jack Jordan, a local merchant. "The basis of our business is an attractive community. People who might shop in Baysville don't want to see ugly billboards on their way into town. Billboards are hurting our ability to earn a living."

Jack Jordan's remarks suggest that he is misinterpreting which one of the following words used by Mary Simms?

(A) billboards
(B) basis
(C) our
(D) ability
(E) damaged

9. It is even more important that we criticize democracies that have committed human rights violations than that we criticize dictatorships that have committed more violent human rights offenses. Human rights violations are always inexcusable, but those committed by governments that represent the will of the people are even more reprehensible than those committed by dictators. Further, our criticism is more likely to have an effect on the former than on the latter.

   Which one of the following is a proper inference from the passage?

   (A) All governments commit some inexcusable and reprehensible acts.
   (B) Some human rights violations are more reprehensible than other, more violent human rights violations.
   (C) Criticism of human rights violations is certain to have no effect on a dictatorship.
   (D) Human rights violations are more likely to occur in democracies than in dictatorships.
   (E) Those who do represent the will of the people are less likely to be moved by criticism than are those who merely claim to represent the will of the people.

10. The press reports on political campaigns these days as if they were chess games. One candidate's campaign advisor makes a move; the other candidate's advisor makes a countermove. The press then reports on the campaign advisors and not on the candidates. The losers in this chess game are the voters. They are deprived of the information they need to make informed decisions because the press is ignoring substantive policy issues and reporting only on the process of the campaign. It is clear that the campaign advisors should stay out of the limelight and let the press report on the most revealing positions on substantive issues the candidates have taken.

    Which one of the following can be inferred from the passage?

    (A) The candidates prefer that the press report on substantive policy issues.
    (B) The press enjoys being in the limelight during political campaigns.
    (C) The candidates believe political campaigning is analogous to a chess game.
    (D) The reporters find it easier to report on the processes and personalities of a campaign than on substantive policy issues.
    (E) Reporting on the campaign advisors is not providing all of the information the voters need in order to make informed decisions.

11. Several cosmetics firms are committed to the active development, validation, and adoption of new product-safety tests that use cultures of human cells. They argue that the new tests serve to reduce the need for tests on live animals.

    The statements above most strongly support which one of the following conclusions?

    (A) The pressure on cosmetics firms to cease conducting experiments that use live animals was initiated by groups of social activists.
    (B) Consumers are no more likely to buy products whose safety was tested on cultures of human cells than they are to buy products whose safety was tested on animals.
    (C) Financial consultants for the cosmetics firms believe that using human cell cultures rather than live animals to test product safety will cost the firm less in actual product-development costs.
    (D) Researchers in the cosmetics firms believe that fewer tests of products will be needed if cell cultures rather than live animals are used.
    (E) Managers of the cosmetics firms believe that it is better for their firms not to perform tests on live animals if there is an acceptable alternative way of determining product safety.

12. One method of dating the emergence of species is to compare the genetic material of related species. Scientists theorize that the more genetically similar two species are to each other, the more recently they diverged from a common ancestor. After comparing genetic material from giant pandas, red pandas, raccoons, coatis, and all seven bear species, scientists concluded that bears and raccoons diverged 30 to 50 million years ago. They further concluded that red pandas separated from the ancestor of today's raccoons and coatis a few million years later, some 10 million years before giant pandas diverged from the other bears.

    Which one of the following can be properly inferred from the passage?

    (A) Giant pandas and red pandas are more closely related than scientists originally thought they were.
    (B) Scientists now count the giant panda as the eighth species of bear.
    (C) It is possible to determine, within a margin of just a few years, the timing of divergence of various species.
    (D) Scientists have found that giant pandas are more similar genetically to bears than to raccoons.
    (E) There is substantial consensus among scientists that giant pandas and red pandas are equally related to raccoons.

13. The teeth of some mammals show "growth rings" that result from the constant depositing of layers of cementum as opaque bands in summer and translucent bands in winter. Cross sections of pigs' teeth found in an excavated Stone Age trash pit revealed bands of remarkably constant width except that the band deposited last, which was invariably translucent, was only about half the normal width.

    The statements above most strongly support the conclusion that the animals died

    (A) in an unusually early winter
    (B) at roughly the same age
    (C) roughly in midwinter
    (D) in a natural catastrophe
    (E) from starvation

14. Measurements of the extent of amino-acid decomposition in fragments of eggshell found at archaeological sites in such places as southern Africa can be used to obtain accurate dates for sites up to 200,000 years old. Because the decomposition is slower in cool climates, the technique can be used to obtain accurate dates for sites almost a million years old in cooler regions.

    The information above provides the most support for which one of the following conclusions?

    (A) The oldest archaeological sites are not in southern Africa, but rather in cooler regions of the world.
    (B) The amino-acid decomposition that enables eggshells to be used in dating does not take place in other organic matter found at ancient archaeological sites.
    (C) If the site being dated has been subject to large unsuspected climatic fluctuations during the time the eggshell has been at the site, application of the technique is less likely to yield accurate results.
    (D) After 200,000 years in a cool climate, less than one-fifth of the amino acids in a fragment of eggshell that would provide material for dating with the technique will have decomposed and will thus no longer be suitable for examination by the technique.
    (E) Fragments of eggshell are more likely to be found at ancient archaeological sites in warm regions of the world than at such sites in cooler regions.

15. Some cleaning fluids, synthetic carpets, wall paneling, and other products release toxins, such as formaldehyde and benzene, into the household air supply. This is not a problem in well-ventilated houses, but it is a problem in houses that are so well insulated that they trap toxins as well as heat. Recent tests, however, demonstrate that houseplants remove some household toxins from the air and thereby eliminate their danger. In one test, 20 large plants eliminated formaldehyde from a small, well-insulated house.

    Assume that a person who lives in a small, well-insulated house that contains toxin-releasing products places houseplants, such as those tested, in the house.

    Which one of the following can be expected as a result?

    (A) There will no longer be any need to ventilate the house.
    (B) The concentration of toxins in the household air supply will remain the same.
    (C) The house will be warm and have a safe air supply.
    (D) If there is formaldehyde in the household air supply, its level will decrease.
    (E) If formaldehyde and benzene are being released into the household air supply, the quantities released of each will decrease.

16. An advertisement states:
    Like Danaxil, all headache pills can stop your headache. But when you are in pain, you want relief right away. Danaxil is for you—no headache pill stops pain more quickly.

    Evelyn and Jane are each suffering from a headache. Suppose Evelyn takes Danaxil and Jane takes its leading competitor. Which one of the following can be properly concluded from the claims in the advertisement?

    (A) Evelyn's headache pain will be relieved, but Jane's will not.
    (B) Evelyn's headache pain will be relieved more quickly than Jane's.
    (C) Evelyn's headache will be relieved at least as quickly as Jane's.
    (D) Jane's headache pain will be relieved at the same time as is Evelyn's.
    (E) Jane will be taking Danaxil for relief from headache pain.

17. People with serious financial problems are so worried about money that they cannot be happy. Their misery makes everyone close to them—family, friends, colleagues—unhappy as well. Only if their financial problems are solved can they and those around them be happy.

    Which one of the following statements can be properly inferred from the passage?

    (A) Only serious problems make people unhappy.
    (B) People who solve their serious financial problems will be happy.
    (C) People who do not have serious financial problems will be happy.
    (D) If people are unhappy, they have serious financial problems.
    (E) If people are happy, they do not have serious financial problems.

18. The translator of poetry must realize that word-for-word equivalents do not exist across languages, any more than piano sounds exist in the violin. The violin can, however, play recognizably the same music as the piano, but only if the violinist is guided by the nature and possibilities of the violin as well as by the original composition.

    As applied to the act of translating poetry from one language into another, the analogy above can best be understood as saying that

    (A) poetry cannot be effectively translated because, unlike music, it is composed of words with specific meanings
    (B) some languages are inherently more musical and more suitable to poetic composition than others
    (C) the translator should be primarily concerned with reproducing the rhythms and sound patterns of the original, not with transcribing its meaning exactly
    (D) the translator must observe the spirit of the original and also the qualities of expression that characterize the language into which the original is translated
    (E) poetry is easier to translate if it focuses on philosophical insights or natural descriptions rather than on subjective impressions

19. The mind and the immune system have been shown to be intimately linked, and scientists are consistently finding that doing good deeds benefits one's immune system. The bone marrow and spleen, which produce the white blood cells needed to fight infection, are both connected by neural pathways to the brain. Recent research has shown that the activity of these white blood cells is stimulated by beneficial chemicals produced by the brain as a result of magnanimous behavior.

    The statements above, if true, support the view that

    (A) good deeds must be based on unselfish motives
    (B) lack of magnanimity is the cause of most serious illnesses
    (C) magnanimous behavior can be regulated by the presence or absence of certain chemicals in the brain
    (D) magnanimity is beneficial to one's own interests
    (E) the number of white blood cells will increase radically if behavior is consistently magnanimous

20. An easy willingness to tell funny stories or jokes about oneself is the surest mark of supreme self-confidence. This willingness, often not acquired until late in life, is even more revealing than is good-natured acquiescence in having others poke fun at one.

    Which one of the following inferences is most supported by the statements above?

    (A) A person who lacks self-confidence will enjoy neither telling nor hearing funny stories about himself or herself.
    (B) People with high self-confidence do not tell funny stories or jokes about others.
    (C) Highly self-confident people tell funny stories and jokes in order to let their audience know that they are self-confident.
    (D) Most people would rather tell a funny story or a joke than listen to one being told.
    (E) Telling funny stories or jokes about people in their presence is a way of expressing one's respect for them.

21. Nature constantly adjusts the atmospheric carbon level. An increase in the level causes the atmosphere to hold more heat, which causes more water to evaporate from the oceans, which causes increased rain. Rain washes some carbon from the air into the oceans, where it eventually becomes part of the seabed. A decrease in atmospheric carbon causes the atmosphere to hold less heat, which causes decreased evaporation from the oceans, which causes less rain, and thus less carbon is washed into the oceans. Yet some environmentalists worry that burning fossil fuels may raise atmospheric carbon to a dangerous level. It is true that a sustained increase would threaten human life. But the environmentalists should relax—nature will continually adjust the carbon level.

    Each of the following can be inferred from the information in the passage EXCEPT:

    (A) A decrease in the level of atmospheric heat causes a decrease in the amount of carbon that rain washes into the oceans from the air.
    (B) An increase in the level of carbon in the atmosphere causes increased evaporation of ocean water.
    (C) An increase in the level of atmospheric heat causes increased rainfall.
    (D) A decrease in the level of carbon in the atmosphere causes decreased evaporation of ocean water.
    (E) A decrease in the level of atmospheric heat causes a decrease in the level of carbon in the atmosphere.

22. The public is aware of the possibility of biases in the mass media and distrusts the media as too powerful. The body of information against which the public evaluates the plausibility of each new media report comes, however, from what the public has heard of through the mass media.

If the view above is correct, it provides a reason for accepting which one of the following conclusions?

(A) If there is a pervasive bias in the presentation of news by the mass media, it would be hard for the public to discern that bias.
(B) The mass media tailor their reports to conform to a specific political agenda.
(C) The biases that news media impose on reporting tend not to be conscious distortions but rather part of a sense they share about what is interesting and believable.
(D) News reporters and their public hold largely the same views about what is most important in society, because news reporters come out of that society.
(E) When a news event occurs that contradicts a stereotype formerly incorporated into reporting by the mass media, the public is predisposed to believe reports of the event.

23. Baking for winter holidays is a tradition that may have a sound medical basis. In midwinter, when days are short, many people suffer from a specific type of seasonal depression caused by lack of sunlight. Carbohydrates, both sugars and starches, boost the brain's levels of serotonin, a neurotransmitter that improves the mood. In this respect, carbohydrates act on the brain in the same way as some antidepressants. Thus, eating holiday cookies may provide an effective form of self-prescribed medication.

Which one of the following can be properly inferred from the passage?

(A) Seasonal depression is one of the most easily treated forms of depression.
(B) Lack of sunlight lowers the level of serotonin in the brain.
(C) People are more likely to be depressed in midwinter than at other times of the year.
(D) Some antidepressants act by changing the brain's level of serotonin.
(E) Raising the level of neurotransmitters in the brain effectively relieves depression.

24. The efficiency of microwave ovens in destroying the harmful bacteria frequently found in common foods is diminished by the presence of salt in the food being cooked. When heated in a microwave oven, the interior of unsalted food reaches temperatures high enough to kill bacteria that cause food poisoning, but the interior of salted food does not. Scientists theorize that salt effectively blocks the microwaves from heating the interior.

Which one of the following conclusions is most supported by the information above?

(A) The kinds of bacteria that cause food poisoning are more likely to be found on the exterior of food than in the interior of food.
(B) The incidence of serious food poisoning would be significantly reduced if microwave ovens were not used by consumers to cook or reheat food.
(C) The addition of salt to food that has been cooked or reheated in a microwave oven can increase the danger of food poisoning.
(D) The danger of food poisoning can be lessened if salt is not used to prepare foods that are to be cooked in a microwave oven.
(E) Salt is the primary cause of food poisoning resulting from food that is heated in microwave ovens.

25. In an experiment, two-year-old boys and their fathers made pie dough together using rolling pins and other utensils. Each father-son pair used a rolling pin that was distinctively different from those used by the other father-son pairs, and each father repeated the phrase "rolling pin" each time his son used it. But when the children were asked to identify all of the rolling pins among a group of kitchen utensils that included several rolling pins, each child picked only the one that he had used.

Which one of the following inferences is most supported by the information above?

(A) The children did not grasp the function of a rolling pin.
(B) No two children understood the name "rolling pin" to apply to the same object.
(C) The children understood that all rolling pins have the same general shape.
(D) Each child was able to identify correctly only the utensils that he had used.
(E) The children were not able to distinguish the rolling pins they used from other rolling pins.

26. A scientific theory is a good theory if it satisfies two requirements: It must accurately describe a large class of observations in terms of a model that is simple enough to contain only a few elements, and it must make definite predictions about the results of future observations. For example, Aristotle's cosmological theory, which claimed that everything was made out of four elements—earth, air, fire, and water—satisfied the first requirement, but it did not make any definite predictions. Thus, Aristotle's cosmological theory was not a good theory.

If all the statements in the passage are true, each of the following must also be true EXCEPT:

(A) Prediction about the results of future observations must be made by any good scientific theory.
(B) Observation of physical phenomena was not a major concern in Aristotle's cosmological theory.
(C) Four elements can be the basis of a scientific model that is simple enough to meet the simplicity criterion of a good theory.
(D) A scientific model that contains many elements is not a good theory.
(E) Aristotle's cosmological theory described a large class of observations in terms of only four elements.

27. During construction of the Quebec Bridge in 1907, the bridge's designer, Theodore Cooper, received word that the suspended span being built out from the bridge's cantilever was deflecting downward by a fraction of an inch. Before he could telegraph to freeze the project, the whole cantilever arm broke off and plunged, along with seven dozen workers, into the St. Lawrence River. It was the worst bridge construction disaster in history. As a direct result of the inquiry that followed, the engineering "rules of thumb" by which thousands of bridges had been built went down with the Quebec Bridge. Twentieth-century bridge engineers would thereafter depend on far more rigorous applications of mathematical analysis.

Which one of the following statements can be properly inferred from the passage?

(A) Bridges built before about 1907 were built without thorough mathematical analysis and, therefore, were unsafe for the public to use.
(B) Cooper's absence from the Quebec Bridge construction site resulted in the breaking off of the cantilever.
(C) Nineteenth-century bridge engineers relied on their rules of thumb because analytical methods were inadequate to solve their design problems.
(D) Only a more rigorous application of mathematical analysis to the design of the Quebec Bridge could have prevented its collapse.
(E) Prior to 1907 the mathematical analysis incorporated in engineering rules of thumb was insufficient to completely assure the safety of bridges under construction.

28. It is not known whether bovine spongiform encephalopathy (BSE), a disease of cattle invariably deadly to them, can be transmitted directly from one infected animal to another at all stages of the infection. If it can be, there is now a reservoir of infected cattle incubating the disease. There are no diagnostic tests to identify infected animals before the animals show overt symptoms. Therefore, if such direct transmission occurs, the disease cannot be eradicated by _______________.

    Which one of the following best completes the argument?

    (A) removing from the herd and destroying any diseased animal as soon as it shows the typical symptoms of advanced BSE
    (B) developing a drug that kills the agent that causes BSE, and then treating with that drug all cattle that might have the disease
    (C) destroying all cattle in areas where BSE occurs and raising cattle only in areas to which BSE is known not to have spread
    (D) developing a vaccine that confers lifelong immunity against BSE and giving it to all cattle, destroying in due course all those animals for which the vaccine protection came too late
    (E) developing a diagnostic test that does identify any infected animal and destroying all animals found to be infected

29. There are about 75 brands of microwave popcorn on the market; altogether, they account for a little over half of the money from sales of microwave food products. It takes three minutes to pop corn in the microwave, compared to seven minutes to pop corn conventionally. Yet by weight, microwave popcorn typically costs over five times as much as conventional popcorn. Judging by the popularity of microwave popcorn, many people are willing to pay a high price for just a little additional convenience.

    If the statements in the passage are true, which one of the following must also be true?

    (A) No single brand of microwave popcorn accounts for a large share of microwave food product sales.
    (B) There are more brands of microwave popcorn on the market than there are of any other microwave food product.
    (C) By volume, more microwave popcorn is sold than is conventional popcorn.
    (D) More money is spent on microwave food products that take three minutes or less to cook than on microwave food products that take longer to cook.
    (E) Of the total number of microwave food products on the market, most are microwave popcorn products.

30. All of John's friends say they know someone who has smoked 40 cigarettes a day for the past 40 years and yet who is really fit and well. John does not know anyone like that and it is quite certain that he is not unique among his friends in this respect.

    If the statements in the passage are true, then which one of the following must also be true?

    (A) Smokers often lie about how much they smoke.
    (B) People often knowingly exaggerate without intending to lie.
    (C) All John's friends know the same lifelong heavy smoker.
    (D) Most of John's friends are not telling the truth.
    (E) Some of John's friends are not telling the truth.

31. For democracy to survive, it is imperative that the average citizen be able to develop informed opinions about important policy issues. In today's society, this means that citizens must be able to develop informed opinions on many scientific subjects, from ecosystems to defense system. Yet, as scientific knowledge advances, the average citizen is increasingly unable to absorb enough information to develop informed opinions on many important issues.

    Of the following, which one follows logically from the passage?

    (A) Scientists have a duty to educate the public.
    (B) The survival of democracy is threatened by the advance of scientific knowledge.
    (C) Every citizen has a duty to and can become scientifically literate.
    (D) The most effective democracy is one that is the most scientifically unsophisticated.
    (E) Democracy will survive if there are at least some citizens who are capable of developing informed opinions on important scientific issues.

32. Using clean-coal technologies to "repower" existing factories promises ultimately a substantial reduction of polluting emissions, and will affect the full range of pollutants implicated in acid rain. The strategy of using these technologies could cut sulfur dioxide emissions by more than 80 percent and nitrogen oxide emissions by more than 50 percent. The emission of a smaller quantity of nitrogen pollutants would in turn reduce the formation of noxious ozone in the troposphere.

Which one of the following statements is an inference that can be drawn from the information given in the passage?

(A) Sulfur dioxide emissions are the most dangerous pollutants implicated in acid rain.
(B) Noxious ozone is formed in factories by chemical reactions involving sulfur dioxide.
(C) Twenty percent of the present level of sulfur dioxide emissions in the atmosphere is not considered a harmful level.
(D) A substantial reduction of polluting emissions will be achieved by the careful design of new factories.
(E) The choice of technologies in factories could reduce the formation of noxious ozone in the troposphere.

33. From a book review: The authors blithely claim that there are "three basic ways to store energy: as heat, as electricity, or as kinetic energy." However, I cannot call to mind any effective ways to store energy as electricity, whereas any capable student of physics could readily suggest a few more ways to store energy: chemical, gravitational, nuclear.

The reviewer makes which one of the following criticisms of a claim that appears in the book under review?

(A) There is no reason to consider any particular way to store energy any more basic than any other.
(B) The list given of ways to store energy is possibly inaccurate and certainly not exhaustive.
(C) It is overly limiting to treat basic ways to store energy as a question unrelated to the question of effective ways to use energy.
(D) What needs to be considered is not whether various ways to store energy are basic but whether they are effective.
(E) Except possibly for electricity, all ways to store energy are equally effective and therefore equally basic.

34. Book Review: When I read a novel set in a city I know well, I must see that the writer knows the city at least as well as I do if I am to take that writer seriously. If the writer is faking, I know immediately and do not trust that writer. When a novelist demonstrates the required knowledge, I trust the storyteller, so I trust the tale. This trust increases my enjoyment of a good novel. Peter Lee's second novel is set in San Francisco. In this novel, as in his first, Lee passes my test with flying colors.

Which one of the following can be properly inferred from the passage?

(A) The book reviewer enjoys virtually any novel written by a novelist whom she trusts.
(B) If the book reviewer trusts the novelist as a storyteller, the novel in question must be set in a city the book reviewer knows well.
(C) Peter Lee's first novel was set in San Francisco.
(D) The book reviewer does not trust any novel set in a city that she does not know well.
(E) The book reviewer does not believe that she knows San Francisco better than Peter Lee does.

35. Four randomly chosen market research companies each produced population estimates for three middle-sized cities; the estimates of each company were then compared with those of the other companies. Two of the cities had relatively stable populations, and for them estimates of current population and of projected population in five years varied little from company to company. However, for the third city, which was growing rapidly, estimates varied greatly from company to company.

The passage provides the most support for which one of the following?

(A) It is more difficult to estimate the population of middle-sized cities than of smaller cities.
(B) Population estimates for rapidly growing cities can be accurate enough to be useful for marketing.
(C) The rate of change in population of rapidly growing cities does not fluctuate.
(D) The market research companies are likely to be equally reliable in estimating the population of stable cities.
(E) Estimates of a city's future population are likely to be more accurate than are estimates of that city's current population.

36. Harry: Airlines have made it possible for anyone to travel around the world in much less time than was formerly possible.

Judith: That is not true. Many flights are too expensive for all but the rich.

Judith's response shows that she interprets Harry's statement to imply that

(A) the majority of people are rich
(B) everyone has an equal right to experience world travel
(C) world travel is only possible via routes serviced by airlines
(D) most forms of world travel are not affordable for most people
(E) anyone can afford to travel long distances by air

37. Coherent solutions for the problem of reducing health-care costs cannot be found within the current piecemeal system of paying these costs. The reason is that this system gives health-care providers and insurers every incentive to shift, wherever possible, the costs of treating illness onto each other or any other party, including the patient. That clearly is the lesson of the various reforms of the 1980s: push in on one part of this pliable spending balloon and an equally expensive bulge pops up elsewhere. For example, when the government health-care insurance program for the poor cut costs by disallowing payments for some visits to physicians, patients with advanced illness later presented themselves at hospital emergency rooms in increased numbers.

The argument provides the most support for which one of the following?

(A) Under the conditions in which the current system operates, the overall volume of health-care costs could be shrunk, if at all, only by a comprehensive approach.
(B) Relative to the resources available for health-care funding, the income of the higher-paid health-care professionals is too high.
(C) Health-care costs are expanding to meet additional funds that have been made available for them.
(D) Advances in medical technology have raised the expected standards of medical care but have proved expensive.
(E) Since unfilled hospital beds contribute to overhead charges on each patient's bill, it would be unwise to hold unused hospital capacity in reserve for large-scale emergencies.

38. The commercial news media emphasize exceptional events such as airplane crashes at the expense of those such as automobile accidents, which occur far more frequently and represent a far greater risk to the public. Yet the public tends to interpret the degree of emphasis the news media give to these occurrences as indicating the degree of risk they represent.

If the statements above are true, which one of the following conclusions is most strongly supported by them?

(A) Print media, such as newspapers and magazines, are a better source of information than are broadcast media.
(B) The emphasis given in the commercial news media to major catastrophes is dictated by the public's taste for the extraordinary.
(C) Events over which people feel they have no control are generally perceived as more dangerous than those which people feel they can avert or avoid.
(D) Where commercial news media constitute the dominant source of information, public perception of risk does not reflect actual risk.
(E) A massive outbreak of cholera will be covered more extensively by the news media than will the occurrence of a rarer but less serious disease.

39. The initial causes of serious accidents at nuclear power plants have not so far been flaws in the advanced technology portion of the plants. Rather, the initial causes have been attributed to human error, as when a worker at the Browns Mills reactor in the United States dropped a candle and started a fire, or to flaws in the plumbing, exemplified in a recent incident in Japan. Such everyday events cannot be thought unlikely to occur over the long run.

Which one of the following is most strongly supported by the statements above?

(A) Now that nuclear power generation has become a part of everyday life, an ever increasing yearly incidence of serious accidents at the plants can be expected.
(B) If nuclear power plants continue in operation, a serious accident at such a plant is not improbable.
(C) The likelihood of human error at the operating consoles of nuclear power generators cannot be lessened by thoughtful design of dials, switches, and displays.
(D) The design of nuclear power plants attempts to compensate for possible failures of the materials used in their construction.
(E) No serious accident will be caused in the future by some flaw in the advanced-technology portion of a nuclear power plant.

40. When individual students are all treated equally in that they have identical exposure to curriculum material, the rate, quality, and quantity of learning will vary from student to student. If all students are to master a given curriculum, some of them need different types of help than others, as any experienced teacher knows.

If the statements above are both true, which one of the following conclusions can be drawn on the basis of them?

(A) Unequal treatment, in a sense, of individual students is required in order to ensure equality with respect to the educational tasks they master.
(B) The rate and quality of learning, with learning understood as the acquiring of the ability to solve problems within a given curriculum area, depend on the quantity of teaching an individual student receives in any given curriculum.
(C) The more experienced the teacher is, the more the students will learn.
(D) All students should have identical exposure to learn the material being taught in any given curriculum.
(E) Teachers should help each of their students to learn as much as possible.

41. Famous personalities found guilty of many types of crimes in well-publicized trials are increasingly sentenced to the performance of community service, though unknown defendants convicted of similar crimes almost always serve prison sentences. However, the principle of equality before the law rules out using fame and publicity as relevant considerations in the sentencing of convicted criminals.

The statements above, if true, most strongly support which one of the following conclusions?

(A) The principle of equality before the law is rigorously applied in only a few types of criminal trials.
(B) The number of convicted celebrities sentenced to community service should equal the number of convicted unknown defendants sentenced to community service.
(C) The principle of equality before the law can properly be overridden by other principles in some cases.
(D) The sentencing of celebrities to community service instead of prison constitutes a violation of the principle of equality before the law in many cases.
(E) The principle of equality before the law does not allow for leniency in sentencing.

42. The consistency of ice cream is adversely affected by even slight temperature changes in the freezer. To counteract this problem, manufacturers add stabilizers to ice cream. Unfortunately, stabilizers, though inexpensive, adversely affect flavor. Stabilizers are less needed if storage temperatures are very low. However, since energy costs are constantly going up, those costs constitute a strong incentive in favor of relatively high storage temperatures.

Which one of the following can be properly inferred from the passage?

(A) Even slight deviations from the proper consistency for ice cream sharply impair its flavor.
(B) Cost considerations favor sacrificing consistency over sacrificing flavor.
(C) It would not be cost-effective to develop a new device to maintain the constancy of freezer temperatures.
(D) Stabilizers function well only at very low freezer temperatures.
(E) Very low, stable freezer temperatures allow for the best possible consistency and flavor of ice cream.

43. It takes 365.25 days for the Earth to make one complete revolution around the Sun. Long-standing convention makes a year 365 days long, with an extra day added every fourth year, and the year is divided into 52 seven-day weeks. But since 52 times 7 is only 364, anniversaries do not fall on the same day of the week each year. Many scheduling problems could be avoided if the last day of each year and an additional day every fourth year belonged to no week, so that January 1 would be a Sunday every year.

The proposal above, once put into effect, would be most likely to result in continued scheduling conflicts for which one of the following groups?

(A) people who have birthdays or other anniversaries on December 30 or 31
(B) employed people whose strict religious observances require that they refrain from working every seventh day
(C) school systems that require students to attend classes a specific number of days each year
(D) employed people who have three-day breaks from work when holidays are celebrated on Mondays or Fridays
(E) people who have to plan events several years before those events occur

44. Complaints that milk bottlers take enormous markups on the bottled milk sold to consumers are most likely to arise when least warranted by the actual spread between the price that bottlers pay for raw milk and the price at which they sell bottled milk. The complaints occur when the bottled-milk price rises, yet these price increases most often merely reflect the rising price of the raw milk that bottlers buy from dairy farmers. When the raw-milk price is rising, the bottlers' markups are actually smallest proportionate to the retail price. When the raw-milk price is falling, however, the markups are greatest.

If all of the statements above are true, which one of the following must also be true on the basis of them?

(A) Consumers pay more for bottled milk when raw-milk prices are falling than when these prices are rising.
(B) Increases in dairy farmers' cost of producing milk are generally not passed on to consumers.
(C) Milk bottlers take substantially greater markups on bottled milk when its price is low for an extended period than when it is high for an extended period.
(D) Milk bottlers generally do not respond to a decrease in raw-milk prices by straightaway proportionately lowering the price of the bottled milk they sell.
(E) Consumers tend to complain more about the price they pay for bottled milk when dairy farmers are earning their smallest profits.

45. Economist: Some policymakers believe that our country's continued economic growth requires a higher level of personal savings than we currently have. A recent legislative proposal would allow individuals to set up savings accounts in which interest earned would be exempt from taxes until money is withdrawn from the account. Backers of this proposal claim that its implementation would increase the amount of money available for banks to loan at a relatively small cost to the government in lost tax revenues. Yet, when similar tax-incentive programs were tried in the past, virtually all of the money invested through them was diverted from other personal savings, and the overall level of personal savings was unchanged.

The passage as a whole provides the most support for which one of the following conclusions?

(A) Backers of the tax-incentive proposal undoubtedly have some motive other than their expressed aim of increasing the amount of money available for banks to loan.
(B) The proposed tax incentive is unlikely to attract enough additional money into personal savings accounts to make up for the attendant loss in tax revenues.
(C) A tax-incentive program that resulted in substantial loss of tax revenues would be likely to generate a large increase in personal savings.
(D) The economy will be in danger unless some alternative to increased personal savings can be found to stimulate growth.
(E) The government has no effective means of influencing the amount of money that people are willing to put into savings accounts.

46. Criticism that the press panders to public sentiment neglects to consider that the press is a profit-making institution. Like other private enterprises, it has to make money to survive. If the press were not profit-making, who would support it? The only alternative is subsidy and, with it, outside control. It is easy to get subsidies for propaganda, but no one will subsidize honest journalism.

It can be properly inferred from the passage that if the press is

(A) not subsidized, it is in no danger of outside control
(B) not subsidized, it will not produce propaganda
(C) not to be subsidized, it cannot be a profit-making institution
(D) to produce honest journalism, it must be a profit-making institution
(E) to make a profit, it must produce honest journalism

47. The incidence in Japan of most types of cancer is remarkably low compared to that in North America, especially considering that Japan has a modern life-style, industrial pollution included. The cancer rates, however, for Japanese people who immigrate to North America and adopt the diet of North Americans approximate the higher cancer rates prevalent in North America.

If the statements above are true, they provide the most support for which one of the following?

(A) The greater the level of industrial pollution in a country, the higher that country's cancer rate will tend to be.
(B) The stress of life in North America is greater than that of life in Japan and predisposes to cancer.
(C) The staple foods of the Japanese diet contain elements that cure cancer.
(D) The relatively low rate of cancer among people in Japan does not result from a high frequency of a protective genetic trait among Japanese people.
(E) The higher cancer rates of Japanese immigrants to North America are caused by fats in the North American diet.

48. This summer, Jennifer, who has worked at KVZ Manufacturing for just over three years, plans to spend with her family the entire four weeks of paid vacation to which she is entitled this year. Anyone who has worked at KVZ Manufacturing for between one and four years is automatically entitled to exactly three weeks paid vacation each year but can apply up to half of any vacation time that remains unused at the end of one year to the next year's vacation.

If the statements above are all true, which one of the following must also be true on the basis of them?

(A) Jennifer did not use two weeks of the paid vacation time to which she was entitled last year.
(B) If Jennifer continues to work for KVZ Manufacturing, she will only be entitled to three weeks paid vacation next year.
(C) The majority of KVZ's employees use each year all of the paid vacation time to which they are entitled.
(D) Last year Jennifer took only one week of the paid vacation time to which she was entitled.
(E) KVZ Manufacturing sometimes allows extra vacation time to employees who need to spend more time with their families.

49. G: The group of works exhibited in this year's Metropolitan Art Show reveals a bias in favor of photographers. Equal numbers of photographers, sculptors, and painters submitted works that met the traditional criteria for the show, yet more photographs were exhibited than either sculptures or paintings. As you know, each artist was allowed to submit work in one medium only.

H: How could there have been bias? All submitted works that met the traditional criteria—and only those works—were exhibited in the show.

If both G's assertions and H's assertion are true, which one of the following must also be true?

(A) More photographers than sculptors or painters submitted works to be considered for exhibition in the Metropolitan Art Show.
(B) All the works submitted for the Metropolitan Art Show met the traditional criteria for the show.
(C) The quality of photographs exhibited in the Metropolitan Art Show was inferior to the quality of the sculptures or paintings exhibited.
(D) Some of the photographs submitted for the Metropolitan Art Show did not meet the traditional criteria for the show.
(E) More works that met the traditional criteria for the Metropolitan Art Show were submitted by photographers than by sculptors or painters.

50. Farm animals have certain behavioral tendencies that result from the evolutionary history of these species. By imposing on these animals a type of organization that conflicts with their behavioral tendencies, current farm-management practices cause the animals more pain and distress than do practices that more closely conform to the animals' behavioral tendencies. Because the animals tend to resist this type of organization, current practices can also be less efficient than those other farm-management practices.

If the statements above are true, which one of the following can be properly inferred from them?

(A) Some of the behavioral tendencies of farm animals can be altered by efficient farm-management practices.
(B) In order to implement efficient farm-management practices, it is necessary to be familiar with the evolutionary history of farm animals.
(C) In order to create farm-management practices that cause less pain and distress to farm animals, a significant loss of efficiency will be required.
(D) Farm-management practices that cause the least amount of pain and distress to farm animals are also the most efficient management practices.
(E) Some changes in farm-management practices that lessen the pain and distress experienced by farm animals can result in gains in efficiency.

51. People cannot be morally responsible for things over which they have no control. Therefore, they should not be held morally responsible for any inevitable consequences of such things, either. Determining whether adults have any control over the treatment they are receiving can be difficult. Hence in some cases it can be difficult to know whether adults bear any moral responsibility for the way they are treated. Everyone, however, sometimes acts in ways that are an inevitable consequence of treatment received as an infant, and infants clearly cannot control, and so are not morally responsible for, the treatment they receive.

Anyone making the claims above would be logically committed to which one of the following further claims?

(A) An infant should never be held morally responsible for an action that infant has performed.
(B) There are certain commonly performed actions for which no one performing those actions should ever be held morally responsible.
(C) Adults who claim that they have no control over the treatment they are receiving should often be held at least partially responsible for being so treated.
(D) If a given action is within a certain person's control that person should be held morally responsible for the consequences of that action.
(E) No adult should be held morally responsible for every action he or she performs.

52. No one knows what purposes, if any, dreams serve, although there are a number of hypotheses. According to one hypothesis, dreams are produced when the brain is erasing "parasitic connections" (meaningless, accidental associations between ideas), which accumulate during the day and which would otherwise clog up our memories. Interestingly, the only mammal that does not have rapid eye movement sleep, in which we humans typically have our most vivid dreams, is the spiny anteater, which has been seen as anomalous in that it has a very large brain relative to the animal's size. This fact provides some confirmation for the parasitic-connection hypothesis, since the hypothesis predicts that for an animal that did not dream to have an effective memory that animal would need extra memory space for the parasitic connections.

The parasitic-connection hypothesis, if true, most strongly supports which one of the following?

(A) The animals with the smallest brains spend the most time sleeping.
(B) Immediately after a person awakens from normal sleep, her or his memory contains virtually no accidental associations between ideas.
(C) When a mammal that would normally dream is prevented from dreaming, the functioning of its memory will be impaired.
(D) Insofar as a person's description of a dream involves meaningful associations between ideas, it is an inaccurate description.
(E) All animals other than the spiny anteater dream.

53. The body of anyone infected by virus X will, after a week, produce antibodies to fight the virus; the antibodies will increase in number for the next year or so. There is now a test that reliably indicates how many antibodies are present in a person's body. If positive, this test can be used during the first year of infection to estimate to within a month how long that person has had the virus.

Which one of the following conclusions is best supported by the statements above?

(A) Antibodies increase in number only until they have defeated the virus.
(B) Without the test for antibodies, there is no way of establishing whether a person has virus X.
(C) Antibodies are produced only for viral infections that cannot be fought by any other body defenses.
(D) If a person remains infected by virus X indefinitely, there is no limit to the number of antibodies that can be present in the person's body.
(E) Anyone infected by virus X will for a time fail to exhibit infection if tested by the antibody test.

54. People often pronounce a word differently when asked to read written material aloud than when speaking spontaneously. These differences may cause problems for those who develop computers that recognize speech. Usually the developers "train" the computers by using samples of written material read by the people who will be using the computer.

The observations above provide most evidence for the conclusion that

(A) it will be impossible to develop computers that decode spontaneous speech
(B) when reading written material, people who have different accents pronounce the same word in the same way as one another
(C) computers may be less reliable in decoding spontaneous speech than in decoding samples that have been read aloud
(D) a "trained" computer never correctly decodes the spontaneous speech of a person whose voice sample was used to train it
(E) computers are now able to interpret oral speech without error

55. Decision makers tend to have distinctive styles. One such style is for the decision maker to seek the widest possible input from advisers and to explore alternatives while making up his or her mind. In fact, decision makers of this sort will often argue vigorously for a particular idea, emphasizing its strong points and downplaying its weaknesses, not because they actually believe in the idea but because they want to see if their real reservations about it are idiosyncratic or are held independently by their advisers.

Which one of the following is most strongly supported by the statements above?

(A) If certain decision makers' statements are quoted accurately and at length, the content of the quote could nonetheless be greatly at variance with the decision eventually made.

(B) Certain decision makers do not know which ideas they do not really believe in until after they have presented a variety of ideas to their advisers.

(C) If certain decision makers dismiss an idea out of hand, it must be because its weaknesses are more pronounced than any strong points it may have.

(D) Certain decision makers proceed in a way that makes it likely that they will frequently decide in favor of ideas in which they do not believe.

(E) If certain decision makers' advisers know the actual beliefs of those they advise, those advisers will give better advice than they would if they did not know those beliefs.

56. The Gulches is an area of volcanic rock that is gashed by many channels that lead downhill from the site of a prehistoric glacier to a river. The channels clearly were cut by running water. It was once accepted as fact that the cutting occurred gradually, as the glacier melted. But one geologist theorized that the channels were cut in a short time by an enormous flood. The channels do show physical evidence of having been formed quickly, but the flood theory was originally rejected because scientists knew of no natural process that could melt so much ice so quickly. Paradoxically, today the scientific community accepts the flood theory even though scientists still do not know of a process that can melt so much ice so quickly.

Which one of the following is supported by the information in the passage?

(A) Only running water can cause deep channels in volcanic rock.

(B) The river did not exist before the channels were cut.

(C) Geologists cannot determine the amount of heat required to melt a glacier quickly.

(D) The physical effects of water on rock vary with the speed with which those effects are produced.

(E) Geologists are compelled to reject physical evidence when it leads to an unexplainable conclusion.

57. Some flowering plant species, entirely dependent on bees for pollination, lure their pollinators with abundant nectar and pollen, which are the only source of food for bees. Often the pollinating species is so highly adapted that it can feed from—and thus pollinate—only a single species of plant. Similarly, some plant species have evolved flowers that only a single species of bee can pollinate—an arrangement that places the plant species at great risk of extinction. If careless applications of pesticides destroy the pollinating bee species, the plant species itself can no longer reproduce.

The information above, if true, most strongly supports which one of the following?

(A) The earliest species of flowering plants appeared on Earth contemporaneously with the earliest bee species.
(B) If the sole pollinator of a certain plant species is in no danger of extinction, the plant species it pollinates is also unlikely to become extinct.
(C) Some bees are able to gather pollen and nectar from any species of plant.
(D) The blossoms of most species of flowering plants attract some species of bees and do not attract others.
(E) The total destruction of the habitat of some plant species could cause some bee species to become extinct.

58. When the rate of inflation exceeds the rate of return on the most profitable investment available, the difference between those two rates will be the percentage by which, at a minimum, the value of any investment will decline. If in such a circumstance the value of a particular investment declines by more than that percentage, it must be true that ______________.

Which one of the following logically completes the argument?

(A) the rate of inflation has risen
(B) the investment in question is becoming less profitable
(C) the investment in question is less profitable than the most profitable investment available
(D) the rate of return on the most profitable investment available has declined
(E) there has been a change in which a particular investment happens to be the most profitable available

59. Body temperature varies over a 24-hour period, with a low point roughly between 4 a.m. and 5 a.m. Speed of reaction varies in line with body temperature, such that whenever body temperature is low, speed of reaction is low. If low body temperature caused slow reaction, the speed of reaction should increase if we artificially raised body temperature during the period 4 a.m. to 5 a.m. But the speed of reaction does not increase.

Which one of the following conclusions can properly be drawn from the above statements?

(A) Low speeds of reaction cause low body temperature.
(B) Low speeds of reaction do not cause low body temperature.
(C) Low body temperatures do not cause low speeds of reaction.
(D) Low body temperatures cause low speeds of reaction.
(E) Artificially raising body temperature causes increased speed of reaction.

60. A recent report on an environmental improvement program was criticized for focusing solely on pragmatic solutions to the large number of significant problems that plague the program instead of seriously trying to produce a coherent vision for the future of the program. In response the report's authors granted that the critics had raised a valid point but explained that, to do anything at all, the program needed continued government funding, and that to get such funding the program first needed to regain a reputation for competence.

The basic position taken by the report's authors on the criticism leveled against the report is that

(A) addressing the critics' concern now would be premature
(B) the critics' motives are self-serving
(C) the notion of a coherent vision would be inappropriate to a program of the sort at issue
(D) the authors of the report are more knowledgeable than its critics
(E) giving the report a single focus is less desirable than the critics claim

61. Cooking teacher: Lima beans generally need about an hour of boiling to reach the proper degree of doneness. The precise amount of time it takes depends on size: larger beans require a longer cooking time than smaller beans do. It is important that lima beans not be overcooked since overcooking robs beans of many of their nutrients. Undercooking should also be avoided, since undercooked beans cannot be completely digested.

If the statements above are true, they most strongly support which one of the following?

(A) Lima beans that are completely digestible have lost many of their nutrients in cooking.
(B) The nutrients that are lost when lima beans are overcooked are the same as those that the body fails to assimilate when lima beans are not completely digested.
(C) Large lima beans, even when fully cooked, are more difficult to digest than small lima beans.
(D) Lima beans that are added to the pot together should be as close to the same size as possible if they are to yield their full nutritional value.
(E) From the standpoint of good nutrition, it is better to overcook than to undercook lima beans.

62. In the 1960s paranoia was viewed by social scientists as ungrounded fear of powerlessness, and the theme of paranoia as it relates to feelings of powerlessness was dominant in films of that period. In the 1970s paranoia instead was viewed by social scientists as a response to real threats from society. Films of this period portray paranoia as a legitimate response to a world gone mad.

Which one of the following is a conclusion that the statements above, if true, most strongly support?

(A) Images of paranoia presented in films made in a period reflect trends in social science of that period.
(B) Responses to real threats can, and often do, degenerate into groundless fears.
(C) The world is becoming more and more threatening.
(D) Paranoia is a condition that keeps changing along with changes in society.
(E) The shift in perception by social scientists from the 1960s to the 1970s resulted from an inability to find a successful cure for paranoia.

63. When glass products are made from recycled glass, the resulting products can be equal in quality to glass products made from quartz sand, the usual raw material. When plastics are recycled, however, the result is inevitably a plastic of a lower grade than the plastic from which it is derived. Moreover, no applications have been found for grades of plastic that are lower than the currently lowest commercial grade.

Which one of the following is a conclusion that can be properly drawn from the statements above?

(A) Products cannot presently be made out of plastic recycled entirely from the currently lowest commercial grade.
(B) It is impossible to make glass products from recycled glass that are equal in quality to the best glass products made from the usual raw material.
(C) Glass products made from recycled glass are less expensive than comparable products made from quartz sand.
(D) Unless recycled plastic bears some symbol revealing its origin, not even materials scientists can distinguish it from virgin plastic.
(E) The difference in quality between different grades of glass is not as great as that between different grades of plastic.

64. The new perfume Aurora smells worse to Joan than any comparably priced perfume, and none of her friends likes the smell of Aurora as much as the smell of other perfumes. However, she and her friends must have a defect in their sense of smell, since Professor Jameson prefers the smell of Aurora to that of any other perfume and she is one of the world's foremost experts on the physiology of smell.

From the information presented in support of the conclusion, it can be properly inferred that

(A) none of Joan's friends is an expert on the physiology of smell
(B) Joan prefers all other perfumes to Aurora
(C) Professor Jameson is not one of Joan's friends
(D) none of Joan's friends likes Aurora perfume
(E) Joan and her friends all like the same kinds of perfumes

65. Most regular coffee is made from arabica coffee beans because the great majority of consumers prefer its generally richer flavor to that of coffee made from robusta beans. Coffee drinkers who switch to decaffeinated coffee, however, overwhelmingly prefer coffee made from robusta beans, which are unlike arabica beans in that their flavor is not as greatly affected by decaffeination. Depending on the type of bean involved, decaffeination reduces or removes various substances, most of which are flavor-neutral but one of which contributes to the richness of the coffee's flavor.

    The statements above provide the most support for which one of the following conclusions?

    (A) The annual world crop of arabica beans is not large enough to satisfy completely the world demand for regular coffee.
    (B) Arabica beans contain more caffeine per unit of weight than do robusta beans.
    (C) Coffee drinkers who drink decaffeinated coffee almost exclusively are the ones who prefer regular coffee made from robusta beans to regular coffee made from arabica beans.
    (D) Decaffeination of arabica beans extracts more of the substance that enhances a coffee's flavor than does decaffeination of robusta beans.
    (E) There are coffee drinkers who switch from drinking regular coffee made from arabica beans to drinking decaffeinated coffee made from arabica beans because coffee made from arabica beans is less costly.

66. Insectivorous plants, which unlike other plants have the ability to trap and digest insects, can thrive in soils that are too poor in minerals to support noninsectivorous plants. Yet the mineral requirements of insectivorous plants are not noticeably different from the mineral requirements of noninsectivorous plants.

    The statements above, if true, most strongly support which one of the following hypotheses?

    (A) The insects that insectivorous plants trap and digest are especially abundant where the soil is poor in minerals.
    (B) Insectivorous plants thrive only in soils that are too poor in minerals to support noninsectivorous plants.
    (C) The types of minerals required by noninsectivorous plants are more likely than are the types of minerals required by insectivorous plants to be found in soils poor in minerals.
    (D) The number of different environments in which insectivorous plants thrive is greater than the number of different environments in which noninsectivorous plants thrive.
    (E) Insectivorous plants can get some of the minerals they require from the insects they trap and digest.

67. Chlorofluorocarbons are the best possible solvents to have in car engines for cleaning the electronic sensors in modern automobile ignition systems. These solvents have contributed significantly to automakers' ability to meet legally mandated emission standards. Now automakers will have to phase out the use of chlorofluorocarbons at the same time that emission standards are becoming more stringent.

If under the circumstances described above cars continue to meet emission standards, which one of the following is the most strongly supported inference?

(A) As emission standards become more stringent, automakers will increasingly cooperate with each other in the area of emission control.
(B) Car engines will be radically redesigned so as to do away with the need for cleaning the electronic ignition sensors.
(C) There will be a marked shift toward smaller, lighter cars that will have less powerful engines but will use their fuel more efficiently.
(D) The solvents developed to replace chlorofluorocarbons in car engines will be only marginally less effective than the chlorofluorocarbons themselves.
(E) Something other than the cleansers for electronic ignition sensors will make a relatively greater contribution to meeting emission standards than at present.

68. Conservationists have established land reserves to preserve the last remaining habitat for certain species whose survival depends on the existence of such habitat. A grove of trees in Mexico that provide habitat for North American monarch butterflies in winter is a typical example of such a land reserve. If global warming occurs as predicted, however, the temperature bands within which various types of vegetation can grow will shift into regions that are currently cooler.

If the statements above are true, they provide the most support for which one of the following?

(A) If global warming occurs as predicted, the conservation land reserves will cease to serve their purpose.
(B) Monarch butterflies will succeed in adapting to climatic change by shortening their migration.
(C) If global warming occurs, it will melt polar ice and so will cause the sea level to rise so high that many coastal plants and animals will become extinct.
(D) The natural world has adapted many times in the past to drastic global warming and cooling.
(E) If global warming occurs rapidly, species of plants and animals now protected in conservation land reserves will move to inhabit areas that are currently used for agriculture.

69. The distance that animals travel each day and the size of the groups in which they live are highly correlated with their diets. And diet itself depends in large part on the sizes and shapes of animals' teeth and faces.

The statements above provide the most support for which one of the following?

(A) Animals that eat meat travel in relatively small groups and across relatively small ranges compared to animals that eat plants.
(B) Animals that have varied diets can be expected to be larger and more robust than animals that eat only one or two kinds of food.
(C) When individual herd animals lose their teeth through age or injury, those animals are likely to travel at the rear of their herd.
(D) Information about the size and shape of an animal's face is all that is needed to identify the species to which that animal belongs.
(E) Information about the size and shape of an extinct animal's teeth and face can establish whether that animal is likely to have been a herd animal.

70. Every political philosopher of the early twentieth century who was either a socialist or a communist was influenced by Rosa Luxemburg. No one who was influenced by Rosa Luxemburg advocated a totalitarian state.

If the statements above are true, which one of the following must on the basis of them also be true?

(A) No early-twentieth-century socialist political philosopher advocated a totalitarian state.
(B) Every early-twentieth-century political philosopher who did not advocate a totalitarian state was influenced by Rosa Luxemburg.
(C) Rosa Luxemburg was the only person to influence every early-twentieth-century political philosopher who was either socialist or communist.
(D) Every early-twentieth-century political philosopher who was influenced by Rosa Luxemburg and was not a socialist was a communist.
(E) Every early-twentieth-century political philosopher who did not advocate a totalitarian state was either socialist or communist.

71. Each year, an official estimate of the stock of cod in the Grand Banks is announced. This estimate is obtained by averaging two separate estimates of how many cod are available, one based on the number of cod caught by research vessels during a once-yearly sampling of the area and the other on the average number of tons of cod caught by various commercial vessels per unit of fishing effort expended there in the past year—a unit of fishing effort being one kilometer of net set out in the water for one hour. In previous decades, the two estimates usually agreed closely. However, for the last decade the estimate based on commercial tonnage has been increasing markedly, by about the same amount as the sampling based estimate has been decreasing.

If the statements in the passage are true, which one of the following is most strongly supported by them?

(A) Last year's official estimate was probably not much different from the official estimate ten years ago.
(B) The number of commercial vessels fishing for cod in the Grand Banks has increased substantially over the past decade.
(C) The sampling-based estimate is more accurate than the estimate based on commercial tonnage in that the data on which it relies is less likely to be inaccurate.
(D) The once-yearly sampling by research vessels should be used as the sole basis for arriving at the official estimate of the stock of cod.
(E) Twenty years ago, the overall stock of cod in the Grand Banks was officially estimated to be much larger than it is estimated to be today.

72. Orthodox medicine is ineffective at both ends of the spectrum of ailments. At the more trivial end, orthodox medicine is largely ineffective in treating aches, pains, and allergies, and, at the other extreme, it has yet to produce a cure for serious, life-threatening diseases such as advanced cancer and lupus. People turn to alternative medicine when orthodox medicine fails to help them and when it produces side effects that are unacceptable to them. One of the reasons alternative medicine is free of such side effects is that it does not have any effects at all.

If the statements above are true, which one of the following can be properly inferred from them?

(A) Practitioners of alternative medicine are acting in bad faith.
(B) There are some medical conditions for which no orthodox or alternative treatment is effective.
(C) There are some trivial illnesses that can be treated effectively by the methods of alternative medicine.
(D) There are no effective medical treatments that are free from unacceptable side effects.
(E) Orthodox medicine will eventually produce a solution for the diseases that are currently incurable.

73. The town of Greenfield recently instituted a substantial supplementary tax on all households, whereby each household is taxed in proportion to the volume of the trash that it puts out for trash collectors to pick up, as measured by the number of standard-sized garbage bags put out. In order to reduce the volume of the trash on which their tax bill is based, Greenfield households can deliver their recyclable trash to a conveniently located local commercial recycling center, where such trash is accepted free of charge.

The supplementary tax provides some financial incentive to Greenfield households to do each of the following EXCEPT

(A) sort out recyclable trash thoroughly from their other trash
(B) dump nonrecyclable trash illegally at parks and roadsides
(C) compress and nest items of nonrecyclable trash before putting them out for pickup
(D) deliver recyclable materials to the recycling center instead of passing them on to neighbors who want to reuse them
(E) buy products without packaging or with recyclable rather than nonrecyclable packaging

74. Unless they are used as strictly temporary measures, rent-control ordinances (municipal regulations placing limits on rent increases) have several negative effects for renters. One of these is that the controls will bring about a shortage of rental units. This disadvantage for renters occurs over the long run, but the advantage—smaller rent increases—occurs immediately. In many municipalities, specifically in all those where tenants of rent-control units have a secure hold on political power and can get rent-control ordinances enacted or repealed, it is invariably the desire for short-term gain that guides those tenants in the exercise of that power.

If the statements above are true, which one of the following can be properly inferred from them?

(A) It is impossible for landlords to raise rents when rent controls are in effect.
(B) In many municipalities rent-control ordinances are repealed as soon as shortages of rental units arise.
(C) The only negative effect of rent control for renters is that it brings about a shortage of rental units.
(D) In many municipalities there is now, or eventually will be, a shortage of rental units.
(E) In the long term, a shortage of rental units will raise rents substantially.

75. A county airport, designed to serve the needs of private aircraft owners, planned to cover its operating expenses in part by charging user fees to private aircraft using the airport. The airport was unable to pay its operating expenses because the revenue from user fees was lower than expected.

If the statements above are true, which one of the following must also be true?

(A) Most of the county's citizens live a convenient distance from one or another airport now offering commercial airline services.
(B) Private aircraft owners were unwilling to pay the user fees charged at the airport.
(C) The airport's construction was financed exclusively by private funds.
(D) The airport's operating expenses were greater than the revenue raised from sources other than the airport user fees for private planes.
(E) The number of owners of private aircraft who use the county's airport facilities will not change appreciably in the future.

76. Only some strains of the tobacco plant are naturally resistant to tobacco mosaic virus, never becoming diseased even when infected. When resistant strains were experimentally infected with the virus, levels of naturally occurring salicylic acid in these plants increased fivefold; no such increase occurred in the nonresistant plants. In a second experiment, 50 nonresistant tobacco plants were exposed to tobacco mosaic virus, and 25 of them were injected with salicylic acid. None of these 25 plants showed signs of infection; however, the other 25 plants succumbed to the disease.

    Which one of the following conclusions is most strongly supported by the results of the experiments?

    (A) Tobacco plants that have become diseased by infection with tobacco mosaic virus can be cured by injecting them with salicylic acid.
    (B) Producing salicylic acid is at least part of the mechanism by which some tobacco plants naturally resist the disease caused by tobacco mosaic virus.
    (C) Salicylic acid is not produced in strains of tobacco plants that are not resistant to tobacco mosaic virus.
    (D) It is possible to test an uninfected tobacco plant for resistance to tobacco mosaic virus by measuring the level of salicylic acid it contains.
    (E) The production of salicylic acid in certain strains of tobacco plants can be increased and thus the strains made resistant to tobacco mosaic virus.

77. On completing both the course in experimental design and the developmental psychology course, Angela will have earned a degree in psychology. Since experimental design, which must be completed before taking developmental psychology, will not be offered until next term, it will be at least two terms before Angela gets her psychology degree.

    If the statements above are all true, which one of the following must also be true?

    (A) The developmental psychology course Angela needs to take requires two terms to complete.
    (B) The course in experimental design is an easier course than the course in developmental psychology.
    (C) There are no prerequisites for the course in experimental design.
    (D) Anyone who earns a degree in psychology from the university Angela attends will have completed the course in experimental design.
    (E) Once Angela completes the developmental psychology course, she will have earned a degree in psychology.

78. Over the past twenty-five years the introduction of laborsaving technologies has greatly reduced the average amount of time a worker needs to produce a given output, potentially both reducing the number of hours each worker works each week and increasing workers' leisure time correspondingly. The average amount of leisure time per worker, however, has increased at only half the rate at which the average hourly output per worker has grown.

    If the statements above are true, which one of the following is most strongly supported by them?

    (A) Workers, on average, spend more money on leisure activities today than they did twenty-five years ago.
    (B) Labor-saving technologies have created fewer jobs than they have eliminated.
    (C) The percentage of the population that is in the work force has grown over the past twenty-five years.
    (D) The average hourly output per worker has not risen as much as had been anticipated when modern labor-saving technologies were first introduced.
    (E) Twenty-five years ago the average weekly output per worker was less than it is today.

79. Individual pyrrole molecules readily join together into larger molecules called polypyrroles. If polypyrroles form from pyrrole in the presence of zeolites, they do so by attaching to the zeolite either in lumps on the outer surface of the zeolite or in delicate chains within the zeolite's inner channels. When zeolite changes color from yellow to black, it means that on or in that zeolite polypyrroles have formed from pyrrole. Yellow zeolite free of any pyrrole was submerged in dissolved pyrrole. The zeolite turned black even though no polypyrroles formed on its outer surface.

If the statements above are true, which one of the following must on the basis of them be true?

(A) Polypyrroles had already formed on or in the zeolite before it was submerged.
(B) Lumps of polypyrrole attached to the zeolite were responsible for its color change.
(C) At least some of the pyrrole in which the zeolite was submerged formed polypyrrole chains.
(D) None of the pyrrole in which the zeolite was submerged attached itself to the zeolite.
(E) Little, if any, of the pyrrole in which the zeolite was submerged reached the zeolite's inner channels.

80. In rheumatoid arthritis, the body's immune system misfunctions by attacking healthy cells in the joints, causing the release of a hormone that in turn causes pain and swelling. This hormone is normally activated only in reaction to injury or infection. A new arthritis medication will contain a protein that inhibits the functioning of the hormone that causes pain and swelling in the joints.

The statements above, if true, most strongly support which one of the following conclusions?

(A) Unlike aspirin and other medications that reduce pain and swelling and that are currently available, the new medication would repair existing cell damage that had been caused by rheumatoid arthritis.
(B) The benefits to rheumatoid arthritis sufferers of the new medication would outweigh the medication's possible harmful side effects.
(C) A patient treated with the new medication for rheumatoid arthritis could sustain a joint injury without becoming aware of it.
(D) The new medication could be adapted for use against a variety of immune system disorders, such as diabetes and lupus.
(E) Joint diseases other than rheumatoid arthritis would not be affected by the new medication.

81. The frequently expressed view that written constitutions are inherently more liberal than unwritten ones is false. No written constitution is more than a paper with words on it until those words are both interpreted and applied. Properly understood, then, a constitution is the sum of those procedures through which the power of the state is legitimately exercised and limited. Therefore, even a written constitution becomes a liberal constitution only when it is interpreted and applied in a liberal way.

If the statements in the argument are all true, which one of the following must also be true on the basis of them?

(A) A careful analysis of the written text of a constitution can show that the constitution is not a liberal one.
(B) It is impossible to determine that a written constitution is liberal merely through careful analysis of the written text.
(C) There are no advantages to having a written rather than an unwritten constitution.
(D) Constitutions that are not written are more likely to be liberal than are constitutions that are written.
(E) A constitution is a liberal constitution if it is possible to interpret it in a liberal way.

82. Politician: Unless our nation redistributes wealth, we will be unable to alleviate economic injustice and our current system will lead inevitably to intolerable economic inequities. If the inequities become intolerable, those who suffer from the injustice will resort to violence to coerce social reform. It is our nation's responsibility to do whatever is necessary to alleviate conditions that would otherwise give rise to violent attempts at social reform.

The statements above logically commit the politician to which one of the following conclusions?

(A) The need for political reform never justifies a resort to violent remedies.
(B) It is our nation's responsibility to redistribute wealth.
(C) Politicians must base decisions on political expediency rather than on abstract moral principles.
(D) Economic injustice need not be remedied unless it leads to intolerable social conditions.
(E) All that is required to create conditions of economic justice is the redistribution of wealth.

83. When a person with temporal lobe epilepsy is having an epileptic seizure, part of the brain's temporal lobe produces abnormal electrical impulses, which can often, but not always, be detected through a test called an electroencephalogram (EEG). Therefore, although a positive EEG reading—that is, evidence of abnormal electrical impulses—during an apparent seizure is a reasonably reliable indicator of temporal lobe epilepsy, _____________.

Of the following, which one logically completes the conclusion above?

(A) a positive reading is just as reliable an indicator of the absence of temporal lobe epilepsy
(B) a positive reading can also indicate the presence of other forms of epilepsy
(C) a positive reading is more frequently an erroneous reading than is a negative one
(D) a negative reading does not mean that temporal lobe epilepsy can be ruled out
(E) a negative reading is just as reliable an indicator of the presence of temporal lobe epilepsy

84. When the manufacturers in a given country are slower to adopt new technologies than their foreign competitors are, their production costs will fall more slowly than their foreign competitors' costs will. But if manufacturers' production costs fall less rapidly than their foreign competitors' costs do, those manufacturers will be unable to lower their prices as rapidly as their foreign competitors can; and when a country's manufacturers cannot lower their prices as rapidly as their foreign competitors can, that country gets squeezed out of the global market.

If the statements above are true, which one of the following must also be true on the basis of them?

(A) If the manufacturers in one country raise their prices, it is because they have squeezed their foreign competitors out of the global market.
(B) If manufacturers in one country have been squeezed out of the global market, this shows that their foreign competitors have adopted new technologies more rapidly than they have.
(C) If a country's foreign competitors can lower their production costs more rapidly than the country's own manufacturers can, then their foreign competitors must have adopted new manufacturing techniques.
(D) If a country's manufacturers adopt new technologies at the same rate as their foreign competitors, neither group will be able to squeeze the other out of the global market.
(E) If a country's manufacturers can lower their prices as rapidly as their foreign competitors can, this shows that they adopt new technology at least as fast as their foreign competitors do.

85. Although water in deep aquifers does not contain disease-causing bacteria, when public water supplies are drawn from deep aquifers, chlorine is often added to the water as a disinfectant because contamination can occur as a result of flaws in pipes or storage tanks. Of 50 municipalities that all pumped water from the same deep aquifer, 30 chlorinated their water and 20 did not. The water in all of the municipalities met the regional government's standards for cleanliness, yet the water supplied by the 20 municipalities that did not chlorinate had less bacterial contamination than the water supplied by the municipalities that added chlorine.

Which one of the following can properly be concluded from the information given above?

(A) A municipality's initial decision whether or not to use chlorine is based on the amount of bacterial contamination in the water source.
(B) Water in deep aquifers does not contain any bacteria of any kind.
(C) Where accessible, deep aquifers are the best choice as a source for a municipal water supply.
(D) The regional government's standards allow some bacteria in municipal water supplies.
(E) Chlorine is the least effective disinfecting agent.

86. If the needle on an industrial sewing machine becomes badly worn, the article being sewn can be ruined. In traditional apparel factories, the people who operate the sewing machines monitor the needles and replace those that begin to wear out. Industrial sewing operations are becoming increasingly automated, however, and it would be inefficient for a factory to hire people for the sole purpose of monitoring needles. Therefore a sophisticated new acoustic device that detects wear in sewing machine needles is expected to become standard equipment in the automated apparel factories of the future.

Which one of the following is most strongly supported by the information above?

(A) In automated apparel factories, items will be ruined by faulty needles less frequently than happens in traditional apparel factories.
(B) In the automated apparel factories of the future, each employee will perform only one type of task.
(C) Traditional apparel factories do not use any automated equipment.
(D) The needles of industrial sewing machines wear out at unpredictable rates.
(E) As sewing machine needles become worn, the noise they make becomes increasingly loud.

87. It is commonly held among marketing experts that in a nonexpanding market a company's best strategy is to go after a bigger share of the market and that the best way to do this is to run comparative advertisements that emphasize weaknesses in the products of rivals. In the stagnant market for food oil, soybean-oil and palm-oil producers did wage a two-year battle with comparative advertisements about the deleterious effect on health of each other's products. These campaigns, however, had little effect on respective market shares; rather, they stopped many people from buying any edible oils at all.

The statements above most strongly support the conclusion that comparative advertisements

(A) increase a company's market share in all cases in which that company's products are clearly superior to the products of rivals
(B) should not be used in a market that is expanding or likely to expand
(C) should under no circumstances be used as a retaliatory measure
(D) carry the risk of causing a contraction of the market at which they are aimed
(E) yield no long-term gains unless consumers can easily verify the claims made

88. The similarity between ichthyosaurs and fish is an example of convergence, a process by which different classes of organisms adapt to the same environment by independently developing one or more similar external body features. Ichthyosaurs were marine reptiles and thus do not belong to the same class of organisms as fish. However, ichthyosaurs adapted to their marine environment by converging on external body features similar to those of fish. Most strikingly, ichthyosaurs, like fish, had fins.

If the statements above are true, which one of the following is an inference that can be properly drawn on the basis of them?

(A) The members of a single class of organisms that inhabit the same environment must be identical in all their external body features.
(B) The members of a single class of organisms must exhibit one or more similar external body features that differentiate that class from all other classes of organisms.
(C) It is only as a result of adaptation to similar environments that one class of organisms develops external body features similar to those of another class of organisms.
(D) An organism does not necessarily belong to a class simply because the organism has one or more external body features similar to those of members of that class.
(E) Whenever two classes of organisms share the same environment, members of one class will differ from members of the other class in several external body features.

89. The basic ingredients from which cement is made are both cheap and plentiful. Materials as common as limestone and clay will do. Nevertheless, the price of cement is influenced by the price of oil, because turning the basic ingredients into cement in high-temperature kilns uses large amounts of energy.

Which one of the following can be logically inferred from the passage?

(A) Oil is one of the basic ingredients that make up cement.
(B) Oil is a source of energy for some of the kilns used in the making of cement.
(C) The higher the price of cement rises, the higher the price of clay rises.
(D) Whenever oil prices rise, cement prices drop.
(E) A given amount of cement costs no more than the total cost of its basic ingredients.

90. Until about 400 million years ago, fishes—the first true swimmers—were jawless. Their feeding methods were limited to either sucking in surface plankton or sucking in food particles from bottom mud. With the development of biting jaws, however, the life of fishes changed dramatically, since jaws allowed them actively to pursue prey, to seize it in their jaws, and to manipulate it between their teeth. The jawed fishes then developed along two main lines: one retained cartilage for its skeletons, for example, sharks and rays; the other adopted bone as its principal skeletal material. From the latter group evolved the most abundant and diverse of all of today's vertebrate groups, the "teleosts," some 21,000 species, which vary from barracudas to sea horses.

If all of the statements in the passage are true, which one of the following must also be true?

(A) Fish are the primary prey of all jawed fishes.
(B) The jawless fishes did not prey upon other fish.
(C) Teleosts do not feed upon particles found in bottom mud.
(D) Jawless fishes did not have cartilage as their skeletal material.
(E) Jawless fishes became extinct approximately 400 million years ago.

91. If a country's manufacturing capacity is fully utilized, there can be no industrial growth without new capital investment. Any reduction in interest rates produces new capital investment.

Which one of the following can be properly concluded from the statements above?

(A) Interest rates might in exceptional cases be reduced without there being any subsequent investment of new capital.
(B) A reduction in interest rates might cause a precondition for industrial growth to be met.
(C) If a country's manufacturing capacity is underutilized, interest rates should be held constant.
(D) New capital investment that takes place while interest rates are rising cannot lead to industrial growth.
(E) Manufacturing capacity newly created by capital investment needs to be fully utilized if it is to lead to industrial growth.

92. Unless the residents of Glen Hills band together, the proposal to rezone that city will be approved. If it is, the city will be able to build the water and sewer systems that developers need in order to construct apartment houses there. These buildings would attract new residents, and the increased population would probably result in overcrowded schools and would certainly result in roads so congested that new roads would be built. Neither new roads nor additional schools could be built without substantial tax increases for the residents of Glen Hills. Ultimately, this growth might even destroy the rural atmosphere that makes Glen Hills so attractive.

Which one of the following can be properly concluded from the passage?

(A) If the citizens of Glen Hills band together, developers will not build apartment houses.
(B) If developers build apartment houses in Glen Hills, there will be substantial tax increases for the residents of Glen Hills.
(C) If the rezoning proposal does not pass, the rural atmosphere in Glen Hills will not be lost.
(D) If developers do not build apartment houses in Glen Hills, the taxes of the residents of Glen Hills will not increase substantially.
(E) If developers do not build apartment houses in Glen Hills, the schools of Glen Hills will not be overcrowded and roads will not be congested.

93. Professor: Members of most species are able to communicate with other members of the same species, but it is not true that all communication can be called "language." The human communication system unquestionably qualifies as language. In fact, using language is a trait without which we would not be human.

Student: I understand that communication by itself is not language, but how do you know that the highly evolved communication systems of songbirds, dolphins, honeybees, and apes, for example, are not languages?

The student has interpreted the professor's remarks to mean that

(A) different species can have similar defining traits
(B) every human trait except using language is shared by at least one other species
(C) not all languages are used to communicate
(D) using language is a trait humans do not share with any other species
(E) humans cannot communicate with members of other species

94. Oxygen-18 is a heavier-than-normal isotope of oxygen. In a rain cloud, water molecules containing oxygen-18 are rarer than water molecules containing normal oxygen. But in rainfall, a higher proportion of all water molecules containing oxygen-18 than of all water molecules containing ordinary oxygen descends to earth. Consequently, scientists were surprised when measurements along the entire route of rain clouds' passage from above the Atlantic Ocean, the site of their original formation, across the Amazon forests, where it rains almost daily, showed that the oxygen-18 content of each of the clouds remained fairly constant.

Which one of the following inferences about an individual rain cloud is supported by the passage?

(A) Once it is formed over the Atlantic, the rain cloud contains more ordinary oxygen than oxygen-18.
(B) Once it has passed over the Amazon, the rain cloud contains a greater-than-normal percentage of oxygen-18.
(C) The cloud's rainfall contains more oxygen-18 than ordinary oxygen.
(D) During a rainfall, the cloud must surrender the same percentage of its ordinary oxygen as of its oxygen-18.
(E) During a rainfall, the cloud must surrender more of its oxygen-18 than it retains.

95. People who listen to certain recordings of music are in danger of being unduly influenced by spoken messages that have been recorded backwards on the records or tapes.

A consequence of the view above is that

(A) the spoken messages must be louder than the music on the recordings
(B) backwards messages can be added to a recording while still preserving all of the musical qualities of the recorded performance
(C) the recordings on which such messages appear are chosen for this purpose either because they are especially popular or because they induce a trancelike state
(D) if such messages must be comprehended to exert influence, then people must be able to comprehend spoken messages recorded backwards
(E) when people listen to recorded music, they pay full attention to the music as it plays

96. Almost all of the books published in the past 150 years were printed on acidic paper. Unfortunately, every kind of acidic paper gradually destroys itself due to its very acidity. This process of deterioration can be slowed if the books are stored in a cool, dry environment. Techniques, which are now being developed, to deacidify books will probably be applied only to books with historical significance.

If all of the statements in the passage above are true, which one of the following must also be true?

(A) If a book was published in the past 150 years and is historically insignificant, it will probably deteriorate completely.
(B) Almost all of the books published in the past 150 years will gradually destroy themselves.
(C) Almost all of the books that gradually deteriorate are made of acidic paper.
(D) If a book is of historical significance and was printed before 150 years ago, it will be deacidified.
(E) Books published on acidic paper in 1900 should now all be at about the same state of deterioration.

97. The only fossilized bones of large prey found in and around settlements of early humans bear teeth marks of nonhuman predators on areas of the skeleton that had the most meat, and cut marks made by humans on the areas that had the least meat. The predators that hunted large prey invariably ate the meatiest parts of the carcasses, leaving uneaten remains behind.

If the information above is true, it provides the most support for which one of the following?

(A) Early humans were predators of small prey, not of large prey.
(B) Early humans ate fruits and edible roots as well as meat.
(C) Early humans would have been more effective hunters of large prey if they had hunted in large groups rather than individually.
(D) Early humans were not hunters of large prey but scavenged the uneaten remains of prey killed by other predators.
(E) Early humans were nomadic, and their settlements followed the migratory patterns of predators of large prey.

98. In a recession, a decrease in consumer spending causes many businesses to lay off workers or even to close. Workers who lose their jobs in a recession usually cannot find new jobs. The result is an increase in the number of people who are jobless. Recovery from a recession is defined by an increase in consumer spending and an expansion of business activity that creates a need for additional workers. But businesspeople generally have little confidence in the economy after a recession and therefore delay hiring additional workers as long as possible.

The statements above, if true, provide most support for which one of the following conclusions?

(A) Recessions are usually caused by a decrease in businesspeople's confidence in the economy.
(B) Governmental intervention is required in order for an economy to recover from a recession.
(C) Employees of businesses that close during a recession make up the majority of the workers who lose their jobs during that recession.
(D) Sometimes recovery from a recession does not promptly result in a decrease in the number of people who are jobless.
(E) Workers who lose their jobs during a recession are likely to get equally good jobs when the economy recovers.

99. The United States ranks far behind countries such as Sweden and Canada when it comes to workplace safety. In all three countries, joint labor-management committees that oversee workplace safety conditions have been very successful in reducing occupational injuries. In the United States, such committees are found only in the few companies that have voluntarily established them. However, in Sweden and several Canadian provinces, joint safety committees are required by law and exist in all medium-sized and large workplaces.

Which one of the following is supported by the information above?

(A) The establishment of joint safety committees in all medium-sized and large workplaces in the United States would result in a reduction of occupational injuries.
(B) A joint safety committee that is required by law is more effective at reducing occupational injuries than is a joint safety committee that is voluntarily established.
(C) Workplace safety in Sweden and Canada was superior to that in the United States even prior to the passage of laws requiring joint safety committees in all medium-sized and large workplaces.
(D) Joint safety committees had been voluntarily established in most medium-sized and large workplaces in Sweden and several Canadian provinces prior to the passage of laws requiring such committees.
(E) The United States would surpass Sweden and Canada in workplace safety if joint safety committees were required in all medium-sized and large workplaces in the United States.

100. On their way from their nest to a food source, ants of most species leave a trail of chemicals called pheromones. The ants use the scent of the pheromones to guide themselves between the food and their nest. All pheromones evaporate without a trace almost immediately when temperatures rise above 45 degrees Celsius (113 degrees Fahrenheit), as is typical during afternoons in places such as the Sahara Desert.

The statements above, if true, most strongly support which one of the following?

(A) Most ants forage for food either only in the morning or only during the night.
(B) Most ants that do not use pheromones to mark the paths they take between their nest and food live in the Sahara Desert.
(C) If any ants live in the Sahara Desert and forage for food at no time but in the afternoon, those ants generally do not use pheromones to guide themselves between food and their nest.
(D) If any ants do not use pheromones to navigate between food and their nest, those ants use a different substance that does not evaporate in temperatures above 45 degrees Celsius.
(E) If any Saharan ants forage for food in the afternoon, those ants forage for food less efficiently when temperatures are above 45 degrees Celsius than they do when temperatures are lower.

101. Sponges attach to the ocean floor, continually filtering seawater for food and ejecting water they have just filtered to avoid reingesting it. Tubular and vase-shaped sponges can eject filtered water without assistance from surrounding ocean currents and thus are adapted to slow-moving, quiet waters. Because of their shape, however, these sponges cannot live in strong currents, since strong currents would dislodge them. Both of these varieties of sponge were widespread during the late Jurassic period.

The statements above, if true, most strongly support which one of the following claims?

(A) Few tubular or vase-shaped sponges lived before the late Jurassic period.
(B) Tubular and vase-shaped sponges were more common during the late Jurassic period than in succeeding geological eras.
(C) During the late Jurassic period there were many areas of the ocean floor where currents were weak.
(D) All sponges that are neither tubular nor vase-shaped inhabit areas of the ocean floor where there are extremely strong currents.
(E) No types of sponge live in large colonies, since sponges do not flourish in areas where much of the water has been filtered by other sponges.

102. French divers recently found a large cave along the coast of the Mediterranean Sea. The cave is accessible only through an underwater tunnel. The interior of the cave is completely filled with seawater and contains numerous large stalagmites, which are stony pillars that form when drops of water fall repeatedly on a single spot on a cave floor, leaving behind mineral deposits that accumulate over time.

The information above most strongly supports which one of the following?

(A) The Mediterranean Sea was at a higher level in the past than it is now.
(B) The water level within the cave is higher now than it once was.
(C) The French divers were the first people who knew that the tunnel leading to the cave existed.
(D) There was once an entrance to the cave besides the underwater tunnel.
(E) Seawater in the Mediterranean has a lower mineral content now than it had when the stalagmites were being formed.

103. Besides laying eggs in her own nest, any female wood duck will lay an egg in the nest of another female wood duck if she sees the other duck leaving her nest. Under natural nesting conditions, this parasitic behavior is relatively rare because the ducks' nests are well hidden. However, when people put up nesting boxes to help the ducks breed, they actually undercut the ducks' reproductive efforts. These nesting boxes become so crowded with extra eggs that few, if any, of the eggs in those boxes hatch.

The statements above, if true, most strongly support which one of the following?

(A) Female wood ducks will establish nests in nest boxes only when natural nesting sites are not available.
(B) Nesting female wood ducks who often see other female wood ducks are the most successful in their breeding efforts.
(C) The nesting boxes for wood ducks have less space for eggs than do natural nesting sites.
(D) The nesting boxes would be more effective in helping wood ducks breed if they were less visible to other wood ducks than they currently are.
(E) Nesting boxes are needed to supplement the natural nesting sites of wood ducks because of the destruction of much of the ducks' habitat.

104. The crux of creativity resides in the ability to manufacture variations on a theme. If we look at the history of science, for instance, we see that every idea is built upon a thousand related ideas. Careful analysis leads us to understand that what we choose to call a new theme or a new discovery is itself always and without exception some sort of variation, on a deep level, of previous themes.

If all of the statements in the passage are true, each of the following must also be true EXCEPT:

(A) A lack of ability to manufacture a variation on a previous theme connotes a lack of creativity
(B) No scientific idea is entirely independent of all other ideas.
(C) Careful analysis of a specific variation can reveal previous themes of which it is a variation.
(D) All great scientific discoverers have been able to manufacture a variation on a theme.
(E) Some new scientific discoveries do not represent, on a deep level, a variation on previous themes.

105. Chronic back pain is usually caused by a herniated or degenerated spinal disk. In most cases the disk will have been damaged years before chronic pain develops, and in fact an estimated one in five people over the age of 30 has a herniated or degenerated disk that shows no chronic symptoms. If chronic pain later develops in such a case, it is generally brought about by a deterioration of the abdominal and spinal muscles caused by insufficient exercise.

The statements above, if true, most strongly support which one of the following?

(A) Four out of five people over the age of 30 can be sure they will never develop chronic back pain.
(B) People who exercise their abdominal and spinal muscles regularly are sure to be free from chronic back pain.
(C) Patients rarely suffer even mild and fleeting back pain at the time that a spinal disk first becomes herniated or degenerated.
(D) Doctors can accurately predict which people who do not have chronic back pain will develop it in the future.
(E) There is a strategy that can be effective in delaying or preventing the onset of pain from a currently asymptomatic herniated or degenerated spinal disk.

106. The *Rienzi*, a passenger ship, sank as a result of a hole in its hull, possibly caused by sabotage. Normally, when a holed ship sinks as rapidly as the *Rienzi* did, water does not enter the ship quickly enough for the ship to be fully flooded when it reaches the ocean floor. Full flooding can be achieved, however, by sabotage. Any ship that sinks deep into the ocean when not fully flooded will implode. Deep-sea photographs, taken of the sunken *Rienzi* where it rests on the ocean floor, reveal that the *Rienzi* did not implode.

Which one of the following must be true on the basis of the information above?

(A) The *Rienzi* was so constructed as to reduce the risk of sinking by impact.
(B) If the *Rienzi* became fully flooded, it did so only after it reached the ocean floor.
(C) If the *Rienzi* was not sunk by sabotage, water flooded into it unusually fast.
(D) If the *Rienzi* had sunk more slowly, it would have imploded.
(E) The *Rienzi* was so strongly constructed as to resist imploding under deep-sea pressure.

107. Curator: The decision to restore the cloak of the central figure in Veronese's painting from its present red to the green found underneath is fully justified. Reliable x-ray and chemical tests show that the red pigment was applied after the painting had been completed, and that the red paint was not mixed in Veronese's workshop. Hence it appears likely that an artist other than Veronese tampered with Veronese's painting after its completion.

Art critic: But in a copy of Veronese's painting made shortly after Veronese died, the cloak is red. It is highly unlikely that a copyist would have made so major a change so soon after Veronese's death.

The art critic's response to the curator would provide the strongest support for which one of the following conclusions?

(A) The copy of Veronese's painting that was made soon after the painter's death is indistinguishable from the original.
(B) No painting should be restored before the painting is tested with technologically sophisticated equipment.
(C) The proposed restoration will fail to restore Veronese's painting to the appearance it had at the end of the artist's lifetime.
(D) The value of an artist's work is not necessarily compromised when that work is tampered with by later artists.
(E) Veronese did not originally intend the central figure's cloak to be green.

108. Mature white pines intercept almost all the sunlight that shines on them. They leave a deep litter that dries readily, and they grow to prodigious height so that, even when there are large gaps in a stand of such trees, little light reaches the forest floor. For this reason white pines cannot regenerate in their own shade. Thus, when in a dense forest a stand of trees consists of nothing but mature white pines, it is a fair bet that ___________.

Which one of the following most logically concludes the argument?

(A) the ages of the trees in the stand do not differ from each other by much more than the length of time it takes a white pine to grow to maturity
(B) the land on which the stand is now growing had been cleared of all trees at the time when the first of the white pines started growing
(C) competition among the trees in the stand for sunlight will soon result in some trees dying and the stand thus becoming thinner
(D) other species of trees will soon begin to colonize the stand, eventually replacing all of the white pines
(E) any differences in the heights of the trees in the stand are attributable solely to differences in the ages of the trees

Chapter Three: Main Point Questions

1. The term "pit bull" does not designate a breed of dog, as do the terms "German shepherd" and "poodle." It is like the terms "Seeing-Eye dog" and "Police dog," which designate dogs according to what they do. If you take two German shepherds and place them side by side, you cannot tell by appearance alone which is the police dog and which is the Seeing-Eye dog.

   Which one of the following is the main point of the passage?

   (A) German shepherds can be pit bulls.
   (B) Pit bulls can be distinguished from other kinds of dogs by appearance alone.
   (C) A dog is a pit bull because of what it does, not because of its breed.
   (D) German shepherds can function both as police dogs and as Seeing-Eye dogs.
   (E) Some breeds of dogs cannot be distinguished from other breeds of dogs by appearance alone.

2. Can any research be found to validate the contention that those who spend time plucking out their gray hairs have more negative attitudes toward the elderly than those who shrug their shoulders about their gray hairs? Unless a person's psychopathology leads him or her to overgeneralize, there is no necessary connection. Certainly it is reasonable to like the elderly yet dislike the idea of impaired eyesight and hearing. Furthermore, holding negative attitudes toward older people merely because they are old is immoral, according to nearly universally accepted ethical standards. But there is nothing immoral about disliking some concomitants of the aging process.

   Which one of the following best expresses the main point of the passage?

   (A) It cannot be assumed that people who dislike some of the physical concomitants of growing old necessarily have negative feelings toward the elderly.
   (B) To dislike some of the physical concomitants of growing old is reasonable, while to dislike the elderly is immoral.
   (C) Since no one likes the physical concomitants of growing old, it is wrong to dislike the elderly merely because of their physical characteristics.
   (D) Being elderly is fine, but the process of becoming elderly is not; and people need to understand this distinction between the two.
   (E) To dislike the elderly is immoral, and to do so just because one dislikes some of the physical concomitants of growing old is unreasonable.

3. As symbols of the freedom of the wilderness, bald eagles have the unique capacity to inspire people and foster in them a sympathetic attitude toward the needs of other threatened species. Clearly, without that sympathy and the political will it engenders, the needs of more obscure species will go unmet. The conservation needs of many obscure species can only be met by beginning with the conservation of this symbolic species, the bald eagle.

   Which one of the following is the main point of the passage as a whole?

   (A) Because bald eagles symbolize freedom, conservation efforts should be concentrated on them rather than on other, more obscure species.
   (B) The conservation of bald eagles is the first necessary step in conserving other endangered species.
   (C) Without increased public sympathy for conservation, the needs of many symbolic species will go unmet.
   (D) People's love of the wilderness can be used to engender political support for conservation efforts.
   (E) Other threatened species do not inspire people or foster sympathy as much as do bald eagles.

4. Some cleaning fluids, synthetic carpets, wall paneling, and other products release toxins, such as formaldehyde and benzene, into the household air supply. This is not a problem in well-ventilated houses, but it is a problem in houses that are so well insulated that they trap toxins as well as heat. Recent tests, however, demonstrate that houseplants remove some household toxins from the air and thereby eliminate their danger. In one test, 20 large plants eliminated formaldehyde from a small, well-insulated house.

   Assume that a person who lives in a small, well-insulated house that contains toxin-releasing products places houseplants, such as those tested, in the house.

   The passage is structured to lead to which one of the following conclusions?

   (A) Houseplants can remove benzene from the air.
   (B) Nonsynthetic products do not release toxins into houses.
   (C) Keeping houseplants is an effective means of trapping heat in a poorly insulated house.
   (D) Keeping houseplants can compensate for some of the negative effects of poor ventilation.
   (E) The air in a well-insulated house with houseplants will contain fewer toxins than the air in a well-ventilated house without houseplants.

5. Like a number of other articles, Ian Raghnall's article relied on a recent survey in which over half the couples applying for divorces listed "money" as a major problem in their marriages. Raghnall's conclusion from the survey data is that financial problems are the major problem in marriages and an important factor contributing to the high divorce rate. Yet couples often express other types of marital frustrations in financial terms. Despite appearances, the survey data do not establish that financial problems are the major problem in contemporary marriages.

   Which one of the following sentences best expresses the main point of the passage?

   (A) Financial problems are not an important factor contributing to the divorce rate.
   (B) Marital problems are more easily solved by marriage counselors than by married couples on their own.
   (C) The conclusion drawn in Raghnall's article is inadequately justified.
   (D) Over half the couples applying for divorces listed money as a major problem in their marriages.
   (E) Many articles wrongly claim that financial problems are the major factor contributing to the divorce rate.

6. Anthropologists assert that cultures advance only when independence replaces dependence—that is, only when imposition by outsiders is replaced by initiative from within. In other words, the natives of a culture are the only ones who can move that culture forward. Non-natives may provide valuable advice, but any imposition of their views threatens independence and thus progress. If one looks at individual schools as separate cultures, therefore, the key to educational progress is obvious: ______.

   Which one of the following best completes the passage?

   (A) individual schools must be independent of outside imposition
   (B) some schools require more independence than others, depending on the initiative of their staffs and students
   (C) school system officials must tailor their initiatives for change to each individual school in the system
   (D) outsiders must be prevented from participation in schools' efforts to advance
   (E) the more independent a school is, the more educational progress it will make

7. The United States government generally tries to protect valuable natural resources. But one resource has been ignored for too long. In the United States, each bushel of corn produced might result in the loss of as much as two bushels of topsoil. Moreover, in the last 100 years, the topsoil in many states, which once was about fourteen inches thick, has been eroded to only six or eight inches. Nonetheless, federal expenditures for nationwide soil conservation programs have remained at ridiculously low levels. Total federal expenditures for nationwide soil conservation programs have been less than the allocations of some individual states.

   Which one of the following best expresses the main point of the argument?

   (A) Corn is not a cost-effective product and substitutes should be found where possible.
   (B) A layer of topsoil only six to eight inches thick cannot support the continued cultivation of corn.
   (C) Soil conservation is a responsibility of the federal government, not the states.
   (D) The federal government's expenditures for soil conservation in the various states have been inequitable.
   (E) The federal government should spend much more on soil conservation than it has been spending.

8. A law that is not consistently enforced does not serve its purpose. Law without enforcement is not law; it is merely statute—the promise of law. To institute real law is not merely to declare that such and such behavior is forbidden; it is also to punish those who violate that edict. Furthermore, those who enforce law must punish without favor for their friends or malice for their enemies. To punish only those one dislikes while forgiving others is not to enforce law but to engage in the arbitrary and unjust exercise of power.

   The main point of the passage is that instituting real law consists in

   (A) the exercise of power
   (B) authorizing the enforcement of punishments
   (C) the unbiased punishment of prohibited behavior
   (D) understanding the purpose of law
   (E) clearly defining unacceptable behavior

MP

9. There is no mystery as to why figurative painting revived in the late 1970s. People want to look at recognizable images. Sorting out art theories reflected in abstract paintings is no substitute for the sense of empathy that comes from looking at a realistic painting of a figure in a landscape. Perhaps members of the art-viewing public resented abstract art because they felt that its lack of realistic subject matter was a rejection of the viewers and their world.

Which one of the following most accurately expresses the main point of the passage?

(A) Abstract paintings often include shapes or forms that are suggestive of real objects or emotions.
(B) The art-viewing public wished to see traditional subjects treated in a non-traditional manner.
(C) Paintings that depict a recognizable physical world rather than the emotional world of the artist's life require more artistic talent to create.
(D) The general public is unable to understand the theories on which abstract painting is based.
(E) The artistic preferences of the art-viewing public stimulated the revival.

10. Arguing that there was no trade between Europe and East Asia in the early Middle Ages because there are no written records of such trade is like arguing that the yeti, an apelike creature supposedly existing in the Himalayas, does not exist because there have been no scientifically confirmed sightings. A verifiable sighting of the yeti would prove that the creature does exist, but the absence of sightings cannot prove that it does not.

Which one of the following best expresses the point of the argument?

(A) Evidence for the existence of trade between Europe and East Asia in the early Middle Ages is, like evidence for the existence of the yeti, not scientifically confirmed.
(B) In order to prove that in the early Middle Ages there was trade between Europe and East Asia it is necessary to find both Asian and European evidence that such trade existed.
(C) That trade between Europe and East Asia did not exist in the early Middle Ages cannot be established simply by the absence of a certain sort of evidence that this trade existed.
(D) The view that there was trade between Europe and East Asia in the early Middle Ages can only be disproved by showing that no references to this trade exist in surviving records.
(E) There is no more evidence that trade between Europe and East Asia existed in the early Middle Ages than there is that the yeti exists.

11. Some legislators refuse to commit public funds for new scientific research if they cannot be assured that the research will contribute to the public welfare. Such a position ignores the lessons of experience. Many important contributions to the public welfare that resulted from scientific research were never predicted as potential outcomes of that research. Suppose that a scientist in the early twentieth century had applied for public funds to study molds: who would have predicted that such research would lead to the discovery of antibiotics—one of the greatest contributions ever made to the public welfare?

Which one of the following most accurately expresses the main point of the argument?

(A) The committal of public funds for new scientific research will ensure that the public welfare will be enhanced.

(B) If it were possible to predict the general outcome of a new scientific research effort, then legislators would not refuse to commit public funds for that effort.

(C) Scientific discoveries that have contributed to the public welfare would have occurred sooner if public funds had been committed to the research that generated those discoveries.

(D) In order to ensure that scientific research is directed toward contributing to the public welfare, legislators must commit public funds to new scientific research.

(E) Lack of guarantees that new scientific research will contribute to the public welfare is not sufficient reason for legislators to refuse to commit public funds to new scientific research.

12. Balance is particularly important when reporting the background of civil wars and conflicts. Facts must not be deliberately manipulated to show one party in a favorable light, and the views of each side should be fairly represented. This concept of balance, however, does not justify concealing or glossing over basic injustices in an effort to be even-handed. If all the media were to adopt such a perverse interpretation of balanced reporting, the public would be given a picture of a world where each party in every conflict had an equal measure of justice on its side, contrary to our experience of life and, indeed, our common sense.

Which one of the following best expresses the main point of the argument?

(A) Balanced reporting presents the public with a picture of the world in which all sides to a conflict have equal justification.

(B) Balanced reporting requires impartially revealing injustices where they occur no less than fairly presenting the views of each party in a conflict.

(C) Our experience of life shows that there are indeed cases in which conflicts arise because of an injustice, with one party clearly in the wrong.

(D) Common sense tells us that balance is especially needed when reporting the background of civil wars and conflicts.

(E) Balanced reporting is an ideal that cannot be realized, because judgments of balance are necessarily subjective.

13. Marcus: For most ethical dilemmas the journalist is likely to face, traditional journalistic ethics is clear, adequate, and essentially correct. For example, when journalists have uncovered newsworthy information, they should go to press with it as soon as possible. No delay motivated by the journalists' personal or professional interests is permissible.

Anita: Well, Marcus, of course interesting and important information should be brought before the public—that is a journalist's job. But in the typical case, where a journalist has some information but is in a quandary about whether it is yet important or "newsworthy," this guidance is inadequate.

The point made by Anita's statements is most accurately expressed by which one of the following?

(A) Marcus' claim that traditional journalistic ethics is clear for most ethical dilemmas in journalism is incorrect.
(B) A typical case illustrates that Marcus is wrong in claiming that traditional journalistic ethics is essentially correct for most ethical dilemmas in journalism.
(C) The ethical principle that Marcus cites does not help the journalist in a typical kind of situation in which a decision needs to be made.
(D) There are common situations in which a journalist must make a decision and in which no principle of journalistic ethics can be of help.
(E) Traditional journalistic ethics amounts to no more than an unnecessarily convoluted description of the journalist's job.

14. The fire that destroyed the Municipal Building started before dawn this morning, and the last fire fighters did not leave until late this afternoon. No one could have been anywhere in the vicinity of a fire like that one and fail to notice it. Thomas must have seen it, whatever he now says to the contrary. He admits that, as usual, he went from his apartment to the library this morning, and there is no way for him to get from his apartment to the library without going past the Municipal Building.

The main conclusion of the argument is that

(A) Thomas was in the vicinity of the fire this morning
(B) Thomas claimed not to have seen the fire
(C) Thomas saw the fire this morning
(D) Thomas went directly from his apartment to the library this morning
(E) Thomas went by the Municipal Building this morning

15. That long-term cigarette smoking can lead to health problems including cancer and lung disease is a scientifically well established fact. Contrary to what many people seem to believe, however, it is not necessary to deny this fact in order to reject the view that tobacco companies should be held either morally or legally responsible for the poor health of smokers. After all, excessive consumption of candy undeniably leads to such health problems as tooth decay, but no one seriously believes that candy eaters who get cavities should be able to sue candy manufacturers.

The main point of the argument is that

(A) no one should feel it necessary to deny the scientifically well-established fact that long-term cigarette smoking can lead to health problems
(B) people who get cavities should not be able to sue candy manufacturers
(C) the fact that smokers' health problems can be caused by their smoking is not enough to justify holding tobacco companies either legally or morally responsible for those problems
(D) excessive consumption of candy will lead to health problems just as surely as long-term cigarette smoking will
(E) if candy manufacturers were held responsible for tooth decay among candy eaters then tobacco companies should also be held responsible for health problems suffered by smokers

16. It is probably within the reach of human technology to make the climate of Mars inhabitable. It might be several centuries before people could live there, even with breathing apparatuses, but some of the world's great temples and cathedrals took centuries to build. Research efforts now are justified if there is even a chance of making another planet inhabitable. Besides, the intellectual exercise of understanding how the Martian atmosphere might be changed could help in understanding atmospheric changes inadvertently triggered by human activity on Earth.

    The main point of the argument is that

    (A) it is probably technologically possible for humankind to alter the climate of Mars
    (B) it would take several centuries to make Mars even marginally inhabitable
    (C) making Mars inhabitable is an effort comparable to building a great temple or cathedral
    (D) research efforts aimed at discovering how to change the climate of Mars are justified
    (E) efforts to change the climate of Mars could facilitate understanding of the Earth's climate

17. Since multinational grain companies operate so as to maximize profits, they cannot be relied to initiate economic changes that would reform the world's food-distribution system. Although it is true that the actions of multinational companies sometimes do result in such economic change, this result is incidental, arising not from the desire for reform but from the desire to maximize profits. The maximization of profits normally depends on a stable economic environment, one that discourages change.

    The main point of the argument is that

    (A) the maximization of profits depends on a stable economic environment
    (B) when economic change accompanies business activity, that change is initiated by concern for the profit motive
    (C) multinational grain companies operates so as to maximize profits
    (D) the world's current food-distribution system is not in need of reform
    (E) multinational grain companies cannot be relied on to initiate reform of the world's food-distribution system

18. Household indebtedness, which some theorists regard as causing recession, was high preceding the recent recession, but so was the value of assets owned by households. Admittedly, if most of the assets were owned by quite affluent households, and most of the debt was owed by low-income households, high household debt levels could have been the cause of the recession despite high asset values: low-income households might have decreased spending in order to pay off debts while the quite affluent ones might simply have failed to increase spending. But, in fact, quite affluent people must have owed most of the household debt, since money is not lent to those without assets. Therefore, the real cause must lie elsewhere.

    The argument is structured to lead to which one of the following conclusions?

    (A) High levels of household debt did not cause the recent recession.
    (B) Low-income households succeeded in paying off their debts despite the recent recession.
    (C) Affluent people probably increased their spending levels during the recent recession.
    (D) High levels of household debt have little impact on the economy.
    (E) When people borrowed money prior to the recent recession, they did not use it to purchase assets.

19. Kim: Some people claim that the battery-powered electric car represents a potential solution to the problem of air pollution. But they forget that it takes electricity to recharge batteries and that most of our electricity is generated by burning polluting fossil fuels. Increasing the number of electric cars on the road would require building more generating facilities since current facilities are operating at maximum capacity. So even if all of the gasoline-powered cars on the roads today were replaced by electric cars, it would at best be an exchange of one source of fossil-fuel pollution for another.

    The main point made in Kim's argument is that

    (A) replacing gasoline-powered cars with battery--powered electric cars will require building more generating facilities
    (B) a significant reduction in air pollution cannot be achieved unless people drive less
    (C) all forms of automobile transportation are equally harmful to the environment in terms of the air pollution they produce
    (D) battery-powered electric cars are not a viable solution to the air-pollution problem
    (E) gasoline-powered cars will probably remain a common means of transportation for the foreseeable future

20. Zachary: One would have to be blind to the reality of moral obligation to deny that people who believe a course of action to be morally obligatory for them have both the right and the duty to pursue that action, and that no one else has any right to stop them from doing so.

Cynthia: But imagine an artist who feels morally obliged to do whatever she can to prevent works of art from being destroyed confronting a morally committed antipornography demonstrator engaged in destroying artworks he deems pornographic. According to your principle that artist has, simultaneously, both the right and the duty to stop the destruction and no right whatsoever to stop it.

Cynthia's response to Zachary's claim is structured to demonstrate that

(A) the concept of moral obligation is incoherent
(B) the ideas of right and duty should not be taken seriously since doing so leads to morally undesirable consequences
(C) Zachary's principle is untenable on its own terms
(D) because the term "moral obligation" is understood differently by different people, it is impossible to find a principle concerning moral rights and duties that applies to everyone
(E) Zachary's principle is based on an understanding of moral obligation that is too narrow to encompass the kind of moral obligation artists feel toward works of art

21. A report on the likely effects of current levels of air pollution on forest growth in North America concluded that, since nitrogen is a necessary nutrient for optimal plant growth, the nitrogen deposited on forest soil as a result of air pollution probably benefits eastern forests. However, European soil scientists have found that in forests saturated with sulfate and nitrate, trees begin to die when the nitrogen deposited exceeds the amount of nitrogen absorbed by the forest system. Since this finding is likely to apply to forests everywhere, large areas of eastern forests of North America are, undoubtedly, already being affected adversely.

Which one of the following most accurately expresses the main point of the passage?

(A) The implication of the report cited is that the amount of nitrogen reaching eastern forests by way of polluted air is approximately what those forests need for optimal growth.
(B) If large areas of eastern forests were increasingly saturated with sulfate and nitrate, the capacity of those forest systems for absorbing nitrogen would also increase.
(C) The type of analysis used by European soil scientists does not necessarily apply to eastern forests of North America.
(D) The eastern forests are the only forests of North America currently affected by polluted air.
(E) Contrary to the report cited, the nitrogen pollution now in the air is more likely to cause trees to die in eastern forests than to benefit them.

22. Would it be right for the government to abandon efforts to determine at what levels to allow toxic substances in our food supply? Only if it can reasonably be argued that the only acceptable level of toxic substances in food is zero. However, virtually all foods contain perfectly natural substances that are toxic but cause no harm because they do not occur in food in toxic concentrations. Furthermore, we can never be certain of having reduced the concentration of any substance to zero; all we can ever know is that it has been reduced to below the threshold of detection of current analytical methods

The main conclusion of the argument is that

(A) the government should continue trying to determine acceptable levels for toxic substances in our food supply
(B) the only acceptable level of toxic substances in food is zero
(C) naturally occurring toxic substances in food present little danger because they rarely occur in toxic concentrations
(D) the government will never be able to determine with certainty that a food contains no toxic substances
(E) the government needs to refine its methods of detecting toxic substances in our food supply

23. Should a journalist's story begin with the set phrase "in a surprise development," as routinely happens? Well, not if the surprise was merely the journalist's, since journalists should not intrude themselves into their stories, and not if the surprise was someone else's, because if some person's surprise was worth mentioning at all, it should have been specifically attributed. The one possibility remaining is that lots of people were surprised; in that case, however, there is no point in belaboring the obvious.

Which one of the following most accurately states the conclusion of the argument above?

(A) Journalists should reserve use of the phrase "in a surprise development" for major developments that are truly unexpected.
(B) The phrase "in a surprise development" is appropriately used only where someone's being surprised is itself interesting.
(C) The phrase "in a surprise development" is used in three distinct sorts of circumstances.
(D) Journalists should make the point that a development comes as a surprise when summing up, not when introducing, a story.
(E) Introducing stories with the phrase "in a surprise development" is not good journalistic practice.

24. Those who support the continued reading and performance of Shakespeare's plays maintain that in England appreciation for his work has always extended beyond educated elites and that ever since Shakespeare's own time his plays have always been known and loved by comparatively uneducated people. Skepticism about this claim is borne out by examining early eighteenth century editions of the plays. These books, with their fine paper and good bindings, must have been far beyond the reach of people of ordinary means.

The main point of the argument is to

(A) suggest that knowledge of Shakespeare's plays is a suitable criterion for distinguishing the educated elite from other members of English society
(B) provide evidence that at some time in the past appreciation for Shakespeare's plays was confined to educated elites
(C) prove that early eighteenth century appreciation for Shakespeare's works rested on aspects of the works that are less appreciated today
(D) demonstrate that since Shakespeare's time the people who have known and loved his work have all been members of educated elites
(E) confirm the skepticism of the educated elite concerning the worth of Shakespeare's plays

25. The frequently expressed view that written constitutions are inherently more liberal than unwritten ones is false. No written constitution is more than a paper with words on it until those words are both interpreted and applied. Properly understood, then, a constitution is the sum of those procedures through which the power of the state is legitimately exercised and limited. Therefore, even a written constitution becomes a liberal constitution only when it is interpreted and applied in a liberal way.

The main point of the argument above is that

(A) written constitutions are no more inherently liberal than are unwritten constitutions
(B) the idea of a written constitution, properly understood, is inherently self-contradictory
(C) unwritten constitutions are less subject to misinterpretation than are constitutions that have been written down
(D) liberal constitutions are extremely difficult to preserve
(E) there are criteria for evaluating the interpretation and application of a constitution

MP

26. Maria: Calling any state totalitarian is misleading: it implies total state control of all aspects of life. The real world contains no political entity exercising literally total control over even one such aspect. This is because any system of control is inefficient, and, therefore, its degree of control is partial.

James: A one-party state that has tried to exercise control over most aspects of a society and that has, broadly speaking, managed to do so is totalitarian. Such a system's practical inefficiencies do not limit the aptness of the term, which does not describe a state's actual degree of control as much as it describes the nature of a state's ambitions.

Which one of the following most accurately expresses Maria's main conclusion?

(A) No state can be called totalitarian without inviting a mistaken belief.
(B) To be totalitarian, a state must totally control society.
(C) The degree of control exercised by a state is necessarily partial.
(D) No existing state currently has even one aspect of society under total control.
(E) Systems of control are inevitably inefficient.

27. Engineer: Some people argue that the world's energy problems could be solved by mining the Moon for helium-3, which could be used for fuel in fusion reactors. But this is nonsense. Even if it were possible to mine the Moon for helium-3, the technology needed to build viable fusion reactors that could use such fuel is at least 50 years away. If the world's energy problems are not solved before then, it will be too late to solve those problems.

The main point of the argument is that

(A) mining the Moon for helium-3 is currently not feasible
(B) fusion reactors that are now being planned are not designed to use helium-3 as fuel
(C) people who advocate mining the Moon for helium-3 do not realize that fusion reactors could be designed to use fuels other than helium-3
(D) mining the Moon for helium-3 is not a possible solution to the world's energy problems
(E) if the world's energy problems are not solved within the next 50 years, it will be too late to solve those problems

28. Some people claim that elected officials must avoid even the appearance of impropriety in office. Yet since actions that give the appearance of impropriety are not necessarily improper, the only reason for an elected official to avoid the appearance of impropriety is to maintain public approval and popularity. No one, however, not even a public official, has an obligation to be popular or to maintain public approval.

The argument is structured so as to lead to which one of the following conclusions?

(A) No elected official has an obligation to avoid the appearance of impropriety.
(B) All elected officials have a vested interest in maintaining a high public approval rating.
(C) Elected officials who have been scrupulous in satisfying the obligations of their office should ensure that the public is aware of this fact.
(D) The public never approves of an elected official who appears to have behaved improperly in office.
(E) Elected officials who abuse the power of their office have an obligation at least to appear to be fulfilling the obligations of their office.

29. Dillworth: More and more people are deciding not to have children because of the personal and economic sacrifices children require and because so often children are ungrateful for the considerable sacrifices their parents do make for them. However, such considerations have no bearing on the fact that their children provide the best chance most people have of ensuring that their values live on after them. Therefore, for anyone with deeply held values, foregoing parenthood out of reluctance to make sacrifices for which little gratitude can be expected would probably be a mistake.

Travers: Your reasoning ignores another fact that deserves consideration: children's ingratitude for parental sacrifices usually stems from a wholesale rejection of parental values.

The point of Travers' rejoinder to Dillworth's argument is that

(A) Dillworth's assumption that children acquire values only from their parents is mistaken
(B) it is a mistake to dismiss as irrelevant the personal and economic sacrifices people are called on to make for the sake of their children
(C) Dillworth has overlooked the well-known fact that people with deeply held values not infrequently reject opposing values that are deeply held by others
(D) the desire to perpetuate their values should not be a factor in people's decision to have children
(E) the fact that children are often ungrateful for parental sacrifices is not irrelevant to deciding whether to have children in order to perpetuate one's values

30. Most people are indignant at the suggestion that they are not reliable authorities about their real wants. Such self-knowledge, however, is not the easiest kind of knowledge to acquire. Indeed, acquiring it often requires hard and even potentially risky work. To avoid such effort, people unconsciously convince themselves that they want what society says they should want.

The main point of the argument is that

(A) acquiring self-knowledge can be risky
(B) knowledge of what one really wants is not as desirable as it is usually thought to be
(C) people cannot really want what they should want
(D) people usually avoid making difficult decisions
(E) people are not necessarily reliable authorities about what they really want

31. The television documentary went beyond the save-the-wildlife pieties of some of those remote from East Africa and showed that in a country pressed for food, the elephant is a pest, and an intelligent pest at that. There appears to be no way to protect East African farms from the voracious foraging of night-raiding elephant herds. Clearly this example illustrates that ________.

Which one of the following most logically completes the paragraph?

(A) the preservation of wildlife may endanger human welfare
(B) it is time to remove elephants from the list of endangered species
(C) television documentaries are incapable of doing more than reiterating accepted pieties
(D) farmers and agricultural agents should work closely with wildlife conservationists before taking measures to control elephants
(E) it is unfair that people in any country should have to endure food shortages

32. Zoo director: The city is in a financial crisis and must reduce its spending. Nevertheless, at least one reduction measure in next year's budget, cutting City Zoo's funding in half, is false economy. The zoo's current budget equals less than 1 percent of the city's deficit, so withdrawing support from the zoo does little to help the city's financial situation. Furthermore, the zoo, which must close if its budget is cut, attracts tourists and tax dollars to the city. Finally, the zoo adds immeasurably to the city's cultural climate and thus makes the city an attractive place for business to locate.

Which one of the following is the main conclusion of the zoo director's argument?

(A) Reducing spending is the only means the city has of responding to the current financial crisis.
(B) It would be false economy for the city to cut the zoo's budget in half.
(C) City Zoo's budget is only a very small portion of the city's entire budget.
(D) The zoo will be forced to close if its budget is cut.
(E) The city's educational and cultural climate will be irreparably damaged if the zoo is forced to close.

33. People cannot devote themselves to the study of natural processes unless they have leisure, and people have leisure when resources are plentiful, not when resources are scarce. Although some anthropologists claim that agriculture, the cultivation of crops, actually began under conditions of drought and hunger, the early societies that domesticated plants must first have discovered how the plants they cultivated reproduced themselves and grew to maturity. These complex discoveries were the result of the active study of natural processes.

    The argument is structured to lead to the conclusion that

    (A) whenever a society has plentiful resources, some members of that society devote themselves to the study of natural processes
    (B) plants cannot be cultivated by someone lacking theoretical knowledge of the principles of plant generation and growth
    (C) agriculture first began in societies that at some time in their history had plentiful resources
    (D) early agricultural societies knew more about the natural sciences than did early nonagricultural societies
    (E) early societies could have discovered by accident how the plants they cultivated reproduced and grew

34. When an ordinary piece of steel is put under pressure, the steel compresses: that is, its volume slightly decreases. Glass, however, is a fluid, so rather than compressing, it flows when put under pressure; its volume remains unchanged. Any portion of a sheet of glass that is under sustained pressure will very slowly flow to areas under less pressure. Therefore, if a single, extremely heavy object is placed in the middle of a horizontal sheet of glass of uniform thickness and if the glass is able to support the weight without cracking, the sheet of glass will eventually______.

    Which one of the following most logically completes the argument?

    (A) become larger in size yet still be of uniform thickness
    (B) flow toward the point at which the pressure of the object is greatest
    (C) compress, although not as much as a piece of steel would
    (D) divide into exactly two pieces that are equal in neither size nor shape to the original piece of glass
    (E) be thinner in the portion of the glass that is under the pressure of the object than in those portions of the glass that are not under that pressure

4

Chapter Four: Weaken Questions

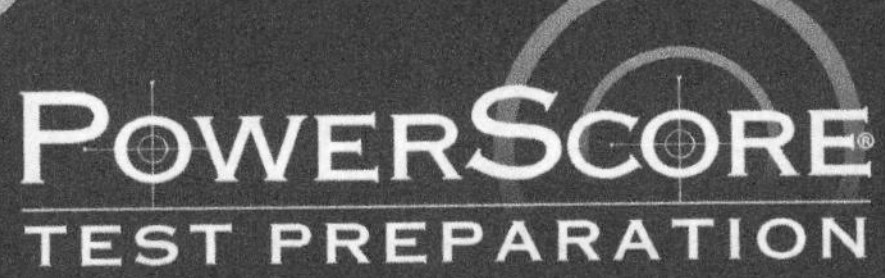

1. To the editor:

In 1960, an astronomer proposed a mathematical model for determining whether extraterrestrial life exists. It was based on the assumptions that life as we know it could exist only on a planet and that many stars are, like our Sun, orbited by planets. On the basis that there are nine planets in our solar system and one of them has life as we know it, the astronomer predicted that there are as many as one million extraterrestrial civilizations across all solar systems. Yet astronomers to date have not detected even one planet outside our solar system. This indicates that the astronomer's model is wrong, and life as we know it exists only on the planet Earth.

Clay Moltz

Which one of the following, if accepted by Clay Moltz, would require him to reconsider his conclusion?

(A) Forms of life other than life as we know it exist on other planets.
(B) There are many stars that are not orbited by planets.
(C) Detecting planets outside our solar system requires more sophisticated instruments than are currently available.
(D) The soundness of the conclusion reached by applying a mathematical model depends on the soundness of the assumptions on which the model is based.
(E) Due to sheer distances and expanses of space involved, any extraterrestrial civilization would have great difficulty communicating with ours.

2. Fines levied against those responsible for certain environmentally damaging accidents are now so high that it costs a company responsible for such an accident more to pay the fine than it would have cost to adopt measures that would have prevented the accident. Therefore, since businesses value their profits, those that might have such accidents will now install adequate environmental safeguards.

Which one of the following, if true, most seriously weakens the argument?

(A) Businesses generally greatly underestimate the risk of future accidents.
(B) Businesses are as concerned with long-term as they are with short-term strategies for maximizing profits.
(C) Businesses generally do the environmentally "right" thing only if doing so makes good business sense.
(D) Businesses treat fines that are levied against them as an ordinary business expense.
(E) Businesses are learning to exploit the public's environmental awareness in promoting themselves.

3. Radioactive waste from nuclear power plants has been temporarily stored on-site, but this is not a satisfactory kind of place for long-range storage. Since no suitable plan of safe permanent storage of such waste from the nation's existing and planned nuclear plants has been devised, some people propose that we should stop trying to develop such a plan and instead should shut down all present nuclear plants and build no new nuclear plants.

The proposal mentioned above falls short of offering a complete solution to the problem it addresses because

(A) it would prevent the development of safe technologies for producing electric power
(B) it does not distinguish between nuclear plants that have, and plants that do not have, a reputation for operating safely
(C) it does not provide for the permanent storage of already-existing waste
(D) the generation of electric power from fossil fuels is relatively safe
(E) the risks of unsafe disposal of waste from nuclear power plants lie in the future, but the benefits from such plants are in the present

4. There is no reason why the work of scientists has to be officially confirmed before being published. There is a system in place for the confirmation or disconfirmation of scientific findings, namely, the replication of results by other scientists. Poor scientific work on the part of any one scientist, which can include anything from careless reporting practices to fraud, is not harmful. It will be exposed and rendered harmless when other scientists conduct the experiments and obtain disconfirmatory results.

   Which one of the following, if true, would weaken the argument?

   (A) Scientific experiments can go unchallenged for many years before they are replicated.
   (B) Most scientists work in universities, where their work is submitted to peer review before publication.
   (C) Most scientists are under pressure to make their work accessible to the scrutiny of replication.
   (D) In scientific experiments, careless reporting is more common than fraud.
   (E) Most scientists work as part of a team rather than alone.

5. The "suicide wave" that followed the United States stock market crash of October 1929 is more legend than fact. Careful examination of the monthly figures on the causes of death in 1929 shows that the number of suicides in October and in November was comparatively low. In only three other months were the monthly figures lower. During the summer months, when the stock market was flourishing, the number of suicides was substantially higher.

   Which one of the following, if true, would best challenge the conclusion of the passage?

   (A) The suicide rate is influenced by many psychological, interpersonal, and societal factors during any given historical period.
   (B) October and November have almost always had relatively high suicide rates, even during the 1920s and 1930s.
   (C) The suicide rate in October and November of 1929 was considerably higher than the average for those months during several preceding and following years.
   (D) During the years surrounding the stock market crash, suicide rates were typically lower at the beginning of any calendar year than toward the end of that year.
   (E) Because of seasonal differences, the number of suicides in October and November of 1929 would not be expected to be the same as those for other months.

6. A government agency publishes ratings of airlines, ranking highest the airlines that have the smallest proportion of late flights. The agency's purpose is to establish an objective measure of the relative efficiency of different airlines' personnel in meeting published flight schedules.

   Which one of the following, if true, would tend to invalidate use of the ratings for the agency's purpose?

   (A) Travelers sometimes have no choice of airlines for a given trip at a given time.
   (B) Flights are often made late by bad weather conditions that affect some airlines more than others.
   (C) The flight schedules of all airlines allow extra time for flights that go into or out of very busy airports.
   (D) Airline personnel are aware that the government agency is monitoring all airline flights for lateness.
   (E) Flights are defined as "late" only if they arrive more than fifteen minutes past their scheduled arrival time, and a record is made of how much later than fifteen minutes they are.

7. Nuclear fusion is a process whereby the nuclei of atoms are joined, or "fused," and in which energy is released. One of the by-products of fusion is helium-4 gas. A recent fusion experiment was conducted using "heavy" water contained in a sealed flask. The flask was, in turn, contained in an air-filled chamber designed to eliminate extraneous vibration. After the experiment, a measurable amount of helium-4 gas was found in the air of the chamber. The experimenters cited this evidence in support of their conclusion that fusion had been achieved.

   Which one of the following, if true, would cast doubt on the experimenters' conclusion?

   (A) Helium-4 was not the only gas found in the experiment chamber.
   (B) When fusion is achieved, it normally produces several by-products, including tritium and gamma rays.
   (C) The amount of helium-4 found in the chamber's air did not exceed the amount of helium-4 that is found in ordinary air.
   (D) Helium-4 gas rapidly breaks down, forming ordinary helium gas after a few hours.
   (E) Nuclear fusion reactions are characterized by the release of large amounts of heat.

WEAKEN

8. For a television program about astrology, investigators went into the street and found twenty volunteers born under the sign of Gemini who were willing to be interviewed on the program and to take a personality test. The test confirmed the investigators' personal impressions that each of the volunteers was more sociable and extroverted than people are on average. This modest investigation thus supports the claim that one's astrological birth sign influences one's personality.

Which one of the following, if true, indicates the most serious flaw in the method used by the investigators?

(A) The personality test was not administered or scored personally by the investigators.
(B) People born under astrological signs other than Gemini have been judged by astrologers to be much less sociable than those born under Gemini.
(C) The personal impressions the investigators first formed of other people have tended to be confirmed by the investigators' later experience of those people.
(D) There is not likely to be a greater proportion of people born under the sign of Gemini on the street than in the population as a whole.
(E) People who are not sociable and extroverted are not likely to agree to participate in such an investigation.

9. Pamela: Physicians training for a medical specialty serve as resident staff physicians in hospitals. They work such long hours—up to 36 consecutive hours—that fatigue impairs their ability to make the best medical decisions during the final portion of their shifts.

Quincy: Thousands of physicians now practicing have been trained according to the same regimen, and records show they generally made good medical decisions during their training periods. Why should what has worked in the past be changed now?

Which one of the following, if true, is the most effective counter Pamela might make to Quincy's argument?

(A) The basic responsibilities of resident staff physicians in hospitals have not changed substantially over the past few decades.
(B) Because medical reimbursement policies now pay for less recuperation time in hospitals, patients in hospitals are, on the average, more seriously ill during their stays than in the past.
(C) It is important that emergency-room patients receive continuity of physician care, insofar as possible, over the critical period after admission, generally 24 hours.
(D) The load of work on resident physicians-in-training varies according to the medical specialty for which each is being trained.
(E) The training of physicians should include observation and recognition of the signs indicating a hospitalized patient's progress or decline over a period of at least 36 hours.

10. In Brazil, side-by-side comparisons of Africanized honeybees and the native honeybees have shown that the Africanized bees are far superior honey producers. Therefore, there is no reason to fear that domestic commercial honey production will decline in the United States if local honeybees are displaced by Africanized honeybees.

Each of the following, if true, would weaken the argument EXCEPT:

(A) The honeybees native to Brazil are not of the same variety as those most frequently used in the commercial beekeeping industry in the United States.

(B) Commercial honey production is far more complicated and expensive with Africanized honeybees than it is with the more docile honeybees common in the United States.

(C) If Africanized honeybees replace local honeybees, certain types of ornamental trees will be less effectively pollinated.

(D) In the United States a significant proportion of the commercial honey supply comes from hobby beekeepers, many of whom are likely to abandon beekeeping with the influx of Africanized bees.

(E) The area of Brazil where the comparative study was done is far better suited to the foraging habits of the Africanized honeybees than are most areas of the United States.

11. "DNA fingerprinting" is a recently-introduced biochemical procedure that uses a pattern derived from a person's genetic material to match a suspect's genetic material against that of a specimen from a crime scene. Proponents have claimed astronomically high odds against obtaining a match by chance alone. These odds are based on an assumption that there is independence between the different characteristics represented by a single pattern.

Which one of the following, if true, casts the most doubt on the claim of the proponents of DNA fingerprinting?

(A) The large amount of genetic material that people share with all other people and with other animals is not included in the DNA fingerprinting procedure.

(B) There is a generally accepted theoretical basis for interpreting the patterns produced by the procedure.

(C) In the whole population there are various different subgroups, within each of which certain sets of genetic characteristics are shared.

(D) The skill required of laboratory technicians performing the DNA fingerprinting procedure is not extraordinary.

(E) In the investigation of certain genetic diseases, the techniques used in DNA fingerprinting have traced the transmission of the diseases among the living members of very large families.

12. Behind the hope that computers can replace teachers is the idea that the student's understanding of the subject being taught consists in knowing facts and rules, the job of a teacher being to make the facts and rules explicit and convey them to the student, either by practice drills or by coaching. If that were indeed the way the mind works, the teacher could transfer facts and rules to the computer, which would replace the teacher as drillmaster and coach. But since understanding does not consist merely of knowing facts and rules, but of the grasp of the general concepts underlying them, the hope that the computer will eventually replace the teacher is fundamentally misguided.

    Which one of the following, if true, would most seriously undermine the author's conclusion that computers will not eventually be able to replace teachers?

    (A) Computers are as good as teachers at drilling students on facts and rules.
    (B) The job of a teacher is to make students understand the general concepts underlying specific facts and rules.
    (C) It is possible to program computers so that they can teach the understanding of general concepts that underlie specific facts and rules.
    (D) Because they are not subject to human error, computers are better than teachers at conveying facts and rules.
    (E) It is not possible for students to develop an understanding of the concepts underlying facts and rules through practice drills and coaching.

13. The high cost of production is severely limiting which operas are available to the public. These costs necessitate reliance on large corporate sponsors, who in return demand that only the most famous operas be produced. Determining which operas will be produced should rest only with ticket purchasers at the box office, not with large corporate sponsors. If we reduce production budgets so that operas can be supported exclusively by box-office receipts and donations from individuals, then the public will be able to see less famous operas.

    Which one of the following, if true, would weaken the argument?

    (A) A few opera ticket purchasers go to the opera for the sake of going to the opera, not to see specific operatic productions.
    (B) The reduction of opera production budgets would not reduce the desire of large corporate sponsors to support operas.
    (C) Without the support of large corporate sponsors, opera companies could not afford to produce any but the most famous of operas.
    (D) Large corporate sponsors will stop supporting opera productions if they are denied control over which operas will be produced.
    (E) The combination of individual donations and box-office receipts cannot match the amounts of money obtained through sponsorship by large corporations.

14. Nature constantly adjusts the atmospheric carbon level. An increase in the level causes the atmosphere to hold more heat, which causes more water to evaporate from the oceans, which causes increased rain. Rain washes some carbon from the air into the oceans, where it eventually becomes part of the seabed. A decrease in atmospheric carbon causes the atmosphere to hold less heat, which causes decreased evaporation from the oceans, which causes less rain, and thus less carbon is washed into the oceans. Yet some environmentalists worry that burning fossil fuels may raise atmospheric carbon to a dangerous level. It is true that a sustained increase would threaten human life. But the environmentalists should relax—nature will continually adjust the carbon level.

    Which one of the following, if true, would most weaken the argument in the passage?

    (A) Plant life cannot survive without atmospheric carbon.
    (B) It is not clear that breathing excess carbon in the atmosphere will have a negative effect on human life.
    (C) Carbon is part of the chemical "blanket" that keeps the Earth warm enough to sustain human life.
    (D) Breathing by animals releases almost 30 times as much carbon as does the burning of fossil fuels.
    (E) The natural adjustment process, which occurs over millions of years, allows wide fluctuations in the carbon level in the short term.

15. Rita: The original purpose of government farm-subsidy programs was to provide income stability for small family farmers, but most farm-subsidy money goes to a few farmers with large holdings. Payments to farmers whose income, before subsidies, is greater than $100,000 a year should be stopped.

    Thomas: It would be impossible to administer such a cutoff point. Subsidies are needed during the planting and growing season, but farmers do not know their income for a given calendar year until tax returns are calculated and submitted the following April.

    Which one of the following, if true, is the strongest counter Rita can make to Thomas' objection?

    (A) It has become difficult for small farmers to obtain bank loans to be repaid later by money from subsidies.
    (B) Having such a cutoff point would cause some farmers whose income would otherwise exceed $100,000 to reduce their plantings.
    (C) The income of a farmer varies because weather and market prices are not stable from year to year.
    (D) If subsidy payments to large farmers were eliminated, the financial condition of the government would improve.
    (E) Subsidy cutoffs can be determined on the basis of income for the preceding year.

16. Oil analysts predict that if the price of oil falls by half, the consumer's purchase price for gasoline made from this oil will also fall by half.

    Which one of the following, if true, would cast the most serious doubt on the prediction made by the oil analysts?

    (A) Improved automobile technology and new kinds of fuel for cars have enabled some drivers to use less gasoline.
    (B) Gasoline manufacturers will not expand their profit margins.
    (C) There are many different gasoline companies that compete with each other to provide the most attractive price to consumers.
    (D) Studies in several countries show that the amount of gasoline purchased by consumers initially rises after the price of gasoline has fallen.
    (E) Refining costs, distribution costs, and taxes, none of which varies significantly with oil prices, constitute a large portion of the price of gasoline.

17. A survey was recently conducted among ferry passengers on the North Sea. Among the results was this: more of those who had taken anti-seasickness medication before their trip reported symptoms of seasickness than those who had not taken such medication. It is clear, then, that despite claims by drug companies that clinical tests show the contrary, people would be better off not taking anti-seasickness medications.

Which one of the following, if true, would most weaken the conclusion above?

(A) Given rough enough weather, most ferry passengers will have some symptoms of seasickness.
(B) The clinical tests reported by the drug companies were conducted by the drug companies' staffs.
(C) People who do not take anti-seasickness medication are just as likely to respond to a survey on seasickness as people who do.
(D) The seasickness symptoms of the people who took anti-seasickness medication would have been more severe had they not taken the medication.
(E) People who have spent money on anti-seasickness medication are less likely to admit symptoms of seasickness than those who have not.

18. The soaring prices of scholarly and scientific journals have forced academic libraries used only by academic researchers to drastically reduce their list of subscriptions. Some have suggested that in each academic discipline subscription decisions should be determined solely by a journal's usefulness in that discipline, measured by the frequency with which it is cited in published writings by researchers in the discipline.

Which one of the following, if true, most seriously calls into question the suggestion described above?

(A) The nonacademic readership of a scholarly or scientific journal can be accurately gauged by the number of times articles appearing in it are cited in daily newspapers and popular magazines.
(B) The average length of a journal article in some sciences, such as physics, is less than half the average length of a journal article in some other academic disciplines, such as history.
(C) The increasingly expensive scholarly journals are less and less likely to be available to the general public from nonacademic public libraries.
(D) Researchers often will not cite a journal article that has influenced their work if they think that the journal in which it appears is not highly regarded by the leading researchers in the mainstream of the discipline.
(E) In some academic disciplines, controversies which begin in the pages of one journal spill over into articles in other journals that are widely read by researchers in the discipline.

19. With the passage of the new tax reform laws, the annual tax burden on low-income taxpayers will be reduced, on average, by anywhere from $100 to $300. Clearly, tax reform is in the interest of low-income taxpayers.

    Which one of the following, if true, most undermines the conclusion above?

    (A) Tax reform, by simplifying the tax code, will save many people the expense of having an accountant do their taxes.
    (B) Tax reform, by eliminating tax incentives to build rental housing, will push up rents an average of about $40 per month for low income taxpayers.
    (C) Low-income taxpayers have consistently voted for those political candidates who are strong advocates of tax reform.
    (D) The new tax reform laws will permit low- and middle-income taxpayers to deduct child-care expenses from their taxes.
    (E) Under the new tax reform laws, many low income taxpayers who now pay taxes will no longer be required to do so.

20. It is more desirable to have some form of socialized medicine than a system of medical care relying on the private sector. Socialized medicine is more broadly accessible than is a private-sector system. In addition, since countries with socialized medicine have a lower infant mortality rate than do countries with a system relying entirely on the private sector, socialized medicine seems to be technologically superior.

    Which one of the following best indicates a flaw in the argument about the technological superiority of socialized medicine?

    (A) The lower infant mortality rate might be due to the system's allowing greater access to medical care.
    (B) There is no necessary connection between the economic system of socialism and technological achievement.
    (C) Infant mortality is a reliable indicator of the quality of medical care for children.
    (D) No list is presented of the countries whose infant mortality statistics are summarized under the two categories, "socialized" and "private-sector."
    (E) The argument presupposes the desirability of socialized medicine, which is what the argument seeks to establish.

21. Prominent business executives often play active roles in United States presidential campaigns as fund raisers or backroom strategists, but few actually seek to become president themselves. Throughout history the great majority of those who have sought to become president have been lawyers, military leaders, or full-time politicians. This is understandable, for the personality and skills that make for success in business do not make for success in politics. Business is largely hierarchical, whereas politics is coordinative. As a result, business executives tend to be uncomfortable with compromises and power-sharing, which are inherent in politics.

    Which one of the following, if true, most seriously weakens the proposed explanation of why business executives do not run for president?

    (A) Many of the most active presidential fund raisers and backroom strategists are themselves politicians.
    (B) Military leaders are generally no more comfortable with compromises and power sharing than are business executives.
    (C) Some of the skills needed to become a successful lawyer are different from some of those needed to become a successful military leader.
    (D) Some former presidents have engaged in business ventures after leaving office.
    (E) Some hierarchically structured companies have been major financial supporters of candidates for president.

22. Compared to nonprofit hospitals of the same size, investor-owned hospitals require less public investment in the form of tax breaks, use fewer employees, and have higher occupancy levels. It can therefore be concluded that investor-owned hospitals are a better way of delivering medical care than are nonprofit hospitals.

    Which one of the following, if true, most undermines the conclusion drawn above?

    (A) Nonprofit hospitals charge more per bed than do investor-owned hospitals.
    (B) Patients in nonprofit hospitals recover more quickly than do patients with comparable illnesses in investor-owned hospitals.
    (C) Nonprofit hospitals do more fundraising than do investor-owned hospitals.
    (D) Doctors at nonprofit hospitals earn higher salaries than do similarly-qualified doctors at investor-owned hospitals.
    (E) Nonprofit hospitals receive more donations than do investor-owned hospitals.

23. Two paleontologists, Dr. Tyson and Dr. Rees, disagree over the interpretation of certain footprints that were left among other footprints in hardened volcanic ash at site G. Dr. Tyson claims they are clearly early hominid footprints since they show human characteristics: a squarish heel and a big toe immediately adjacent to the next toe. However, since the footprints indicate that if hominids made those prints they would have had to walk in an unexpected cross-stepping manner, by placing the left foot to the right of the right foot, Dr. Rees rejects Dr. Tyson's conclusion.

Which one of the following, if true, most seriously undermines Dr. Tyson's conclusion?

(A) The footprints showing human characteristics were clearly those of at least two distinct individuals.
(B) Certain species of bears had feet very like human feet, except that the outside toe on each foot was the biggest toe and the innermost toe was the smallest toe.
(C) Footprints shaped like a human's that do not show a cross-stepping pattern exist at site M, which is a mile away from site G, and the two sets of footprints are contemporaneous.
(D) When the moist volcanic ash became sealed under additional layers of ash before hardening, some details of some of the footprints were erased.
(E) Most of the other footprints at site G were of animals with hooves.

24. Auto industry executive: Statistics show that cars that were built smaller after 1977 to make them more fuel-efficient had a higher incidence of accident-related fatalities than did their earlier, larger counterparts. For this reason we oppose recent guidelines that would require us to produce cars with higher fuel efficiency.

Which one of the following, if true, would constitute the strongest objection to the executive's argument?

(A) Even after 1977, large automobiles were frequently involved in accidents that caused death or serious injury.
(B) Although fatalities in accidents involving small cars have increased since 1977, the number of accidents has decreased.
(C) New computerized fuel systems can enable large cars to meet fuel efficiency standards established by the recent guidelines.
(D) Modern technology can make small cars more fuel-efficient today than at any other time in their production history.
(E) Fuel efficiency in models of large cars rose immediately after 1977 but has been declining ever since.

25. Older United States automobiles have been identified as contributing disproportionately to global air pollution. The requirement in many jurisdictions that automobiles pass emission-control inspections has had the effect of taking many such automobiles out of service in the United States, as they fail inspection and their owners opt to buy newer automobiles. Thus the burden of pollution such older United States automobiles contribute to the global atmosphere will be gradually reduced over the next decade.

Which one of the following, if true, most seriously weakens the argument?

(A) It is impossible to separate the air of one country or jurisdiction from that of others, since air currents circle the globe.
(B) When automobiles that are now new become older, they will, because of a design change, cause less air pollution than older automobiles do now.
(C) There is a thriving market for used older United States automobiles that are exported to regions that have no emission-control regulations.
(D) The number of jurisdictions in the United States requiring automobiles to pass emission-control inspections is no longer increasing.
(E) Even if all the older automobiles in the United States were retired from service, air pollution from United States automobiles could still increase if the total number of automobiles in use should increase significantly.

26. There are about 75 brands of microwave popcorn on the market; altogether, they account for a little over half of the money from sales of microwave food products. It takes three minutes to pop corn in the microwave, compared to seven minutes to pop corn conventionally. Yet by weight, microwave popcorn typically costs over five times as much as conventional popcorn. Judging by the popularity of microwave popcorn, many people are willing to pay a high price for just a little additional convenience.

Which one of the following statements, if true, would call into question the conclusion in the passage?

(A) More than 50 percent of popcorn purchasers buy conventional popcorn rather than microwave popcorn.
(B) Most people who prefer microwave popcorn do so because it is less fattening than popcorn that is popped conventionally in oil.
(C) The price of microwave popcorn reflects its packaging more than it reflects the quality of the popcorn contained in the package.
(D) The ratio of unpopped kernels to popped kernels is generally the same whether popcorn is popped in a microwave or conventionally in oil.
(E) Because microwave popcorn contains additives not contained in conventional popcorn, microwave popcorn weighs more than a equal volume of conventional popcorn.

27. Valitania's long-standing practice of paying high salaries to its elected politicians has had a disastrous effect on the level of integrity among politicians in that country. This is because the prospect of earning a high salary is always attractive to anyone whose primary aim in life is to make money, so that inevitably the wrong people must have been attracted into Valitanian politics: people who are more interested in making money than in serving the needs of the nation.

Which one of the following, if true, would weaken the argument?

(A) Many Valitanian candidates for elected office spend some of their own money to finance their campaigns.
(B) Most Valitanian elective offices have four-year terms.
(C) No more people compete for elected office when officeholders are paid well than when they are paid poorly.
(D) Only politicians who rely on their offices for income tend to support policies that advance their own selfish interests.
(E) Most of those who are currently Valitanian politicians could have obtained better-paid work outside politics.

28. The use of money causes a civilization to decline. That this is true is shown by the way the troubles of Western civilization began with the invention of money. While real money (gold and silver) is bad enough, imitation money (paper money) is a horror. The decline of Western civilization exactly parallels the increasing use of money—both real money and worthless paper money—as a substitute for things of intrinsic value.

Which one of the following, if true, could contribute most to a refutation of the argument?

(A) People prefer using money to having a system in which goods are bartered for other goods of equal intrinsic value.
(B) Eastern cultures have used money, and Eastern civilizations have not declined.
(C) The use of paper money encourages disregard for the value of work because the money itself has no intrinsic value.
(D) The rate of exchange between gold and paper money has fluctuated greatly in Western civilization.
(E) Some employers exchange goods for their employees' services in order to avoid the exchange of money.

29. In an attempt to counter complaints that a certain pesticide is potentially hazardous to humans if absorbed into edible plants, the pesticide manufacturer has advertised that "ounce for ounce, the active ingredient in this pesticide is less toxic than the active ingredient in mouthwash."

Which one of the following, if true, indicates a weakness in the manufacturer's argument?

(A) The ounce-for-ounce toxicity of the active ingredient in mouthwash is less than that of most products meant for external use by humans, such as nail polish or other cosmetics.
(B) The quantity of toxins humans ingest by consuming plants treated with the pesticide is, on average, much higher than the quantity of toxins humans ingest by using mouthwash.
(C) The container in which the pesticide is packaged clearly identifies the toxic ingredients and carries warnings about their potential danger to humans.
(D) On average, the toxins present in the pesticide take longer than the toxins present in mouthwash to reach harmful levels in the human body.
(E) Since the government began to regulate the pesticide industry over ten years ago, there has been a growing awareness of the dangers of toxins used in pesticides.

30. Arguing that there was no trade between Europe and East Asia in the early Middle Ages because there are no written records of such trade is like arguing that the yeti, an apelike creature supposedly existing in the Himalayas, does not exist because there have been no scientifically confirmed sightings. A verifiable sighting of the yeti would prove that the creature does exist, but the absence of sightings cannot prove that it does not.

    Which one of the following considerations, if true, best counters the argument?

    (A) Most of the evidence for the existence of trade between Europe and East Asia in the early Middle Ages is archaeological and therefore does not rely on written records.
    (B) Although written records of trade in East Asia in the early Middle Ages survived, there are almost no European documents from that period that mention trade at all.
    (C) Any trade between Europe and East Asia in the early Middle Ages would necessarily have been of very low volume and would have involved high-priced items, such as precious metals and silk.
    (D) There have been no confirmed sightings of the yeti, but there is indirect evidence, such as footprints, which if it is accepted as authentic would establish the yeti's existence.
    (E) There are surviving European and East Asian written records from the early Middle Ages that do not mention trade between the two regions but would have been very likely to do so if this trade had existed.

31. Samples from the floor of a rock shelter in Pennsylvania were dated by analyzing the carbon they contained. The dates assigned to samples associated with human activities formed a consistent series, beginning with the present and going back in time, a series that was correlated with the depth from which the samples came. The oldest and deepest sample was dated at 19,650 years before the present, plus or minus 2,400 years. Skeptics, viewing that date as too early and inconsistent with the accepted date of human migration into North America, suggested that the samples could have been contaminated by dissolved "old carbon" carried by percolating groundwater from nearby coal deposits.

    Which one of the following considerations, if true, argues most strongly against the suggestion of the skeptics?

    (A) No likely mechanism of contamination involving percolating groundwater would have affected the deeper samples from the site without affecting the uppermost sample.
    (B) Not every application of the carbon-dating procedure has led to results that have been generally acceptable to scientists.
    (C) There is no evidence that people were using coal for fuel at any time when the deepest layer might have been laid down.
    (D) No sample in the series, when retested by the carbon-dating procedure, was assigned an earlier date than that assigned to a sample from a layer above it.
    (E) No North American site besides the one in Pennsylvania has ever yielded a sample to which the carbon-dating procedure assigned a date that was comparably ancient.

32. Before the printing press, books could be purchased only in expensive manuscript copies. The printing press produced books that were significantly less expensive than the manuscript editions. The public's demand for printed books in the first years after the invention of the printing press was many times greater than demand had been for manuscript copies. This increase demonstrates that there was a dramatic jump in the number of people who learned how to read in the years after publishers first started producing books on the printing press.

Which one of the following statements, if true, casts doubt on the argument?

(A) During the first years after the invention of the printing press, letter writing by people who wrote without the assistance of scribes or clerks exhibited a dramatic increase.

(B) Books produced on the printing press are often found with written comments in the margins in the handwriting of the people who owned the books.

(C) In the first years after the printing press was invented, printed books were purchased primarily by people who had always bought and read expensive manuscripts but could afford a greater number of printed books for the same money.

(D) Books that were printed on the printing press in the first years after its invention often circulated among friends in informal reading clubs or libraries.

(E) The first printed books published after the invention of the printing press would have been useless to illiterate people, since the books had virtually no illustrations.

33. Our tomato soup provides good nutrition: for instance, a warm bowl of it contains more units of vitamin C than does a serving of apricots or fresh carrots!

The advertisement is misleading if which one of the following is true?

(A) Few people depend exclusively on apricots and carrots to supply vitamin C to their diets.

(B) A liquid can lose vitamins if it stands in contact with the air for a protracted period of time.

(C) Tomato soup contains important nutrients other than vitamin C.

(D) The amount of vitamin C provided by a serving of the advertised soup is less than the amount furnished by a serving of fresh strawberries.

(E) Apricots and fresh carrots are widely known to be nutritious, but their contribution consists primarily in providing a large amount of vitamin A, not a large amount of vitamin C.

34. In a study of the effect of radiation from nuclear weapons plants on people living in areas near them, researchers compared death rates in the areas near the plants with death rates in areas that had no such plants. Finding no difference in these rates, the researchers concluded that radiation from the nuclear weapons plants poses no health hazards to people living near them.

Which one of the following, if true, most seriously weakens the researchers' argument?

(A) Nuclear power plants were not included in the study.

(B) The areas studied had similar death rates before and after the nuclear weapons plants were built.

(C) Exposure to nuclear radiation can cause many serious diseases that do not necessarily result in death.

(D) Only a small number of areas have nuclear weapons plants.

(E) The researchers did not study the possible health hazards of radiation on people who were employed at the nuclear weapons plants if those employees did not live in the study areas.

35. If the public library shared by the adjacent towns of Redville and Glenwood were relocated from the library's current, overcrowded building in central Redville to a larger, available building in central Glenwood, the library would then be within walking distance of a larger number of library users. That is because there are many more people living in central Glenwood than in central Redville, and people generally will walk to the library only if it is located close to their homes.

Which one of the following, if true, most seriously weakens the argument?

(A) Many more people who currently walk to the library live in central Redville than in central Glenwood.
(B) The number of people living in central Glenwood who would use the library if it were located there is smaller than the number of people living in central Redville who currently use the library.
(C) The number of people using the public library would continue to increase steadily if the library were moved to Glenwood.
(D) Most of the people who currently either drive to the library or take public transportation to reach it would continue to do so if the library were moved to central Glenwood.
(E) Most of the people who currently walk to the library would remain library users if the library were relocated to central Glenwood.

36. Most disposable plastic containers are now labeled with a code number (from 1 to 9) indicating the type or quality of the plastic. Plastics with the lowest code numbers are the easiest for recycling plants to recycle and are thus the most likely to be recycled after use rather than dumped in landfills. Plastics labeled with the highest numbers are only rarely recycled. Consumers can make a significant long-term reduction in the amount of waste that goes unrecycled, therefore, by refusing to purchase those products packaged in plastic containers labeled with the highest code numbers.

Which one of the following, if true, most seriously undermines the conclusion above?

(A) The cost of collecting, sorting, and recycling discarded plastics is currently higher than the cost of manufacturing new plastics from virgin materials.
(B) Many consumers are unaware of the codes that are stamped on the plastic containers.
(C) A plastic container almost always has a higher code number after it is recycled than it had before recycling because the recycling process causes a degradation of the quality of the plastic.
(D) Products packaged in plastics with the lowest code numbers are often more expensive than those packaged in the higher-numbered plastics.
(E) Communities that collect all discarded plastic containers for potential recycling later dump in landfills plastics with higher-numbered codes only when it is clear that no recycler will take them.

37. Purebred dogs are prone to genetically determined abnormalities. Although such abnormalities often can be corrected by surgery, the cost can reach several thousand dollars. Since nonpurebred dogs rarely suffer from genetically determined abnormalities, potential dog owners who want to reduce the risk of incurring costly medical bills for their pets would be well advised to choose nonpurebred dogs.

Which one of the following, if true, most seriously weakens the argument?

(A) Most genetically determined abnormalities in dogs do not seriously affect a dog's general well-being.
(B) All dogs, whether purebred or nonpurebred, are subject to the same common nongenetically determined diseases.
(C) Purebred dogs tend to have shorter natural life spans than do nonpurebred dogs.
(D) The purchase price of nonpurebred dogs tends to be lower than the purchase price of purebred dogs.
(E) A dog that does not have genetically determined abnormalities may nevertheless have offspring with such abnormalities.

38. When a study of aspirin's ability to prevent heart attacks in humans yielded positive results, researchers immediately submitted those results to a medical journal, which published them six weeks later. Had the results been published sooner, many of the heart attacks that occurred during the delay could have been prevented.

The conclusion drawn above would be most undermined if it were true that

(A) the medical journal's staff worked overtime in order to publish the study's results as soon as possible
(B) studies of aspirin's usefulness in reducing heart attacks in laboratory animals remain inconclusive
(C) people who take aspirin regularly suffer a higher-than-average incidence of stomach ulcers
(D) the medical journal's official policy is to publish articles only after an extensive review process
(E) a person's risk of suffering a heart attack drops only after that person has taken aspirin regularly for two years

39. When butterfat was considered nutritious and healthful, a law was enacted requiring that manufacturers use the term "imitation butter" to indicate butter whose butterfat content had been diminished through the addition of water. Today, it is known that the high cholesterol content of butterfat makes it harmful to human health. Since the public should be encouraged to eat foods with lower rather than higher butterfat content and since the term "imitation" with its connotations of falsity deters many people from purchasing products so designated, manufacturers who wish to give reduced-butterfat butter the more appealing name of "lite butter" should be allowed to do so.

Which one of the following, if true, most seriously undermines the argument?

(A) The manufacturers who prefer to use the word "lite" instead of "imitation" are motivated principally by the financial interest of their stockholders.
(B) The manufacturers who wish to call their product "lite butter" plan to change the composition of the product so that it contains more water than it now does.
(C) Some individuals who need to reduce their intake of cholesterol are not deterred from using the reduced-butterfat product by the negative connotations of the term "imitation."
(D) Cholesterol is only one of many factors that contribute to the types of health problems with which the consumption of excessive amounts of cholesterol is often associated.
(E) Most people deterred from eating "imitation butter" because of its name choose alternatives with a lower butterfat content than this product has.

40. A favored theory to explain the extinction of dinosaurs, together with many other species, has been the globally catastrophic collision of a large asteroid with the Earth. Supporting evidence is an extraterrestrial chemical element in a layer of dust found worldwide at a geological level laid down contemporaneously with the supposed event. A new competing theory contends that any asteroid impact was irrelevant, because it was massive volcanic activity that caused the extinctions by putting enough dust into the atmosphere to cool the planet. The Deccan region of India contains extensive volcanic flows that occurred within the same time period as the supposed asteroid impact and the extinctions.

Which one of the following, if true, most strongly indicates that the asteroid-impact theory is at least incomplete, if not false?

(A) Large concentrations of dinosaur nests with fossil eggs found in Alberta indicate that at least some species of dinosaurs congregated in large groups during some part of their lives.
(B) Dinosaur remains indicate that some species of dinosaur could have migrated in herds over wide ranges, so that they could have traveled to escape the local effects of certain catastrophes.
(C) Legends from many cultures, such as the Greek legend that Cadmus raised an army by sowing dragons' teeth in the ground, show that various ancient peoples worldwide were familiar with the fossils of dinosaurs.
(D) In the Gobi desert in China, where now only small animals can eke out an existence, fossil dinosaur skeletons 27 feet long were found in circumstances indicating that the climate there was as dry when the dinosaurs lived as it is now.
(E) The fossil record in Montana from below the layer of extraterrestrial dust shows a diminution over time in dinosaur species from 35 to 13, and dinosaur teeth found above the dust layer show a diminution in species from 13 to 5.

41. Fares on the city-run public buses in Greenville are subsidized by city tax revenues, but among the beneficiaries of the low fares are many people who commute from outside the city to jobs in Greenville. Some city councillors argue that city taxes should be used primarily to benefit the people who pay them, and therefore that bus fares should be raised enough to cover the cost of the service.

Each of the following, if true, would weaken the argument advanced by the city councillors EXCEPT:

(A) Many businesses whose presence in the city is beneficial to the city's taxpayers would relocate outside the city if public-transit fares were more expensive.
(B) By providing commuters with economic incentives to drive to work, higher transit fares would worsen air pollution in Greenville and increase the cost of maintaining the city's streets.
(C) Increasing transit fares would disadvantage those residents of the city whose low incomes make them exempt from city taxes, and all city councillors agree that these residents should be able to take advantage of city-run services.
(D) Voters in the city, many of whom benefit from the low transit fares, are strongly opposed to increasing local taxes.
(E) People who work in Greenville and earn wages above the nationally mandated minimum all pay the city wage tax of 5 percent.

42. A physician who is too thorough in conducting a medical checkup is likely to subject the patient to the discomfort and expense of unnecessary tests. One who is not thorough enough is likely to miss some serious problem and therefore give the patient a false sense of security. It is difficult for physicians to judge exactly how thorough they should be. Therefore, it is generally unwise for patients to have medical checkups when they do not feel ill.

Which one of the following, if true, would most seriously weaken the argument in the passage?

(A) Some serious diseases in their early stages have symptoms that physicians can readily detect, although patients are not aware of any problem.
(B) Under the pressure of reduced reimbursements, physicians have been reducing the average amount of time they spend on each medical checkup.
(C) Patients not medically trained are unable to judge for themselves what degree of thoroughness is appropriate for physicians in conducting medical checkups.
(D) Many people are financially unable to afford regular medical checkups.
(E) Some physicians sometimes exercise exactly the right degree of thoroughness in performing a medical checkup.

43. The labeling of otherwise high-calorie foods as "sugar-free," based on the replacement of all sugar by artificial sweeteners, should be prohibited by law. Such a prohibition is indicated because many consumers who need to lose weight will interpret the label "sugar-free" as synonymous with "low in calories" and harm themselves by building weight-loss diets around foods labeled "sugar-free." Manufacturers of sugar-free foods are well aware of this tendency on the part of consumers.

Which one of the following, if true, provides the strongest basis for challenging the conclusion in the passage?

(A) Food manufacturers would respond to a ban on the label "sugar-free" by reducing the calories in sugar-free products by enough to be able to promote those products as diet foods.
(B) Individuals who are diabetic need to be able to identify products that contain no sugar by reference to product labels that expressly state that the product contains no sugar.
(C) Consumers are sometimes slow to notice changes in product labels unless those changes are themselves well advertised.
(D) Consumers who have chosen a particular weight-loss diet tend to persist with this diet if they have been warned not to expect very quick results.
(E) Exactly what appears on a product label is less important to consumer behavior than is the relative visual prominence of the different pieces of information that the label contains.

44. The format of network television news programs generally allows advocates of a point of view only 30 seconds to convey their message. Consequently, regular watchers become accustomed to thinking of issues in terms only of slogans and catch phrases, and so the expectation of careful discussion of public issues gradually disappears from their awareness. The format of newspaper stories, on the other hand, leads readers to pursue details of stories headed by the most important facts and so has the opposite effect on regular readers, that of maintaining the expectation of careful discussion of public issues. Therefore, in contrast to regular newspaper reading, regular watching of network television news programs increases the tendency to think of public issues in oversimplified terms.

Which one of the following, if true, most seriously weakens the argument?

(A) Regular watchers of network television news programs are much more likely than other people to be habitual readers of newspapers.

(B) Including any 30-second quotations from proponents of diverse views, the total amount of time devoted to a single topic on regular network television news programs averages less than one and a half minutes.

(C) The format of network television news programs does not include roundtable discussion of issues among informed proponents of diverse views.

(D) Television news reports tend to devote equal time to discussion of opposing views.

(E) People who watch the most television, measured in average number of hours of watching per week, tend not to be regular readers of newspapers.

45. A recent report on an environmental improvement program was criticized for focusing solely on pragmatic solutions to the large number of significant problems that plague the program instead of seriously trying to produce a coherent vision for the future of the program. In response the report's authors granted that the critics had raised a valid point but explained that, to do anything at all, the program needed continued government funding, and that to get such funding the program first needed to regain a reputation for competence.

Which one of the following, if true, would best serve the critics of the report in their attempt to undermine the position taken by the report's authors?

(A) The government does not actually provide a full 100 percent of the program's funding.

(B) The program will continue to have numerous serious problems precisely because it lacks a coherent vision for its future.

(C) The program had a coherent vision at its inception, but that vision has proved impossible to sustain.

(D) The government has threatened to cut off funding for the program but has not acted yet on this threat.

(E) The program has acquired a worse reputation for incompetence than it deserves.

WEAKEN

46. Why should the government, rather than industry or universities, provide the money to put a network of supercomputers in place? Because there is a range of problems that can be attacked only with the massive data-managing capacity of a supercomputer network. No business or university has the resources to purchase by itself enough machines for a whole network, and no business or university wants to invest in a part of a network if no mechanism exists for coordinating establishment of the network as a whole.

Which one of the following indicates a weakness in the argument?

(A) It does not furnish a way in which the dilemma concerning the establishment of the network can be resolved.
(B) It does not establish the impossibility of creating a supercomputer network as an international network.
(C) It fails to address the question of who would maintain the network if the government, rather than industry or universities, provides the money for establishing it.
(D) It takes for granted and without justification that it would enhance national preeminence in science for the government to provide the network.
(E) It overlooks the possibility that businesses or universities, or both, could cooperate to build the network.

47. Large quantities of lead dust can be released during renovations in houses with walls painted with lead-based paint. Because the dust puts occupants at high risk of lead poisoning, such renovations should be done only in unoccupied houses by contractors who are experienced in removing all traces of lead from houses and who have the equipment to protect themselves from lead dust. Even when warned, however, many people will not pay to have someone else do renovations they believe they could do less expensively themselves. Therefore, Homeowners' Journal should run an article giving information to homeowners on how to reduce the risk of lead poisoning associated with do-it-yourself renovation.

Which one of the following, if true, argues most strongly against the passage's recommendation about an article?

(A) Most homeowners know whether or not the walls of their houses are painted with lead-based paint, even if the walls were painted by previous owners.
(B) Most people who undertake do-it-yourself renovation projects do so for the satisfaction of doing the work themselves and so are unlikely to hire a professional to do that sort of work.
(C) Whenever information on do-it-yourself home renovation is published, many people who would otherwise hire professionals decide to perform the renovations themselves, even when there are risks involved.
(D) In many areas, it is difficult to find professional renovators who have the equipment and qualifications to perform safely renovations involving lead dust.
(E) When professionally done home renovations are no more expensive than do-it-yourself renovations, most people choose to have their homes renovated by professionals.

48. Logging industry official: Harvesting trees from old-growth forests for use in manufacture can reduce the amount of carbon dioxide in the atmosphere, since when large old trees die in the forest they decompose, releasing their stored carbon dioxide. Harvesting old-growth forests would, moreover, make room for rapidly growing young trees, which absorb more carbon dioxide from the atmosphere than do trees in old-growth forests.

Which one of the following, if true, most seriously weakens the official's argument?

(A) Many old-growth forests are the home of thousands of animal species that would be endangered if the forests were to be destroyed.
(B) Much of the organic matter from old-growth trees, unusable as lumber, is made into products that decompose rapidly.
(C) A young tree contains less than half the amount of carbon dioxide that is stored in an old tree of the same species.
(D) Much of the carbon dioxide present in forests is eventually released when wood and other organic debris found on the forest floor decompose.
(E) It can take many years for the trees of a newly planted forest to reach the size of those found in existing old-growth forests.

49. When the supply of a given resource dwindles, alternative technologies allowing the use of different resources develop, and demand for the resource that was in short supply naturally declines. Then the existing supplies of that resource satisfy whatever demand remains. Among the once-dwindling resources that are now in more than adequate supply are flint for arrowheads, trees usable for schooner masts, and good mules. Because new technologies constantly replace old ones, we can never run out of important natural resources.

Which one of the following, if true, most seriously undermines the conclusion?

(A) The masts and hulls of some sailing ships built today are still made of wood.
(B) There are considerably fewer mules today than there were 100 years ago.
(C) The cost of some new technologies is often so high that the companies developing them might actually lose money at first.
(D) Dwindling supplies of a natural resource often result in that resource's costing more to use.
(E) The biological requirements for substances like clean air and clean water are unaffected by technological change.

50. Morris High School has introduced a policy designed to improve the working conditions of its new teachers. As a result of this policy, only one-quarter of all part-time teachers now quit during their first year. However, a third of all full-time teachers now quit during their first year. Thus, more full-time than part-time teachers at Morris now quit during their first year.

The argument's reasoning is questionable because the argument fails to rule out the possibility that

(A) before the new policy was instituted, more part-time than full-time teachers at Morris High School used to quit during their first year
(B) before the new policy was instituted, the same number of full-time teachers as part-time teachers at Morris High School used to quit during their first year
(C) Morris High School employs more new full-time teachers than new part-time teachers
(D) Morris High School employs more new part-time teachers than new full-time teachers
(E) Morris High School employs the same number of new part-time as new full-time teachers

51. *Salmonella* is a food-borne microorganism that can cause intestinal illness. The illness is sometimes fatal, especially if not identified quickly and treated. Conventional *Salmonella* tests on food samples are slow and can miss unusual strains of the microorganism. A new test identifies the presence or absence of *Salmonella* by the one piece of genetic material common to all strains. Clearly, public health officials would be well advised to replace the previous *Salmonella* tests with the new test.

Which one of the following, if true, most substantially weakens the argument?

(A) The new test identifies genetic material from *Salmonella* organisms only and not from similar bacteria.
(B) The new test detects the presence of *Salmonella* at levels that are too low to pose a health risk to people.
(C) *Salmonella* is only one of a variety of food-borne microorganisms that can cause intestinal illness.
(D) The new test has been made possible only recently by dramatic advances in biological science.
(E) Symptoms of *Salmonella* poisoning are often mistaken for those of other common intestinal illness.

52. The region's water authority is responding to the current drought by restricting residential water use. Yet reservoir levels are now at the same height they were during the drought ten years ago when no restrictions were put into effect and none proved necessary. Therefore, imposing restrictions now is clearly premature.

Which one of the following, if true, most seriously calls the conclusion above into question?

(A) There are now more water storage reservoirs in the region than there were ten years ago.
(B) The population of the region is approximately three times greater than it was ten years ago.
(C) The region currently has more sources outside the drought-stricken area from which to draw water than it did ten years ago.
(D) The water-consuming home appliances and fixtures sold today are designed to use water more efficiently than those sold ten years ago.
(E) The price of water for residential use is significantly higher in the region than it is in regions that are not drought-stricken.

53. Household indebtedness, which some theorists regard as causing recession, was high preceding the recent recession, but so was the value of assets owned by households. Admittedly, if most of the assets were owned by quite affluent households, and most of the debt was owed by low-income households, high household debt levels could have been the cause of the recession despite high asset values: low-income households might have decreased spending in order to pay off debts while the quite affluent ones might simply have failed to increase spending. But, in fact, quite affluent people must have owed most of the household debt, since money is not lent to those without assets. Therefore, the real cause must lie elsewhere.

Which one of the following, if true, casts the most doubt on the argument?

(A) Prior to the recent recession, middle-income households owed enough debt that they had begun to decrease spending.
(B) The total value of the economy's household debt is exceeded by the total value of assets held by households.
(C) Low-income households somewhat decreased their spending during the recent recession.
(D) During a recession the affluent usually borrow money only in order to purchase assets.
(E) Household debt is the category of debt least likely to affect the economy.

54. Some people fear that global warming will cause the large ice formations in the polar seas to melt, thereby warming the waters of those seas and threatening the plankton that is crucial to the marine food chain. Some scientists contend that it is unlikely that the melting process has begun, since water temperatures in the polar seas are the same today as they were a century ago.

Which one of the following, if true, most seriously undermines the scientists' contention?

(A) Much of the marine plant life that flourishes in the polar seas will die in the event that the water temperatures rise above their present levels.
(B) The overall effect of the melting process will be an increase in global sea levels.
(C) The mean air temperature above both land and water in the polar regions has not varied significantly over the past 100 years.
(D) The temperature of water that contains melting ice tends to remain constant until all of the ice in the ice-and-water mixture has melted.
(E) The mean temperature of ocean waters near the equator has remained constant over the past 100 years.

55. Paperback books wear out more quickly than hardcover books do, but paperback books cost much less. Therefore, users of public libraries would be better served if public libraries bought only paperback books, since by so doing these libraries could increase the number of new book titles added to their collections without increasing their budgets.

Which one of the following, if true, most seriously weakens the argument?

(A) If a public library's overall budget is cut, the budge for new acquisitions is usually cut back more than is that for day-to-day operations.
(B) Paperback books can very inexpensively have their covers reinforced in order to make them last longer.
(C) Many paperback books are never published in hardcover.
(D) Library users as a group depend on their public library for access to a wide variety of up-to-date reference books that are published in hardcover only.
(E) People are more likely to buy for themselves a copy of a book they had previously borrowed from the public library if that book is available in paperback.

56. From an analysis of broken pottery and statuary, archaeologists have estimated that an ancient settlement in southwestern Arabia was established around 1000 B.C. However, new evidence suggests that the settlement is considerably older: tests show that a piece of building timber recently uncovered at the site is substantially older than the pottery and statuary.

Which one of the following, if true, most seriously undermines the conclusion drawn from the new evidence?

(A) The building timber bore marks suggesting that it had been salvaged from an earlier settlement.
(B) The pieces of pottery and fragments of statues that were analyzed come from several parts of the site.
(C) The tests used to determine the age of the pottery and statuary had been devised more recently than those used to determine the age of the building timber.
(D) The site has yielded many more samples of pottery and statuary than of building timber.
(E) The type of pottery found at the site is similar to a type of pottery associated with civilizations that existed before 1000 B.C.

57. Mark: Plastic-foam cups, which contain environmentally harmful chlorofluorocarbons, should no longer be used; paper cups are preferable. Styrene, a carcinogenic by-product, is generated in foam production, and foam cups, once used, persist indefinitely in the environment.

Tina: You overlook the environmental effects of paper cups. A study done 5 years ago showed that making paper for their production burned more petroleum than was used for foam cups and used 12 times as much steam, 36 times as much electricity, and twice as much cooling water. Because paper cups weigh more, their transportation takes more energy. Paper mills produce water pollution, and when the cups decay they produce methane, a gas that contributes to harmful global warming. So they are a worse choice.

Which one of the following, if true, could Mark cite to counter evidence offered by Tina?

(A) The use of energy for chain saws that cut down trees and for trucks that haul logs is part of the environmental cost of manufacturing paper.
(B) Foam cups are somewhat more acceptable to consumers than paper cups because of their better insulating qualities.
(C) The production and transportation of petroleum occasions serious environmental pollution, but the energy that runs paper mills now comes from burning waste wood rather than petroleum.
(D) The amount of styrene escaping into the environment or remaining in foam cups after their manufacture is negligible.
(E) Acre for acre, tree farms for the production of wood for paper have fewer beneficial effects on the environment than do natural forests than remain uncut.

WEAKEN

58. Beverage company representative: The plastic rings that hold six-packs of beverage cans together pose a threat to wild animals, which often become entangled in the discarded rings and suffocate as a result. Following our lead, all beverage companies will soon use only those rings consisting of a new plastic that disintegrates after only three days' exposure to sunlight. Once we all complete the switchover from the old to the new plastic rings, therefore, the threat of suffocation that plastic rings pose to wild animals will be eliminated.

Which one of the following, if true, most seriously weakens the representative's argument?

(A) The switchover to the new plastic rings will take at least two more years to complete.
(B) After the beverage companies have switched over to the new plastic rings, a substantial number of the old plastic rings will persist in most aquatic and woodland environments.
(C) The new plastic rings are slightly less expensive than the old rings.
(D) The new plastic rings rarely disintegrate during shipping of beverage six-packs because most trucks that transport canned beverages protect their cargo from sunlight.
(E) The new plastic rings disintegrate into substances that are harmful to aquatic animals when ingested in substantial quantities by them.

59. Recent research shows that hesitation, shifting posture, and failure to maintain eye contact are not reliable indicators in discriminating between those who are lying and those who are telling the truth. The research indicates that behavior that cannot be controlled is a much better clue, at least when the lie is important to the liar. Such behavior includes the dilation of eye pupils, which indicates emotional arousal, and small movements of facial muscles, which indicate distress, fear or anger.

Which one of the following provides the strongest reason for exercising caution when relying on the "better" clues mentioned above in order to discover whether someone is lying?

(A) A person who is lying might be aware that he or she is being closely observed for indications of lying.
(B) Someone who is telling the truth might nevertheless have a past history of lying.
(C) A practiced liar might have achieved great control over body posture and eye contact.
(D) A person telling the truth might be affected emotionally by being suspected of lying or by some other aspect of the situation.
(E) Someone who is lying might exhibit hesitation and shifting posture as well as dilated pupils.

60. Orthodox medicine is ineffective at both ends of the spectrum of ailments. At the more trivial end, orthodox medicine is largely ineffective in treating aches, pains, and allergies, and, at the other extreme, it has yet to produce a cure for serious, life-threatening diseases such as advanced cancer and lupus. People turn to alternative medicine when orthodox medicine fails to help them and when it produces side effects that are unacceptable to them. One of the reasons alternative medicine is free of such side effects is that it does not have any effects at all.

The charge made above against alternative medicine is most seriously weakened if it is true that

(A) predictions based on orthodox medicine have sometimes failed, as when a patient has recovered despite the judgment of doctors that an illness is fatal
(B) alternative medicine relies on concepts of the body and of the nature of healing that differ from those on which orthodox medicine is based
(C) alternative medicine provides hope to those for whom orthodox medicine offers no cure
(D) a patient's belief in the medical treatment the patient is receiving can release the body's own chemical painkillers, diminish allergic reactions, and promote healing
(E) many treatments used for a time by orthodox medicine have later been found to be totally ineffective

61. In many languages other than English there is a word for "mother's brother" which is different from the word for "father's brother," whereas English uses the word "uncle" for both. Thus, speakers of these languages evidence a more finely discriminated kinship system than English speakers do. The number of basic words for colors also varies widely from language to language. Therefore, speakers of languages that have fewer basic words for colors than English has must be perceptually unable to distinguish as many colors as speakers of English can distinguish.

Which one of the following, if true, undermines the conclusion concerning words for colors?

(A) Speakers of English are able to distinguish between lighter and darker shades of the color they call "blue," for which Russian has two different basic words.
(B) Almost every language distinguishes red from the other colors.
(C) Khmer uses a basic word corresponding to English "blue" for most leaves, but uses its basic word corresponding to English "green" for unripe bananas.
(D) The word "orange" in English has the same origin as the equivalent word in Spanish.
(E) Most languages do not have a basic word that distinguishes gray from other colors, although gray is commonly found in nature.

62. In response to high mortality in area hospitals, surgery was restricted to emergency procedures during a five-week period. Mortality in these hospitals was found to have fallen by nearly one-third during the period. The number of deaths rose again when elective surgery (surgery that can be postponed) was resumed. It can be concluded that, before the five-week period, the risks of elective surgery had been incurred unnecessarily often in the area.

Which one of the following, if true, most seriously undermines the conclusion above?

(A) The conditions for which elective surgery was performed would in the long run have been life-threatening, and surgery for them would have become riskier with time.
(B) The physicians planning elective surgery performed before the five-week period had fully informed the patients who would undergo it of the possible risks of the procedures.
(C) Before the suspension of elective surgery, surgical operations were performed in area hospitals at a higher rate, per thousand residents of the area, than was usual elsewhere.
(D) Elective surgery is, in general, less risky than is emergency surgery because the conditions requiring or indicating surgery are often less severe.
(E) Even if a surgical procedure is successful, the patient can die of a hospital-contracted infection with a bacterium that is resistant to antibiotic treatment.

63. Many economically useful raw materials are nonrenewable and in limited supply on Earth. Therefore, unless those materials can be obtained somewhere other than Earth, people will eventually be unable to accomplish what they now accomplish using those materials.

Which one of the following, if true, most seriously weakens the argument?

(A) Some economically useful resources are renewable.
(B) It is extremely difficult to get raw materials from outer space.
(C) Functionally equivalent renewable substitutes could be found for nonrenewable resources that are in limited supply.
(D) What is accomplished now using nonrenewable resources is sometimes not worth accomplishing.
(E) It will be a few hundred years before the Earth is depleted of certain nonrenewable resources that are in limited supply.

64. The number of hospital emergency room visits by heroin users grew by more than 25 percent during the 1980s. Clearly, then, the use of heroin rose in that decade.

Which one of the following, if true, would account for the statistic above without supporting the author's conclusion?

(A) Widespread use of automatic weapons in the drug trade during the 1980s raised the incidence of physical injury to heroin users.
(B) The introduction of a smokable type of heroin during the 1980s removed the need for heroin to be injected intravenously and thus reduced the users' risk of infection.
(C) Many hospital emergency rooms were barely able to accommodate the dramatic increase in the number of medical emergencies related to drug abuse during the 1980s.
(D) Heroin use increased much more than is reflected in the rate of heroin-linked hospital emergency room visits.
(E) Viral and bacterial infections, malnourishment, and overdoses account for most hospital emergency room visits linked to heroin.

65. "This company will not be training any more pilots in the foreseeable future, since we have 400 trained pilots on our waiting list who are seeking employment. The other five major companies each have roughly the same number of trained pilots on their waiting lists, and since the projected requirement of each company is for not many more than 100 additional pilots, there will be no shortage of personnel despite the current upswing in the aviation industry."

Which one of the following, if true, casts the most doubt on the accuracy of the above conclusion?

(A) Most of the trained pilots who are on a waiting list for a job are on the waiting lists of all the major companies.
(B) In the long run, pilot training will become necessary to compensate for ordinary attrition.
(C) If no new pilots are trained, there will be an age imbalance in the pilot work force.
(D) The quoted personnel projections take account of the current upswing in the aviation industry.
(E) Some of the other major companies are still training pilots but with no presumption of subsequent employment.

66. Workers may complain about many things at work, but stress is not high on the list. In fact, in a recent survey a majority placed boredom at the top of their list of complaints. The assumption that job-related stress is the most serious problem for workers in the corporate world is thus simply not warranted.

Which one of the following, if true, most seriously weakens the argument?

(A) Those workers who are responsible for the planning and supervision of long-term projects are less likely to complain of either boredom or stress.
(B) Workers who complain of boredom exhibit more stress-related symptoms than do those who claim their work is interesting.
(C) Workers responding to opinion surveys tend to emphasize those experiences that have happened most recently.
(D) Workers who feel that their salaries are commensurate with the amount of work they do are less likely to complain of boredom.
(E) Workers are less likely to complain about work if they feel that their jobs are secure.

67. When volcanic lava solidifies, it becomes uniformly magnetized in the direction in which the Earth's magnetic field points. There are significant differences in the direction of magnetization among solidified lava flows from different volcanoes that erupted at different times over the past several million years. Therefore, it must be that the direction of the Earth's magnetic field has changed over time. Since lava flows differing by thousands of years in age often have very similar directions of magnetization, the change in the direction of the Earth's magnetic field must take place very gradually over hundreds of thousands of years.

Which one of the following, if true, most seriously undermines the conclusion that the change in the direction of the Earth's magnetic field happened very slowly?

(A) The changes in the direction of the Earth's magnetic field are determined by the chaotic movement of iron-containing liquids in the Earth's outer core.
(B) There has not been a change in the direction of the Earth's magnetic field since scientists have begun measuring the direction of magnetization of lava flows.
(C) The direction of the Earth's magnetic field has undergone a complete reversal several times over the past few million years.
(D) A lava flow has been found in which the direction of magnetization in the center of the flow differs significantly from that on the surface, even though the flow took only two weeks to solidify completely.
(E) Since the rate at which molten lava solidifies depends on the temperature and altitude of the environment, some lava flows from volcanoes in certain areas will take years to solidify completely.

68. Recently, reviewers of patent applications decided against granting a patent to a university for a genetically engineered mouse developed for laboratory use in studying cancer. The reviewers argued that the mouse was a new variety of animal and that rules governing the granting of patents specifically disallow patents for new animal varieties.

Which one of the following, if true, most weakens the patent reviewers' argument?

(A) The restrictions the patent reviewers cited pertain only to domesticated farm animals.
(B) The university's application for a patent for the genetically engineered mouse was the first such patent application made by the university.
(C) The patent reviewers had reached the same decision on all previous patent requests for new animal varieties.
(D) The patent reviewers had in the past approved patents for genetically engineered plant varieties.
(E) The patent reviewers had previously decided against granting patents for new animal varieties that were developed through conventional breeding programs rather than through genetic engineering.

69. The painted spider spins webs that are much stickier than the webs spun by the other species of spiders that share the same habitat. Stickier webs are more efficient at trapping insects that fly into them. Spiders prey on insects by trapping them in their webs; therefore, it can be concluded that the painted spider is a more successful predator than its competitors.

Which one of the following, if true, most seriously weakens the argument?

(A) Not all of the species of insects living in the painted spider's habitat are flying insects.
(B) Butterflies and moths, which can shed scales, are especially unlikely to be trapped by spider webs that are not very sticky.
(C) Although the painted spider's venom does not kill insects quickly, it paralyzes them almost instantaneously.
(D) Stickier webs reflect more light, and so are more visible to insects, than are less-sticky webs.
(E) The webs spun by the painted spider are no larger than the webs spun by the other species of spiders in the same habitat.

70. Recent unexpectedly heavy rainfalls in the metropolitan area have filled the reservoirs and streams; water rationing, therefore, will not be necessary this summer.

Which one of the following, if true, most undermines the author's prediction?

(A) Water rationing was imposed in the city in three of the last five years.
(B) A small part of the city's water supply is obtained from deep underground water systems that are not reached by rainwater.
(C) The water company's capacity to pump water to customers has not kept up with the increased demand created by population growth in the metropolitan area.
(D) The long-range weather forecast predicts lower-than-average temperatures for this summer.
(E) In most years the city receives less total precipitation in the summer than it receives in any other season.

71. Because dinosaurs were reptiles, scientists once assumed that, like all reptiles alive today, dinosaurs were cold-blooded. The recent discovery of dinosaur fossils in the northern arctic, however, has led a number of researchers to conclude that at least some dinosaurs might have been warm-blooded. These researchers point out that only warm-blooded animals could have withstood the frigid temperatures that are characteristic of arctic winters, whereas cold-blooded animals would have frozen to death in the extreme cold.

Which one of the following, if true, weakens the researchers' argument?

(A) Today's reptiles are generally confined to regions of temperate or even tropical climates.
(B) The fossils show the arctic dinosaurs to have been substantially smaller than other known species of dinosaurs.
(C) The arctic dinosaur fossils were found alongside fossils of plants known for their ability to withstand extremely cold temperatures.
(D) The number of fossils found together indicates herds of dinosaurs so large that they would need to migrate to find a continual food supply.
(E) Experts on prehistoric climatic conditions believe that winter temperatures in the prehistoric northern arctic were not significantly different from what they are today.

72. The fishing industry cannot currently be relied upon to help the government count the seabirds killed by net fishing, since an accurate count might result in restriction of net fishing. The government should therefore institute a program under which tissue samples from the dead birds are examined to determine the amount of toxins in the fish eaten by the birds. The industry would then have a reason to turn in the bird carcasses, since the industry needs to know whether the fish it catches are contaminated with toxins.

Which one of the following, if true, most strongly indicates that the government program would not by itself provide an accurate count of the seabirds killed by net fishing?

(A) The seabirds killed by net fishing might be contaminated with several different toxins even if the birds eat only one kind of fish.
(B) The fishing industry could learn whether the fish it catches are contaminated with toxins if only a few of the seabirds killed by the nets were examined.
(C) The government could gain valuable information about the source of toxins by examining tissue samples of the seabirds caught in the nets.
(D) The fish caught in a particular net might be contaminated with the same toxins as those in the seabirds caught in that net.
(E) The government would be willing to certify that the fish caught by the industry are not contaminated with toxins if tests done on the seabirds showed no contamination.

73. Public health will improve more quickly in the wake of new medical discoveries if medical researchers abandon their practice of waiting until their findings are published in peer-reviewed journals before informing the press of important research results. That is because the public release of new medical information allows people to use that information in order to improve their health, but the peer-review process is unavoidably very slow.

Which one of the following, if true, most seriously weakens the argument?

(A) Peer review often prevents the publication of false conclusions drawn on the basis of poorly conducted medical research.
(B) People often alter their life-styles on the basis of new medical information made available through the press.
(C) Some improvements in public health are due to factors other than the discovery of new medical information.
(D) Some newspapers would be willing to publish the results of medical research before those results have appeared in peer-reviewed journals.
(E) Most peer-reviewed scientific journals would refuse to give up the practice of peer review.

74. Although tales of wonder and the fantastic are integral to all world literatures, only recently has the fantasy genre had a commercial resurgence in North America. During the last 20 years, sales of fantasy-fiction books written for adults have gone from 1 to 10 percent of total adult-fiction sales. At the same time, the number of favorable reviews of fantasy books has increased markedly. Some booksellers say that the increased sales of fantasy books written for adults can be traced to the increased favorable attention given the genre by book reviewers.

Which one of the following, if true, undermines the booksellers' explanation of the growth in sales of fantasy-fiction books for adults?

(A) Publishers often select a manuscript on the basis of whether they think that the published book will receive favorable reviews by book reviewers.
(B) Few readers of fantasy fiction read book reviews, and even fewer select books to purchase on the basis of those reviews.
(C) Most booksellers are aware of what major book reviewers have written about recently published books.
(D) Although the increase in the percentage of fantasy books sold has been substantial, publishers estimate that sales could increase even further.
(E) Many of the book reviews of new fantasy-fiction novels also mention great fantasy novels of the past.

75. During the 1980s the homicide rate in Britain rose by 50 percent. The weapon used usually was a knife. Potentially lethal knives are sold openly and legally in many shops. Most homicide deaths occur as a result of unpremeditated assaults within the family. Even if these are increasing, they would probably not result in deaths if it were not for the prevalence of such knives. Thus the blame lies with the permissiveness of the government that allows such lethal weapons to be sold.

Which one of the following is the strongest criticism of the argument above?

(A) There are other means besides knives, such as guns or poison, that can be used to accomplish homicide by a person who intends to cause the death of another.
(B) It is impossible to know how many unpremeditated assaults occur within the family, since many are not reported to the authorities.
(C) Knives are used in other homicides besides those that result from unpremeditated assaults within the family.
(D) The argument assumes without justification that the knives used to commit homicide are generally purchased as part of a deliberate plan to commit murder or to inflict grievous harm on a family member.
(E) If the potentially lethal knives referred to are ordinary household knives, such knives were common before the rise in the homicide rate; but if they are weaponry, such knives are not generally available in households.

76. It is very difficult to prove today that a painting done two or three hundred years ago, especially one without a signature or with a questionably authentic signature, is indubitably the work of this or that particular artist. This fact gives the traditional attribution of a disputed painting special weight, since that attribution carries the presumption of historical continuity. Consequently, an art historian arguing for a deattribution will generally convince other art historians only if he or she can persuasively argue for a specific reattribution.

Which one of the following, if true, most strongly supports the position that the traditional attribution of a disputed painting should not have special weight?

(A) Art dealers have always been led by economic self-interest to attribute any unsigned paintings of merit to recognized masters rather than to obscure artists.
(B) When a painting is originally created, there are invariably at least some eyewitnesses who see the artist at work, and thus questions of correct attribution cannot arise at that time.
(C) There are not always clearly discernible differences between the occasional inferior work produced by a master and the very best work produced by a lesser talent.
(D) Attribution can shape perception inasmuch as certain features that would count as marks of greatness in a master's work would be counted as signs of inferior artistry if a work were attributed to a minor artist.
(E) Even though some masters had specialists assist them with certain detail work, such as depicting lace, the resulting works are properly attributed to the masters alone.

77. Dr. Ruiz: Dr. Smith has expressed outspoken antismoking views in public. Even though Dr. Smith is otherwise qualified, clearly she cannot be included on a panel that examines the danger of secondhand cigarette smoke. As an organizer of the panel, I want to ensure that the panel examines the issue in an unbiased manner before coming to any conclusion.

Which one of the following, if true, provides the strongest basis for countering Dr. Ruiz' argument that Dr. Smith should not be included on the panel?

(A) A panel composed of qualified people with strong but conflicting views on a particular topic is more likely to reach an unbiased conclusion than a panel composed of people who have kept their views, if any, private.
(B) People who hold strong views on a particular topic tend to accept new evidence on that topic only if it supports their views.
(C) A panel that includes one qualified person with publicly known strong views on a particular topic is more likely to have lively discussions than a panel that includes only people with no well-defined views on that topic.
(D) People who have expressed strong views in public on a particular topic are better at raising funds to support their case than are people who have never expressed strong views in public.
(E) People who have well-defined strong views on a particular topic prior to joining a panel are often able to impose their views on panel members who are not committed at the outset to any conclusion.

WEAKEN

78. Advertisement: Over 80 percent of the people who test-drive a Zenith car end up buying one. So be warned: you should not test-drive a Zenith unless you are prepared to buy one, because if you so much as drive a Zenith around the block, there is a better than 80 percent chance you will choose to buy it.

If the advertisement is interpreted as implying that the quality of the car is unusually impressive, which one of the following, if true, most clearly casts doubt on that implication?

(A) Test-drives of Zenith cars are, according to Zenith sales personnel, generally more extensive than a drive around the block and encounter varied driving conditions.

(B) Usually dealers have enough Zenith models in stock that prospective purchasers are able to test-drive the exact model that they are considering for purchase.

(C) Those who take test-drives in cars are, in overwhelming proportions, people who have already decided to buy the model driven unless some fault should become evident.

(D) Almost 90 percent of the people who purchase a car do not do so on the day they take a first test-drive but do so after another test-drive.

(E) In some Zenith cars, a minor part has broken within the first year, and Zenith dealers have issued notices to owners that the dealers will replace the part with a redesigned one at no cost to owners.

79. Scientists analyzing air bubbles that had been trapped in Antarctic ice during the Earth's last ice age found that the ice-age atmosphere had contained unusually large amounts of ferrous material and surprisingly small amounts of carbon dioxide. One scientist noted that algae absorb carbon dioxide from the atmosphere. The scientist hypothesized that the ferrous material, which was contained in atmospheric dust, had promoted a great increase in the population of Antarctic algae such as diatoms.

Which one of the following, if true, would most seriously undermine the scientist's hypothesis?

(A) Diatoms are a microscopic form of algae that has remained largely unchanged since the last ice age.

(B) Computer models suggest that a large increase in ferrous material today could greatly promote the growth of oceanic algae.

(C) The dust found in the air bubbles trapped in Antarctic ice contained other minerals in addition to the ferrous material.

(D) Sediment from the ocean floor near Antarctica reflects no increase, during the last ice age, in the rate at which the shells that diatoms leave when they die accumulated.

(E) Algae that currently grow in the oceans near Antarctica do not appear to be harmed by even a large increase in exposure to ferrous material.

80. Carl: Researchers who perform operations on animals for experimental purposes are legally required to complete detailed pain protocols indicating whether the animals will be at risk of pain and, if so, what steps will be taken to minimize or alleviate it. Yet when human beings undergo operations, such protocols are never required. If lawmakers were as concerned about human beings as they seem to be about animals, there would be pain protocols for human beings too.

Debbie: But consider this: a person for whom a doctor wants to schedule surgery can simply be told what pain to expect and can then decide whether or not to undergo the operation. So you see, pain protocols are unnecessary for human beings.

Which one of the following, if true, most seriously weakens the argument made by Debbie in response to Carl's argument?

(A) Not all operations that are performed on human beings are painful.
(B) Some experimentation that is now done on animals need not be done at all.
(C) Preparing pain protocols is not a time-consuming or costly procedure.
(D) Some surgical operations performed on infants are painful.
(E) Unalleviated pain after an operation tends to delay the healing process.

81. Audiences find a speaker more convincing if the speaker begins a speech by arguing briefly against his or her position before providing reasons for accepting it. The reason this technique is so effective is that it makes the speaker appear fair-minded and trustworthy. Therefore, candidates for national political office who wish to be successful in winning votes should use this argumentative technique in their speeches.

Which one of the following, if true, most seriously limits the effectiveness of adopting the argument's recommendation?

(A) Political candidates typically have no control over which excerpts from their speeches will be reported by the news media.
(B) Many people do not find arguments made by politicians convincing, since the arguments are often one-sided or oversimplify the issues.
(C) People decide which political candidate to vote for more on the basis of their opinions of the candidate's character than on the exact positions of the candidate.
(D) People regard a political candidate more favorably if they think that the candidate respects an opponent's position even while disagreeing with it.
(E) Political candidates have to address audiences of many different sizes and at many different locations in the course of a political campaign.

WEAKEN

82. Sasha: Handwriting analysis should be banned in court as evidence of a person's character: handwriting analysts called as witnesses habitually exaggerate the reliability of their analyses.

Gregory: You are right that the current use of handwriting analysis as evidence is problematic. But this problem exists only because there is no licensing board to set professional standards and thus deter irresponsible analysts from making exaggerated claims. When such a board is established, however, handwriting analysis by licensed practitioners will be a legitimate courtroom tool for character assessment.

Which one of the following, if true, would provide Sasha with the strongest counter to Gregory's response?

(A) Courts routinely use means other than handwriting analysis to provide evidence of a person's character.
(B) Many people can provide two samples of their handwriting so different that only a highly trained professional could identify them as having been written by the same person.
(C) A licensing board would inevitably refuse to grant licenses to some responsible handwriting analysts for reasons having nothing to do with their reliability.
(D) The only handwriting analysts who claim that handwriting provides reliable evidence of a person's character are irresponsible.
(E) The number of handwriting analysts who could conform to professional standards set by a licensing board is very small.

83. A director of the Rexx Pharmaceutical Company argued that the development costs for new vaccines that the health department has requested should be subsidized by the government, since the marketing of vaccines promised to be less profitable than the marketing of any other pharmaceutical product. In support of this claim the director argued that sales of vaccines are likely to be lower since each vaccine is administered to a patient only once, whereas medicines that combat diseases and chronic illnesses are administered many times to each patient.

Which one of the following, if true, most weakens the support offered by the company director for the claim concerning the marketing of vaccines?

(A) Vaccines are administered to many more people than are most other pharmaceutical products.
(B) Many of the diseases that vaccines are designed to prevent can be successfully treated by medicines.
(C) Pharmaceutical companies occasionally market products that are neither medicines nor vaccines.
(D) Pharmaceutical companies other than the Rexx Pharmaceutical Company produce vaccines.
(E) The cost of administering a vaccine is rarely borne by the pharmaceutical company that manufactures that vaccine.

84. Opponents of allowing triple-trailer trucks to use the national highway system are wrong in claiming that these trucks are more dangerous than other commercial vehicles. In the western part of the country, in areas where triple-trailers are now permitted on some highways, for these vehicles the rate of road accident fatalities per mile of travel is lower than the national rate for other types of commercial vehicles. Clearly, triple-trailers are safer than other commercial vehicles.

Which one of the following, if true, most substantially weakens the argument?

(A) It takes two smaller semitrailers to haul as much weight as a single triple-trailer can.
(B) Highways in the sparsely populated West are much less heavily traveled and consequently are far safer than highways in the national system as a whole.
(C) Opponents of the triple-trailers also once opposed the shorter twin-trailers, which are now common on the nation's highways.
(D) In areas where the triple-trailers are permitted, drivers need a special license to operate them.
(E) For triple-trailers the rate of road accident fatalities per mile of travel was higher last year than in the two previous years.

85. Using fossil energy more efficiently is in the interest of the nation and the global environment, but major improvements are unlikely unless proposed government standards are implemented to eliminate products or practices that are among the least efficient in their class.

Objection: Decisions on energy use are best left to the operation of the market.

Which one of the following, if true, most directly undermines the objection above?

(A) It would be unrealistic to expect society to make the changes necessary to achieve maximum energy efficiency all at once.
(B) There are products, such as automobiles, that consume energy at a sufficient rate that persons who purchase and use them will become conscious of any unusual energy inefficiency in comparison with other products in the same class.
(C) Whenever a new mode of generating energy, such as a new fuel, is introduced, a number of support systems, such as a fuel-distribution system, must be created or adapted.
(D) When energy prices rise, consumers of energy tend to look for new ways to increase energy efficiency, such as by adding insulation to their houses.
(E) Often the purchaser of a product, such as a landlord buying an appliance, chooses on the basis of purchase price because the purchaser is not the person who will pay for energy used by the product.

WEAKEN

86. Marianne is a professional chess player who hums audibly while playing her matches, thereby distracting her opponents. When ordered by chess officials to cease humming or else be disqualified from professional chess, Marianne protested the order. She argued that since she was unaware of her humming, her humming was involuntary and that therefore she should not be held responsible for it.

Which one of the following, if true, most undermines Marianne's argument against the order?

(A) The officials of chess have little or no authority to control the behavior of its professional players outside of matches.
(B) Many of the customs of amateur chess matches are not observed by professional chess players.
(C) Not all of a person's involuntary actions are actions of which that person is unaware.
(D) A person who hums involuntarily can easily learn to notice it and can thereby come to control it.
(E) Not all of Marianne's opponents are distracted by her humming during chess matches.

Chapter Five: Strengthen Questions

STRENGTHEN

1. Computer operating system software has become increasingly standardized. But when a large business with multiple, linked computer systems uses identical operating system software on all of its computers, a computer vandal who gains access to one computer automatically has access to the data on all the computers. Using a program known as a "virus," the vandal can then destroy much of the data on all the computers. If such a business introduced minor variations into its operating system software, unauthorized access to all the computers at the same time could be virtually eliminated. Furthermore, variations in operating system software can be created without any loss of computer compatibility to the business. Therefore, it is advisable for businesses to implement such variations.

   Which one of the following, if true, supports the conclusion in the passage?

   (A) Standardization of computer operating system software has increased computer compatibility among different businesses.
   (B) Correcting any damage resulting from an invasion by a computer virus program is more expensive than preventing the damage.
   (C) It is not costly for a business to maintain incompatible computer operating systems.
   (D) There are other kinds of destructive computer programs that do not depend on intercomputer links.
   (E) Not all businesses need to share data among their internal computer systems.

2. State researchers have found that since the oil price increases of the 1970s, there has been a decline in home energy consumption. They concluded that almost all of the decline has been achieved through reduced standards of living and changes in the way people spend their time.

   Each of the following, if true, would support the conclusion above EXCEPT:

   (A) Sales of portable heaters rose as families concentrated their winter activities in a limited number of rooms.
   (B) During the winter months, more people frequented public places such as libraries and community centers and, on the average, spent considerably longer periods in them than they had previously.
   (C) More than 39 percent of households were able to decrease energy costs substantially by having relatively inexpensive work done to improve the efficiency of their existing heating systems.
   (D) At least 59 percent of households maintained a lower indoor temperature than they had been accustomed to maintain on very cold days.
   (E) Members of at least 60 percent of households showered for shorter periods of time than they had previously.

3. Mr. Blatt: Expert consultants are sought after by management because they help executives make better decisions. That is why they are worth the substantial fees they charge.

Ms. Fring: Nonsense. Expert consultants are hired in order to enable executives to avoid responsibility. The more the experts cost, the more they can be blamed when things go wrong.

Which one of the following, if it occurred, would be the strongest evidence favoring Ms. Fring's position over Mr. Blatt's position?

(A) A company that is trying to decide whether to move its manufacturing plant hires an expensive expert to conduct a cost/benefit analysis.
(B) Two competing companies faced with very similar problems adopt different solutions, one with the help of a consultant, one without.
(C) A successful firm of expert consultants seeks to increase its volume of business by reducing its fees, but its volume of business drops.
(D) An expert consultant builds up a successful business by charging clients a substantial percentage of the amount an independent assessor judges that the consultant saved the company.
(E) A company follows a consultant's advice to open two new stores, but both stores are only marginally profitable at first.

4. Advertisers are often criticized for their unscrupulous manipulation of people's tastes and wants. There is evidence, however, that some advertisers are motivated by moral as well as financial considerations. A particular publication decided to change its image from being a family newspaper to concentrating on sex and violence, thus appealing to a different readership. Some advertisers withdrew their advertisements from the publication, and this must have been because they morally disapproved of publishing salacious material.

Which one of the following, if true, would most strengthen the argument?

(A) The advertisers switched their advertisements to other family newspapers.
(B) Some advertisers switched from family newspapers to advertise in the changed publication.
(C) The advertisers expected their product sales to increase if they stayed with the changed publication, but to decrease if they withdrew.
(D) People who generally read family newspapers are not likely to buy newspapers that concentrate on sex and violence.
(E) It was expected that the changed publication would appeal principally to those in a different income group.

STRENGTHEN

5. Marine biologists have long thought that variation in the shell color of aquatic snails evolved as a protective camouflage against birds and other predators. Brown shells seem to be more frequent when the underlying seafloor is dark-colored and white shells more frequent when the underlying seafloor is light-colored. A new theory has been advanced, however, that claims that shell color is related to physiological stress associated with heat absorption. According to this theory, brown shells will be more prevalent in areas where the wave action of the sea is great and thus heat absorption from the Sun is minimized, whereas white shells will be more numerous in calmer waters where the snails will absorb more heat from the Sun's rays.

   Evidence that would strongly favor the new theory over the traditional theory would be the discovery of a large majority of

   (A) dark-shelled snails in a calm inlet with a dark, rocky bottom and many predators
   (B) dark-shelled snails in a calm inlet with a white, sandy bottom
   (C) light-shelled snails in an inlet with much wave action and a dark, rocky bottom
   (D) light-shelled snails in a calm inlet with a dark, rocky bottom and many predators
   (E) light-shelled snails in a calm inlet with a white, sandy bottom and many predators

6. Even if a crime that has been committed by computer is discovered and reported, the odds of being both arrested and convicted greatly favor the criminal.

   Each of the following, if true, supports the claim above EXCEPT:

   (A) The preparation of computer-fraud cases takes much more time than is required for average fraud cases, and the productivity of prosecutors is evaluated by the number of good cases made.
   (B) In most police departments, officers are rotated through different assignments every two or three years, a shorter time than it takes to become proficient as a computer-crime investigator.
   (C) The priorities of local police departments, under whose jurisdiction most computer crime falls, are weighted toward visible street crime that communities perceive as threatening.
   (D) Computer criminals have rarely been sentenced to serve time in prison, because prisons are overcrowded with violent criminals and drug offenders.
   (E) The many police officers who are untrained in computers often inadvertently destroy the physical evidence of computer crime.

7. The mayor boasts that the average ambulance turnaround time, the time from summons to delivery of the patient, has been reduced this year for top priority emergencies. This is a serious misrepresentation. This "reduction" was produced simply by redefining "top priority." Such emergencies used to include gunshot wounds and electrocutions, the most time-consuming cases. Now they are limited strictly to heart attacks and strokes.

   Which one of the following would strengthen the author's conclusion that it was the redefinition of "top priority" that produced the reduction in turnaround time?

   (A) The number of heart attacks and strokes declined this year.
   (B) The mayor redefined the city's financial priorities this year.
   (C) Experts disagree with the mayor's definition of "top-priority emergency."
   (D) Other cities include gunshot wound cases in their category of top-priority emergencies.
   (E) One half of all of last year's top-priority emergencies were gunshot wounds and electrocution cases.

8. In opposing the 1970 Clean Air Act, the United States automobile industry argued that meeting the act's standards for automobile emissions was neither economically feasible nor environmentally necessary. However, the catalytic converter, invented in 1967, enabled automakers to meet the 1970 standards efficiently. Currently, automakers are lobbying against the government's attempt to pass legislation that would tighten restrictions on automobile emissions. The automakers contend that these new restrictions would be overly expensive and unnecessary to efforts to curb air pollution. Clearly, the automobile industry's position should not be heeded.

Which one of the following, if true, lends the most support to the automakers' current position?

(A) The more stringent the legislation restricting emissions becomes, the more difficult it becomes for automakers to provide the required technology economically.
(B) Emissions-restriction technology can often be engineered so as to avoid reducing the efficiency with which an automobile uses fuel.
(C) Not every new piece of legislation restricting emissions requires new automotive technology in order for automakers to comply with it.
(D) The more automobiles there are on the road, the more stringent emission restrictions must be to prevent increased overall air pollution.
(E) Unless forced to do so by the government, automakers rarely make changes in automotive technology that is not related to profitability.

9. A society's infant mortality rate is an accepted indicator of that society's general health status. Even though in some localities in the United States the rate is higher than in many developing countries, in the United States overall the rate has been steadily declining. This decline does not necessarily indicate, however, that babies in the United States are now, on the average, healthier at birth than they were in the past.

Which one of the following reasons, if true, most strongly supports the claim made above about the implications of the decline?

(A) The figure for infant mortality is compiled as an overall rate and thus masks deficiencies in particular localities.
(B) Low birth weight is a contributing factor in more than half of the infant deaths in the United States.
(C) The United States has been developing and has achieved extremely sophisticated technology for saving premature and low-birth-weight babies, most of whom require extended hospital stays.
(D) In eleven states of the United States, the infant mortality rate declined last year.
(E) Babies who do not receive adequate attention from a caregiver fail to thrive and so they gain weight slowly.

STRENGTHEN

10. Leona: If the average consumption of eggs in the United States were cut in half, an estimated 5,000 lives might be saved each year.

Thomas: How can that be? That would mean that if people adopt this single change in diet for ten years, the population ten years from now will be greater by 50,000 people than it otherwise would have been.

Which one of the following is a statement that Leona could offer Thomas to clarify her own claim and to address the point he has made?

(A) It is possible for the population to grow by 5,000 people for every year if the base year chosen for purposes of comparison is one with unusually low population growth.
(B) It is accurate to say that 5,000 lives have been saved as long as 5,000 people who would have died in a given year as a result of not changing their diet, did not do so,even if they died for some other reason.
(C) If egg consumption were reduced by more than half, the estimated number of lives saved each year could be even more than 5,000.
(D) The actual rate of population growth depends not only on the birth rate, but also on changes in life expectancy.
(E) For the average consumption of eggs to be cut by half, many individual consumers would have to cut their own consumption by much more than half.

11. As air-breathing mammals, whales must once have lived on land and needed hind limbs capable of supporting the mammals' weight. Whales have the bare remnants of a pelvis. If animals have a pelvis, we expect them to have hind limbs. A newly discovered fossilized whale skeleton has very fragile hind limbs that could not have supported the animal's weight on land. This skeleton had a partial pelvis.

If the statements above are true, which one of the following, if also true, would most strongly support the conclusion that the fragile hind limbs are remnants of limbs that land-dwelling whales once had?

(A) Whale bones older than the fossilized hind limbs confirm that ancient whales had full pelvises.
(B) No skeletons of ancient whales with intact hind limbs capable of supporting the mammals' weight have ever been found.
(C) Scientists are uncertain whether the apparently nonfunctioning limbs of other early mammals derived from once-functioning limbs of their ancestors.
(D) Other large-bodied mammals like seals and sea lions maneuver on beaches and rocky coasts without fully functioning hind limbs.
(E) Some smaller sea-dwelling mammals, such as modern dolphins, have no visible indications of hind limbs.

12. Policy Adviser: Freedom of speech is not only a basic human right; it is also the only rational policy for this government to adopt. When ideas are openly aired, good ideas flourish, silly proposals are easily recognized as such, and dangerous ideas can be responded to by rational argument. Nothing is ever gained by forcing citizens to disseminate their thoughts in secret.

Which one of the following, if true, would most strengthen the argument?

(A) Most citizens would tolerate some limits on the freedom of speech.
(B) With or without a policy of freedom of speech, governments respond to dangerous ideas irrationally.
(C) Freedom of religion and freedom of assembly are also basic human rights that governments must recognize.
(D) Governments are less likely to be overthrown if they openly adopt a policy allowing freedom of speech.
(E) Great ideas have flourished in societies that repress free speech as often as in those that permit it.

13. If the public library shared by the adjacent towns of Redville and Glenwood were relocated from the library's current, overcrowded building in central Redville to a larger, available building in central Glenwood, the library would then be within walking distance of a larger number of library users. That is because there are many more people living in central Glenwood than in central Redville, and people generally will walk to the library only if it is located close to their homes.

Which one of the following, if true, most strengthens the argument?

(A) The public library was located between Glenwood and Redville before being moved to its current location in central Redville.
(B) The area covered by central Glenwood is approximately the same size as that covered by central Redville.
(C) The building that is available in Glenwood is smaller than an alternative building that is available in Redville.
(D) Many of the people who use the public library do not live in either Glenwood or Redville.
(E) The distance that people currently walk to get to the library is farther than what is generally considered walking distance.

14. A distemper virus has caused two-thirds of the seal population in the North Sea to die since May 1988. The explanation for the deaths cannot rest here, however. There must be a reason the normally latent virus could prevail so suddenly: clearly the severe pollution of the North Sea waters must have weakened the immune system of the seals so that they could no longer withstand the virus.

Which one of the following, if true, most strongly supports the explanation given in the argument?

(A) At various times during the last ten years, several species of shellfish and seabirds in the North Sea have experienced unprecedentedly steep drops in population.
(B) By reducing pollution at its source, Northern Europe and Scandinavia have been taking the lead in preventing pollution from reaching the waters of the North Sea.
(C) For many years, fish for human consumption have been taken from the waters of the North Sea.
(D) There are two species of seal found throughout the North Sea area, the common seal and the gray seal.
(E) The distemper caused by the virus was a disease that was new to the population of North Sea seals in May 1988, and so the seals' immune systems were unprepared to counter it.

Questions 15-16

The number of aircraft collisions on the ground is increasing because of the substantial increase in the number of flights operated by the airlines. Many of the fatalities that occur in such collisions are caused not by the collision itself, but by an inherent flaw in the cabin design of most aircraft, in which seats, by restricting access to emergency exits, impede escape. Therefore, to reduce the total number of fatalities that result annually from such collisions, the airlines should be required to remove all seats that restrict access to emergency exits.

15. Which one of the following, if true, provides the most support for the proposal?

(A) The number of deaths that occurred in theater fires because theater patrons could not escape was greatly reduced when theaters were required to have aisles leading to each exit.
(B) Removing the seats that block emergency exits on aircraft will require a costly refitting of aircraft cabins.
(C) In the event of fire, public buildings equipped with smoke detectors have fewer fatalities than do public buildings not so equipped.
(D) In the event of collision, passengers on planes with a smaller passenger capacity generally suffer more serious injury than do passengers on planes with a larger passenger capacity.
(E) The safety belts attached to aircraft seats function to protect passengers from the full force of impact in the event of a collision.

16. Which one of the following proposals, if implemented together with the proposal made in the passage, would improve the prospects for achieving the stated objective of reducing fatalities?

A) The airlines should be required, when buying new planes, to buy only planes with unrestricted access to emergency exits.
(B) The airlines should not be permitted to increase further the number of flights in order to offset the decrease in the number of seats on each aircraft.
(C) Airport authorities should be required to streamline their passenger check-in procedures to accommodate the increased number of passengers served by the airlines.
(D) Airport authorities should be required to refine security precautions by making them less conspicuous without making them less effective.
(E) The airlines should not be allowed to increase the ticket price for each passenger to offset the decrease in the number of seats on each aircraft.

17. G: The group of works exhibited in this year's Metropolitan Art Show reveals a bias in favor of photographers. Equal numbers of photographers, sculptors, and painters submitted works that met the traditional criteria for the show, yet more photographs were exhibited than either sculptures or paintings. As you know, each artist was allowed to submit work in one medium only.

H: How could there have been bias? All submitted works that met the traditional criteria—and only those works—were exhibited in the show.

Which one of the following, if true, most strongly supports G's allegation of bias?

(A) If an artist has had one of his or her works exhibited in the Metropolitan Art Show, that artist has an advantage in getting commissions and selling works over artists who have never had a work exhibited in the show.

(B) The fee for entering photographs in the Metropolitan Art Show was $25 per work submitted, while the fee for each painting or sculpture submitted was $75.

(C) The committee that selected from the submitted works the ones to be exhibited in this year's Metropolitan Art Show had four members: one photographer, one sculptor, one painter, and one who works in all three media but is the least known of the four members.

(D) Reviews of this year's Metropolitan Art Show that appeared in major newspapers and magazines tended to give more coverage to the photographs in the show than to the sculptures and paintings that were exhibited.

(E) In previous years, it has often happened that more paintings or more sculptures were exhibited in the Metropolitan Art Show than photographs, even though the total number of works exhibited each year does not vary widely.

18. Paleontologists have discovered fossils of centipedes that are 414 million years old. These fossils are at least 20 million years older than the earliest land-dwelling animals previously identified. The paleontologists are confident that these centipedes lived on land, even though the fossilized centipedes were discovered in rock that also contained fossilized remains of animals known to be water-dwelling.

The paleontologists' view would be LEAST supported by the truth of which one of the following?

(A) The legs of the fossilized centipedes were particularly suited to being a means of locomotion on land.

(B) All of the centipedes that had previously been discovered were land dwellers.

(C) The rock in which the fossilized centipedes were found was formed from mud flats that were occasionally covered by river water.

(D) Fossils of the earliest land-dwelling animals that had previously been identified were found in rock that did not contain fossilized remains of water-dwelling animals.

(E) Fossils of spiders with respiratory systems adapted only to breathing air were found in the same rock as the centipede fossils.

19. A physician who is too thorough in conducting a medical checkup is likely to subject the patient to the discomfort and expense of unnecessary tests. One who is not thorough enough is likely to miss some serious problem and therefore give the patient a false sense of security. It is difficult for physicians to judge exactly how thorough they should be. Therefore, it is generally unwise for patients to have medical checkups when they do not feel ill.

Which one of the following, if true, would provide the most support for the conclusion in the passage?

(A) Not all medical tests entail significant discomfort.

(B) Sometimes, unnecessary medical tests cause healthy people to become ill.

(C) Some patients refuse to accept a physician's assurance that the patient is healthy.

(D) The more complete the series of tests performed in a medical checkup, the more likely it is that a rare disease, if present, will be discovered.

(E) Physicians can eliminate the need to order certain tests by carefully questioning patients and rejecting some possibilities on that basis.

20. The foreign minister of Zeria announced today that her country was severing diplomatic relations with Nandalo because of Nandalo's flagrant violations of human rights. But Zeria continues to maintain diplomatic relations with many countries that the minister knows to have far worse human-rights records than Nandalo does. Therefore, despite the foreign minister's claim, this latest diplomatic move cannot be explained exclusively by Zeria's commitment to upholding human rights.

Which one of the following, if true, provides the most support for the argument in the passage?

(A) The country that currently buys most of Zeria's exports recently suggested that it might severely restrict its imports from Zeria unless Zeria broke off diplomatic relations with Nandalo.

(B) Two weeks after the Zerian minister's announcement, several other countries cited human-rights violations as a reason for severing diplomatic relations with Nandalo.

(C) More countries have expressed concern over reported human-rights violations in Nandalo than have expressed concern over human-rights violations in Zeria.

(D) Nandalo has considered accusing Zeria of violating the human rights of Nandalo citizens living in Zeria.

(E) The opposition party in Zeria has long advocated severing trade relations with countries that systematically violate human rights but has opposed severing diplomatic relations.

21. Teacher: Journalists who conceal the identity of the sources they quote stake their professional reputations on what may be called the logic of anecdotes. This is so because the statements reported by such journalists are dissociated from the precise circumstances in which they were made and thus will be accepted for publication only if the statements are high in plausibility or originality or interest to a given audience—precisely the properties of a good anecdote.

Student: But what you are saying, then, is that the journalist need not bother with sources in the first place. Surely, any reasonably resourceful journalist can invent plausible, original, or interesting stories faster than they can be obtained from unidentified sources.

Which one of the following, if true, most strengthens the teacher's argument?

(A) A journalist undermines his or her own professional standing by submitting for publication statements that, not being attributed to a named source, are rejected for being implausible, unoriginal, or dull.

(B) Statements that are attributed to a fully identified source make up the majority of reported statements included by journalists in stories submitted for publication.

(C) Reported statements that are highly original will often seem implausible unless submitted by a journalist who is known for solid, reliable work.

(D) Reputable journalists sometimes do not conceal the identity of their sources from their publishers but insist that the identity of those sources be concealed from the public.

(E) Journalists who have special access to sources whose identity they must conceal are greatly valued by their publishers.

22. The demand for used cars has risen dramatically in Germany in recent years. Most of this demand is generated by former East Germans who cannot yet afford new cars and for whom cars were generally unavailable prior to unification. This demand has outstripped supply and thus has exerted an upward pressure on the prices of used cars. Consequently, an increasing number of former West Germans, in order to take advantage of the improved market, will be selling the cars they have owned for several years. Hence, the German new-car market will most likely improve soon as well.

Which one of the following, if true, would most help to support the conclusion about the German new-car market?

(A) The demand for old cars in former West Germany is greater than the demand for new cars in former East Germany.
(B) In most European countries, the sale of a used car is subject to less tax than is the sale of a new car.
(C) Most Germans own very few cars in the course of their lives.
(D) Most former West Germans purchase new cars once they sell their used cars.
(E) Many former East Germans prefer to buy cars imported from North America because they are generally larger than European cars.

23. *Salmonella* is a food-borne microorganism that can cause intestinal illness. The illness is sometimes fatal, especially if not identified quickly and treated. Conventional *Salmonella* tests on food samples are slow and can miss unusual strains of the microorganism. A new test identifies the presence or absence of *Salmonella* by the one piece of genetic material common to all strains. Clearly, public health officials would be well advised to replace the previous *Salmonella* tests with the new test.

Which one of the following, if true, most strengthens the argument?

(A) The level of skill required for laboratory technicians to perform the new test is higher than that required to perform previous tests for *Salmonella*.
(B) The new test returns results very soon after food samples are submitted for testing.
(C) A proposed new treatment for *Salmonella* poisoning would take effect faster than the old treatment.
(D) *Salmonella* poisoning is becoming less frequent in the general population.
(E) Some remedies for *Salmonella* poisoning also cure intestinal disorders caused by other microorganisms.

24. Financial success does not guarantee happiness. This claim is not mere proverbial wisdom but a fact verified by statistics. In a recently concluded survey, only one-third of the respondents who claimed to have achieved financial success reported that they were happy.

Which one of the following, if true, most strongly supports the conclusion drawn from the survey results?

(A) The respondents who reported financial success were, for the most part, financially successful.
(B) Financial success was once thought to be necessary for happiness but is no longer considered a prerequisite for happiness.
(C) Many of the respondents who claimed not to have achieved financial success reported that they were happy five years ago.
(D) Many of the respondents who failed to report financial success were in fact financially successful.
(E) Most of the respondents who reported they were unhappy were in fact happy.

25. In a mature tourist market such as Bellaria there are only two ways hotel owners can increase profits: by building more rooms or by improving what is already there. Rigid land-use laws in Bellaria rule out construction of new hotels or, indeed, any expansion of hotel capacity. It follows that hotel owners cannot increase their profits in Bellaria since Bellarian hotels _________.

Which one of the following logically completes the argument?

(A) are already operating at an occupancy rate approaching 100 percent year-round
(B) could not have been sited any more attractively than they are even in the absence of land-use laws
(C) have to contend with upward pressures on the cost of labor which stem from an incipient shortage of trained personnel
(D) already provide a level of luxury that is at the limits of what even wealthy patrons are prepared to pay for
(E) have shifted from serving mainly Bellarian tourists to serving foreign tourists traveling in organized tour groups

26. Some scientists believe that the relationship between mice and humans has, over time, diminished the ability of mice to survive in nature, so that now they must depend upon human civilization for their continued existence. This opinion, however, ignores significant facts. Despite numerous predators and humanity's enmity, mice have distributed themselves more widely across the planet than any other mammal except humans. Mice reproduce rapidly and, more important to their survival, they have the ability to adapt to an extraordinary range of habitats. Should the environment ever become too extreme to support human life, naturalists predict that mice would be able to adapt and survive.

Which one of the following, if true, would most support the naturalists' prediction?

(A) The size of the mouse population is limited by the availability of food.
(B) Under optimum conditions, mice reproduce every four weeks, with five to seven pups per litter.
(C) Fossil remains prove that mice inhabited North America prior to the arrival of humans.
(D) Mice have colonized an island near Antarctica which is too bleak and harsh to support human life.
(E) A significant percentage of the world's mouse population lives in urban areas.

27. All zebras have stripes, and the most widespread subspecies has the best-defined stripes. The stripes must therefore be of importance to the species. Since among these grassland grazers the stripes can hardly function as camouflage, they must serve as some sort of signal for other zebras.

Which one of the following, if true, most strongly supports the conclusion regarding a signaling function?

(A) The subspecies of zebras with the best-defined stripes is also characterized by exceptional size and vigor.
(B) In certain tall grasses zebras can be harder to spot than grazing animals with a coat of uniform color.
(C) A visual signal transmitted among the members of a species can consist of a temporary change of color perceptible to other members of the species.
(D) Zebras react much faster to moving shapes that have stripes than they do to moving shapes that are otherwise identical but lack stripes.
(E) Zebras have a richer repertoire of vocal signals than do similar species such as horses.

28. In Peru, ancient disturbances in the dark surface material of a desert show up as light-colored lines that are the width of a footpath and stretch for long distances. One group of lines branching out like rays from a single point crosses over curved lines that form a very large bird figure. Interpreting the lines in the desert as landing strips for spaceship-traveling aliens, an investigator argues that they could hardly have been Inca roads, asking, "What use to the Inca would have been closely spaced roads that ran parallel? That intersected in a sunburst pattern? That came abruptly to an end in the middle of an uninhabited plain?"

For someone who interprets the lines as referring to astronomical phenomena, which one of the following, if true, most effectively counters an objection that the crossing of the straight-line pattern over the bird figure shows that the two kinds of line pattern served unrelated purposes?

(A) In areas that were inhabited by ancient native North American peoples, arrangements of stones have been found that mark places where sunlight falls precisely on the spring solstice, an astronomically determined date.
(B) The straight lines are consistent with sight lines to points on the horizon where particular astronomical events could have been observed at certain plausible dates, and the figure could represent a constellation.
(C) The straight-line pattern is part of a large connected complex of patterns of straight-line rays connecting certain points with one another.
(D) Native Central American cultures, such as that of the Maya, left behind elaborate astronomical calendars that were engraved on rocks.
(E) There is evidence that the bird figure was made well before the straight-line pattern.

29. Delta green ground beetles sometimes remain motionless for hours at a stretch, although they are more active in wet years than in dry years. In 1989 an observer spotted ten delta green ground beetles in nine hours; in 1985 the same observer at the same location had counted 38 in about two hours. This difference probably does not reflect a drop in the population of these rare beetles over this period, however, because 1985 was a wet year and 1989 was relatively dry.

Which one of the following, if true, most strongly supports the conclusion drawn above?

(A) Because of their excellent camouflage, delta green ground beetles are almost impossible to see if they are not moving.
(B) The only habitat of delta green ground beetles is around pools formed by the collection of winter rains in low-lying areas.
(C) Delta green ground beetles move about very little to get food; most of their moving from one place to another is related to their reproductive behavior.
(D) Delta green ground beetles are so rare that, although the first specimen was found in 1878, a second was not found until 1974.
(E) No predator relies on the delta green ground beetle for a major portion of its food supply.

30. Consumer advocate: The toy-labeling law should require manufacturers to provide explicit safety labels on toys to indicate what hazards the toys pose. The only labels currently required by law are labels indicating the age range for which a toy is intended. For instance, a "three and up" label is required on toys that pose a choking hazard for children under three years of age. Although the current toy-labeling law has indeed reduced the incidence of injuries to children from toys, parents could prevent such injuries almost entirely if toy labels provided explicit safety information.

Which one of the following, if true, most strengthens the consumer advocate's argument?

(A) Certain types of toys have never been associated with injury to children.
(B) Most parents believe that the current labels are recommendations regarding level of cognitive skill.
(C) The majority of children injured by toys are under three years of age.
(D) Many parents do not pay attention to manufacturers' labels when they select toys for their children.
(E) Choking is the most serious hazard presented to children by toys.

31. Asbestos, an almost indestructible mineral once installed as building insulation, poses no health risk unless the asbestos is disturbed and asbestos fibers are released into the environment. Since removing asbestos from buildings disturbs it, thereby releasing asbestos fibers, the government should not require removal of all asbestos insulation.

Which one of the following, if true, most strengthens the argument?

(A) Asbestos poses far less risk to health than does smoking, drug and alcohol abuse, improper diet, or lack of exercise.
(B) Asbestos can pose a health threat to workers who remove it without wearing required protective gear.
(C) Some kinds of asbestos, when disturbed, pose greater health risks than do other kinds.
(D) Asbestos is inevitably disturbed by building renovations or building demolition.
(E) Much of the time, removed asbestos is buried in landfills and forgotten, with no guarantee that it will not be disturbed again.

32. Winston: The Public Transportation Authority (PTA) cannot fulfill its mandate to operate without a budget deficit unless it eliminates service during late-night periods of low ridership. Since the fares collected during these periods are less than the cost of providing the service, these cuts would reduce the deficit and should be made. Transit law prohibits unauthorized fare increases, and fare-increase authorization would take two years.

Ping: Such service cuts might cost the PTA more in lost fares than they would save in costs, for the PTA would lose those riders who leave home during the day but must return late at night. Thus the PTA would lose two fares, while realizing cost savings for only one leg of such trips.

Which one of the following, if true, most strongly supports Ping's conclusion?

(A) Over 23 percent of the round trips made by PTA riders are either initiated or else completed during late-night periods.
(B) Reliable survey results show that over 43 percent of the PTA's riders oppose any cut in PTA services.
(C) The last time the PTA petitioned for a 15 percent fare increase, the petition was denied.
(D) The PTA's budget deficit is 40 percent larger this year than it was last year.
(E) The PTA's bus drivers recently won a new contract that guarantees them a significant cash bonus each time they work the late-night shifts.

33. The fishing industry cannot currently be relied upon to help the government count the seabirds killed by net fishing, since an accurate count might result in restriction of net fishing. The government should therefore institute a program under which tissue samples from the dead birds are examined to determine the amount of toxins in the fish eaten by the birds. The industry would then have a reason to turn in the bird carcasses, since the industry needs to know whether the fish it catches are contaminated with toxins.

Which one of the following, if true, most strengthens the argument?

(A) The seabirds that are killed by net fishing do not eat all of the species of fish caught by the fishing industry.
(B) The government has not in the past sought to determine whether fish were contaminated with toxins by examining tissue samples of seabirds.
(C) The government cannot gain an accurate count of the number of seabirds killed by net fishing unless the fishing industry cooperates.
(D) If the government knew that fish caught by the fishing industry were contaminated by toxins, the government would restrict net fishing.
(E) If net fishing were restricted by the government, then the fishing industry would become more inclined to reveal the number of seabirds killed by net fishing.

34. Three major laundry detergent manufacturers have concentrated their powdered detergents by reducing the proportion of inactive ingredients in the detergent formulas. The concentrated detergents will be sold in smaller packages. In explaining the change, the manufacturers cited the desire to reduce cardboard packaging and other production costs. Market analysts predict that the decision of these three manufacturers, who control 80 percent of the laundry detergent market, will eventually bring about the virtual disappearance of old-style bulky detergents.

Which one of the following, if true, most strongly supports the prediction made by the market analysts?

(A) Most smaller manufacturers of laundry detergents will consider it too expensive to retool factories for the production of the smaller detergent packages.
(B) Many consumers will be skeptical initially that the recommended small amount of concentrated detergent will clean laundry as effectively as the larger amount of the old-style detergent did.
(C) Some analysts believe that consumers will have to pay a greater cost per load of laundry to use the new concentrated detergent than they did to use the old-style detergent.
(D) Major supermarkets have announced that they will not charge the detergent manufacturers less to display their detergents, even though the detergents will take up less shelf space.
(E) Consumers are increasingly being persuaded by environmental concerns to buy concentrated detergents when available in order to reduce cardboard waste.

STRENGTHEN

35. Although tales of wonder and the fantastic are integral to all world literatures, only recently has the fantasy genre had a commercial resurgence in North America. During the last 20 years, sales of fantasy-fiction books written for adults have gone from 1 to 10 percent of total adult-fiction sales. At the same time, the number of favorable reviews of fantasy books has increased markedly. Some booksellers say that the increased sales of fantasy books written for adults can be traced to the increased favorable attention given the genre by book reviewers.

Which one of the following, if true, most strongly supports the booksellers' explanation of the growth in sales of fantasy-fiction books for adults?

(A) Many experts report that on average the reading level of book buyers has declined over the past 20 years.
(B) Because life during the past 20 years has become complex and difficult, many readers have come to prefer the happy endings that fantasy fiction often provides.
(C) Some fantasy publishers take advantage of the popularity of certain books by commissioning similar books.
(D) Because few readers of mystery novels were buying fantasy fiction, 10 years ago the major publishers of fantasy fiction created an advertising campaign directed specifically at those readers.
(E) After fantasy fiction began to be favorably reviewed by respected critics 20 years ago, book buyers began to regard fantasy books as suitable reading for adults.

36. Environmentalist: An increased number of oil spills and the consequent damage to the environment indicate the need for stricter safety standards for the oil industry. Since the industry refuses to take action, it is the national government that must regulate industry safety standards. In particular, the government has to at least require oil companies to put double hulls on their tankers and to assume financial responsibility for accidents.

Industry representative: The industry alone should be responsible for devising safety standards because of its expertise in handling oil and its understanding of the cost entailed. Implementing the double-hull proposal is not currently feasible because it creates new safety issues. Furthermore, the cost would be burdensome to the industry and consumers.

Which one of the following, if true, most strongly supports the industry representative's position against the environmentalist's position?

(A) Recently a double-hulled tanker loaded with oil was punctured when it ran aground, but no oil was released.
(B) Proposed government regulation would mandate the creation of regional response teams within the Coast Guard to respond to oil spills and coordinate cleanup activities.
(C) Proposed legislation requires that new tankers have double hulls but that existing tankers either be refitted with double hulls in the next 20 years or else be retired.
(D) Fumes can become trapped between the two hull layers of double-hulled tankers, and the risk of explosions that could rupture the tanker's hull is thereby increased.
(E) From now on, the oil industry will be required by recent legislation to finance a newly established oil-spill cleanup fund.

37. Until recently, anthropologists generally agreed that higher primates originated about 30 million years ago in the Al Fayyum region of Egypt. However, a 40-million-year-old fossilized fragment of a lower jawbone discovered in Burma (now called Myanmar) in 1978 was used to support the theory that the earliest higher primates originated in Burma. However, the claim is premature, for __________.

Which one of the following, if true, is the most logical completion of the paragraph above?

(A) there are no more primate species in Burma than there are in Egypt
(B) several anthropologists, using different dating methods, independently confirmed the estimated age of the jawbone fragment
(C) higher primates cannot be identified solely by their lower jawbones
(D) several prominent anthropologists do not believe that higher primates could have originated in either Egypt or Burma
(E) other archaeological expeditions in Burma have unearthed higher-primate fossilized bone fragments that are clearly older than 40 million years

38. The cumbersome spears that were the principal weapons used by certain tribes in the early Bronze Age precluded widespread casualties during intertribal conflicts. But the comparatively high number of warrior tombs found in recent excavations of the same tribes' late Bronze Age settlements indicates that in the late Bronze Age, wars between these tribes were frequent, and the casualty rate was high. Hence some archaeologists claim that by the late Bronze Age, these tribes had developed new methods of warfare designed to inflict many casualties.

Which one of the following, if true, most supports the archaeologists' claim?

(A) A royal tomb dating to the early Bronze Age contained pottery depicting battle scenes in which warriors use spears.
(B) There is evidence that many buildings dating to the late Bronze Age were built by prisoners of war taken in battles between enemy tribes.
(C) Scenes of violent warfare, painted in bright hues, frequently appear on pottery that has been found in some early Bronze Age tombs of warriors.
(D) Some tombs of warriors dating to the late Bronze Age contain armor and weapons that anthropologists believe were trophies taken from enemies in battle.
(E) The marks on the bones of many of the late Bronze Age warriors whose tombs were excavated are consistent with the kind of wounds inflicted by arrowheads also found in many late Bronze Age settlements.

39. Someone who gets sick from eating a meal will often develop a strong distaste for the one food in the meal that had the most distinctive flavor, whether or not that food caused the sickness. This phenomenon explains why children are especially likely to develop strong aversions to some foods.

Which one of the following, if true, provides the strongest support for the explanation?

(A) Children are more likely than adults to be given meals composed of foods lacking especially distinctive flavors.
(B) Children are less likely than adults to see a connection between their health and the foods they eat.
(C) Children tend to have more acute taste and to become sick more often than adults do.
(D) Children typically recover more slowly than adults do from sickness caused by food.
(E) Children are more likely than are adults to refuse to eat unfamiliar foods.

STRENGTHEN

40. A newly developed light bulb is much more cost effective than conventional light bulbs: it costs only about 3 times what a conventional light bulb costs but it lasts up to 10 times as long as a conventional light bulb. Despite the manufacturer's intense efforts to publicize the advantages of the new bulb, one analyst predicts that these new bulbs will prove to sell very poorly.

Each of the following, if true, provides support for the analyst's prediction EXCEPT:

(A) The light generated by the new bulb is in the yellow range of the spectrum, a type of artificial light most people find unappealing.

(B) Most people who purchase light bulbs prefer to buy inexpensive light bulbs rather than more durable but expensive light bulbs.

(C) A manufacturer of one brand of conventional light bulb has advertised claims that the new light bulb uses more electricity than do conventional light bulbs.

(D) The new bulb is to be marketed in several different quantities, ranging from packages containing one bulb to packages containing four bulbs.

(E) A competing manufacturer is about to introduce a light bulb that lasts 10 times as long as a conventional bulb but costs less than a conventional bulb.

6

Chapter Six: Justify the Conclusion Questions

JUSTIFY

1. A fourteen-year study of finches on the Galapagos islands concluded that there is a definite relationship between climate and the population size of finch species that thrive at various times. During droughts, more members of large finch species survive because their bills are large enough to crack large, hard seeds, giving them a food supply unavailable to smaller birds. In rainy years, fewer members of the large finch species survive because the additional moisture fosters the growth of plants that produce small seeds. The larger finch varieties have to consume enormous numbers of small seeds to meet their energy demands, and some just cannot eat them fast enough.

   Which one of the following must be assumed in order to justify the conclusion that climatic variations cause a major difference in survival rates of small and large finches?

   (A) During drought conditions, the weather promotes the growth of plants that produce small, hard seeds.
   (B) A lengthy period of rainy weather results in fewer large, hard seeds being produced.
   (C) In rainy periods, the small finches gather enough food to grow much larger and heavier, but their ultimate size is limited by their inability to eat small seeds fast.
   (D) The Galapagos climate during this fourteen-year period had about as much dry weather as it had wet weather.
   (E) Small seeds do not have to be cracked open in order to be digested by any of the finch varieties.

2. "Though they soon will, patients should not have a legal right to see their medical records. As a doctor, I see two reasons for this. First, giving them access will be time-wasting because it will significantly reduce the amount of time that medical staff can spend on more important duties, by forcing them to retrieve and return files. Second, if my experience is anything to go by, no patients are going to ask for access to their records anyway."

   Which one of the following, if true, establishes that the doctor's second reason does not cancel out the first?

   (A) The new law will require that doctors, when seeing a patient in their office, must be ready to produce the patient's records immediately, not just ready to retrieve them.
   (B) The task of retrieving and returning files would fall to the lowest-paid member of a doctor's office staff.
   (C) Any patients who asked to see their medical records would also insist on having details they did not understand explained to them.
   (D) The new law does not rule out that doctors may charge patients for extra expenses incurred specifically in order to comply with the new law.
   (E) Some doctors have all along had a policy of allowing their patients access to their medical records, but those doctors' patients took no advantage of this policy.

3. Every photograph, because it involves the light rays that something emits hitting film, must in some obvious sense be true. But because it could always have been made to show things differently than it does, it cannot express the whole truth and, in that sense, is false. Therefore, nothing can ever be definitively proved with a photograph.

   Which one of the following is an assumption that would permit the conclusion above to be properly drawn?

   (A) Whatever is false in the sense that it cannot express the whole truth cannot furnish definitive proof.
   (B) The whole truth cannot be known.
   (C) It is not possible to determine the truthfulness of a photograph in any sense.
   (D) It is possible to use a photograph as corroborative evidence if there is additional evidence establishing the truth about the scene photographed.
   (E) If something is being photographed, then it is possible to prove definitively the truth about it.

4. Photovoltaic power plants produce electricity from sunlight. As a result of astonishing recent technological advances, the cost of producing electric power at photovoltaic power plants, allowing for both construction and operating costs, is one-tenth of what it was 20 years ago, whereas the corresponding cost for traditional plants, which burn fossil fuels, has increased. Thus, photovoltaic power plants offer a less expensive approach to meeting demand for electricity than do traditional power plants.

   The conclusion of the argument is properly drawn if which one of the following is assumed?

   (A) The cost of producing electric power at traditional plants has increased over the past 20 years.
   (B) Twenty years ago, traditional power plants were producing 10 times more electric power than were photovoltaic plants.
   (C) None of the recent technological advances in producing electric power at photovoltaic plants can be applied to producing power at traditional plants.
   (D) Twenty years ago, the cost of producing electric power at photovoltaic plants was less than 10 times the cost of producing power at traditional plants.
   (E) The cost of producing electric power at photovoltaic plants is expected to decrease further, while the cost of producing power at traditional plants is not expected to decrease.

5. In a bureaucracy, all decisions are arrived at by a process that involves many people. There is no one person who has the authority to decide whether a project will proceed or not. As a consequence, in bureaucracies, risky projects are never undertaken.

   The conclusion follows logically from the premises if which one of the following is assumed?

   (A) All projects in a bureaucracy require risk.
   (B) Decisive individuals choose not to work in a bureaucracy.
   (C) An individual who has decision-making power will take risks.
   (D) The only risky projects undertaken are those for which a single individual has decision-making power.
   (E) People sometimes take risks as individuals that they would not take as part of a group.

6. Modern physicians often employ laboratory tests, in addition to physical examinations, in order to diagnose diseases accurately. Insurance company regulations that deny coverage for certain laboratory tests therefore decrease the quality of medical care provided to patients.

   Which one of the following is an assumption that would serve to justify the conclusion above?

   (A) Physical examinations and the uncovered laboratory tests together provide a more accurate diagnosis of many diseases than do physical examinations alone.
   (B) Many physicians generally oppose insurance company regulations that, in order to reduce costs, limit the use of laboratory tests.
   (C) Many patients who might benefit from the uncovered laboratory tests do not have any form of health insurance.
   (D) There are some illnesses that experienced physicians can diagnose accurately from physical examination alone.
   (E) Laboratory tests are more costly to perform than are physical examinations.

7. Impact craters caused by meteorites smashing into Earth have been found all around the globe, but they have been found in the greatest density in geologically stable regions. This relatively greater abundance of securely identified craters in geologically stable regions must be explained by the lower rates of destructive geophysical processes in those regions.

   The conclusion is properly drawn if which one of the following is assumed?

   (A) A meteorite that strikes exactly the same spot as an earlier meteorite will obliterate all traces of the earlier impact.
   (B) Rates of destructive geophysical processes within any given region vary markedly throughout geological time.
   (C) The rate at which the Earth is struck by meteorites has greatly increased in geologically recent times.
   (D) Actual meteorite impacts have been scattered fairly evenly over the Earth's surface in the course of Earth's geological history.
   (E) The Earth's geologically stable regions have been studied more intensively by geologists than have its less stable regions.

JUSTIFY

8. The seventeenth-century physicist Sir Isaac Newton is remembered chiefly for his treatises on motion and gravity. But Newton also conducted experiments secretly for many years based on the arcane theories of alchemy, trying unsuccessfully to transmute common metals into gold and produce rejuvenating elixirs. If the alchemists of the seventeenth century had published the results of their experiments, chemistry in the eighteenth century would have been more advanced than it actually was.

Which one of the following assumptions would allow the conclusion concerning eighteenth-century chemistry to be properly drawn?

(A) Scientific progress is retarded by the reluctance of historians to acknowledge the failures of some of the great scientists.
(B) Advances in science are hastened when reports of experiments, whether successful or not, are available for review by other scientists.
(C) Newton's work on motion and gravity would not have gained wide acceptance if the results of his work in alchemy had also been made public.
(D) Increasing specialization within the sciences makes it difficult for scientists in one field to understand the principles of other fields.
(E) The seventeenth-century alchemists could have achieved their goals only if their experiments had been subjected to public scrutiny.

9. The workers at Bell Manufacturing will shortly go on strike unless the management increases their wages. As Bell's president is well aware, however, in order to increase the workers' wages, Bell would have to sell off some of its subsidiaries. So, some of Bell's subsidiaries will be sold.

The conclusion above is properly drawn if which one of the following is assumed?

(A) Bell Manufacturing will begin to suffer increased losses.
(B) Bell's management will refuse to increase its workers' wages.
(C) The workers at Bell Manufacturing will not be going on strike.
(D) Bell's president has the authority to offer the workers their desired wage increase.
(E) Bell's workers will not accept a package of improved benefits in place of their desired wage increase.

10. A person can develop or outgrow asthma at any age. In children under ten, asthma is twice as likely to develop in boys. Boys are less likely than girls to outgrow asthma, yet by adolescence the percentage of boys with asthma is about the same as the percentage of girls with asthma because a large number of girls develop asthma in early adolescence.

Assuming the truth of the passage, one can conclude from it that the number of adolescent boys with asthma is approximately equal to the number of adolescent girls with asthma, if one also knows that

(A) a tendency toward asthma is often inherited
(B) children who develop asthma before two years of age are unlikely to outgrow it
(C) there are approximately equal numbers of adolescent boys and adolescent girls in the population
(D) the development of asthma in childhood is not closely related to climate or environment
(E) the percentage of adults with asthma is lower than the percentage of adolescents with asthma

11. It can safely be concluded that there are at least as many trees in Seclee as there are in Martown.

From which one of the following does the conclusion logically follow?

(A) More trees were planted in Seclee in the past two years than in Martown.
(B) Seclee is the region within which Martown is located.
(C) Martown is suffering from an epidemic of tree-virus infection.
(D) The average annual rainfall for Seclee is greater than the average annual rainfall for Martown.
(E) The average number of trees cut down annually in Martown is higher than in Seclee.

12. A poor farmer was fond of telling his children: "In this world, you are either rich or poor, and you are either honest or dishonest. All poor farmers are honest. Therefore, all rich farmers are dishonest."

The farmer's conclusion is properly drawn if the argument assumes that

(A) every honest farmer is poor
(B) every honest person is a farmer
(C) everyone who is dishonest is a rich farmer
(D) everyone who is poor is honest
(E) every poor person is a farmer

13. Some accountants calculate with simple adding machines, and some use complex computers. One can perform more calculations in less time with a computer than with an adding machine. Therefore, assuming the costs of using the two types of machines are equal, an accountant who uses a computer generally can earn more per hour than an accountant who uses an adding machine.

Which one of the following is an assumption that would make the conclusion in the passage a logical one?

(A) More accountants use computers than use adding machines.
(B) The more hours an accountant spends on the job, the more money he or she will earn.
(C) The more calculations an accountant performs, the more money he or she will earn.
(D) An accountant who uses an adding machine can charge a higher hourly rate than one who uses a computer.
(E) In general, accountants vary in terms of the number of calculations they make and the amount of money they earn.

14. Oil company representative: We spent more money on cleaning the otters affected by our recent oil spill than has been spent on any previous marine mammal rescue project. This shows our concern for the environment.

Environmentalist: You have no such concern. Your real concern is evident in your admission to the press that news photographs of oil-covered otters would be particularly damaging to your public image, which plays an important role in your level of sales.

The environmentalist's conclusion would be properly drawn if it were true that the

(A) oil company cannot have more than one motive for cleaning the otters affected by the oil spill
(B) otter population in the area of the oil spill could not have survived without the cleaning project
(C) oil company has always shown a high regard for its profits in choosing its courses of action
(D) government would have spent the money to clean the otters if the oil company had not agreed to do it
(E) oil company's efforts toward cleaning the affected otters have been more successful than have such efforts in previous projects to clean up oil spills

15. A new gardening rake with an S-shaped handle reduces compression stress on the spine during the pull stroke to about one-fifth of what it is with a straight-handled rake. During the push stroke, however, compression stress is five times more with the new rake than with a straight-handled rake. Neither the push stroke nor the pull stroke with a straight-handled rake produces enough compression stress to cause injury, but compression stress during the push stroke with the new rake is above the danger level. Therefore, straight-handled rakes are better than the new rakes for minimizing risk of spinal injury.

The conclusion above is properly drawn from the premises given if which one of the following is true?

(A) Compression stress resulting from pushing is the only cause of injuries to the spine that occur as a result of raking.
(B) Raking is a frequent cause of spinal injury among gardeners.
(C) The redesign of a tool rarely results in a net gain of efficiency, since gains tend to be counterbalanced by losses.
(D) A garden rake can never be used in such a way that all the strokes with that rake are push strokes.
(E) It is not possible to design a garden rake with a handle that is other than straight or S-shaped.

JUSTIFY

16. In many languages other than English there is a word for "mother's brother" which is different from the word for "father's brother," whereas English uses the word "uncle" for both. Thus, speakers of these languages evidence a more finely discriminated kinship system than English speakers do. The number of basic words for colors also varies widely from language to language. Therefore, speakers of languages that have fewer basic words for colors than English has must be perceptually unable to distinguish as many colors as speakers of English can distinguish.

    The conclusion concerning words for colors would be properly drawn if which one of the following were assumed?

    (A) Most languages have distinct words for "sister" and "brother."
    (B) Each language has a different basic word for each sensory quality that its speakers can perceptually distinguish.
    (C) Every language makes some category distinctions that no other language makes.
    (D) In any language short, frequently used words express categories that are important for its speakers to distinguish perceptually from each other.
    (E) Speakers of languages with relatively few basic words for colors live in geographical regions where flora and fauna do not vary greatly in color.

17. The number of hospital emergency room visits by heroin users grew by more than 25 percent during the 1980s. Clearly, then, the use of heroin rose in that decade.

    The author's conclusion is properly drawn if which one of the following is assumed?

    (A) Those who seek medical care because of heroin use usually do so in the later stages of addiction.
    (B) Many heroin users visit hospital emergency rooms repeatedly.
    (C) The number of visits to hospital emergency rooms by heroin users is proportional to the incidence of heroin usage.
    (D) The methods of using heroin have changed since 1980, and the new methods are less hazardous.
    (E) Users of heroin identify themselves as such when they come to hospital emergency rooms.

18. A car's antitheft alarm that sounds in the middle of the night in a crowded city neighborhood may stop an attempted car theft. On the other hand, the alarm might signal only a fault in the device, or a response to some harmless contact, such as a tree branch brushing the car. But whatever the cause, the sleep of many people in the neighborhood is disturbed. Out of consideration for others, people who have these antitheft alarms on their cars should deactivate them when they park in crowded city neighborhoods at night.

    Which one of the following, if assumed by the author of the passage, would allow her properly to draw her conclusion that the owners of alarm-equipped cars should deactivate the alarms when parking in crowded city neighborhoods at night?

    (A) The inconvenience of false alarms is a small price to pay for the security of a neighborhood.
    (B) In most cases when a car alarm sounds at night, it is a false alarm.
    (C) Allowing the residents of a crowded city neighborhood to sleep undisturbed is more important than preventing car theft.
    (D) People who equip their cars with antitheft alarms are generally inconsiderate of others.
    (E) The sounding of car antitheft alarms during the daytime does not disturb the residents of crowded city neighborhoods.

19. In experiments in which certain kinds of bacteria were placed in a generous supply of nutrients, the populations of bacteria grew rapidly, and genetic mutations occurred at random in the populations. These experiments show that all genetic mutation is random.

    Which one of the following, if true, enables the conclusion to be properly drawn?

    (A) Either all genetic mutations are random or none are random.
    (B) The bacteria tested in the experiments were of extremely common forms.
    (C) If all genetic mutations in bacteria are random, then all genetic mutations in every other life form are random also.
    (D) The kind of environment in which genetic mutation takes place has no effect on the way genetic mutation occurs.
    (E) The nutrients used were the same as those that nourish the bacteria in nature.

20. The ends of modern centuries have been greeted with both apocalyptic anxieties and utopian fantasies. It is not surprising that both reactions have consistently proven to be misplaced. After all, the precise time when a century happens to end cannot have any special significance, since the Gregorian calendar though widely used, is only one among many that people have devised.

Which one of the following, if true, could be substituted for the reason cited above while still preserving the force of the argument?

(A) It is logically impossible for both reactions to be correct at the same time.
(B) What is a utopian fantasy to one group of people may well be, for another group of people, a realization of their worst fears.
(C) The number system based on the number ten, in the absence of which one hundred years would not have the appearance of being a significant period of time, is by no means the only one that people have created.
(D) The firm expectation that something extraordinary is about to happen can make people behave in a manner that makes it less likely that something extraordinary will happen.
(E) Since a century far exceeds the normal human life span, people do not live long enough to learn from mistakes that they themselves made one hundred years before.

21. Although most species of nondomestic mammals in Australia are marsupials, over 100 species—including seals, bats, and mice—are not marsupials but placentals. It is clear, however, that these placentals are not native to this island continent: all nonhuman placentals except the dingo, a dog introduced by the first humans that settled Australia, are animals whose ancestors could swim long distances, fly, or float on driftwood.

The conclusion above is properly drawn if which one of the following is assumed?

(A) Some marsupials now found in Australia might not be native to that continent, but rather might have been introduced to Australia by some other means.
(B) Humans who settled Australia probably introduced many of the placental mammal species now present on that continent.
(C) The only Australian placentals that could be native to Australia would be animals whose ancestors could not have reached Australia from elsewhere.
(D) No marsupials now found in Australia can swim long distances, fly, or float on driftwood.
(E) Seals, bats, and mice are typically found only in areas where there are no native marsupials.

22. In the past decade, a decreasing percentage of money spent on treating disease X went to pay for standard methods of treatment, which are known to be effective though they are expensive and painful. An increasing percentage is being spent on nonstandard treatments, which cause little discomfort. Unfortunately the nonstandard treatments have proved to be ineffective. Obviously, less money is being spent now on effective treatments of disease X than was spent ten years ago.

Which one of the following, if assumed, allows the conclusion above to be properly drawn?

(A) Varieties of disease X requiring expensive special treatment have become less common during the past decade.
(B) Nonstandard methods of treating disease X are more expensive now than they were a decade ago.
(C) Of total medical expenditures, the percentage that is due to treatment of disease X increased during the past decade.
(D) Most of the money spent on treating disease X during the last decade went to pay for nonstandard treatments.
(E) The total amount of money spent on treating disease X slowly declined during the past decade.

JUSTIFY

Chapter Seven: Assumption Questions

ASSUMPTION

1. Even in a democracy, it is necessary to restrict the dissemination of advanced technological knowledge that is of commercial or national-security value. Dissemination to certain countries, those that are or will be competitors or enemies, should be selectively prohibited. There must, however, be free exchange of scientific information.

In order to act in accordance with the position above, it would be necessary to be able to rely on each of the following EXCEPT:

(A) It is possible to distinguish with confidence, despite any changes in the international environment, friendly or noncompetitive from hostile or competitive nations.
(B) In a democracy, it is not necessary that the public have detailed knowledge of the country's advanced technology in order, for example, to make informed decisions about the direction public policy should take.
(C) In most fields of science, basic scientific research is further advanced in countries that are democracies than in countries that are not democracies.
(D) In each field of science, it is possible to distinguish scientific information from advanced technological knowledge that is of commercial or national-security value.
(E) In cases where a company that uses advanced technology is a multinational organization, it is possible to keep information about the technology from being passed across designated national boundaries.

2. It is the mark of a superior conductor that he or she has the authority to insist, even with a top orchestra, that rehearsal work must be intensified. This authority cannot be simply claimed; the conductor must earn it by winning the orchestra's respect for the artistic interpretations he or she is currently pursuing.

In taking the position outlined, the author presupposes which one of the following?

(A) Superior conductors devise different interpretations of a composition for each orchestra with which they perform.
(B) Superior conductors are perfectionists who are never satisfied with any performance even by a top orchestra.
(C) Top orchestras are always ready to put in additional work on rehearsals if the conductor considers additional rehearsing necessary.
(D) Top orchestras can appreciate the merits of an interpretation even before they have brought it to full realization.
(E) Even top orchestras are not always led by superior conductors.

3. Train service suffers when a railroad combines commuter and freight service. By dividing its attention between its freight and commuter customers, a railroad serves neither particularly well. Therefore, if a railroad is going to be a successful business, then it must concentrate exclusively on one of these two markets.

For the argument to be logically correct it must make which one of the following assumptions?

(A) Commuter and freight service have little in common with each other.
(B) The first priority of a railroad is to be a successful business.
(C) Unless a railroad serves its customers well, it will not be a successful business.
(D) If a railroad concentrates on commuter service, it will be a successful business.
(E) Railroad commuters rarely want freight service.

4. The energy an animal must expend to move uphill is proportional to its body weight, whereas the animal's energy output available to perform this task is proportional to its surface area. This is the reason that small animals, like squirrels, can run up a tree trunk almost as fast as they can move on level ground, whereas large animals tend to slow down when they are moving uphill.

Which one of the following is an assumption on which the explanation above depends?

(A) The amount of energy needed to move uphill is no greater for large animals than it is for small animals.
(B) Small animals can move more rapidly than large animals can.
(C) The ratio of surface area to body weight is smaller in large animals than it is in small animals.
(D) There is little variation in the ratio of energy output to body weight among animals.
(E) The amount of energy needed to run at a given speed is proportional to the surface area of the running animal.

5. In 1860 Bavarian quarry workers discovered the impression of a feather in a limestone slab dating to the Mesozoic era. It had previously been assumed that birds developed only after the close of the Mesozoic era and after the disappearance of pterosaurs, a species characteristic of that era. But there in limestone lay the imprint of a fully aerodynamic, three-inch-long feather. This, therefore, must have been the earliest bird (certainly, the earliest found to that date).

The argument assumes which one of the following?

(A) The creature to which the feather belonged was a descendant of the pterosaurs.
(B) Birds with such feathers were preceded by species of birds with less-developed feathers.
(C) In the Mesozoic era, no creatures other than birds had such feathers.
(D) The feather belonged to a Mesozoic creature that was neither a pterosaur nor a bird, but intermediate between them.
(E) The earliest bird flew in an awkward manner.

6. When Cortez arrived in Mexico in A.D. 1519, he observed the inhabitants playing a ceremonial game with a rubber ball. The pre-Columbian inhabitants of Mexico began to use rubber around A.D. 1000. Thus, we can be sure that the game must have originated sometime between approximately A.D. 1000 and Cortez' arrival.

The conclusion reached above depends on which one of the following assumptions?

(A) The pre-Columbian inhabitants of Mexico played games on all ceremonial occasions.
(B) The making of rubber balls was one of the earliest uses of rubber by the inhabitants of Mexico.
(C) The ceremonial game referred to was popular throughout Mexico.
(D) The game had been played since its inception with a rubber ball.
(E) The dating of the first use of rubber in Mexico was due to Cortez.

7. The press reports on political campaigns these days as if they were chess games. One candidate's campaign advisor makes a move; the other candidate's advisor makes a countermove. The press then reports on the campaign advisors and not on the candidates. The losers in this chess game are the voters. They are deprived of the information they need to make informed decisions because the press is ignoring substantive policy issues and reporting only on the process of the campaign. It is clear that the campaign advisors should stay out of the limelight and let the press report on the most revealing positions on substantive issues the candidates have taken.

Which one of the following is an assumption upon which the argument in the passage depends?

(A) Chess is the most appropriate analogy to reporting on political campaigns.
(B) The candidates in the election are taking positions on substantive policy issues.
(C) How the press reports politics determines the substantive issues in the campaign.
(D) The voters are not paying enough attention to the election to be able to make informed decisions.
(E) There is no difference between reporting on the political process and reporting on substantive issues.

8. More than a year ago, the city announced that police would crack down on illegally parked cars and that resources would be diverted from writing speeding tickets to ticketing illegally parked cars. But no crackdown has taken place. The police chief claims that resources have had to be diverted from writing speeding tickets to combating the city's staggering drug problem. Yet the police are still writing as many speeding tickets as ever. Therefore, the excuse about resources being tied up in fighting drug-related crime simply is not true.

The conclusion in the passage depends on the assumption that

(A) every member of the police force is qualified to work on combating the city's drug problem
(B) drug-related crime is not as serious a problem for the city as the police chief claims it is
(C) writing speeding tickets should be as important a priority for the city as combating drug related crime
(D) the police could be cracking down on illegally parked cars and combating the drug problem without having to reduce writing speeding tickets
(E) the police cannot continue writing as many speeding tickets as ever while diverting resources to combating drug-related crime

9. How do the airlines expect to prevent commercial plane crashes? Studies have shown that pilot error contributes to two-thirds of all such crashes. To address this problem, the airlines have upgraded their training programs by increasing the hours of classroom instruction and emphasizing communication skills in the cockpit. But it is unrealistic to expect such measures to compensate for pilots' lack of actual flying time. Therefore, the airlines should rethink their training approach to reducing commercial crashes.

Which one of the following is an assumption upon which the argument depends?

(A) Training programs can eliminate pilot errors.
(B) Commercial pilots routinely undergo additional training throughout their careers.
(C) The number of airline crashes will decrease if pilot training programs focus on increasing actual flying time.
(D) Lack of actual flying time is an important contributor to pilot error in commercial plane crashes.
(E) Communication skills are not important to pilot training programs.

10. Advertisement: Clark brand-name parts are made for cars manufactured in this country. They satisfy all of our government automotive tests—the toughest such tests in the world. With foreign-made parts, you never know which might be reliable and which are cheap look-alikes that are poorly constructed and liable to cost you hundreds of dollars in repairs. Therefore, be smart and insist on brand-name parts by Clark for your car.

The argument requires the assumption that

(A) Clark parts are available only in this country
(B) foreign-made parts are not suitable for cars manufactured in this country
(C) no foreign-made parts satisfy our government standards
(D) parts that satisfy our government standards are not as poorly constructed as cheap foreign-made parts
(E) if parts are made for cars manufactured in our country, they are not poorly constructed

11. In Europe, schoolchildren devote time during each school day to calisthenics. North American schools rarely offer a daily calisthenics program. Tests prove that North American children are weaker, slower, and shorter-winded than European children. We must conclude that North American children can be made physically fit only if they participate in school calisthenics on a daily basis.

Which of the following is assumed in the passage?

(A) All children can be made physically fit by daily calisthenics.
(B) All children can be made equally physically fit by daily calisthenics.
(C) Superior physical fitness produces superior health.
(D) School calisthenics are an indispensable factor in European children's superior physical fitness.
(E) North American children can learn to eat a more nutritious diet as well as to exercise daily.

12. The public is well aware that high blood cholesterol levels raise the risk of stroke caused by blood clots. But a recent report concludes that people with low blood cholesterol levels are at increased risk of the other lethal type of stroke—cerebral hemorrhage, caused when a brain artery bursts. The report suggests that because blood cholesterol plays a vital role in maintaining cell membranes, low blood cholesterol weakens artery walls, making them prone to rupture. The conclusion thus supports a long-standing contention by Japanese researchers that Western diets better protect against cerebral hemorrhage than do non-Western diets.

The argument is based on which one of the following assumptions?

(A) Western diets are healthier than non-Western diets.
(B) Western diets result in higher blood cholesterol levels than do non-Western diets.
(C) High blood cholesterol levels preclude the weakening of artery walls.
(D) Cerebral hemorrhages are more dangerous than strokes caused by blood clots.
(E) People who have low blood pressure are at increased risk of cerebral hemorrhage.

13. Because a large disparity in pay between the public and private sectors has developed in recent years, many experienced and extremely capable government administrators have quit their posts and taken positions in private-sector management. Government will be able to recapture these capable administrators by raising salaries to a level comparable to those of the private sector. In that way, the functioning of public agencies will be improved.

The position taken above presupposes which one of the following?

(A) Experience gained from private-sector management will be very valuable in government administration.
(B) The most important factor determining how well government agencies function is the amount of experience the administrators have.
(C) Unless government action is taken, the disparity in pay between government administration and private-sector management will continue to increase.
(D) People who moved from jobs in government administration to private-sector management would choose to change careers again.
(E) If the disparity in pay between government administration and private-sector management increases, administrators will move to the public sector in large numbers.

14. Economic considerations color every aspect of international dealings, and nations are just like individuals in that the lender sets the terms of its dealings with the borrower. That is why a nation that owes money to another nation cannot be a world leader.

The reasoning in the passage assumes which one of the following?

(A) A nation that does not lend to any other nation cannot be a world leader.
(B) A nation that can set the terms of its dealings with other nations is certain to be a world leader.
(C) A nation that has the terms of its dealings with another nation set by that nation cannot be a world leader.
(D) A nation that is a world leader can borrow from another nation as long as that other nation does not set the terms of the dealings between the two nations.
(E) A nation that has no dealings with any other nation cannot be a world leader.

15. Rotelle: You are too old to address effectively the difficult issues facing the country, such as nuclear power, poverty, and pollution.

Sims: I don't want to make age an issue in this campaign, so I will not comment on your youth and inexperience.

Rotelle is committed to which one of the following?

(A) Many old people cannot effectively address the difficult issues facing the country.
(B) Those at least as old as Sims are the only people who cannot effectively address the difficult issues facing the country.
(C) Some young people can effectively address the difficult issues facing the country.
(D) If anyone can effectively address the difficult issues facing the country, that person must be younger than Sims.
(E) Addressing the difficult issues facing the country requires an understanding of young people's points of view.

ASSUMPTION

16. *Rhizobium* bacteria living in the roots of bean plants or other legumes produce fixed nitrogen, which is one of the essential plant nutrients and which for non legume crops, such as wheat, normally must be supplied by applications of nitrogen-based fertilizer. So if biotechnology succeeds in producing wheat strains whose roots will play host to *Rhizobium* bacteria, the need for artificial fertilizers will be reduced.

The argument above makes which one of the following assumptions?

(A) Biotechnology should be directed toward producing plants that do not require artificial fertilizer.
(B) Fixed nitrogen is currently the only soil nutrient that must be supplied by artificial fertilizer for growing wheat crops.
(C) There are no naturally occurring strains of wheat or other grasses that have *Rhizobium* bacteria living in their roots.
(D) Legumes are currently the only crops that produce their own supply of fixed nitrogen.
(E) *Rhizobium* bacteria living in the roots of wheat would produce fixed nitrogen.

17. Scientific research that involves international collaboration has produced papers of greater influence, as measured by the number of times a paper is cited in subsequent papers, than has research without any collaboration. Papers that result from international collaboration are cited an average of seven times, whereas papers with single authors are cited only three times on average. This difference shows that research projects conducted by international research teams are of greater importance than those conducted by single researchers.

Which one of the following is an assumption on which the argument depends?

(A) Prolific writers can inflate the number of citations they receive by citing themselves in subsequent papers.
(B) It is possible to ascertain whether or not a paper is the product of international collaboration by determining the number of citations it has received.
(C) The number of citations a paper receives is a measure of the importance of the research it reports.
(D) The collaborative efforts of scientists who are citizens of the same country do not produce papers that are as important as papers that are produced by international collaboration.
(E) International research teams tend to be more generously funded than are single researchers.

18. Millions of irreplaceable exhibits in natural history museums are currently allowed to decay. Yet without analyses of eggs from museums, the studies linking pesticides with the decline of birds of prey would have been impossible. Therefore, funds must be raised to preserve at least those exhibits that will be most valuable to science in the future.

The argument presupposes that

(A) if a museum exhibit is irreplaceable, its preservation is of an importance that overrides economic considerations
(B) the scientific analysis of museum exhibits can be performed in a nondestructive way
(C) eggs of extinct species should be analyzed to increase knowledge of genetic relationships among species
(D) it can be known at this time what data will be of most use to scientific investigators in the future
(E) the decay of organic material in natural history exhibits is natural and cannot be prevented

19. Mayor of Plainsville: In order to help the economy of Plainsville, I am using some of our tax revenues to help bring a major highway through the town and thereby attract new business to Plainsville.

Citizens' group: You must have interests other than our economy in mind. If you were really interested in helping our economy, you would instead allocate the revenues to building a new business park, since it would bring in twice the business that your highway would.

The argument by the citizens' group relies on which one of the following assumptions?

(A) Plainsville presently has no major highways running through it.
(B) The mayor accepts that a new business park would bring in more new business than would the new highway.
(C) The new highway would have no benefits for Plainsville other than attracting new business.
(D) The mayor is required to get approval for all tax revenue allocation plans from the city council.
(E) Plainsville's economy will not be helped unless a new business park of the sort envisioned by the citizens' group is built.

20. Animals with a certain behavioral disorder have unusually high levels of aluminum in their brain tissue. Since a silicon-based compound binds to aluminum and prevents it from affecting the brain tissue, animals can be cured of the disorder by being treated with the compound.

The argument is based on which one of the following assumptions?

(A) Animals with the disorder have unusually high but invariable levels of aluminum in their brain tissue.
(B) Aluminum is the cause of the disorder rather than merely an effect of it.
(C) Introducing the compound into the brain tissue has no side effects.
(D) The amount of the compound needed to neutralize the aluminum in an animal's brain issue varies depending upon the species.
(E) Aluminum is never present in normal brain tissue.

21. The stated goal of the government's funding program for the arts is to encourage the creation of works of artistic excellence. Senator Beton claims, however, that a government-funded artwork can never reflect the independent artistic conscience of the artist because artists, like anyone else who accepts financial support, will inevitably try to please those who control the distribution of that support. Senator Beton concludes that government funding of the arts not only is a burden on taxpayers but also cannot lead to the creation of works of true artistic excellence.

Which one of the following is an assumption on which Senator Beton's argument is based?

(A) Most taxpayers have little or no interest in the creation of works of true artistic excellence.
(B) Government funding of the arts is more generous than other financial support most artists receive.
(C) Distribution of government funds for the arts is based on a broad agreement as to what constitutes artistic excellence.
(D) Once an artist has produced works of true artistic excellence, he or she will never accept government funding.
(E) A contemporary work of art that does not reflect the independent artistic conscience of the artist cannot be a work of true artistic excellence.

22. The reforms to improve the quality of public education that have been initiated on the part of suppliers of public education have been insufficient. Therefore, reforms must be demanded by consumers. Parents should be given government vouchers with which to pay for their children's education and should be allowed to choose the schools at which the vouchers will be spent. To attract students, academically underachieving schools will be forced to improve their academic offerings.

The argument assumes that

(A) in selecting schools parents would tend to prefer a reasonable level of academic quality to greater sports opportunities or more convenient location
(B) improvement in the academic offerings of schools will be enforced by the discipline of the job market in which graduating students compete
(C) there is a single best way to educate students
(D) children are able to recognize which schools are better and would influence their parents' decisions
(E) schools would each improve all of their academic offerings and would not tend to specialize in one particular field to the exclusion of others

23. School superintendent: It is a sad fact that, until now, entry into the academically best high school in our district has been restricted to the children of people who were wealthy enough to pay the high tuition. Parents who were previously denied the option of sending their children to this school now have this option, since I am replacing the tuition requirement with a requirement that allows only those who live in the neighborhood of the school to attend.

The superintendent's claim about the effect of replacing the tuition requirement relies on the assumption that

(A) the residents of the school's neighborhood tend to be wealthy
(B) people other than those wealthy enough to have paid the old tuition are able to live in the neighborhood of the school
(C) people less wealthy than those who were able to pay the old tuition are in the majority in the district
(D) there are no high schools in the district other than the one referred to by the superintendent
(E) there are many people not wealthy enough to have paid the old tuition who wish to have their children attend the school

ASSUMPTION

24. Being articulate has been equated with having a large vocabulary. Actually, however, people with large vocabularies have no incentive for, and tend not to engage in, the kind of creative linguistic self-expression that is required when no available words seem adequate. Thus a large vocabulary is a hindrance to using language in a truly articulate way.

Which one of the following is an assumption made in the argument?

(A) When people are truly articulate, they have the capacity to express themselves in situations in which their vocabularies seem inadequate.
(B) People who are able to express themselves creatively in new situations have little incentive to acquire large vocabularies.
(C) The most articulate people are people who have large vocabularies but also are able to express themselves creatively when the situation demands it.
(D) In educating people to be more articulate, it would be futile to try to increase the size of their vocabularies.
(E) In unfamiliar situations, even people with large vocabularies often do not have specifically suitable words available.

25. Mary Ann: Our country should, above all, be strong. Strength gains the respect of other countries and makes a country admirable.

Inez: There are many examples in history of countries that were strong but used their strength to commit atrocities. We should judge a country by the morality of its actions, not by its strength. If the actions are morally good, the country is admirable.

Which one of the following is a presupposition that underlies Inez' argument?

(A) At least one country is admirable.
(B) Countries cannot be both strong and moral.
(C) It is possible to assign moral weight to the actions of countries.
(D) The citizens of any country believe that whatever their country does is good.
(E) Countries should impose their standards of morality on other countries by whatever means necessary.

26. J.J. Thomson, the discoverer of the electron and a recipient of the Nobel Prize in physics, trained many physicists, among them seven Nobel Prize winners, 32 fellows of the Royal Society of London, and 83 professors of physics. This shows that the skills needed for creative research can be taught and learned.

Which one of the following is an assumption on which the argument depends?

(A) J. J. Thomson was an internationally known physicist, and scientists came from all over the world to work with him.
(B) All the scientists trained by J. J. Thomson were renowned for their creative scientific research.
(C) At least one of the eminent scientists trained by J. J. Thomson was not a creative researcher before coming to study with him.
(D) Creative research in physics requires research habits not necessary for creative research in other fields.
(E) Scientists who go on to be the most successful researchers often receive their scientific education in classes taught by renowned research scientists.

27. Fire ants from Brazil now infest the southern United States. Unlike queen fire ants in Brazil, two queens in the United States share a nest. Ants from these nests are more aggressive than those from single-queen nests. By destroying virtually all insects in the nest area, these aggressive ants gain sole access to food sources, and the ant population skyrockets. Since certain predator insects in Brazil limit the fire-ant population there, importing such predator insects into the United States would be of overall benefit to the environment by stopping the increase of the fire-ant population in the United States.

Each of the following is an assumption made in the argument EXCEPT:

(A) The imported insects would not prove more damaging to the environment in the United States than are the fire ants themselves.
(B) The predator insects from Brazil could survive in the ecological environment found in the United States.
(C) The especially aggressive fire ants from the two-queen nests would not be able to destroy the Brazilian predator insects.
(D) The predator insects would stop the increase of the ant population before the ants spread to states that are farther north.
(E) The rate of increase of the fire-ant population would not exceed the rate at which the predator insects could kill the ants.

28. Head injury is the most serious type of injury sustained in motorcycle accidents. The average cost to taxpayers for medical care for nonhelmeted motorcycle-accident victims is twice that for their helmeted counterparts. Jurisdictions that have enacted motorcycle-helmet laws have reduced the incidence and severity of accident-related head injuries, thereby reducing the cost to taxpayers. Therefore, to achieve similar cost reductions, other jurisdictions should enact motorcycle-helmet laws. For the same reason jurisdictions should also require helmets for horseback riders, since horseback-riding accidents are even more likely to cause serious head injury than motorcycle accidents are.

Which one of the following is an assumption upon which the author's conclusion concerning helmets for horseback riders depends?

(A) Medical care for victims of horseback-riding accidents is a financial drain on tax funds.
(B) The higher rate of serious head injury suffered by victims of horseback-riding accidents is due to the difference in size between horses and motorcycles.
(C) The medical costs associated with treating head injuries are higher than those for other types of injury.
(D) Most fatalities resulting from horseback-riding and motorcycle accidents could have been prevented if the victims had been wearing helmets.
(E) When deciding whether to enact helmet laws for motorcyclists and horseback riders, the jurisdiction's primary concern is the safety of its citizens.

29. Twenty years ago the Republic of Rosinia produced nearly 100 million tons of potatoes, but last year the harvest barely reached 60 million tons. Agricultural researchers, who have failed to develop new higher-yielding strains of potatoes, are to blame for this decrease, since they have been concerned only with their own research and not with the needs of Rosinia.

Which one of the following is an assumption on which the argument depends?

(A) Any current attempts by agricultural researchers to develop higher-yielding potato strains are futile.
(B) Strains of potatoes most commonly grown in Rosinia could not have produced the yields last year that they once did.
(C) Agricultural researchers often find concrete solutions to practical problems when investigating seemingly unrelated questions.
(D) Wide fluctuations in the size of the potato crop over a twenty-year period are not unusual.
(E) Agricultural research in Rosinia is funded by government grants.

30. Bevex, an artificial sweetener used only in soft drinks, is carcinogenic for mice, but only when it is consumed in very large quantities. To ingest an amount of Bevex equivalent to the amount fed to the mice in the relevant studies, a person would have to drink 25 cans of Bevex-sweetened soft drinks per day. For that reason, Bevex is in fact safe for people.

In order for the conclusion that Bevex is safe for people to be properly drawn, which one of the following must be true?

(A) Cancer from carcinogenic substances develops more slowly in mice than it does in people.
(B) If all food additives that are currently used in foods were tested, some would be found to be carcinogenic for mice.
(C) People drink fewer than 25 cans of Bevex-sweetened soda per day.
(D) People can obtain important health benefits by controlling their weight through the use of artificially sweetened soft drinks.
(E) Some of the studies done on Bevex were not relevant to the question of whether or not Bevex is carcinogenic for people.

31. Marine biologists had hypothesized that lobsters kept together in lobster traps eat one another in response to hunger. Periodic checking of lobster traps, however, has revealed instances of lobsters sharing traps together for weeks. Eight lobsters even shared one trap together for two months without eating one another. The marine biologists' hypothesis, therefore, is clearly wrong.

The argument against the marine biologists' hypothesis is based on which one of the following assumptions?

(A) Lobsters not caught in lobster traps have been observed eating one another.
(B) Two months is the longest known period during which eight or more lobsters have been trapped together.
(C) It is unusual to find as many as eight lobsters caught together in one single trap.
(D) Members of other marine species sometimes eat their own kind when no other food sources are available.
(E) Any food that the eight lobsters in the trap might have obtained was not enough to ward off hunger.

32. Many major scientific discoveries of the past were the product of serendipity, the chance discovery of valuable findings that investigators had not purposely sought. Now, however, scientific research tends to be so costly that investigators are heavily dependent on large grants to fund their research. Because such grants require investigators to provide the grant sponsors with clear projections of the outcome of the proposed research, investigators ignore anything that does not directly bear on the funded research. Therefore, under the prevailing circumstances, serendipity can no longer play a role in scientific discovery.

Which one of the following is an assumption on which the argument depends?

(A) Only findings that an investigator purposely seeks can directly bear on that investigator's research.
(B) In the past few scientific investigators attempted to make clear predictions of the outcome of their research.
(C) Dependence on large grants is preventing investigators from conducting the type of scientific research that those investigators would personally prefer.
(D) All scientific investigators who provide grant sponsors with clear projections of the outcome of their research receive at least some of the grants for which they apply.
(E) In general the most valuable scientific discoveries are the product of serendipity.

33. The government provides insurance for individuals' bank deposits, but requires the banks to pay the premiums for this insurance. Since it is depositors who primarily benefit from the security this insurance provides, the government should take steps to ensure that depositors who want this security bear the cost of it and thus should make depositors pay the premiums for insuring their own accounts.

Which one of the following is assumed by the argument?

(A) Banks are not insured by the government against default on the loans the banks make.
(B) Private insurance companies do not have the resources to provide banks or individuals with deposit insurance.
(C) Banks do not always cover the cost of the deposit-insurance premiums by paying depositors lower interest rates on insured deposits than the banks would on uninsured deposits.
(D) The government limits the insurance protection it provides by insuring accounts up to a certain legally defined amount only.
(E) The government does not allow banks to offer some kinds of accounts in which deposits are not insured.

34. One sure way you can tell how quickly a new idea—for example, the idea of "privatization"—is taking hold among the population is to monitor how fast the word or words expressing that particular idea are passing into common usage. Professional opinions of whether or not words can indeed be said to have passed into common usage are available from dictionary editors, who are vitally concerned with this question.

The method described above for determining how quickly a new idea is taking hold relies on which one of the following assumptions?

(A) Dictionary editors are not professionally interested in words that are only rarely used.
(B) Dictionary editors have exact numerical criteria for telling when a word has passed into common usage.
(C) For a new idea to take hold, dictionary editors have to include the relevant word or words in their dictionaries.
(D) As a word passes into common usage, its meaning does not undergo any severe distortions in the process.
(E) Words denoting new ideas tend to be used before the ideas denoted are understood.

35. Between 1971 and 1975, the government office that monitors drug companies issued an average of 60 citations a year for serious violations of drug-promotion laws. Between 1976 and 1980, the annual average for issuance of such citations was only 5. This decrease indicates that the government office was, on average, considerably more lax in enforcing drug-promotion laws between 1976 and 1980 than it was between 1971 and 1975.

The argument assumes which one of the following?

(A) The decrease in the number of citations was not caused by a decrease in drug companies' violations of drug-promotion laws.
(B) A change in enforcement of drug-promotion laws did not apply to minor violations.
(C) The enforcement of drug-promotion laws changed in response to political pressure.
(D) The government office should not issue more than an average of 5 citations a year to drug companies for serious violations of drug-promotion laws.
(E) Before 1971 the government office issued more than 60 citations a year to drug companies for serious violations of drug-promotion laws.

36. Harry Trevalga: You and your publication have unfairly discriminated against my poems. I have submitted thirty poems in the last two years and you have not published any of them! It is all because I won the Fenner Poetry Award two years ago and your poetry editor thought she deserved it.

Publisher: Ridiculous! Our editorial policy and practice is perfectly fair, since our poetry editor judges all submissions for publication without ever seeing the names of the poets, and hence cannot possibly have known who wrote your poems.

The publisher makes which one of the following assumptions in replying to Trevalga's charges of unfair discrimination?

(A) The poetry editor does not bear a grudge against Harry Trevalga for his winning the Fenner Poetry Award.
(B) It is not unusual for poets to contribute many poems to the publisher's publication without ever having any accepted for publication.
(C) The poetry editor cannot recognize the poems submitted by Harry Trevalga as his unless Trevalga's name is attached to them.
(D) The poetry editor's decisions on which poems to publish are not based strictly on judgments of intrinsic merit.
(E) Harry Trevalga submitted his poems to the publisher's publication under his pen name.

ASSUMPTION

37. Light utility trucks have become popular among consumers who buy them primarily for the trucks' rugged appearance. Yet although these trucks are tough-looking, they are exempt from the government's car-safety standards that dictate minimum roof strength and minimum resistance to impact. Therefore, if involved in a serious high-impact accident, a driver of one of these trucks is more likely to be injured than is a driver of a car that is subject to these government standards.

The argument depends on the assumption that

(A) the government has established safety standards for the construction of light utility trucks
(B) people who buy automobiles solely for their appearance are more likely than other people to drive recklessly
(C) light utility trucks are more likely than other kinds of vehicles to be involved in accidents that result in injuries
(D) the trucks' rugged appearance is deceptive in that their engines are not especially powerful
(E) light utility trucks are less likely to meet the car-safety standards than are cars that are subject to the standards

38. A distemper virus has caused two-thirds of the seal population in the North Sea to die since May 1988. The explanation for the deaths cannot rest here, however. There must be a reason the normally latent virus could prevail so suddenly: clearly the severe pollution of the North Sea waters must have weakened the immune system of the seals so that they could no longer withstand the virus.

The argument concerning the immune system of the seals presupposes which one of the following?

(A) There has been a gradual decline in the seal population of the North Sea during the past two centuries.
(B) No further sources of pollution have been added since May 1988 to the already existing sources of pollution in the North Sea.
(C) There was no sudden mutation in the distemper virus which would have allowed the virus successfully to attack healthy North Sea seals by May 1988.
(D) Pollution in the North Sea is no greater than pollution in the Mediterranean Sea, off the coast of North America, or in the Sea of Japan.
(E) Some species that provide food for the seals have nearly become extinct as a result of the pollution.

39. The dean of computing must be respected by the academic staff and be competent to oversee the use of computers on campus. The only deans whom academics respect are those who hold doctoral degrees, and only someone who really knows about computers can competently oversee the use of computers on campus. Furthermore, the board of trustees has decided that the dean of computing must be selected from among this university's staff. Therefore, the dean of computing must be a professor from this university's computer science department.

Which one of the following is an assumption on which the argument depends?

(A) Academics respect only people who hold doctoral degrees.
(B) All of this university's professors have obtained doctoral degrees.
(C) At this university, every professor who holds a doctoral degree in computer science really knows about computers.
(D) All academics who hold doctoral degrees are respected by their academic colleagues.
(E) Among this university's staff members with doctoral degrees, only those in the computer science department really know about computers.

40. In order to control the deer population, a biologist has proposed injecting female deer during breeding season with 10 milligrams of a hormone that would suppress fertility. Critics have charged that the proposal poses health risks to people who might eat the meat of treated deer and thereby ingest unsafe quantities of the hormone. The biologist has responded to these critics by pointing out that humans can ingest up to 10 milligrams of the hormone a day without any adverse effects, and since no one would eat even one entire deer a day, the treatment would be safe.

The biologist's response to critics of the proposal is based on which one of the following assumptions?

(A) People would be notified of the time when deer in their area were to be treated with the hormone.
(B) The hormone that would be injected into the deer is chemically similar to hormones used in human contraceptives.
(C) Hunting season for deer could be scheduled so that it would not coincide with breeding season.
(D) The hormone in question does not occur naturally in the female deer that would be injected.
(E) Most people do not consider deer meat to be part of their daily diet and eat it only on rare occasions.

41. So-called environmentalists have argued that the proposed Golden Lake Development would interfere with bird-migration patterns. However, the fact that these same people have raised environmental objections to virtually every development proposal brought before the council in recent years indicates that their expressed concern for bird-migration patterns is nothing but a mask for their antidevelopment, antiprogress agenda. Their claim, therefore, should be dismissed without further consideration.

For the claim that the concern expressed by the so-called environmentalists is not their real concern to be properly drawn on the basis of the evidence cited, which one of the following must be assumed?

(A) Not every development proposal opposed in recent years by these so-called environmentalists was opposed because they believed it to pose a threat to the environment.
(B) People whose real agenda is to block development wherever it is proposed always try to disguise their true motives.
(C) Anyone who opposes unrestricted development is an opponent of progress.
(D) The council has no reason to object to the proposed Golden Lake Development other than concern about the development's effect on bird-migration patterns.
(E) When people say that they oppose a development project solely on environmental grounds, their real concern almost always lies elsewhere.

42. A university should not be entitled to patent the inventions of its faculty members. Universities, as guarantors of intellectual freedom, should encourage the free flow of ideas and the general dissemination of knowledge. Yet a university that retains the right to patent the inventions of its faculty members has a motive to suppress information about a potentially valuable discovery until the patent for it has been secured. Clearly, suppressing information concerning such discoveries is incompatible with the university's obligation to promote the free flow of ideas.

Which one of the following is an assumption that the argument makes?

(A) Universities are the only institutions that have an obligation to guarantee intellectual freedom.
(B) Most inventions by university faculty members would be profitable if patented.
(C) Publication of reports on research is the only practical way to disseminate information concerning new discoveries.
(D) Universities that have a motive to suppress information concerning discoveries by their faculty members will occasionally act on that motive.
(E) If the inventions of a university faculty member are not patented by that university, then they will be patented by the faculty member instead.

43. English and the Austronesian language Mbarbaram both use the word "dog" for canines. These two languages are unrelated, and since speakers of the two languages only came in contact with one another long after the word "dog" was first used in this way in either language, neither language could have borrowed the word from the other. Thus this case shows that sometimes when languages share words that are similar in sound and meaning the similarity is due neither to language relatedness nor to borrowing.

The argument requires that which one of the following be assumed?

(A) English and Mbarbaram share no words other than "dog."
(B) Several languages besides English and Mbarbaram use "dog" as the word for canines.
(C) Usually when two languages share a word, those languages are related to each other.
(D) There is no third language from which both English and Mbarbaram borrowed the word dog.
(E) If two unrelated languages share a word, speakers of those two languages must have come in contact with one another at some time.

44. Medical research findings are customarily not made public prior to their publication in a medical journal that has had them reviewed by a panel of experts in a process called peer review. It is claimed that this practice delays public access to potentially beneficial information that, in extreme instances, could save lives. Yet prepublication peer review is the only way to prevent erroneous and therefore potentially harmful information from reaching a public that is ill equipped to evaluate medical claims on its own. Therefore, waiting until a medical journal has published the research findings that have passed peer review is the price that must be paid to protect the public from making decisions based on possibly substandard research.

The argument assumes that

(A) unless medical research findings are brought to peer review by a medical journal, peer review will not occur

(B) anyone who does not serve on a medical review panel does not have the necessary knowledge and expertise to evaluate medical research findings

(C) the general public does not have access to the medical journals in which research findings are published

(D) all medical research findings are subjected to prepublication peer review

(E) peer review panels are sometimes subject to political and professional pressures that can make their judgments less than impartial

45. The economies of some industrialized countries face the prospect of large labor shortages in the decades ahead. Meanwhile, these countries will have a vast number of experienced and productive older workers who, as things stand, will be driven from the work force upon reaching the age of sixty-five by the widespread practice of requiring workers to retire at that age. Therefore, if the discriminatory practice of mandatory retirement at age sixty-five were eliminated, the labor shortages facing these economies would be averted.

The argument assumes that

(A) older workers have acquired skills that are extremely valuable and that their younger colleagues lack

(B) workers in industrialized countries are often unprepared to face the economic consequences of enforced idleness

(C) a large number of workers in some industrialized countries would continue working beyond the age of sixty-five if workers in those countries were allowed to do so

(D) mandatory retirement at age sixty-five was first instituted when life expectancy was considerably lower than it is today

(E) a substantial proportion of the population of officially retired workers is actually engaged in gainful employment

46. Myrna: People should follow diets in which fat represents no more than 30 percent of total calories, not the 37 percent the average diet in this country contains.

Roland: If everyone in the country followed your recommendation during his or her entire life, just 0.7 percent would lengthen their lives at all, and then only by an average of 3 months. Modifying our diet is not worthwhile. A lifetime of sacrifice spent eating an unappealing low-fat diet is too high a price to pay for the chance of extending that sacrifice for 3 months.

Myrna: But for everyone who dies early from a high-fat diet, many more people suffer from serious chronic diseases because they followed such diets.

Roland's argument assumes that

(A) it is desirable to live in such a way as to lengthen life as much as possible
(B) a low-fat diet cannot readily be made appealing and satisfying to a person who follows it regularly
(C) diet is the only relevant factor to consider in computing influences on length of time
(D) the difference in tastiness between a diet in which fat represents 30 percent of total calories and one in which it represents 37 percent is not noticeable
(E) not everyone in the country eats the average diet

47. Marcus: For most ethical dilemmas the journalist is likely to face, traditional journalistic ethics is clear, adequate, and essentially correct. For example, when journalists have uncovered newsworthy information, they should go to press with it as soon as possible. No delay motivated by the journalists' personal or professional interests is permissible.

Anita: Well, Marcus, of course interesting and important information should be brought before the public—that is a journalist's job. But in the typical case, where a journalist has some information but is in a quandary about whether it is yet important or "newsworthy," this guidance is inadequate.

In order to conclude properly from Anita's statements that Marcus' general claim about traditional journalistic ethics is incorrect, it would have to be assumed that

(A) whether a piece of information is or is not newsworthy can raise ethical dilemmas for journalists
(B) there are circumstances in which it would be ethically wrong for a journalist to go to press with legitimately acquired, newsworthy information
(C) the most serious professional dilemmas that a journalist is likely to face are not ethical dilemmas
(D) there are no ethical dilemmas that a journalist is likely to face that would not be conclusively resolved by an adequate system of journalistic ethics
(E) for a system of journalistic ethics to be adequate it must be able to provide guidance in every case in which a journalist must make a professional decision

48. Scientists attempting to replicate certain controversial results reported by a group of experienced researchers failed to get the same results as those reported. The conclusion drawn from this by the scientists who conducted the replication experiments was that the originally reported results had been due to faulty measurements.

The argument of the scientists who conducted the replication experiments assumes that

(A) the original experiments had not been described in sufficient detail to make an exact replication possible
(B) the fact that the originally reported results aroused controversy made it highly likely that they were in error
(C) the theoretical principles called into question by the originally reported results were themselves based on weak evidence
(D) the replication experiments were not so likely as the original experiments to be marred by faulty measurements
(E) the researchers who originally reported the controversial results had themselves observed those results only once

49. Educational television is a contradiction in terms. While a classroom encourages social interaction, television encourages solitude. School is centered on the development of language, but television depends upon constantly changing visual images. And in a classroom, fun is merely a means to an end, but on television it is the end in itself.

Upon which one of the following assumptions does the author rely in the passage?

(A) The classroom should not be a place where anyone has fun.
(B) Only experiences that closely resemble what takes place in the school environment can be educational.
(C) Television programs reinforce some of the values of the school environment.
(D) Educational television programs are qualitatively better than most other television programs.
(E) The potential of television as a powerful learning tool has not yet been realized.

50. Sally: I cannot study at a university where there is an alcohol problem, so unless something is done about the alcohol problem at this university, I'll have to transfer to a university where there are no fraternities.

Yolanda: I don't agree that fraternities are responsible for the alcohol problem at this university. Alcohol problems exist at all universities, including those where there are no fraternities. We all should become more aware of alcohol abuse. It's not simply a fraternity problem; it's a cultural problem.

Which one of the following is an assumption on which Sally's argument depends?

(A) Most universities have fraternities.
(B) Nothing will be done about the alcohol problem at Sally's university.
(C) Alcohol problems are becoming more widespread at universities.
(D) Some fraternity members who drink alcoholic beverages are too young to do so legally.
(E) There could be universities that have no alcohol problems.

51. Slash-and-burn agriculture involves burning several acres of forest, leaving vegetable ash that provides ample fertilizer for three or four years of bountiful crops. On the cleared land nutrients leach out of the soil, however, and the land becomes too poor to support agriculture. New land is then cleared by burning and the process starts again. Since most farming in the tropics uses this method, forests in this region will eventually be permanently eradicated.

The argument depends on the assumption that

(A) forests in the tropics do not regenerate well enough to restore themselves once they have been cleared by the slash-and-burn method
(B) some other methods of agriculture are not as destructive to the environment in tropical regions as the slash-and-burn method is
(C) forests in the tropics are naturally deficient in nutrients that are needed to support the growth of plants that are not native to those regions
(D) slash-and-burn agriculture is particularly suitable for farming in tropical areas
(E) slash-and-burn agriculture produces a more bountiful crop than do other agriculture methods for the first year

52. A favored theory to explain the extinction of dinosaurs, together with many other species, has been the globally catastrophic collision of a large asteroid with the Earth. Supporting evidence is an extraterrestrial chemical element in a layer of dust found worldwide at a geological level laid down contemporaneously with the supposed event. A new competing theory contends that any asteroid impact was irrelevant, because it was massive volcanic activity that caused the extinctions by putting enough dust into the atmosphere to cool the planet. The Deccan region of India contains extensive volcanic flows that occurred within the same time period as the supposed asteroid impact and the extinctions.

The new theory assumes that

(A) the massive volcanic activity was not caused by the impact of an asteroid
(B) no individual dinosaurs survived the impact of the asteroid, if it occurred
(C) the extinctions took place over a longer time period than they would have if caused by the impact of an asteroid
(D) other volcanic eruptions were not occurring at the same time as those in the Deccan region
(E) it is not possible to determine which would have occurred first, the volcanic flows in the Deccan region or the supposed impact of an asteroid

53. One of the requirements for admission to the Lunnville Roller Skating Club is a high degree of skill in roller skating. The club president has expressed concern that the club may have discriminated against qualified women in its admissions this year. Yet half of the applicants admitted to the club this year were women. This proves that there was no discrimination against qualified women applicants in the club's admissions this year.

Which one of the following is an assumption on which the conclusion of the argument depends?

(A) Only a few applicants were found to be qualified and were admitted to the club this year.
(B) No more than half of all the roller skaters in Lunnville are women.
(C) No more than half of all the roller skaters in Lunnville are men.
(D) This year no more than half of the applicants who met all the qualifications for admission to the club were women.
(E) This year no more than half of the members of the club's committee that makes decisions about applicants' qualifications were men.

54. X: Since many chemicals useful for agriculture and medicine derive from rare or endangered plant species, it is likely that many plant species that are now extinct could have provided us with substances that would have been a boon to humanity. Therefore, if we want to ensure that chemicals from plants are available for use in the future, we must make more serious efforts to preserve for all time our natural resources.

Y: But living things are not our "resources." Yours is a selfish approach to conservation. We should rather strive to preserve living species because they deserve to survive, not because of the good they can do us.

X's argument relies on which one of the following assumptions?

(A) Medicine would now be more advanced than it is if there had been a serious conservation policy in the past.
(B) All living things exist to serve humankind.
(C) The use of rare and endangered plant species as a source for chemicals will not itself render those species extinct.
(D) The only way to persuade people to preserve natural resources is to convince them that it is in their interest to do so.
(E) Few, if any, plant species have been saved from extinction through human efforts.

55. Advertisement: Attention pond owners! Ninety-eight percent of mosquito larvae in a pond die within minutes after the pond has been treated with BTI. Yet BTI is not toxic to fish, birds, animals, plants, or beneficial insects. So by using BTI regularly to destroy their larvae, you can greatly reduce populations of pesky mosquitoes that hatch in your pond, and you can do so without diminishing the populations of fish, frogs, or beneficial insects in and around the pond.

Which one of the following is an assumption on which the argument depends?

(A) The most effective way to control the numbers of mosquitoes in a given area is to destroy the mosquito larvae in that area.
(B) Populations of mosquitoes are not dependent on a single body of water within an area as a place for their larvae to hatch and develop.
(C) There are no insect pests besides mosquitoes that pond owners might want to eliminate from in and around their ponds.
(D) The effectiveness of BTI in destroying mosquito larvae in a pond does not require the pond owner's strict adherence to specific application procedures.
(E) The fish, frogs, and beneficial insects in and around a pond-owner's pond do not depend on mosquito larvae as an important source of food.

56. The government has proposed a plan requiring young people to perform services to correct various current social ills, especially those in education and housing. Government service, however, should be compelled only in response to a direct threat to the nation's existence. For that reason, the proposed program should not be implemented.

Which one of the following is an assumption on which the argument depends?

(A) Government-required service by young people cannot correct all social ills.
(B) The nation's existence is directly threatened only in times of foreign attack.
(C) Crises in education and housing constitute a threat to the nation's existence.
(D) The nation's young people believe that current social ills pose no direct threat to the nation's existence.
(E) Some of the social ills that currently afflict the nation do not pose a direct threat to the nation's existence.

57. The format of network television news programs generally allows advocates of a point of view only 30 seconds to convey their message. Consequently, regular watchers become accustomed to thinking of issues in terms only of slogans and catch phrases, and so the expectation of careful discussion of public issues gradually disappears from their awareness. The format of newspaper stories, on the other hand, leads readers to pursue details of stories headed by the most important facts and so has the opposite effect on regular readers—that of maintaining the expectation of careful discussion of public issues. Therefore, in contrast to regular newspaper reading, regular watching of network television news programs increases the tendency to think of public issues in oversimplified terms.

The argument assumes which one of the following?

(A) Viewers of network television news programs would be interested in seeing advocates of opposing views present their positions at length.
(B) Since it is not possible to present striking images that would symbolize events for viewers, and since images hold sway over words in television, television must oversimplify.
(C) It is not possible for television to present public issues in a way that allows for the nuanced presentation of diverse views and a good-faith interchange between advocates of opposing views.
(D) In network television news reports, it is not usual for a reporter to offer additional factual evidence and background information to develop a story in which opposing views are presented briefly by their advocates.
(E) Television news reporters introduce more of their own biases into news stories than do newspaper reporters.

58. Since Mayor Drabble always repays her political debts as soon as possible, she will almost certainly appoint Lee to be the new head of the arts commission. Lee has wanted that job for a long time, and Drabble owes Lee a lot for his support in the last election.

Which one of the following is an assumption on which the argument depends?

(A) Mayor Drabble has no political debt that is both of longer standing than the one she owes to Lee and could as suitably be repaid by an appointment to be the new head of the arts commission.
(B) There is no one to whom Mayor Drabble owes a greater political debt for support in the last election than the political debt she owes to Lee.
(C) Lee is the only person to whom Mayor Drabble owes a political debt who would be willing to accept an appointment from her as the new head of the arts commission.
(D) Whether Lee is qualified to head the arts commission is irrelevant to Mayor Drabble's decision.
(E) The only way that Mayor Drabble can adequately repay her political debt to Lee is by appointing him to head the arts commission.

59. The scientific theory of evolution has challenged the view of human origin as divine creation and sees us as simply descended from the same ancestors as the apes. While science and technology have provided brilliant insights into our world and eased our everyday life, they have simultaneously deprived us of a view in which our importance is assured. Thus, while science has given us many things, it has taken away much that is also greatly valued.

Which one of the following is assumed in the passage?

(A) Science and technology are of less value than religion.
(B) People have resisted the advances of science and technology.
(C) The assurance that people are important is highly valued.
(D) The world was a better place before the advent of science and technology.
(E) The need of people to feel important is now met by science and technology.

60. There are tests to detect some of the rare genetic flaws that increase the likelihood of certain diseases. If these tests are performed, then a person with a rare genetic flaw that is detected can receive the appropriate preventive treatment. Since it costs the health-care system less to prevent a disease than to treat it after it has occurred, widespread genetic screening will reduce the overall cost of health care.

The argument assumes which one of the following?

(A) The cost of treating patients who would, in the absence of screening, develop diseases that are linked to rare genetic flaws would be more than the combined costs of widespread screening and preventive treatment.
(B) Most diseases linked to rare genetic flaws are preventable.
(C) The resources allocated by hospitals to the treatment of persons with diseases linked to genetic flaws will increase once screening is widely available.
(D) Even if the genetic tests are performed, many people whose rare genetic flaws are detected will develop diseases linked to the flaws as a consequence of not receiving the appropriate preventive treatment.
(E) If preventive treatment is given to patients with rare genetic flaws, additional funds will be available for treating the more common diseases.

61. A certain experimental fungicide causes no harm to garden plants, though only if it is diluted at least to ten parts water to one part fungicide. Moreover, this fungicide is known to be so effective against powdery mildew that it has the capacity to eliminate it completely from rose plants. Thus this fungicide, as long as it is sufficiently diluted, provides a means of eliminating powdery mildew from rose plants that involves no risk of harming the plants.

Which one of the following is an assumption on which the argument depends?

(A) There is not an alternative method, besides application of this fungicide, for eliminating powdery mildew from rose plants without harming the plants.
(B) When the fungicide is sufficiently diluted, it does not present any risk of harm to people, animals, or beneficial insects.
(C) Powdery mildew is the only fungal infection that affects rose plants.
(D) If a fungicide is to be effective against powdery mildew on rose plants, it must eliminate the powdery mildew completely.
(E) The effectiveness of the fungicide does not depend on its being more concentrated than one part in ten parts of water.

62. Adults have the right to vote; so should adolescents. Admittedly, adolescents and adults are not the same. But to the extent that adolescents and adults are different, adults cannot be expected to represent the interests of adolescents. If adults cannot represent the interests of adolescents, then only by giving adolescents the vote will these interests represented.

The argument relies on which one of the following assumptions?

(A) The right to vote is a right that all human beings should have.
(B) Adolescents and adults differ in most respects that are important.
(C) Adolescents should have their interests represented.
(D) Anyone who has the right to vote has all the right an adult has.
(E) Adolescents have never enjoyed the right to vote.

63. Stage performances are judged to be realistic to the degree that actors reproduce on stage the behaviors generally associated by audiences with the emotional states of the characters portrayed. Traditional actors imitate those behaviors, whereas Method actors, through recollection of personal experience, actually experience the same emotions that their characters are meant to be experiencing. Audiences will therefore judge the performances of Method actors to be more realistic than the performances of traditional actors.

Which one of the following is an assumption on which the argument depends?

(A) Performances based on an actor's own experience of emotional states are more likely to affect an audience's emotions than are performances based on imitations of the behaviors generally associated with those emotional states.
(B) The behavior that results when a Method actor feels a certain emotion will conform to the behavior that is generally associated by audiences with that emotion.
(C) Realism is an essential criterion for evaluating the performances of both traditional actors and Method actors.
(D) Traditional actors do not aim to produce performances that are realistic representations of a character's emotional states.
(E) In order to portray a character, a Method actor need not have had experiences identical to those of the character portrayed.

64. The tiny country of Minlandia does not produce its own television programming. Instead, the citizens of Minlandia, who generally are fluent not only in their native Minlandian, but also in Boltese, watch Boltese-language television programs from neighboring Bolta. Surveys show that the Minlandians spend on average more hours per week reading for pleasure and fewer hours per week watching television than people anywhere else in the world. A prominent psychologist accounts for the survey results by explaining that people generally prefer to be entertained in their native language even if they are perfectly fluent in other languages.

The explanation offered by the psychologist accounts for the Minlandian's behavior only if which one of the following is assumed?

(A) Some Minlandians derive no pleasure from watching television in a language other than their native Minlandian.
(B) The study of Boltese is required of Minlandian children as part of their schooling.
(C) The proportion of bilingual residents to total population is greater in Minlandia than anywhere else in the world.
(D) At least some of what the Minlandians read for pleasure is in the Minlandian language.
(E) When Minlandians watch Boltese television programs, they tend to ignore the fact that they are hearing a foreign language spoken.

65. For the past 13 years, high school guidance counselors nationwide have implemented an aggressive program to convince high school students to select careers requiring college degrees. The government reported that the percentage of last year's high school graduates who went on to college was 15 percent greater than the percentage of those who graduated 10 years ago and did so. The counselors concluded from this report that the program had been successful.

The guidance counselors' reasoning depends on which one of the following assumptions about high school graduates?

(A) The number of graduates who went on to college remained constant each year during the 10-year period.
(B) Any college courses that the graduates take will improve their career prospects.
(C) Some of the graduates who went on to college never received guidance from a high school counselor.
(D) There has been a decrease in the number of graduates who go on to college without career plans.
(E) Many of last year's graduates who went on to college did so in order to prepare for careers requiring college degrees.

66. Chronic fatigue syndrome is characterized by prolonged fatigue, muscular pain, and neurological problems. It is not known whether these symptoms are all caused by a single virus or whether each symptom is the result of a separate viral infection. A newly synthesized drug has been tested on those who suffer from chronic fatigue syndrome. Although the specific antiviral effects of this drug are unknown, it has lessened the severity of all of the symptoms of chronic fatigue syndrome. Thus there is evidence that chronic fatigue syndrome is, in fact, caused by one virus.

The argument assumes which one of the following?

(A) All those who suffer from prolonged fatigue also suffer from neurological problems.
(B) It is more likely that the new drug counteracts one virus than that it counteracts several viruses.
(C) The symptoms of chronic fatigue syndrome are dissimilar to those of any other syndrome.
(D) Most syndromes that are characterized by related symptoms are each caused by a single viral infection.
(E) An antiviral medication that eliminates the most severe symptoms of chronic fatigue syndrome thereby cures chronic fatigue syndrome.

67. A history book written hundreds of years ago contains several inconsistencies. Some scholars argue that because the book contains inconsistencies, the author must have been getting information from more than one source.

The conclusion cited does not follow unless

(A) authors generally try to reconcile discrepancies between sources
(B) the inconsistencies would be apparent to the average reader of the history book at the present time
(C) the history book's author used no source that contained inconsistencies repeated in the history book
(D) the author of the history book was aware of the kinds of inconsistencies that can arise when multiple sources are consulted
(E) the author of the history book was familiar with all of the available source material that was relevant to the history book

68. Harris: Currently, hybrid animals are not protected by international endangered-species regulations. But new techniques in genetic research suggest that the red wolf, long thought to be an independent species, is a hybrid of the coyote and the gray wolf. Hence, since the red wolf clearly deserves protection, these regulations should be changed to admit the protection of hybrids.

Vogel: Yet hybrids do not need protection. Since a breeding population that arises through hybridization descends from independent species, if any such population were to die out, it could easily be revived by interbreeding members of the species from which the hybrid is descended.

Which one of the following is an assumption on which Vogel's argument relies?

(A) The techniques currently being used to determine whether a population of animals is a hybrid of other species have proven to be reliable.
(B) The international regulations that protect endangered species and subspecies are being enforced successfully.
(C) The gray wolf has been successfully bred in captivity.
(D) All hybrids are the descendants of species that are currently extant.
(E) The coyote and the red wolf are not related genetically.

69. The book *To Save the Earth* is so persuasive that no one who reads it can fail to heed its environmentalist message. Members of the Earth Association have given away 2,000 copies in the last month. Thus the Earth Association can justly claim credit for at least 2,000 people in one month converted to the environmentalist cause.

Which one of the following is an assumption on which the argument depends?

(A) No other environmental organization gave away copies of *To Save the Earth* during the month in which the Earth Association gave away its 2,000 copies.
(B) The people to whom the Earth Association gave copies of *To Save the Earth* would not have been willing to pay to receive it from the Earth Association.
(C) The copies of *To Save the Earth* given away by members of the Earth Association were printed on recycled paper.
(D) None of those who received *To Save the Earth* from a member of the Earth Association were already committed to the environmentalist cause when they received this book.
(E) Every recipient of *To Save the Earth* will embrace the environmental program advocated by the Earth Association.

70. Kim: Some people claim that the battery-powered electric car represents a potential solution to the problem of air pollution. But they forget that it takes electricity to recharge batteries and that most of our electricity is generated by burning polluting fossil fuels. Increasing the number of electric cars on the road would require building more generating facilities since current facilities are operating at maximum capacity. So even if all of the gasoline-powered cars on the roads today were replaced by electric cars, it would at best be an exchange of one source of fossil-fuel pollution for another.

Which one of the following is an assumption on which Kim's argument depends?

(A) Replacing gasoline-powered cars with battery-powered electric cars will not lead to a net increase in the total number of cars on the road.
(B) Gasoline-powered cars are currently not the most significant source of fossil-fuel pollution.
(C) Replacing gasoline-powered cars with battery-powered electric cars is justified only if electric cars produce less air pollution.
(D) While it is being operated, a battery-powered electric car does not cause any significant air pollution.
(E) At least some of the generating facilities built to meet the demand for electricity for battery-powered electric cars would be of a type that burns fossil fuel.

71. Oscar: Emerging information technologies will soon make speed of information processing the single most important factor in the creation of individual, corporate, and national wealth. Consequently, the division of the world into northern countries—in general rich—and southern countries—in general poor—will soon be obsolete. Instead, there simply will be fast countries and slow countries, and thus a country's economic well-being will not be a function of its geographical position but just a matter of its relative success in incorporating those new technologies.

Sylvia: But the poor countries of the south lack the economic resources to acquire those technologies and will therefore remain poor. The technologies will thus only widen the existing economic gap between north and south.

Sylvia's reasoning depends on the assumption that

(A) the prosperity of the rich countries of the north depends, at least in part, on the natural resources of the poor countries of the south
(B) the emergence of new information technologies will not result in a significant net increase in the total amount of global wealth
(C) there are technologies other than information technologies whose development could help narrow the existing economic gap between north and south
(D) at least some of the rich countries of the north will be effective in incorporating new information technologies into their economies
(E) the speed at which information processing takes place will continue to increase indefinitely

72. Beverage company representative: The plastic rings that hold six-packs of beverage cans together pose a threat to wild animals, which often become entangled in the discarded rings and suffocate as a result. Following our lead, all beverage companies will soon use only those rings consisting of a new plastic that disintegrates after only three days' exposure to sunlight. Once we all complete the switchover from the old to the new plastic rings, therefore, the threat of suffocation that plastic rings pose to wild animals will be eliminated.

The argument depends on which one of the following assumptions?

(A) None of the new plastic rings can disintegrate after only two days' exposure to sunlight.
(B) The switchover to the new plastic rings can be completed without causing significant financial hardship to the beverage companies.
(C) Wild animals will not become entangled in the new plastic rings before the rings have had sufficient exposure to sunlight to disintegrate.
(D) Use of the old plastic rings poses no substantial threat to wild animals other than that of suffocation.
(E) Any wild animal that becomes entangled in the old plastic rings will suffocate as a result.

ASSUMPTION

Questions 73-74

Consumer activist: By allowing major airlines to abandon, as they promptly did, all but their most profitable routes, the government's decision to cease regulation of the airline industry has worked to the disadvantage of everyone who lacks access to a large metropolitan airport.

Industry representative: On the contrary, where major airlines moved out, regional airlines have moved in and, as a consequence, there are more flights into and out of most small airports now than before the change in regulatory policy.

73. The industry representative's argument will not provide an effective answer to the consumer activist's claim unless which one of the following is true?

(A) No small airport has fewer flights now than it did before the change in policy regarding regulation of the airline industry.
(B) When permitted to do so by changes in regulatory policy, each major airline abandoned all but large metropolitan airports.
(C) Policies that result in an increase in the number of flights to which consumers have easy access do not generally work to the disadvantage of consumers.
(D) Regional airlines charge less to fly a given route now than the major airlines charged when they flew the same route.
(E) Any policy that leads to an increase in the number of competitors in a given field works to the long-term advantage of consumers.

74. Which one of the following is an assumption on which the consumer activist's argument depends?

(A) Before the recent change in regulatory policy, there was no advantage in having easy access to a large metropolitan airport.
(B) When any sizable group of consumers is seriously disadvantaged by a change in government policy, that change should be reversed.
(C) Government regulation of industry almost always works to the advantage of consumers.
(D) At the time of the regulatory change, the major airlines were maintaining their less profitable routes at least in part because of government requirements.
(E) Regional airlines lack the resources to provide consumers with service of the same quality as that provided by the major airlines.

75. Railroad spokesperson: Of course it is a difficult task to maintain quality of service at the same time that the amount of subsidy the taxpayers give the railroad network is reduced. Over recent years, however, the number of passengers has increased in spite of subsidy reductions. This fact leads to the conclusion that our quality of service has been satisfactory.

The spokesperson's argument is based on which one of the following assumptions?

(A) Taxpayers do not wish to have their taxes raised to subsidize the railroads.
(B) Some people refuse to travel by train if they are dissatisfied with the quality of service.
(C) The quality of service on the trains must have improved in spite of subsidy reductions.
(D) It is impossible to reduce subsidies to the railroad network without some effect on the quality of service
(E) The increase in the number of passengers will increase revenue sufficiently to offset the subsidy reductions.

76. "Addiction" has been defined as "dependence on and abuse of a psychoactive substance." Dependence and abuse do not always go hand in hand, however. For example, cancer patients can become dependent on morphine to relieve their pain, but this is not abusing the drug. Correspondingly, a person can abuse a drug without being dependent on it. Therefore, the definition of "addiction" is incorrect.

The relevance of the example of cancer patients to the argument depends on the assumption that

(A) cancer patients never abuse morphine
(B) cancer patients often become dependent on morphine
(C) cancer patients who are dependent on morphine are addicted to it
(D) cancer patients who abuse a drug are dependent on it
(E) cancer patients cannot depend on morphine without abusing it

77. When permits for the discharge of chemicals into a waterway are issued, they are issued in terms of the number of pounds of each chemical that can be discharged into the waterway per day. These figures, calculated separately for each chemical for which a permit is issued, are based on an estimate of the effect of the dilution of the chemical by the amount of water flowing through the waterway. The waterway is therefore protected against being adversely affected by chemicals discharged under the permits.

The argument depends on the assumption that

(A) relatively harmless chemicals do not interact with each other in the water to form harmful compounds
(B) there is a swift flow of water in the waterway that ensures rapid dispersion of chemicals discharged
(C) there are no chemicals for which discharge into waterways is entirely prohibited
(D) those who receive the permits do not always discharge the entire quantity of chemicals that the permits allow
(E) the danger of chemical pollution of waterways is to be evaluated in terms of human health only and not in terms of the health of both human beings and wildlife

78. A primate jawbone found in Namibia in southern Africa has been identified by anthropologists as that of an ape that lived between 10 million and 15 million years ago. Researchers generally agree that such ancient primates lived only in dense forests. Consequently, the dry, treeless expanses now dominating the landscape in and around Namibia must have replaced an earlier, heavily forested terrain.

The argument assumes which one of the following?

(A) Modern apes also tend to live only in heavily forested terrain.
(B) The ape whose jawbone was found lived in or near the area that is now Namibia.
(C) There were no apes living in the area that is now Namibia prior to 15 million years ago.
(D) The ape whose jawbone was found was adapted to a diet that was significantly different from that of any modern ape.
(E) The ancient primates were numerous enough to have caused severe damage to the ecology of the forests in which they lived.

79. In their native habitat, amaryllis plants go dormant when the soil in which they are growing dries out during the dry season. Therefore, if amaryllis plants kept as houseplants are to thrive, water should be withheld from them during part of the year so that the plants go dormant.

Which one of the following is an assumption on which the argument depends?

(A) Most kinds of plants go dormant at some time or other during the year.

(B) Amaryllis are more difficult to keep as houseplants than other kinds of plants are.

(C) Water should be withheld from amaryllis plants kept as houseplants during the exact time of year that corresponds to the dry season in their native habitat.

(D) Any amaryllis plant that fails to thrive is likely to have been dormant for too short a time.

(E) Going dormant benefits amaryllis plants in their native habitat in some way other than simply preventing death during overly dry periods.

80. No computer will ever be able to do everything that some human minds can do, for there are some problems that cannot be solved by following any set of mechanically applicable rules. Yet computers can only solve problems by following some set of mechanically applicable rules.

Which one of the following is an assumption on which the argument depends?

(A) At least one problem solvable by following some set of mechanically applicable rules is not solvable by any human mind.

(B) At least one problem not solvable by following any set of mechanically applicable rules is solvable by at least one human mind.

(C) At least one problem solvable by following some set of mechanically applicable rules is solvable by every human mind.

(D) Every problem that is solvable by following more than one set of mechanically applicable rules is solvable by almost every human mind.

(E) Every problem that is solvable by following at least one set of mechanically applicable rules is solvable by at least one human mind.

81. Organization president: The stationery and envelopes used in all of the mailings from our national headquarters are made from recycled paper, and we never put anything but letters in the envelopes. When the envelopes have windows, these windows are also made from recycled material. Therefore the envelopes, and thus these mailings, are completely recyclable.

Which one of the following is an assumption on which the organization president's argument depends?

(A) All the paper used by the organization for purposes other than mailings is recycled.

(B) The mailings from the organization's national headquarters always use envelopes that have windows.

(C) The envelope windows made from recycled material are recyclable.

(D) The envelopes and stationery used in the organization's mailings are always recycled.

(E) The organization sends mailings only from its national headquarters.

82. Proponents of organic farming claim that using chemical fertilizers and pesticides in farming is harmful to local wildlife. To produce the same amount of food, however, more land must be under cultivation when organic farming techniques are used than when chemicals are used. Therefore, organic farming leaves less land available as habitat for local wildlife.

Which one of the following is an assumption on which the author's argument depends?

(A) Chemical fertilizers and pesticides pose no health threat to wildlife.

(B) Wildlife living near farms where chemicals are used will not ingest any food or water containing those chemicals.

(C) The only disadvantage to using chemicals in farming is their potential effect on wildlife.

(D) The same crops are grown on organic farms as on farms where chemicals are used.

(E) Land cultivated by organic farming methods no longer constitutes a habitat for wildlife.

83. When volcanic lava solidifies, it becomes uniformly magnetized in the direction in which the Earth's magnetic field points. There are significant differences in the direction of magnetization among solidified lava flows from different volcanoes that erupted at different times over the past several million years. Therefore, it must be that the direction of the Earth's magnetic field has changed over time. Since lava flows differing by thousands of years in age often have very similar directions of magnetization, the change in the direction of the Earth's magnetic field must take place very gradually over hundreds of thousands of years.

The argument that the direction of the Earth's magnetic field has changed over time requires the assumption that

(A) only lava can be used to measure the direction of the Earth's magnetic field as it existed in the distant past
(B) a single volcano can produce lava of differing consistencies during different eruptions
(C) not all solidified lava has changed the direction of its magnetization unpredictably
(D) there are fewer volcanic eruptions now than there were millions of years ago
(E) as lava flows down the side of a volcano, it picks up magnetized rocks

84. The introduction of symbols for numbers is an event lost in prehistory, but the earliest known number symbols, in the form of simple grooves and scratches on bones and stones, date back 20,000 years or more. Nevertheless, since it was not until 5,500 years ago that systematic methods for writing numerals were invented, it was only then that any sort of computation became possible.

Which one of the following is an assumption on which the argument relies?

(A) Grooves and scratches found on bones and stones were all made by people, and none resulted from natural processes.
(B) Some kinds of surfaces upon which numeric symbols could have been made in the period before 5,500 years ago were not used for that purpose.
(C) Grooves and scratches inscribed on bones and stones do not date back to the time of the earliest people.
(D) Computation of any sort required a systematic method for writing numerals.
(E) Systematic methods for writing numerals were invented only because the need for computation arose.

85. Bart: A mathematical problem that defied solution for hundreds of years has finally yielded to a supercomputer. The process by which the supercomputer derived the result is so complex, however, that no one can fully comprehend it. Consequently, the result is unacceptable.

Anne: In scientific research, if the results of a test can be replicated in other tests, the results are acceptable even though the way they were derived might not be fully understood. Therefore, if a mathematical result derived by a supercomputer can be reproduced by other supercomputers following the same procedure, it is acceptable.

Bart's argument requires which one of the following assumptions?

(A) The mathematical result in question is unacceptable because it was derived with the use of a supercomputer.
(B) For the mathematical result in question to be acceptable, there must be someone who can fully comprehend the process by which it was derived.
(C) To be acceptable, the mathematical result in question must be reproduced on another supercomputer.
(D) Making the mathematical result in question less complex would guarantee its acceptability.
(E) The supercomputer cannot derive an acceptable solution to the mathematical problem in question.

86. The retina scanner, a machine that scans the web of tiny blood vessels in the retina, stores information about the pattern formed by the blood vessels. This information allows it to recognize any pattern it has previously scanned. No two eyes have identical patterns of blood vessels in the retina. A retina scanner can therefore be used successfully to determine for any person whether it has ever scanned a retina of that person before.

The reasoning in the argument depends upon assuming that

(A) diseases of the human eye do not alter the pattern of blood vessels in the retina in ways that would make the pattern unrecognizable to the retina scanner
(B) no person has a different pattern of blood vessels in the retina of the left eye than in the retina of the right eye
(C) there are enough retina scanners to store information about every person's retinas
(D) the number of blood vessels in the human retina is invariant, although the patterns they form differ from person to person
(E) there is no person whose retinas have been scanned by two or more different retina scanners

87. Caffeine can kill or inhibit the growth of the larvae of several species of insects. One recent experiment showed that tobacco hornworm larvae die when they ingest a preparation that consists, in part, of finely powdered tea leaves, which contain caffeine. This result is evidence for the hypothesis that the presence of non-negligible quantities of caffeine in various parts of many diverse species of plants is not accidental but evolved as a defense for those plants.

The argument assumes that

(A) caffeine-producing plants are an important raw material in the manufacture of commercial insecticides
(B) caffeine is stored in leaves and other parts of caffeine-producing plants in concentrations roughly equal to the caffeine concentration of the preparation fed to the tobacco hornworm larvae
(C) caffeine-producing plants grow wherever insect larvae pose a major threat to indigenous plants or once posed a major threat to the ancestors of those plants
(D) the tobacco plant is among the plant species that produce caffeine for their own defense
(E) caffeine-producing plants or their ancestors have at some time been subject to being fed upon by creatures sensitive to caffeine

88. Cafeteria patron: The apples sold in this cafeteria are greasy. The cashier told me that the apples are in that condition when they are delivered to the cafeteria and that the cafeteria does not wash the apples it sells. Most fruit is sprayed with dangerous pesticides before it is harvested, and is dangerous until it is washed. Clearly, the cafeteria is selling pesticide-covered fruit, thereby endangering its patrons.

Which one of the following is an assumption on which the argument depends?

(A) The apples that the cafeteria sells are not thoroughly washed after harvest but before reaching the cafeteria.
(B) Most pesticides that are sprayed on fruit before harvest leave a greasy residue on the fruit.
(C) Many of the cafeteria's patrons are unaware that the cafeteria does not wash the apples it sells.
(D) Only pesticides that leave a greasy residue on fruit can be washed off.
(E) Fruits other than apples also arrive at the cafeteria in a greasy condition.

89. Public health will improve more quickly in the wake of new medical discoveries if medical researchers abandon their practice of waiting until their findings are published in peer-reviewed journals before informing the press of important research results. That is because the public release of new medical information allows people to use that information in order to improve their health, but the peer-review process is unavoidably very slow.

Which one of the following is an assumption on which the argument depends?

(A) Many medical researchers do not agree to serve as reviewers when their own research is in a critical phase.
(B) Reviewers for many medical journals are not themselves medical researchers.
(C) People would use new medical information even if it were not first published in peer-reviewed journals.
(D) The peer-review process could be speeded up enough to produce a significant improvement in public health.
(E) New medical information that is first published in peer-reviewed journals does not usually receive public attention.

90. Nuclear reactors are sometimes built in "geologically quiet" regions, so called by geologists because such regions are distant from plate boundaries and contain only minor faults. Since no minor fault in a geologically quiet region produces an earthquake more often than once in any given 100,000-year period, it follows that of all potential nuclear reactor sites in such a region, those that are least likely to be struck by an earthquake are ones located near a fault that has produced an earthquake within living memory.

Which one of the following is an assumption on which the argument depends?

(A) Geologically quiet regions are the least dangerous regions in which to build nuclear reactors.
(B) For any potential nuclear reactor site, the likelihood of being struck by an earthquake is the primary determinant of site safety.
(C) In a geologically quiet region, every potential nuclear reactor site is near at least one minor fault.
(D) Nuclear reactors that are located in geologically quiet regions are built to withstand at least one but not necessarily more than one earthquake of minor to moderate force.
(E) Earthquake faults in geologically quiet regions produce earthquakes at least once in 100,000 years.

91. Magazine editor: I know that some of our regular advertisers have been pressuring us to give favorable mention to their products in our articles, but they should realize that for us to yield to their wishes would actually be against their interests. To remain an effective advertising vehicle we must have loyal readership, and we would soon lose that readership if our readers suspect that our editorial integrity has been compromised by pandering to advertisers.

Advertising-sales director: You underestimate the sophistication of our readers. They recognize that the advertisements we carry are not articles, so their response to the advertisements has never depended on their opinion of the editorial integrity of the magazine as a whole.

The magazine editor's argument assumes which one of the following?

(A) A magazine editor should never be influenced in the performance of his or her professional duties by the wishes of the companies that regularly advertise in the magazine.
(B) The magazine cannot give any favorable mention in its articles to its regular advertisers without compromising its reputation for editorial integrity.
(C) Favorable mention of their products in the magazine's articles is of less value to the advertisers than is the continued effectiveness of the magazine as an advertising vehicle.
(D) Giving favorable mention to a product in a magazine article is a more effective form of advertising than is an explicit advertisement for the product in the same magazine.
(E) Carrying paid advertisements can never pose any threat to the magazine's reputation for editorial integrity nor to the loyalty of its readership.

92. The current move to patent computer programs is a move in the wrong direction and should be stopped. The patent system was originally designed solely to protect small-time inventors from exploitation, not to give large corporations control over a methodology. Any computer program is merely the implementation of a methodology.

Which one of the following is an assumption on which the argument depends?

(A) Computer programs should be developed not only by large corporations but by small-time inventors as well.
(B) Implementing a methodology always requires less creative effort than does true invention.
(C) The issue of whether or not to patent computer programs presents the patent system with problems that have never before arisen.
(D) Large corporations should not hold patents for implementations of methodologies.
(E) Small-time inventors who support the move to patent computer programs act contrary to their own best interests.

93. Even the earliest known species of land animals, known from fossils dating from the late Silurian period, 400 million years ago, show highly evolved adaptations to life on land. Since neither aquatic nor amphibious animals exhibit these adaptations, early species of land animals must have evolved very rapidly after leaving an aquatic environment.

Which one of the following is an assumption on which the argument depends?

(A) Known fossils of early land animals include fossils of animals that lived relatively soon after the first emergence of land animals.
(B) Fossils from the late Silurian period represent only a small number of the animal species that were alive at that time.
(C) No plants were established on land before the late Silurian period.
(D) No present-day species of aquatic animal is descended from a species of animal that once lived on land.
(E) All animals alive in the late Silurian period lived either exclusively on land or exclusively in the water.

94. By examining fossilized beetles, a research team has produced the most detailed description yet of temperatures in Britain over the past 22,000 years. Fossils of species that still exist were selected and dated. When individuals of several species found in the same place were found to date to the same period, the known temperature tolerances of the existing beetle species were used to determine the maximum summer temperature that could have existed at that place and period.

The procedure of the researchers assumes which one of the following?

(A) Beetles can tolerate warm weather better than cold weather.
(B) Fossils of different species found in the same place belonged to different periods.
(C) The process of dating is more accurate for beetles than for other organisms.
(D) The highest actual summer temperature at a place and period equaled the average of the highest temperatures that could have been tolerated by each of the beetle species found there and dated to that period.
(E) The temperature tolerances of the beetle species did not change significantly during the 22,000-year period.

95. Citizen of Mooresville: Mooresville's current city council is having a ruinous effect on municipal finances. Since a majority of the incumbents are running for reelection, I am going to campaign against all these incumbents in the upcoming city council election. The only incumbent I will support and vote for is the one who represents my own neighborhood, because she has the experience necessary to ensure that our neighborhood's interests are served. If everyone in Mooresville would follow my example, we could substantially change the council's membership.

Assuming that each citizen of Mooresville is allowed to vote only for a city council representative from his or her own neighborhood, for the council's membership to be changed substantially, it must be true that

(A) at least some other voters in Mooresville do not make the same exception for their own incumbent in the upcoming election
(B) most of the eligible voters in Mooresville vote in the upcoming election
(C) few of the incumbents on the Mooresville city council have run for reelection in previous elections
(D) all of the seats on the Mooresville city council are filled by incumbents whose terms are expiring
(E) none of the challengers in the upcoming election for seats on Mooresville's city council are better able to serve the interests of their neighborhoods than were the incumbents

96. Nutritionist: Vitamins synthesized by chemists are exactly the same as vitamins that occur naturally in foods. Therefore, it is a waste of money to pay extra for brands of vitamin pills that are advertised as made of higher-quality ingredients or more natural ingredients than other brands are.

The nutritionist's advice is based on which one of the following assumptions?

(A) It is a waste of money for people to supplement their diets with vitamin pills.
(B) Brands of vitamin pills made of natural ingredients always cost more money than brands that contain synthesized vitamins.
(C) All brands of vitamin pills contain some synthesized vitamins.
(D) Some producers of vitamin pills are guilty of false advertising.
(E) There is no nonvitamin ingredient in vitamin pills whose quality makes one brand worth more money than another brand.

97. Environmentalist: An increased number of oil spills and the consequent damage to the environment indicate the need for stricter safety standards for the oil industry. Since the industry refuses to take action, it is the national government that must regulate industry safety standards. In particular, the government has to at least require oil companies to put double hulls on their tankers and to assume financial responsibility for accidents.

Industry representative: The industry alone should be responsible for devising safety standards because of its expertise in handling oil and its understanding of the cost entailed. Implementing the double-hull proposal is not currently feasible because it creates new safety issues. Furthermore, the cost would be burdensome to the industry and consumers.

Which one of the following is an assumption on which the argument of the environmentalist depends?

(A) The only effective sources of increased stringency in safety standards for oil tankers are action by the industry itself or national government regulation.
(B) The requirement of two hulls on oil tankers, although initially costly, will save money over time by reducing cleanup costs.
(C) The oil industry's aging fleet of tankers must either be repaired or else replaced.
(D) Government safety regulations are developed in a process of negotiation with industry leaders and independent experts.
(E) Environmental concerns outweigh all financial considerations when developing safety standards

ASSUMPTION

98. In Malsenia sales of classical records are soaring. The buyers responsible for this boom are quite new to classical music and were drawn to it either by classical scores from television commercials or by theme tunes introducing major sports events on television. Audiences at classical concerts, however, are continually shrinking in Malsenia. It can be concluded from this that the new Malsenian converts to classical music, having initially experienced this music as recorded music, are most comfortable with classical music as recorded music and really have no desire to hear live performances.

The argument assumes which one of the following?

(A) To sell well in Malsenia, a classical record must include at least one piece familiar from television.
(B) At least some of the new Malsenian buyers of classical records have available to them the option of attending classical concerts.
(C) The number of classical concerts performed in Malsenia has not decreased in response to smaller audiences.
(D) The classical records available in Malsenia are, for the most part, not recordings of actual public concerts.
(E) Classical concerts in Malsenia are not limited to music that is readily available on recordings.

99. Professor Hartley's new book on moral philosophy contains numerous passages that can be found verbatim in an earlier published work by Hartley's colleague, Professor Lawrence. Therefore, in view of the fact that these passages were unattributed in Hartley's book, Hartley has been dishonest in not acknowledging the intellectual debt owed to Lawrence.

Which one of the following is an assumption on which the argument is based?

(A) Hartley could not have written the new book without the passages in question.
(B) While writing the new book, Hartley had access to the manuscript of Lawrence's book.
(C) A book on moral philosophy should contain only material representing the author's own convictions.
(D) Lawrence did not get the ideas in the passages in question or did not get their formulations originally from Hartley.
(E) Hartley considered the passages in question to be the best possible expressions of the ideas they contain.

100. A large number of drivers routinely violate highway speed limits. Since driving at speeds that exceed posted limits is a significant factor in most accidents, installing devices in all cars that prevent those cars from traveling faster than the speed limit would prevent most accidents.

Which one of the following is an assumption on which the argument depends?

(A) A person need not be a trained mechanic to install the device properly.
(B) Most accidents are caused by inexperienced drivers.
(C) A driver seldom needs to exceed the speed limit to avoid an accident when none of the other drivers involved are violating the speed limit.
(D) Most drivers who exceed the speed limit do so unintentionally.
(E) Even if the fines for speed-limit violations were increased, the number of such violations would still not be reduced.

101. Ornithologist: The curvature of the claws of modem tree-dwelling birds enables them to perch in trees. The claws of Archeopteryx, the earliest known birdlike creature, show similar curvature that must have enabled the creature to perch on tree limbs. Therefore, Archeopteryx was probably a tree-dwelling creature.

Paleontologist: No, the ability to perch in trees is not good evidence that Archeopteryx was a tree-dwelling bird. Chickens also spend time perched in trees, yet chickens are primarily ground-dwelling.

Which one of the following is an assumption on which the ornithologist's reasoning depends?

(A) Modem tree-dwelling birds are the direct descendants of Archeopteryx.
(B) Archeopteryx made use of the curvature of its claws.
(C) There have never been tree-dwelling birds without curved claws.
(D) Archeopteryx was in fact the earliest birdlike creature.
(E) The curvature of the claws is the only available evidence for the claim that Archeopteryx was tree-dwelling.

102. A company with long-outstanding bills owed by its customers can assign those bills to a collection agency that pays the company a fraction of their amount and then tries to collect payment from the customers. Since these agencies pay companies only 15 percent of the total amount of the outstanding bills, a company interested in reducing losses from long-outstanding bills would be well advised to pursue its debtors on its own.

The argument depends on the assumption that

(A) a company that pursues its debtors on its own typically collects more than 15 percent of the total amount of the long-outstanding bills that it is owed
(B) the cost to a company of pursuing its debtors on its own for payment of long-outstanding bills does not exceed 15 percent of the total amount of those bills
(C) collection agencies that are assigned bills for collection by companies are unsuccessful in collecting, on average, only 15 percent of the total amount of those bills
(D) at least 15 percent of the customers that owe money to companies eventually pay their bills whether or not those bills are assigned to a collection agency
(E) unless most of the customers of a company pay their bills, that company in the long run will not be profitable

103. Because of the lucrative but illegal trade in rhinoceros horns, a certain rhinoceros species has been hunted nearly to extinction. Therefore an effective way to ensure the survival of that species would be to periodically trim off the horns of all rhinoceroses, thereby eliminating the motivation for poaching.

Which one of the following is an assumption required by the argument?

(A) Most poachers who are discouraged from hunting rhinoceroses are not likely to hunt other animals for their horns.
(B) At least some rhinoceroses whose horns are periodically trimmed off will be able to attract mates.
(C) Poachers hunt at least some immature rhinoceroses whose horns have not yet started to develop.
(D) The demand for rhinoceros horns will remain constant even if the supply decreases after the periodic trimming-off of the rhinoceros horns has begun.
(E) Rhinoceroses whose horns have been trimmed off are unable to defend themselves against predators.

104. In order to increase production, ABC Company should implement a flextime schedule, which would allow individual employees some flexibility in deciding when to begin and end their workday. Studies have shown that working under flextime schedules is associated with increased employee morale.

The argument depends on the assumption that

(A) the employees who prefer a flextime schedule are the most productive employees at ABC Company
(B) an increase in the morale of ABC Company's employees could lead to increased production
(C) flextime schedules tend to be associated with reduced lateness and absenteeism
(D) employees are most productive during the part of the day when all employees are present
(E) companies that are in competition with ABC Company also use a flextime schedule

105. Based on data collected from policyholders, life insurance companies have developed tables that list standard weight ranges for various heights. Policyholders whose weight fell within the range given for their height lived longer than those whose weight fell outside their given range. Therefore, if people whose weight falls outside their given range modified their weight to fall within that range, their overall life expectancies would improve.

Which one of the following is an assumption on which the argument relies?

(A) Some people would be unwilling to modify their weights solely to increase the general population's overall life expectancies.
(B) Life insurance companies intended their tables to guide individuals in adjusting their weights in order to increase their life spans.
(C) The tables include data gathered from policyholders whose deaths resulted from accidents in addition to those whose deaths resulted from natural causes.
(D) Holders of life insurance policies do not have longer overall life expectancies than the general population.
(E) People's efforts to modify their weight to conform to a given range would not damage their health enough to decrease their overall life expectancies.

106. The Biocarb Company wants to build a sterilization plant to treat contaminated medical waste in a city neighborhood where residents and environmental activists fear that such a facility will pollute the area. Biocarb's president argues that the operation of the plant cannot cause pollution because the waste would be sterile after processing by the plant. He claims that after exposure for an hour to superheated steam in the autoclave, such refuse would be far cleaner than food prepared in the cleanest kitchen.

The president's argument depends on which one of the following assumptions?

(A) Environmental activists believe that waste treated with steam will not pollute.
(B) Handling of the waste before treatment in the proposed facility will not pose a threat of pollution to the area.
(C) Fear of pollution is the only argument against construction of an autoclave facility for medical waste.
(D) No others besides environmental activists are concerned about pollution hazards that can result from processing medical waste.
(E) Treatment by superheated steam represents the surest method of sterilization.

107. Manager: Our new computer network, the purpose of which is to increase productivity, can be installed during the day, which would disrupt our employees' work, or else at night, which would entail much higher installation charges. Since saving money is important, we should have the network installed during the day.

The manager's argument assumes which one of the following?

(A) The monetary value of the network equipment would not exceed the cost of having the equipment installed at night.
(B) The monetary value of any productivity lost during a daytime installation would be less than the difference between daytime and nighttime installation costs.
(C) A daytime installation would be completed by no larger a crew and would take the crew no more time than would a nighttime installation.
(D) Once the network has been installed, most of the company's employees will be able to use it immediately to increase their productivity.
(E) Most of the company's employees would be able to work productively while a daytime installation is in progress.

108. A certain credit-card company awards its customers bonus points for using its credit card. Customers can use accumulated points in the purchase of brand name merchandise by mail at prices lower than the manufacturers' suggested retail prices. At any given time, therefore, customers who purchase merchandise using the bonus points spend less than they would spend if they purchased the same merchandise in retail stores.

Which one of the following is an assumption on which the argument depends?

(A) The merchandise that can be ordered by mail using the bonus points is not offered at lower prices by other credit-card companies that award bonus points.
(B) The bonus points cannot be used by the credit card customers in the purchase of brand name merchandise that is not available for purchase in retail stores.
(C) The credit-card company does not require its customers to accumulate a large number of bonus points before becoming eligible to order merchandise at prices lower than the manufacturers' suggested retail price.
(D) The amount credit-card customers pay for shipping the merchandise ordered by mail does not increase the amount customers spend to an amount greater than they would spend if they purchased the same merchandise in retail stores.
(E) The merchandise available to the company's credit-card customers using the bonus points is frequently sold in retail stores at prices that are higher than the manufacturers' suggested retail prices.

109. Brown dwarfs—dim red stars that are too cool to burn hydrogen—are very similar in appearance to red dwarf stars, which are just hot enough to burn hydrogen. Stars, when first formed, contain substantial amounts of the element lithium. All stars but the coolest of the brown dwarfs are hot enough to destroy lithium completely by converting it to helium. Accordingly, any star found that contains no lithium is not one of these coolest brown dwarfs.

The argument depends on assuming which one of the following?

(A) None of the coolest brown dwarfs has ever been hot enough to destroy lithium.
(B) Most stars that are too cool to burn hydrogen are too cool to destroy lithium completely.
(C) Brown dwarfs that are not hot enough to destroy lithium are hot enough to destroy helium.
(D) Most stars, when first formed, contain roughly the same percentage of lithium.
(E) No stars are more similar in appearance to red dwarfs than are brown dwarfs.

110. Some people have been promoting a new herbal mixture as a remedy for the common cold. The mixture contains, among other things, extracts of the plants purple cone-flower and goldenseal. A cold sufferer, skeptical of the claim that the mixture is an effective cold remedy, argued, "Suppose that the mixture were an effective cold remedy. Since most people with colds wish to recover quickly, it follows that almost everybody with a cold would be using it. Therefore, since there are many people who have colds but do not use the mixture, it is obviously not effective."

Each of the following is an assumption required by the skeptical cold sufferer's argument EXCEPT:

(A) Enough of the mixture is produced to provide the required doses to almost everybody with a cold.
(B) The mixture does not have side effects severe enough to make many people who have colds avoid using it.
(C) The mixture is powerful enough to prevent almost everybody who uses it from contracting any further colds.
(D) The mixture is widely enough known that almost everybody with a cold is aware of it.
(E) There are no effective cold remedies available that many people who have colds prefer to the mixture.

111. Critic: People today place an especially high value on respect for others; yet, in their comedy acts, many of today's most popular comedians display blatant disrespect for others. But when people fail to live up to the very ideals they hold in highest esteem, exaggeration of such failings often forms the basis of successful comedy. Thus the current popularity of comedians who display disrespect in their acts is hardly surprising.

The critic's argument depends on which one of the following assumptions?

(A) People who enjoy comedians who display disrespect in their acts do not place a high value on respect for others.
(B) Only comedians who display blatant disrespect in their acts are currently successful.
(C) Many people disapprove of the portrayal of blatant disrespect for others in comedy acts.
(D) People who value an ideal especially highly do not always succeed in living up to this ideal.
(E) People today fail to live up to their own ideals more frequently than was the case in the past.

112. John works five days each week except when on vacation or during weeks in which national holidays occur. Four days a week he works in an insurance company; on Fridays he works as a blacksmith. Last week there were no holidays, and John was not on vacation. Therefore, he must have worked in the insurance company on Monday, Tuesday, Wednesday, and Thursday last week.

Which one of the following is an assumption on which the argument depends?

(A) John never takes a vacation of more than one week in length.
(B) Every day last week that John worked, he worked for an entire workday.
(C) John does not take vacations in weeks in which national holidays occur.
(D) Last week John worked neither on Saturday nor on Sunday.
(E) There were no days last week on which John both worked in the insurance company and also worked as a blacksmith.

ASSUMPTION

113. Private industry is trying to attract skilled research scientists by offering them high salaries. As a result, most research scientists employed in private industry now earn 50 percent more than do comparably skilled research scientists employed by the government. So, unless government-employed research scientists are motivated more by a sense of public duty than by their own interests, the government is likely to lose its most skilled research scientists to private industry, since none of these scientists would have problems finding private sector jobs.

Which one of the following is an assumption on which the argument depends?

(A) Government research scientists are less likely to receive acknowledgment for their research contributions than are research scientists in the private sector.
(B) None of the research scientists currently employed by the government earns more than the highest-paid researchers employed in the private sector.
(C) The government does not employ as many research scientists who are highly skilled as does any large company in the private sector which employs research scientists.
(D) The government does not provide its research scientists with unusually good working conditions or fringe benefits that more than compensate for the lower salaries they receive.
(E) Research scientists employed in the private sector generally work longer hours than do researchers employed by the government.

Chapter Eight: Resolve the Paradox Questions

1. It is difficult to keep deep wounds free of bacteria. Even strong antibiotics fail to kill the bacteria that live in such wounds. However, many physicians have succeeded in eliminating bacteria from deep wounds by packing the wound with a sweet substance like sugar.

   Which one of the following, if true, most helps to explain why treating deep wounds with sugar as described above is successful?

   (A) Bacteria that live in deep wounds thrive in a moist environment, and sugar has a dehydrating effect.
   (B) Sugar that is nearly pure is readily available for use in medical treatments.
   (C) Many kinds of bacteria can use sugar as a nutrient and will reproduce rapidly when sugar is available to them.
   (D) Some foods that contain sugar can weaken the effects of certain antibiotics.
   (E) Strong antibiotics were developed only recently, but the use of sugar as a treatment for wounds dates back to ancient times.

2. In the United States proven oil reserves—the amount of oil considered extractable from known fields—are at the same level as they were ten years ago. Yet over this same period no new oil fields of any consequence have been discovered, and the annual consumption of domestically produced oil has increased.

   Which one of the following, if true, best reconciles the discrepancy described above?

   (A) Over the past decade the annual consumption of imported oil has increased more rapidly than that of domestic oil in the United States.
   (B) Conservation measures have lowered the rate of growth of domestic oil consumption from what it was a decade ago.
   (C) Oil exploration in the United States has slowed due to increased concern over the environmental impact of such exploration.
   (D) The price of domestically produced oil has fallen substantially over the past decade.
   (E) Due to technological advances over the last decade, much oil previously considered unextractable is now considered extractable.

3. A recent survey of brand preferences showed that R-Bar Beans are considered the best of all brands among all age groups, leading both Texas T Beans and Aunt Sally's Beans by a wide margin. However, the national sales figures show that Texas T and Aunt Sally's each sold many more cans of beans last year than did R-Bar.

   Each of the following would, by itself, help to resolve the apparent paradox described in the passage EXCEPT:

   (A) Texas T Beans and Aunt Sally's Beans are each much less expensive than R-Bar Beans.
   (B) Some of the surveyed age groups showed more of a preference for R-Bar Beans than did others.
   (C) The survey was carried out only in the small geographic area where R-Bar distributes its beans, not nationwide.
   (D) Most food stores refuse to carry R-Bar Beans because the manufacturer demands that R-Bar Beans be carried exclusively.
   (E) R-Bar Beans were only introduced to the market three months prior to the calculation of sales figures, while Texas T Beans and Aunt Sally's Beans had been available for years.

4. Dried grass clippings mixed into garden soil gradually decompose, providing nutrients for beneficial soil bacteria. This results in better-than-average plant growth. Yet mixing fresh grass clippings into garden soil usually causes poorer-than-average plant growth.

   Which one of the following, if true, most helps to explain the difference in plant growth described above?

   (A) The number of beneficial soil bacteria increases whenever any kind of plant material is mixed into garden soil.
   (B) Nutrients released by dried grass clippings are immediately available to beneficial soil bacteria.
   (C) Some dried grass clippings retain nutrients originally derived from commercial lawn fertilizers, and thus provide additional enrichment to the soil.
   (D) Fresh grass clippings mixed into soil decompose rapidly, generating high levels of heat that kill beneficial soil bacteria.
   (E) When a mix of fresh and dried grass clippings is mixed into garden soil, plant growth often decreases.

5. Although nondairy coffee lighteners made with coconut oil contain 2 grams of saturated fat per tablespoon, or 7 times more than does whole milk, those lighteners usually contain no cholesterol. Yet one tablespoon of such lighteners causes the consumer's blood cholesterol to rise to a higher level than does an identical amount of whole milk, which contains 2 milligrams of cholesterol per tablespoon.

   Which one of the following, if true, contributes most to an explanation of the apparent discrepancy noted above?

   (A) Nutritionists recommend that adults consume as little saturated fat as possible and no more than 250 milligrams of cholesterol a day.
   (B) One gram of saturated fat in food has roughly the same effect on blood cholesterol as 25 milligrams of cholesterol in food.
   (C) Light cream, a dairy product that contains 5 times more cholesterol than does whole milk, is often chosen as a lightener by consumers who normally prefer whole milk.
   (D) Certain nondairy coffee lighteners made without coconut oil contain less saturated fat and less cholesterol than does whole milk.
   (E) The lower the saturated fat content of dairy products, the less cholesterol they usually contain.

6. On the basis of incontestable proof that car safety seats will greatly reduce the number of serious injuries sustained by children in car accidents, laws have been passed mandating the use of these seats. Unexpectedly, it has since been found that a large number of children who are riding in safety seats continue to receive serious injuries that safety seats were specifically designed to avoid, and in the prevention of which they in fact have proven to be effective.

   Which one of the following, if true, could by itself adequately explain the unexpected finding reported in the passage?

   (A) Many parents are defying the law by not using safety seats for their children.
   (B) Children are more likely to make automobile trips now than they were before the introduction of the safety seat.
   (C) The high cost of child safety seats has caused many parents to delay purchasing them.
   (D) The car safety seat was not designed to prevent all types of injuries, so it is not surprising that some injuries are sustained.
   (E) The protection afforded by child safety seats depends on their being used properly, which many parents fail to do.

7. The average level of fat in the blood of people suffering from acute cases of disease W is lower than the average level for the population as a whole. Nevertheless, most doctors believe that reducing blood-fat levels is an effective way of preventing acute W.

   Which one of the following, if true, does most to justify this apparently paradoxical belief?

   (A) The blood level of fat for patients who have been cured of W is on average the same as that for the population at large.
   (B) Several of the symptoms characteristic of acute W have been produced in laboratory animals fed large doses of a synthetic fat substitute, though acute W itself has not been produced in this way.
   (C) The progression from latent to acute W can occur only when the agent that causes acute W absorbs large quantities of fat from the patient's blood.
   (D) The levels of fat in the blood of patients who have disease W respond abnormally slowly to changes in dietary intake of fat.
   (E) High levels of fat in the blood are indicative of several diseases that are just as serious as W.

8. If we are to expand the exploration of our solar system, our next manned flight should be to Phobos, one of Mars's moons, rather than to Mars itself. The flight times to each are the same, but the Phobos expedition would require less than half the fuel load of a Mars expedition and would, therefore, be much less costly. So, it is clear that Phobos should be our next step in space exploration.

   Which one of the following, if true, would most help to explain the difference in fuel requirements?

   (A) More equipment would be required to explore Phobos than to explore Mars.
   (B) Smaller spaceships require less fuel than larger spaceships.
   (C) Information learned during the trip to Phobos can be used during a subsequent trip to Mars.
   (D) The shortest distance between Phobos and Mars is less than half the shortest distance between Earth and Mars.
   (E) Lift-off for the return trip from Phobos requires much less fuel than that from Mars because of Phobos' weaker gravitational pull.

9. Sixty adults were asked to keep a diary of their meals, including what they consumed, when, and in the company of how many people. It was found that at meals with which they drank alcoholic beverages, they consumed about 175 calories more from nonalcoholic sources than they did at meals with which they did not drink alcoholic beverages.

   Each of the following, if true, contributes to an explanation of the difference in caloric intake EXCEPT:

   (A) Diners spent a much longer time at meals served with alcohol than they did at those served without alcohol.
   (B) The meals eaten later in the day tended to be larger than those eaten earlier in the day, and later meals were more likely to include alcohol.
   (C) People eat more when there are more people present at the meal, and more people tended to be present at meals served with alcohol than at meals served without alcohol.
   (D) The meals that were most carefully prepared and most attractively served tended to be those at which alcoholic beverages were consumed.
   (E) At meals that included alcohol, relatively more of the total calories consumed came from carbohydrates and relatively fewer of them came from fats and proteins.

10. A tree's age can be determined by counting the annual growth rings in its trunk. Each ring represents one year, and the ring's thickness reveals the relative amount of rainfall that year. Archaeologists successfully used annual rings to determine the relative ages of ancient tombs at Pazyryk. Each tomb was constructed from freshly cut logs, and the tombs' builders were constrained by tradition to use only logs from trees growing in the sacred Pazyryk Valley.

    Which one of the following, if true, contributes most to an explanation of the archaeologists' success in using annual rings to establish the relative ages of the tombs at the Pazyryk site?

    (A) The Pazyryk tombs were all robbed during ancient times, but breakage of the tombs' seals allowed the seepage of water, which soon froze permanently, thereby preserving the tombs' remaining artifacts.
    (B) The Pazyryk Valley, surrounded by extremely high mountains, has a distinctive yearly pattern of rainfall, and so trees growing in the Pazyryk Valley have annual rings that are quite distinct from trees growing in nearby valleys.
    (C) Each log in the Pazyryk tombs has among its rings a distinctive sequence of twelve annual rings representing six drought years followed by three rainy years and three more drought years.
    (D) The archaeologists determined that the youngest tree used in any of the tombs was 90 years old and that the oldest tree was 450 years old.
    (E) All of the Pazyryk tombs contained cultural artifacts that can be dated to roughly 2300 years ago.

RESOLVE

11. In essence, all rent-control policies involve specifying a maximum rent that a landlord may charge for a dwelling. The rationale for controlling rents is to protect tenants in situations where limited supply will cause rents to rise sharply in the face of increased demand. However, although rent control may help some tenants in the short run, it affects the rental-housing market adversely in the long run because landlords become reluctant to maintain the quality of their existing properties and even more reluctant to have additional rental-housing units built.

Which one of the following, if true, best explains the landlords' reluctance described above?

(A) Tenants prefer low-quality accommodations with rent control to high-quality accommodations without it.
(B) Rent control makes it very difficult for landlords to achieve reasonable returns on any investments in maintenance or in new construction.
(C) Rent control is a common practice even though it does nothing to alleviate shortages in rental housing.
(D) Rent control is generally introduced for political reasons and it takes political action to have it lifted again.
(E) Tenants prefer rent control to the alternative of receiving direct government subsidies toward rents they cannot afford.

12. Economist: Money, no matter what its form and in almost every culture in which it has been used, derives its value from its scarcity, whether real or perceived.

Anthropologist: But cowrie shells formed the major currency in the Solomon Island economy of the Kwara'ae, and unlimited numbers of these shells washed up daily on the beaches to which the Kwara'ae had access.

Which one of the following, if true about the Kwara'ae, best serves to resolve the apparently conflicting positions cited above?

(A) During festivals they exchanged strings of cowrie-shell money with each other as part of a traditional ritual that honored their elders.
(B) They considered porpoise teeth valuable, and these were generally threaded on strings to be worn as jewelry.
(C) The shells used as money by men were not always from the same species of cowrie as those used as money by women.
(D) They accepted as money only cowrie shells that were polished and carved by a neighboring people, and such shell preparation required both time and skilled labor.
(E) After Western traders brought money in the form of precious-metal coins to the Solomon Islands, cowrie-shell money continued to be used as one of the major media of exchange for both goods and services.

13. A certain viral infection is widespread among children, and about 30 percent of children infected with the virus develop middle ear infections. Antibiotics, although effective in treating bacterial infections, have no effect on the virus. Yet when middle ear infections in children infected with the virus are treated with antibiotics, the ear infections often clear up.

Which one of the following most helps to explain the success of the treatments with antibiotics?

(A) Although some types of antibiotics fail to clear up certain infections, other types of antibiotics might provide effective treatment for those infections.
(B) Children infected with the virus are particularly susceptible to bacteria that infect the middle ear.
(C) Many children who develop middle ear infections are not infected with the virus.
(D) Most viral infections are more difficult to treat than are most bacterial infections.
(E) Among children not infected with the virus, fewer than 30 percent develop middle ear infections.

14. Some companies in fields where skilled employees are hard to find make signing an "agreement not to compete" a condition of employment. In such an agreement the employee promises not to go to work for a competing firm for a set period after leaving his or her current employer. Courts are increasingly ruling that these agreements are not binding. Yet paradoxically, for people who signed such agreements when working for competing firms, many firms are unwilling to consider hiring them during the period covered by the agreement.

Which one of the following, if true, most helps to resolve the paradox?

(A) Many companies will not risk having to become involved in lawsuits, even suits that they expect to have a favorable outcome, because of the associated costs and publicity.
(B) In some industries, for example the broadcast media, companies' main source of new employees tends to be people who are already employed by competing firms.
(C) Most companies that require their employees to sign agreements not to compete are aware that these documents are not legally binding.
(D) Many people who have signed agreements not to compete are unwilling to renege on a promise by going to work for a competing firm.
(E) Many companies consider their employees' established relationships with clients and other people outside the company to be valuable company assets.

15. By dating fossils of pollen and beetles, which returned after an Ice Age glacier left an area, it is possible to establish an approximate date when a warmer climate developed. In one glacial area, it appears from the insect record that a warm climate developed immediately after the melting of the glacier. From the pollen record, however, it appears that the warm climate did not develop until long after the glacier disappeared.

Each one of the following, if true, helps to explain the apparent discrepancy EXCEPT:

(A) Cold-weather beetle fossils can be mistaken for those of beetles that live in warm climates.
(B) Warm-weather plants cannot establish themselves as quickly as can beetles in a new environment.
(C) Beetles can survive in a relatively barren postglacial area by scavenging.
(D) Since plants spread unevenly in a new climate, researchers can mistake gaps in the pollen record as evidence of no new overall growth.
(E) Beetles are among the oldest insect species and are much older than many warm-weather plants.

16. The ancient Romans understood the principles of water power very well, and in some outlying parts of their empire they made extensive and excellent use of water as an energy source. This makes it all the more striking that the Romans made do without water power in regions dominated by large cities.

Which one of the following, if true, contributes most to an explanation of the difference described above in the Romans' use of water power?

(A) The ancient Romans were adept at constructing and maintaining aqueducts that could carry quantities of water sufficient to supply large cities over considerable distances.
(B) In the areas in which water power was not used, water flow in rivers and streams was substantial throughout the year but nevertheless exhibited some seasonal variation.
(C) Water power was relatively vulnerable to sabotage, but any damage could be quickly and inexpensively repaired.
(D) In most areas to which the use of water power was not extended, other, more traditional sources of energy continued to be used.
(E) In heavily populated areas the introduction of water power would have been certain to cause social unrest by depriving large numbers of people of their livelihood.

17. Four randomly chosen market research companies each produced population estimates for three middle-sized cities; the estimates of each company were then compared with those of the other companies. Two of the cities had relatively stable populations, and for them estimates of current population and of projected population in five years varied little from company to company. However, for the third city, which was growing rapidly, estimates varied greatly from company to company.

Which one of the following, if true, would best help explain why estimates of the current population of the rapidly growing city varied more than did current population estimates for the two other cities?

(A) Population changes over time are more uniform from one district to another in the rapidly growing city than in the two other cities.
(B) The population of the rapidly growing city is increasing largely as a result of a high birth rate.
(C) The population of the rapidly growing city has a lower average age than the populations of either of the two other cities.
(D) All population estimates of the rapidly growing city were produced first by estimating the current populations of the city's districts and then by adding those estimates.
(E) Whereas the companies used different methods for estimating the current population of the rapidly growing city, the companies used the same method for the two other cities.

18. Since the introduction of the Impanian National Health scheme, Impanians (or their private insurance companies) have had to pay only for the more unusual and sophisticated medical procedures. When the scheme was introduced, it was hoped that private insurance to pay for these procedures would be available at modest cost, since the insurers would no longer be paying for the bulk of health care costs, as they had done previously. Paradoxically, however, the cost of private health insurance did not decrease but has instead increased dramatically in the years since the scheme's introduction.

Which one of the following, if true, does most to explain the apparently paradoxical outcome?

(A) The National Health scheme has greatly reduced the number of medical claims handled annually by Impania's private insurers, enabling these firms to reduce overhead costs substantially.
(B) Before the National Health scheme was introduced, more than 80 percent of all Impanian medical costs were associated with procedures that are now covered by the scheme.
(C) Impanians who previously were unable to afford regular medical treatment now use the National Health scheme, but the number of Impanians with private health insurance has not increased.
(D) Impanians now buy private medical insurance only at times when they expect that they will need care of kinds not available in the National Health scheme.
(E) The proportion of total expenditures within Impania that is spent on health care has declined since the introduction of the National Health scheme.

19. In clinical trials of new medicines, half of the subjects receive the drug being tested and half receive a physiologically inert substance—a placebo. Trials are designed with the intention that neither subjects nor experimenters will find out which subjects are actually being given the drug being tested. However, this intention is frequently frustrated because ____________.

Which one of the following, if true, most appropriately completes the explanation?

(A) often the subjects who receive the drug being tested develop symptoms that the experimenters recognize as side effects of the physiologically active drug
(B) subjects who believe they are receiving the drug being tested often display improvements in their conditions regardless of whether what is administered to them is physiologically active or not
(C) in general, when the trial is intended to establish the experimental drug's safety rather than its effectiveness, all of the subjects are healthy volunteers
(D) when a trial runs a long time, few of the experimenters will work on it from inception to conclusion
(E) the people who are subjects for clinical trials must, by law, be volunteers and must be informed of the possibility that they will receive a placebo

RESOLVE

20. Of all of the surgeons practicing at the city hospital, the chief surgeon has the worst record in terms of the percentage of his patients who die either during or immediately following an operation performed by him. Paradoxically, the hospital's administrators claim that he is the best surgeon currently working at the hospital.

Which one of the following, if true, goes farthest toward showing that the administrators' claim and the statistic cited might both be correct?

(A) Since the hospital administrators appoint the chief surgeon, the administrators are strongly motivated to depict the chief surgeon they have chosen as a wise choice.
(B) In appointing the current chief surgeon, the hospital administrators followed the practice, well established at the city hospital, of promoting one of the surgeons already on staff.
(C) Some of the younger surgeons on the city hospital's staff received part of their training from the current chief surgeon.
(D) At the city hospital those operations that inherently entail the greatest risk to the life of the patient are generally performed by the chief surgeon.
(E) The current chief surgeon has a better record of patients' surviving surgery than did his immediate predecessor.

21. When old-growth forests are cleared of tall trees, more sunlight reaches the forest floor. This results in a sharp increase in the population of leafy shrubs on which the mule deer depend for food. Yet mule deer herds that inhabit cleared forests are less well-nourished than are herds living in old-growth forests.

Which one of the following, if true, most helps to resolve the apparent paradox?

(A) Mule deer have enzyme-rich saliva and specialized digestive organs that enable the deer to digest tough plants inedible to other deer species.
(B) Mule deer herds that inhabit cleared forests tend to have more females with young offspring and fewer adult males than do other mule deer populations.
(C) Mule deer populations are spread throughout western North America and inhabit hot, sunny climates as well as cool, wet climates.
(D) As plants receive more sunlight, they produce higher amounts of tannins, compounds that inhibit digestion of the plants' proteins.
(E) Insect parasites, such as certain species of ticks, that feed primarily on mule deer often dwell in trees, from which they drop onto passing deer.

22. All people residing in the country of Gradara approve of legislation requiring that certain hazardous wastes be disposed of by being burned in modern high-temperature incinerators. However, waste disposal companies planning to build such incinerators encounter fierce resistance to their applications for building permits from the residents of every Gradaran community that those companies propose as an incinerator site.

Which one of the following, if true, most helps to explain the residents' simultaneously holding both of the positions ascribed to them?

(A) High-temperature incineration minimizes the overall risk to the human population of the country from the wastes being disposed of, but it concentrates the remaining risk in a small number of incineration sites.
(B) High-temperature incineration is more expensive than any of the available alternatives would be, and the higher costs would be recovered through higher product prices.
(C) High-temperature incineration will be carried out by private companies rather than by a government agency so that the government will not be required to police itself.
(D) The toxic fumes generated within a high-temperature incinerator can be further treated so that all toxic residues from a properly operating incinerator are solids.
(E) The substantial cost of high-temperature incineration can be partially offset by revenue from sales of electric energy generated as a by-product of incineration.

RESOLVE

23. A recent survey conducted in one North American city revealed widespread concern about the problems faced by teenagers today. Seventy percent of the adults surveyed said they would pay higher taxes for drug treatment programs, and 60 percent said they were willing to pay higher taxes to improve the city's schools. Yet in a vote in that same city, a proposition to increase funding for schools by raising taxes failed by a narrow margin to win majority approval.

Which one of the following factors, if true, would LEAST contribute to an explanation of the discrepancy described above?

(A) The survey sample was not representative of the voters who voted on the proposition.
(B) Many of the people who were surveyed did not respond truthfully to all of the questions put to them.
(C) The proposition was only part of a more expensive community improvement program that voters had to accept or reject in total.
(D) A proposition for increasing funds for local drug treatment centers also failed to win approval.
(E) The proposition to raise taxes for schools was couched in terminology that many of the voters found confusing.

24. In the summer of 1936 a polling service telephoned 10,000 United States voters and asked how they planned to vote in the coming presidential election. The survey sample included a variety of respondents—rural and urban, male and female, from every state. The poll predicted that Alfred Landon would soundly defeat Franklin Roosevelt. Nevertheless, Roosevelt won in a landslide.

Which one of the following, if true, best explains why the poll's prediction was inaccurate?

(A) The interviewers did not reveal their own political affiliation to the respondents.
(B) Only people who would be qualified to vote by election time were interviewed, so the survey sample was not representative of the overall United States population.
(C) The survey sample was representative only of people who could afford telephones at a time when phone ownership was less common than it is today.
(D) No effort was made to determine the respondents' political affiliations.
(E) Because the poll asked only for respondents' candidate preference, it collected no information concerning their reasons for favoring Landon or Roosevelt.

25. Most of the ultraviolet radiation reaching the Earth's atmosphere from the Sun is absorbed by the layer of stratospheric ozone and never reaches the Earth's surface. Between 1969 and 1986, the layer of stratospheric ozone over North America thinned, decreasing by about 3 percent. Yet, the average level of ultraviolet radiation measured at research stations across North America decreased over the same period.

Which one of the following, if true, best reconciles the apparently discrepant facts described above?

(A) Ultraviolet radiation increases the risk of skin cancer and cataracts; the incidence of skin cancer and cataracts increased substantially between 1969 and 1986.
(B) Between 1969 and 1986, the layer of stratospheric ozone over Brazil thinned, and the average level of ultraviolet radiation reaching the Earth's surface in Brazil increased.
(C) Manufactured chlorine chemicals thin the layer of stratospheric ozone.
(D) Ozone pollution, which absorbs ultraviolet radiation, increased dramatically between 1969 and 1986.
(E) Thinning of the layer of stratospheric ozone varies from one part of the world to another and from year to year.

26. It might seem that an airline could increase profits by reducing airfares on all its flights in order to encourage discretionary travel and thus fill planes. Offers of across-the-board discount fares have, indeed, resulted in the sale of large numbers of reduced-price tickets. Nevertheless such offers have, in the past, actually cut the airline's profits.

Which one of the following, if true, most helps to resolve the apparent discrepancy described above?

(A) Fewer than 10 percent of all air travelers make no attempt to seek out discount fares.
(B) Fares for trips between a large city and a small city are higher than those for trips between two large cities even when the distances involved are the same.
(C) Across-the-board discounts in fares tend to decrease revenues on flights that are normally filled, but they fail to attract passengers to unpopular flights.
(D) Only a small number of people who have never before traveled by air are persuaded to do so on the basis of across-the-board discount fares.
(E) It is difficult to devise an advertising campaign that makes the public aware of across-the-board discount fares while fully explaining the restrictions applied to those discount fares.

27. Switching to "low-yield" cigarettes, those that yield less nicotine, tar, and carbon monoxide than regular cigarettes when tested on a standard machine, does not, in general, reduce the incidence of heart attack. This result is surprising, since nicotine and carbon monoxide have been implicated as contributing to heart disease.

Which one of the following, if true, most helps to resolve the apparent discrepancy?

(A) Smoking low-yield cigarettes has become fashionable, as relatively healthier styles of life have become more popular than those that have been identified as risky.
(B) For those who are themselves smokers, inhaling the smoke of others is not generally a significant factor contributing to an increased risk of heart disease.
(C) Nicotine does not contribute as much to heart disease as does carbon monoxide.
(D) Carbon monoxide and cigarette tar are not addictive substances.
(E) People who switch from high-yield to low-yield cigarettes often compensate by increasing the number and depth of puffs in order to maintain their accustomed nicotine levels.

28. Once consumers recognize that a period of inflation has begun, there is generally an increase in consumer spending. This increase can be readily explained by consumers' desire not to postpone purchases that will surely increase in price. But during protracted periods of inflation, consumers eventually begin to put off making even routine purchases, despite the fact that consumers continue to expect prices to rise and despite the fact that salaries also rise during inflationary periods.

Which one of the following, if true, most helps to explain the apparent inconsistency in consumer behavior described above?

(A) During times of inflation consumers save more money than they do in noninflationary periods.
(B) There is usually a lag between the leading economic indicators' first signaling the onset of an inflationary period and consumers' recognition of its onset.
(C) No generalization that describes human behavior will be true of every type of human behavior.
(D) If significant numbers of consumers are unable to make purchases, prices will eventually fall but salaries will not be directly affected.
(E) Consumers' purchasing power decreases during periods of protracted inflation since salaries do not keep pace with prices.

29. The Gulches is an area of volcanic rock that is gashed by many channels that lead downhill from the site of a prehistoric glacier to a river. The channels clearly were cut by running water. It was once accepted as fact that the cutting occurred gradually, as the glacier melted. But one geologist theorized that the channels were cut in a short time by an enormous flood. The channels do show physical evidence of having been formed quickly, but the flood theory was originally rejected because scientists knew of no natural process that could melt so much ice so quickly. Paradoxically, today the scientific community accepts the flood theory even though scientists still do not know of a process that can melt so much ice so quickly.

Which one of the following, if true, most helps to resolve the apparent paradox in the passage?

(A) Ripples, which indicate that the channels were cut by water, have been discovered in the floors of the channels.
(B) The Gulches is known to be similar in certain respects to many other volcanic rock formations.
(C) More than one glacier was present in the area during prehistoric times.
(D) Volcanic rock is more easily cut by water than are other forms of rock.
(E) Scientists now believe that the prehistoric glacier dammed a source of water, created a huge lake in the process, and then retreated.

RESOLVE

30. Throughout European history famines have generally been followed by periods of rising wages, because when a labor force is diminished, workers are more valuable in accordance with the law of supply and demand. The Irish potato famine of the 1840s is an exception; it resulted in the death or emigration of half of Ireland's population, but there was no significant rise in the average wages in Ireland in the following decade.

Which one of the following, if true, would LEAST contribute to an explanation of the exception to the generalization?

(A) Improved medical care reduced the mortality rate among able-bodied adults in the decade following the famine to below prefamine levels.
(B) Eviction policies of the landowners in Ireland were designed to force emigration of the elderly and infirm, who could not work, and to retain a high percentage of able-bodied workers.
(C) Advances in technology increased the efficiency of industry and agriculture, and so allowed maintenance of economic output with less demand for labor.
(D) The birth rate increased during the decade following the famine, and this compensated for much of the loss of population that was due to the famine.
(E) England, which had political control of Ireland, legislated artificially low wages to provide English-owned industry and agriculture in Ireland with cheap labor.

31. A group of scientists studying calcium metabolism in laboratory rats discovered that removing the rats' parathyroid glands resulted in the rats' having substantially lower than normal levels of calcium in their blood. This discovery led the scientists to hypothesize that the function of the parathyroid gland is to regulate the level of calcium in the blood by raising that level when it falls below the normal range. In a further experiment, the scientists removed not only the parathyroid gland but also the adrenal gland from rats. They made the surprising discovery that the level of calcium in the rats' blood decreased much less sharply than when the parathyroid gland alone was removed.

Which one of the following, if true, explains the surprising discovery in a way most consistent with the scientists' hypothesis?

(A) The adrenal gland acts to lower the level of calcium in the blood.
(B) The adrenal gland and the parathyroid gland play the same role in regulating calcium blood levels.
(C) The absence of a parathyroid gland causes the adrenal gland to increase the level of calcium in the blood.
(D) If the adrenal gland, and no other gland, of a rat were removed, the rat's calcium level would remain stable.
(E) The only function of the parathyroid gland is to regulate the level of calcium in the blood.

32. Megatrash Co., the country's largest waste-disposal company, has been sued by environmental groups who have accused the firm of negligent handling of hazardous waste. The fines and legal fees that have resulted from the legal attacks against Megatrash have cost the company substantial amounts of money. Surprisingly, as successful lawsuits against the company have increased in number, the company has grown stronger and more profitable.

Which one of the following, if true, does the most to resolve the apparent paradox?

(A) Although waste-disposal firms merely handle but do not generate toxic waste, these firms have been held legally responsible for environmental damage caused by this waste.
(B) Megatrash has made substantial contributions to environmental causes, as have other large waste-disposal companies.
(C) Some of the judgments against Megatrash have legally barred it from entering the more profitable areas of the waste-management business.
(D) The example of Megatrash's legal entanglements has driven most of the company's competitors from the field and deterred potential rivals from entering it.
(E) In cases in which Megatrash has been acquitted of charges of negligence, the company has paid more in legal fees than it would have been likely to pay in fines.

RESOLVE

33. When deciding where to locate or relocate, businesses look for an educated work force, a high level of services, a low business-tax rate, and close proximity to markets and raw materials. However, although each of these considerations has approximately equal importance, the lack of proximity either to markets or to raw materials often causes municipalities to lose prospective business, whereas having a higher-than-average business-tax rate rarely has this effect.

    Which one of the following, if true, most helps to resolve the apparent discrepancy in the statements above?

    (A) Taxes paid by businesses constitute only a part of the tax revenue collected by most municipalities.

    (B) In general, the higher the rate at which municipalities tax businesses, the more those municipalities spend on education and on providing services to businesses.

    (C) Businesses sometimes leave a municipality after that municipality has raised its taxes on businesses.

    (D) Members of the work force who are highly educated are more likely to be willing to relocate to secure work than are less highly educated workers.

    (E) Businesses have sometimes tried to obtain tax reductions from municipalities by suggesting that without such a reduction the business might be forced to relocate elsewhere.

34. Soil scientists studying the role of compost in horticulture have found that, while compost is useful for building soil structure, it does not supply large enough quantities of the nutrients essential for plant growth to make it a replacement for fertilizer. Many home gardeners, however, have found they can grow healthy and highly productive plants in soil that lacked essential nutrients by enriching the soil with nothing but compost.

    Which one of the following, if true, most helps to explain the discrepant findings of the soil scientists and the home gardeners?

    (A) The findings of soil scientists who are employed by fertilizer manufacturers do not differ widely from those of scientists employed by the government or by universities.

    (B) Compost used in research projects is usually made from leaves and grass clipping only, whereas compost used in home gardens is generally made from a wide variety of ingredients.

    (C) Most plants grown in home gardens and in scientists' test plots need a favorable soil structure, as well as essential nutrients, in order to thrive.

    (D) The soil in test plots, before it is adjusted in the course of experiments, tends to contain about the same quantities of plant nutrients as does soil in home gardens to which no compost or fertilizer has been added.

    (E) Some of the varieties of plants grown by home gardeners require greater quantities of nutrients in order to be healthy than do the varieties of plants generally grown by the soil scientists in test plots.

35. In 1980 health officials began to publicize the adverse effects of prolonged exposure to the sun, and since then the number of people who sunbathe for extended periods of time has decreased considerably each year. Nevertheless, in 1982 there was a dramatic rise in newly reported cases of melanoma, a form of skin cancer found mostly in people who have had prolonged exposure to the sun.

Which one of the following, if true, helps to resolve the apparent discrepancy in the information above?

(A) Before 1980 a considerable number of the people who developed melanoma as a result of prolonged exposure to the sun were over forty years of age.
(B) Before 1980, when most people had not yet begun to avoid prolonged exposure to the sun, sunbathing was widely thought to be healthful.
(C) In 1982 scientists reported that the body's need for exposure to sunlight in order to produce vitamin D, which helps prevent the growth of skin cancers, is less than was previously though.
(D) In 1982 medical researchers perfected a diagnostic technique that allowed them to detect the presence of melanoma much earlier than had previously been possible.
(E) Since 1980, those people who have continued to sunbathe for extended periods of time have used sunblocks that effectively screen out the ultraviolet rays that help cause melanoma.

36. Fossil-fuel emissions, considered a key factor in the phenomenon known as global warming, contain two gases, carbon dioxide and sulfur dioxide, that have opposite effects on atmospheric temperatures. Carbon dioxide traps heat, tending to warm the atmosphere, whereas sulfur dioxide turns into sulfate aerosols that reflect sunlight back toward space, thereby tending to cool the atmosphere. Given that the heat-trapping effect is stronger than the cooling effect, cutting fossil-fuel emissions might be expected to slow the rise in global temperatures. Yet, surprisingly, if fossil-fuel emissions were cut today, global warming would actually be enhanced for more than three decades before the temperature rise began to slow.

Which one of the following, if true, most helps to explain the claim made in the last sentence above?

(A) Carbon dioxide stays in the atmosphere for many decades, while the sulfate aerosols fall out within days.
(B) Sulfur pollution is not spread evenly around the globe but is concentrated in the Northern Hemisphere, where there is a relatively high concentration of industry.
(C) While it has long been understood that sulfur dioxide is a harmful pollutant, it has been understood only recently that carbon dioxide might also be a harmful pollutant.
(D) Carbon dioxide is produced not only by automobiles but also by power plants that burn fossil fuels.
(E) Because fossil-fuel emissions contain sulfur dioxide, they contribute not only to global warming but also to acid rain.

RESOLVE

37. A long-term health study that followed a group of people who were age 35 in 1950 found that those whose weight increased by approximately half a kilogram or one pound per year after the age of 35 tended, on the whole, to live longer than those who maintained the weight they had at age 35. This finding seems at variance with other studies that have associated weight gain with a host of health problems that tend to lower life expectancy.

Which one of the following, if true, most helps to resolve the apparently conflicting findings?

(A) As people age, muscle and bone tissue tends to make up a smaller and smaller proportion of total body weight.
(B) Individuals who reduce their cholesterol levels by losing weight can thereby also reduce their risk of dying from heart attacks or strokes.
(C) Smokers, who tend to be leaner than nonsmokers, tend to have shorter life spans than nonsmokers.
(D) The normal deterioration of the human immune system with age can be slowed down by a reduction in the number of calories consumed.
(E) Diets that tend to lead to weight gain often contain not only excess fat but also unhealthful concentrations of sugar and sodium.

38. When compact discs first entered the market, they were priced significantly higher than vinyl records. Manufacturers attributed the difference in price to the difference in production costs, saying that compact disc production was expensive because the technology was new and unfamiliar. As the technology became more efficient, the price of the discs did indeed come down. But vinyl records, whose production technology has long been established then went up in price to approach that of compact discs.

Which one of the following most helps to explain why the price of vinyl records went up?

(A) Consumers were so enthusiastic about the improved sound quality offered by compact disc technology that they were willing to pay higher price to obtain it.
(B) Some consumers who continued to buy vinyl records instead of compact discs did so because they were unwilling to pay a higher price for compact discs.
(C) As consumers bought compact discs instead of vinyl records, the number of vinyl records produced decreased, making their production less cost-efficient.
(D) Compact disc player technology continued to change and develop even after compact discs first entered the market.
(E) When compact discs first entered the market, many consumers continued to buy vinyl records rather than buying the equipment necessary to play compact discs.

39. Smokers of pipes or cigars run a distinctly lower risk to their health than do cigarette smokers. However, whereas cigarette smokers who quit smoking altogether sharply reduce their risk of smoking related health problems, those who give up cigarettes and take up pipes or cigars remain in as much danger as before.

    Which one of the following, if true, offers the best prospects for an explanation of why the two changes in smoking habits do not both result in reduced health risks?

    (A) Smokers of pipes or cigars who quit smoking thereby reduce their risk of smoking-related health problems.
    (B) Cigarette smokers who quit smoking for a time and who then resume cigarette smoking do not necessarily reduce their risk of smoking related health problems.
    (C) The kinds of illnesses that smokers run an increased risk of contracting develop no earlier in cigarette smokers than they do in smokers of pipes or cigars.
    (D) At any given period in their lives, virtually all smokers smoke either cigarettes exclusively or cigars exclusively or pipes exclusively, rather than alternating freely among various ways of smoking.
    (E) People who switch from cigarette smoking to smoking pipes or cigars inhale smoke in a way that those who have never smoked cigarettes do not.

40. Each year, an official estimate of the stock of cod in the Grand Banks is announced. This estimate is obtained by averaging two separate estimates of how many cod are available, one based on the number of cod caught by research vessels during a once-yearly sampling of the area and the other on the average number of tons of cod caught by various commercial vessels per unit of fishing effort expended there in the past year—a unit of fishing effort being one kilometer of net set out in the water for one hour. In previous decades, the two estimates usually agreed closely. However, for the last decade the estimate based on commercial tonnage has been increasing markedly, by about the same amount as the sampling based estimate has been decreasing.

    Which one of the following, if true, most helps to account for the growing discrepancy between the estimate based on commercial tonnage and the research-based estimate?

    (A) Fishing vessels often exceed their fishing quotas for cod and therefore often underreport the number of tons of cod that they catch.
    (B) More survey vessels are now involved in the yearly sampling effort than were involved 10 years ago.
    (C) Improvements in technology over the last 10 years have allowed commercial fishing vessels to locate and catch large schools of cod more easily.
    (D) Survey vessels count only those cod caught during a 30-day survey period, whereas commercial fishing vessels report all cod caught during the course of a year.
    (E) Because of past overfishing of cod, fewer fishing vessels now catch the maximum tonnage of cod each vessel is allowed by law to catch.

41. The company that produces XYZ, a computer spreadsheet program, estimates that millions of illegally reproduced copies of XYZ are being used. If legally purchased, this number of copies would have generated millions of dollars in sales for the company, yet despite a company-wide effort to boost sales, the company has not taken available legal measures to prosecute those who have copied the program illegally.

Which one of the following, if true, most helps to explain why the company has not taken available legal measures?

(A) XYZ is very difficult to copy illegally, because a sophisticated anticopying mechanism in the program must first be disabled.
(B) The legal measures that the company that produces XYZ could take against those who have copied its product became available several years before XYZ came on the market.
(C) Many people who purchase a software program like XYZ are willing to purchase that program only after they have already used it.
(D) The number of illegally reproduced copies of XYZ currently in use exceeds the number of legally reproduced copies currently in use.
(E) The company that produces ABC, the spreadsheet program that is XYZ's main rival in the marketplace, is well known for taking legal action against people who have copied ABC illegally.

RESOLVE

42. At the beginning of each month, companies report to the federal government their net loss or gain in jobs over the past month. These reports are then consolidated by the government and reported as the total gain or loss for the past month. Despite accurate reporting by companies and correct tallying by the government, the number of jobs lost was significantly underestimated in the recent recession.

Which one of the following, if true, contributes most to a resolution of the apparent discrepancy described?

(A) More jobs are lost in a recession than in a period of growth.
(B) The expenses of collecting and reporting employment data have steadily increased.
(C) Many people who lose their jobs start up their own businesses.
(D) In the recent recession a large number of failing companies abruptly ceased all operations.
(E) The recent recession contributed to the growing preponderance of service jobs over manufacturing jobs.

43. Alcohol consumption has been clearly linked to high blood pressure, which increases the likelihood of developing heart disease. Yet in a study of the effects of alcohol consumption, the incidence of heart disease was lower among participants who drank moderate quantities of alcohol every day than it was among participants identified as nondrinkers.

Which one of the following, if true, most helps to resolve the apparent discrepancy in the information above?

(A) Because many people who do not drink alcohol are conscious of their health habits, they are likely to engage in regular exercise and to eat nutritionally well-balanced meals.
(B) Many of the participants identified as nondrinkers were people who had been heavy drinkers but had stopped drinking alcohol prior to participating in the study.
(C) Some of the participants who drank moderate quantities of alcohol every day said that they occasionally drank large quantities of alcohol.
(D) Some of the participants who drank moderate quantities of alcohol every day had high blood pressure.
(E) The two groups of participants were similar to each other with respect to the participants' age, sex, geographical origin, and economic background.

44. Rainfall in the drought-plagued metropolitan area was heavier than usual for the month of June. Nevertheless, by the first of July the city's water shortage was more severe than ever, and officials proposed drastic restrictions on the use of water.

Which one of the following, if true, helps to explain why the city's water shortage was not alleviated by the first of July?

(A) Moderate restrictions on the industrial use of water had gone into effect in the metropolitan area several months earlier.
(B) Because of the heavier rainfall, people watered their lawns much less in June than they usually do in the metropolitan area during that month.
(C) People in the metropolitan area who had voluntarily reduced their use of water in earlier months when officials voiced alarm used greater than normal amounts of water when rainfall seemed plentiful in June.
(D) During the drought most residents of the metropolitan area had been informed about water conservation methods that would help them to reduce their water consumption significantly with a minimal reduction in their standard of living.
(E) The per capita rate of the use of water in the metropolitan area was slightly lower in June than in each of the three previous months and significantly lower than in June of the previous year.

45. Deer mice normally do not travel far from their nests, and deer mice that are moved more than half a kilometer from their nests generally never find their way back. Yet in one case, when researchers camped near a deer mouse nest and observed a young deer mouse for several weeks before moving it to an area over two kilometers away, the deer mouse found its way back to its nest near their camp in less than two days.

Which one of the following, if true, most helps to explain how the deer mouse might have found its way back to its nest?

(A) The area to which the deer mouse was moved was dryer and more rocky than the area in which its nest was located.
(B) The researchers released the deer mouse in a flat area across which their campfire smoke drifted.
(C) There were very few deer mice in the area to which the deer mouse was moved.
(D) The researchers had moved the deer mouse in a small dark box, keeping the mouse calm before it was released.
(E) Animals that prey on deer mice were common in the area to which the deer mouse was moved.

46. In a yearlong study, half of the participants were given a simple kit to use at home for measuring the cholesterol level of their blood. They reduced their cholesterol levels on average 15 percent more than did participants without the kit. Participants were selected at random from among people with dangerously high cholesterol levels.

Which one of the following, if true, most helps to explain the study's finding?

(A) The lower a blood-cholesterol level is, the less accurate are measurements made by the kit.
(B) Participants with the kit were more likely to avoid foods that lower cholesterol level.
(C) Participants with the kit used it more frequently during the first two months of the study.
(D) All the participants in the study showed some lowering of cholesterol levels, the most striking decreases having been achieved in the first three months.
(E) Participants using the kit reported that each reading reinforced their efforts to reduce their cholesterol levels.

47. The government recently released a study of drinking water, in which it was reported that consumers who bought bottled water were in many cases getting water that was less safe than what they could obtain much more cheaply from the public water supply. In spite of the enormous publicity that the study received, sales of bottled water have continued to rise.

Which one of the following, if true, is most helpful in resolving the apparent paradox?

(A) Bottled water might contain levels of potentially harmful contaminants that are not allowed in drinking water.
(B) Most consumers who habitually drink the bottled water discussed in the study cannot differentiate between the taste of their usual brand of bottled water and that of water from public sources.
(C) Increased consumption of the five best-selling brands of bottled water, which the report said were safer than both public water and most other brands of bottled water, accounted for the increase in sales.
(D) The rate of increase in the sales of bottled water has slowed since the publication of the government study.
(E) Government health warnings concerning food have become so frequent that consumers have begun to doubt the safety of many everyday foods.

RESOLVE

48. Of the five bill collectors at Apex Collection Agency, Mr. Young has the highest rate of unsuccessful collections. Yet Mr. Young is the best bill collector on the agency's staff.

Which one of the following, if true, most helps to resolve the apparent discrepancy?

(A) Mr. Young is assigned the majority of the most difficult cases at the agency.
(B) The other four bill collectors at the agency all consider Mr. Young to be a very capable bill collector.
(C) Mr. Young's rate of collections per year has remained fairly steady in the last few years.
(D) Before joining the agency, Mr. Young was affiliated with the credit department of a large department store.
(E) None of the bill collectors at the agency has been on the agency's staff longer than Mr. Young has.

49. Ten thousand years ago many communities in western Asia stopped procuring food by hunting and gathering and began instead to cultivate food. Archaeological evidence reveals that, compared to their hunter-gatherer forebears, the early agricultural peoples ate a poorly balanced diet and had diet-related health problems, yet these peoples never returned to hunting and gathering

Which one of the following, if true, most helps to explain why the agricultural peoples of western Asia never returned to hunting and gathering?

(A) The plants and animals that the agricultural peoples began to cultivate continued to exist in the wild.
(B) Both hunter-gatherers and agriculturalists sometimes depended on stored and preserved foods instead of fresh foods.
(C) An increase in population density at the time required a higher food production rate than hunting and gathering could provide.
(D) Thousands of years ago similar shifts from hunting and gathering to agriculture occurred in many other parts of the world.
(E) The physical labor involved in agriculture burns more calories than does that needed for hunting and gathering.

50. Calories consumed in excess of those with which the body needs to be provided to maintain its weight are normally stored as fat and the body gains weight. Alcoholic beverages are laden with calories. However, those people who regularly drink two or three alcoholic beverages a day and thereby exceed the caloric intake necessary to maintain their weight do not in general gain weight.

Which one of the following, if true, most helps to resolve the apparent discrepancy?

(A) Some people who regularly drink two or three alcoholic beverages a day avoid exceeding the caloric intake necessary to maintain their weight by decreasing caloric intake from other sources.
(B) Excess calories consumed by people who regularly drink two or three alcoholic beverages a day tend to be dissipated as heat.
(C) Some people who do not drink alcoholic beverages but who eat high-calorie foods do not gain weight.
(D) Many people who regularly drink more than three alcoholic beverages a day do not gain weight.
(E) Some people who take in fewer calories than are normally necessary to maintain their weight do not lose weight.

51. Although water in deep aquifers does not contain disease-causing bacteria, when public water supplies are drawn from deep aquifers, chlorine is often added to the water as a disinfectant because contamination can occur as a result of flaws in pipes or storage tanks. Of 50 municipalities that all pumped water from the same deep aquifer, 30 chlorinated their water and 20 did not. The water in all of the municipalities met the regional government's standards for cleanliness, yet the water supplied by the 20 municipalities that did not chlorinate had less bacterial contamination than the water supplied by the municipalities that added chlorine.

Which one of the following, if true, most helps explain the difference in bacterial contamination in the two groups of municipalities?

(A) Chlorine is considered by some experts to be dangerous to human health, even in the small concentrations used in municipal water supplies.
(B) When municipalities decide not to chlorinate their water supplies, it is usually because their citizens have voiced objections to the taste and smell of chlorine.
(C) The municipalities that did not add chlorine to their water supplies also did not add any of the other available water disinfectants, which are more expensive than chlorine.
(D) Other agents commonly added to public water supplies, such as fluoride and sodium hydroxide, were not used by any of the 50 municipalities.
(E) Municipalities that do not chlorinate their water supplies are subject to stricter regulation by the regional government in regard to pipes and water tanks than are municipalities that use chlorine.

52. Municipal officials originally estimated that it would be six months before municipal road crews could complete repaving a stretch of road. The officials presumed that private contractors could not finish any sooner. However, when the job was assigned to a private contractor, it was completed in just 28 days.

Which one of the following, if true, does most to resolve the discrepancy between the time estimated for completion of the repaving job, and the actual time taken by the private contractor?

(A) Road repaving work can only be done in the summer months of June, July, and August.
(B) The labor union contract for road crews employed by both municipal agencies and private contractors stipulates that employees can work only eight hours a day, five days a week, before being paid overtime.
(C) Many road-crew workers for private contractors have previously worked for municipal road crews, and vice versa.
(D) Private contractors typically assign 25 workers to each road-repaving job site, whereas the number assigned to municipal road crews is usually 30.
(E) Municipal agencies must conduct a lengthy bidding process to procure supplies after repaving work is ordered and before they can actually start work, whereas private contractors can obtain supplies readily as needed.

RESOLVE

53. Michelangelo's sixteenth-century Sistine Chapel paintings are currently being restored. A goal of the restorers is to uncover Michelangelo's original work, and so additions made to Michelangelo's paintings by later artists are being removed. However, the restorers have decided to make one exception: to leave intact additions that were painted by da Volterra.

Which one of the following, if true, most helps to reconcile the restorers' decision with the goal stated in the passage?

(A) The restorers believe that da Volterra stripped away all previous layers of paint before he painted his own additions to the Sistine Chapel.
(B) Because da Volterra used a type of pigment that is especially sensitive to light, the additions to the Sistine Chapel that da Volterra painted have relatively muted colors.
(C) Da Volterra's additions were painted in a style that was similar to the style used by Michelangelo.
(D) Michelangelo is famous primarily for his sculptures and only secondarily for his paintings, whereas da Volterra is known exclusively for his paintings.
(E) Da Volterra's work is considered by certain art historians to be just as valuable as the work of some of the other artists who painted additions to Michelangelo's work.

54. A new silencing device for domestic appliances operates by producing sound waves that cancel out the sound waves produced by the appliance. The device, unlike conventional silencers, actively eliminates the noise the appliance makes, and for that reason vacuum cleaners designed to incorporate the new device will operate with much lower electricity consumption than conventional vacuum cleaners.

Which one of the following, if true, most helps to explain why the new silencing device will make lower electricity consumption possible?

(A) Designers of vacuum cleaner motors typically have to compromise the motors' efficiency in order to reduce noise production.
(B) The device runs on electricity drawn from the appliance's main power supply.
(C) Conventional vacuum cleaners often use spinning brushes to loosen dirt in addition to using suction to remove dirt.
(D) Governmental standards for such domestic appliances as vacuum cleaners allow higher electricity consumption when vacuum cleaners are quieter.
(E) The need to incorporate silencers in conventional vacuum cleaners makes them heavier and less mobile than they might otherwise be.

55. A certain type of insect trap uses a scented lure to attract rose beetles into a plastic bag from which it is difficult for them to escape. If several of these traps are installed in a backyard garden, the number of rose beetles in the garden will be greatly reduced. If only one trap is installed, however, the number of rose beetles in the garden will actually increase.

Which one of the following, if true, most helps to resolve the apparent discrepancy?

(A) The scent of a single trap's lure usually cannot be detected throughout a backyard garden by rose beetles.
(B) Several traps are better able to catch a large number of rose beetles than is one trap alone, since any rose beetles that evade one trap are likely to encounter another trap if there are several traps in the garden.
(C) When there are several traps in a garden, they each capture fewer rose beetles than any single trap would if it were the only trap in the garden.
(D) The presence of any traps in a backyard garden will attract more rose beetles than one trap can catch, but several traps will not attract significantly more rose beetles to a garden than one trap will.
(E) When there is only one trap in the garden, the plastic bag quickly becomes filled to capacity, allowing some rose beetles to escape.

56. Since 1945 pesticide use in the United States has increased tenfold despite an overall stability in number of acres planted. During the same period, crop loss from insects has approximately doubled, from about seven to thirteen percent.

Which one of the following, if true, contributes most to explaining the paradoxical findings above?

(A) Extension agents employed by state governments to advise farmers have recently advocated using smaller amounts of pesticide, though in past years they promoted heavy pesticide use.
(B) While pesticide-resistant strains of insects were developing, crop rotation, which for insects disrupts a stable food supply, was gradually abandoned because farmers' eligibility to receive government crop subsidies depended on continuing to plant the same crop.
(C) Since 1970 the pesticides most lethal to people have generally been replaced by less-lethal chemicals that are equally effective against insects and have a less-damaging effect on the fish in streams fed by water that runs off from treated agricultural fields.
(D) Because farmers' decisions about how much land to plant are governed by their expectations about crop prices at harvest time, the amount of pesticide they apply also depends in part on expected crop prices.
(E) Although some pesticides can be removed from foodstuffs through washing, others are taken up into the edible portion of plants, and consumers have begun to boycott foods containing pesticides that cannot be washed off.

RESOLVE

57. Oxygen-18 is a heavier-than-normal isotope of oxygen. In a rain cloud, water molecules containing oxygen-18 are rarer than water molecules containing normal oxygen. But in rainfall, a higher proportion of all water molecules containing oxygen-18 than of all water molecules containing ordinary oxygen descends to earth. Consequently, scientists were surprised when measurements along the entire route of rain clouds' passage from above the Atlantic Ocean, the site of their original formation, across the Amazon forests, where it rains almost daily, showed that the oxygen-18 content of each of the clouds remained fairly constant.

    Which one of the following statements, if true, best helps to resolve the conflict between scientists' expectations, based on the known behavior of oxygen-18, and the result of their measurements of the rain clouds' oxygen-18 content?

    (A) Rain clouds above tropical forests are poorer in oxygen-18 than rain clouds above unforested regions.
    (B) Like the oceans, tropical rain forests can create or replenish rain clouds in the atmosphere above them.
    (C) The amount of rainfall over the Amazon rain forests is exactly the same as the amount of rain originally collected in the clouds formed above the Atlantic Ocean.
    (D) The amount of rain recycled back into the atmosphere from the leaves of forest vegetation is exactly the same as the amount of rain in river runoffs that is not recycled into the atmosphere.
    (E) Oxygen-18 is not a good indicator of the effect of tropical rain forests on the atmosphere above them.

58. Much of the best scientific research of today shows that many of the results of earlier scientific work that was regarded in its time as good are in fact mistaken. Yet despite the fact that scientists are above all concerned to discover the truth, it is valuable for today's scientists to study firsthand accounts of earlier scientific work.

    Which one of the following, if true, would best reconcile the two statements above?

    (A) Many firsthand accounts of earlier, flawed scientific work are not generally known to be mistaken.
    (B) Lessons in scientific methodology can be learned by seeing how earlier scientific work was carried out, sometimes especially when the results of that work are known to be incorrect.
    (C) Scientists can make valuable contributions to the scientific work of their time even if the results of their work will later be shown to be mistaken.
    (D) There are many scientists today who are not thoroughly familiar with earlier scientific research.
    (E) Some of the better scientific research of today does not directly address earlier scientific work.

59. I. Room air conditioners produced by Japanese manufacturers tend to be more reliable than those produced by United States manufacturers.

    II. The average lifetime of room air conditioners produced by United States manufacturers is about fifteen years, the same as that of room air conditioners produced by Japanese manufacturers.

    Which one of the following, if true, would best reconcile the two statements above?

    (A) Reliability is a measure of how long a product functions without needing repair.
    (B) Production facilities of firms designated as United States manufacturers are not all located in the United States.
    (C) Damage to room air conditioners during shipping and installation does not occur with great frequency in the United States or in Japan.
    (D) Room air conditioners have been manufactured for a longer time in the United States than in Japan.
    (E) Japanese manufacturers often use more reliable components in their room air conditioners than do United States manufacturers.

60. Goodbody, Inc., is in the process of finding tenants for its newly completed Parrot Quay commercial development, which will make available hundreds of thousands of square feet of new office space on what was formerly derelict property outside the financial center of the city. Surprisingly enough, the coming recession, though it will hurt most of the city's businesses, should help Goodbody to find tenants.

Which one of the following, if true, does most to help resolve the apparent paradox?

(A) Businesses forced to economize by the recession will want to take advantage of the lower rents available outside the financial center.
(B) Public transportation links the financial center with the area around Parrot Quay.
(C) The area in which the Parrot Quay development is located became derelict after the heavy industry that used to be there closed down in a previous recession.
(D) Many of Goodbody's other properties are in the financial center and will become vacant if the recession is severe enough to force Goodbody's tenants out of business.
(E) The recession is likely to have the most severe effect not on service industries, which require a lot of office space, but on manufacturers.

61. Adults who work outside the home spend, on average, 100 minutes less time each week in preparing dinner than adults who do not work outside the home. But, contrary to expectation, comparisons show that the dinners eaten at home by the two groups of adults do not differ significantly with respect to nutritional value, variety of menus, or number of courses.

Which one of the following, if true, most helps to resolve the apparent discrepancy in the information above?

(A) The fat content of the dinners eaten at home by adults who do not work outside the home is 25 percent higher than national guidelines recommend.
(B) Adults who do not work outside the home tend to prepare breakfast more often than adults who work outside the home.
(C) Adults who work outside the home spend 2 hours less time per day on all household responsibilities, including dinner preparation, than do adults who do not work outside the home.
(D) Adults who work outside the home eat dinner at home 20 percent less often than do adults who do not work outside the home.
(E) Adults who work outside the home are less likely to plan dinner menus well in advance than are adults who do not work outside the home.

62. There is strong evidence that the cause of migraines (severe recurrent headaches) is not psychological but instead is purely physiological. Yet several studies have found that people being professionally treated for migraines rate higher on a standard psychological scale of anxiety than do people not being professionally treated for migraines.

Which one of the following, if true, most helps to resolve the apparent discrepancy in the information above?

(A) People who have migraine headaches tend to have relatives who also have migraine headaches.
(B) People who have migraine headaches often suffer these headaches when under emotional stress.
(C) People who rate higher on the standard psychological scale of anxiety are more likely to seek professional treatment than are people who rate lower on the scale.
(D) Of the many studies done on the cause of migraine headaches, most of those that suggest that psychological factors such as anxiety cause migraines have been widely publicized.
(E) Most people who have migraines and who seek professional treatment remain in treatment until they stop having migraines, whether their doctors consider the cause to be physiological or psychological.

63. Construction contractors working on the cutting edge of technology nearly always work on a "cost-plus" basis only. One kind of cost-plus contract stipulates the contractor's profit as a fixed percentage of the contractor's costs; the other kind stipulates a fixed amount of profit over and above costs. Under the first kind of contract, higher costs yield higher profits for the contractor, so this is where one might expect final costs in excess of original cost estimates to be more common. Paradoxically, such cost overruns are actually more common if the contract is of the fixed-profit kind.

Which one of the following, if true, most helps to resolve the apparent paradox in the situation described above?

(A) Clients are much less likely to agree to a fixed-profit type of cost-plus contract when it is understood that under certain conditions the project will be scuttled than they are when there is no such understanding.
(B) On long-term contracts, cost projections take future inflation into account, but since the figures used are provided by the government, they are usually underestimated.
(C) On any sizable construction project, the contractor bills the client monthly or quarterly, so any tendency for original cost estimates to be exceeded can be detected early.
(D) Clients billed under a cost-plus contract are free to review individual billings in order to uncover wasteful expenditures, but they do so only when the contractor's profit varies with cost.
(E) The practice of submitting deliberately exaggerated cost estimates is most common in the case of fixed-profit contracts, because it makes the profit, as a percentage of estimated cost, appear modest.

RESOLVE

64. In recent years the climate has been generally cool in northern Asia. But during periods when the average daily temperature and humidity in northern Asia were slightly higher than their normal levels the yields of most crops grown there increased significantly. In the next century, the increased average daily temperature and humidity attained during those periods are expected to become the norm. Yet scientists predict that the yearly yields of most of the region's crops will decrease during the next century.

Which one of the following, if true, most helps to resolve the apparent paradox in the information above?

(A) Crop yields in southern Asia are expected to remain constant even after the average daily temperature and humidity there increase from recent levels.
(B) Any increases in temperature and humidity would be accompanied by higher levels of atmospheric carbon dioxide, which is vital to plant respiration.
(C) The climate in northern Asia has generally been too cool and dry in recent years for populations of many crop insect pests to become established.
(D) In many parts of Asia, the increased annual precipitation that would result from warmer and wetter climates would cause most edible plant species to flourish.
(E) The recent climate of northern Asia prevents many crops from being farmed there during the winter.

65. Smoking in bed has long been the main cause of home fires. Despite a significant decline in cigarette smoking in the last two decades, however, there has been no comparable decline in the number of people killed in home fires.

Each one of the following statements, if true over the last two decades, helps to resolve the apparent discrepancy above EXCEPT:

(A) Compared to other types of home fires, home fires caused by smoking in bed usually cause relatively little damage before they are extinguished.
(B) Home fires caused by smoking in bed often break out after the home's occupants have fallen asleep.
(C) Smokers who smoke in bed tend to be heavy smokers who are less likely to quit smoking than are smokers who do not smoke in bed.
(D) An increasing number of people have been killed in home fires that started in the kitchen.
(E) Population densities have increased, with the result that one home fire can cause more deaths than in previous decades.

RESOLVE

Chapter Nine: Method of Reasoning Questions

Please Note: In this chapter, Method—AP questions appear first, followed by general Method questions.

1. Politician: Homelessness is a serious social problem, but further government spending to provide low-income housing is not the cure for homelessness. The most cursory glance at the real-estate section of any major newspaper is enough to show that there is no lack of housing units available to rent. So the frequent claim that people are homeless because of a lack of available housing is wrong.

That homelessness is a serious social problem figures in the argument in which one of the following ways?

(A) It suggests an alternative perspective to the one adopted in the argument.
(B) It sets out a problem the argument is designed to resolve.
(C) It is compatible either with accepting the conclusion or with denying it.
(D) It summarizes a position the argument as a whole is directed toward discrediting.
(E) It is required in order to establish the conclusion.

2. When Alicia Green borrowed a neighbor's car without permission, the police merely gave her a warning. However, when Peter Foster did the same thing, he was charged with automobile theft. Peter came to the attention of the police because the car he was driving was hit by a speeding taxi. Alicia was stopped because the car she was driving had defective taillights. It is true that the car Peter took got damaged and the car Alicia took did not, but since it was the taxi that caused the damage this difference was not due to any difference in the blameworthiness of their behavior. Therefore Alicia should also have been charged with automobile theft.

The statement that the car Peter took got damaged and the car Alicia took did not plays which one of the following roles in the argument?

(A) It presents a reason that directly supports the conclusion.
(B) It justifies the difference in the actual outcome in the two cases.
(C) It demonstrates awareness of a fact on which a possible objection might be based.
(D) It illustrates a general principle on which the argument relies.
(E) It summarizes a position against which the argument is directed.

3. A university should not be entitled to patent the inventions of its faculty members. Universities, as guarantors of intellectual freedom, should encourage the free flow of ideas and the general dissemination of knowledge. Yet a university that retains the right to patent the inventions of its faculty members has a motive to suppress information about a potentially valuable discovery until the patent for it has been secured. Clearly, suppressing information concerning such discoveries is incompatible with the university's obligation to promote the free flow of ideas.

The claim that a university should not be entitled to patent the inventions of its faculty members plays which one of the following roles in the argument?

(A) It is the conclusion of the argument.
(B) It is a principle from which the conclusion is derived.
(C) It is an explicit assumption.
(D) It is additional but nonessential information in support of one of the premises.
(E) It is a claim that must be demonstrated to be false in order to establish the conclusion.

4. Of every 100 burglar alarms police answer, 99 are false alarms. This situation causes an enormous and dangerous drain on increasingly scarce public resources. Each false alarm wastes an average of 45 minutes of police time. As a result police are consistently taken away from responding to other legitimate calls for service, and a disproportionate share of police service goes to alarm system users, who are mostly businesses and affluent homeowners. However, burglar alarm systems, unlike car alarm systems, are effective in deterring burglaries, so the only acceptable solution is to fine burglar alarm system owners the cost of 45 minutes of police time for each false alarm their systems generate.

The statement that burglar alarm systems, unlike car alarm systems, are effective in deterring burglaries plays which one of the following roles in the argument?

(A) It justifies placing more restrictions on owners of burglar alarms than on owners of car alarms.
(B) It provides background information needed to make plausible the claim that the number of burglar alarms police are called on to answer is great enough to be a drain on public resources.
(C) It provides a basis for excluding as unacceptable one obvious alternative to the proposal of fining owners of burglar alarm systems for false alarms.
(D) It gives a reason why police might be more inclined to respond to burglar alarms than to car alarms.
(E) It explains why a disproportionate number of the burglar alarms responded to by police come from alarm systems owned by businesses.

5. Few politicians will support legislation that conflicts with their own self-interest. A case in point is August Frenson, who throughout his eight terms in office consistently opposed measures limiting the advantage incumbents enjoy over their challengers. Therefore, if such measures are to be enacted, they must result from direct popular vote rather from legislative action.

The case of August Frenson plays which one of the following roles in the argument?

(A) It provides evidence, the falsity of which would guarantee the falsity of the author's conclusion.
(B) It is cited as an example illustrating the generalization that is invoked.
(C) It gives essential background information concerning a measure being advocated.
(D) It demonstrates the extent to which incumbents have the advantage over challengers.
(E) It gives an example of the limits of direct popular vote.

6. Mainstream economic theory holds that manufacturers, in deciding what kinds of products to manufacture and what form those products should have, simply respond to the needs and desires of consumers. However, most major manufacturers manipulate and even create consumer demand, as anyone who watches television knows. Since even mainstream economic theorists watch television, their motive in advancing this theory must be something other than disinterested concern for scientific truth.

The claim that manufacturers manipulate and create consumer demand plays which one of the following roles in the argument?

(A) It is one of the claims on which the conclusion is based.
(B) It is the conclusion of the argument.
(C) It states the position argued against.
(D) It states a possible objection to the argument's conclusion.
(E) It provides supplementary background information.

7. Adults have the right to vote; so should adolescents. Admittedly, adolescents and adults are not the same. But to the extent that adolescents and adults are different, adults cannot be expected to represent the interests of adolescents. If adults cannot represent the interests of adolescents, then only by giving adolescents the vote will these interests represented.

The statement that adolescents and adults are not the same plays which one of the following roles in the argument?

(A) It presents the conclusion of the argument.
(B) It makes a key word in the argument more precise.
(C) It illustrates a consequence of one of the claims that are used to support the conclusion.
(D) It distracts attention from the point at issue.
(E) It concedes a point that is then used to support the conclusion.

8. Ph.D. programs are valuable only if they inculcate good scholarship and expedite the student's full participation in the field. Hence, doctoral dissertations should not be required in the humanities. Undertaking a quality book-length dissertation demands an accumulation of knowledge virtually impossible for those relatively new to their disciplines. The student consequently either seeks to compensate for poor quality with quantity or ends up spending years producing a work of quality. Either way, the dissertation is counterproductive and frustrates the appropriate goals of the doctoral program.

The claim that doctoral dissertations should not be required in the humanities plays which one of the following roles in the argument?

(A) It provides essential support for the conclusion.
(B) It is an example illustrative of a general principle concerning the goals of Ph.D. programs.
(C) It is what the argument is attempting to establish.
(D) It provides evidence for the assumption that requirements for degrees in the humanities differ from requirements for degrees in other disciplines.
(E) It confirms the observation that the requirement for a dissertation can frustrate the goals of a doctoral program.

9. Pedigreed dogs, including those officially classified as working dogs, must conform to standards set by organizations that issue pedigrees. Those standards generally specify the physical appearance necessary for a dog to be recognized as belonging to a breed but stipulate nothing about other genetic traits, such as those that enable breeds originally developed as working dogs to perform the work for which they were developed. Since dog breeders try to maintain only those traits specified by pedigree organizations, and traits that breeders do not try to maintain risk being lost, certain traits like herding ability risk being lost among pedigreed dogs. Therefore, pedigree organizations should set standards requiring working ability in pedigreed dogs classified as working dogs.

The phrase "certain traits like herding ability risk being lost among pedigreed dogs" serves which one of the following functions in the argument?

(A) It is a claim on which the argument depends but for which no support is given.
(B) It is a subsidiary conclusion used in support of the main conclusion.
(C) It acknowledges a possible objection to the proposal put forth in the argument.
(D) It summarizes the position that the argument as a whole is directed toward discrediting.
(E) It provides evidence necessary to support a claim stated earlier in the argument.

10. Consumer advocate: The toy-labeling law should require manufacturers to provide explicit safety labels on toys to indicate what hazards the toys pose. The only labels currently required by law are labels indicating the age range for which a toy is intended. For instance, a "three and up" label is required on toys that pose a choking hazard for children under three years of age. Although the current toy-labeling law has indeed reduced the incidence of injuries to children from toys, parents could prevent such injuries almost entirely if toy labels provided explicit safety information.

The statement that the law should require explicit safety labels on toys serves which one of the following functions in the consumer advocate's argument?

(A) It is a general principle supporting the conclusion of the argument.
(B) It is a proposed compromise between two conflicting goals.
(C) It is the conclusion of the argument.
(D) It is evidence that must be refuted in order to establish the conclusion of the argument.
(E) It is a particular instance of the general position under discussion.

11. Henry: Some scientists explain the dance of honeybees as the means by which honeybees communicate the location of whatever food source they have just visited to other members of the hive. But honeybees do not need so complicated a mechanism to communicate that information. Forager honeybees returning to their hive simply leave a scent trail from the food source they have just visited. There must therefore be some other explanation for the honeybees' dance.

Winifred: Not necessarily. Most animals have several ways of accomplishing critical tasks. Bees of some species can navigate using either the position of the Sun or the memory of landmarks. Similarly, for honeybees, scent trails are a supplementary not an exclusive means of communicating.

In Winifred's response to Henry, the statement about how bees of some species navigate plays which one of the following roles?

(A) It addresses an ambiguity in Henry's use of the expression "communicate the location."

(B) It provides evidence in support of a general claim.

(C) It calls into question the accuracy of key evidence cited by Henry.

(D) It points out that Henry's conclusion directly contradicts one of his premises.

(E) It proposes an alternative explanation for the honeybees' dance.

12. Curator: The decision to restore the cloak of the central figure in Veronese's painting from its present red to the green found underneath is fully justified. Reliable x-ray and chemical tests show that the red pigment was applied after the painting had been completed, and that the red paint was not mixed in Veronese's workshop. Hence it appears likely that an artist other than Veronese tampered with Veronese's painting after its completion.

Art critic: But in a copy of Veronese's painting made shortly after Veronese died, the cloak is red. It is highly unlikely that a copyist would have made so major a change so soon after Veronese's death.

The assertion that a later artist tampered with Veronese's painting serves which one of the following functions in the curator's argument?

(A) It is the main point toward which the argument as a whole is directed.

(B) It is a subsidiary conclusion that supports the argument's main conclusion.

(C) It is a clarification of a key term of the argument.

(D) It is a particular instance of the general position to be defended.

(E) It is a reiteration of the main point that is made for the sake of emphasis.

METHOD

1. Senator Strongwood reported that, contrary to a study cited by the administration, a thorough study by his own party concluded that a reduction in the capital gains tax would lead to an increase in the federal deficit. "Hooray for common sense," he said. "Everyone knows that when you cut taxes you lose revenue." He concluded that the administration's plan for reducing the capital gains tax was now dead, because he could not imagine any senator voting to increase the deficit.

   Which one of the following accurately describes something Senator Strongwood does in advancing his argument?

   (A) He implies that increasing the capital gains tax would decrease the federal deficit.
   (B) He assumes senators will believe his party's report instead of the administration's.
   (C) He resorts to name-calling by expressly stating that his opponents lack common sense.
   (D) He assumes that senators will rarely vote for unpopular legislation.
   (E) He assumes that a study commissioned by his party must be more objective than one commissioned by the administration.

2. Can any research be found to validate the contention that those who spend time plucking out their gray hairs have more negative attitudes toward the elderly than those who shrug their shoulders about their gray hairs? Unless a person's psychopathology leads him or her to overgeneralize, there is no necessary connection. Certainly it is reasonable to like the elderly yet dislike the idea of impaired eyesight and hearing. Furthermore, holding negative attitudes toward older people merely because they are old is immoral, according to nearly universally accepted ethical standards. But there is nothing immoral about disliking some concomitants of the aging process.

   In order to advance her point of view, the author does all of the following EXCEPT

   (A) dismiss an assertion as unfounded
   (B) appeal to reason
   (C) appeal to a general principle
   (D) discredit a common stereotype about the elderly
   (E) make a distinction about attitudes

3. Alice: Quotas on automobile imports to the United States should be eliminated. Then domestic producers would have to compete directly with Japanese manufacturers and would be forced to produce higher-quality cars. Such competition would be good for consumers.

   David: You fail to realize, Alice, that quotas on automobile imports are pervasive worldwide. Since Germany, Britain, and France have quotas, so should the United States.

   Which one of the following most accurately characterizes David's response to Alice's statement?

   (A) David falsely accuses Alice of contradicting herself.
   (B) David unfairly directs his argument against Alice personally.
   (C) David uncovers a hidden assumption underlying Alice's position.
   (D) David takes a position that is similar to the one Alice has taken.
   (E) David fails to address the reasons Alice cites in favor of her conclusion.

4. People have long been fascinated by the paranormal. Over the years, numerous researchers have investigated telepathy only to find that conclusive evidence for its existence has persistently evaded them. Despite this, there are still those who believe that there must be "something in it" since some research seems to support the view that telepathy exists. However, it can often be shown that other explanations that do comply with known laws can be given. Therefore, it is premature to conclude that telepathy is an alternative means of communication.

   In the passage, the author

   (A) supports the conclusion by pointing to the inadequacy of evidence for the opposite view
   (B) supports the conclusion by describing particular experiments
   (C) supports the conclusion by overgeneralizing from a specific piece of evidence
   (D) draws a conclusion that is not supported by the premises
   (E) rephrases the conclusion without offering any support for it

5. The United States has never been a great international trader. It found most of its raw materials and customers for finished products within its own borders. The terrible consequences of this situation have become apparent, as this country now owes the largest foreign debt in the world and is a playground for wealthy foreign investors. The moral is clear: a country can no more live without foreign trade than a dog can live by eating its own tail.

   In order to advance her point of view, the author does each of the following EXCEPT

   (A) draw on an analogy
   (B) appeal to historical fact
   (C) identify a cause and an effect
   (D) suggest a cause of the current economic situation
   (E) question the ethical basis of an economic situation

6. In opposing the 1970 Clean Air Act, the United States automobile industry argued that meeting the act's standards for automobile emissions was neither economically feasible nor environmentally necessary. However, the catalytic converter, invented in 1967, enabled automakers to meet the 1970 standards efficiently. Currently, automakers are lobbying against the government's attempt to pass legislation that would tighten restrictions on automobile emissions. The automakers contend that these new restrictions would be overly expensive and unnecessary to efforts to curb air pollution. Clearly, the automobile industry's position should not be heeded.

   Which one of the following most accurately expresses the method used to counter the automakers' current position?

   (A) The automakers' premises are shown to lead to a contradiction.
   (B) Facts are mentioned that show that the automakers are relying on false information.
   (C) A flaw is pointed out in the reasoning used by the automakers to reach their conclusion.
   (D) A comparison is drawn between the automakers' current position and a position they held in the past.
   (E) Evidence is provided that the new emissions legislation is both economically feasible and environmentally necessary.

7. The Transit Authority's proposal to increase fares by 40 percent must be implemented. Admittedly, this fare increase will impose a hardship on some bus and subway riders. But if the fare is not increased, service will have to be cut severely and that would result in an unacceptably large loss of ridership.

   The passage employs which one of the following argumentative strategies?

   (A) It offers evidence that the recommended course of action would have no undesirable consequences.
   (B) It shows that a proponent of any alternative position would be force into a contradiction.
   (C) It arrives at its conclusion indirectly by providing reasons for rejecting an alternative course of action.
   (D) It explains why the recommended course of action would not be subject to the objections raised against the alternative.
   (E) It justifies the conclusion by showing that such a course of action has proven effective in the past.

8. It is often said that people should be rewarded for doing a given job in proportion to the effort it costs them to do it. However, a little reflection will show that this is, in fact, a very bad idea, since it would mean that those people with the least skill or natural aptitude for a particular task would be the ones given the most incentive to do it.

   Which one of the following argumentative strategies is used above?

   (A) stating a general principle and then presenting reasons in favor of adopting it
   (B) providing evidence that where the principle under discussion has been adopted, the results usually have been undesirable
   (C) demonstrating that a consequence that had been assumed to follow from the principle under consideration need not follow from it
   (D) attempting to undermine a general principle by arguing that undesirable consequences would follow from it
   (E) showing that, in practice, the principle under consideration could not be uniformly applied

9. Like a number of other articles, Ian Raghnall's article relied on a recent survey in which over half the couples applying for divorces listed "money" as a major problem in their marriages. Raghnall's conclusion from the survey data is that financial problems are the major problem in marriages and an important factor contributing to the high divorce rate. Yet couples often express other types of marital frustrations in financial terms. Despite appearances, the survey data do not establish that financial problems are the major problem in contemporary marriages.

In the passage, the author does which one of the following?

(A) undermines a conclusion drawn from statistical data by offering a specific counterexample
(B) undermines a conclusion drawn from statistical data by offering an alternative explanation for some of the data
(C) undermines a conclusion drawn from statistical data by showing that one cannot prove the presence of an emotion by using statistical methods
(D) undermines a conclusion drawn from statistical data by criticizing the survey for which the data was gathered
(E) undermines a conclusion by showing that couples cannot accurately describe their own problems

10. Rotelle: You are too old to address effectively the difficult issues facing the country, such as nuclear power, poverty, and pollution.

Sims: I don't want to make age an issue in this campaign, so I will not comment on your youth and inexperience.

Sims does which one of the following?

(A) demonstrates that Rotelle's claim is incorrect
(B) avoids mentioning the issue of age
(C) proposes a way to decide which issues are important
(D) shows that Rotelle's statement is self-contradictory
(E) fails to respond directly to Rotelle's claim

11. The question whether intelligent life exists elsewhere in the universe is certainly imprecise, because we are not sure how different from us something might be and still count as "intelligent life." Yet we cannot just decide to define "intelligent life" in some more precise way since it is likely that we will find and recognize intelligent life elsewhere in the universe only if we leave our definitions open to new, unimagined possibilities.

The passage, if seen as an objection to an antecedent claim, challenges that claim by

(A) showing the claim to be irrelevant to the issue at hand
(B) citing examples that fail to fit a proposed definition of "intelligent life"
(C) claiming that "intelligent life" cannot be adequately defined
(D) arguing that the claim, if acted on, would be counterproductive
(E) maintaining that the claim is not supported by the available evidence

12. Pedro: Unlike cloth diapers, disposable diapers are a threat to the environment. Sixteen billion disposable diapers are discarded annually, filling up landfills at an alarming rate. So people must stop buying disposable diapers and use cloth diapers.

Maria: But you forget that cloth diapers must be washed in hot water, which requires energy. Moreover, the resulting wastewater pollutes our rivers. When families use diaper services, diapers must be delivered by fuel-burning trucks that pollute the air and add to traffic congestion.

Maria objects to Pedro's argument by

(A) claiming that Pedro overstates the negative evidence about disposable diapers in the course of his argument in favor of cloth diapers
(B) indicating that Pedro draws a hasty conclusion, based on inadequate evidence about cloth diapers
(C) pointing out that there is an ambiguous use of the word "disposable" in Pedro's argument
(D) demonstrating that cloth diapers are a far more serious threat to the environment than disposable diapers are
(E) suggesting that the economic advantages of cloth diapers outweigh whatever environmental damage they may cause

13. Concetta: Franchot was a great writer because she was ahead of her time in understanding that industrialization was taking an unconscionable toll on the family structure of the working class.

Alicia: Franchot was not a great writer. The mark of a great writer is the ability to move people with the power of the written word, not the ability to be among the first to grasp a social issue. Besides, the social consequences of industrialization were widely understood in Franchot's day.

In her disagreement with Concetta, Alicia does which one of the following?

(A) accepts Concetta's criterion and then adds evidence to Concetta's case
(B) discredits Concetta's evidence and then generalizes from new evidence
(C) rejects Concetta's criterion and then disputes a specific claim
(D) disputes Concetta's conclusion and then presents facts in support of an alternative criterion
(E) attacks one of Concetta's claims and then criticizes the structure of her argument

14. Historian: Alexander the Great should not be judged by appeal to current notions of justice. Alexander, an ancient figure of heroic stature, should be judged by the standards of his own culture. That is, did he live up to his culture's ideals of leadership? Did Alexander elevate the contemporary standards of justice? Was he, in his day, judged to be a just and wise ruler?

Student: But you cannot tell whether or not Alexander raised the contemporary standards of justice without invoking standards other than those of his own culture.

Which one of the following argumentative strategies does the student use in responding to the historian?

(A) arguing that applying the historian's principle would require a knowledge of the past that is necessarily inaccessible to current scholarship
(B) attempting to undermine the historian's principle by showing that some of its consequences are inconsistent with each other
(C) showing that the principle the historian invokes, when applied to Alexander, does not justify the assertion that he was heroic
(D) questioning the historian's motivation for determining whether a standard of behavior has been raised or lowered
(E) claiming that one of the historian's criteria for judging Alexander is inconsistent with the principle that the historian has advanced

15. The United States government generally tries to protect valuable natural resources. But one resource has been ignored for too long. In the United States, each bushel of corn produced might result in the loss of as much as two bushels of topsoil. Moreover, in the last 100 years, the topsoil in many states, which once was about fourteen inches thick, has been eroded to only six or eight inches. Nonetheless, federal expenditures for nationwide soil conservation programs have remained at ridiculously low levels. Total federal expenditures for nationwide soil conservation programs have been less than the allocations of some individual states.

In stating the argument, the author does which one of the following?

(A) makes a detailed statistical projection of future topsoil loss
(B) makes a generalization about total reduction in topsoil depth in all states
(C) assumes that the United States government does not place a high value on its natural resources
(D) refrains from using slanted language concerning the level of federal expenditures
(E) compares state expenditures with federal expenditures

16. Dr. Schilling: Those who advocate replacing my country's private health insurance system with nationalized health insurance because of the rising costs of medical care fail to consider the high human costs that consumers pay in countries with nationalized insurance: access to high-technology medicine is restricted. Kidney transplants and open-heart surgery,familiar life-saving procedures,are rationed. People are denied their right to treatments they want and need.

Dr. Laforte: Your country's reliance on private health insurance denies access even to basic, conventional medicine to the many people who cannot afford adequate health coverage. With nationalized insurance, rich and poor have equal access to life-saving medical procedures, and people's right to decent medical treatment regardless of income is not violated.

In responding to Dr. Schilling, Dr. Laforte employs which one of the following argumentative strategies?

(A) showing that the objections raised by Dr. Schilling have no bearing on the question of which of the two systems under consideration is the superior system
(B) calling into question Dr. Schilling's status as an authority on the issue of whether consumers' access to medical treatments is restricted in countries with nationalized health insurance
(C) producing counterexamples to Dr. Schilling's claims that nationalized health insurance schemes extract high human costs from consumers
(D) demonstrating that Dr. Schilling's reasoning is persuasive only because of his ambiguous use of the key word "consumer"
(E) showing that the force of Dr. Schilling's criticism depends on construing the key notion of access in a particular limited way

17. Policy Adviser: Freedom of speech is not only a basic human right; it is also the only rational policy for this government to adopt. When ideas are openly aired, good ideas flourish, silly proposals are easily recognized as such, and dangerous ideas can be responded to by rational argument. Nothing is ever gained by forcing citizens to disseminate their thoughts in secret.

The policy adviser's method of persuasion, in recommending a policy of free speech to the government, is best described by which one of the following?

(A) a circular justification of the idea of free speech as an idea that flourishes when free speech is allowed
(B) advocating respect for basic rights of citizens for its own sake
(C) a coupling of moral ideals with self-interest
(D) a warning about the difficulty of suppressing the truth
(E) a description of an ideal situation that cannot realistically be achieved

18. Joel: A myth is a narrative told to convey a community's traditional wisdom. Myths are not generally told in the modern world because there are no longer bodies of generally accepted truths that can be conveyed in this way.

Giselle: Of course there are myths in the modern world. For example, there is the myth of the machine: we see the human body as a machine, to be fixed by mending defective parts. This may not be a narrative, but what medically trained specialist can deny the existence of that myth?

Which one of the following most accurately characterizes Giselle's response to Joel's statement?

(A) It offers a scientific explanation to a problem of literary theory.
(B) It points out a weakness in Joel's position by advancing an analogous position.
(C) It is based on an unsupported distinction between traditional societies and the modern world.
(D) It assumes that Joel is a medically trained specialist.
(E) It offers a counterexample that calls into question part of Joel's definition of myth.

19. Proposals for extending the United States school year to bring it more in line with its European and Japanese counterparts are often met with the objection that curtailing the schools' three-month summer vacation would violate an established United States tradition dating from the nineteenth century. However, this objection misses its mark. True, in the nineteenth century the majority of schools closed for three months every summer, but only because they were in rural areas where successful harvests depended on children's labor. If any policy could be justified by those appeals to tradition, it would be the policy of determining the length of the school year according to the needs of the economy.

The argument counters the objection by

(A) providing evidence to show that the objection relies on a misunderstanding about the amount of time each year United States schools traditionally have been closed
(B) calling into question the relevance of information about historical practices to current disputes about proposed social change
(C) arguing for an alternative understanding of the nature of the United States tradition regarding the length of the school year
(D) showing that those who oppose extending the school year have no genuine concern for tradition
(E) demonstrating that tradition justifies bringing the United States school year in line with that of the rest of the industrialized world

20. Advertisement: Anyone who exercises knows from firsthand experience that exercise leads to better performance of such physical organs as the heart and the lungs, as well as to improvement in muscle tone. And since your brain is a physical organ, your actions can improve its performance, too. Act now. Subscribe to *Stimulus*: read the magazine that exercises your brain.

The advertisement employs which one of the following argumentative strategies?

(A) It cites experimental evidence that subscribing to the product being advertised has desirable consequences.
(B) It ridicules people who do not subscribe to *Stimulus* by suggesting that they do not believe that exercise will improve brain capacity.
(C) It explains the process by which the product being advertised brings about the result claimed for its use.
(D) It supports its recommendation by a careful analysis of the concept of exercise.
(E) It implies that brains and muscle are similar in one respect because they are similar in another respect.

21. Coherent solutions for the problem of reducing health-care costs cannot be found within the current piecemeal system of paying these costs. The reason is that this system gives health-care providers and insurers every incentive to shift, wherever possible, the costs of treating illness onto each other or any other party, including the patient. That clearly is the lesson of the various reforms of the 1980s: push in on one part of this pliable spending balloon and an equally expensive bulge pops up elsewhere. For example, when the government health-care insurance program for the poor cut costs by disallowing payments for some visits to physicians, patients with advanced illness later presented themselves at hospital emergency rooms in increased numbers.

The argument proceeds by

(A) showing that shifting costs onto the patient contradicts the premise of health-care reimbursement
(B) attributing without justification fraudulent intent to people
(C) employing an analogy to characterize interrelationships
(D) denying the possibility of a solution by disparaging each possible alternative system
(E) demonstrating that cooperation is feasible by citing an instance

22. Edwina: True appreciation of Mozart's music demands that you hear it exactly as he intended it to be heard; that is, exactly as he heard it. Since he heard it on eighteenth-century instruments, it follows that so should we.

Alberto: But what makes you think that Mozart ever heard his music played as he had intended it to be played? After all, Mozart was writing at a time when the performer was expected, as a matter of course, not just to interpret but to modify the written score.

Alberto adopts which one of the following strategies in criticizing Edwina's position?

(A) He appeals to an academic authority in order to challenge the factual basis of her conclusion.
(B) He attacks her judgment by suggesting that she does not recognize the importance of the performer's creativity to the audience's appreciation of a musical composition.
(C) He defends a competing view of musical authenticity.
(D) He attacks the logic of her argument by suggesting that the conclusion she draws does not follow from the premises she sets forth.
(E) He offers a reason to believe that one of the premises of her argument is false.

23. Graphologists claim that it is possible to detect permanent character traits by examining people's handwriting. For example, a strong cross on the "t" is supposed to denote enthusiasm. Obviously, however, with practice and perseverance people can alter their handwriting to include this feature. So it seems that graphologists must hold that permanent character traits can be changed.

The argument against graphology proceeds by

(A) citing apparently incontestable evidence that leads to absurd consequences when conjoined with the view in question
(B) demonstrating that an apparently controversial and interesting claim is really just a platitude
(C) arguing that a particular technique of analysis can never be effective when the people analyzed know that it is being used
(D) showing that proponents of the view have no theoretical justification for the view
(E) attacking a technique by arguing that what the technique is supposed to detect can be detected quite readily without it

METHOD

24. Historian: There is no direct evidence that timber was traded between the ancient nations of Poran and Nayal, but the fact that a law setting tariffs on timber imports from Poran was enacted during the third Nayalese dynasty does suggest that during that period a timber trade was conducted.

Critic: Your reasoning is flawed. During its third dynasty, Nayal may well have imported timber from Poran, but certainly on today's statute books there remain many laws regulating activities that were once common but in which people no longer engage.

The critic's response to the historian's reasoning does which one of the following?

(A) It implies an analogy between the present and the past.
(B) It identifies a general principle that the historian's reasoning violates.
(C) It distinguishes between what has been established as a certainty and what has been established as a possibility.
(D) It establishes explicit criteria that must be used in evaluating indirect evidence.
(E) It points out the dissimilar roles that law plays in societies that are distinct from one another.

25. The case of the French Revolution is typically regarded as the best evidence for the claim that societies can reap more benefit than harm from a revolution. But even the French Revolution serves this role poorly, since France at the time of the Revolution had a unique advantage. Despite the Revolution, the same civil servants and functionaries remained in office, carrying on the day-to-day work of government, and thus many of the disruptions that revolutions normally bring were avoided.

Which one of the following most accurately characterizes the argumentative strategy used in the passage?

(A) demonstrating that the claim argued against is internally inconsistent
(B) supporting a particular position on the basis of general principles
(C) opposing a claim by undermining evidence offered in support of that claim
(D) justifying a view through the use of a series of persuasive examples
(E) comparing two positions in order to illustrate their relative strengths and weaknesses

26. Economist: Some policymakers believe that our country's continued economic growth requires a higher level of personal savings than we currently have. A recent legislative proposal would allow individuals to set up savings accounts in which interest earned would be exempt from taxes until money is withdrawn from the account. Backers of this proposal claim that its implementation would increase the amount of money available for banks to loan at a relatively small cost to the government in lost tax revenues. Yet, when similar tax-incentive programs were tried in the past, virtually all of the money invested through them was diverted from other personal savings, and the overall level of personal savings was unchanged.

The author criticizes the proposed tax-incentive program by

(A) challenging a premise on which the proposal is based
(B) pointing out a disagreement among policymakers
(C) demonstrating that the proposal's implementation is not feasible
(D) questioning the judgment of the proposal's backers by citing past cases in which they had advocated programs that have proved ineffective
(E) disputing the assumption that a program to encourage personal savings is needed

27. Jones: Prehistoric wooden tools found in South America have been dated to 13,000 years ago. Although scientists attribute these tools to peoples whose ancestors first crossed into the Americas from Siberia to Alaska, this cannot be correct. In order to have reached a site so far south, these peoples must have been migrating southward well before 13,000 years ago. However, no such tools dating to before 13,000 years ago have been found anywhere between Alaska and South America.

Smith: Your evidence is inconclusive. Those tools were found in peat bogs, which are rare in the Americas. Wooden tools in soils other than peat bogs usually decompose within only a few years.

Smith responds to Jones by

(A) citing several studies that invalidate Jones's conclusion
(B) accusing Jones of distorting the scientists' position
(C) disputing the accuracy of the supporting evidence cited by Jones
(D) showing that Jones's evidence actually supports the denial of Jones's conclusion
(E) challenging an implicit assumption in Jones's argument

28. Certain items—those with that hard-to-define quality called exclusivity—have the odd property, when they become available for sale, of selling rapidly even though they are extremely expensive. In fact, trying to sell such an item fast by asking too low a price is a serious error, since it calls into question the very thing—exclusivity—that is supposed to be the item's chief appeal. Therefore, given that a price that will prove to be right is virtually impossible for the seller to gauge in advance, the seller should make sure that any error in the initial asking price is in the direction of setting the price too high.

The argument recommends a certain pricing strategy on the grounds that

(A) this strategy lacks a counterproductive feature of the rejected alternative
(B) this strategy has all of the advantages of the rejected alternative, but fewer of its disadvantages
(C) experience has proven this strategy to be superior, even though the reasons for this superiority elude analysis
(D) this strategy does not rely on prospective buyers' estimates of value
(E) the error associated with this strategy, unlike the error associated with the rejected alternative, is likely to go unnoticed

29. Recently discovered fossil evidence casts doubt on the evolutionary theory that dinosaurs are more closely related to reptiles than to other classes of animals. Fossils show that some dinosaurs had hollow bones—a feature found today only in warm-blooded creatures, such as birds, that have a high metabolic rate. Dinosaurs had well-developed senses of sight and hearing, which is not true of present-day cold-blooded creatures like reptiles. The highly arched mouth roof of some dinosaurs would have permitted them to breathe while eating, as fast-breathing animals, such as birds, need to do. Today, all fast-breathing animals are warm-blooded. Finally, fossils reveal that many dinosaurs had a pattern of growth typical of warm-blooded animals.

The argument in the passage proceeds by

(A) attempting to justify one position by demonstrating that an opposing position is based on erroneous information
(B) establishing a general principle that it then uses to draw a conclusion about a particular case
(C) dismissing a claim made about the present on the basis of historical evidence
(D) assuming that if all members of a category have a certain property then all things with that property belong to the category
(E) presenting evidence that a past phenomenon is more similar to one rather than the other of two present-day phenomena

30. Lucien: Public-housing advocates claim that the many homeless people in this city are proof that there is insufficient housing available to them and therefore that more low-income apartments are needed. But that conclusion is absurd. Many apartments in my own building remain unrented and my professional colleagues report similar vacancies where they live. Since apartments clearly are available, homelessness is not a housing problem. Homelessness can, therefore, only be caused by people's inability or unwillingness to work to pay the rent.

Maria: On the contrary, all recent studies show that a significant percentage of this city's homeless people hold regular jobs. These are people who lack neither will nor ability.

Maria responds to Lucien's argument by

(A) challenging the accuracy of the personal experiences he offers in support of his position
(B) showing that a presupposition of his argument is false
(C) presenting evidence that calls into question his motives for adopting the view he holds
(D) demonstrating that the evidence he offers supports a conclusion other than the conclusion he draws from it
(E) offering an alternative explanation for the facts he cites as evidence supporting his conclusion

31. Myrna: People should follow diets in which fat represents no more than 30 percent of total calories, not the 37 percent the average diet in this country contains.

Roland: If everyone in the country followed your recommendation during his or her entire life, just 0.7 percent would lengthen their lives at all, and then only by an average of 3 months. Modifying our diet is not worthwhile. A lifetime of sacrifice spent eating an unappealing low-fat diet is too high a price to pay for the chance of extending that sacrifice for 3 months.

Myrna: But for everyone who dies early from a high-fat diet, many more people suffer from serious chronic diseases because they followed such diets.

Myrna responds to Roland by

(A) disputing the correctness of the facts cited by Roland and offering facts that she considers correct
(B) showing that the factors considered by Roland are not the only ones relevant in evaluating her recommendation
(C) demonstrating that the statistics used by Roland to dispute her recommendation are inaccurate
(D) suggesting that Roland's evidence derives from unreliable sources
(E) pointing out that Roland's argument assumes the very proposition it sets out to prove

32. Sally: I cannot study at a university where there is an alcohol problem, so unless something is done about the alcohol problem at this university, I'll have to transfer to a university where there are no fraternities.

Yolanda: I don't agree that fraternities are responsible for the alcohol problem at this university. Alcohol problems exist at all universities, including those where there are no fraternities. We all should become more aware of alcohol abuse. It's not simply a fraternity problem; it's a cultural problem.

In the conversation, Yolanda does which one of the following?

(A) She argues that if people become more aware of alcohol abuse, fewer people will themselves abuse alcohol.
(B) She makes an overly broad generalization from one university to all universities.
(C) She concludes that because alcohol problems are cultural problems, they cannot be fraternity problems.
(D) She tries to undermine what she supposes to be Sally's position by pointing out that alcohol problems occur even at universities where there are no fraternities.
(E) She suggests that even if alcohol problems existed only at universities with fraternities, she would still conclude that alcoholism is a cultural rather than a fraternity problem.

METHOD

33. The fire that destroyed the Municipal Building started before dawn this morning, and the last fire fighters did not leave until late this afternoon. No one could have been anywhere in the vicinity of a fire like that one and fail to notice it. Thomas must have seen it, whatever he now says to the contrary. He admits that, as usual, he went from his apartment to the library this morning, and there is no way for him to get from his apartment to the library without going past the Municipal Building.

The argument employs which one of the following reasoning techniques?

(A) presenting several different pieces of evidence, each of which by itself would allow the conclusion to be properly drawn
(B) establishing that one thing occurred by showing that another thing occurred and that this second thing was enough to ensure the occurrence of the first thing
(C) justifying a claim that a view held by someone else is false by explaining why that view, despite its falsity, is a tempting one for that person to hold under the circumstances
(D) relying on evidence that a certain kind of event has regularly occurred in the past as a basis for concluding that an event of that kind occurred in the present case
(E) drawing a general conclusion about what is possible in a certain kind of situation on the basis of firsthand experience with one such situation

34. Philosopher: The eighteenth-century thesis that motion is absolute asserts that the change in an object's position over time could be measured without reference to the position of any other object. A well-respected physicist, however, claims that this thesis is incoherent. Since a thesis that is incoherent cannot be accepted as a description of reality, motion cannot be absolute.

The argument uses which one of the following argumentative techniques?

(A) attempting to persuade by the mere use of technical terminology
(B) using experimental results to justify a change in definition
(C) relying on the authority of an expert to support a premise
(D) inferring from what has been observed to be the case under experimental conditions to what is in principle true
(E) generalizing from what is true in one region of space to what must be true in all regions of space

35. For Juanita to get to the zoo she must take either the number 12 bus or else the subway. Everyone knows that the number 12 bus is not running this week; so although Juanita generally avoids using the subway, she must have used it today, since she was seen at the zoo this afternoon.

The method of the argument is to

(A) assert that if something is true, it will be known to be true
(B) demonstrate that certain possibilities are not exclusive
(C) show that something is the case by ruling out the only alternative
(D) explain why an apparent exception to a general rule is not a real exception
(E) substitute a claim about what invariably occurs for a claim about what typically occurs

36. S: Our nation is becoming too averse to risk. We boycott any food reported to contain a toxic chemical, even though the risk, as a mathematical ratio, might be minimal. With this mentality, Columbus would never have sailed west.

T: A risk-taker in one context can be risk-averse in another: the same person can drive recklessly, but refuse to eat food not grown organically.

T responds to S by showing that

(A) a distinction should be made between avoidable and unavoidable risks
(B) aversion to risk cannot be reliably assessed without reference to context
(C) there is confusion about risk in the minds of many members of the public
(D) mathematical odds concerning risk give an unwarranted impression of precision
(E) risk cannot be defined in relation to perceived probable benefit

37. Dr. Libokov: Certain islands near New Zealand are home to the tuatara, reptiles that are the sole surviving members of the sphenodontidans. Sphenodontidans were plentiful throughout the world during the age of the dinosaurs. But the survival of sphenodontidans near New Zealand, and their total disappearance elsewhere, is no mystery. New Zealand and nearby islands have no native land mammals. Land mammals, plentiful elsewhere, undoubtedly became major predators of sphenodontidans and their eggs, leading to their extinction.

Dr. Santos: In fact, the tuatara thrive only on a few islands near New Zealand. On all those where land mammals, such as rats, dogs, or cats, have been introduced in recent years, the tuatara are now extinct or nearly so.

Which one of the following most accurately characterizes Dr. Santos' response to the hypothesis advanced by Dr. Libokov?

(A) It identifies a flaw in Dr. Libokov's reasoning.
(B) It restates Dr. Libokov's major hypothesis and thus adds nothing to it.
(C) It contradicts one of Dr. Libokov's assertions.
(D) It offers a hypothesis that is incompatible with Dr. Libokov's position.
(E) It provides additional evidence in support of Dr. Libokov's hypothesis.

38. Lydia: Each year, thousands of seabirds are injured when they become entangled in equipment owned by fishing companies. Therefore, the fishing companies should assume responsibility for funding veterinary treatment for the injured birds.

Jonathan: Your feelings for the birds are admirable. Your proposal, however, should not be adopted because treatment of the most seriously injured birds would inhumanely prolong the lives of animals no longer able to live in the wild, as all wildlife should.

Jonathan uses which one of the following techniques in his response to Lydia?

(A) He directs a personal attack against her rather than addressing the argument she advances.
(B) He suggests that her proposal is based on self-interest rather than on real sympathy for the injured birds.
(C) He questions the appropriateness of interfering with wildlife in any way, even if the goal of the interference is to help.
(D) He attempts to discredit her proposal by discussing its implications for only those birds that it serves least well.
(E) He evades discussion of her proposal by raising the issue of whether her feelings about the birds are justified.

39. Oscar: I have been accused of plagiarizing the work of Ethel Myers in my recent article. But that accusation is unwarranted. Although I admit I used passages from Myers's book without attribution, Myers gave me permission in private correspondence to do so.

Millie: Myers cannot give you permission to plagiarize. Plagiarism is wrong, not only because it violates author's rights to their own words, but also because it misleads readers: it is fundamentally a type of lie. A lie is no less a lie if another person agrees to the deception.

Millie uses which one of the following argumentative strategies in contesting Oscar's position?

(A) analyzing plagiarism in a way that undermines Oscar's position
(B) invoking evidence to show that Oscar did quote Myers' work without attribution
(C) challenging Oscar's ability to quote Myers' work without attribution
(D) citing a theory of rights that prohibits plagiarism and suggesting that Oscar is committed to that theory
(E) showing that Oscar's admission demonstrates his lack of credibility

40. Science Academy study: It has been demonstrated that with natural methods, some well-managed farms are able to reduce the amounts of synthetic fertilizer and pesticide and also of antibiotics they use without necessarily decreasing yields; in some cases yields can be increased.

Critics: Not so. The farms the academy selected to study were the ones that seemed most likely to be successful in using natural methods. What about the farmers who have tried such methods and failed?

Which one of the following is the most adequate evaluation of the logical force of the critics' response?

(A) Success and failure in farming are rarely due only to luck, because farming is the management of chance occurrences.
(B) The critics show that the result of the study would have been different if twice as many farms had been studied.
(C) The critics assume without justification that the failures were not due to soil quality.
(D) The critics demonstrate that natural methods are not suitable for the majority of farmers.
(E) The issue is only to show that something is possible, so it is not relevant whether the instances studied were representative.

41. Ingrid: Rock music has produced no songs as durable as the songs of the 1940s, which continue to be recorded by numerous performers.

Jerome: True, rock songs are usually recorded only once. If the original recording continues to be popular, however, that fact can indicate durability, and the best rock songs will prove to be durable.

Jerome responds to Ingrid's claim by

(A) intentionally misinterpreting the claim
(B) showing that the claim necessarily leads to a contradiction
(C) undermining the truth of the evidence that Ingrid presents
(D) suggesting an alternative standard for judging the point at issue
(E) claiming that Ingrid's knowledge of the period under discussion is incomplete

METHOD

42. The problem that environmental economics aims to remedy is the following: people making economic decisions cannot readily compare environmental factors, such as clean air and the survival of endangered species, with other costs and benefits. As environmental economists recognize, solving this problem requires assigning monetary values to environmental factors. But monetary values result from people comparing costs and benefits in order to arrive at economic decisions. Thus, environmental economics is stymied by what motivates it.

If the considerations advanced in its support are true, the passage's conclusion is supported

(A) strongly, on the assumption that monetary values for environmental factors cannot be assigned unless people make economic decisions about these factors
(B) strongly, unless economic decision-making has not yet had any effect on the things categorized as environmental factors
(C) at best weakly, because the passage fails to establish that economic decision-makers do not by and large take adequate account of environmental factors
(D) at best weakly, because the argument assumes that pollution and other effects on environmental factors rarely result from economic decision-making
(E) not at all, since the argument is circular, taking that conclusion as one of its premises

43. Garbage in this neighborhood probably will not be collected until Thursday this week. Garbage is usually collected here on Wednesdays, and the garbage collectors in this city are extremely reliable. However, Monday was a public holiday, and after a public holiday that falls on a Monday, garbage throughout the city is supposed to be collected one day later than usual.

The argument proceeds by

(A) treating several pieces of irrelevant evidence as though they provide support for the conclusion
(B) indirectly establishing that one thing is likely to occur by directly ruling out all of the alternative possibilities
(C) providing information that allows application of a general rule to a specific case
(D) generalizing about all actions of a certain kind on the basis of a description of one such action
(E) treating something that is probable as though it were inevitable

44. Production manager: The building materials that we produce meet industry safety codes but pose some safety risk. Since we have recently developed the technology to make a safer version of our product, we should stop producing our current product and sell only the safer version in order to protect public safety.

Sales manager: If we stop selling our current product, we will have no money to develop and promote the safer product. We need to continue to sell the less-safe product in order to be in a position to market the safer product successfully.

The sales manager counters the production manager's argument by

(A) pointing out that one part of the production manager's proposal would have consequences that would prevent successful execution of another part
(B) challenging the production manager's authority to dictate company policy
(C) questioning the product manager's assumption that a product is necessarily safe just because it is safer than another product
(D) proposing a change in the standards by which product safety is judged
(E) presenting evidence to show that the production manager has overestimated the potential impact of the new technology

45. James: In my own house, I do what I want. In banning smoking on passenger airlines during domestic flights, the government has ignored the airlines' right to set smoking policies on their own property.

Eileen: Your house is for your own use. Because a passenger airline offers a service to the public, the passengers' health must come first.

The basic step in Eileen's method of attacking James' argument is to

(A) draw a distinction
(B) offer a definition
(C) establish an analogy
(D) derive a contradiction from it
(E) question its motivation

46. Patient: Pharmacists maintain that doctors should not be permitted to sell the medicine that they prescribe because doctors would then be tempted to prescribe unnecessary medicines in order to earn extra income. But pharmacists have a financial interest in having a monopoly on the sale of prescription medicines, so their objection to the sale of medicines by doctors cannot be taken seriously.

The patient's argument proceeds by

(A) pointing out an unstated assumption on which the pharmacists' argument relies and then refuting it
(B) attempting to discredit a position by questioning the motives of the proponents of that position
(C) undermining the pharmacists' conclusion by demonstrating that one of the statements used to support the conclusion is false
(D) rejecting a questionable position on the grounds that the general public does not support that position
(E) asserting that pharmacists lack the appropriate knowledge to have informed opinions on the subject under discussion

47. Some years ago, an editorial defended United States government restrictions on academic freedom, arguing that scientists who receive public funding cannot rightly "detach themselves from the government's policies on national security." Yet the same editorial criticized the Soviet government for not allowing scientists to "detach themselves from politics." If there is a significant difference between the principles involved in each case, the editorial should have explained what that difference is.

The author of the passage criticizes the editorial by

(A) disputing certain factual claims made in the editorial
(B) pointing out an apparent inconsistency in the editorial
(C) describing an alleged exception to a general claim made in the editorial
(D) refuting an assumption on which the argument of the editorial appears to have been based
(E) drawing a conclusion from the editorial different from the conclusion drawn by the writer of the editorial

48. It is not reasonable to search out "organic" foods—those grown without the application of synthetic chemicals—as the only natural foods. A plant will take up the molecules it needs from the soil and turn them into the same natural compounds, whether or not those molecules come from chemicals applied to the soil. All compounds made by plants are part of nature, so all are equally natural.

The argument proceeds by

(A) redefining a term in a way that is favorable to the argument
(B) giving a reason why a recommended course of action would be beneficial
(C) appealing to the authority of scientific methods
(D) showing that a necessary condition for correctly applying the term "organic" is not satisfied
(E) reinterpreting evidence presented as supporting the position being rejected

49. In Peru, ancient disturbances in the dark surface material of a desert show up as light-colored lines that are the width of a footpath and stretch for long distances. One group of lines branching out like rays from a single point crosses over curved lines that form a very large bird figure. Interpreting the lines in the desert as landing strips for spaceship-traveling aliens, an investigator argues that they could hardly have been Inca roads, asking, "What use to the Inca would have been closely spaced roads that ran parallel? That intersected in a sunburst pattern? That came abruptly to an end in the middle of an uninhabited plain?"

The argumentative strategy of the investigator quoted is to

(A) reject out of hand direct counterevidence to the investigator's own interpretation
(B) introduce evidence newly discovered by the investigator which discredits the alternative interpretation
(C) support one interpretation by calling into question the plausibility of the alternative interpretation
(D) challenge the investigative methods used by those who developed the alternative interpretation
(E) show that the two competing interpretations can be reconciled with one another

METHOD

50. People were asked in a survey how old they felt. They replied, almost unanimously despite a great diversity of ages, with a number that was 75 percent of their real age. There is, however, a problem in understanding this sort of response. For example, suppose it meant that a 48-year-old man was claiming to feel as he felt at 36. But at age 36 he would have said he felt like a man of 27, and at 27 he would have said he felt just over 20, and so on into childhood. And surely, that 48-year-old man did not mean to suggest that he felt like a child!

Which one of the following techniques of reasoning is employed in the argument?

(A) projecting from responses collected at one time from many individuals of widely different ages to hypothetical earlier responses of a single individual at some of those ages

(B) reinterpreting what certain people actually said in the light of what would, in the circumstances, have been the most reasonable thing for them to say

(C) qualifying an overly sweeping generalization in light of a single, well chosen counterexample

(D) deriving a contradiction from a pair of statements in order to prove that at least one of those statements is false

(E) analyzing an unexpected unanimity among respondents as evidence, not of a great uniformity of opinion among those respondents, but of their successful manipulation by their questioners

51. X: Medical research on animals should not be reduced in response to a concern for animals, because results of such research serve to avert human suffering. In such research a trade-off between human and animal welfare is always inevitable, but we should give greater weight to human welfare.

Y: With technology that is currently available, much of the research presently performed on animals could instead be done with computer modeling or human subjects without causing any suffering.

The relationship of Y's response to X's argument is that Y's response

(A) contradicts a premise on which X's argument relies

(B) disagrees with X about the weight to be given to animal suffering as opposed to human suffering

(C) presents a logical consequence of the premises of X's argument

(D) strengthens X's argument by presenting evidence not mentioned by X

(E) supplies a premise to X's argument that was not explicitly stated

52. Winston: The Public Transportation Authority (PTA) cannot fulfill its mandate to operate without a budget deficit unless it eliminates service during late-night periods of low ridership. Since the fares collected during these periods are less than the cost of providing the service, these cuts would reduce the deficit and should be made. Transit law prohibits unauthorized fare increases, and fare-increase authorization would take two years.

Ping: Such service cuts might cost the PTA more in lost fares than they would save in costs, for the PTA would lose those riders who leave home during the day but must return late at night. Thus the PTA would lose two fares, while realizing cost savings for only one leg of such trips.

The relationship of Ping's response to Winston's argument is that Ping's response

(A) carefully redefines a term used in Winston's argument
(B) questions Winston's proposal by raising considerations not addressed by Winston
(C) supplies a premise that could have been used as part of the support for Winston's argument
(D) introduces detailed statistical evidence that is more persuasive than that offered by Winston
(E) proposes a solution to the PTA's dilemma by contradicting Winston's conclusion

53. S: People who are old enough to fight for their country are old enough to vote for the people who make decisions about war and peace. This government clearly regards 17-year-olds as old enough to fight, so it should acknowledge their right to vote.

T: Your argument is a good one only to the extent that fighting and voting are the same kind of activity. Fighting well requires strength, muscular coordination, and in a modern army, instant and automatic response to orders. Performed responsibly, voting, unlike fighting, is essentially a deliberative activity requiring reasoning power and knowledge of both history and human nature.

T responds to S's argument by

(A) citing evidence overlooked by S that would have supported S's conclusion
(B) calling into question S's understanding of the concept of rights
(C) showing that S has ignored the distinction between having a right to do something and having an obligation to do that thing
(D) challenging the truth of a claim on which S's conclusion is based
(E) arguing for a conclusion opposite to the one drawn by S

54. Maria: Calling any state totalitarian is misleading: it implies total state control of all aspects of life. The real world contains no political entity exercising literally total control over even one such aspect. This is because any system of control is inefficient, and, therefore, its degree of control is partial.

James: A one-party state that has tried to exercise control over most aspects of a society and that has, broadly speaking, managed to do so is totalitarian. Such a system's practical inefficiencies do not limit the aptness of the term, which does not describe a state's actual degree of control as much as it describes the nature of a state's ambitions.

James responds to Maria's argument by

(A) pointing out a logical inconsistency between two statements she makes in support of her argument
(B) offering an alternative explanation for political conditions she mentions
(C) rejecting some of the evidence she presents without challenging what she infers from it
(D) disputing the conditions under which a key term of her argument can be appropriately applied
(E) demonstrating that her own premises lead to a conclusion different from hers

55. The government has no right to tax earnings from labor. Taxation of this kind requires the laborer to devote a certain percentage of hours worked to earning money for the government. Thus, such taxation forces the laborer to work, in part, for another's purpose. Since involuntary servitude can be defined as forced work for another's purpose, just as involuntary servitude is pernicious, so is taxing earnings from labor.

The argument uses which one of the following argumentative techniques?

(A) deriving a general principle about the rights of individuals from a judgment concerning the obligations of governments
(B) inferring what will be the case merely from a description of what once was the case
(C) inferring that since two institutions are similar in one respect, they are similar in another respect
(D) citing the authority of an economic theory in order to justify a moral principle
(E) presupposing the inevitability of a hierarchical class system in order to oppose a given economic practice

56. Wife: The work of the artist who painted the portrait of my grandparents 50 years ago has become quite popular lately, so the portrait has recently become valuable. But since these sorts of artistic fads fade rapidly, the practical thing to do would be to sell the portrait while it is still worth something, and thereby enable our daughter to attend the college she has chosen.

Husband: How could you make such a suggestion? That painting is the only thing you own that belonged to your grandparents. I don't think it's a very good painting, but it has great sentimental value. Besides, you owe it to our daughter to keep it in the family as a link to her family's past.

The husband uses which one of the following argumentative techniques in replying to the wife's suggestion?

(A) taking issue with the practicality of her suggestion
(B) questioning her aesthetic judgment
(C) claiming that the reasons she gives are based on emotions rather than on rational considerations
(D) asserting that the evidence she cites in support of her suggestion is false
(E) invoking a competing obligation that he judges to override her practical considerations

57. Dillworth: More and more people are deciding not to have children because of the personal and economic sacrifices children require and because so often children are ungrateful for the considerable sacrifices their parents do make for them. However, such considerations have no bearing on the fact that their children provide the best chance most people have of ensuring that their values live on after them. Therefore, for anyone with deeply held values, foregoing parenthood out of reluctance to make sacrifices for which little gratitude can be expected would probably be a mistake.

Travers: Your reasoning ignores another fact that deserves consideration: children's ingratitude for parental sacrifices usually stems from a wholesale rejection of parental values.

Dillworth employs which one of the following argumentative strategies?

(A) showing that considerations cited as drawbacks to a given course of action are not really drawbacks at all
(B) exposing as morally suspect the motives of people who would make the choice that Dillworth rejects
(C) indirectly establishing that a given course of action is obligatory by arguing that the alternative course of action is prohibited
(D) distinguishing a category of person for whom the reason presented in favor of a given course of action is more telling than the reasons cited against that course of action
(E) using evidence that a certain course of action would be appropriate under one set of conditions to arrive at a general conclusion about what would be appropriate in all cases

58. Magazine editor: I know that some of our regular advertisers have been pressuring us to give favorable mention to their products in our articles, but they should realize that for us to yield to their wishes would actually be against their interests. To remain an effective advertising vehicle we must have loyal readership, and we would soon lose that readership if our readers suspect that our editorial integrity has been compromised by pandering to advertisers.

Advertising-sales director: You underestimate the sophistication of our readers. They recognize that the advertisements we carry are not articles, so their response to the advertisements has never depended on their opinion of the editorial integrity of the magazine as a whole.

Which one of the following is the most accurate assessment of the advertising-sales director's argument as a response to the magazine editor's argument?

(A) It succeeds because it shows that the editor's argument depends on an unwarranted assumption about factors affecting an advertisement's effectiveness.
(B) It succeeds because it exposes as mistaken the editor's estimation of the sophistication of the magazine's readers.
(C) It succeeds because it undermines the editor's claim about how the magazine's editorial integrity would be affected by allowing advertisers to influence articles.
(D) It fails because the editor's argument does not depend on any assumption about readers' response to the advertisements they see in the magazine.
(E) It fails because it is based on a misunderstanding of the editor's view about how readers respond to advertisements they see in the magazine.

METHOD

59. S: It would be premature to act to halt the threatened "global warming trend," since that alleged trend might not be real. After all, scientists disagree about it, some predicting over twice as much warming as others, so clearly their predictions cannot be based on firm evidence.

W: Most scientists consider discussions of accepted ideas boring, and prefer to argue about what is not known. According to the International Science Council, there is a consensus among reputable investigators that average global warming in the next century will be from 1.5° to 4.5°C.

W's rejoinder proceeds by

(A) denying the existence of the disagreements cited by S
(B) accepting S's conclusion while disputing the reasons offered for it
(C) relying on authorities whose views conflict with the views of the authorities cited by S
(D) putting disagreements cited by S in perspective by emphasizing similarities
(E) reasoning in a circle by accepting evidence only if it agrees with a desired conclusion

60. Walter: For the economically privileged in a society to tolerate an injustice perpetrated against one of society's disadvantaged is not just morally wrong but also shortsighted: a system that inflicts an injustice on a disadvantaged person today can equally well inflict that same injustice on a well-to-do person tomorrow.

Larissa: In our society, the wealthy as well as the well-educated can protect themselves against all sorts of injustices suffered by the less well-off. Allowing such injustices to persist is bad policy not because it places everyone at equal risk of injustice but because it is a potent source of social unrest.

Larissa responds to Walter by doing which one of the following?

(A) giving reason to doubt the truth of Walter's conclusion
(B) drawing implausible consequences from Walter's assumptions
(C) questioning Walter's authority to address matters of social policy
(D) providing an alternative reason for accepting the truth of Walter's conclusion
(E) charging Walter with stopping short of recognizing the full implications of his position

61. Political advocate: Campaigns for elective office should be subsidized with public funds. One reason is that this would allow politicians to devote less time to fund-raising, thus giving campaigning incumbents more time to serve the public. A second reason is that such subsidies would make it possible to set caps on individual campaign contributions, thereby reducing the likelihood that elected officials will be working for the benefit not of the public but of individual large contributors.

Critic: This argument is problematic: the more the caps constrain contributions, the more time candidates have to spend finding more small contributors.

The critic objects that the advocate's argument is flawed because

(A) any resourceful large contributor can circumvent caps on individual contributions by sending in smaller amounts under various names
(B) one of the projected results cited in support of the proposal made is entailed by the other and therefore does not constitute independent support of the proposal
(C) of the two projected results cited in support of the proposal made, one works against the other
(D) it overlooks the possibility that large contributors will stop contributing if they cannot contribute at will
(E) it overlooks the possibility that incumbents with a few extremely generous contributors will be hit harder by caps than incumbents with many moderately generous contributors

62. Psychologists have claimed that many people are more susceptible to psychological problems in the winter than in the summer; the psychologists call this condition seasonal affective disorder. Their claim is based on the results of surveys in which people were asked to recall how they felt at various times in the past. However, it is not clear that people are able to report accurately on their past psychological states. Therefore, these survey results do not justify the psychologists' claim that there is any such condition as seasonal affective disorder.

The author criticizes the psychologists' claim by

(A) offering an alternative explanation of the variation in the occurrence of psychological problems across seasons
(B) questioning whether any seasonal variation in the occurrence of psychological problems could properly be labeled a disorder
(C) questioning the representativeness of the population sample surveyed by the psychologists
(D) questioning an assumption that the author attributes to the psychologists
(E) demonstrating that fewer people actually suffer from seasonal affective disorder than psychologists had previously thought

63. From a magazine article: Self-confidence is a dangerous virtue: it often degenerates into the vice of arrogance. The danger of arrogance is evident to all who care to look. How much more humane the twentieth century would have been without the arrogant self-confidence of a Hitler or a Stalin!

The author attempts to persuade by doing all of the following EXCEPT

(A) using extreme cases to evoke an emotional response
(B) introducing value-laden terms, such as "vice"
(C) illustrating the danger of arrogance
(D) appealing to authority to substantiate an assertion
(E) implying that Hitler's arrogance arose from self-confidence

64. Scientists are sometimes said to assume that something is not the case until there is proof that it is the case. Now suppose the question arises whether a given food additive is safe. At that point, it would be neither known to be safe nor known not to be safe. By the characterization above, scientists would assume the additive not to be safe because it has not been proven safe. But they would also assume it to be safe because it has not been proven otherwise. But no scientist could assume without contradiction that a given substance is both safe and not safe; so this characterization of scientists is clearly wrong.

Which one of the following describes the technique of reasoning used above?

(A) A general statement is argued to be false by showing that it has deliberately been formulated to mislead.
(B) A statement is argued to be false by showing that taking it to be true leads to implausible consequences.
(C) A statement is shown to be false by showing that it directly contradicts a second statement that is taken to be true.
(D) A general statement is shown to be uninformative by showing that there are as many specific instances in which it is false as there are instances in which it is true.
(E) A statement is shown to be uninformative by showing that it supports no independently testable inferences.

65. In discussing the pros and cons of monetary union among several European nations, some politicians have claimed that living standards in the countries concerned would first have to converge if monetary union is not to lead to economic chaos. This claim is plainly false, as is demonstrated by the fact that living standards diverge widely between regions within countries that nevertheless have stable economies.

In attempting to refute the politicians' claim, the author does which one of the following?

(A) argues that those making the claim are mistaken about a temporal relationship that has been observed
(B) presents an earlier instance of the action being considered in which the predicted consequences did not occur
(C) argues that the feared consequence would occur regardless of what course of action was followed
(D) gives an example of a state of affairs, assumed to be relevantly similar, in which the allegedly incompatible elements coexist
(E) points out that if an implicit recommendation is followed, the claim can be neither shown to be true nor shown to be false

66. Jane: Professor Harper's ideas for modifying the design of guitars are of no value because there is no general agreement among musicians as to what a guitar should sound like and, consequently, no widely accepted basis for evaluating the merits of a guitar's sound.

Mark: What's more, Harper's ideas have had enough time to be adopted if they really resulted in superior sound. It took only ten years for the Torres design for guitars to be almost universally adopted because of the improvement it makes in tonal quality.

Which one of the following most accurately describes the relationship between Jane's argument and Mark's argument?

(A) Mark's argument shows how a weakness in Jane's argument can be overcome.
(B) Mark's argument has a premise in common with Jane's argument.
(C) Mark and Jane use similar techniques to argue for different conclusions.
(D) Mark's argument restates Jane's argument in other terms.
(E) Mark's argument and Jane's argument are based on conflicting suppositions.

METHOD

67. Ornithologist: The curvature of the claws of modern tree dwelling birds enables them to perch in trees. The claws of Archeopteryx, the earliest known birdlike creature, show similar curvature that must have enabled the creature to perch on tree limbs. Therefore, Archeopteryx was probably a tree-dwelling creature.

Paleontologist: No, the ability to perch in trees is not good evidence that Archeopteryx was a tree-dwelling bird. Chickens also spend time perched in trees, yet chickens are primarily ground-dwelling.

In responding to the ornithologist's hypothesis that Archeopteryx was tree-dwelling, the paleontologist

(A) questions the qualifications of the ornithologist to evaluate the evidence
(B) denies the truth of the claims the ornithologist makes in support of the hypothesis
(C) uses a parallel case to illustrate a weakness in the ornithologist's argument
(D) shows that the hypothesis contradicts one of the pieces of evidence used to support it
(E) provides additional evidence to support the ornithologist's argument

68. There are rumors that the Premier will reshuffle the cabinet this week. However, every previous reshuffle that the Premier has made was preceded by meetings between the Premier and senior cabinet members. No such meetings have occurred or are planned. Therefore the rumors are most likely false.

Which one of the following most accurately expresses a principle of reasoning employed by the argument?

(A) When a conclusion follows logically from a set of premises, the probability that the conclusion is true cannot be any less than the probability that the premises are all true.
(B) A hypothesis is undermined when a state of affairs does not obtain that would be expected to obtain if the hypothesis were true.
(C) It is possible for a hypothesis to be false even though it is supported by all the available data.
(D) Even if in the past a phenomenon was caused by particular circumstances, it is erroneous to assume that the phenomenon will recur only under the circumstances in which it previously occurred.
(E) If two statements are known to be inconsistent with each other and if one of the statements is known to be false, it cannot be deduced from these known facts that the other statement is true

69. Carl: Researchers who perform operations on animals for experimental purposes are legally required to complete detailed pain protocols indicating whether the animals will be at risk of pain and, if so, what steps will be taken to minimize or alleviate it. Yet when human beings undergo operations, such protocols are never required. If lawmakers were as concerned about human beings as they seem to be about animals, there would be pain protocols for human beings too.

Debbie: But consider this: a person for whom a doctor wants to schedule surgery can simply be told what pain to expect and can then decide whether or not to undergo the operation. So you see, pain protocols are unnecessary for human beings.

Debbie attempts to counter Carl's argument by

(A) showing that one of the claims on which Carl bases his conclusion is inaccurate
(B) pointing out a relevant difference to undermine an analogy on which Carl bases his conclusion
(C) claiming that Carl's argument should be rejected because it is based on an appeal to sentimentality rather than on reasoned principles
(D) drawing an analogy that illustrates a major flaw in Carl's argument
(E) offering a specific example to demonstrate that Carl's argument is based on a claim that can be neither confirmed nor disproved

METHOD

70. Lambert: The proposal to raise gasoline taxes to support mass transit networks is unfair. Why should drivers who will never use train or bus lines be forced to pay for them?

Keziah: You have misunderstood. The government has always spent far more, per user, from general revenue sources to fund highways than to fund mass transit. The additional revenue from the gasoline tax will simply allow the government to make its distribution of transportation funds more equitable.

Keziah uses which one of the following argumentative strategies in replying to Lambert?

(A) elaborating the context of the issue in order to place the proposal in a more favorable light
(B) appealing to the principle that what benefits society as a whole benefits all individuals within that society
(C) challenging the presupposition that fairness is an appropriate criterion on which to judge the matter
(D) demonstrating that the proposed tax increase will not result in increased expenses for drivers
(E) declining to argue a point with someone who is poorly informed on the matter under discussion

71. Attorneys for a criminal defendant charged that the government, in a coverup, had destroyed evidence that would have supported the defendant in a case. The government replied that there is no evidence that would even tend to support the defendant in the case.

Which one of the following is the most accurate evaluation of the government's reply?

(A) It leaves open the question of whether the government had destroyed such evidence.
(B) It establishes that the attorneys' charge is an exaggeration.
(C) It shows that the attorneys did not know whether their charge was true.
(D) It demonstrates the government's failure to search for evidence in its files.
(E) If true, it effectively disproves the charge made on behalf of the defendant.

72. Politician: A government that taxes incomes at a rate of 100 percent will generate no revenue because all economic activity will cease. So it follows that the lower the rate of income tax, the more revenue the government will generate by that tax.

Economist: Your conclusion cannot be correct, since it would mean that an income tax of 0 percent would generate the maximum revenue.

Which one of the following argumentative strategies is used by the economist in responding to the politician?

(A) stating a general principle that is incompatible with the conclusion the politician derives
(B) providing evidence that where the politician's advice has been adopted, the results have been disappointing
(C) arguing that the principle derived by the politician, if applied in the limiting case, leads to an absurdly false conclusion
(D) undermining the credibility of the politician by openly questioning the politician's understanding of economics
(E) attacking the politician's argument by giving reason to doubt the truth of a premise

73. Sasha: Handwriting analysis should be banned in court as evidence of a person's character: handwriting analysts called as witnesses habitually exaggerate the reliability of their analyses.

Gregory: You are right that the current use of handwriting analysis as evidence is problematic. But this problem exists only because there is no licensing board to set professional standards and thus deter irresponsible analysts from making exaggerated claims. When such a board is established, however, handwriting analysis by licensed practitioners will be a legitimate courtroom tool for character assessment.

Gregory does which one of the following in responding to Sasha's argument?

(A) He ignores evidence introduced as support for Sasha's recommendation.
(B) He defends a principle by restricting the class to which it is to be applied.
(C) He abstracts a general principle from specific evidence.
(D) He identifies a self-contradictory statement in Sasha's argument.
(E) He shows that Sasha's argument itself manifests the undesirable characteristic that it condemns.

74. Millions of female bats rear their pups in Bracken Cave. Although the mothers all leave the cave nightly, on their return each mother is almost always swiftly reunited with her own pup. Since the bats' calls are their only means of finding one another, and a bat pup cannot distinguish the call of its mother from that of any other adult bat, it is clear that each mother bat can recognize the call of her pup.

The argument seeks to do which one of the following?

(A) derive a general conclusion about all members of a group from facts known about representative members of that group
(B) establish the validity of one explanation for a phenomenon by excluding alternative explanations
(C) support, by describing a suitable mechanism, the hypothesis that a certain phenomenon can occur
(D) conclude that members of two groups are likely to share a certain ability because of other characteristics they share
(E) demonstrate that a general rule applies in a particular case

75. Some people have been promoting a new herbal mixture as a remedy for the common cold. The mixture contains, among other things, extracts of the plants purple coneflower and goldenseal. A cold sufferer, skeptical of the claim that the mixture is an effective cold remedy, argued, "Suppose that the mixture were an effective cold remedy. Since most people with colds wish to recover quickly, it follows that almost everybody with a cold would be using it. Therefore, since there are many people who have colds but do not use the mixture, it is obviously not effective."

Which one of the following most accurately describes the method of reasoning the cold sufferer uses to reach the conclusion of the argument?

(A) finding a claim to be false on the grounds that it would if true have consequences that are false
(B) accepting a claim on the basis of public opinion of the claim
(C) showing that conditions necessary to establish the truth of a claim are met
(D) basing a generalization on a representative group of instances
(E) showing that a measure claimed to be effective in achieving a certain effect would actually make achieving the effect more difficult

76. Tom: Employers complain that people graduating from high school too often lack the vocational skills required for full-time employment. Therefore, since these skills are best acquired on the job, we should require high school students to work at part-time jobs so that they acquire the skills needed for today's job market.

Mary: There are already too few part-time jobs for students who want to work, and simply requiring students to work will not create jobs for them.

Which one of the following most accurately describes how Mary's response is related to Tom's argument?

(A) It analyzes an undesirable result of undertaking the course of action that Tom recommends.
(B) It argues that Tom has mistaken an unavoidable trend for an avoidable one.
(C) It provides information that is inconsistent with an explicitly stated premise in Tom's argument.
(D) It presents a consideration that undercuts an assumption on which Tom's argument depends.
(E) It defends an alternative solution to the problem that Tom describes.

77. Whittaker: There can be no such thing as the number of medical school students who drop out before their second year, because if they drop out, they never have a second year.

Hudson: By your reasoning I cannot help but become rich, because there is similarly no such thing as my dying before my first million dollars is in the bank.

Hudson responds to Whittaker by

(A) showing that a relevantly analogous argument leads to an untenable conclusion
(B) citing a specific example to counter Whittaker's general claim
(C) pointing out that Whittaker mistakes a necessary situation for a possible situation
(D) claiming that what Whittaker says cannot be true because Whittaker acts as if it were false
(E) showing that Whittaker's argument relies on analyzing an extreme and unrepresentative case

78. Wirth: All efforts to identify a gene responsible for predisposing people to manic-depression have failed. In fact, nearly all researchers now agree that there is no "manic-depression gene." Therefore, if these researchers are right, any claim that some people are genetically predisposed to manic-depression is simply false.

Chang: I do not dispute your evidence, but I take issue with your conclusion. Many of the researchers you refer to have found evidence that a set of several genes is involved and that complex interactions among these genes produce a predisposition to manic-depression.

Which one of the following most accurately expresses Chang's criticism of Wirth's argument?

(A) It presupposes only one possibility where more than one exists.
(B) It depends on separate pieces of evidence that contradict each other.
(C) It relies on the opinion of experts in an area outside the experts' field of expertise.
(D) It disallows in principle any evidence that would disconfirm its conclusion.
(E) It treats something that is merely unlikely as though it were impossible.

10

Chapter Ten: Flaw in the Reasoning Questions

1. The common procedure for determining whether a food additive should be banned from use is to compare its health-related benefits with its potential risks. Yellow Dye No. 5, an additive used to color lemon soda, might cause allergic reactions in a few consumers. For most consumers of lemon soda, however, the coloring enhances their enjoyment of the beverage. This particular additive should not be banned, therefore, because its benefits greatly outweigh its risks.

   A flaw in the argument is that the author

   (A) implies that the dye entails no health-related risks
   (B) treats enjoyment of a beverage as a health-related benefit
   (C) ignores the possibility that some food additives are harmful to most people
   (D) bases the argument on an unproven claim regarding a danger in using Yellow Dye No. 5
   (E) presumes that most consumers heed the warning labels on beverage containers

2. Some of the most prosperous nations in the world have experienced a pronounced drop in national savings rates—the percentage of after-tax income an average household saves. This trend will undoubtedly continue if the average age of these nations' populations continues to rise, since older people have fewer reasons to save than do younger people.

   Which one of the following indicates an error in the reasoning leading to the prediction above?

   (A) It fails to specify the many reasons younger people have for saving money, and it fails to identify which of those reasons is the strongest.
   (B) It assumes that a negative savings rate—the result of the average household's spending all of its after-tax income as well as some of its existing savings—cannot ever come about in any nation.
   (C) It fails to cite statistics showing that the average age of the population of certain nations is rising.
   (D) It only takes into account the comparative number of reasons older and younger people, respectively, have for saving, and not the comparative strength of those reasons.
   (E) It uses after-tax income as the base for computing the national savings rate without establishing by argument that after-tax income is a more appropriate base than before-tax income.

3. The 1980s have been characterized as a period of selfish individualism that threatens the cohesion of society. But this characterization is true of any time. Throughout history all human actions have been motivated by selfishness. When the deeper implications are considered, even the simplest "unselfish" acts prove to be instances of selfish concern for the human species.

   Which one of the following is a flaw in the argument?

   (A) The claim that selfishness has been present throughout history is not actually relevant to the argument.
   (B) No statistical evidence is provided to show that humans act selfishly more often than they act unselfishly.
   (C) The argument assumes that selfishness is unique to the present age.
   (D) The argument mentions only humans and does not consider the behavior of other species.
   (E) The argument relies on two different uses of the term "selfish."

4. A gas tax of one cent per gallon would raise one billion dollars per year at current consumption rates. Since a tax of fifty cents per gallon would therefore raise fifty billion dollars per year, it seems a perfect way to deal with the federal budget deficit. This tax would have the additional advantage that the resulting drop in the demand for gasoline would be ecologically sound and would keep our country from being too dependent on foreign oil producers.

   Which one of the following most clearly identifies an error in the author's reasoning?

   (A) The author cites irrelevant data.
   (B) The author relies on incorrect current consumption figures.
   (C) The author makes incompatible assumptions.
   (D) The author mistakes an effect for a cause.
   (E) The author appeals to conscience rather than reason.

5. Giselle: The government needs to ensure that the public consumes less petroleum. When things cost more, people buy and use less of them. Therefore, the government should raise the sales tax on gasoline, a major petroleum product.

Antoine: The government should not raise the sales tax on gasoline. Such an increase would be unfair to gasoline users. If taxes are to be increased, the increases should be applied in such a way that they spread the burden of providing the government with increased revenues among many people, not just the users of gasoline.

As a rebuttal of Giselle's argument, Antoine's response is ineffective because

(A) he ignores the fact that Giselle does not base her argument for raising the gasoline sales tax on the government's need for increased revenues
(B) he fails to specify how many taxpayers there are who are not gasoline users
(C) his conclusion is based on an assertion regarding unfairness, and unfairness is a very subjective concept
(D) he mistakenly assumes that Giselle wants a sales tax increase only on gasoline
(E) he makes the implausible assumption that the burden of increasing government revenues can be more evenly distributed among the people through other means besides increasing the gasoline sales tax

6. Although this bottle is labeled "vinegar," no fizzing occurred when some of the liquid in it was added to powder from this box labeled "baking soda." But when an acidic liquid such as vinegar is added to baking soda the resulting mixture fizzes, so this bottle clearly has been mislabeled.

A flaw in the reasoning in the argument above is that this argument

(A) ignores the possibility that the bottle contained an acidic liquid other than vinegar
(B) fails to exclude an alternative explanation for the observed effect
(C) depends on the use of the imprecise term "fizz"
(D) does not take into account the fact that scientific principles can be definitively tested only under controlled laboratory conditions
(E) assumes that the fact of a labeling error is proof of an intention to deceive

7. Every week, the programming office at an FM radio station reviewed unsolicited letters from listeners who were expressing comments on the station's programs. One week, the station received 50 letters with favorable comments about the station's news reporting and music selection and 10 letters with unfavorable comments on the station's new movie review segment of the evening program. Faced with this information, the programming director assumed that if some listeners did not like the movie review segment, then there must be other listeners who did like it. Therefore, he decided to continue the movie review segment of the evening program.

Which one of the following identifies a problem with the programming director's decision process?

(A) He failed to recognize that people are more likely to write letters of criticism than of praise.
(B) He could not properly infer from the fact that some listeners did not like the movie review segment that some others did.
(C) He failed to take into consideration the discrepancy in numbers between favorable and unfavorable letters received.
(D) He failed to take into account the relation existing between the movie review segment and the news.
(E) He did not wait until he received at least 50 letters with unfavorable comments about the movie review segment before making his decision.

8. Observatory director: Some say that funding the megatelescope will benefit only the astronomers who will work with it. This dangerous point of view, applied to the work of Maxwell, Newton, or Einstein, would have stifled their research and deprived the world of beneficial applications, such as the development of radio, that followed from that research.

If the statements above are put forward as an argument in favor of development of the megatelescope, which one of the following is the strongest criticism of that argument?

(A) It appeals to the authority of experts who cannot have known all the issues involved in construction of the megatelescope.
(B) It does not identify those opposed to development of the megatelescope.
(C) It launches a personal attack on opponents of the megatelescope by accusing them of having a dangerous point of view.
(D) It does not distinguish between the economic and the intellectual senses of "benefit."
(E) It does not show that the proposed megatelescope research is worthy of comparison with that of eminent scientists in its potential for applications.

FLAW

9. The public in the United States has in the past been conditioned to support a substantial defense budget by the threat of confrontation with the Eastern bloc. Now that that threat is dissolving, along with the Eastern bloc itself, it is doubtful whether the public can be persuaded to support an adequate defense budget.

Which one of the following indicates a weakness in the position expressed above?

(A) It presupposes that public opinion can be manipulated indefinitely, without the public's becoming aware of that manipulation.
(B) It refers to past and present events that do not have a causal connection with public support of the budget.
(C) It assumes as fact what it seeks to establish by reasoning.
(D) It fails to give any reason for the judgment it reaches.
(E) It hinges on the term "adequate," the precise meaning of which requires reevaluation in the new context.

10. Extinction is the way of nature. Scientists estimate that over half of the species that have ever come into existence on this planet were already extinct before humans developed even the most primitive of tools. This constant natural process of species emergence and extinction, however, is ignored by those who wish to trace the blame for more recent extinctions to humanity's use of technology, with its consequent effects on the environment. These people must be made to understand that the species that have become extinct in modern times would have become extinct by now even if humans had never acquired technology.

Which one of the following identifies a reasoning error in the passage?

(A) The author mistakenly assumes that technology has not caused any harm to the environment.
(B) The author ignores the fact that some species that are not yet extinct are in danger of extinction.
(C) The author fails to consider that there are probably species in existence that have not yet been identified and studied by scientists.
(D) The author cites scientists who support the theory that over half of all species that ever existed have become extinct, but fails to mention any scientists who do not support that theory.
(E) The author provides no specific evidence that the species that have become extinct in modern times are the same species that would have become extinct in the absence of human technology.

11. "Physicalists" expect that ultimately all mental functions will be explainable in neurobiological terms. Achieving this goal requires knowledge of neurons and their basic functions, a knowledge of how neurons interact, and a delineation of the psychological faculties to be explained. At present, there is a substantial amount of fundamental knowledge about the basic functions of neurons, and the scope and character of such psychological capacities as visual perception and memory are well understood. Thus, as the physicalists claim, mental functions are bound to receive explanations in neurobiological terms in the near future.

Which one of the following indicates an error in the reasoning in the passage?

(A) The conclusion contradicts the claim of the physicalists.
(B) The passage fails to describe exactly what is currently known about the basic functions of neurons.
(C) The word "neurobiological" is used as though it had the same meaning as the word "mental."
(D) The argument does not indicate whether it would be useful to explain mental functions in neurobiological terms.
(E) The passage does not indicate that any knowledge has been achieved about how neurons interact.

12. The current proposal to give college students a broader choice in planning their own courses of study should be abandoned. The students who are supporting the proposal will never be satisfied, no matter what requirements are established. Some of these students have reached their third year without declaring a major. One first-year student has failed to complete four required courses. Several others have indicated a serious indifference to grades and intellectual achievement.

A flaw in the argument is that it does which one of the following?

(A) avoids the issue by focusing on supporters of the proposal
(B) argues circularly by assuming the conclusion is true in stating the premises
(C) fails to define the critical term "satisfied"
(D) distorts the proposal advocated by opponents
(E) uses the term "student" equivocally

13. The ancient Egyptian pharaoh Akhenaten, who had a profound effect during his lifetime on Egyptian art and religion, was well loved and highly respected by his subjects. We know this from the fierce loyalty shown to him by his palace guards, as documented in reports written during Akhenaten's reign.

A questionable technique used in the argument is to

(A) introduce information that actually contradicts the conclusion
(B) rely on evidence that in principle would be impossible to challenge
(C) make a generalization based on a sample that is likely to be unrepresentative
(D) depend on the ambiguity of the term "ancient"
(E) apply present-day standards in an inappropriate way to ancient times

14. Smith: Meat in the diet is healthy, despite what some people say. After all, most doctors do eat meat, and who knows more about health than doctors do?

Which one of the following is a flaw in Smith's reasoning?

(A) attacking the opponents' motives instead of their argument
(B) generalizing on the basis of a sample consisting of atypical cases
(C) assuming at the outset what the argument claims to establish through reasoning
(D) appealing to authority, even when different authorities give conflicting advice about an issue
(E) taking for granted that experts do not act counter to what, according to their expertise, is in their best interest

15. College professor: College students do not write nearly as well as they used to. Almost all of the papers that my students have done for me this year have been poorly written and ungrammatical.

Which one of the following is the most serious weakness in the argument made by the professor?

(A) It requires confirmation that the change in the professor's students is representative of a change among college students in general.
(B) It offers no proof to the effect that the professor is an accurate judge of writing ability.
(C) It does not take into account the possibility that the professor is a poor teacher.
(D) It fails to present contrary evidence.
(E) It fails to define its terms sufficiently.

16. No one who lacks knowledge of a subject is competent to pass judgment on that subject. Since political know-how is a matter, not of adhering to technical rules, but of insight and style learned through apprenticeship and experience, only seasoned politicians are competent to judge whether a particular political policy is fair to all.

A major weakness of the argument is that it

(A) relies on a generalization about the characteristic that makes someone competent to pass judgment

(B) fails to give specific examples to illustrate how political know-how can be acquired

(C) uses the term "apprenticeship" to describe what is seldom a formalized relationship

(D) equates political know-how with understanding the social implications of political policies

(E) assumes that when inexperienced politicians set policy they are guided by the advice of more experienced politicians

17. Certain minor peculiarities of language are used unconsciously by poets. If such peculiarities appear in the works of more than one poet, they are likely to reflect the language in common use during the poets' time. However, if they appear in the work of only one poet, they are likely to be personal idiosyncrasies. As such, they can provide a kind of "fingerprint" that allows scholars, by comparing a poem of previously unknown authorship to the work of a particular known poet, to identify the poem as the work of that poet.

For which one of the following reasons can the test described above never provide conclusive proof of the authorship of any poem?

(A) The labor of analyzing peculiarities of language both in the work of a known poet and in a poem of unknown authorship would not be undertaken unless other evidence already suggested that the poem of unknown authorship was written by the known poet.

(B) A peculiarity of language that might be used as an identifying mark is likely to be widely scattered in the work of a poet, so that a single poem not known to have been written by that poet might not include that peculiarity.

(C) A peculiarity of language in a poem of unknown authorship could be evidence either that the poem was written by the one author known to use that peculiarity or that the peculiarity was not unique to that author.

(D) Minor peculiarities of language contribute far less to the literary effect of any poem than such factors as poetic form, subject matter, and deliberately chosen wording.

(E) A poet's use of some peculiarities of language might have been unconscious in some poems and conscious in other poems, and the two uses would be indistinguishable to scholars at a later date.

18. The journalistic practice of fabricating remarks after an interview and printing them within quotation marks, as if they were the interviewee's own words, has been decried as a form of unfair misrepresentation. However, people's actual spoken remarks rarely convey their ideas as clearly as does a distillation of those ideas crafted, after an interview, by a skilled writer. Therefore, since this practice avoids the more serious misrepresentation that would occur if people's exact words were quoted but their ideas only partially expressed, it is entirely defensible.

Which one of the following is a questionable technique used in the argument?

(A) answering an exaggerated charge by undermining the personal authority of those who made that charge
(B) claiming that the prestige of a profession provides ample grounds for dismissing criticisms of that profession
(C) offering as an adequate defense of a practice an observation that discredits only one of several possible alternatives to that practice
(D) concluding that a practice is right on the grounds that it is necessary
(E) using the opponent's admission that a practice is sometimes appropriate as conclusive proof that that practice is never inappropriate

19. Professor Smith published a paper arguing that a chemical found in minute quantities in most drinking water had an adverse effect on the human nervous system. Existing scientific theory held that no such effect was possible because there was no neural mechanism for bringing it about. Several papers by well-known scientists in the field followed, unanimously purporting to prove Professor Smith wrong. This clearly shows that the scientific establishment was threatened by Professor Smith's work and conspired to discredit it.

Which one of the following is the central flaw in the argument given by the author of the passage?

(A) The author passes over the possibility that Professor Smith had much to gain should Professor Smith's discovery have found general acceptance.
(B) The author fails to mention whether or not Professor Smith knew that the existence of the alleged new effect was incompatible with established scientific theory.
(C) The author fails to show why the other scientists could not have been presenting evidence in order to establish the truth of the matter.
(D) The author neglects to clarify what his or her relationship to Professor Smith is.
(E) The author fails to indicate what, if any, effect the publication of Professor Smith's paper had on the public's confidence in the safety of most drinking water.

20. Approximately 7.6 million women who earn incomes have preschool-age children, and approximately 6.4 million women are the sole income earners for their families. These figures indicate that there are comparatively few income-earning women who have preschool-age children but are not the sole income earners for their families.

A major flaw in the reasoning is that it

(A) relies on figures that are too imprecise to support the conclusion drawn
(B) overlooks the possibility that there is little or no overlap between the two populations of women cited
(C) fails to indicate whether the difference between the two figures cited will tend to remain stable over time
(D) ignores the possibility that families with preschool-age children might also have older children
(E) provides no information on families in which men are the sole income earners

21. Lenore: It is naive to think that historical explanations can be objective. In evaluating evidence, historians are always influenced by their national, political, and class loyalties.

Victor: Still, the very fact that cases of biased thinking have been detected and sources of bias identified shows that there are people who can maintain objectivity.

Victor's response does not succeed as a rebuttal of Lenore's argument because his response

(A) displays the same kind of biased thinking as that against which Lenore's argument is directed
(B) does not address the special case of historians who purposely distort evidence in order to promote their own political objectives
(C) fails to provide examples of cases in which biased thinking has been detected and the source of that bias identified
(D) does not consider sources of bias in historical explanation other than those that are due to national, political, and class loyalties
(E) overlooks the possibility that those who detect and identify bias are themselves biased in some way

FLAW

22. Joshua Smith's new novel was criticized by the book editor for *The Daily Standard* as implausible. That criticism, like so many other criticisms from the same source in the past, is completely unwarranted. As anyone who has actually read the novel would agree, each one of the incidents in which Smith's hero gets involved is the kind of incident that could very well have happened to someone or other.

Which one of the following is the most serious error of reasoning in the argument?

(A) It relies on the assumption that a criticism can legitimately be dismissed as unwarranted if it is offered by someone who had previously displayed questionable judgment.
(B) It ignores the fact that people can agree about something even though what they agree about is not the case.
(C) It calls into question the intellectual integrity of the critic in order to avoid having to address the grounds on which the criticism is based.
(D) It takes for granted that a whole story will have a given characteristic if each of its parts has that characteristic.
(E) It attempts to justify its conclusion by citing reasons that most people would find plausible only if they were already convinced that the conclusion was true.

23. The senator has long held to the general principle that no true work of art is obscene, and thus that there is no conflict between the need to encourage free artistic expression and the need to protect the sensibilities of the public from obscenity. When well-known works generally viewed as obscene are cited as possible counterexamples, the senator justifies accepting the principle by saying that if these works really are obscene then they cannot be works of art.

The senator's reasoning contains which one of the following errors?

(A) It seeks to persuade by emotional rather than intellectual means.
(B) It contains an implicit contradiction.
(C) It relies on an assertion of the senator's authority.
(D) It assumes what it seeks to establish.
(E) It attempts to justify a position by appeal to an irrelevant consideration.

24. Those influenced by modern Western science take it for granted that a genuine belief in astrology is proof of a credulous and unscientific mind. Yet, in the past, people of indisputable intellectual and scientific brilliance accepted astrology as a fact. Therefore, there is no scientific basis for rejecting astrology.

The argument is most vulnerable to criticism on which one of the following grounds?

(A) A belief can be consistent with the available evidence and accepted scientific theories at one time but not with the accepted evidence and theories of a later time.
(B) Since it is controversial whether astrology has a scientific basis, any argument that attempts to prove that it has will be specious.
(C) Although the conclusion is intended to hold in all cultures, the evidence advanced in its support is drawn only from those cultures strongly influenced by modern Western science.
(D) The implicit assumption that all practitioners of Western science believe in astrology is false.
(E) The fact that there might be legitimate nonscientific reasons for rejecting astrology has been overlooked.

25. Psychotherapy has been described as a form of moral coercion. However, when people are coerced, their ability to make choices is restricted, and the goal of psychotherapy is to enhance people's ability to make choices. Hence, psychotherapy cannot possibly be a form of coercion.

Which one of the following describes a flaw in the argument?

(A) The position being argued against is redefined unfairly in order to make it an easier target.
(B) Psychotherapy is unfairly criticized for having a single goal, rather than having many complex goals.
(C) No allowance is made for the fact that the practice or results of psychotherapy might run counter to its goals.
(D) The goals of psychotherapy are taken to justify any means that are used to achieve those goals.
(E) It offers no argument to show that moral coercion is always undesirable.

26. The true scientific significance of a group of unusual fossils discovered by the paleontologist Charles Walcott is more likely to be reflected in a recent classification than it was in Walcott's own classification. Walcott was, after all, a prominent member of the scientific establishment. His classifications are thus unlikely to have done anything but confirm what established science had already taken to be true.

Which one of the following most accurately describes a questionable technique used in the argument?

(A) It draws conclusions about the merit of a position and about the content of that position from evidence about the position's source.
(B) It cites two pieces of evidence, each of which is both questionable and unverifiable, and uses this evidence to support its conclusions.
(C) It bases a conclusion on two premises that contradict each other and minimizes this contradiction by the vagueness of the terms employed.
(D) It attempts to establish the validity of a claim, which is otherwise unsupported, by denying the truth of the opposite of that claim.
(E) It analyzes the past on the basis of social and political categories that properly apply only to the present and uses the results of this analysis to support its conclusion.

27. A large group of hyperactive children whose regular diets included food containing large amounts of additives was observed by researchers trained to assess the presence or absence of behavior problems. The children were then placed on a low-additive diet for several weeks, after which they were observed again. Originally nearly 60 percent of the children exhibited behavior problems; after the change in diet, only 30 percent did so. On the basis of these data, it can be concluded that food additives can contribute to behavior problems in hyperactive children.

The evidence cited fails to establish the conclusion because

(A) there is no evidence that the reduction in behavior problems was proportionate to the reduction in food-additive intake
(B) there is no way to know what changes would have occurred without the change of diet, since only children who changed to a low-additive diet were studied
(C) exactly how many children exhibited behavior problems after the change in diet cannot be determined, since the size of the group studied is not precisely given
(D) there is no evidence that the behavior of some of the children was unaffected by additives
(E) the evidence is consistent with the claim that some children exhibit more frequent behavior problems after being on the low-additive diet than they had exhibited when first observed

28. Office manager: I will not order recycled paper for this office. Our letters to clients must make a good impression, so we cannot print them on inferior paper.

Stationery supplier: Recycled paper is not necessarily inferior. In fact, from the beginning, the finest paper has been made of recycled material. It was only in the 1850s that paper began to be made from wood fiber, and then only because there were no longer enough rags to meet the demand for paper.

In which one of the following ways does the stationer's response fail to address the office manager's objection to recycled paper?

(A) It does not recognize that the office manager's prejudice against recycled paper stems from ignorance.
(B) It uses irrelevant facts to justify a claim about the quality of the disputed product.
(C) It assumes that the office manager is concerned about environmental issues.
(D) It presupposes that the office manager understands the basic technology of paper manufacturing.
(E) It ignores the office manager's legitimate concern about quality.

29. When workers do not find their assignments challenging, they become bored and so achieve less than their abilities would allow. On the other hand, when workers find their assignments too difficult, they give up and so again achieve less than what they are capable of achieving. It is, therefore, clear that no worker's full potential will ever be realized.

Which one of the following is an error of reasoning contained in the argument?

(A) mistakenly equating what is actual and what is merely possible
(B) assuming without warrant that a situation allows only two possibilities
(C) relying on subjective rather than objective evidence
(D) confusing the coincidence of two events with a causal relation between the two
(E) depending on the ambiguous use of a key term

30. Student representative: Our university, in expelling a student who verbally harassed his roommate, has erred by penalizing the student for doing what he surely has a right to do: speak his mind!

Dean of students: But what you're saying is that our university should endorse verbal harassment. Yet surely if we did that, we would threaten the free flow of ideas that is the essence of university life.

Which one of the following is a questionable technique that the dean of students uses in attempting to refute the student representative?

(A) challenging the student representative's knowledge of the process by which the student was expelled
(B) invoking a fallacious distinction between speech and other sorts of behavior
(C) misdescribing the student representative's position, thereby making it easier to challenge
(D) questioning the motives of the student representative rather than offering reasons for the conclusion defended
(E) relying on a position of power to silence the opposing viewpoint with a threat

31. Scientific research at a certain university was supported in part by an annual grant from a major foundation. When the university's physics department embarked on weapons-related research, the foundation, which has a purely humanitarian mission, threatened to cancel its grant. The university then promised that none of the foundation's money would be used for the weapons research, whereupon the foundation withdrew its threat, concluding that the weapons research would not benefit from the foundation's grant.

Which one of the following describes a flaw in the reasoning underlying the foundation's conclusion?

(A) It overlooks the possibility that the availability of the foundation's money for humanitarian uses will allow the university to redirect other funds from humanitarian uses to weapons research.
(B) It overlooks the possibility that the physics department's weapons research is not the only one of the university's research activities with other than purely humanitarian purposes.
(C) It overlooks the possibility that the university made its promise specifically in order to induce the foundation to withdraw its threat.
(D) It confuses the intention of not using a sum of money for a particular purpose with the intention of not using that sum of money at all.
(E) It assumes that if the means to achieve an objective are humanitarian in character, then the objective is also humanitarian in character.

32. Historian: There is no direct evidence that timber was traded between the ancient nations of Poran and Nayal, but the fact that a law setting tariffs on timber imports from Poran was enacted during the third Nayalese dynasty does suggest that during that period a timber trade was conducted.

Critic: Your reasoning is flawed. During its third dynasty, Nayal may well have imported timber from Poran, but certainly on today's statute books there remain many laws regulating activities that were once common but in which people no longer engage.

The critic's response to the historian is flawed because it

(A) produces evidence that is consistent with there not having been any timber trade between Poran and Nayal during the third Nayalese dynasty
(B) cites current laws without indicating whether the laws cited are relevant to the timber trade
(C) fails to recognize that the historian's conclusion was based on indirect evidence rather than direct evidence
(D) takes no account of the difference between a law's enactment at a particular time and a law's existence as part of a legal code at a particular time
(E) accepts without question the assumption about the purpose of laws that underlies the historian's argument

33. Sheila: Health experts generally agree that smoking a tobacco product for many years is very likely to be harmful to the smoker's health.

Tim: On the contrary, smoking has no effect on health at all: although my grandfather smoked three cigars a day from the age of fourteen, he died at age ninety-six.

A major weakness of Tim's counterargument is that his counterargument

(A) attempts to refute a probabilistic conclusion by claiming the existence of a single counterexample
(B) challenges expert opinion on the basis of specific information unavailable to experts in the field
(C) describes an individual case that is explicitly discounted as an exception to the experts' conclusion
(D) presupposes that longevity and health status are unrelated to each other in the general population
(E) tacitly assumes that those health experts who are in agreement on this issue arrived at that agreement independently of one another

34. Saunders: Everyone at last week's neighborhood association meeting agreed that the row of abandoned and vandalized houses on Carlton Street posed a threat to the safety of our neighborhood. Moreover, no one now disputes that getting the houses torn down eliminated that threat. Some people tried to argue that it was unnecessary to demolish what they claimed were basically sound buildings, since the city had established a fund to help people in need of housing buy and rehabilitate such buildings. The overwhelming success of the demolition strategy, however, proves that the majority, who favored demolition, were right and that those who claimed that the problem could and should be solved by rehabilitating the houses were wrong.

Saunders' reasoning is flawed because it

(A) relies on fear rather than on argument to persuade the neighborhood association to reject the policy advocated by Saunders' opponents
(B) fails to establish that there is anyone who could qualify for city funds who would be interested in buying and rehabilitating the houses
(C) mistakenly equates an absence of vocal public dissent with the presence of universal public support
(D) offers no evidence that the policy advocated by Saunders' opponents would not have succeeded if it had been given the chance
(E) does not specify the precise nature of the threat to neighborhood safety supposedly posed by the vandalized houses

35. Mayor Smith, one of our few government officials with a record of outspoken, informed, and consistent opposition to nuclear power plant construction projects, has now declared herself in favor of building the nuclear power plant at Littletown. If someone with her past antinuclear record now favors building this power plant, then there is good reason to believe that it will be safe and therefore should be built.

The argument is vulnerable to criticism on which one of the following grounds?

(A) It overlooks the possibility that not all those who fail to speak out on issues of nuclear power are necessarily opposed to it.
(B) It assumes without warrant that the qualities enabling a person to be elected to public office confer on that person a grasp of the scientific principles on which technical decisions are based.
(C) It fails to establish that a consistent and outspoken opposition is necessarily an informed opposition.
(D) It leads to the further but unacceptable conclusion that any project favored by Mayor Smith should be sanctioned simply on the basis of her having spoken out in favor of it.
(E) It gives no indication of either the basis of Mayor Smith's former opposition to nuclear power plant construction or the reasons for her support for the Littletown project.

36. So-called environmentalists have argued that the proposed Golden Lake Development would interfere with bird-migration patterns. However, the fact that these same people have raised environmental objections to virtually every development proposal brought before the council in recent years indicates that their expressed concern for bird-migration patterns is nothing but a mask for their antidevelopment, antiprogress agenda. Their claim, therefore, should be dismissed without further consideration.

Which one of the following questionable argumentative techniques is employed in the passage?

(A) taking the failure of a given argument to establish its conclusion as the basis for claiming that the view expressed by that conclusion is false
(B) rejecting the conclusion of an argument on the basis of a claim about the motives of those advancing the argument
(C) using a few exceptional cases as the basis for a claim about what is true in general
(D) misrepresenting evidence that supports the position the argument is intended to refute
(E) assuming that what is true of a group as a whole is necessarily true of each member of that group

37. Lucien: Public-housing advocates claim that the many homeless people in this city are proof that there is insufficient housing available to them and therefore that more low-income apartments are needed. But that conclusion is absurd. Many apartments in my own building remain unrented and my professional colleagues report similar vacancies where they live. Since apartments clearly are available, homelessness is not a housing problem. Homelessness can, therefore, only be caused by people's inability or unwillingness to work to pay the rent.

Maria: On the contrary, all recent studies show that a significant percentage of this city's homeless people hold regular jobs. These are people who lack neither will nor ability.

Lucien's argument against the public-housing advocates' position is most vulnerable to which one of the following criticisms?

(A) It offers no justification for dismissing as absurd the housing advocates' claim that there are many homeless people in the city.
(B) It treats information acquired through informal conversations as though it provided evidence as strong as information acquired on the basis of controlled scientific studies.
(C) It responds to a claim in which "available" is used in the sense of "affordable" by using "available" in the sense of "not occupied."
(D) It overlooks the possibility that not all apartment buildings have vacant apartments for rent.
(E) It fails to address the issue, raised by the public-housing advocates' argument, of who would pay for the construction of more low-income housing.

38. People who accuse the postal service of incompetence and inefficiency while complaining of the proposed five-cent increase in postal rates do not know a bargain when they see one. Few experiences are more enjoyable than reading a personal letter from a friend. Viewed in this way, postal service is so underpriced that a five-cent increase is unworthy of serious debate.

The reasoning in the argument is flawed because the argument

(A) suggests that the postal service is both competent and efficient, but does not establish how competence and efficiency should be measured
(B) claims that the proposed increase is insignificant but does not say at what level the increase would be worthy of serious debate
(C) confuses the value of the object delivered with the value of delivering that object
(D) appeals to an outside authority for support of a premise that should be established by argument
(E) fails to establish whether or not the critics of the postal service are employees of the postal service

39. Infants younger than six months who have normal hearing can readily distinguish between acoustically similar sounds that are used as part of any language—not only those used in the language spoken by the people who raise them. Young adults can readily distinguish between such sounds only in languages that they regularly use. It is known that the physiological capacity to hear begins to deteriorate after infancy. So the observed difference in the abilities of infants and young adults to distinguish between acoustically similar speech sounds must be the result of the physiological deterioration of hearing.

The reasoning in the argument is flawed because the argument

(A) sets an arbitrary cutoff point of six months for the age below which infants are able to distinguish acoustically similar speech sounds
(B) does not explain the procedures used to measure the abilities of two very different populations
(C) ignores the fact that certain types of speech sounds occur in almost all languages
(D) assumes that what is true of a group of people taken collectively is also true of any individual within that group
(E) takes a factor that might contribute to an explanation of the observed difference as a sufficient explanation for that difference

40. A careful review of hospital fatalities due to anesthesia during the last 20 years indicates that the most significant safety improvements resulted from better training of anesthetists. Equipment that monitors a patient's oxygen and carbon dioxide levels was not available in most operating rooms during the period under review. Therefore, the increased use of such monitoring equipment in operating rooms will not significantly cut fatalities due to anesthesia.

A flaw in the argument is that

(A) the evidence cited to show that one factor led to a certain result is not sufficient to show that a second factor will not also lead to that result
(B) the reasons given in support of the conclusion presuppose the truth of that conclusion
(C) the evidence cited to show that a certain factor was absent when a certain result occurred does not show that the absence of that factor caused that result
(D) the evidence cited in support of the conclusion is inconsistent with other information that is provided
(E) the reason indicated for the claim that one event caused a second more strongly supports the claim that both events were independent effects of a third event

41. Some people have questioned why the Homeowners Association is supporting Cooper's candidacy for mayor. But if the Association wants a mayor who will attract more businesses to the town, Cooper is the only candidate it could support. So, since the Association is supporting Cooper, it must have a goal of attracting more businesses to the town.

The reasoning in the argument is in error because

(A) the reasons the Homeowners Association should want to attract more businesses to the town are not given
(B) the Homeowners Association could be supporting Cooper's candidacy for reasons unrelated to attracting businesses to the town
(C) other groups besides the Homeowners Association could be supporting Cooper's candidacy
(D) the Homeowners Association might discover that attracting more businesses to the town would not be in the best interest of its members
(E) Cooper might not have all of the skills that are needed by a mayor who wants to attract businesses to a town

42. Of 2,500 people who survived a first heart attack, those who did not smoke had their first heart attack at a median age of 62. However, of those 2,500, people who smoked two packs of cigarettes a day had their first heart attack at a median age of 51. On the basis of this information, it can be concluded that nonsmokers tend to have a first heart attack eleven years later than do people who smoke two packs of cigarettes a day.

The conclusion is incorrectly drawn from the information given because this information does not include

(A) the relative severity of heart attacks suffered by smokers and nonsmokers
(B) the nature of the different medical treatments that smokers and nonsmokers received after they had survived their first heart attack
(C) how many of the 2,500 people studied suffered a second heart attack
(D) the earliest age at which a person who smoked two packs a day had his or her first heart attack
(E) data on people who did not survive a first heart attack

43. Broadcaster: Our radio station has a responsibility to serve the public interest. Hence, when our critics contend that our recent exposé of events in the private lives of local celebrities was excessively intrusive, we can only reply that the overwhelming public interest in these matters makes it our responsibility to publicize them.

Which one of the following is a flaw in the broadcaster's defense of the radio station's practice?

(A) assuming without argument that there is a right to privacy
(B) ignoring grounds for criticism of the exposé aside from intrusion into people's private lives
(C) intentionally failing to specify what is meant by "excessively intrusive"
(D) confusing legal responsibility with moral obligation
(E) improperly exploiting an ambiguity in the phrase "public interest"

44. Editorial: In rejecting the plan proposed by parliament to reform the electoral process, the president clearly acted in the best interests of the nation. Anyone who thinks otherwise should remember that the president made this decision knowing it would be met with fierce opposition at home and widespread disapproval abroad. All citizens who place the nation's well-being above narrow partisan interests will applaud this courageous action.

The reasoning in the editorial is in error because

(A) it confuses a quality that is merely desirable in a political leader with a quality that is essential to effective political decision-making
(B) it fails to distinguish between evidence concerning the courage required to make a certain decision and evidence concerning the wisdom of making that decision
(C) it ignores the likelihood that many citizens have no narrow partisan interest in the proposed election reform plan
(D) it overlooks the possibility that there was strong opposition to the parliament's plan among members of the president's own party
(E) it depends on the unwarranted assumption that any plan proposed by a parliament will necessarily serve only narrow partisan interests

45. A contract, whether expressed or unexpressed, exists when two parties engage with each other for the reciprocal transfer of benefits. Thus, in accepting support from public funds, an artist creates at least an unexpressed contract between himself or herself and the public, and the public can rightly expect to benefit from the artist's work.

Which one of the following most accurately describes an error in reasoning in the passage?

(A) attempting to justify a rule of conduct on the grounds that it confers benefits on all of the parties involved
(B) concluding that a definition is fully applicable to a situation when it is known only that the situation conforms partially to that definition
(C) speaking only in abstract terms about matters that involve contingencies and that must be judged on a case-by-case basis
(D) confusing the type of mental or emotional activity in which an individual can engage with the mental or emotional states that can characterize groups of individuals
(E) treating an issue that requires resolution through political processes as if it were merely a matter of opinion

46. The Japanese *haiku* is defined as a poem of three lines with five syllables in the first line, seven syllables in the second line, and five syllables in the third line. English poets tend to ignore this fact. Disregarding syllable count, they generally call any three-line English poem with a "*haiku* feel" a *haiku*. This demonstrates that English poets have little respect for foreign traditions, even those from which some of their own poetry derives.

The reasoning is flawed because it

(A) confuses matters of objective fact with matters of subjective feeling
(B) draws a conclusion that is broader in scope than is warranted by the evidence advanced
(C) relies on stereotypes instead of presenting evidence
(D) overlooks the possibility that the case it cites is not unique
(E) fails to acknowledge that ignoring something implies a negative judgment about that thing

47. In a learning experiment a researcher ran rats through a maze. Some of the rats were blind, others deaf, others lacked a sense of smell, and others had no sensory deficiencies; yet all the rats learned the task in much the same amount of time. Of the senses other than sight, hearing, and smell, only kinesthesia had not previously been shown to be irrelevant to maze-learning. The researcher concluded on the basis of these facts that kinesthesia, the sensation of bodily movement, is sufficient for maze-learning.

The researcher's reasoning is most vulnerable to which one of the following criticisms?

(A) The small differences in proficiency found by the researcher did not appear to fall into a systematic pattern by group.
(B) The possibility that the interaction of kinesthesia with at least one other sense is required for maze-learning cannot be ruled out on the basis of the data above.
(C) It can be determined from the data that rats who are deprived of one of their sources of sensory stimulation become more reliant on kinesthesia than they had been, but the data do not indicate how such a transference takes place.
(D) It can be determined from the data that rats can learn to run mazes by depending on kinesthesia alone, but the possibility that rats respond to nonkinesthetic stimulation is not ruled out.
(E) It can be determined from the data that maze-learning in rats depends on at least two sources of sensory stimulation, one of which is kinesthesia, but which of the remaining sources must also be employed is not determinable.

FLAW

48. Many people change their wills on their own every few years, in response to significant changes in their personal or financial circumstances. This practice can create a problem for the executor when these people are careless and do not date their wills: the executor will then often know neither which one of several undated wills is the most recent, nor whether the will drawn up last has ever been found. Therefore, people should not only date their wills but also state in any new will which will it supersedes, for then there would not be a problem to begin with.

The reasoning in the argument is flawed because the argument

(A) treats a partial solution to the stated problem as though it were a complete solution
(B) fails to distinguish between prevention of a problem and successful containment of the adverse effects that the problem might cause
(C) proposes a solution to the stated problem that does not actually solve the problem but merely makes someone else responsible for solving the problem
(D) claims that a certain action would be a change for the better without explicitly considering what negative consequences the action might have
(E) proposes that a certain action be based on information that would be unavailable at the time proposed for that action

49. The proper way to plan a scientific project is first to decide its goal and then to plan the best way to accomplish that goal. The United States space station project does not conform to this ideal. When the Cold War ended, the project lost its original purpose, so another purpose was quickly grafted onto the project, that of conducting limited-gravity experiments, even though such experiments can be done in an alternative way. It is, therefore, abundantly clear that the space station should not be built.

The reasoning in the argument is flawed because the argument

(A) attacks the proponents of a claim rather than arguing against the claim itself
(B) presupposes what it sets out to prove
(C) faults planners for not foreseeing a certain event, when in fact that event was not foreseeable
(D) contains statements that lead to a self-contradiction
(E) concludes that a shortcoming is fatal, having produced evidence only of the existence of that shortcoming

50. A standard problem for computer security is that passwords that have to be typed on a computer keyboard are comparatively easy for unauthorized users to steal or guess. A new system that relies on recognizing the voices of authorized users apparently avoids this problem. In a small initial trial, the system never incorrectly accepted someone seeking access to the computer's data. Clearly, if this result can be repeated in an operational setting, then there will be a way of giving access to those people who are entitled to access and to no one else.

The reasoning above is flawed because it

(A) makes a faulty comparison, in that a security system based on voice recognition would not be expected to suffer from the same problems as one that relied on passwords entered from a keyboard
(B) bases a general conclusion on a small amount of data
(C) fails to recognize that a security system based on voice recognition could easily have applications other than computer security
(D) ignores the possibility that the system sometimes denies access to people who are entitled to access
(E) states its conclusion in a heavily qualified way

51. A group of scientists who have done research on the health effects of food irradiation has discovered no evidence challenging its safety. Supporters of food irradiation have cited this research as certain proof that food irradiation is a safe practice.

A flaw in the reasoning of the supporters of food irradiation is that they

(A) assume that the scientists doing the research set out to prove that food irradiation is an unsafe practice
(B) are motivated by a biased interest in proving the practice to be safe
(C) overlook the possibility that objections about safety are not the only possible objections to the practice
(D) neglect to provide detailed information about the evidence used to support the conclusion
(E) use the lack of evidence contradicting a claim as conclusive evidence for that claim

52. That long-term cigarette smoking can lead to health problems including cancer and lung disease is a scientifically well established fact. Contrary to what many people seem to believe, however, it is not necessary to deny this fact in order to reject the view that tobacco companies should be held either morally or legally responsible for the poor health of smokers. After all, excessive consumption of candy undeniably leads to such health problems as tooth decay, but no one seriously believes that candy eaters who get cavities should be able to sue candy manufacturers.

The reasoning in the argument is most vulnerable to criticism on the grounds that it

(A) fails to establish that the connection between tooth decay and candy eating is as scientifically well documented as that between smoking and the health problems suffered by smokers
(B) depends on the obviously false assumption that everyone who gets cavities does so only as a result of eating too much candy
(C) leaves undefined such critical qualifying terms as "excessive" and "long-term"
(D) attributes certain beliefs to "many people" without identifying the people who allegedly hold those beliefs
(E) fails to address the striking differences in the nature of the threat to health posed by tooth decay on the one hand and cancer and lung disease on the other

53. Teacher: Journalists who conceal the identity of the sources they quote stake their professional reputations on what may be called the logic of anecdotes. This is so because the statements reported by such journalists are dissociated from the precise circumstances in which they were made and thus will be accepted for publication only if the statements are high in plausibility or originality or interest to a given audience—precisely the properties of a good anecdote.

Student: But what you are saying, then, is that the journalist need not bother with sources in the first place. Surely, any reasonably resourceful journalist can invent plausible, original, or interesting stories faster than they can be obtained from unidentified sources.

The student's response contains which one of the following reasoning flaws?

(A) confusing a marginal journalistic practice with the primary work done by journalists
(B) ignoring the possibility that the teacher regards as a prerequisite for the publication of an unattributed statement that the statement have actually been made
(C) confusing the characteristics of reported statements with the characteristics of the situations in which the statements were made
(D) judging the merits of the teacher's position solely by the most extreme case to which the position applies
(E) falsely concluding that if three criteria, met jointly, assure an outcome, then each criterion, met individually, also assures that outcome

54. The proposal to extend clinical trials, which are routinely used as systematic tests of pharmaceutical innovations, to new surgical procedures should not be implemented. The point is that surgical procedures differ in one important respect from medicinal drugs: a correctly prescribed drug depends for its effectiveness only on the drug's composition, whereas the effectiveness of even the most appropriate surgical procedure is transparently related to the skills of the surgeon who uses it.

The reasoning in the argument is flawed because the argument

(A) does not consider that new surgical procedures might be found to be intrinsically more harmful than the best treatment previously available
(B) ignores the possibility that the challenged proposal is deliberately crude in a way designed to elicit criticism to be used in refining the proposal
(C) assumes that a surgeon's skills remain unchanged throughout the surgeon's professional life
(D) describes a dissimilarity without citing any scientific evidence for the existence of that dissimilarity
(E) rejects a proposal presumably advanced in good faith without acknowledging any such good faith

FLAW

55. A study of adults who suffer from migraine headaches revealed that a significant proportion of the study participants suffer from a complex syndrome characterized by a set of three symptoms. Those who suffer from the syndrome experienced excessive anxiety during early childhood. As adolescents, these people began experiencing migraine headaches. As these people approached the age of 20, they also began to experience recurring bouts of depression. Since this pattern is invariant, always with excessive anxiety at its beginning, it follows that excessive anxiety in childhood is one of the causes of migraine headaches and depression in later life.

The reasoning in the argument is vulnerable to criticism on which one of the following grounds?

(A) It does not specify the proportion of those in the general population who suffer from the syndrome.
(B) It fails to rule out the possibility that all of the characteristic symptoms of the syndrome have a common cause.
(C) It makes a generalization that is inconsistent with the evidence.
(D) It fails to demonstrate that the people who participated in the study are representative of migraine sufferers.
(E) It does not establish why the study of migraine sufferers was restricted to adult participants.

56. Frieda: Lightning causes fires and damages electronic equipment. Since lightning rods can prevent any major damage, every building should have one.

Erik: Your recommendation is pointless. It is true that lightning occasionally causes fires, but faulty wiring and overloaded circuits cause far more fires and damage to equipment than lightning does.

Erik's response fails to establish that Frieda's recommendation should not be acted on because his response

(A) does not show that the benefits that would follow from Frieda's recommendation would be offset by any disadvantage
(B) does not offer any additional way of lessening the risk associated with lightning
(C) appeals to Frieda's emotions rather than to her reason
(D) introduces an irrelevant comparison between overloaded circuits and faulty wiring
(E) confuses the notion of preventing damage with that of causing inconvenience

57. The new perfume Aurora smells worse to Joan than any comparably priced perfume, and none of her friends likes the smell of Aurora as much as the smell of other perfumes. However, she and her friends must have a defect in their sense of smell, since Professor Jameson prefers the smell of Aurora to that of any other perfume and she is one of the world's foremost experts on the physiology of smell.

The reasoning is flawed because it

(A) calls into question the truthfulness of the opponent rather than addressing the point at issue
(B) ignores the well-known fact that someone can prefer one thing to another without liking either very much
(C) fails to establish that there is widespread agreement among the experts in the field
(D) makes an illegitimate appeal to the authority of an expert
(E) misrepresents the position against which it is directed

58. Until recently it was thought that ink used before the sixteenth century did not contain titanium. However, a new type of analysis detected titanium in the ink of the famous Bible printed by Johannes Gutenberg and in that of another fifteenth-century Bible known as B-36, though not in the ink of any of numerous other fifteenth-century books analyzed. This finding is of great significance, since it not only strongly supports the hypothesis that B-36 was printed by Gutenberg but also shows that the presence of titanium in the ink of the purportedly fifteenth century Vinland Map can no longer be regarded as a reason for doubting the map's authenticity.

The reasoning in the passage is vulnerable to criticism on the ground that

(A) the results of the analysis are interpreted as indicating that the use of titanium as an ingredient in fifteenth-century ink both was, and was not, extremely restricted
(B) if the technology that makes it possible to detect titanium in printing ink has only recently become available, it is unlikely that printers or artists in the fifteenth century would know whether their ink contained titanium or not
(C) it is unreasonable to suppose that determination of the date and location of a document's printing or drawing can be made solely on the basis of the presence or absence of a single element in the ink used in the document
(D) both the B-36 Bible and the Vinland Map are objects that can be appreciated on their own merits whether or not the precise date of their creation or the identity of the person who made them is known
(E) the discovery of titanium in the ink of the Vinland Map must have occurred before titanium was discovered in the ink of the Gutenberg Bible and the B-36 Bible

59. Montgomery, a biologist who is also well read in archaeology, has recently written a book on the origin and purpose of ancient monumental architecture. This book has received much positive attention in the popular press but has been severely criticized by many professional archaeologists for being too extreme. Montgomery's views do not deserve a negative appraisal, however, since those views are no more extreme than the views of some professional archaeologists.

The argument is most vulnerable to which one of the following criticisms?

(A) It fails to establish that professional archaeologists' views that are at least as extreme as Montgomery's views do not deserve negative appraisal for that reason.
(B) It assumes without warrant that many professional archaeologists consider biologists unqualified to discuss ancient architecture.
(C) It overlooks the possibility that many professional archaeologists are unfamiliar with Montgomery's views.
(D) It provides no independent evidence to show that the majority of professional archaeologists do not support Montgomery's views.
(E) It attempts to support its position by calling into question the motives of anyone who supports an opposing position.

60. Health insurance insulates patients from the expense of medical care, giving doctors almost complete discretion in deciding the course of most medical treatments. Moreover, with doctors being paid for each procedure performed, they have an incentive to overtreat patients. It is thus clear that medical procedures administered by doctors are frequently prescribed only because these procedures lead to financial rewards.

The argument uses which one of the following questionable techniques?

(A) assigning responsibility for a certain result to someone whose involvement in the events leading to that result was purely coincidental
(B) inferring the performance of certain actions on no basis other than the existence of both incentive and opportunity for performing those actions
(C) presenting as capricious and idiosyncratic decisions that are based on the rigorous application of well-defined principles
(D) depicting choices as having been made arbitrarily by dismissing without argument reasons that have been given for these choices
(E) assuming that the irrelevance of a consideration for one participant in a decision makes that consideration irrelevant for each participant in the decision

61 Two alternative drugs are available to prevent blood clots from developing after a heart attack. According to two major studies, drug Y does this no more effectively than the more expensive drug Z, but drug Z is either no more or only slightly more effective than drug Y. Drug Z's manufacturer, which has engaged in questionable marketing practices such as offering stock options to doctors who participate in clinical trials of drug Z, does not contest the results of the studies but claims that they do not reveal drug Z's advantages. However, since drug Z does not clearly treat the problem more effectively than drug Y, there is no established medical reason for doctors to use drug Z rather than drug Y on their heart-attack victims.

A major flaw in the argument is that the argument

(A) does not consider drugs or treatments other than drug Y and Z that may be used to prevent blood clotting in heart-attack patients
(B) neglects to compare the marketing practices of drug Y's manufacturer with those of drug Z's manufacturer
(C) fails to recognize that there may be medical criteria relevant to the choice between the two drugs other than their effectiveness as a treatment
(D) assumes without proof that the two drugs are similar in their effectiveness as treatments because they are similar in their chemical composition
(E) confuses economic reasons for selecting a treatment with medical reasons

62. Jane: According to an article in this news magazine, children's hand-eye coordination suffers when they spend a great amount of time watching television. Therefore, we must restrict the amount of time Jacqueline and Mildred are allowed to watch television.

Alan: Rubbish! The article says that only children under three are affected in that way. Jacqueline is ten and Mildred is eight. Therefore, we need not restrict their television viewing.

Alan's argument against Jane's conclusion makes which one of the following errors in reasoning?

(A) It relies on the same source that Jane cited in support of her conclusion.
(B) It confuses undermining an argument in support of a given conclusion with showing that the conclusion itself is false.
(C) It does not address the main point of Jane's argument and focuses instead on a side issue.
(D) It makes an irrelevant appeal to an authority.
(E) It fails to distinguish the consequences of a certain practice from the causes of the practice.

63. It is not correct that the people of the United States, relative to comparable countries, are the most lightly taxed. True, the United States has the lowest tax, as percent of gross domestic product, of the Western industrialized countries, but tax rates alone do not tell the whole story. People in the United States pay out of pocket for many goods and services provided from tax revenues elsewhere. Consider universal health care, which is an entitlement supported by tax revenues in every other Western industrialized country. United States government health-care expenditures are equivalent to about 5 percent of the gross domestic product, but private health-care expenditures represent another 7 percent. This 7 percent, then, amounts to a tax.

The argument concerning whether the people of the United States are the most lightly taxed is most vulnerable to which one of the following criticisms?

(A) It bases a comparison on percentages rather than on absolute numbers.
(B) It unreasonably extends the application of a key term.
(C) It uses negatively charged language instead of attempting to give a reason.
(D) It generalizes from only a few instances.
(E) It sets up a dichotomy between alternatives that are not exclusive.

64. A certain airport security scanner designed to detect explosives in luggage will alert the scanner's operator whenever the piece of luggage passing under the scanner contains an explosive. The scanner will erroneously alert the operator for only one percent of the pieces of luggage that contain no explosives. Thus in ninety-nine out of a hundred alerts explosives will actually be present.

The reasoning in the argument is flawed because the argument

(A) ignores the possibility of the scanner's failing to signal an alert when the luggage does contain an explosive
(B) draws a general conclusion about reliability on the basis of a sample that is likely to be biased
(C) ignores the possibility of human error on the part of the scanner's operator once the scanner has alerted him or her
(D) fails to acknowledge the possibility that the scanner will not be equally sensitive to all kinds of explosives
(E) substitutes one group for a different group in the statement of a percentage

65. Oscar: Emerging information technologies will soon make speed of information processing the single most important factor in the creation of individual, corporate, and national wealth. Consequently, the division of the world into northern countries—in general rich—and southern countries—in general poor—will soon be obsolete. Instead, there simply will be fast countries and slow countries, and thus a country's economic well-being will not be a function of its geographical position but just a matter of its relative success in incorporating those new technologies.

Sylvia: But the poor countries of the south lack the economic resources to acquire those technologies and will therefore remain poor. The technologies will thus only widen the existing economic gap between north and south.

The reasoning that Oscar uses in supporting his prediction is vulnerable to criticism on the ground that it

(A) overlooks the possibility that the ability of countries to acquire new technologies at some time in the future will depend on factors other than those countries' present economic status
(B) fails to establish that the division of the world into rich countries and poor countries is the single most important problem that will confront the world economy in the future
(C) ignores the possibility that, in determining a country's future wealth, the country's incorporation of information-processing technologies might be outweighed by a combination of other factors
(D) provides no reason to believe that faster information processing will have only beneficial effects on countries that successfully incorporate new information technologies into their economies
(E) makes no distinction between those of the world's rich countries that are the wealthiest and those that are less wealthy

66. The government's proposed 8 percent cut in all subsidies to arts groups will be difficult for those groups to absorb. As can be seen, however, from their response to last year's cut, it will not put them out of existence. Last year there was also an 8 percent cut, and though private fund-raising was very difficult for the arts groups in the current recessionary economy, they did survive.

The reasoning in the argument is flawed because the argument

(A) relies without warrant on the probability that the economy will improve
(B) does not raise the issue of whether there should be any government subsidies to arts groups at all
(C) equates the mere survival of the arts groups with their flourishing
(D) does not take into account that the dollar amount of the proposed cut is lower than the dollar amount of last year's cut
(E) overlooks the possibility that the cumulative effect of the cuts will be more than the arts groups can withstand

67. The government of Penglai, an isolated island, proposed eliminating outdoor advertising except for small signs of standard shape that identify places of business. Some island merchants protested that the law would reduce the overall volume of business in Penglai, pointing to a report done by the government indicating that in every industry the Penglai businesses that used outdoor advertising had a larger market share than those that did not.

Which one of the following describes an error of reasoning in the merchants' argument?

(A) presupposing that there are no good reasons for restricting the use of outdoor advertising in Penglai
(B) assuming without giving justification that the outdoor advertising increased market share by some means other than by diverting trade from competing businesses
(C) ignoring the question of whether the government's survey of the island could be objective
(D) failing to establish whether the market-share advantage enjoyed by businesses employing outdoor advertising was precisely proportionate to the amount of advertising
(E) disregarding the possibility that the government's proposed restrictions are unconstitutional

68. Gallery owner: Because this painting appears in no catalog of van Gogh's work, we cannot guarantee that he painted it. But consider: the subject is one he painted often, and experts agree that in his later paintings van Gogh invariably used just such broad brushstrokes and distinctive combinations of colors as we find here. Internal evidence, therefore, makes it virtually certain that this is a previously uncataloged, late van Gogh, and as such, a bargain at its price.

The reasoning used by the gallery owner is flawed because it

(A) ignores the fact that there can be general agreement that something is the case without its being the case
(B) neglects to cite expert authority to substantiate the claim about the subject matter of the painting
(C) assumes without sufficient warrant that the only reason anyone would want to acquire a painting is to make a profit
(D) provides no evidence that the painting is more likely to be an uncataloged van Gogh than to be a painting by someone else who painted that particular subject in van Gogh's style
(E) attempts to establish a particular conclusion because doing so is in the reasoner's self-interest rather than because of any genuine concern for the truth of the matter

69. Interviewer: You have shown that biofeedback, dietary changes, and adoption of proper sleep habits all succeed in curing insomnia. You go so far as to claim that, with rigorous adherence to the proper treatment, any case of insomnia is curable. Yet in fact some patients suffering from insomnia do not respond to treatment.

Therapist: If patients do not respond to treatment, this just shows that they are not rigorous in adhering to their treatment.

The therapist's reply to the interviewer is most vulnerable to which one of the following criticisms?

(A) It precludes the possibility of disconfirming evidence.
(B) It depends on the ambiguous use of the term "treatment."
(C) It fails to acknowledge that there may be different causes for different cases of insomnia.
(D) It does not provide statistical evidence to back up its claim.
(E) It overlooks the possibility that some cases of insomnia might improve without any treatment.

70. Magazine article: The Environmental Commissioner's new proposals are called "Fresh Thinking on the Environment," and a nationwide debate on them has been announced. Well, "fresh thinking" from such an unlikely source as the commissioner does deserve closer inspection. Unfortunately we discovered that these proposals are virtually identical to those issued three months ago by Tsarque Inc. under the heading "New Environmentalism" (Tsarque Inc.'s chief is a close friend of the commissioner). Since Tsarque Inc.'s polluting has marked it as an environmental nightmare, in our opinion the "nationwide debate" can end here.

A flaw in the magazine article's reasoning is that it

(A) assumes without any justification that since two texts are similar one of them must be influenced by the other
(B) gives a distorted version of the commissioner's proposals and then attacks this distorted version
(C) dismisses the proposals because of their source rather than because of their substance
(D) uses emotive language in labeling the proposals
(E) appeals to the authority of Tsarque Inc.'s chief without giving evidence that this person's opinion should carry special weight

71. According to a government official involved in overseeing airplane safety during the last year, over 75 percent of the voice-recorder tapes taken from small airplanes involved in relatively minor accidents record the whistling of the pilot during the fifteen minutes immediately preceding the accident. Even such minor accidents pose some safety risk. Therefore, if passengers hear the pilot start to whistle they should take safety precautions, whether instructed by the pilot to do so or not.

The argument is most vulnerable to criticism on the grounds that it

(A) accepts the reliability of the cited statistics on the authority of an unidentified government official
(B) ignores the fact that in nearly one-quarter of these accidents following the recommendation would not have improved passengers' safety
(C) does not indicate the criteria by which an accident is classified as "relatively minor"
(D) provides no information about the percentage of all small airplane flights during which the pilot whistles at some time during that flight
(E) fails to specify the percentage of all small airplane flights that involve relatively minor accidents

72. Physicist: The claim that low-temperature nuclear fusion can be achieved entirely by chemical means is based on chemical experiments in which the measurements and calculations are inaccurate.

Chemist: But your challenge is ineffectual, since you are simply jealous at the thought that chemists might have solved a problem that physicists have been unable to solve.

Which one of the following is the strongest criticism of the chemist's response to the physicist's challenge?

(A) It restates a claim in different words instead of offering evidence for this claim.
(B) It fails to establish that perfect accuracy of measurements and calculations is possible.
(C) It confuses two different meanings of the word "solve."
(D) It is directed against the proponent of a claim rather than against the claim itself.
(E) It rests on a contradiction.

73. Most people believe that yawning is most powerfully triggered by seeing someone else yawn. This belief about yawning is widespread not only today, but also has been commonplace in many parts of the world in the past, if we are to believe historians of popular culture. Thus, seeing someone else yawn must be the most irresistible cause of yawning.

The argument is most vulnerable to which one of the following criticisms?

(A) It attempts to support its conclusion solely by restating that conclusion in other words.
(B) It cites the evidence of historians of popular culture in direct support of a claim that lies outside their area of expertise.
(C) It makes a sweeping generalization about yawning based on evidence drawn from a limited number of atypical cases.
(D) It supports its conclusion by appealing solely to opinion in a matter that is largely factual.
(E) It takes for granted that yawns have no cause other than the one it cites.

74. Without information that could only have come from someone present at the secret meeting between the finance minister and the leader of the opposition party, the newspaper story that forced the finance minister to resign could not have been written. No one witnessed the meeting, however, except the minister's aide. It is clear, therefore, that the finance minister was ultimately brought down, not by any of his powerful political enemies, but by his own trusted aide.

The argument commits which one of the following errors of reasoning?

(A) drawing a conclusion on the basis of evidence that provides equally strong support for a competing conclusion
(B) assuming without warrant that if one thing cannot occur without another thing's already having occurred, then the earlier thing cannot occur without bringing about the later thing
(C) confusing evidence that a given outcome on one occasion was brought about in a certain way with evidence that the same outcome on a different occasion was brought about in that way
(D) basing its conclusion on evidence that is almost entirely irrelevant to the point at issue
(E) treating evidence that a given action contributed to bringing about a certain effect as though that evidence established that the given action by itself was sufficient to bring about that effect

75. S. R. Evans: A few critics have dismissed my poems as not being poems and have dismissed me as not being a poet. But one principle of criticism has it that only true poets can recognize poetic creativity or function as critics of poetry—and that the only true poets are those whose work conveys genuine poetic creativity. But I have read the work of these critics; none of it demonstrated poetic creativity. These critics' judgments should be rejected, since these critics are not true poets.

The argument above is vulnerable to criticism on the grounds that it

(A) presupposes what it sets out to conclude, since the principle requires that only true poets can determine whether the critics' work demonstrates poetic creativity
(B) uses the distinction between poets and critics as though everyone fell into one category or the other
(C) gives no justification for the implicit claim that the standing of a poet can be judged independently of his or her poetry
(D) makes an unjustifiable distinction, since it is possible that some critics are also poets
(E) inevitably leads to the conclusion that poets can never learn to improve their poetry, since no poet is in a position to criticize his or her own work

76. Those who support the continued reading and performance of Shakespeare's plays maintain that in England appreciation for his work has always extended beyond educated elites and that ever since Shakespeare's own time his plays have always been known and loved by comparatively uneducated people. Skepticism about this claim is borne out by examining early eighteenth-century editions of the plays. These books, with their fine paper and good bindings, must have been far beyond the reach of people of ordinary means.

Which one of the following describes a reasoning error in the argument?

(A) The argument uses the popularity of Shakespeare's plays as a measure of their literary quality.
(B) The argument bases an aesthetic conclusion about Shakespeare's plays on purely economic evidence.
(C) The argument anachronistically uses the standards of the twentieth century to judge events that occurred in the early eighteenth century.
(D) The argument judges the literary quality of a book's text on the basis of the quality of the volume in which the text is printed.
(E) The argument does not allow for the possibility that people might know Shakespeare's plays without having read them.

77. Although inflated government spending for weapons research encourages waste at weapons research laboratories, weapons production plants must be viewed as equally wasteful of taxpayer dollars. After all, by the government's own admission, the weapons plant it plans to reopen will violate at least 69 environmental, health, and safety laws. The government has decided to reopen the plant and exempt it from compliance, even though the weapons to be produced there could be produced at the same cost at a safer facility.

The reasoning in the argument is most vulnerable to criticism on which one of the following grounds?

(A) It offers no evidence that the "safer" alternative production site actually complies with any of the laws mentioned.
(B) It concedes a point regarding weapons research laboratories that undermines its conclusion about weapons production plants.
(C) It relies on evidence that does not directly address the issue of wasteful spending.
(D) It confuses necessary expenditures for research with wasteful spending on weapons.
(E) It fails to establish that research laboratories and weapons production plants are similar enough to be meaningfully compared.

78. Thomas: The club president had no right to disallow Jeffrey's vote. Club rules say that only members in good standing may vote. You've admitted that club rules also say that all members whose dues are fully paid are members in good standing. And since, as the records indicate, Jeffrey has always paid his dues on time, clearly the president acted in violation of club rules.

Althea: By that reasoning my two-year-old niece can legally vote in next month's national election since she is a citizen of this country, and only citizens can legally vote in national elections.

The reasoning in Thomas' argument is flawed because his argument

(A) fails to take into account the distinction between something not being prohibited and its being authorized
(B) offers evidence that casts doubt on the character of the club president and thereby ignores the question of voting eligibility
(C) wrongly assumes that if a statement is not actually denied by someone, that statement must be regarded as true
(D) does not specify the issue with respect to which the disputed vote was cast
(E) overlooks the possibility that Althea is not an authority on the club's rules

79. A fundamental illusion in robotics is the belief that improvements in robots will liberate humanity from "hazardous and demeaning work." Engineers are designing only those types of robots that can be properly maintained with the least expensive, least skilled human labor possible. Therefore, robots will not eliminate demeaning work—only substitute one type of demeaning work for another.

The reasoning in the argument is most vulnerable to the criticism that it

(A) ignores the consideration that in a competitive business environment some jobs might be eliminated if robots are not used in the manufacturing process
(B) assumes what it sets out to prove, that robots create demeaning work
(C) does not specify whether or not the engineers who design robots consider their work demeaning
(D) attempts to support its conclusion by an appeal to the emotion of fear, which is often experienced by people faced with the prospect of losing their jobs to robots
(E) fails to address the possibility that the amount of demeaning work eliminated by robots might be significantly greater than the amount they create

80. Director of personnel: Ms. Tours has formally requested a salary adjustment on the grounds that she was denied merit raises to which she was entitled. Since such grounds provide a possible basis for adjustments, an official response is required. Ms. Tours presents compelling evidence that her job performance has been both excellent in itself and markedly superior to that of others in her department who were awarded merit raises. Her complaint that she was treated unfairly thus appears justified. Nevertheless, her request should be denied. To raise Ms. Tours's salary because of her complaint would jeopardize the integrity of the firm's merit-based reward system by sending the message that employees can get their salaries raised if they just complain enough.

The personnel director's reasoning is most vulnerable to criticism on the grounds that it

(A) fails to consider the possibility that Ms. Tours's complaint could be handled on an unofficial basis
(B) attempts to undermine the persuasiveness of Ms. Tours's evidence by characterizing it as "mere complaining"
(C) sidesteps the issue of whether superior job performance is a suitable basis for awarding salary increases
(D) ignores the possibility that some of the people who did receive merit increases were not entitled to them
(E) overlooks the implications for the integrity of the firm's merit-based reward system of denying Ms. Tour' s request

81. The role of the Uplandian supreme court is to protect all human rights against abuses of government power. Since the constitution of Uplandia is not explicit about all human rights, the supreme court must sometimes resort to principles outside the explicit provisions of the constitution in justifying its decisions. However, human rights will be subject to the whim of whoever holds judicial power unless the supreme court is bound to adhere to a single objective standard, namely, the constitution. Therefore, nothing but the explicit provisions of the constitution can be used to justify the court's decisions. Since these conclusions are inconsistent with each other, it cannot be true that the role of the Uplandian supreme court is to protect all human rights against abuses of government power.

The reasoning that leads to the conclusion that the first sentence in the passage is false is flawed because the argument

(A) ignores data that offer reasonable support for a general claim and focuses on a single example that argues against that claim
(B) seeks to defend a view on the grounds that the view is widely held and that decisions based on that view are often accepted as correct
(C) rejects a claim as false on the grounds that those who make that claim could profit if that claim is accepted by others
(D) makes an unwarranted assumption that what is true of each member of a group taken separately is also true of the group as a whole
(E) concludes that a particular premise is false when it is equally possible for that premise to be true and some other premise false

82. Despite the best efforts of astronomers, no one has yet succeeded in exchanging messages with intelligent life on other planets or in other solar systems. In fact, no one has even managed to prove that any kind of extraterrestrial life exists. Thus, there is clearly no intelligent life anywhere but on Earth.

The argument's reasoning is flawed because the argument

(A) fails to consider that there might be extraterrestrial forms of intelligence that are not living beings
(B) confuses an absence of evidence for a hypothesis with the existence of evidence against the hypothesis
(C) interprets a disagreement over a scientific theory as a disproof of that theory
(D) makes an inference that relies on the vagueness of the term "life"
(E) relies on a weak analogy rather than on evidence to draw a conclusion

83. Theater critic: The theater is in a dismal state. Audiences are sparse and revenue is down. Without the audience and the revenue, the talented and creative people who are the lifeblood of the theater are abandoning it. No wonder standards are deteriorating.

Producer: It's not true that the theater is in decline. Don't you realize that your comments constitute a self-fulfilling prophecy? By publishing these opinions, you yourself are discouraging new audiences from emerging and new talent from joining the theater.

Which one of the following is a questionable technique employed by the producer in responding to the critic?

(A) focusing on the effects of the critic's evaluation rather than on its content
(B) accusing the critic of relying solely on opinion unsupported by factual evidence
(C) challenging the motives behind the critic's remarks rather than the remarks themselves
(D) relying on emphasis rather than on argument
(E) invoking authority in order to intimidate the critic

84. A controversial program rewards prison inmates who behave particularly well in prison by giving them the chance to receive free cosmetic plastic surgery performed by medical students. The program is obviously morally questionable, both in its assumptions about what inmates might want and in its use of the prison population to train future surgeons. Putting these moral issues aside, however, the surgery clearly has a powerful rehabilitative effect, as is shown by the fact that, among recipients of the surgery, the proportion who are convicted of new crimes committed after release is only half that for the prison population as a whole.

A flaw in the reasoning of the passage is that it

(A) allows moral issues to be a consideration in presenting evidence about matters of fact
(B) dismisses moral considerations on the grounds that only matters of fact are relevant
(C) labels the program as "controversial" instead of discussing the issues that give rise to controversy
(D) asserts that the rehabilitation of criminals is not a moral issue
(E) relies on evidence drawn from a sample that there is reason to believe is unrepresentative

85. A birth is more likely to be difficult when the mother is over the age of 40 than when she is younger. Regardless of the mother's age, a person whose birth was difficult is more likely to be ambidextrous than is a person whose birth was not difficult. Since other causes of ambidexterity are not related to the mother's age, there must be more ambidextrous people who were born to women over 40 than there are ambidextrous people who were born to younger women.

The argument is most vulnerable to which one of the following criticisms?

(A) It assumes what it sets out to establish.
(B) It overlooks the possibility that fewer children are born to women over 40 than to women under 40.
(C) It fails to specify what percentage of people in the population as a whole are ambidextrous.
(D) It does not state how old a child must be before its handedness can be determined.
(E) It neglects to explain how difficulties during birth can result in a child's ambidexterity.

86. The government has no right to tax earnings from labor. Taxation of this kind requires the laborer to devote a certain percentage of hours worked to earning money for the government. Thus, such taxation forces the laborer to work, in part, for another's purpose. Since involuntary servitude can be defined as forced work for another's purpose, just as involuntary servitude is pernicious, so is taxing earnings from labor.

Which one of the following is an error of reasoning committed by the argument?

(A) It ignores a difference in how the idea of forced work for another's purpose applies to the two cases.
(B) It does not take into account the fact that labor is taxed at different rates depending on income.
(C) It mistakenly assumes that all work is taxed.
(D) It ignores the fact that the government also taxes income from investment.
(E) It treats definitions as if they were matters of subjective opinion rather than objective facts about language.

87. Many people do not understand themselves, nor do they try to gain self-understanding. These people might try to understand others, but these attempts are sure to fail, because without self-understanding it is impossible to understand others. It is clear from this that anyone who lacks self-understanding will be incapable of understanding others.

The reasoning in the argument is flawed because the argument

(A) mistakes something that is necessary to bring about a situation for something that in itself is enough to bring about that situation
(B) fails to take into account the possibility that not everyone wants to gain a thorough understanding of himself or herself
(C) blames people for something for which they cannot legitimately be held responsible
(D) makes use of the inherently vague term "self-understanding" without defining that term
(E) draws a conclusion that simply restates a claim given in support of that conclusion

88. Questions have arisen regarding the accuracy of the reports the university's archaeological museum issues on its sales and acquisitions for the year. To forestall controversy, this year's report is being reviewed by three archaeologists from other universities. Since these archaeologists will be given full access to all documents on which the report is based, they will be able to determine whether it is indeed accurate.

The reasoning in the argument is flawed because the argument

(A) does not specify whether the reviewers will have access to data about objects that have been in the museum's collection for many years
(B) provides no information regarding the size or quality of the archaeological museum's collection
(C) omits any mention of whether the museum's collection is on display or is available only to researchers
(D) ignores the possibility that there might have been some sales or acquisitions during the past year that were not mentioned in the documents on which the report was based
(E) does not describe what will occur if the reviewers discover discrepancies between the report and the documents on which it was based

89. Politician: Critics of the wetlands-protection bill are delaying passage of this important legislation merely on the grounds that they disagree with its new, more restrictive definition of the term "wetlands." But this bill will place stricter limits on the development of wetlands than the existing regulations do. Therefore, in quibbling over semantics, critics of this bill show that they care little about what really happens to our wetlands.

The politician's reply to the opponents of the wetlands-protection bill is most vulnerable to which one of the following criticisms?

(A) It falsely identifies the motives of those who have criticized the wetlands-protection bill with the motives of all those who are opposed to conservation.
(B) It does not adequately recognize the possibility that the definition of the word "wetlands" determines the impact of the legislation.
(C) It assumes without justification that those who criticized the wetlands-protection bill stand to profit if the bill is defeated.
(D) It fails to provide a defense for a less restrictive definition of "wetlands."
(E) It attempts to defend the credibility of the author of the bill rather than defending the bill itself.

90. Novice bird-watcher: I don't know much about animal tracks, but I do know that birds typically have four toes, and most birds have three toes pointing forward and one toe pointing backward. Since this track was made by an animal with four toes, of which three point forward and one points backward, we can conclude it was made by some kind of bird.

The argument is flawed because it

(A) relies on the vagueness of the term "track"
(B) does not define birds as animals with four toes
(C) fails to identify what kind of bird might have made the track
(D) does not establish that only a bird could have made the track
(E) depends on evidence about an individual bird rather than about birds in general

91. Each of the elements of Girelli's recently completed design for a university library is copied from a different one of several historic libraries. The design includes various features from Classical Greek, Islamic, Mogul, and Romanesque structures. Since no one element in the design is original, it follows that the design of the library cannot be considered original.

Which one of the following is a reasoning error made in the argument?

(A) assuming that because something is true of each of the parts of a whole it is true of the whole itself
(B) generalizing illegitimately from a few instances of a certain kind to all instances of that kind
(C) concluding that an unknown instance of a phenomenon must have all the properties of the known instances
(D) presupposing that alternatives that can be true separately cannot be true together
(E) deriving a factual conclusion from evidence derived from reports of aesthetic preferences

92. Morton: In order to succeed in today's society, one must have a college degree. Skeptics have objected that there are many people who never completed any education beyond high school but who are nevertheless quite successful. This success is only apparent, however, because without a college degree a person does not have enough education to be truly successful.

Morton's argument is flawed because it

(A) assumes what it sets out to conclude
(B) mistakes a correlation for a cause
(C) draws a highly general conclusion from evidence about individual cases
(D) fails to consider the status of alleged counterexamples
(E) bases its conclusion on the supposition that most people believe in that conclusion

93. On Saturday Melvin suggested that Jerome take the following week off from work and accompany him on a trip to the mountains. Jerome refused, claiming that he could not afford the cost of the trip added to the wages he would forfeit by taking off without notice. It is clear, however, that cost cannot be the real reason for Jerome's unwillingness to go with Melvin to the mountains, since he makes the same excuse every time Melvin asks him to take an unscheduled vacation regardless of where Melvin proposes to go.

The reasoning is most vulnerable to which one of the following criticisms?

(A) It attempts to forestall an attack on Melvin's behavior by focusing attention on the behavior of Jerome.
(B) It fails to establish that Melvin could no more afford to take an unscheduled vacation trip to the mountains than could Jerome.
(C) It overlooks the possibility that Jerome, unlike Melvin, prefers vacations that have been planned far in advance.
(D) It assumes that if Jerome's professed reason is not his only reason, then it cannot be a real reason for Jerome at all.
(E) It does not examine the possibility that Jerome's behavior is adequately explained by the reason he gives for it.

FLAW

94. Marianna: The problem of drunk driving has been somewhat ameliorated by public education and stricter laws. Additional measures are nevertheless needed. People still drive after drinking, and when they do the probability is greatly increased that they will cause an accident involving death or serious injury.

David: I think you exaggerate the dangers of driving while drunk. Actually, a driver who is in an automobile accident is slightly less likely to be seriously injured if drunk than if sober.

In responding to Marianna's argument, David makes which one of the following errors of reasoning?

(A) He contradicts himself.
(B) He assumes what he is seeking to establish.
(C) He contradicts Marianna's conclusion without giving any evidence for his point of view.
(D) He argues against a point that is not one that Marianna was making.
(E) He directs his criticism against the person making the argument rather than directing it against the argument itself.

95. Civil libertarian: The categorical prohibition of any nonviolent means of expression inevitably poisons a society's intellectual atmosphere. Therefore, those advocating censorship of all potentially offensive art are pursuing a course that is harmful to society.

Censorship advocate: You're wrong, because many people are in agreement about what constitutes potentially offensive art.

The censorship advocate's rebuttal is flawed because it

(A) attempts to extract a general rule from a specific case
(B) extracts an erroneous principle from a commonly held belief
(C) attacks the civil libertarian's character instead of the argument
(D) relies on an irrelevant reason for rejecting the civil libertarian's argument
(E) uses hyperbolic, inflammatory language that obscures the issue at hand

96. Dr. Kim: Electronic fetal monitors, now routinely used in hospital delivery rooms to check fetal heartbeat, are more intrusive than ordinary stethoscopes and do no more to improve the chances that a healthy baby will be born. Therefore, the additional cost of electronic monitoring is unjustified and such monitoring should be discontinued.

Dr. Anders: I disagree. Although you and I know that both methods are capable of providing the same information, electronic monitoring has been well worth the cost. Doctors now know the warning signs they need to listen for with stethoscopes, but only because of what was learned from using electronic monitors.

As a reply to Dr. Kim's argument, Dr. Anders' response is inadequate because it

(A) misses the point at issue
(B) assumes what it sets out to prove
(C) confuses high cost with high quality
(D) overestimates the importance of technology to modern medicine
(E) overlooks the fact that a procedure can be extensively used without being the best procedure available

97. George: A well-known educator claims that children who are read to when they are very young are more likely to enjoy reading when they grow up than are children who were not read to. But this claim is clearly false. My cousin Emory was regularly read to as a child and as an adult he seldom reads for pleasure, whereas no one read to me and reading is now my favorite form of relaxation.

Ursula: You and Emory prove nothing in this case. Your experience is enough to refute the claim that all avid adult readers were read to as children, but what the educator said about reading to children is not that sort of claim.

Which one of the following describes a flaw in George's reasoning?

(A) He treats his own experience and the experiences of other members of his own family as though they have more weight as evidence than do the experiences of other people.
(B) He does not distinguish between the quality and the quantity of the books that adults read to Emory when Emory was a child.
(C) He overlooks the well-known fact that not all reading is equally relaxing.
(D) He fails to establish that the claim made by this particular educator accurately reflects the position held by the majority of educators.
(E) He attempts to refute a general claim by reference to nonconforming cases, although the claim is consistent with the occurrence of such cases.

98. Director of Ace Manufacturing Company: Our management consultant proposes that we reassign staff so that all employees are doing both what they like to do and what they do well. This, she says, will "increase productivity by fully exploiting our available resources." But Ace Manufacturing has a long-standing commitment not to exploit its workers. Therefore, implementing her recommendations would cause us to violate our own policy.

The director's argument for rejecting the management consultant's proposal is most vulnerable to criticism on which one of the following grounds?

(A) failing to distinguish two distinct senses of a key term
(B) attempting to defend an action on the ground that it is frequently carried out
(C) defining a term by pointing to an atypical example of something to which the term applies
(D) drawing a conclusion that simply restates one of the premises of the argument
(E) calling something by a less offensive term than the term that is usually used to name that thing

99. Herbalist: Many of my customers find that their physical coordination improves after drinking juice containing certain herbs. A few doctors assert that the herbs are potentially harmful, but doctors are always trying to maintain a monopoly over medical therapies. So there is no reason not to try my herb juice.

The reasoning in the herbalist's argument is flawed because the argument

(A) attempts to force acceptance of a claim by inducing fear of the consequences of rejecting that claim
(B) bases a conclusion on claims that are inconsistent with each other
(C) rejects a claim by attacking the proponents of the claim rather than addressing the claim itself
(D) relies on evidence presented in terms that presuppose the truth of the claim for which the evidence is offered
(E) mistakes the observation that one thing happens after another for proof that the second thing is the result of the first

100. A museum director, in order to finance expensive new acquisitions, discreetly sold some paintings by major artists. All of them were paintings that the director privately considered inferior. Critics roundly condemned the sale, charging that the museum had lost first-rate pieces, thereby violating its duty as a trustee of art for future generations. A few months after being sold by the museum, those paintings were resold, in an otherwise stagnant art market, at two to three times the price paid to the museum. Clearly, these prices settle the issue, since they demonstrate the correctness of the critics' evaluation.

The reasoning in the argument is vulnerable to the criticism that the argument does which one of the following?

(A) It concludes that a certain opinion is correct on the grounds that it is held by more people than hold the opposing view.
(B) It rejects the judgment of the experts in an area in which there is no better guide to the truth than expert judgment.
(C) It rejects a proven means of accomplishing an objective without offering any alternative means of accomplishing that objective.
(D) It bases a firm conclusion about a state of affairs in the present on somewhat speculative claims about a future state of affairs.
(E) It bases its conclusion on facts that could, in the given situation, have resulted from causes other than those presupposed by the argument.

101. Three-year-old Sara and her playmate Michael are both ill and have the same symptoms. Since they play together every afternoon, Sara probably has the same illness as Michael does. Since Michael definitely does not have a streptococcal infection, despite his having some symptoms of one, the illness that Sara has is definitely not a streptococcal infection either.

The reasoning in the argument is flawed because the argument

(A) presupposes what it sets out to prove
(B) mistakes the cause of a particular phenomenon for the effect of that phenomenon
(C) fails to distinguish between acute streptococcal infections on the one hand, and less severe streptococcal infections on the other
(D) treats evidence that the conclusion is probably true as if that evidence establishes the certainty of the conclusion
(E) makes a general claim based on particular examples that do not adequately represent the respective groups that they are each intended to represent

102. The number of calories in a gram of refined cane sugar is the same as in an equal amount of fructose, the natural sugar found in fruits and vegetables. Therefore, a piece of candy made with a given amount of refined cane sugar is no higher in calories than a piece of fruit that contains an equal amount of fructose.

The reasoning in the argument is flawed because the argument

(A) fails to consider the possibility that fruit might contain noncaloric nutrients that candy does not contain
(B) presupposes that all candy is made with similar amounts of sugar
(C) confuses one kind of sugar with another
(D) presupposes what it sets out to establish, that fruit does not differ from sugar-based candy in the number of calories each contains
(E) overlooks the possibility that sugar might not be the only calorie-containing ingredient in candy or fruit

103. Yolanda: Gaining access to computers without authorization and manipulating the data and programs they contain is comparable to joyriding in stolen cars; both involve breaking into private property and treating it recklessly. Joyriding however, is the more dangerous crime because it physically endangers people, whereas only intellectual property is harmed in the case of computer crimes.

Arjun: I disagree! For example, unauthorized use of medical records systems in hospitals could damage data systems on which human lives depend, and therefore computer crimes also cause physical harm to people.

The reasoning in Arjun's response is flawed because he

(A) fails to maintain a distinction made in Yolanda's argument
(B) denies Yolanda's conclusion without providing evidence against it
(C) relies on the actuality of a phenomenon that he has only shown to be possible
(D) mistakes something that leads to his conclusion for something that is necessary for his conclusion
(E) uses as evidence a phenomenon that is inconsistent with his own conclusion

104. A report of a government survey concluded that Center City was among the ten cities in the nation with the highest dropout rate from its schools. The survey data were obtained by asking all city residents over the age of 19 whether they were high school graduates and computing the proportion who were not. A city school official objected that the result did not seem accurate according to the schools' figures.

The school official can most properly criticize the reasoning by which the survey report reached its result for failure to do which one of the following?

(A) take into account instances of respondents' dropping out that occurred before the respondents reached high school
(B) ask residents whether they had completed their high school work in fewer than the usual number of years
(C) distinguish between residents who had attended the city's schools and those who had received their schooling elsewhere
(D) predict the effect of the information contained in the report on future high school dropout rates for the city
(E) consider whether a diploma from the city's high schools signaled the same level of achievement over time

105. To hold criminals responsible for their crimes involves a failure to recognize that criminal actions, like all actions, are ultimately products of the environment that forged the agent's character. It is not criminals but people in the law-abiding majority who by their actions do most to create and maintain this environment. Therefore, it is law-abiding people whose actions, and nothing else, make them alone truly responsible for crime.

The reasoning in the argument is most vulnerable to criticism on the grounds that

(A) it exploits an ambiguity in the term "environment" by treating two different meanings of the word as though they were equivalent
(B) it fails to distinguish between actions that are socially acceptable and actions that are socially unacceptable
(C) the way it distinguishes criminals from crimes implicitly denies that someone becomes a criminal solely in virtue of having committed a crime
(D) its conclusion is a generalization of statistical evidence drawn from only a small minority of the population
(E) its conclusion contradicts an implicit principle on which an earlier part of the argument is based

106. The law firm of Sutherlin, Pérez, and Associates is one of the most successful law firms whose primary specialization is in criminal defense cases. In fact, the firm has a better than 90 percent acquittal rate in such cases. Dalton is an attorney whose primary specialization is in divorce cases, so Dalton certainly cannot be a member of Sutherlin, Pérez, and Associates.

The reasoning in the argument is flawed because the argument

(A) offers in support of its conclusion pieces of evidence that are mutually contradictory
(B) overlooks the possibility that a person can practice law without being a member of a law firm
(C) concludes that someone is not a member of a group on the grounds that that person does not have a characteristic that the group as a whole has
(D) takes a high rate of success among the members of a group to indicate that the successes are evenly spread among the members
(E) states a generalization based on a selection that is not representative of the group about which the generalization is supposed to hold true

107. Dobson: Some historians claim that the people who built a ring of stones thousands of years ago in Britain were knowledgeable about celestial events. The ground for this claim is that two of the stones determine a line pointing directly to the position of the sun at sunrise at the spring equinox. There are many stones in the ring, however, so the chance that one pair will point in a celestially significant direction is large. Therefore, the people who built the ring were not knowledgeable about celestial events.

Which one of the following is an error of reasoning in Dobson's argument?

(A) The failure of cited evidence to establish a statement is taken as evidence that that statement is false.
(B) Dobson's conclusion logically contradicts some of the evidence presented in support of it.
(C) Statements that absolutely establish Dobson's conclusion are treated as if they merely give some support to that conclusion.
(D) Something that is merely a matter of opinion is treated as if it were subject to verification as a matter of fact.
(E) Dobson's drawing the conclusion relies on interpreting a key term in two different ways.

FLAW

Chapter Eleven: Parallel Reasoning Questions

Please Note: In this chapter, Parallel Reasoning and Parallel Flaw questions are commingled.

1. The formation of hurricanes that threaten the United States mainland is triggered by high atmospheric winds off the western coast of Africa. When abundant rain falls in sub-Saharan Africa, hurricanes afterward hit the United States mainland with particular frequency. Therefore, the abundant rains must somehow promote the ability of the winds to form hurricanes.

Which one of the following arguments contains a flaw that is most similar to one in the argument above?

(A) People who exercise vigorously tend to sleep well. Therefore, people who exercise vigorously tend to be healthy.
(B) Cars drive faster on long city blocks than on short city blocks. Long blocks are thus more dangerous for pedestrians than short blocks.
(C) Many people who later become successful entrepreneurs played competitive sports in college. Therefore, playing competitive sports must enhance a person's entrepreneurial ability.
(D) The blossoms of the chicory plant close up in full sun. Therefore, the chicory plant's blossoms must open up in the dark.
(E) Events in Eastern Europe can affect the political mood in Central America. Therefore, liberalization in Eastern Europe will lead to liberalization in Central America.

2. Some people believe that witnessing violence in movies will discharge aggressive energy. Does watching someone else eat fill one's own stomach?

In which one of the following does the reasoning most closely parallel that employed in the passage?

(A) Some people think appropriating supplies at work for their own personal use is morally wrong. Isn't shoplifting morally wrong?
(B) Some people think nationalism is defensible. Hasn't nationalism been the excuse for committing abominable crimes?
(C) Some people think that boxing is fixed just because wrestling usually is. Are the two sports managed by the same sort of people?
(D) Some people think that economists can control inflation. Can meteorologists make the sun shine?
(E) Some people think workaholics are compensating for a lack of interpersonal skills. However, aren't most doctors workaholics?

3. A well-known sports figure found that combining publicity tours with playing tours led to problems, so she stopped combining the two. She no longer allows bookstore appearances and playing in competition to occur in the same city within the same trip. This week she is traveling to London to play in a major competition, so during her stay in London she will not be making any publicity appearances at any bookstore in London.

Which one of the following most closely parallels the reasoning used in the passage?

(A) Wherever there is an Acme Bugkiller, many wasps are killed. The Z family garden has an Acme Bugkiller, so any wasps remaining in the garden will soon be killed.
(B) The only times that the hospital's emergency room staff attends to relatively less serious emergencies are times when there is no critical emergency to attend to. On Monday night the emergency room staff attended to a series of fairly minor emergencies, so there must not have been any critical emergencies to take care of at the time.
(C) Tomato plants require hot summers to thrive. Farms in the cool summers of country Y probably do not have thriving tomato plants.
(D) Higher grades lead to better job opportunities, and studying leads to higher grades. Therefore, studying will lead to better job opportunities.
(E) Butter knives are not sharp. Q was not murdered with a sharp blade, so suspect X's butter knife may have been the murder weapon.

PARALLEL

4. Pamela: Business has an interest in enabling employees to care for children, because those children will be the customers, employees, and managers of the future. Therefore, businesses should adopt policies, such as day-care benefits, that facilitate parenting.

Lee: No individual company, though, will be patronized, staffed, and managed only by its own employees' children, so it would not be to a company's advantage to provide such benefits to employees when other companies do not.

In which one of the following pairs consisting of argument and objection does the objection function most similarly to the way Lee's objection functions in relation to Pamela's argument?

(A) New roads will not serve to relieve this area's traffic congestion, because new roads would encourage new construction and generate additional traffic.
Objection: Failure to build new roads would mean that traffic congestion would strangle the area even earlier.

(B) Humanity needs clean air to breathe, so each person should make an effort to avoid polluting the air.
Objection: The air one person breathes is affected mainly by pollution caused by others, so it makes no sense to act alone to curb air pollution.

(C) Advertised discounts on products draw customers' attention to the products, so advertised discounts benefit sales.
Objection: Customers already planning to purchase a product accelerate buying to take advantage of advertised discounts, and thus subsequent sales suffer.

(D) If people always told lies, then no one would know what the truth was, so people should always tell the truth.
Objection: If people always told lies, then everyone would know that the truth was the opposite of what was said.

(E) Human social institutions have always changed, so even if we do not know what those changes will be, we do know that the social institutions of the future will differ from those of the past.
Objection: The existence of change in the past does not ensure that there will always be change in the future.

5. People who take what others regard as a ridiculous position should not bother to say, "I mean every word!" For either their position truly is ridiculous, in which case insisting that they are serious about it only exposes them to deeper embarrassment, or else their position has merit, in which case they should meet disbelief with rational argument rather than with assurances of their sincerity.

Which one of the following arguments is most similar in its reasoning to the argument above?

(A) A practice that has been denounced as a poor practice should not be defended on the grounds that "this is how we have always done it." If the practice is a poor one, so much the worse that it has been extensively used; if it is not a poor one, there must be a better reason for engaging in it than inertia.

(B) People who are asked why they eat some of the unusual foods they eat should not answer, "because that is what I like." This sort of answer will sound either naive or evasive and thus will satisfy no one.

(C) People whose taste in clothes is being criticized should not reply, "Every penny I spent on these clothes I earned honestly." For the issue raised by the critics is not how the money was come by but rather whether it was spent wisely.

(D) Scholars who champion unpopular new theories should not assume that the widespread rejection of their ideas shows that they "must be on the right track." The truth is that few theories of any consequence are either wholly right or wholly wrong and thus there is no substitute for patient work in ascertaining which parts are right.

(E) People who set themselves goals that others denounce as overly ambitious do little to silence their critics if they say, "I can accomplish this if anyone can." Rather, those people should either admit that their critics are right or not dignify the criticism with any reply.

6. Experienced gardeners advise against planting snap peas after late April because peas do not develop properly in warm weather. This year, however, the weather was unusually cool into late June, and therefore the fact that these snap peas were planted in mid-May is unlikely to result in crop failure despite the experts' warnings.

   The pattern of reasoning displayed above is most closely paralleled in which one of the following?

   (A) According to many gardening authorities, tomatoes should not be planted near dill because doing so is likely to affect their taste adversely; however, since these tomatoes were grown near dill and taste fine, there is clearly no reason to pay much attention to the so-called experts' advice.
   (B) Since African violets do not thrive in direct sunlight, it is said that in this region these plants should be placed in windows facing north rather than south; however, since these south-facing windows are well shaded by evergreen trees, the African violets placed in them are likely to grow satisfactorily.
   (C) Where flowers are to be planted under shade trees, gardening experts often advise using impatiens since impatiens does well in conditions of shade; however, it is unlikely to do well under maple trees since maple tree roots are so near the surface that they absorb all available moisture.
   (D) Most seeds tend to germinate at much higher rates when planted in warm soil than when planted in cold soil; spinach seeds, however, are unlikely to germinate properly if the soil is too warm, and therefore experts advise that spinach should be planted earlier than most vegetables.
   (E) House plants generally grow best in pots slightly larger than their existing root systems, so the usual advice is to repot when roots first reach the sides of the pot; this rule should not be followed with amaryllis plants, however, because they are likely to do best with tightly compressed roots.

7. The Scorpio Miser with its special high-efficiency engine costs more to buy than the standard Scorpio sports car. At current fuel prices, a buyer choosing the Miser would have to drive it 60,000 miles to make up the difference in purchase price through savings on fuel. It follows that, if fuel prices fell, it would take fewer miles to reach the break-even point.

   Which one of the following arguments contains an error of reasoning similar to that in the argument above?

   (A) The true annual rate of earnings on an interest-bearing account is the annual rate of interest less the annual rate of inflation. Consequently, if the rate of inflation drops, the rate of interest can be reduced by an equal amount without there being a change in the true rate of earnings.
   (B) For retail food stores, the Polar freezer, unlike the Arctic freezer, provides a consistent temperature that allows the store to carry premium frozen foods. Though the Polar freezer uses more electricity, there is a bigger profit on premium foods. Thus, if electricity rates fell, a lower volume of premium-food sales could justify choosing the Polar freezer.
   (C) With the Roadmaker, a crew can repave a mile of decayed road in less time than with the competing model, which is, however, much less expensive. Reduced staffing levels made possible by the Roadmaker eventually compensate for its higher price. Therefore, the Roadmaker is especially advantageous where average wages are low.
   (D) The improved strain of the Northland apple tree bears fruit younger and lives longer than the standard strain. The standard strain does grow larger at maturity, but to allow for this, standard trees must be spaced farther apart. Therefore, new plantings should all be of the improved strain.
   (E) Stocks pay dividends, which vary from year to year depending on profits made. Bonds pay interest, which remains constant from year to year. Therefore, since the interest earned on bonds does not decrease when economic conditions decline, investors interested in a reliable income should choose bonds.

PARALLEL

8. Situation: In the island nation of Bezun, the government taxes gasoline heavily in order to induce people not to drive. It uses the revenue from the gasoline tax to subsidize electricity in order to reduce prices charged for electricity.

Analysis: The greater the success achieved in meeting the first of these objectives, the less will be the success achieved in meeting the second.

The analysis provided for the situation above would be most appropriate in which one of the following situations?

(A) A library charges a late fee in order to induce borrowers to return books promptly. The library uses revenue from the late fee to send reminders to tardy borrowers in order to reduce the incidence of overdue books.

(B) A mail-order store imposes a stiff surcharge for overnight delivery in order to limit use of this option. The store uses revenue from the surcharge to pay the extra expenses it incurs for providing the overnight delivery service.

(C) The park management charges an admission fee so that a park's users will contribute to the park's upkeep. In order to keep admission fees low, the management does not finance any new projects from them.

(D) A restaurant adds a service charge in order to spare customers the trouble of individual tips. The service charge is then shared among the restaurant's workers in order to augment their low hourly wages.

(E) The highway administration charges a toll for crossing a bridge in order to get motorists to use other routes. It uses the revenue from that toll to generate a reserve fund in order to be able one day to build a new bridge.

9. The museum's night security guard maintains that the thieves who stole the portrait did not enter the museum at any point at or above ground level. Therefore, the thieves must have gained access to the museum from below ground level.

The flawed pattern of reasoning in the argument above is most similar to that in which one of the following?

(A) The rules stipulate the participants in the contest be judged on both form and accuracy. The eventual winner was judged highest in neither category, so there must be a third criterion that judges were free to invoke.

(B) The store's competitors claim that the store, in selling off the shirts at those prices, neither made any profit nor broke even. Consequently, the store's customers must have been able to buy shirts there at less than the store's cost.

(C) If the census is to be believed, the percentage of men who are married is higher than the percentage of women who are married. Thus, the census must show a higher number of men than of women overall.

(D) The product label establishes that this insecticide is safe for both humans and pets. Therefore, the insecticide must also be safe for such wild mammals as deer and rabbits.

(E) As had generally been expected, not all questionnaires were sent in by the official deadline. It follows that plans must have been made for the processing of questionnaires received late.

10. Certain governments subsidize certain basic agricultural products in order to guarantee an adequate domestic production of them. But subsidies encourage more intensive farming, which eventually leads to soil exhaustion and drastically reduced yields.

The situation above is most nearly similar to which one of the following situations with respect to the relationship between the declared intent of a governmental practice and a circumstance relevant to it?

(A) Certain governments subsidize theaters in order to attract foreign tourists. But tourists rarely choose a destination for the theatrical performances it has to offer.
(B) Certain governments restrict imports in order to keep domestic producers in business. But, since domestic producers do not have to face the full force of foreign competition, some domestic producers are able to earn inordinately high profits.
(C) Certain governments build strong armed forces in order to forestall armed conflict. But in order to maintain the sort of discipline and morale that keeps armed forces strong, those forces must be used in actual combat periodically.
(D) Certain governments reduce taxes on businesses in order to stimulate private investment. But any investment is to some extent a gamble, and new business ventures are not always as successful as their owners hoped.
(E) Certain governments pass traffic laws in order to make travel safer. But the population-driven growth in volumes of traffic often has the effect of making travel less safe despite the passage of new traffic laws.

11. According to sources who can be expected to know, Dr. Maria Esposito is going to run in the mayoral election. But if Dr. Esposito runs, Jerome Krasman will certainly not run against her. Therefore Dr. Esposito will be the only candidate in the election.

The flawed reasoning in the argument above most closely parallels that in which one of the following?

(A) According to its management, Brown's Stores will move next year. Without Brown's being present, no new large store can be attracted to the downtown area. Therefore the downtown area will no longer be viable as a shopping district.
(B) The press release says that the rock group Rollercoaster is playing a concert on Saturday. It won't be playing on Friday if it plays on Saturday. So Saturday will be the only day this week on which Rollercoaster will perform.
(C) Joshua says the interviewing panel was impressed by Marilyn. But if they were impressed by Marilyn, they probably thought less of Sven. Joshua is probably right, and so Sven will probably not get the job.
(D) An informant says that Rustimann was involved in the bank robbery. If Rustimann was involved, Jones was certainly not involved. Since these two are the only people who could have been involved, Rustimann is the only person the police need to arrest.
(E) The review said that this book is the best one for beginners at programming. If this book is the best, that other one can't be as good. So this one is the book we should buy.

PARALLEL

12. Advertisement: HomeGlo Paints, Inc., has won the prestigious Golden Paintbrush Award—given to the one paint manufacturer in the country that has increased the environmental safety of its product most over the past three years—for HomeGlo Exterior Enamel. The Golden Paintbrush is awarded only on the basis of thorough tests by independent testing laboratories. So when you choose HomeGlo Exterior Enamel, you will know that you have chosen the most environmentally safe brand of paint manufactured in this country today.

The flawed reasoning in the advertisement most closely parallels that in which one of the following?

(A) The ZXC audio system received the overall top ranking for looks, performance, durability, and value in *Listeners Report* magazine's ratings of currently produced systems. Therefore, the ZXC must have better sound quality than any other currently produced sound system.

(B) Morning Sunshine breakfast cereal contains, ounce for ounce, more of the nutrients needed for a healthy diet than any other breakfast cereal on the market today. Thus, when you eat Morning Sunshine, you will know you are eating the most nutritious food now on the market.

(C) The number of consumer visits increased more at Countryside Market last year than at any other market in the region. Therefore, Countryside's profits must also have increased more last year than those of any other market in the region.

(D) Jerrold's teachers recognize him as the student who has shown more academic improvement than any other student in the junior class this year. Therefore, if Jerrold and his classmates are ranked according to their current academic performance, Jerrold must hold the highest ranking.

(E) Margaret Durring's short story "The Power Lunch" won three separate awards for best short fiction of the year. Therefore, any of Margaret Durring's earlier stories certainly has enough literary merit to be included in an anthology of the best recent short fiction.

13. Because migrant workers are typically not hired by any one employer for longer than a single season, migrant workers can legally be paid less than the minimum hourly wage that the government requires employers to pay all their permanent employees. Yet most migrant workers work long hours each day for eleven or twelve months a year and thus are as much full-time workers as are people hired on a year-round basis. Therefore, the law should require that migrant workers be paid the same minimum hourly wage that other full-time workers must be paid.

The pattern of reasoning displayed above most closely parallels that displayed in which one of the following arguments?

(A) Because day-care facilities are now regulated at the local level, the quality of care available to children in two different cities can differ widely. Since such differences in treatment clearly are unfair, day care should be federally rather than locally regulated.

(B) Because many rural areas have few restrictions on development, housing estates in such areas have been built where no adequate supply of safe drinking water could be ensured. Thus, rural areas should adopt building codes more like those large cities have.

(C) Because some countries regulate gun sales more strictly than do other countries, some people can readily purchase a gun, whereas others cannot. Therefore, all countries should cooperate in developing a uniform international policy regarding gun sales.

(D) Because it is a democratic principle that laws should have the consent of those affected by them, liquor laws should be formulated not by politicians but by club and restaurant owners, since such laws directly affect the profitability of their businesses.

(E) Because food additives are not considered drugs, they have not had to meet the safety standards the government applies to drugs. But food additives can be as dangerous as drugs. Therefore, food additives should also be subject to safety regulations as stringent as those covering drugs.

14. Genevieve: Increasing costs have led commercial airlines to cut back on airplane maintenance. Also, reductions in public spending have led to air traffic control centers being underfunded and understaffed. For these and other reasons it is becoming quite unsafe to fly, and so one should avoid doing it.

Harold: Your reasoning may be sound, but I can hardly accept your conclusion when you yourself have recently been flying on commercial airlines even more than before.

Which one of the following relies on a questionable technique most similar to that used in Harold's reply to Genevieve?

(A) David says that the new film is not very good, but he has not seen it himself, so I don't accept his opinion.
(B) A long time ago Maria showed me a great way to cook lamb, but for medical reasons she no longer eats red meat, so I'll cook something else for dinner tonight.
(C) Susan has been trying to persuade me to go rock climbing with her, claiming that it's quite safe, but last week she fell and broke her collarbone, so I don't believe her.
(D) Pat has shown me research that proves that eating raw green vegetables is very beneficial and that one should eat them daily, but I don't believe it, since she hardly ever eats raw green vegetables.
(E) Gabriel has all the qualifications we have specified for the job and has much relevant work experience, but I don't believe we should hire him, because when he worked in a similar position before his performance was mediocre.

15. Crimes in which handguns are used are more likely than other crimes to result in fatalities. However, the majority of crimes in which handguns are used do not result in fatalities. Therefore, there is no need to enact laws that address crimes involving handguns as distinct from other crimes.

The pattern of flawed reasoning displayed in the argument above most closely resembles that in which one of the following?

(A) Overweight people are at higher risk of developing heart disease than other people. However, more than half of all overweight people never develop heart disease. Hence it is unnecessary for physicians to be more careful to emphasize the danger of heart disease to their overweight patients than to their other patients.
(B) Many people swim daily in order to stay physically fit. Yet people who swim daily increase their risk of developing ear infections. Hence people who want to remain in good health are better off not following fitness programs that include swimming daily.
(C) Most physicians recommend a balanced diet for those who want to remain in good health. Yet many people find that nontraditional dietary regimens such as extended fasting do their health no serious harm. Therefore, there is no need for everyone to avoid nontraditional dietary regimens.
(D) Foods rich in cholesterol and fat pose a serious health threat to most people. However, many people are reluctant to give up eating foods that they greatly enjoy. Therefore, people who refuse to give up rich foods need to spend more time exercising than do other people.
(E) Many serious health problems are the result of dietary disorders. Yet these disorders are often brought about by psychological factors. Hence people suffering from serious health problems should undergo psychological evaluation.

PARALLEL

16. Journalist: Can you give me a summary of the novel you are working on?

Novelist: Well, I assume that by summary you mean something brief and not a version of the novel itself. The reason I write novels is that what I want to communicate can be communicated only in the form of a novel. So I am afraid I cannot summarize my novel for you in a way that would tell you what I am trying to communicate with this novel.

Which one of the following exhibits a pattern of reasoning that is most parallel to that used by the novelist?

(A) Only if a drawing can be used as a guide by the builder can it be considered a blueprint. This drawing of the proposed building can be used as a guide by the builder, so it can be considered a blueprint.

(B) Only a statement that does not divulge company secrets can be used as a press release. This statement does not divulge company secrets, but it is uninformative and therefore cannot be used as a press release.

(C) Watching a travelog is not the same as traveling. But a travelog confers some of the benefits of travel without the hardships of travel. So many people just watch travelogs and do not undergo the hardships of travel.

(D) Only a three-dimensional representation of a landscape can convey the experience of being in that landscape. A photograph taken with a traditional camera is not three-dimensional. Therefore a photograph taken with a traditional camera can never convey the experience of being in a landscape.

(E) A banquet menu foretells the content of a meal, but some people collect menus in order to remind themselves of great meals they have eaten. Thus a banquet menu has a function not only before, but also after, a meal has been served.

17. New types of washing machines designed to consume less energy also extract less water from laundry during their final spin cycles than do washing machines that consume somewhat more energy. The wetter the laundry, the more energy required to dry it in an automatic dryer. Thus using these new types of washing machines could result in an overall increase in the energy needed to wash and dry a load of laundry.

In which one of the following is the pattern of reasoning most parallel to that in the argument above?

(A) The more skill required to operate a machine, the harder it is to find people able to do it, and thus the more those people must be paid. Therefore, if a factory installs machines that require highly skilled operators, it must be prepared to pay higher wages.

(B) There are two routes between Centerville and Mapletown, and the scenic route is the longer route. Therefore, a person who is not concerned with how long it will take to travel between Centerville and Mapletown will probably take the scenic route.

(C) The more people who work in the library's reading room, the noisier the room becomes; and the noisier the working environment, the less efficiently people work. Therefore, when many people are working in the reading room, those people are working less efficiently.

(D) Pine is a less expensive wood than cedar but is more susceptible to rot. Outdoor furniture made from wood susceptible to rot must be painter with more expensive paint. Therefore, building outdoor furniture from pine rather than cedar could increase the total cost of building and painting the furniture.

(E) The more weights added to an exercise machine, the greater the muscle strength needed to work out on the machine. Up to a point, using more muscle strength can make a person stronger. Thus an exercise machine with more weights can, but does not necessarily, make a person stronger.

18. It now seems clear that the significant role initially predicted for personal computers in the classroom has not become fact. One need only look to the dramatic decline in sales of computers for classroom use in the past year for proof that the fad has passed.

Which one of the following arguments contains flawed reasoning parallel to that in the argument above?

(A) Clearly, government legislation mandating the reduction of automobile emissions has been at least partially successful, as is demonstrated by the fact that the air of the 20 largest cities now contains smaller amounts of the major pollutants mentioned in the legislation than it did before the legislation was passed.

(B) Mechanical translation from one language into another, not merely in narrow contexts such as airline reservations but generally, is clearly an idea whose time has come. Since experts have been working on the problem for 40 years, it is now time for the accumulated expertise to achieve a breakthrough.

(C) Sales of computers for home use will never reach the levels optimistically projected by manufacturers. The reason is that home use was envisioned as encompassing tasks, such as menu planning and checkbook reconciliation, that most homemakers perform in much simpler ways than using a computer would require.

(D) It is apparent that consumers have tired of microwave ovens as quickly as they initially came to accept this recent invention. In contrast to several years of increasing sales following the introduction of microwave ovens, sales of microwave ovens flattened last year, indicating that consumers have found relatively little use for these devices.

(E) Creating incentives for a particular kind of investment inevitably engenders boom-and-bust cycles. The evidence is in the recent decline in the value of commercial real estate, which shows that, although the government can encourage people to put up buildings, it cannot guarantee that those buildings will be fully rented or sold.

19. Government official: Clearly, censorship exists if we, as citizens, are not allowed to communicate what we are ready to communicate at our own expense or if other citizens are not permitted access to our communications at their own expense. Public unwillingness to provide funds for certain kinds of scientific, scholarly, or artistic activities cannot, therefore, be described as censorship.

The flawed reasoning in the government official's argument is most parallel to that in which one of the following?

(A) All actions that cause unnecessary harm to others are unjust; so if a just action causes harm to others, that action must be necessary.

(B) Since there is more to good manners than simply using polite forms of address, it is not possible to say on first meeting a person whether or not that person has good manners.

(C) Acrophobia, usually defined as a morbid fear of heights, can also mean a morbid fear of sharp objects. Since both fears have the same name, they undoubtedly have the same origin.

(D) There is no doubt that a deed is heroic if the doer risks his or her own life to benefit another person. Thus an action is not heroic if the only thing it endangers is the reputation of the doer.

(E) Perception of beauty in an object is determined by past and present influences on the mind of the beholder. Thus no object can be called beautiful, since not everyone will see beauty in it.

PARALLEL

20. Large inequalities in wealth always threaten the viability of true democracy, since wealth is the basis of political power, and true democracy depends on the equal distribution of political power among all citizens.

The reasoning in which one of the following arguments most closely parallels the reasoning in the argument above?

(A) Consumer culture and an emphasis on technological innovation are a dangerous combination, since together they are uncontrollable and lead to irrational excess.

(B) If Sara went to the bookstore every time her pocket was full, Sara would never have enough money to cover her living expenses, since books are her love and they are getting very expensive.

(C) It is very difficult to write a successful science fiction novel that is set in the past, since historical fiction depends on historical accuracy, whereas science fiction does not.

(D) Honesty is important in maintaining friendships. But sometimes honesty can lead to arguments, so it is difficult to predict the effect a particular honest act will have on a friendship.

(E) Repeated encroachments on one's leisure time by a demanding job interfere with the requirements of good health. The reason is that good health depends on regular moderate exercise, but adequate leisure time is essential to regular exercise.

21. The foreign minister of Zeria announced today that her country was severing diplomatic relations with Nandalo because of Nandalo's flagrant violations of human rights. But Zeria continues to maintain diplomatic relations with many countries that the minister knows to have far worse human-rights records than Nandalo does. Therefore, despite the foreign minister's claim, this latest diplomatic move cannot be explained exclusively by Zeria's commitment to upholding human rights.

The argumentative structure of which one of the following most closely parallels that of the argument in the passage?

(A) Henry's parents insist that he eat breakfast before leaving for school because not doing so would be bad for his health. But his parents themselves almost never eat breakfast, so their insistence cannot be completely explained by their concern for his health.

(B) Professor Walsh says that only typed term papers will be accepted because most handwriting is difficult to read. But since she lectures from handwritten notes, her policy cannot be exclusively explained by any difficulty she has with handwritten material.

(C) James claims that he stole only because he was hungry. But although hunger could account for stealing if food could not be readily obtained in any other way, in this case food was otherwise readily available, and so James' theft cannot be completely explained by his hunger.

(D) Armand declined Helen's invitation to dinner on the grounds that socializing with coworkers is imprudent. But since Armand went to a movie with another coworker, Maria, that same evening, his expressed concern for prudence cannot fully explain his refusal.

(E) It is often asserted that there are fewer good teachers than there used to be because teachers' salaries have reached a new low. But teachers have always been poorly paid, so low salaries cannot fully explain this perceived decline in the effectiveness of teachers.

22. Of the two proposals for solving the traffic problems on Main Street, Chen's plan is better for the city as a whole, as is clear from the fact that the principal supporter of Ripley's plan is Smith Stores. Smith Stores, with its highly paid consultants, knows where its own interest lies and, moreover, has supported its own interests in the past, even to the detriment of the city as a whole.

The faulty reasoning in which one of the following is most parallel to that in the argument above?

(A) Surely Centreville should oppose adoption of the regional planning commission's new plan since it is not in Centreville's interest, even though it might be in the interest of some towns in the region.
(B) The school board should support the plan for the new high school since this plan was recommended by the well qualified consultants whom the school board hired at great expense.
(C) Of the two budget proposals, the mayor's is clearly preferable to the city council's, since the mayor's budget addresses the needs of the city as a whole, whereas the city council is protecting special interests.
(D) Nomura is clearly a better candidate for college president than Miller, since Nomura has the support of the three deans who best understand the president's job and with whom the president will have to work most closely.
(E) The planned light-rail system will clearly serve suburban areas well, since its main opponent is the city government, which has always ignored the needs of the suburbs and sought only to protect the interests of the city.

23. The fact that tobacco smoke inhaled by smokers harms the smokers does not prove that the much smaller amount of tobacco smoke inhaled by nonsmokers who share living space with smokers harms the nonsmokers to some degree. Many substances, such as vitamin A, are toxic in large quantities but beneficial in small quantities.

In which one of the following is the pattern of reasoning most similar to that in the argument above?

(A) The fact that a large concentration of bleach will make fabric very white does not prove that a small concentration of bleach will make fabric somewhat white. The effect of a small concentration of bleach may be too slight to change the color of the fabric.
(B) Although a healthful diet should include a certain amount of fiber, it does not follow that a diet that includes large amounts of fiber is more healthful than one that includes smaller amounts of fiber. Too much fiber can interfere with proper digestion.
(C) The fact that large amounts of chemical fertilizers can kill plants does not prove that chemical fertilizers are generally harmful to plants. It proves only that the quantity of chemical fertilizer used should be adjusted according to the needs of the plants and the nutrients already in the soil.
(D) From the fact that five professional taste testers found a new cereal product tasty, it does not follow that everyone will like it. Many people find broccoli a tasty food, but other people have a strong dislike for the taste of broccoli.
(E) Although watching television for half of every day would be a waste of time, watching television briefly every day is not necessarily even a small waste of time. After all, it would be a waste to sleep half of every day, but some sleep every day is necessary.

24. On average, city bus drivers who are using the new computerized fare-collection system have a much better on-time record than do drivers using the old fare-collection system. Millicent Smith has the best on-time record of any bus driver in the city. Therefore, she must be using the computerized fare-collection system.

Which one of the following contains flawed reasoning most similar to that contained in the argument above?

(A) All the city's solid-waste collection vehicles acquired after 1988 have a large capacity than any of those acquired before 1988. This vehicle has the largest capacity of any the city owns, so it must have been acquired after 1988.

(B) The soccer players on the blue team are generally taller than the players on the gold team. Since Henri is a member of the blue team, he is undoubtedly taller than most of the members of the gold team.

(C) This tomato is the largest of this year's crop. Since the tomatoes in the experimental plot are on average larger than those grown in the regular plots, this tomato must have been grown in the experiment plot.

(D) Last week's snowstorm in Toronto was probably an average storm for the area. It was certainly heavier than any snowstorm known to have occurred in Miami, but any average snowstorm in Toronto leaves more snow than ever falls in Miami.

(E) Lawn mowers powered by electricity generally require less maintenance than do lawn mowers powered by gasoline. This lawn mower is powered by gasoline, so it will probably require a lot of maintenance.

25. The capture of a wild animal is justified only as a last resort to save that animal's life. But many wild animals are captured not because their lives are in any danger but so that they can be bred in captivity. Hence, many animals that have been captured should not have been captured.

Which one of the following arguments is most similar in its pattern of reasoning to the argument above?

(A) Punishing a child is justified if it is the only way to reform poor behavior. But punishment is never the only way to reform poor behavior. Hence, punishing a child is never justified.

(B) Parents who never punish a child are not justified in complaining if the child regularly behaves in ways that disturb them. But many parents who prefer not to punish their children complain regularly about their children's behavior. Hence, many parents who complain about their children have no right to complain.

(C) Punishing a young child is justified only if it is done out of concern for the child's future welfare. But many young children are punished not in order to promote their welfare but to minimize sibling rivalry. Hence, many children who are punished should not have been punished.

(D) A teacher is entitled to punish a child only if the child's parents have explicitly given the teacher the permission to do so. But many parents never give their child's teacher the right to punish their child. Hence, many teachers should not punish their pupils.

(E) Society has no right to punish children for deeds that would be crimes if the children were adults. But society does have the right to protect itself from children who are known threats. Hence, confinement of such children does not constitute punishment.

26. Some games, such as chess and soccer, are competitive and played according to rules, but others, such as children's games of make believe, are neither. Therefore, being competitive and involving rules are not essential to being a game.

Which one of the following is most similar in its logical features to the argument above?

(A) Both the gourmet and the glutton enjoy eating. However, one can be a glutton, but not a gourmet, without having an educated palate. Therefore, having an educated palate is essential to being a gourmet, but enjoying food is not.

(B) All North American bears eat meat. Some taxonomists, however, have theorized that the giant panda, which eats only bamboo shoots, is a kind of bear. Either these taxonomists are wrong or eating meat is not essential to being a bear.

(C) It is true that dogs occasionally eat vegetation, but if dogs were not carnivorous they would be shaped quite differently from the way they are. Therefore, being carnivorous is essential to being a dog.

(D) Most automobiles, and nearly all of those produced today, are gasoline-fueled and four-wheeled, but others, such as some experimental electric cars, are neither. Therefore, being gasoline-fueled and having four wheels are not essential to being an automobile.

(E) Montréal's most vaunted characteristics, such as its cosmopolitanism and its vitality, are all to be found in many other cities. Therefore, cosmopolitanism and vitality are not essential properties of Montréal.

27. Insurance industry statistics demonstrate that cars with alarms or other antitheft devices are more likely to be stolen or broken into than cars without such devices or alarms. Therefore antitheft devices do not protect cars against thieves.

The pattern of flawed reasoning in the argument above is most similar to that in which one of the following?

(A) Since surveys reveal that communities with flourishing public libraries have, on average, better-educated citizens, it follows that good schools are typically found in communities with public libraries.

(B) Most public libraries are obviously intended to serve the interests of the casual reader, because most public libraries contain large collections of fiction and relatively small reference collections.

(C) Studies reveal that people who are regular users of libraries purchase more books per year than do people who do not use libraries regularly. Hence using libraries regularly does not reduce the number of books that library patrons purchase.

(D) Since youngsters who read voraciously are more likely to have defective vision than youngsters who do not read very much, it follows that children who do not like to read usually have perfect vision.

(E) Societies that support free public libraries are more likely to support free public universities than are societies without free public libraries. Hence a society that wishes to establish a free public university should first establish a free public library.

28. Various mid-fourteenth-century European writers show an interest in games, but no writer of this period mentions the playing of cards. Nor do any of the mid-fourteenth-century statutes that proscribe or limit the play of games mention cards, though they do mention dice, chess, and other games. It is therefore likely that, contrary to what is sometimes claimed, at that time playing cards was not yet common in Europe.

The pattern of reasoning in which one of the following is most similar to that in the argument above?

(A) Neither today's newspapers nor this evening's television news mentioned a huge fire that was rumored to have happened in the port last night. Therefore, there probably was no such fire.
(B) This evening's television news reported that the cruise ship was only damaged in the fire last night, whereas the newspaper reported that it was destroyed. The television news is based on more recent information, so probably the ship was not destroyed.
(C) Among the buildings that are near the port is the newspaper's printing plant. Early editions of this morning's paper were very late. Therefore, the fire at the port probably affected areas beyond the port itself.
(D) The newspaper does not explicitly say that the port reopened after the fire, but in its listing of newly arrived ships it mentions some arrival times after the fire. Therefore, the port was probably not closed for long.
(E) The newspaper is generally more reliable than the television news, and the newspaper reported that the damage from last night's fire in the port was not severe. Therefore, the damage probably was not severe.

29. At Flordyce University any student who wants to participate in a certain archaeological dig is eligible to do so but only if the student has taken at least one archaeology course and has shown an interest in the field. Many students who have shown an interest in archaeology never take even one archaeology course. Therefore, many students who want to participate in the dig will be ineligible to do so.

The flawed reasoning of which one of the following arguments is most similar to that of the argument above?

(A) Theoretically, any jar is worth saving regardless of its size, but only if it has a lid. Therefore, since some jars are sure not to have lids, there are certain sizes of jar that are actually not worth saving.
(B) For a horse that is well schooled to be ideal for beginning riders that horse must also be surefooted and gentle. Many horses that are surefooted are not gentle. Therefore many well-schooled horses are not ideal for beginning riders.
(C) If an author's first novel has a romantic setting and a suspenseful plot, it will become a best-seller. Since many authors' first novels have neither, not many first novels become best-sellers.
(D) Any automobile that is more than a few years old is eventually sure to need repairs if it is not regularly maintained. Many automobiles are more than a few years old, but still do not need repairs. Therefore, many automobiles are regularly maintained.
(E) An expensive new building will prove to be a good investment only if it is aesthetically pleasing or provides lots of office space. However, since many expensive new buildings are not aesthetically pleasing, few expensive new buildings will prove to be good investments.

30. From the observation that each member of a group could possess a characteristic, it is fallacious to conclude immediately that it is possible for all the group's members to possess the characteristic. An example in which the fallacy is obvious: arguing that because each of the players entering a tennis tournament has a possibility of winning it, there is therefore a possibility that all will win the tournament.

Which one of the following commits the fallacy described above?

(A) You can fool some of the people all of the time and all of the people some of the time, but you cannot fool all of the people all of the time.
(B) Each of the candidates for mayor appears at first glance to possess the necessary qualifications. It would therefore be a mistake to rule out any of them without more careful examination.
(C) Each of the many nominees could be appointed to any one of the three openings on the committee. Therefore it is possible for all of the nominees to be appointed to the openings on the committee.
(D) If a fair coin is tossed five times, then on each toss the chance of heads being the result is half. Therefore the chance of heads being the result on all five tosses is also half.
(E) It is estimated that ten million planets capable of supporting life exist in our galaxy. Thus to rule out the possibility of life on worlds other than Earth, ten million planetary explorations would be needed.

31. Plant species differ in that renewed growth in spring can be triggered by day length or by temperature or else by a combination of both. Day length is the same, year after year, for any given date. Therefore, any plant species that starts to grow again on widely different dates in different years resumes growth at least in part in response to temperature.

Which one of the following arguments is most similar in its pattern of reasoning to the argument above?

(A) In Xandia, medical assistant trainees must either complete a formal training course or work for one year under the close supervision of a physician. Since few physicians are willing to act as supervisors, it must be true that most medical assistant trainees in Xandia take the training course.
(B) In the Crawford area, easterly winds mean rain will come and westerly winds mean dry weather will come; winds from other directions do not occur. Therefore, since it is currently raining in Crawford, there must be an easterly wind blowing there now.
(C) Some landfills charge garbage companies by volume only, some charge by weight only, and all others use a formula sensitive to both volume and weight. So if at a particular landfill the charges for two particular loads of equal volume dumped on the same day are different, weight must determine, or help determine, charges at that landfill.
(D) Depending on volume of business, either one or two or three store detectives are needed for adequate protection against shoplifting. Therefore, if on any particular day store management has decided that three detectives will be needed, it must be because business that day is expected to be heavy.
(E) A call is more likely to be heard if it is loud rather than soft, if it is high-pitched rather than low-pitched, and especially if it is both loud and high-pitched. Therefore, anyone whose call goes unheard in spite of being at maximum loudness should try to raise the pitch of the call.

32. Zachary: One would have to be blind to the reality of moral obligation to deny that people who believe a course of action to be morally obligatory for them have both the right and the duty to pursue that action, and that no one else has any right to stop them from doing so.

Cynthia: But imagine an artist who feels morally obliged to do whatever she can to prevent works of art from being destroyed confronting a morally committed antipornography demonstrator engaged in destroying artworks he deems pornographic. According to your principle that artist has, simultaneously, both the right and the duty to stop the destruction and no right whatsoever to stop it.

Which one of the following, if substituted for the scenario invoked by Cynthia, would preserve the force of her argument?

(A) a medical researcher who feels a moral obligation not to claim sole credit for work that was performed in part by someone else confronting another researcher who feels no such moral obligation
(B) a manufacturer who feels a moral obligation to recall potentially dangerous products confronting a consumer advocate who feels morally obliged to expose product defects
(C) an investment banker who believes that governments are morally obliged to regulate major industries confronting an investment banker who holds that governments have a moral obligation not to interfere with market forces
(D) an architect who feels a moral obligation to design only energy-efficient buildings confronting, as a potential client, a corporation that believes its primary moral obligation is to maximize shareholder profits
(E) a health inspector who feels morally obliged to enforce restrictions on the number of cats a householder may keep confronting a householder who, feeling morally obliged to keep every stray that comes along, has over twice that number of cats

33. The commissioner has announced that Judge Khalid, who was on the seven-member panel appointed to resolve the Amlec labor dispute, will have sole responsibility for resolving the Simdon labor dispute. Since in its decision the Amlec panel showed itself both reasonable and fair, the two sides in the Simdon dispute are undoubtedly justified in the confidence they have expressed in the reasonableness and fairness of the arbitrator assigned to their case.

Which one of the following contains flawed reasoning most parallel to that contained in the passage?

(A) Representing the school board, Marcia Barthes presented to the school's principal a list of recently elected school board members. Since only an elected member of the school board can act as its representative, Ms. Barthes's name undoubtedly appears on that list.
(B) Alan Caldalf, who likes being around young children, has decided to become a pediatrician. Since the one characteristic common to all good pediatricians is that they like young children, Mr. Caldalf will undoubtedly be a very good pediatrician.
(C) Jorge Diaz is a teacher at a music school nationally known for the excellence of its conducting faculty. Since Mr. Diaz has recently been commended for the excellence of his teaching, he is undoubtedly a member of the school's conducting faculty.
(D) Ula Borg, who has sold real estate for Arcande Realty for many years, undoubtedly sold fewer houses last year than she had the year before since the number of houses sold last year by Arcande Realty is far lower than the number sold the previous year.
(E) The members of the local historical society unanimously support designating the First National Bank building a historical landmark. Since Evelyn George is a member of that society, she undoubtedly favors according landmark status to the city hall as well.

34. In Sheldon most bicyclists aged 18 and over have lights on their bicycles, whereas most bicyclists under the age of 18 do not. It follows that in Sheldon most bicyclists who have lights on their bicycles are at least 18 years old.

Which one of the following exhibits a pattern of flawed reasoning most similar to that in the argument above?

(A) Most of the people in Sheldon buy gasoline on Mondays only. But almost everyone in Sheldon buys groceries on Tuesdays only. It follows that fewer than half of the people in Sheldon buy gasoline on the same day on which they buy groceries.
(B) The Sheldon Library lent more books during the week after it began lending videos than it had in the entire preceding month. It follows that the availability of videos was responsible for the increase in the number of books lent.
(C) Most of the residents of Sheldon who voted in the last election are on the Conservative party's mailing list, whereas most of Sheldon's residents who did not vote are not on the list. It follows that most of the residents of Sheldon on the Conservative party's mailing list voted in the last election.
(D) In the county where Sheldon is located, every town that has two or more fire trucks has a town pool, whereas most towns that have fewer than two fire trucks do not have a town pool. It follows that Sheldon, which has a town pool, must have at least two fire trucks.
(E) In Sheldon everyone over the age of 60 who knits also sews, but not everyone over the age of 60 who sews also knits. It follows that among people over the age of 60 in Sheldon there are more who sew than there are who knit.

35. The Volunteers for Literacy Program would benefit if Dolores takes Victor's place as director, since Dolores is far more skillful than Victor is at securing the kind of financial support the program needs and Dolores does not have Victor's propensity for alienating the program's most dedicated volunteers.

The pattern of reasoning in the argument above is most closely paralleled in which one of the following?

(A) It would be more convenient for Dominique to take a bus to school than to take the subway, since the bus stops closer to her house than does the subway and, unlike the subway, the bus goes directly to the school.
(B) Joshua's interest would be better served by taking the bus to get to his parent's house rather than by taking an airplane, since his primary concern is to travel as cheaply as possible and taking the bus is less expensive than going by airplane.
(C) Belinda will get to the concert more quickly by subway than by taxi, since the concert takes place on a Friday evening and on Friday evenings traffic near the concert hall is exceptionally heavy.
(D) Anita would benefit financially by taking the train to work rather than driving her car, since when she drives she has to pay parking fees and the daily fee for parking a car is higher than a round-trip train ticket.
(E) It would be to Fred's advantage to exchange his bus tickets for train tickets, since he needs to arrive at his meeting before any of the other participants and if he goes by bus at least one of the other participants will arrive first.

36. The only plants in the garden were tulips, but they were tall tulips. So the only plants in the garden were tall plants.

Which one of the following exhibits faulty reasoning most similar to the faulty reasoning in the argument above?

(A) The only dogs in the show were poodles, and they were all black poodles. So all the dogs in the show were black.

(B) All the buildings on the block were tall. The only buildings on the block were office buildings and residential towers. So all the office buildings on the block were tall buildings.

(C) All the primates in the zoo were gorillas. The only gorillas in the zoo were small gorillas. Thus the only primates in the zoo were small primates.

(D) The only fruit in the kitchen was pears, but the pears were not ripe. Thus none of the fruit in the kitchen was ripe.

(E) All the grand pianos here are large. All the grand pianos here are heavy. Thus everything large is heavy.

37. Public policy dictates the health risks the public routinely takes. Statistical arguments about health risks are used primarily to deflect public fears, while contributing little to policy debate. For example, statistics are cited to imply that wearing a seat belt reduces one's risk of death in an automobile accident, deflecting attention from the fact that a transportation policy that promotes increasing use of automobiles inherently increases any individual's risk of death in an automobile accident.

The way the example functions above is most closely paralleled in which one of the following?

(A) Statistics indicate that an individual's risk of contracting cancer from radiation emitted by a nuclear power plant is less than that of contracting cancer from sunshine. These statistics draw attention away from the fact that a policy of energy conservation is safer for human health than a policy based on nuclear energy.

(B) Statistics indicate that an urban resident's risk of accidental death from any cause is no greater than that of an individual who lives in a suburban or rural area. These statistics counter the widely held public belief that urban areas are more dangerous than suburban or rural areas.

(C) Statistics indicate that the average life expectancy of males is shorter than that of females. This alone should not influence policies regarding eligibility for life insurance because it is also true that any individual's expectancy can be calculated on the basis of personal characteristics and health practices.

(D) Statistics indicate that the average life expectancy of males is shorter than that of females. When one accounts for the fact that females smoke less and are less likely to work in jobs in the chemical and manufacturing industries, the difference in life expectancy is narrowed.

(E) Statistics indicate that the number of people dependent on alcohol far exceeds the number dependent on illegal addictive drugs; thus, any policy for the control and treatment of substance abuse should provide for treatment of alcoholism.

38. Of all the houses in the city's historic district, the house that once belonged to the Tyler family is the most famous by far. Since the historic district is the most famous district in the city, the Tyler house must be the city's most famous house.

The flawed reasoning in the argument above most closely parallels the flawed reasoning in which one of the following?

(A) Of all the peaks in the coastal mountain range, Mount Williams is the tallest. Since the tallest peaks in the entire region are in the coastal mountain range, Mount Williams must be the region's tallest peak.

(B) Tobacco smoking is the behavior most likely to cause lung cancer in people. Since more tobacco is smoked in Greene County than anywhere else in the world, there must be more lung cancer in Greene County than anywhere else in the world.

(C) Susan Coleman is the oldest of the three children in her family. Since the three Coleman children are each older than any of the other children who live in their building, Susan Coleman must be the oldest child now living in the building.

(D) Of all the fish stores in the harbor area, Miller's Fish Market has the most exotic selection of fish. Since there are many more fish stores in the harbor area than anywhere else in the city, Miller's Fish Market must have the most exotic selection of fish in the city.

(E) Of all the flowers grown in the university's botanical garden, the Oakland roses are the most beautiful. Since the university's botanical garden is the most beautiful garden in the region, the Oakland roses grown in the garden must be the most beautiful flowers grown in the entire region.

39. Because some student demonstrations protesting his scheduled appearance have resulted in violence, the president of the Imperialist Society has been prevented from speaking about politics on campus by the dean of student affairs. Yet to deny anyone the unrestricted freedom to speak is to threaten everyone's right to free expression. Hence, the dean's decision has threatened everyone's right to free expression.

The pattern of reasoning displayed above is most closely paralleled in which one of the following?

(A) Dr. Pacheco saved a child's life by performing emergency surgery. But surgery rarely involves any risk to the surgeon. Therefore, if an act is not heroic unless it requires the actor to take some risk, Dr. Pacheco's surgery was not heroic.

(B) Because anyone who performs an act of heroism acts altruistically rather than selfishly, a society that rewards heroism encourages altruism rather than pure self-interest.

(C) In order to rescue a drowning child, Isabel jumped into a freezing river. Such acts of heroism performed to save the life of one enrich the lives of all. Hence, Isabel's action enriched the lives of all.

(D) Fire fighters are often expected to perform heroically under harsh conditions. But no one is ever required to act heroically. Hence, fire fighters are often expected to perform actions they are not required to perform.

(E) Acts of extreme generosity are usually above and beyond the call of duty. Therefore, most acts of extreme generosity are heroic, since all actions that are above and beyond the call of duty are heroic.

40. Biographer: Arnold's belief that every offer of assistance on the part of his colleagues was a disguised attempt to make him look inadequate and that no expression of congratulations on his promotion should be taken at face value may seem irrational. In fact, this belief was a consequence of his early experiences with an admired older sister who always made fun of his ambitions and achievements. In light of this explanation, therefore, Arnold's stubborn belief that his colleagues were duplicitous emerges as clearly justified.

The flawed reasoning in the biographer's argument is most similar to that in which one of the following?

(A) The fact that top executives generally have much larger vocabularies than do their subordinates explains why Sheldon's belief, instilled in him during his childhood, that developing a large vocabulary is the way to get to the top in the world of business is completely justified.

(B) Emily suspected that apples are unhealthy ever since she almost choked to death while eating an apple when she was a child. Now, evidence that apples treated with certain pesticides can be health hazards shows that Emily's long-held belief is fully justified.

(C) As a child, Joan was severely punished whenever she played with her father's prize Siamese cat. Therefore, since this information makes her present belief that cats are not good pets completely understandable, that belief is justified.

(D) Studies show that when usually well-behaved children become irritable, they often exhibit symptoms of viral infections the next day. The suspicion, still held by many adults, that misbehavior must always be paid for is thus both explained and justified.

(E) Sumayia's father and mother were both concert pianists, and as a child, Sumayia knew several other people trying to make careers as musicians. Thus Sumayia's opinion that her friend Anthony lacks the drive to be a successful pianist is undoubtedly justified.

41. Last year the county park system failed to generate enough revenue to cover its costs. Any business should be closed if it is unprofitable, but county parks are not businesses. Therefore, the fact that county parks are unprofitable does not by itself justify closing them.

The pattern of reasoning in the argument above is most closely paralleled in which one of the following?

(A) A prime-time television series should be canceled if it fails to attract a large audience, but the small audience attracted by the documentary series is not sufficient reason to cancel it, since it does not air during prime time.

(B) Although companies that manufacture and market automobiles in the United States must meet stringent air-quality standards, the OKESA company should be exempt from these standards since it manufactures bicycles in addition to automobiles.

(C) Although the province did not specifically intend to prohibit betting on horse races when it passed a law prohibiting gambling, such betting should be regarded as being prohibited because it is a form of gambling.

(D) Even though cockatiels are not, strictly speaking, members of the parrot family, they should be fed the same diet as most parrots since the cockatiel's dietary needs are so similar to those of parrots.

(E) Since minors are not subject to the same criminal laws as are adults, they should not be subject to the same sorts of punishments as those that apply to adults.

42. Anyone who insists that music videos are an art form should also agree that television gave rise to an art form, since television gave rise to music videos.

The pattern of reasoning displayed in the argument above most closely parallels that displayed in which one of the following?

(A) Anyone who claims that all vegetables are nutritious should also agree that some vegetables are harmful if eaten in large quantities.
(B) Anyone who holds that avocados are a fruit should also hold that pound cake is lower in fat than some fruit, since pound cake is lower in fat than avocados.
(C) Anyone who dislikes tomatoes should also agree that some people do like tomatoes, if that person agrees that no taste is universal.
(D) A person who eats a variety of vegetables is probably well nourished, since most people who eat a variety of vegetables generally eat well-balanced meals.
(E) A person who claims to prefer fruit to vegetables should also prefer cake to bread, since fruit is sweeter than vegetables and cake is sweeter than bread.

43. No one in the French department to which Professor Alban belongs is allowed to teach more than one introductory level class in any one term. Moreover, the only language classes being taught next term are advanced ones. So it is untrue that both of the French classes Professor Alban will be teaching next term will be introductory level classes.

The pattern of reasoning displayed in the argument above is most closely paralleled by that in which one of the following arguments?

(A) The Morrison Building will be fully occupied by May and since if a building is occupied by May the new tax rates apply to it, the Morrison Building will be taxed according to the new rates.
(B) The revised tax code does not apply at all to buildings built before 1900, and only the first section of the revised code applies to buildings built between 1900 and 1920, so the revised code does not apply to the Norton Building, since it was built in 1873.
(C) All property on Overton Road will be reassessed for tax purposes by the end of the year and the Elnor Company headquarters is on Overton Road, so Elnor's property taxes will be higher next year.
(D) New buildings that include public space are exempt from city taxes for two years and all new buildings in the city's Alton district are exempt for five years, so the building with the large public space that was recently completed in Alton will not be subject to city taxes next year.
(E) Since according to recent statute, a building that is exempt from property taxes is charged for city water at a special rate, and hospitals are exempt from property taxes, Founder's Hospital will be charged for city water at the special rate.

PARALLEL

44. The report released by the interior ministry states that within the past 5 years the national land-reclamation program has resulted in a 19 percent increase in the amount of arable land within the country. If these figures are accurate, the program has been a resounding success. Senator Armand, a distinguished mathematician and a woman of indisputable brilliance, maintains, however, that the reclamation program could not possibly have been successful. Clearly, therefore, the figures cited in the report cannot be accurate.

The argument above exhibits an erroneous pattern of reasoning most similar to that exhibited by which one of the following?

(A) Albert's father claims that Albert does not know where the spare car keys are hidden. Yesterday, however, Albert reported that he had discovered the spare car keys in the garage toolbox, so his father's claim cannot be true.

(B) Gloria's drama teacher claims that her policy is to give each student the opportunity to act in at least one play during the year but, since Gloria, who attended every class, reports that she was not given such an opportunity, the teacher's claim cannot be true.

(C) Amos claims that he can hold his breath under water for a full hour. Dr. Treviso, a cardiopulmonary specialist, has stated that humans are physiologically incapable of holding their breath for even half that long; so Amos' claim cannot be true.

(D) Evelyn reports that she got home before midnight. Robert, who always knows the time, insists that she did not. If Robert is right, Evelyn could not possibly have listened to the late news; since she admits not having listened to the late news, her report cannot be true.

(E) Moira, after observing the finish of the 60-kilometer bicycle race, reports that Lee won with Adams a distant third. Lomas, a bicycle engineering expert, insists, however, that Lee could not have won a race in which Adams competed; so Moira's report cannot be true.

PARALLEL

Chapter Twelve: Evaluate the Argument Questions

1. In a new police program, automobile owners in some neighborhoods whose cars are not normally driven between 1 A.M. and 5 A.M. can display a special decal in the cars' windows and authorize police to stop the cars during those hours to check the drivers' licenses. The theft rate for cars bearing such decals is much lower than had been usual for cars in those neighborhoods.

If it is concluded from the statements above that automobile theft has been reduced by the program, which one of the following would it be most important to answer in evaluating that conclusion?

(A) Are owners who are cautious enough to join the program taking other special measures to protect their cars against theft?
(B) In how many neighborhoods is the police program operating?
(C) Are cars in neighborhoods that are actively participating in the program sometimes stolen during daylight hours?
(D) Will owners who have placed decals on their cars' windows but who find it necessary to drive between 1 A.M. and 5 A.M. be harassed by police?
(E) Are the neighborhoods in which the program has been put into effect a representative cross section of neighborhoods with respect to the types of automobiles owned by residents?

2. There is a widespread belief that people can predict impending earthquakes from unusual animal behavior. Skeptics claim that this belief is based on selective coincidence: people whose dogs behaved oddly just before an earthquake will be especially likely to remember that fact. At any given time, the skeptics say, some of the world's dogs will be behaving oddly.

Clarification of which one of the following issues would be most important to an evaluation of the skeptics' position?

(A) Which is larger, the number of skeptics or the number of people who believe that animal behavior can foreshadow earthquakes?
(B) Are there means other than the observation of animal behavior that nonscientists can use to predict earthquakes?
(C) Are there animals about whose behavior people know too little to be able to distinguish unusual from everyday behavior?
(D) Are the sorts of behavior supposedly predictive of earthquakes as pronounced in dogs as they are in other animals?
(E) Is the animal behavior supposedly predictive of earthquakes specific to impending earthquakes or can it be any kind of unusual behavior?

3. George: Some scientists say that global warming will occur because people are releasing large amounts of carbon dioxide into the atmosphere by burning trees and fossil fuels. We can see, though, that the predicted warming is occurring already. In the middle of last winter, we had a month of springlike weather in our area, and this fall, because of unusually mild temperatures, the leaves on our town's trees were three weeks late in turning color.

Which one of the following would it be most relevant to investigate in evaluating the conclusion of George's argument?

(A) whether carbon dioxide is the only cause of global warming
(B) when leaves on the trees in the town usually change color
(C) what proportion of global emissions of carbon dioxide is due to the burning of trees by humans
(D) whether air pollution is causing some trees in the area to lose their leaves
(E) whether unusually warm weather is occurring elsewhere on the globe more frequently than before

4. Saunders: Everyone at last week's neighborhood association meeting agreed that the row of abandoned and vandalized houses on Carlton Street posed a threat to the safety of our neighborhood. Moreover, no one now disputes that getting the houses torn down eliminated that threat. Some people tried to argue that it was unnecessary to demolish what they claimed were basically sound buildings, since the city had established a fund to help people in need of housing buy and rehabilitate such buildings. The overwhelming success of the demolition strategy, however, proves that the majority, who favored demolition, were right and that those who claimed that the problem could and should be solved by rehabilitating the houses were wrong.

Which one of the following principles, if established, would determine that demolishing the houses was the right decision or instead would determine that the proposal advocated by the opponents of demolition should have been adopted?

(A) When what to do about an abandoned neighborhood building is in dispute, the course of action that would result in the most housing for people who need it should be the one adopted unless the building is believed to pose a threat to neighborhood safety.

(B) When there are two proposals for solving a neighborhood problem, and only one of them would preclude the possibility of trying the other approach if the first proves unsatisfactory, then the approach that does not foreclose the other possibility should be the one adopted.

(C) If one of two proposals for renovating vacant neighborhood buildings requires government funding whereas the second does not, the second proposal should be the one adopted unless the necessary government funds have already been secured.

(D) No plan for eliminating a neighborhood problem that requires demolishing basically sound houses should be carried out until all other possible alternatives have been thoroughly investigated.

(E) No proposal for dealing with a threat to a neighborhood's safety should be adopted merely because a majority of the residents of that neighborhood prefer that proposal to a particular counterproposal.

5. A translation invariably reflects the writing style of the translator. Sometimes when a long document needs to be translated quickly, several translators are put to work on the job, each assigned to translate part of the document. In these cases, the result is usually a translation marked by different and often incompatible writing styles. Certain computer programs for language translation that work without the intervention of human translators can finish the job faster than human translators and produce a stylistically uniform translation with an 80 percent accuracy rate. Therefore, when a long document needs to be translated quickly, it is better to use a computer translation program than human translators.

Which one of the following issues would be LEAST important to resolve in evaluating the argument?

(A) whether the problem of stylistic variety in human translation could be solved by giving stylistic guidelines to human translators

(B) whether numerical comparisons of the accuracy of translations can reasonably be made

(C) whether computer translation programs, like human translators, each have their own distinct writing style

(D) whether the computer translation contains errors of grammar and usage that drastically alter the meaning of the text

(E) how the accuracy rate of computer translation programs compares with that of human translators in relation to the users' needs

6. Advertisement: Most power hedge trimmers on the market do an adequate job of trimming hedges, but many power hedge trimmers are dangerous to operate and can cause serious injury when used by untrained operators. Bolter Industries' hedge trimmer has been tested by National Laboratories, the most trusted name in safety testing. So you know, if you buy a Bolter's, you are buying a power hedge trimmer whose safety is assured.

The answer to which one of the following questions would be most useful in evaluating the truth of the conclusion drawn in the advertisement?

(A) Has National Laboratories performed safety tests on other machines made by Bolter Industries?
(B) How important to the average buyer of a power hedge trimmer is safety of operation?
(C) What were the results of National Laboratories' tests of Bolter Industries' hedge trimmer?
(D) Are there safer ways of trimming a hedge than using a power hedge trimmer?
(E) Does any other power hedge trimmer on the market do a better job of trimming hedges than does Bolter Industries' hedge trimmer?

7. Sea turtles nest only at their own birthplaces. After hatching on the beach, the turtles enter the water to begin their far-ranging migration, only returning to their birthplaces to nest some 15 to 30 years later. It has been hypothesized that newborn sea turtles learn the smell of their birth environment, and it is this smell that stimulates the turtles to return to nest.

Which one of the following would be most important to know in evaluating the hypothesis in the passage?

(A) how long the expected life span of sea turtles is
(B) what the maximum migratory range of mature sea turtles is
(C) whether many beaches on which sea turtles were hatched have since been destroyed by development
(D) whether immediately before returning to nest, sea turtles are outside the area where the smell of their birthplace would be perceptible
(E) whether both sexes of sea turtles are actively involved in the nesting process

EVALUATE

8. Mark: Plastic-foam cups, which contain environmentally harmful chlorofluorocarbons, should no longer be used; paper cups are preferable. Styrene, a carcinogenic by-product, is generated in foam production, and foam cups, once used, persist indefinitely in the environment.

Tina: You overlook the environmental effects of paper cups. A study done 5 years ago showed that making paper for their production burned more petroleum than was used for foam cups and used 12 times as much steam, 36 times as much electricity, and twice as much cooling water. Because paper cups weigh more, their transportation takes more energy. Paper mills produce water pollution, and when the cups decay they produce methane, a gas that contributes to harmful global warming. So they are a worse choice.

To decide the issue between Mark and Tina, it would first be most important to decide

(A) how soon each of the kinds of harm cited by Mark and Tina would be likely to be at its maximum level
(B) whether members of some societies use, on average, more disposable goods than do members of other societies
(C) whether it is necessary to seek a third alternative that has none of the negative consequences cited with respect to the two products
(D) how much of the chains of causation involved in the production, marketing, and disposal of the products should be considered in analyzing their environmental impact
(E) whether paper and foam cups, in their most popular sizes, hold the same quantities of liquid

9. A scientist made three observations: (1) in the world's temperate zones, food is more plentiful in the ocean than it is in fresh water; (2) migratory fish in temperate zones generally mature in the ocean and spawn in fresh water; and (3) migratory fish need much nourishment as they mature but little or none during the part of their lives when they spawn. On the basis of those observations, the scientist formulated the hypothesis that food availability is a determining factor in the migration of migratory fish. Subsequently the scientist learned that in the tropics migratory fish generally mature in fresh water and spawn in the ocean.

Which one of the following would it be most helpful to know in order to judge whether what the scientist subsequently learned calls into question the hypothesis?

(A) whether in the world's temperate zones, the temperatures of bodies of fresh water tend to be lower than those of the regions of the oceans into which they flow
(B) whether the types of foods that migratory fish eat while they inhabit the ocean are similar to those that they eat while they inhabit bodies of fresh water
(C) whether any species of fish with populations in temperate zones also have populations that live in the tropics
(D) whether there are more species of migratory fish in the tropics than there are in temperate zones
(E) whether in the tropics food is less plentiful in the ocean than in fresh water

10. Dr. Godfrey: Now that high school students are allowed to work more than 15 hours per week at part-time jobs, those who actually do so show less interest in school and get lower grades than those who do not work as many hours at part-time jobs. Obviously, working long hours at part-time jobs during the school year contributes to the academic problems that many of our high school students experience.

Dr. Nash: That's not so. Many of our high school students set out to earn as much money as they can simply to compensate for their lack of academic success.

The answer to which one of the following would be the most helpful in determining whether the conclusion that Dr. Godfrey draws could be logically defended against Dr. Nash's counterargument?

(A) whether people who have had academic problems in high school are ultimately less successful in their careers than people who have not had such problems
(B) whether students are allowed to spend more than 15 hours per week at school-sponsored nonacademic extracurricular activities such as team sports or clubs
(C) whether the students who work more than 15 hours per week and have academic problems had such problems before they began to work that many hours
(D) whether employers and high school students typically obey all the laws that regulate the conditions under which young people may legally be employed
(E) whether high school students who have after-school jobs continue to work at those jobs after graduating from high school

11. When a planetary system forms, the chances that a planet capable of supporting life will be formed are high. The chances that a large planet the size of Jupiter or Saturn will be formed, however, are low. Without Jupiter and Saturn, whose gravitational forces have prevented Earth from being frequently struck by large comets, intelligent life would never have arisen on Earth. Since planetary systems are unlikely to contain any large planets, the chances that intelligent life will emerge on a planet are, therefore, low.

Knowing which one of the following would be most useful in evaluating the argument?

(A) whether all planetary systems are formed from similar amounts of matter
(B) whether intelligent species would be likely to survive if a comet struck their planet
(C) whether large comets could be deflected by only one large planet rather than by two
(D) how high the chances are that planetary systems will contain many large comets
(E) how likely it is that planetary systems containing large planets will also contain planets the size of Earth

12. For every 50 dogs that contract a certain disease, one will die from it. A vaccine exists that is virtually 100 percent effective in preventing this disease. Since the risk of death from complications of vaccination is one death per 5,000 vaccinations, it is therefore safer for a dog to receive the vaccine than not to receive it.

Which one of the following would it be most helpful to know in order to evaluate the argument?

(A) the total number of dogs that die each year from all causes taken together
(B) whether the vaccine is effective against the disease in household pets other than dogs
(C) the number of dogs that die each year from diseases other than the disease in question
(D) the likelihood that a dog will contract another disease such as rabies
(E) the likelihood that an unvaccinated dog will contract the disease in question

Chapter Thirteen: Cannot Be True Questions

1. The advanced technology of ski boots and bindings has brought a dramatic drop in the incidence of injuries that occur on the slopes of ski resorts: from 9 injuries per 1,000 skiers in 1950 to 3 in 1980. As a result, the remainder of ski-related injuries, which includes all injuries occurring on the premises of a ski resort but not on the slopes, rose from 10 percent of all ski-related injuries in 1950 to 25 percent in 1980. The incidence of these injuries, including accidents such as falling down steps, increases with the amount of alcohol consumed per skier.

Which one of the following conflicts with information in the passage?

(A) The number of ski injuries that occurred on the slopes was greater in 1980 than in 1950.
(B) A skier was less likely to be injured on the slopes in 1950 than in 1980.
(C) The reporting of ski injuries became more accurate between 1950 and 1980.
(D) The total number of skiers dropped between 1950 and 1980.
(E) Some ski-related injuries occurred in 1980 to people who were not skiing.

2. The only way that bookstores can profitably sell books at below-market prices is to get the books at a discount from publishers. Unless bookstores generate a high sales volume, however, they cannot get discounts from publishers. To generate such volume, bookstores must either cater to mass tastes or have exclusive access to a large specialized market, such as medical textbooks, or both.

If all the statements in the passage are true and if it is also true that a bookstore does not cater to mass tastes, which one of the following CANNOT be true?

(A) The bookstore profitably sells some of its books at below-market prices.
(B) The bookstore does not profitably sell any of its books at below-market prices.
(C) Either the bookstore has exclusive access to a large specialized market or else it does not get a discount from any publishers.
(D) The bookstore does not have exclusive access to a large specialized market but profitably sells some of its books at below-market prices.
(E) The bookstore does not have exclusive access to a large specialized market, nor does it get a discount from any publishers.

3. The question whether intelligent life exists elsewhere in the universe is certainly imprecise, because we are not sure how different from us something might be and still count as "intelligent life." Yet we cannot just decide to define "intelligent life" in some more precise way since it is likely that we will find and recognize intelligent life elsewhere in the universe only if we leave our definitions open to new, unimagined possibilities.

The argument can most reasonably be interpreted as an objection to which one of the following claims?

(A) The question whether intelligent life exists elsewhere in the universe is one that will never be correctly answered.
(B) Whether or not there is intelligent life elsewhere in the universe, our understanding of intelligent life is limited.
(C) The question about the existence of intelligent life elsewhere in the universe must be made more precise if we hope to answer it correctly.
(D) The question whether there is intelligent life elsewhere in the universe is so imprecise as to be meaningless.
(E) The question whether there is intelligent life elsewhere in the universe is one we should not spend our time trying to answer.

4. The brains of identical twins are genetically identical. When only one of a pair of identical twins is a schizophrenic, certain areas of the affected twin's brain are smaller than corresponding areas in the brain of the unaffected twin. No such differences are found when neither twin is schizophrenic. Therefore, this discovery provides definitive evidence that schizophrenia is caused by damage to the physical structure of the brain.

If the statements on which the conclusion above is based are all true, each of the following could be true EXCEPT:

(A) People who lack a genetic susceptibility for the disease will not develop schizophrenia.
(B) Medications can control most of the symptoms of schizophrenia in most patients but will never be able to cure it.
(C) The brains of schizophrenics share many of the characteristics found in those of people without the disorder.
(D) It will eventually be possible to determine whether or not someone will develop schizophrenia on the basis of genetic information alone.
(E) Brain abnormalities associated with schizophrenia are the result of childhood viral infections that inhibit the development of brain cells.

5. M: It is almost impossible to find a person between the ages of 85 and 90 who primarily uses the left hand.

Q: Seventy to ninety years ago, however, children were punished for using their left hands to eat or to write and were forced to use their right hands.

Q's response serves to counter any use by M of the evidence about 85 to 90 year olds in support of which one of the following hypotheses?

(A) Being born right-handed confers a survival advantage.
(B) Societal attitudes toward handedness differ at different times.
(C) Forcing a person to switch from a preferred hand is harmless.
(D) Handedness is a product of both genetic predisposition and social pressures.
(E) Physical habits learned in school often persist in old age.

6. Amy McConnell is considering running for election against the incumbent, Gregory Lutz. If Lutz has a large campaign fund, then he is already far ahead, and McConnell will not run against him. If Lutz does not have a large campaign fund, McConnell will scrutinize Lutz's record for any hints of scandal that she could use against him. Anything of a scandalous nature would increase McConnell's chances of winning, and she would campaign for election. If Lutz has a clean record, however, McConnell will not run against him.

Given the information in the passage, which one of the following must be false?

(A) Lutz does not have a large campaign fund, and McConnell does not run against him.
(B) Lutz's record contains items that would increase McConnell's chances of winning, and she runs against him.
(C) Lutz's record contains scandalous items, and McConnell does not run against him.
(D) Lutz's record contains nothing that would increase McConnell's chances of winning, and she runs against him.
(E) Lutz has a large campaign fund, and McConnell does not run against him.

7. When Alicia Green borrowed a neighbor's car without permission, the police merely gave her a warning. However, when Peter Foster did the same thing, he was charged with automobile theft. Peter came to the attention of the police because the car he was driving was hit by a speeding taxi. Alicia was stopped because the car she was driving had defective taillights. It is true that the car Peter took got damaged and the car Alicia took did not, but since it was the taxi that caused the damage this difference was not due to any difference in the blameworthiness of their behavior. Therefore Alicia should also have been charged with automobile theft.

If all of the claims offered in support of the conclusion are accurate, each of the following could be true EXCEPT:

(A) The interests of justice would have been better served if the police had released Peter Foster with a warning.
(B) Alicia Green had never before driven a car belonging to someone else without first securing the owner's permission.
(C) Peter Foster was hit by the taxi while he was running a red light, whereas Alicia Green drove with extra care to avoid drawing the attention of the police to the car she had taken.
(D) Alicia Green barely missed hitting a pedestrian when she sped through a red light ten minutes before she was stopped by the police for driving a car that had defective taillights.
(E) Peter Foster had been cited for speeding twice in the preceding month, whereas Alicia Green had never been cited for a traffic violation.

8. To suit the needs of corporate clients, advertising agencies have successfully modified a strategy originally developed for political campaigns. This strategy aims to provide clients with free publicity and air time by designing an advertising campaign that is controversial, thus drawing prime-time media coverage and evoking public comment by officials.

The statements above, if true, most seriously undermine which one of the following assertions?

(A) The usefulness of an advertising campaign is based solely on the degree to which the campaign's advertisements persuade their audiences.
(B) Only a small percentage of eligible voters admit to being influenced by advertising campaigns in deciding how to vote.
(C) Campaign managers have transformed political campaigns by making increasing use of strategies borrowed from corporate advertising campaigns.
(D) Corporations are typically more concerned with maintaining public recognition of the corporate name than with enhancing goodwill toward the corporation.
(E) Advertising agencies that specialize in campaigns for corporate clients are not usually chosen for political campaigns.

9. It was once believed that cells grown in laboratory tissue cultures were essentially immortal. That is, as long as all of their needs were met, they would continue dividing forever. However, it has been shown that normal cells have a finite reproductive limit. A human liver cell, for example, divides 60 times and then stops. If such a cell divides 30 times and then is put into a deep freeze for months or even years, it "remembers" where it stopped dividing. After thawing, it divides another 30 times, but no more.

If the information above is accurate, a liver cell in which more than 60 divisions took place in a tissue culture CANNOT be which one of the following?

(A) an abnormal human liver cell
(B) a normal human liver cell that had been frozen after its first division and afterward thawed
(C) a normal cell that came from the liver of an individual of a nonhuman species and had never been frozen
(D) a normal liver cell that came from an individual of a nonhuman species and had been frozen after its first division and afterward thawed
(E) an abnormal cell from the liver of an individual of a nonhuman species

10. Some people take their moral cues from governmental codes of law; for them, it is inconceivable that something that is legally permissible could be immoral.

Those whose view is described above hold inconsistent beliefs if they also believe that

(A) law does not cover all circumstances in which one person morally wrongs another
(B) a legally impermissible action is never morally excusable
(C) governmental officials sometimes behave illegally
(D) the moral consensus of a society is expressed in its laws
(E) some governmental regulations are so detailed that they are burdensome to the economy

11. Certain instruments used in veterinary surgery can be made either of stainless steel or of nylon. In a study of such instruments, 50 complete sterilizations of a set of nylon instruments required 3.4 times the amount of energy used to manufacture that set of instruments, whereas 50 complete sterilizations of a set of stainless steel instruments required 2.1 times the amount of energy required to manufacture that set of instruments.

If the statements above are true, each of the following could be true EXCEPT:

(A) The 50 complete sterilizations of the nylon instruments used more energy than did the 50 complete sterilizations of the stainless steel instruments.
(B) More energy was required for each complete sterilization of the nylon instruments than was required to manufacture the nylon instruments.
(C) More nylon instruments than stainless steel instruments were sterilized in the study.
(D) More energy was used to produce the stainless steel instruments than was used to produce the nylon instruments.
(E) The total cost of 50 complete sterilizations of the stainless steel instruments was greater than the cost of manufacturing the stainless steel instruments.

12. In a survey of consumers in an Eastern European nation, respondents were asked two questions about each of 400 famous Western brands: whether or not they recognized the brand name and whether or not they thought the products bearing that name were of high quality. The results of the survey were a rating and corresponding rank order for each brand based on recognition, and a second rating-plus-ranking based on approval. The brands ranked in the top 27 for recognition were those actually available in that nation. The approval rankings of these 27 brands often differed sharply from their recognition rankings. By contrast, most of the other brands had ratings, and thus rankings, that were essentially the same for recognition as for approval.

Which one of the following, if each is a principle about consumer surveys, is violated by the survey described?

(A) Never ask all respondents a question if it cannot reasonably be answered by respondents who make a particular response to another question in the same survey.
(B) Never ask a question that is likely to generate a large variety of responses that are difficult to group into a manageable number of categories.
(C) Never ask all respondents a question that respondents cannot answer without giving up their anonymity.
(D) It is better to ask the same question about ten different products than to ask ten different questions about a single product.
(E) It is best to ask questions that a respondent can answer without fear of having gotten the answer wrong.

13. Manager: I have circulated a posting for the position of Social Scientific Researcher. Applicants must have either an earned doctorate and a track record of published research, or else five years' work experience. The relevant fields for these requirements are sociology, psychology, and education.

Which one of the applicants, as described below, does NOT meet the manager's requirements?

(A) Joanne Bernstein has worked for the department of education as coordinator of research for the past eleven years. She also served for six years as director of the Save the Children Fund, for which she was awarded an honorary doctorate from the liberal arts college where she earned her bachelor's degree.

(B) Alvin Johnson is a doctoral candidate at a local university and is currently working on a dissertation. Prior to undertaking doctoral studies, he worked as a psychology researcher for seven years.

(C) Edward St. John has worked as a business consultant for the past ten years, during which time he has published six novels. He holds an earned doctorate from one of the nation's foremost business schools.

(D) Michael Roberts has published two highly regarded books on the problems of urban public schools and has a master's degree in special education. He taught special education classes for two years and then for four years served as a research associate with the Mayor's Task Force on Education.

(E) Alicia Arias holds an earned doctorate in sociology from a prestigious university and has published one book and fifteen research articles in sociology.

14. Government-subsidized insurance available to homeowners makes it feasible for anyone to build a house on a section of coastline regularly struck by hurricanes. Each major storm causes billions of dollars worth of damage in such coastal areas, after which owners who have insurance are able to collect an amount of money sufficient to recoup a high percentage of their losses.

The passage provides the most support for an argument against a government bill proposing

(A) that power companies be required to bury power lines in areas of the coastline regularly struck by hurricanes

(B) an increase in funding of weather service programs that provide a hurricane watch and warning system for coastal areas

(C) renewal of federal funding for emergency life-support programs in hurricane-stricken areas

(D) establishment of an agency committed to managing coastal lands in ecologically responsible ways

(E) establishment of a contingency fund protecting owners of uninsured houses in the coastal areas from catastrophic losses due to the hurricane damage

15. Conservative: Socialists begin their arguments with an analysis of history, from which they claim to derive certain trends leading inevitably to a socialist future. But in the day-to-day progress of history there are never such discernible trends. Only in retrospect does inevitability appear, for history occurs through accident, contingency, and individual struggle.

Socialist: If we thought the outcome of history were inevitable, we would not work so hard to transform the institutions of capitalist society. But to transform them we must first understand them, and we can only understand them by an analysis of their history. This is why historical analysis is important in socialist argument.

The socialist's statements imply a conflict with the conservative's view of history if the conservative also holds that

(A) it would have been impossible for anyone to predict a significant period beforehand that the institutions of capitalist society would take the form that they actually took
(B) the apparent inevitability of historical change is deceptive; all historical events could have occurred otherwise than they actually did
(C) in the past, radical changes in social structures have mostly resulted in a deterioration of social conditions
(D) since socialism cannot arise by accident or contingency, it can only arise as a result of individual struggle
(E) because historical changes are mostly accidental, it is impossible for people to direct their efforts sensibly toward achieving large-scale changes in social conditions

16. Because learned patterns of behavior, such as the association of a green light with "go" or the expectation that switches will flip up for "on," become deeply ingrained, designers should make allowances for that fact, in order not to produce machines that are inefficient or dangerous. In which one of the following situations is the principle expressed most clearly violated?

(A) Manufacturers have refused to change the standard order of letters on the typewriter keyboard even though some people who have never learned to type find this arrangement of letters bewildering.
(B) Government regulations require that crucial instruments in airplane cockpits be placed in exactly the same array in all commercial aircraft.
(C) Automobile manufacturers generally design for all of their automobiles a square or oblong ignition key and a round or oval luggage compartment key.
(D) The only traffic signs that are triangular in shape are "yield" signs.
(E) On some tape recorders the "start" button is red and the "stop" button is yellow.

17. Babies who can hear and have hearing parents who expose them to speech begin to babble at a certain age as a precursor to speaking. In the same way, deaf babies with deaf parents who communicate with them and with each other by signing begin to babble in signs at the same age. That is, they make repetitive hand gestures that constitute, within the language system of signs, the analogue of repeated syllables in speech.

The information above, if accurate, can best be used as evidence against which one of the following hypotheses?

(A) Names of persons or things are the simplest words in a language, since babies use them before using the names of actions or processes.
(B) The development of language competency in babies depends primarily on the physical maturation of the vocal tract, a process that requires speech-oriented vocal activity.
(C) In the absence of adults who communicate with each other in their presence, babies develop idiosyncratic languages.
(D) In babbling, babies are unaware that the sound or gesture combinations they use can be employed in a purposive way.
(E) The making of hand gestures by hearing babies who have hearing parents should be interpreted as a part of their developing language.

18. Teachers are effective only when they help their students become independent learners. Yet not until teachers have the power to make decisions in their own classrooms can they enable their students to make their own decisions. Students' capability to make their own decisions is essential to their becoming independent learners. Therefore, if teachers are to be effective, they must have the power to make decisions in their own classrooms.

    According to the argument, each of the following could be true of teachers who have enabled their students to make their own decisions EXCEPT:

    (A) Their students have not become independent learners.
    (B) They are not effective teachers.
    (C) They are effective teachers.
    (D) They have the power to make decisions in their own classrooms.
    (E) They do not have the power to make decisions in their own classrooms.

19. Some people think that in every barrel of politicians there are only a few rotten ones. But if deceit is a quality of rottenness, I believe all effective politicians are rotten. They must be deceitful in order to do the job properly. Someone who is scrupulously honest about obeying the rules of society will never be an effective politician.

    Assuming that the author's statements are accurate, which one of the following statements CANNOT be true?

    (A) Some people think all politicians are rotten.
    (B) Some politicians are scrupulously honest.
    (C) Some people define a politician's job as obeying the rules of society.
    (D) Some deceitful politicians are ineffective.
    (E) Some scrupulously honest politicians are effective.

Chapter Fourteen: Point at Issue Questions

Please Note: A Point of Agreement question appears last in this chapter.

1. Shanna: Owners of any work of art, simply by virtue of ownership, ethically have the right to destroy that artwork if they find it morally or aesthetically distasteful, or if caring for it becomes inconvenient.

Jorge: Ownership of unique artworks, unlike ownership of other kinds of objects, carries the moral right to possess but not to destroy. A unique work of art with aesthetic or historical value belongs to posterity and so must be preserved, whatever the personal wishes of its legal owner.

On the basis of their statements, Shanna and Jorge are committed to disagreeing about the truth of which one of the following statements?

(A) Anyone who owns a portrait presenting his or her father in an unflattering light would for that reason alone be ethically justified in destroying it.
(B) People who own aesthetically valuable works of art have no moral obligation to make them available for public viewing.
(C) Valuable paintings by well-known artists are seldom intentionally damaged or destroyed by their owners.
(D) If a piece of sculpture is not unique, its owner has no ethical obligation to preserve it if doing so proves burdensome.
(E) It is legally permissible for a unique and historically valuable mural to be destroyed by its owner if he or she tires of it.

2. Alia: Hawthorne admits that he has influence with high government officials. He further admits that he sold that influence to an environmental interest group. There can be no justification for this kind of unethical behavior.

Martha: I disagree that he was unethical. The group that retained Hawthorne's services is dedicated to the cause of preventing water pollution. So, in using his influence to benefit this group, Hawthorne also benefited the public.

Alia and Martha disagree on whether

(A) the meaning of ethical behavior has changed over time
(B) the consequences of Hawthorne's behavior can ethically justify that behavior
(C) the standards for judging ethical behavior can be imposed on Hawthorne by another
(D) the meaning of ethical behavior is the same in a public situation as in a private one
(E) the definition of ethical behavior is rooted in philosophy or religion

3. Consumer advocate: Tropical oils are high in saturated fats, which increase the risk of heart disease. Fortunately, in most prepared food tropical oils can be replaced by healthier alternatives without noticeably affecting taste. Therefore, intensive publicity about the disadvantage of tropical oils will be likely to result in dietary changes that will diminish many people's risk of developing heart disease.

Nutritionist: The major sources of saturated fat in the average North American diet are meat, poultry, and dairy products, not tropical oils. Thus, focusing attention on the health hazards of tropical oils would be counterproductive, because it would encourage people to believe that more substantial dietary changes are unnecessary.

Which one of the following is a point at issue between the nutritionist and the consumer advocate?

(A) whether a diet that regularly includes large quantities of tropical oil can increase the risk of heart disease
(B) whether intensive publicity campaigns can be effective as a means of changing people's eating habits
(C) whether more people in North America would benefit from reducing the amount of meat they consume than would benefit from eliminating tropical oils from their diets
(D) whether some people's diets could be made significantly healthier if they replaced all tropical oils with vegetable oils that are significantly lower in saturated fat
(E) whether conducting a publicity campaign that, by focusing on the health hazards of tropical oils, persuades people to replace such oils with healthier alternatives is a good public-health strategy

4. Two paleontologists, Dr. Tyson and Dr. Rees, disagree over the interpretation of certain footprints that were left among other footprints in hardened volcanic ash at site G. Dr. Tyson claims they are clearly early hominid footprints since they show human charac-teristics: a squarish heel and a big toe immediately adjacent to the next toe. However, since the footprints indicate that if hominids made those prints they would have had to walk in an unexpected cross-stepping manner, by placing the left foot to the right of the right foot, Dr. Rees rejects Dr. Tyson's conclusion.

The disagreement between the two paleontologists is over which one of the following?

(A) the relative significance of various aspects of the evidence
(B) the assumption that early hominid footprints are distinguishable from other footprints
(C) the possibility of using the evidence of footprints to determine the gait of the creature that made those footprints
(D) the assumption that evidence from one paleontologic site is enough to support a conclusion
(E) the likelihood that early hominids would have walked upright on two feet

5. Dr. Schilling: Those who advocate replacing my country's private health insurance system with nationalized health insurance because of the rising costs of medical care fail to consider the high human costs that consumers pay in countries with nationalized insurance: access to high-technology medicine is restricted. Kidney transplants and open-heart surgery,familiar life-saving procedures,are rationed. People are denied their right to treatments they want and need.

Dr. Laforte: Your country's reliance on private health insurance denies access even to basic, conventional medicine to the many people who cannot afford adequate health coverage. With nationalized insurance, rich and poor have equal access to life-saving medical procedures, and people's right to decent medical treatment regardless of income is not violated.

Dr. Schilling's and Dr. Laforte's statements provide the most support for holding that they would disagree about the truth of which one of the following?

(A) People's rights are violated less when they are denied an available medical treatment they need because they lack the means to pay for it than when they are denied such treatment on noneconomic grounds.
(B) Where health insurance is provided by private insurance companies, people who are wealthy generally receive better health care than do people who are unable to afford health insurance.
(C) In countries that rely primarily on private health insurance to pay for medical costs, most people who would benefit from a kidney transplant receive one.
(D) In countries with nationalized health insurance, no one who needs a familiar medical treatment in order to stay alive is denied that treatment.
(E) Anyone who wants a particular medical treatment has a right to receive that treatment.

6. Jones: Prehistoric wooden tools found in South America have been dated to 13,000 years ago. Although scientists attribute these tools to peoples whose ancestors first crossed into the Americas from Siberia to Alaska, this cannot be correct. In order to have reached a site so far south, these peoples must have been migrating southward well before 13,000 years ago. However, no such tools dating to before 13,000 years ago have been found anywhere between Alaska and South America.

Smith: Your evidence is inconclusive. Those tools were found in peat bogs, which are rare in the Americas. Wooden tools in soils other than peat bogs usually decompose within only a few years.

The point at issue between Jones and Smith is

(A) whether all prehistoric tools that are 13,000 years or older were made of wood
(B) whether the scientists' attribution of tools could be correct in light of Jones's evidence
(C) whether the dating of the wooden tools by the scientists could be correct
(D) how long ago the peoples who crossed into the Americas from Siberia to Alaska first did so
(E) whether Smith's evidence entails that the wooden tools have been dated correctly

7. Derek: We must exploit available resources in developing effective anticancer drugs such as the one made from mature Pacific yew trees. Although the yew population might be threatened, the trees should be harvested now, since an effective synthetic version of the yew's anticancer chemical could take years to develop.

Lola: Not only are mature yews very rare, but most are located in areas where logging is prohibited to protect the habitat of the endangered spotted owl. Despite our eagerness to take advantage of a new medical breakthrough, we should wait for a synthetic drug rather than threaten the survival of both the yew and the owl, which could have far-reaching consequences for an entire ecosystem.

Which one of the following is the main point at issue between Lola and Derek?

(A) whether the harvesting of available Pacific yews would have far-reaching environmental repercussions
(B) whether the drugs that are effective against potentially deadly diseases should be based on synthetic rather than naturally occurring chemicals
(C) whether it is justifiable to wait until a synthetic drug can be developed when the capacity for producing the yew-derived drug already exists
(D) the extent of the environmental disaster that would result if both the Pacific yew and the spotted owl were to become extinct
(E) whether environmental considerations should ever have any weight when human lives are at stake

8. Consumer advocate: Under the current absence of government standards for food product labeling, manufacturers are misleading or deceiving consumers by their product labeling. For example, a certain brand of juice is labeled "fresh orange juice," yet the product is made from water, concentrate, and flavor enhancers. Since "fresh" as applied to food products is commonly understood to mean pure and unprocessed, labeling that orange juice "fresh" is unquestionably deceptive.

Manufacturer: Using words somewhat differently than they are commonly used is not deceptive. After all, "fresh" can also mean never frozen. We cannot be faulted for failing to comply with standards that have not been officially formulated. When the government sets clear standards pertaining to product labeling, we will certainly comply with them.

On the basis of their statements above, the consumer advocate and the manufacturer are committed to disagreeing about the truth of which one of the following statements?

(A) In the absence of government standards, common understanding is the arbiter of deceptive labeling practices.
(B) Truthful labeling practices that reflect common standards of usage can be established by the government.
(C) The term "fresh" when it is applied to food products is commonly understood to mean pure and unprocessed.
(D) Terms that apply to natural foods can be truthfully applied to packaged foods.
(E) Clear government standards for labeling food products will ensure truthful labeling practices.

9. Sabina: The words used in expressing facts affect neither the facts nor the conclusions those facts will support. Moreover, if the words are clearly defined and consistently used, the actual words chosen make no difference to an argument's soundness. Thus, how an argument is expressed can have no bearing on whether it is a good argument.

Emile: Badly chosen words can make even the soundest argument a poor one. After all, many words have social and political connotations that influence people's response to claims expressed in those words, regardless of how carefully and explicitly those words are defined. Since whether people will acknowledge a fact is affected by how the fact is expressed, the conclusions they actually draw are also affected.

The point at issue between Emile and Sabina is whether

(A) defining words in one way rather than another can alter either the facts or the conclusions the facts will justify
(B) a word can be defined without taking into account its social and political connotations
(C) a sound argument in support of a given conclusion is a better argument than any unsound argument for that same conclusion
(D) it would be a good policy to avoid using words that are likely to lead people either to misunderstand the claims being made or to reason badly about those claims
(E) a factor that affects neither the truth of an argument's premises nor the logical relation between its premises and its conclusion can cause an argument to be a bad one

10. X: Since many chemicals useful for agriculture and medicine derive from rare or endangered plant species, it is likely that many plant species that are now extinct could have provided us with substances that would have been a boon to humanity. Therefore, if we want to ensure that chemicals from plants are available for use in the future, we must make more serious efforts to preserve for all time our natural resources.

Y: But living things are not our "resources." Yours is a selfish approach to conservation. We should rather strive to preserve living species because they deserve to survive, not because of the good they can do us.

Which one of the following is an issue about which X and Y disagree?

(A) whether the benefits humans derive from exploiting nonhuman species provide a good reason for preserving nonhuman species
(B) whether the cost of preserving plant species outweighs the cost of artificially synthesizing chemicals that could otherwise be derived from those species
(C) whether it is prudent to conserve natural resources
(D) whether humans should make efforts to prevent the extinction of living species
(E) whether all nonhuman species are equally valuable as natural resources

11. Lewis: Those who do not learn from past mistakes—their own and those of others—are condemned to repeat them. In order to benefit from the lessons of history, however, we first have to know history. That is why the acquisition of broad historical knowledge is so important.

Morris: The trouble is that the past is infinitely various. From its inexhaustible storehouse of events it is possible to prove anything or its contrary.

The issue that Morris raises in objecting to Lewis' view is whether

(A) there are any uncontested historical facts
(B) historical knowledge can be too narrow to be useful
(C) history teaches any unequivocal lessons
(D) there are conventional criteria for calling a past action a mistake
(E) events in the present are influenced by past events

12. Harris: Currently, hybrid animals are not protected by international endangered-species regulations. But new techniques in genetic research suggest that the red wolf, long thought to be an independent species, is a hybrid of the coyote and the gray wolf. Hence, since the red wolf clearly deserves protection, these regulations should be changed to admit the protection of hybrids.

Vogel: Yet hybrids do not need protection. Since a breeding population that arises through hybridization descends from independent species, if any such population were to die out, it could easily be revived by interbreeding members of the species from which the hybrid is descended.

Which one of the following is a point at issue between Harris and Vogel?

(A) whether the red wolf descends from the gray wolf and the coyote
(B) whether there are some species that are currently considered endangered that are not in fact in any danger
(C) whether the packs of red wolves that currently exist are in danger of dying out
(D) whether there are some hybrids that ought to be protected by endangered-species regulations
(E) whether new techniques in genetic research should be used to determine which groups of animals constitute species and which constitute hybrids

13. Conservative: Socialists begin their arguments with an analysis of history, from which they claim to derive certain trends leading inevitably to a socialist future. But in the day-to-day progress of history there are never such discernible trends. Only in retrospect does inevitability appear, for history occurs through accident, contingency, and individual struggle.

Socialist: If we thought the outcome of history were inevitable, we would not work so hard to transform the institutions of capitalist society. But to transform them we must first understand them, and we can only understand them by an analysis of their history. This is why historical analysis is important in socialist argument.

In the dispute the issue between the socialist and the conservative can most accurately be described as whether

(A) a socialist society is the inevitable consequence of historical trends that can be identified by an analysis of history
(B) the institutions of capitalist society stand in need of transformation
(C) socialists' arguments for the inevitability of socialism are justified
(D) it is possible for people by their own efforts to affect the course of history
(E) socialists analyze history in order to support the view that socialism is inevitable

14. Alexander: The chemical waste dump outside our town should be cleaned up immediately. Admittedly, it will be very costly to convert that site into woodland, but we have a pressing obligation to redress the harm we have done to local forests and wildlife.

Teresa: But our town's first priority is the health of its people. So even if putting the dump there was environmentally disastrous, we should not spend our resources on correcting it unless it presents a significant health hazard to people. If it does, then we only need to remove that hazard.

Which one of the following is the point at issue between Alexander and Teresa?

(A) whether the maintenance of a chemical waste dump inflicts significant damage on forests and wildlife
(B) whether it is extremely costly to clean up a chemical waste dump in order to replace it by a woodland
(C) whether the public should be consulted in determining the public health risk posed by a chemical waste dump
(D) whether the town has an obligation to redress damage to local forests and wildlife if that damage poses no significant health hazard to people
(E) whether destroying forests and wildlife in order to establish a chemical waste dump amounts to an environmental disaster

15. Bart: A mathematical problem that defied solution for hundreds of years has finally yielded to a supercomputer. The process by which the supercomputer derived the result is so complex, however, that no one can fully comprehend it. Consequently, the result is unacceptable.

Anne: In scientific research, if the results of a test can be replicated in other tests, the results are acceptable even though the way they were derived might not be fully understood. Therefore, if a mathematical result derived by a supercomputer can be reproduced by other supercomputers following the same procedure, it is acceptable.

The exchange between Bart and Anne most strongly supports the view that they disagree as to

(A) whether a scientific result that has not been replicated can properly be accepted

(B) whether the result that a supercomputer derives for a mathematical problem must be replicated on another supercomputer before it can be accepted

(C) the criterion to be used for accepting a mathematical result derived by a supercomputer

(D) the level of complexity of the process to which Bart refers in his statements

(E) the relative complexity of mathematical problems as compared to scientific problems

16. Walter: For the economically privileged in a society to tolerate an injustice perpetrated against one of society's disadvantaged is not just morally wrong but also shortsighted: a system that inflicts an injustice on a disadvantaged person today can equally well inflict that same injustice on a well-to-do person tomorrow.

Larissa: In our society, the wealthy as well as the well-educated can protect themselves against all sorts of injustices suffered by the less well-off. Allowing such injustices to persist is bad policy not because it places everyone at equal risk of injustice but because it is a potent source of social unrest.

Walter and Larissa are logically committed by what they say to disagreeing about which one of the following?

(A) whether the poor and the rich are part of the same social fabric

(B) whether the most successful members of a society are that society's least tolerant people

(C) whether the disadvantaged members of society suffer from injustice

(D) whether those who have the most advantages in a society are morally obligated to correct that society's injustices

(E) whether the economically privileged members of a society are less exposed to certain sorts of injustices than are the economically disadvantaged

17. Motorcoach driver: Professional drivers spend much more time driving, on average, than do other people and hence are more competent drivers than are other, less experienced drivers. Therefore, the speed limit on major highways should not be reduced, because that action would have the undesirable effect of forcing some people who are now both law-abiding and competent drivers to break the law.

Police officer: All drivers can drive within the legal speed limit if they wish, so it is not true to say that reducing the speed limit would be the cause of such illegal behavior.

The point at issue between the motorcoach driver and the police officer is whether

(A) it would be desirable to reduce the speed limit on major highways
(B) professional drivers will drive within the legal speed limit if that limit is reduced
(C) reducing the speed limit on major highways would cause some professional drivers to break the law
(D) professional drivers are more competent drivers than are other, less experienced drivers
(E) all drivers wish to drive within the speed limit

18. Henry: Some scientists explain the dance of honeybees as the means by which honeybees communicate the location of whatever food source they have just visited to other members of the hive. But honeybees do not need so complicated a mechanism to communicate that information. Forager honeybees returning to their hive simply leave a scent trail from the food source they have just visited. There must therefore be some other explanation for the honeybees' dance.

Winifred: Not necessarily. Most animals have several ways of accomplishing critical tasks. Bees of some species can navigate using either the position of the Sun or the memory of landmarks. Similarly, for honeybees, scent trails are a supplementary not an exclusive means of communicating.

The point at issue between Henry and Winifred is whether

(A) theories of animal behavior can be established on the basis of evidence about only one species of animal
(B) there is more than one valid explanation for the dance of honeybees
(C) honeybees communicate the location of food sources through their dance
(D) the honeybee is the only species of bee that is capable of communicating navigational information to other hive members
(E) the honeybee's sense of smell plays a role in its foraging strategies

19. Yolanda: Gaining access to computers without authorization and manipulating the data and programs they contain is comparable to joyriding in stolen cars; both involve breaking into private property and treating it recklessly. Joyriding, however, is the more dangerous crime because it physically endangers people, whereas only intellectual property is harmed in the case of computer crimes.

Arjun: I disagree! For example, unauthorized use of medical records systems in hospitals could damage data systems on which human lives depend, and therefore computer crimes also cause physical harm to people.

An issue in dispute between Yolanda and Arjun is

(A) whether joyriding physically endangers human lives
(B) whether the unauthorized manipulation of computer data involves damage to private property
(C) whether damage to physical property is more criminal than damage to intellectual property
(D) whether the unauthorized use of computers is as dangerous to people as is joyriding
(E) whether treating private property recklessly is ever a dangerous crime

20. Wirth: All efforts to identify a gene responsible for predisposing people to manic-depression have failed. In fact, nearly all researchers now agree that there is no "manic-depression gene." Therefore, if these researchers are right, any claim that some people are genetically predisposed to manic-depression is simply false.

Chang: I do not dispute your evidence, but I take issue with your conclusion. Many of the researchers you refer to have found evidence that a set of several genes is involved and that complex interactions among these genes produce a predisposition to manic-depression.

The point at issue between Wirth and Chang is whether

(A) efforts to identify a gene or set of several genes responsible for predisposing people to manic depression have all failed
(B) it is likely that researchers will ever be able to find a single gene that predisposes people to manic-depression
(C) nearly all researchers now agree that there is no manic-depression gene
(D) current research supports the claim that no one is genetically predisposed to manic-depression
(E) the efforts made to find a gene that can produce a predisposition to manic-depression were thorough

1. Murray: You claim Senator Brandon has accepted gifts from lobbyists. You are wrong to make this criticism. That it is motivated by personal dislike is shown by the fact that you deliberately avoid criticizing other politicians who have done what you accuse Senator Brandon of doing.

Jane: You are right that I dislike Senator Brandon, but just because I have not criticized the same failing in others doesn't mean you can excuse the senator's offense.

If Murray and Jane are both sincere in what they say, then it can properly be concluded that they agree that

(A) Senator Brandon has accepted gifts from lobbyists
(B) it is wrong for politicians to accept gifts from lobbyists
(C) Jane's criticism of Senator Brandon is motivated only by personal dislike
(D) Senator Brandon should be criticized for accepting gifts from lobbyists
(E) one or more politicians have accepted gifts from lobbyists

Chapter Fifteen: Principle Questions

1. Shanna: Owners of any work of art, simply by virtue of ownership, ethically have the right to destroy that artwork if they find it morally or aesthetically distasteful, or if caring for it becomes inconvenient.

Jorge: Ownership of unique artworks, unlike ownership of other kinds of objects, carries the moral right to possess but not to destroy. A unique work of art with aesthetic or historical value belongs to posterity and so must be preserved, whatever the personal wishes of its legal owner.

Which one of the following principles, if accepted, would contribute most to Shanna's defense of her position against that of Jorge?

(A) Truly great works of art are never morally or aesthetically distasteful to any serious student of the history of art.
(B) The right of future generations to have their artistic heritage preserved is of greater importance than the rights of any presently living individual.
(C) It would be imprudent to allow the present stock of artworks to be destroyed without some guarantee that the artists of the future will produce works as great as those produced in the past.
(D) There are certain entities over which no one would be ethically justified in claiming absolute rights to ownership.
(E) The autonomy of individuals to do what they wish with what is theirs must not be compromised, in the absence of a threat to anyone's health or safety.

2. A major art theft from a museum was remarkable in that the pieces stolen clearly had been carefully selected. The criterion for selection, however, clearly had not been greatest estimated market value. It follows that the theft was specifically carried out to suit the taste of some individual collector for whose private collection the pieces were destined.

The argument tacitly appeals to which one of the following principles?

(A) Any art theft can, on the evidence of the selection of pieces stolen, be categorized as committed either at the direction of a single known individual or at the direction of a group of known individuals.
(B) Any art theft committed at the direction of a single individual results in a pattern of works taken and works left alone that defies rational analysis.
(C) The pattern of works taken and works left alone can sometimes distinguish one type of art theft from another.
(D) Art thefts committed with no preexisting plan for the disposition of the stolen works do not always involve theft of the most valuable pieces only.
(E) The pattern of works taken and works left alone in an art theft can be particularly damaging to the integrity of the remaining collection.

3. When machines are invented and technologies are developed, they alter the range of choices open to us. The clock, for example, made possible the synchronization of human affairs, which resulted in an increase in productivity. At the same time that the clock opened up some avenues, it closed others. It has become harder and harder to live except by the clock, so that now people have no choice in the matter at all.

Which one of the following propositions is best illustrated by the example presented in the passage?

(A) New machines and technologies can enslave as well as liberate us.
(B) People should make a concerted effort to free themselves from the clock.
(C) Some new machines and technologies bring no improvement to our lives.
(D) The increase in productivity was not worth our dependence on the clock.
(E) Most new machines and technologies make our lives more synchronized and productive.

4. It has been claimed that an action is morally good only if it benefits another person and was performed with that intention; whereas an action that harms another person is morally bad either if such harm was intended or if reasonable forethought would have shown that the action was likely to cause harm.

   Which one of the following judgments most closely conforms to the principle cited above?

   (A) Pamela wrote a letter attempting to cause trouble between Edward and his friend; this action of Pamela's was morally bad, even though the letter, in fact, had an effect directly opposite from the one intended.
   (B) In order to secure a promotion, Jeffrey devoted his own time to resolving a backlog of medical benefits claims; Jeffrey's action was morally good since it alone enabled Sara's claim to be processed in time for her to receive much needed treatment.
   (C) Intending to help her elderly neighbor by clearing his walkway after a snowstorm, Teresa inadvertently left ice on his steps; because of this exposed ice, her neighbor had a bad fall, thus showing that morally good actions can have bad consequences.
   (D) Marilees, asked by a homeless man for food, gave the man her own sandwich; however, because the man tried to talk while he was eating the sandwich, it caused him to choke, and thus Marilees unintentionally performed a morally bad action.
   (E) Jonathan agreed to watch his three-year-old niece while she played but, becoming engrossed in conversation, did not see her run into the street where she was hit by a bicycle; even though he intended no harm, Jonathan's action was morally bad.

5. Current legislation that requires designated sections for smokers and nonsmokers on the premises of privately owned businesses is an intrusion into the private sector that cannot be justified. The fact that studies indicate that nonsmokers might be harmed by inhaling the smoke from others' cigarettes is not the main issue. Rather, the main issue concerns the government's violation of the right of private businesses to determine their own policies and rules.

   Which one of the following is a principle that, if accepted, could enable the conclusion to be properly drawn?

   (A) Government intrusion into the policies and rules of private businesses is justified only when individuals might be harmed.
   (B) The right of individuals to breathe safe air supersedes the right of businesses to be free from government intrusion.
   (C) The right of businesses to self-determination overrides whatever right or duty the government may have to protect the individual.
   (D) It is the duty of private businesses to protect employees from harm in the workplace.
   (E) Where the rights of businesses and the duty of government conflict, the main issue is finding a successful compromise.

PRINCIPLE

6. Physician: The patient is suffering either from disease X or else from disease Y, but there is no available test for distinguishing X from Y. Therefore, since there is an effective treatment for Y but no treatment for X, we must act on the assumption that the patient has a case of Y.

The physician's reasoning could be based on which one of the following principles?

(A) In treating a patient who has one or the other of two diseases, it is more important to treat the diseases than to determine which of the two diseases the patient has.
(B) If circumstances beyond a decision maker's control will affect the outcome of the decision maker's actions, the decision maker must assume that circumstances are unfavorable.
(C) When the soundness of a strategy depends on the truth of a certain assumption, the first step in putting the strategy into effect must be to test the truth of this assumption.
(D) When success is possible only if a circumstance beyond one's control is favorable, then one's strategy must be based on the assumption that this circumstance is in fact favorable.
(E) When only one strategy carries the possibility of success, circumstances must as much as possible be changed to fit this strategy.

7. Most children find it very difficult to explain exactly what the words they use mean when those words do not refer to things that can be seen or touched. Yet, since children are able to use these words to convey the feelings and emotions they are obviously experiencing, understanding what a word means clearly does not depend on being able to explain it.

Which one of the following principles, if accepted, would provide the most justification for the conclusion?

(A) The fact that a task is very difficult for most people does not mean that no one can do it.
(B) Anyone who can provide an exact explanation of a word has a clear understanding of what that word means.
(C) Words that refer to emotions invariably have less narrowly circumscribed conventional meanings than do words that refer to physical objects.
(D) When someone appropriately uses a word to convey something that he or she is experiencing, that person understands what that word means.
(E) Words can be explained satisfactorily only when they refer to things that can be seen or touched.

8. Something must be done to ease traffic congestion. In traditional small towns, people used to work and shop in the same town in which they lived; but now that stores and workplaces are located far away from residential areas, people cannot avoid traveling long distances each day. Traffic congestion is so heavy on all roads that, even on major highways where the maximum speed limit is 55 miles per hour, the actual speed averages only 35 miles per hour.

Which one of the following proposals is most supported by the statements above?

(A) The maximum speed limit on major highways should be increased.
(B) People who now travel on major highways should be encouraged to travel on secondary roads instead.
(C) Residents of the remaining traditional small towns should be encouraged to move to the suburbs.
(D) Drivers who travel well below the maximum speed limit on major highways should be fined.
(E) New businesses should be encouraged to locate closer to where their workers would live.

9. Mayor of Plainsville: In order to help the economy of Plainsville, I am using some of our tax revenues to help bring a major highway through the town and thereby attract new business to Plainsville.

Citizens' group: You must have interests other than our economy in mind. If you were really interested in helping our economy, you would instead allocate the revenues to building a new business park, since it would bring in twice the business that your highway would.

Which one of the following principles, if accepted, would most help the citizens' group to justify drawing its conclusion that the mayor has in mind interests other than Plainsville's economy?

(A) Anyone really pursuing a cause will choose the means that that person believes will advance the cause the farthest.
(B) Any goal that includes helping the economy of a community will require public revenues in order to be achieved.
(C) Anyone planning to use resources collected from a group must consult the members of the group before using the resources.
(D) Any cause worth committing oneself to must include specific goals toward which one can work.
(E) Any cause not pursued by public officials, if it is to be pursued at all, must be pursued by members of the community.

10. Mary, a veterinary student, has been assigned an experiment in mammalian physiology that would require her to take a healthy, anesthetized dog and subject it to a drastic blood loss in order to observe the physiological consequences of shock. The dog would neither regain consciousness nor survive the experiment. Mary decides not to do this assignment.

Mary's decision most closely accords with which one of the following principles?

(A) All other things being equal, gratuitously causing any animal to suffer pain is unjustified.
(B) Taking the life of an animal is not justifiable unless doing so would immediately assist in saving several animal lives or in protecting the health of a person.
(C) The only sufficient justification for experimenting on animals is that future animal suffering is thereby prevented.
(D) Practicing veterinarians have a professional obligation to strive to prevent the unnecessary death of an animal except in cases of severely ill or injured animals whose prospects for recovery are dim.
(E) No one is ever justified in acting with the sole intention of causing the death of a living thing, be it animal or human.

11. Whenever a major political scandal erupts before an election and voters blame the scandal on all parties about equally, virtually all incumbents, from whatever party, seeking reelection are returned to office. However, when voters blame such a scandal on only one party, incumbents from that party are likely to be defeated by challengers from other parties. The proportion of incumbents who seek reelection is high and remarkably constant from election to election.

If the voters' reactions are guided by a principle, which one of the following principles would best account for the contrast in reactions described above?

(A) Whenever one incumbent is responsible for one major political scandal and another incumbent is responsible for another, the consequences for the two incumbents should be the same.
(B) When a major political scandal is blamed on incumbents from all parties, that judgment is more accurate than any judgment that incumbents from only one party are to blame.
(C) Incumbents who are rightly blamed for a major political scandal should not seek reelection, but if they do, they should not be returned to office.
(D) Major political scandals can practically always be blamed on incumbents, but whether those incumbents should be voted out of office depends on who their challengers are.
(E) When major political scandals are less the responsibility of individual incumbents than of the parties to which they belong, whatever party was responsible must be penalized when possible.

12. Naturalist: For decades we have known that the tuatara, a New Zealand reptile, have been approaching extinction on the South Island. But since South Island tuatara were thought to be of the same species as North Island tuatara there was no need to protect them. But new research indicates that the South Island tuatara are a distinct species, found only in that location. Because it is now known that if the South Island tuatara are lost an entire species will thereby be lost, human beings are now obliged to prevent their extinction, even if it means killing many of their unendangered natural predators.

Which one of the following principles most helps to justify the naturalist's argumentation?

(A) In order to maximize the number of living things on Earth, steps should be taken to preserve all local populations of animals.
(B) When an animal is in danger of dying, there is an obligation to help save its life, if doing so would not interfere with the health or well-being of other animals or people.
(C) The threat of local extinction imposes no obligation to try to prevent that extinction, whereas the threat of global extinction does impose such an obligation.
(D) Human activities that either intentionally or unintentionally threaten the survival of an animal species ought to be curtailed.
(E) Species that are found in only one circumscribed geographical region ought to be given more care and attention than are other species because they are more vulnerable to extinction.

PRINCIPLE

13. Someone's benefiting from having done harm to another person is morally justifiable only if the person who was harmed knew that what was done could cause that harm but consented to its being done anyway.

Which one of the following judgments most closely conforms to the principle above?

(A) Attempting to avoid being kept after school as punishment for breaking a window, Sonia falsely claimed that her brother had broken it; Sonia's action was morally unjustifiable since it resulted in both children being kept after school for something only Sonia had done.

(B) Since Ned would not have won the prize for best model airplane if Penny's brother had not inadvertently damaged her entry while playing with it, Ned is morally unjustified in accepting his prize.

(C) Wesley, a doctor, persuaded Max to take part in a medical experiment in which a new drug was being tested; since Wesley failed to warn Max about the serious side effects of the drug and the drug proved to have no other effects, Wesley was morally unjustified in using the results obtained from Max in his report.

(D) Because Roger's mother suffered severe complications as a result of donating a kidney to him for a lifesaving kidney transplant, it was morally unjustifiable for Roger to receive the transplant, even though his mother, herself a doctor, had been eager for the transplant to be performed.

(E) For James, who was convicted of having defrauded a large number of people out of their savings and wrote a book about his scheme while in prison, to be denied the profits from his book would be morally unjustifiable since he has already been punished for his crime.

14. Proposals for extending the United States school year to bring it more in line with its European and Japanese counterparts are often met with the objection that curtailing the schools' three-month summer vacation would violate an established United States tradition dating from the nineteenth century. However, this objection misses its mark. True, in the nineteenth century the majority of schools closed for three months every summer, but only because they were in rural areas where successful harvests depended on children's labor. If any policy could be justified by those appeals to tradition, it would be the policy of determining the length of the school year according to the needs of the economy.

Which one of the following principles, if accepted, would provide the strongest justification for the conclusion?

(A) That a given social policy has traditionally been in force justifies maintaining that policy only if doing so does not conflict with more pressing social needs.

(B) Appeals to its own traditions cannot excuse a country from the obligation to bring its practices in line with the legitimate expectations of the rest of the world.

(C) Because appeals to tradition often serve to mask the real interests at issue, such appeals should be disregarded.

(D) Traditional principles should be discarded when they no longer serve the needs of the economy.

(E) The actual tradition embodied in a given practice can be accurately identified only by reference to the reasons that originally prompted that practice.

15. Many environmentalists have urged environmental awareness on consumers, saying that if we accept moral responsibility for our effects on the environment, then products that directly or indirectly harm the environment ought to be avoided. Unfortunately it is usually impossible for consumers to assess the environmental impact of a product, and thus impossible for them to consciously restrict their purchases to environmentally benign products. Because of this impossibility there can be no moral duty to choose products in the way these environmentalists urge, since ________________.

    Which one of the following principles provides the most appropriate completion for the argument?

    (A) a moral duty to perform an action is never based solely on the effects the action will have on other people
    (B) a person cannot possibly have a moral duty to do what he or she is unable to do
    (C) moral considerations should not be the sole determinants of what products are made available to consumers
    (D) the morally right action is always the one whose effects produce the least total harm
    (E) where a moral duty exists, it supersedes any legal duty and any other kind of duty

16. The government provides insurance for individuals' bank deposits, but requires the banks to pay the premiums for this insurance. Since it is depositors who primarily benefit from the security this insurance provides, the government should take steps to ensure that depositors who want this security bear the cost of it and thus should make depositors pay the premiums for insuring their own accounts.

    Which one of the following principles, if established, would do most to justify drawing the conclusion of the argument on the basis of the reasons offered in its support?

    (A) The people who stand to benefit from an economic service should always be made to bear the costs of that service.
    (B) Any rational system of insurance must base the size of premiums on the degree of risk involved.
    (C) Government-backed security for investors, such as bank depositors, should be provided only when it does not reduce incentives for investors to make responsible investments.
    (D) The choice of not accepting an offered service should always be available, even if there is no charge for the service.
    (E) The government should avoid any actions that might alter the behavior of corporations and individuals in the market.

17. Derek: We must exploit available resources in developing effective anticancer drugs such as the one made from mature Pacific yew trees. Although the yew population might be threatened, the trees should be harvested now, since an effective synthetic version of the yew's anticancer chemical could take years to develop.

    Lola: Not only are mature yews very rare, but most are located in areas where logging is prohibited to protect the habitat of the endangered spotted owl. Despite our eagerness to take advantage of a new medical breakthrough, we should wait for a synthetic drug rather than threaten the survival of both the yew and the owl, which could have far-reaching consequences for an entire Ecosystem.

    Lola's position most closely conforms to which one of the following principles?

    (A) Unless people's well-being is threatened, there should be no higher priority than preserving endangered plant and animal populations.
    (B) Medical researchers should work with environmentalists to come to an agreement about the fate of the Pacific yew and the spotted owl.
    (C) Environmental concerns should play a role in decisions concerning medical research only if human lives are not at stake.
    (D) Only medical breakthroughs that could save human lives would justify threatening the environment.
    (E) Avoiding actions that threaten an entire ecosystem takes precedence over immediately providing advantage to a restricted group of people.

18. Consumer advocate: Under the current absence of government standards for food product labeling, manufacturers are misleading or deceiving consumers by their product labeling. For example, a certain brand of juice is labeled "fresh orange juice," yet the product is made from water, concentrate, and flavor enhancers. Since "fresh" as applied to food products is commonly understood to mean pure and unprocessed, labeling that orange juice "fresh" is unquestionably deceptive.

Manufacturer: Using words somewhat differently than they are commonly used is not deceptive. After all, "fresh" can also mean never frozen. We cannot be faulted for failing to comply with standards that have not been officially formulated. When the government sets clear standards pertaining to product labeling, we will certainly comply with them.

Which one of the following principles, if established, would contribute most to a defense of the manufacturer's position against that of the consumer advocate?

(A) In the absence of government definitions for terms used in product labeling, common standards of understanding alone should apply.
(B) Government standards for truthful labeling should always be designed to reflect common standards of understanding.
(C) People should be free, to the extent that it is legal to do so, to exploit to their advantages the inherent ambiguity and vagueness in language.
(D) When government standards and common standards for truthful labeling are incompatible with each other, the government standards should always take precedence.
(E) In their interpretation of language, consumers should never presume that vagueness indicates an attempt to deceive on the part of manufacturers unless those manufacturers would reap large benefits from successful deception.

19. Psychologists today recognize childhood as a separate stage of life which can only be understood in its own terms, and they wonder why the Western world took so long to see the folly of regarding children simply as small, inadequately socialized adults. Most psychologists, however, persist in regarding people 70 to 90 years old as though they were 35 year olds who just happen to have white hair and extra leisure time. But old age is as fundamentally different from young adulthood and middle age as childhood is,a fact attested to by the organization of modern social and economic life. Surely it is time, therefore, to acknowledge that serious research into the unique psychology of advanced age has become indispensable.

Which one of the following principles, if established, would provide the strongest backing for the argument?

(A) Whenever current psychological practice conflicts with traditional attitudes toward people, those traditional attitudes should be changed to bring them in line with current psychological practice.
(B) Whenever two groups of people are so related to each other that any member of the second group must previously have been a member of the first, people in the first group should not be regarded simply as deviant members of the second group.
(C) Whenever most practitioners of a given discipline approach a particular problem in the same way, that uniformity is good evidence that all similar problems should also be approached in that way.
(D) Whenever a society's economic life is so organized that two distinct times of life are treated as being fundamentally different from one another, each time of life can be understood only in terms of its own distinct psychology.
(E) Whenever psychologists agree that a single psychology is inadequate for two distinct age groups, they should be prepared to show that there are greater differences between the two age groups than there are between individuals in the same age group.

20. A local group had planned a parade for tomorrow, but city hall has not yet acted on its application for a permit. The group had applied for the permit well in advance, had made sure their application satisfied all the requirements, and was clearly entitled to a permit. Although the law prohibits parades without a permit, the group plans to proceed with its parade. The group's leader defended its decision by appealing to the principle that citizens need not refrain from actions that fail to comply with the law if they have made a good-faith effort to comply but are prevented from doing so by government inaction.

Which one of the following actions would be justified by the principle to which the leader of the group appealed in defending the decision to proceed?

(A) A chemical-processing company commissioned an environmental impact report on its plant. The report described foul odors emanating from the plant but found no hazardous wastes being produced. Consequently, the plant did not alter its processing practices.

(B) A city resident applied for rezoning of her property so that she could build a bowling alley in a residential community. She based her application on the need for recreational facilities in the community. Her application was turned down by the zoning board, so she decided to forgo construction.

(C) The law requires that no car be operated without a certain amount of insurance coverage. But since the authorities have been unable to design an effective procedure for prosecuting owners of cars that are driven without insurance, many car owners are allowing their insurance to lapse.

(D) A real-estate developer obtained a permit to demolish a historic apartment building that had not yet been declared a governmentally protected historic landmark. Despite the protests of citizens' groups, the developer then demolished the building.

(E) A physician who had been trained in one country applied for a license to practice medicine in another country. Although he knew he met all the qualifications for this license, he had not yet received it one year after he applied for it. He began to practice medicine without the license in the second country despite the law's requirement for a license.

21. Some critics claim that it is unfair that so many great works of art are housed in huge metropolitan museums, since the populations served by these museums already have access to a wide variety of important artwork. But this criticism is in principle unwarranted because the limited number of masterpieces makes wider distribution of them impractical. Besides, if a masterpiece is to be fully appreciated, it must be seen alongside other works that provide a social and historical context for it.

Which one of the following, if established, could most logically serve as the principle appealed to in the argument countering the critics' claim?

(A) In providing facilities to the public, the goal should be to ensure that as many as possible of those people who could benefit from the facilities are able to do so.

(B) In providing facilities to the public, the goal should be to ensure that the greatest possible number of people gain the greatest benefit possible from them.

(C) It is unreasonable to enforce a redistribution of social goods that involves depriving some members of society of these goods in order to supply others.

(D) For it to be reasonable to criticize an arrangement as unfair, there must be a more equitable arrangement that is practically attainable.

(E) A work of art should be displayed in conditions resembling as closely as possible those in which the work was originally intended to be displayed.

PRINCIPLE

22. Of every 100 burglar alarms police answer, 99 are false alarms. This situation causes an enormous and dangerous drain on increasingly scarce public resources. Each false alarm wastes an average of 45 minutes of police time. As a result police are consistently taken away from responding to other legitimate calls for service, and a disproportionate share of police service goes to alarm system users, who are mostly businesses and affluent homeowners. However, burglar alarm systems, unlike car alarm systems, are effective in deterring burglaries, so the only acceptable solution is to fine burglar alarm system owners the cost of 45 minutes of police time for each false alarm their systems generate.

On the basis of the premises advanced, which one of the following principles, if established, would provide the most justification for the concluding recommendation?

(A) No segment of a community should be permitted to engage in a practice that has been shown to result in a disproportionate share of police service being devoted to that segment of the community.

(B) When public resources are in short supply, any individual who wants special services from public agencies such as police and fire departments should be required to pay for those services if he or she can afford to do so.

(C) Police departments are not justified in improving service to one segment of the community at the expense of other segments of the community unless doing so reduces the crime level throughout the entire area served.

(D) Anyone who directly benefits from a service provided by public employees should be required to reimburse the general public fund an amount equivalent to the average cost of providing that service.

(E) If receipt of a service results in the waste of scarce public resources and people with other legitimate needs are disadvantaged in consequence, the recipient of that service should compensate the public for the resources wasted.

23. No one knows what purposes, if any, dreams serve, although there are a number of hypotheses. According to one hypothesis, dreams are produced when the brain is erasing "parasitic connections" (meaningless, accidental associations between ideas), which accumulate during the day and which would otherwise clog up our memories. Interestingly, the only mammal that does not have rapid eye movement sleep, in which we humans typically have our most vivid dreams, is the spiny anteater, which has been seen as anomalous in that it has a very large brain relative to the animal's size. This fact provides some confirmation for the parasitic-connection hypothesis, since the hypothesis predicts that for an animal that did not dream to have an effective memory that animal would need extra memory space for the parasitic connections.

The reasoning in the argument most closely conforms to which one of the following principles?

(A) Facts about one species of animal can provide confirmation for hypotheses about all species that are similar in all relevant respects to the particular species in question.

(B) A hypothesis from which several predictions can be drawn as logical conclusions is confirmed only when the majority of these predictions turn out to be true.

(C) A hypothesis about the purpose of an action or object is confirmed when it is shown that the hypothesized purpose is achieved with the help of the action or object and could not be achieved without that action or object.

(D) A hypothesis is partially confirmed whenever a prediction derived from that hypothesis provides an explanation for an otherwise unexplained set of facts.

(E) When several competing hypotheses exist, one of them is confirmed only when it makes a correct prediction that its rivals fail to make.

24. In the past century, North America has shifted its main energy source first from wood to coal, then from coal to oil and natural gas. With each transition, the newly dominant fuel has had less carbon and more hydrogen than its predecessor had. It is logical to conclude that in the future the main energy source will be pure hydrogen.

Which one of the following expresses a general principle that could underlie the argument?

(A) If a series of transitions from one state of a system to another state of that system is allowed to continue without interference, the initial state of the series will eventually recur.
(B) If each of two desirable attributes belongs to a useful substance, then the most useful form of that substance will have those two attributes in equal amounts.
(C) If the second stage of a process has been completed more quickly than the first stage, the third stage of that process will be completed more quickly than the second stage.
(D) If each step in a series of changes involves a decrease of one attribute of the thing undergoing the change and an increase of another, the series will terminate with the first attribute eliminated and only the second attribute present.
(E) If one substance is better for a certain purpose than another substance is, then the best substance for that purpose is one that includes among its attributes all of the attributes of the first substance and none of the attributes of the second substance.

25. New legislation would require a seven-day waiting period in the sale of handguns to private individuals, in order that records of prisons could be checked and the sale of handguns to people likely to hurt other people thereby prevented. People opposed to this legislation claim that prison records are so full of errors that the proposed law would prevent as many law-abiding citizens as criminals from having access to handguns.

If the claim made by people opposed to the new legislation is true, which one of the following is a principle that, if established, would do the most to justify opposition to the new legislation on the basis of that claim?

(A) The rights of law-abiding citizens are more worthy of protection than are the rights of criminals.
(B) Nothing should be done to restrict potential criminals at the cost of placing restrictions on law-abiding citizens.
(C) Legislation should not be enacted if no benefit could accrue to society as a result of that legislation.
(D) No restrictions should be placed on the sale of merchandise unless sale of that merchandise could endanger innocent people.
(E) Even citizens who are neither fugitives nor felons should not be permitted to own a handgun unless they have received adequate training.

26. Cigarette smoking has been shown to be a health hazard; therefore, governments should ban all advertisements that promote smoking.

Which one of the following principles, if established, most strongly supports the argument?

(A) Advertisements should not be allowed to show people doing things that endanger their health.
(B) Advertisers should not make misleading claims about the healthfulness of their products.
(C) Advertisements should disclose the health hazards associated with the products they promote.
(D) All products should conform to strict government health and safety standards.
(E) Advertisements should promote only healthful products.

27. The labeling of otherwise high-calorie foods as "sugar-free," based on the replacement of all sugar by artificial sweeteners, should be prohibited by law. Such a prohibition is indicated because many consumers who need to lose weight will interpret the label "sugar-free" as synonymous with "low in calories" and harm themselves by building weight-loss diets around foods labeled "sugar-free." Manufacturers of sugar-free foods are well aware of this tendency on the part of consumers.

Which one of the following principles, if established, most helps to justify the conclusion in the passage?

(A) Product labels that are literally incorrect should be prohibited by law, even if reliance on those labels is not likely to cause harm to consumers.
(B) Product labels that are literally incorrect, but in such an obvious manner that no rational consumer would rely on them, should nevertheless be prohibited by law.
(C) Product labels that are literally correct but cannot be interpreted by the average buyer of the product without expert help should be prohibited by law.
(D) Product labels that are literally correct but will predictably be misinterpreted by some buyers of the product to their own harm should be prohibited by law.
(E) Product labels that are literally correct, but only on one of two equally accurate interpretations, should be prohibited by law if buyers tend to interpret the label in the way that does not match the product's actual properties.

28. Large quantities of lead dust can be released during renovations in houses with walls painted with lead-based paint. Because the dust puts occupants at high risk of lead poisoning, such renovations should be done only in unoccupied houses by contractors who are experienced in removing all traces of lead from houses and who have the equipment to protect themselves from lead dust. Even when warned, however, many people will not pay to have someone else do renovations they believe they could do less expensively themselves. Therefore, Homeowners' Journal should run an article giving information to homeowners on how to reduce the risk of lead poisoning associated with do-it-yourself renovation.

Which one of the following principles most helps to justify the passage's recommendation about an article?

(A) Potentially dangerous jobs should always be left to those who have the training and experience to perform them safely, even if additional expense results.
(B) If people refuse to change their behavior even when warned that they are jeopardizing their health, information that enables them to minimize the risks of that behavior should be made available to them.
(C) A journal for homeowners should provide its readers with information on do-it-yourself projects only if such projects do not entail substantial risks.
(D) No one should be encouraged to perform a potentially dangerous procedure if doing so could place any other people at risk.
(E) People who are willing to do work themselves and who are competent to do so should not be discouraged from doing that work.

29. Oscar: I have been accused of plagiarizing the work of Ethel Myers in my recent article. But that accusation is unwarranted. Although I admit I used passages from Myers's book without attribution, Myers gave me permission in private correspondence to do so.

Millie: Myers cannot give you permission to plagiarize. Plagiarism is wrong, not only because it violates author's rights to their own words, but also because it misleads readers: it is fundamentally a type of lie. A lie is no less a lie if another person agrees to the deception.

Which of the following principles, if established, would justify Oscar's judgment?

(A) A writer has no right to quote passage from another published source if the author of that other source has not granted the writer permission to do so.

(B) The writer of an article must cite the source of all passages that were not written by that writer if those passages are more than a few sentences long.

(C) Plagiarism is never justified, but writers are justified in occasionally quoting without attribution the work of other writers if the work quoted has not been published.

(D) An author is entitled to quote freely without attribution the work of a writer if that writer relinquishes his or her exclusive right to the material.

(E) Authors are entitled to quote without attribution passages that they themselves have written and published in other books or articles.

30. Police published a "wanted" poster for a criminal fugitive in a medical journal, because the fugitive was known to have a certain acute noninfectious skin problem that would eventually require a visit to a doctor. The poster asked for information about the whereabouts of the fugitive. A physician's responding to the poster's request for information would not violate medical ethics, since physicians are already subject to requirements to report gunshot wounds to police and certain infectious diseases to health authorities. These exceptions to confidentiality are clearly ethical.

Which one of the following principles, while remaining compatible with the requirements cited above, supports the view that a physician's responding to the request would violate medical ethics?

(A) Since a physician acts both as a professional person and as a citizen, it is not ethical for a physician to conceal information about patients from duly constituted law enforcement agencies that have proper jurisdiction.

(B) Since a patient comes to a physician with the expectation that the patient's visit and medical condition will remain confidential, it is not ethical for a physician to share this information with anyone except personnel within the physician's office.

(C) Since the primary concern of medicine is individual and public health, it is not ethical for a physician, except in the case of gunshot wounds, to reduce patients' willingness to come for treatment by a policy of disclosing their identities to law-enforcement agencies.

(D) Except as required by the medical treatment of the patient, physicians cannot ethically disclose to others information about a patient's identity or medical condition without the patient's consent.

(E) Except to other medical personnel working to preserve or restore the health of a patient or of other persons, physicians cannot ethically disclose information about the identity of patients or their medical condition.

31. Two alternative drugs are available to prevent blood clots from developing after a heart attack. According to two major studies, drug Y does this no more effectively than the more expensive drug Z, but drug Z is either no more or only slightly more effective than drug Y. Drug Z's manufacturer, which has engaged in questionable marketing practices such as offering stock options to doctors who participate in clinical trials of drug Z, does not contest the results of the studies but claims that they do not reveal drug Z's advantages. However, since drug Z does not clearly treat the problem more effectively than drug Y, there is no established medical reason for doctors to use drug Z rather than drug Y on their heart-attack victims.

Which one of the following principles, if established, would most help to justify a doctor's decision to use drug Z rather than drug Y when treating a patient?

(A) Only patients to whom the cost of an expensive treatment will not be a financial hardship should receive that treatment rather than a less expensive alternative one.
(B) Doctors who are willing to assist in research on the relative effectiveness of drugs by participating in clinical trials deserve fair remuneration for that participation.
(C) The decision to use a particular drug when treating a patient should not be influenced by the marketing practices employed by the company manufacturing that drug.
(D) A drug company's criticism of studies of its product that do not report favorably on that product is unavoidably biased and therefore invalid.
(E) Where alternative treatments exist and there is a chance that one is more effective than the other, the possibly more effective one should be employed, regardless of cost.

32. Production manager: The building materials that we produce meet industry safety codes but pose some safety risk. Since we have recently developed the technology to make a safer version of our product, we should stop producing our current product and sell only the safer version in order to protect public safety.

Sales manager: If we stop selling our current product, we will have no money to develop and promote the safer product. We need to continue to sell the less-safe product in order to be in a position to market the safer product successfully.

Which one of the following principles, if established, most helps to justify the production manager's conclusion?

(A) Companies should be required to develop safer products if such development can be funded from sales of existing products.
(B) That a product does not meet industry safety codes should be taken as sufficient indication that the product poses some safety risks.
(C) Companies should not sell a product that poses safety risks if they are technologically capable of producing a safer version of that product.
(D) Product safety codes should be reviewed whenever an industry replaces one version of a product with a technologically more advanced version of that product.
(E) In order to make building materials safer, companies should continually research new technologies whether or not they are required to do so in order to comply with safety codes.

PRINCIPLE

33. You should not praise an act of apparent generosity unless you believe it is actually performed out of selfless motives, and you should not condemn an act of apparent selfishness unless you believe it is actually performed out of self-centered motives.

Which one of the following judgments conforms to the principle stated above?

(A) Caroline rightly blamed her coworker Monica for failing to assist her in doing a time-consuming project, even though she knew that Monica had offered to help in the project earlier but that her offer had been vetoed by their supervisor.

(B) It was correct for Sarah not to praise Michael for being charitable when he told her that he donates a tenth of his income to charity, since she guessed that he only told that fact in order to impress her.

(C) Enrique justifiably excused his friend William for failing to write or phone after William moved out of town because he realized that William never makes an effort to keep in contact with any of his friends.

(D) Daniel was right not to praise Margaret for offering to share her house with a visiting French family, since he believed that she made the offer only because she hoped it would be reciprocated by an invitation to use the family's apartment in Paris.

(E) Albert correctly criticized Louise for adopting an abandoned dog because he believed that, although she felt sorry for the dog, she did not have sufficient time or space to care for it adequately.

34. Walter: Although cigarette smoking is legal, it should be banned on all airline flights. Cigarette smoking in the confines of an aircraft exposes nonsmokers to harmful secondhand smoke that they cannot avoid.

Which one of the following principles, if established, would justify the proposal put forth by Walter?

(A) People should be prohibited from engaging in an otherwise legal activity in those situations in which that activity would unavoidably expose others to harm.

(B) An activity should be banned only if most situations in which a person engages in that activity would inevitably expose others to harm.

(C) A legal activity that has the potential for causing harm to others in certain situations should be modified in those situations to render it harmless.

(D) People who regularly engage in an activity that has the potential for harming others when that activity takes place in certain situations should be excluded from those situations.

(E) If an activity is legal in some situations in which a person's engaging in that activity could harm others, then that activity should be legal in all situations.

35. Pedigreed dogs, including those officially classified as working dogs, must conform to standards set by organizations that issue pedigrees. Those standards generally specify the physical appearance necessary for a dog to be recognized as belonging to a breed but stipulate nothing about other genetic traits, such as those that enable breeds originally developed as working dogs to perform the work for which they were developed. Since dog breeders try to maintain only those traits specified by pedigree organizations, and traits that breeders do not try to maintain risk being lost, certain traits like herding ability risk being lost among pedigreed dogs. Therefore, pedigree organizations should set standards requiring working ability in pedigreed dogs classified as working dogs.

Which one of the following principles, if valid, justifies the argument's conclusion that pedigree organizations should set standards for working ability in dogs?

(A) Organizations that set standards for products or activities should not set standards calling for a particular characteristic if such standards increase the risk of some other characteristic being lost.
(B) Any standard currently in effect for a product or an activity should be rigorously enforced regardless of when the standard was first set.
(C) Organizations that set standards for products or activities should be responsible for seeing to it that those products or activities conform to all the specifications called for by those standards.
(D) Any standard that is set for a product or an activity should reflect the uses to which that product or activity will eventually be put.
(E) Organizations that set standards for products or activities should attempt to ensure that those products or activities can serve the purposes for which they were originally developed.

36. Claim: Country X's government lowered tariff barriers because doing so served the interests of powerful foreign companies.

Principle: In order for a change to be explained by the advantage some person or group gained from it, it must be shown how the interests of the person or group played a role in bringing about the change.

Which one of the following, if true, can most logically serve as a premise for an argument that uses the principle to counter the claim?

(A) Foreign companies did benefit when Country X lowered tariff barriers, but consumers in Country X benefited just as much.
(B) In the period since tariff barriers were lowered, price competition among importers has severely limited importers' profits from selling foreign companies' products in Country X.
(C) It was impossible to predict how Country X's economic reforms, which included lowering tariff barriers, would affect the economy in the short term.
(D) Many of the foreign companies that benefited from Country X's lowering tariff barriers compete fiercely among themselves both in Country X and in other markets.
(E) Although foreign companies benefited when Country X lowered tariff barriers, there is no other evidence that these foreign companies induced the change.

PRINCIPLE

37. As far as we know, Earth is the only planet on which life has evolved, and all known life forms are carbon-based. Therefore, although there might exist noncarbon-based life on planets very unlike Earth, our scientific estimates of the probability of extraterrestrial life should be generated from estimates of the number of planets like Earth and the likelihood of carbon-based life on those planets.

Which one of the following general principles most strongly supports the recommendation?

(A) There is no good reason to think that unobserved phenomena closely resemble those that have been observed.

(B) A scientific theory that explains a broad range of phenomena is preferable to a competing theory that explains only some of those phenomena.

(C) It is preferable for scientists to restrict their studies to phenomena that are observable and forego making estimates about unobservable things.

(D) A scientific theory that explains observed phenomena on the basis of a few principles that are independent of each other is preferable to a theory that explains those same phenomena on the basis of many independent principles.

(E) Estimations of probability that are more closely tied to what is known are preferable to those that are less closely tied to what is known.

38. Alexander: The chemical waste dump outside our town should be cleaned up immediately. Admittedly, it will be very costly to convert that site into woodland, but we have a pressing obligation to redress the harm we have done to local forests and wildlife.

Teresa: But our town's first priority is the health of its people. So even if putting the dump there was environmentally disastrous, we should not spend our resources on correcting it unless it presents a significant health hazard to people. If it does, then we only need to remove that hazard.

Teresa's statement most closely conforms to which one of the following principles?

(A) Environmental destruction should be redressed only if it is in the economic interest of the community to do so.

(B) Resources should be allocated only to satisfy goals that have the highest priority.

(C) No expense should be spared in protecting the community's health.

(D) Environmental hazards that pose slight health risks to people should be rectified if the technology is available to do so.

(E) It is the community as a whole that should evaluate the importance of eliminating various perceived threats to public health.

PRINCIPLE

39. Reporting on a civil war, a journalist encountered evidence that refugees were starving because the government would not permit food shipments to a rebel-held area. Government censors deleted all mention of the government's role in the starvation from the journalist's report, which had not implicated either nature or the rebels in the starvation. The journalist concluded that it was ethically permissible to file the censored report, because the journalist's news agency would precede it with the notice "Cleared by government censors."

Which one of the following ethical criteria, if valid, would serve to support the journalist's conclusion while placing the least constraint on the flow of reported information?

(A) It is ethical in general to report known facts but unethical to do so while omitting other known facts if the omitted facts would substantially alter an impression of a person or institution that would be congruent with the reported facts.
(B) In a situation of conflict, it is ethical to report known facts and unethical to fail to report known facts that would tend to exonerate one party to the conflict.
(C) In a situation of censorship, it is unethical to make any report if the government represented by the censor deletes from the report material unfavorable to that government.
(D) It is ethical in general to report known facts but unethical to make a report in a situation of censorship if relevant facts have been deleted by the censor, unless the recipient of the report is warned that censorship existed.
(E) Although it is ethical in general to report known facts, it is unethical to make a report from which a censor has deleted relevant facts, unless the recipient of the report is warned that there was censorship and the reported facts do not by themselves give a misleading impression.

40. Wife: The work of the artist who painted the portrait of my grandparents 50 years ago has become quite popular lately, so the portrait has recently become valuable. But since these sorts of artistic fads fade rapidly, the practical thing to do would be to sell the portrait while it is still worth something, and thereby enable our daughter to attend the college she has chosen.

Husband: How could you make such a suggestion? That painting is the only thing you own that belonged to your grandparents. I don't think it's a very good painting, but it has great sentimental value. Besides, you owe it to our daughter to keep it in the family as a link to her family's past.

Which one of the following principles, if established, does most to justify the husband's reply?

(A) Gifts offered as sentimental tokens of affection should not be accepted if the recipient intends to sell them later for profit.
(B) A beautiful work of art is more valuable than the money it could be sold for, whatever the amount.
(C) It is more important for parents to provide their children with tangible links to the family's past than it is to enable them to attend the college of their choice.
(D) Children and grandchildren have a duty to preserve family heirlooms only if they have promised their parents or grandparents that they would do so.
(E) Providing one's children with an education is more important than providing them with material goods, even if the goods have sentimental value.

PRINCIPLE

41. To perform an act that is morally wrong is to offend against humanity, and all offenses against humanity are equally bad. Because murder is morally wrong, it is just as bad to have murdered one person by setting off a bomb as it would have been to have murdered a hundred people by setting off that bomb.

Which one of the following judgments conforms to the principles invoked above?

(A) If lying is morally wrong, telling a lie is as bad as murdering someone.
(B) Risking one's life to save the lives of a hundred people is morally no better than risking one's life to save one person.
(C) If stealing is morally wrong, it is equally important to society to prevent people from stealing as it is to prevent them from committing murder.
(D) Accidentally causing the death of a person is just as bad as murdering that person.
(E) In a situation in which the life of one person can be saved only by killing another person, killing and not killing are equally bad.

42. Political advocate: Campaigns for elective office should be subsidized with public funds. One reason is that this would allow politicians to devote less time to fund-raising, thus giving campaigning incumbents more time to serve the public. A second reason is that such subsidies would make it possible to set caps on individual campaign contributions, thereby reducing the likelihood that elected officials will be working for the benefit not of the public but of individual large contributors.

Critic: This argument is problematic: the more the caps constrain contributions, the more time candidates have to spend finding more small contributors.

Which one of the following principles, if established, provides a basis for the advocate's argument?

(A) If complete reliance on private funding of some activity keeps the public from enjoying a benefit that could be provided if public funds were used, such public funds should be provided.
(B) If election campaigns are to be funded from public funds, terms of office for elected officials should be lengthened.
(C) If in an election campaign large contributions flow primarily to one candidate, public funds should be used to support the campaigns of that candidate's rivals.
(D) If public funding of some activity produces a benefit to the public but also inevitably a special benefit for specific individuals, the activity should not be fully funded publicly but in part by the individuals deriving the special benefit.
(E) If a person would not have run for office in the absence of public campaign subsidies, this person should not be eligible for any such subsidies.

43. Arnold: I was recently denied a seat on an airline flight for which I had a confirmed reservation, because the airline had overbooked the flight. Since I was forced to fly on the next available flight, which did not depart until two hours later, I missed an important business meeting. Even though the flight on which I had a reservation was canceled at the last minute due to bad weather, the airline should still pay me compensation for denying me a seat on the flight.

Jamie: The airline is not morally obligated to pay you any compensation. Even if you had not been denied a seat on the earlier flight, you would have missed your business meeting anyway.

A principle that, if established, justifies Jamie's response to Arnold is that an airline is morally obligated to compensate a passenger who has been denied a seat on a flight for which the passenger has confirmed reservations

(A) if the only reason the passenger is forced to take a later flight is that the airline overbooked the original flight

(B) only if there is a reason the passenger is forced to take a later flight other than the original flight's being canceled due to bad weather

(C) only if the passenger would not have been forced to take a later flight had the airline not overbooked the original flight

(D) even if the only reason the passenger is forced to take a later flight were that the original flight is canceled due to bad weather

(E) even if the passenger would still have been forced to take a later flight had the airline not overbooked the original flight

44. Biotechnology companies say that voluntary guidelines for their industry are sufficient to ensure that no harm will result when a genetically altered organism is released into the environment. It is foolish, however, to rely on assurances from producers of genetically altered organisms that their products will not be harmful. Therefore, a biotechnology company should be required to apply to an independent regulatory board composed of scientists outside the biotechnology industry for the right to sell newly created organisms.

Which one of the following principles, if accepted, most strongly justifies drawing the conclusion above?

(A) Voluntary guidelines are sufficient to regulate activities that pose little danger to the environment.

(B) People who engage in an activity and have a financial stake in that activity should not be the sole regulators of that activity.

(C) Methods that result in harm to the environment must sometimes be used in order to avoid even greater harm.

(D) A company is obligated to ensure the effectiveness of its products but not their environmental safety.

(E) Issues of environmental protection are so important that they should not be left to scientific experts.

45. Dr. Kim: Electronic fetal monitors, now routinely used in hospital delivery rooms to check fetal heartbeat, are more intrusive than ordinary stethoscopes and do no more to improve the chances that a healthy baby will be born. Therefore, the additional cost of electronic monitoring is unjustified and such monitoring should be discontinued.

Dr. Anders: I disagree. Although you and I know that both methods are capable of providing the same information, electronic monitoring has been well worth the cost. Doctors now know the warning signs they need to listen for with stethoscopes, but only because of what was learned from using electronic monitors.

Which one of the following principles, if accepted, would provide the most support for Dr. Kim's contention that the use of electronic fetal monitors should be discontinued?

(A) Hospitals should discontinue the routine use of a monitoring method whenever an alternative method that provides more information becomes available.

(B) Monitoring procedures should be routinely used in delivery rooms only if they provide information of a kind that is potentially useful in ensuring that a healthy baby will be born.

(C) When two methods available to hospitals provide the same kind of information, the more intrusive method should not be used.

(D) When the use of a medical device has enabled doctors to learn something that improves the chances that babies will be born healthy, that device is well worth its cost.

(E) Routinely used medical procedures should be reevaluated periodically to be sure that these procedures provide reliable information.

46. People who receive unsolicited advice from someone whose advantage would be served if that advice is taken should regard the proffered advice with skepticism unless there is good reason to think that their interests substantially coincide with those of the advice giver in the circumstance in question.

This principle, if accepted, would justify which one of the following judgments?

(A) After learning by chance that Harriet is looking for a secure investment for her retirement savings, Floyd writes to her recommending the R&M Company as an especially secure investment. But since Floyd is the sole owner of R&M, Harriet should reject his advice out of hand and invest her savings elsewhere.

(B) While shopping for a refrigerator, Ramón is approached by a salesperson who, on the basis of her personal experience, warns him against the least expensive model. However, the salesperson's commission increases with the price of the refrigerator sold, so Ramón should not reject the least expensive model on the salesperson's advice alone.

(C) Mario wants to bring pastry to Yvette's party, and when he consults her Yvette suggests that he bring his favorite chocolate fudge brownies from the local bakery. However, since Yvette also prefers those brownies to any other pastry, Mario would be wise to check with others before following her recommendation.

(D) Sara overhears Ron talking about a course he will be teaching and interrupts to recommend a textbook for his course. However, even though Sara and Ron each wrote a chapter of this textbook, since the book's editor is a personal friend of Sara's, Ron should investigate further before deciding whether it is the best textbook for his course.

(E) Mei is buying fish for soup. Joel, who owns the fish market where Mei is a regular and valued customer, suggests a much less expensive fish than the fish Mei herself prefers. Since if Mei follows Joel's advice, Joel will make less profit on the sale than he would have otherwise, Mei should follow his recommendation.

PRINCIPLE

47. Archaeologist: A large corporation has recently offered to provide funding to restore an archaeological site and to construct facilities to make the site readily accessible to the general public. The restoration will conform to the best current theories about how the site appeared at the height of the ancient civilization that occupied it. This offer should be rejected, however, because many parts of the site contain unexamined evidence.

Which one of the following principles, if valid, justifies the archaeologist's argument?

(A) The ownership of archaeological sites should not be under the control of business interests.
(B) Any restoration of an archaeological site should represent only the most ancient period of that site's history.
(C) No one should make judgments about what constitutes the height of another civilization.
(D) Only those with a true concern for an archaeological site's history should be involved in the restoration of that site.
(E) The risk of losing evidence relevant to possible future theories should outweigh any advantages of displaying the results of theories already developed.

48. After several attempts to distract his young parrot from chewing on furniture, George reluctantly took an expert's advice and gently hit the parrot's beak whenever the bird started to chew furniture. The bird stopped chewing furniture, but it is now afraid of hands and will sometimes bite. Since chewing on the furniture would not have hurt the bird, George should not have hit it.

When Carla's puppy escaped from her yard, it bounded into a busy street. Although Carla does not generally approve of physical discipline, she hit the puppy sharply with her hand. Now the puppy enters the street only when accompanied by Carla, so Carla was justified in disciplining the puppy.

Which one of the following principles, if established, would justify the judgments about George's and Carla's actions?

(A) When disciplining an animal physically, a trainer should use an object such as a rolled up newspaper to avoid making the animal frightened of hands.
(B) When training an animal, physical discipline should be used only when such discipline is necessary to correct behavior that could result in serious harm to the animal.
(C) Using physical discipline to train an animal is justified only when all alternative strategies for correcting undesirable behavior have failed.
(D) Physical discipline should not be used on immature animals.
(E) Physical discipline should not be used by an animal trainer except to correct persistent behavior problems.

49. Marianne is a professional chess player who hums audibly while playing her matches, thereby distracting her opponents. When ordered by chess officials to cease humming or else be disqualified from professional chess, Marianne protested the order. She argued that since she was unaware of her humming, her humming was involuntary and that therefore she should not be held responsible for it.

Which one of the following principles, if valid, most helps to support Marianne's argument against the order?

(A) Chess players who hum audibly while playing their matches should not protest if their opponents also hum.

(B) Of a player's actions, only those that are voluntary should be used as justification for disqualifying that player from professional chess.

(C) A person should be held responsible for those involuntary actions that serve that person's interests.

(D) Types of behavior that are not considered voluntary in everyday circumstances should be considered voluntary if they occur in the context of a professional chess match.

(E) Chess players should be disqualified from professional chess matches if they regularly attempt to distract their opponents.

Chapter Sixteen: Conditional Reasoning Questions

1. People who are red/green color-blind cannot distinguish between green and brown. Gerald cannot distinguish between green and brown. Therefore Gerald is red/green color-blind.

Which one of the following most closely parallels the reasoning in the argument presented in the passage?

(A) People who are fair-skinned suffer from sunburn. William is fair-skinned. Therefore William suffers from sunburn.
(B) People who are suffering from sinusitis lose their sense of smell. Mary has lost her sense of smell. Therefore Mary is suffering from sinusitis.
(C) People who have suffered from jaundice cannot become blood donors. Jean is a blood donor. Therefore Jean has not suffered from jaundice.
(D) People who are color-blind cannot become airline pilots. Arthur is color-blind. Therefore Arthur cannot become an airline pilot.
(E) People who are diabetic cannot eat large amounts of sugar. Freda is diabetic. Therefore Freda is on a special diet.

2. If Max were guilty, he would not ask the police to investigate. Therefore, his asking the police to investigate shows that he is not guilty.

The logical structure of the argument above is most similar to which one of the following?

(A) If Lucille were in the next room, I would not be able to see her. Therefore, the fact that I can see her shows that she is not in the next room.
(B) If Sam were rich, he would not spend his vacation in Alaska. Therefore, his spending his vacation in the Bahamas shows that he is rich.
(C) If Joe were over 40 he would not want to learn to ski. Therefore, the fact that he does not want to learn to ski shows that he is over 40.
(D) If Mark were a good cook, he would not put cinnamon in the chili. Therefore, the fact that he is not a good cook shows that he put cinnamon in the chili.
(E) If Sally were sociable, she would not avoid her friends. Therefore, the fact that she is sociable shows that she does not avoid her friends.

3. Historically, monetary systems have developed only in population centers with marketplaces. Through the fourth century B.C., Mesopotamian cities engaged in trade, but had never had marketplaces. By that period, however, Greek cities all had marketplaces, or agorae. The Greek cities' agorae were centrally located and goods were traded there either for money or for commodities.

If all of the statements in the passage are true, then which one of the following must also be true?

(A) In the fourth century B.C., Greek cities were the only population centers with monetary systems.
(B) The development of monetary systems has historically led to the development of marketplaces.
(C) In the fourth century B.C., the Greeks and the Mesopotamians traded with each other.
(D) After the fourth century B.C., Mesopotamian cities had marketplaces and monetary systems.
(E) The Mesopotamian cities of the fourth century B.C. did not have monetary systems.

4. Professor: If both parents have type O blood then their children can only have type O blood. This is a genetic law.

Student: But that's not true; my father has type B blood and I have type O blood.

The student has most likely misinterpreted the professor's remark to imply that

(A) only people with type O blood can have children with type O blood
(B) people with type O blood cannot have children with type B blood
(C) people with type B blood invariably have children with type O blood
(D) what is true of one child in the family must also be true of all children in that family
(E) if both parents have type B blood, then their child will have type B blood

5. A society in which there are many crimes, such as thefts and murders, should not be called "lawless." That is an abuse of the meaning of words. As a suffix, " less" means "without," so "lawless" means "without laws." However, a society that has no laws has no crimes, because no laws can be broken. A lawless society would, therefore, be a crimeless society. So what some have termed a lawless society should actually be called "crimeful."

If the statements in the passage are true, which one of the following must also be true?

(A) A society that has laws has crimes.
(B) A society that has no crimes has no laws.
(C) A society that has many laws has many crimes.
(D) A society that has some crimes has some laws.
(E) A society that has many crimes has many laws.

6. Ann: All the campers at Camp Winnehatchee go to Tri-Cities High School.

Bill: That's not true. Some Tri-Cities students are campers at Camp Lakemont.

Bill's answer can be best explained on the assumption that he has interpreted Ann's remark to mean that

(A) most of the campers at Camp Lakemont come from high schools other than Tri-Cities
(B) most Tri-Cities High School students are campers at Camp Winnehatchee
(C) some Tri-Cities High School students have withdrawn from Camp Lakemont
(D) all Tri-Cities High School students attend summer camp
(E) only campers at Camp Winnehatchee are students at Tri-Cities High School

7. Governments have only one response to public criticism of socially necessary services: regulation of the activity of providing those services. But governments inevitably make the activity more expensive by regulating it, and that is particularly troublesome in these times of strained financial resources. However, since public criticism of child care services has undermined all confidence in such services, and since such services are socially necessary, the government is certain to respond.

Which one of the following statements can be inferred from the passage?

(A) The quality of child care will improve.
(B) The cost of providing child-care services will increase.
(C) The government will use funding to foster advances in child care.
(D) If public criticism of policy is strongly voiced, the government is certain to respond.
(E) If child-care services are not regulated, the cost of providing child care will not increase.

8. "If the forest continues to disappear at its present pace, the koala will approach extinction," said the biologist.

"So all that is needed to save the koala is to stop deforestation," said the politician.

Which one of the following statements is consistent with the biologist's claim but not with the politician's claim?

(A) Deforestation continues and the koala becomes extinct.
(B) Deforestation is stopped and the koala becomes extinct.
(C) Reforestation begins and the koala survives.
(D) Deforestation is slowed and the koala survives.
(E) Deforestation is slowed and the koala approaches extinction.

9. If retail stores experience a decrease in revenues during this holiday season, then either attitudes toward extravagant gift-giving have changed or prices have risen beyond the level most people can afford. If attitudes have changed, then we all have something to celebrate this season. If prices have risen beyond the level most people can afford, then it must be that salaries have not kept pace with rising prices during the past year.

Assume the premises above to be true. If salaries have kept pace with rising prices during the past year, which one of the following must be true?

(A) Attitudes toward extravagant gift-giving have changed.
(B) Retail stores will not experience a decrease in retail sales during this holiday season.
(C) Prices in retail stores have not risen beyond the level that most people can afford during this holiday season.
(D) Attitudes toward extravagant gift-giving have not changed, and stores will not experience a decrease in revenues during this holiday season.
(E) Either attitudes toward extravagant gift-giving have changed or prices have risen beyond the level that most people can afford during this holiday season.

10. In a large residential building, there is a rule that no pets are allowed. A group of pet lovers tried to change that rule but failed. The rule-changing procedure outlined in the building's regulations states that only if a group of tenants can obtain the signatures of 10 percent of the tenants on a petition to change a rule will the proposed change be put to a majority vote of all the tenants in the building. It follows that the pet lovers were voted down on their proposal by the majority of the tenants.

The argument depends on which one of the following assumptions?

(A) The pet lovers succeeded in obtaining the signatures of 10 percent of the tenants on their petition.
(B) The signatures of less than 10 percent of the tenants were obtained on the pet lovers' petition.
(C) Ninety percent of the tenants are against changing the rule forbidding pets.
(D) The support of 10 percent of the tenants for a rule change ensures that the rule change will be adopted.
(E) The failure of the pet lovers to obtain the signatures of 10 percent of the tenants on their petition for a rule change ensures that the rule change will be voted down by a majority of the tenants.

11. Normal full-term babies are all born with certain instinctive reflexes that disappear by the age of two months. Because this three-month-old baby exhibits these reflexes, this baby is not a normal full-term baby.

Which one of the following has a logical structure most like that of the argument above?

(A) Because carbon dioxide turns limewater milky and this gas is oxygen, it will not turn limewater milky.
(B) Because no ape can talk and Suzy is an ape, Suzy cannot talk.
(C) Because humans are social animals and Henry is sociable, Henry is normal.
(D) Because opossums have abdominal pouches and this animal lacks any such pouch, this animal is not an opossum.
(E) Because some types of trees shed their leaves annually and this tree has not shed its leaves, it is not normal.

12. Efficiency and redundancy are contradictory characteristics of linguistic systems; however, they can be used together to achieve usefulness and reliability in communication. If a spoken language is completely efficient, then every possible permutation of its basic language sounds can be an understandable word. However, if the human auditory system is an imperfect receptor of sounds, then it is not true that every possible permutation of a spoken language's basic language sounds can be an understandable word.

If all of the statements above are true, which one of the following must also be true?

(A) Efficiency causes a spoken language to be useful and redundancy causes it to be reliable.
(B) Neither efficiency nor redundancy can be completely achieved in spoken language.
(C) If a spoken language were completely redundant, then it could not be useful.
(D) If the human auditory system were a perfect receptor of sounds, then every permutation of language sounds would be an understandable word.
(E) If the human auditory system is an imperfect receptor of sounds, then a spoken language cannot be completely efficient.

13. All intelligent people are nearsighted. I am very nearsighted. So I must be a genius.

Which one of the following exhibits both of the logical flaws exhibited in the argument above?

(A) I must be stupid because all intelligent people are nearsighted and I have perfect eyesight.
(B) All chickens have beaks. This bird has a beak. So this bird must be a chicken.
(C) All pigs have four legs, but this spider has eight legs. So this spider must be twice as big as any pig.
(D) John is extremely happy, so he must be extremely tall because all tall people are happy.
(E) All geniuses are very nearsighted. I must be very nearsighted since I am a genius.

14. If you have a large amount of money in the bank, your spending power is great. If your spending power is great, you are happy. So if you have a large amount of money in the bank, you are happy.

Which one of the following most closely parallels the reasoning in the argument above?

(A) If you have good health, you can earn a lot. If you can earn a lot, you can buy an expensive house. So if you have good health, you can have a comfortable life.
(B) If you drink too much alcohol, you will feel sick. If you drink too much alcohol, you will have no money left. So if you have no money left, you will feel sick.
(C) If you swim energetically, your heart rate increases. If your heart rate increases, you are overexcited. So if you swim energetically, you are overexcited.
(D) If you take a great deal of exercise, you are physically fit. If you take a great deal of exercise, you are exhausted. So if you are physically fit, you are exhausted.
(E) If you have a large amount of money in the bank, you are confident about the future. If you are optimistic by nature, you are confident about the future. So if you have a large amount of money in the bank, you are optimistic by nature.

15. A work of architecture, if it is to be both inviting and functional for public use, must be unobtrusive, taking second place to the total environment. Modern architects, plagued by egoism, have violated this precept. They have let their strong personalities take over their work, producing buildings that are not functional for public use.

Which one of the statements below follows logically from the statements in the passage?

(A) Unobtrusive architecture is both inviting and functional.
(B) Modern architects who let their strong personalities take over their work produce buildings that are not unobtrusive.
(C) An architect with a strong personality cannot produce buildings that functional well for the public.
(D) A work of architecture that takes second place to the environment functions well for public use.
(E) A work of architecture cannot simultaneously express its architect's personality and be functional for public use.

16. If that insect is a bee, it can only sting once. It only did sting once. So it is a bee.

Which one of the following exhibits a pattern of reasoning most similar to that in the argument above?

(A) Spring is here. It has to be, because when it is spring, I cannot stop sneezing; and I just sneezed.
(B) When the sky is clear, the atmospheric pressure is high. At the moment, it is clearing up, so the atmospheric pressure is bound to be high soon.
(C) Old and brittle paintings are always moved with extreme care. That particular painting is never moved with extreme care. So it must not be old and brittle.
(D) Only one more thunderstorm was needed to ruin that roof. But the roof was still fine a month later. There must not have been any thunderstorms over that month.
(E) To survive in the wild requires physical stamina like Mark's. All the same, Mark's fear of spiders would prevent his survival.

17. Public reports by national commissions, governors' conferences, and leadership groups have stressed the great need for better understanding of international affairs by the citizenry. If the country is to remain a leading nation in an era of international competitiveness, the need is undeniable. If there is such a need for the citizenry to have a better understanding of international affairs, then all of our new teachers must be prepared to teach their subject matter with an international orientation.

If all of the statements in the passage are true, which one of the following must also be true?

(A) If the country is to remain a leading nation in an era of international competitiveness, then new teachers must be prepared to teach their subject matter with an international orientation.
(B) If new teachers are prepared to teach their subject matter with an international orientation, then the country will remain a leading nation in an era of international competitiveness.
(C) If there is better understanding of international affairs by the citizenry, then the country will remain a leading nation in an era of international competitiveness.
(D) If the country is to remain a leading nation in an era of international competitiveness, then there is no need for the citizenry to have a better understanding of international affairs.
(E) Public reports from various groups and commissions have stressed the need for a more international orientation in the education of teachers.

18. To become an expert on a musical instrument, a person must practice. If people practice a musical instrument for three hours each day, they will eventually become experts on that instrument. Therefore, if a person is an expert on a musical instrument, that person must have practiced for at least three hours each day.

Which one of the following most accurately describes a flaw in the reasoning above?

(A) The conclusion fails to take into account that people who practice for three hours every day might not yet have reached a degree of proficiency that everyone would consider expert.
(B) The conclusion fails to take into account that practicing for less than three hours each day may be enough for some people to become experts.
(C) The conclusion fails to take into account that if a person has not practiced for at least three hours a day, the person has not become an expert.
(D) The conclusion fails to take into account that three consecutive hours of daily practice is not recommended by all music teachers.
(E) The conclusion fails to take into account that few people have the spare time necessary to devote three hours daily to practice.

19. The only way that bookstores can profitably sell books at below-market prices is to get the books at a discount from publishers. Unless bookstores generate a high sales volume, however, they cannot get discounts from publishers. To generate such volume, bookstores must either cater to mass tastes or have exclusive access to a large specialized market, such as medical textbooks, or both.

Which one of the following can be properly inferred from the passage?

(A) If a bookstore receives discounts from publishers, it will profitably sell books at below-market prices.
(B) A bookstore that caters to mass tastes or has exclusive access to a large specialized market will have a high sales volume.
(C) A bookstore that profitably sells books at below-market prices gets discounts from publishers.
(D) A bookstore that does not sell books at below-market prices does not get discounts from publishers.
(E) A bookstore that not only caters to mass tastes but also has exclusive access to a large specialized market cannot profitably sell books at below-market prices.

20. The United States Food and Drug Administration (FDA) regulates the introduction of new therapeutic agents into the marketplace. Consequently, it plays a critical role in improving health care in the United States. While it is those in the academic and government research communities who engage in the long process of initial discovery and clinical testing of new therapeutic agents, it is the FDA's role and responsibility to facilitate the transfer of new discoveries from the laboratory to the marketplace. Only after the transfer can important new therapies help patients.

Which one of the following statements can be inferred from the passage?

(A) The FDA is responsible for ensuring that any therapeutic agent that is marketed is then regulated.
(B) Before new therapeutic agents reach the marketplace they do not help patients.
(C) The research community is responsible for the excessively long testing period for new drugs, not the FDA.
(D) The FDA should work more closely with researchers to ensure that the quality of therapeutic agents is maintained.
(E) If a new medical discovery has been transferred from the laboratory to the marketplace, it will help patients.

21. Political theorist: The chief foundations of all governments are the legal system and the police force; and as there cannot be a good legal system where the police are not well paid, it follows that where the police are well paid there will be a good legal system.

The reasoning in the argument is not sound because it fails to establish that

(A) many governments with bad legal systems have poorly paid police forces
(B) bad governments with good legal systems must have poorly paid police forces
(C) a well-paid police force cannot be effective without a good legal system
(D) a well-paid police force is sufficient to guarantee a good legal system
(E) some bad governments have good legal systems

22. Leachate is a solution, frequently highly contaminated, that develops when water permeates a landfill site. If and only if the landfill's capacity to hold liquids is exceeded does the leachate escape into the environment, generally in unpredictable quantities. A method must be found for disposing of leachate. Most landfill leachate is sent directly to sewage treatment plants, but not all sewage plants are capable of handling the highly contaminated water.

Which one of the following can be inferred from the passage?

(A) The ability to predict the volume of escaping landfill leachate would help solve the disposal problem.
(B) If any water permeates a landfill, leachate will escape into the environment.
(C) No sewage treatment plants are capable of handling leachate.
(D) Some landfill leachate is sent to sewage treatment plants that are incapable of handling it.
(E) If leachate does not escape from a landfill into the environment, then the landfill's capacity to hold liquids has not been exceeded.

SN

23. If a society encourages freedom of thought and expression, then, during the time when it does so, creativity will flourish in that society. In the United States creativity flourished during the eighteenth century. It is clear, therefore, that freedom of thought was encouraged in the United States during the eighteenth century.

An error of reasoning of the same kind as one contained in the passage is present in each of the following arguments EXCEPT:

(A) According to the airline industry, airfares have to rise if air travel is to be made safer; since airfares were just raised, we can rest assured that air travel will therefore become safer.

(B) We can conclude that the Hillside police department has improved its efficiency, because crime rates are down in Hillside, and it is an established fact that crime rates go down when police departments increase their efficiency.

(C) People who are really interested in the preservation of wildlife obviously do not go hunting for big game; since Gerda has never gone hunting for big game and intends never to do so, it is clear that she is really interested in the preservation of wildlife.

(D) If the contents of a bottle are safe to drink, the bottle will not be marked "poison," so, since the bottle is not marked "poison," its contents will be safe to drink.

(E) None of the so-called Western democracies is really democratic, because, for a country to be democratic, the opinion of each of its citizens must have a meaningful effect on government, and in none of these countries does each citizen's opinion have such an effect.

24. A certain retailer promotes merchandise by using the following policy:

> At all times there is either a "manager's sale" or a "holiday sale" or both going on. All sales are run for exactly one calendar month. In any given month, if a manager wishes to clear out a particular line of merchandise, then a manager's sale is declared. If a holiday falls within the calendar month and there is excess merchandise in the warehouse, then a holiday sale is declared.

However, there is no holiday that falls within the month of August and, in that month, the warehouse never contains excess merchandise.

Which one of the following can be concluded from the passage?

(A) If a holiday falls within a given month and there is no extra merchandise in the warehouse that month, then a holiday sale is declared.

(B) If a holiday sale is not being run, then it is the month of August.

(C) If a manager's sale is being run in some month, then there is no excess merchandise in the warehouse in that month.

(D) If there is not a manager's sale being run in some month, then there is a holiday sale being run in that month.

(E) If there is no excess merchandise in the warehouse, then it is the month of August.

NS

Questions 25-26

Zelda: Dr. Ladlow, a research psychologist, has convincingly demonstrated that his theory about the determinants of rat behavior generates consistently accurate predictions about how rats will perform in a maze. On the basis of this evidence, Dr. Ladlow has claimed that his theory is irrefutably correct.

Anson: Then Dr. Ladlow is not a responsible psychologist. Dr. Ladlow's evidence does not conclusively prove that his theory is correct. Responsible psychologists always accept the possibility that new evidence will show that their theories are incorrect.

25. Which one of the following can be properly inferred from Anson's argument?

(A) Dr. Ladlow's evidence that his theory generates consistently accurate predictions about how rats will perform in a maze is inaccurate.
(B) Psychologists who can derive consistently accurate predictions about how rats will perform in a maze from their theories cannot responsibly conclude that those theories cannot be disproved.
(C) No matter how responsible psychologists are, they can never develop correct theoretical explanations.
(D) Responsible psychologists do not make predictions about how rats will perform in a maze.
(E) Psychologists who accept the possibility that new evidence will show that their theories are incorrect are responsible psychologists.

26. Anson bases his conclusion about Dr. Ladlow on which one of the following?

(A) an attack on Dr. Ladlow's character
(B) the application of a general principle
(C) the use of an ambiguous term
(D) the discrediting of facts
(E) the rejection of a theoretical explanation

27. Once people habitually engaged in conversation; now the television competes for their attention. When the television is on, communication between family members stops. Where there is no communication, family ties become frayed and eventually snap. Therefore, the only solution is to get rid of the television.

Which one of the following is most closely parallel in its reasoning to the flawed reasoning in the argument above?

(A) Once friendships thrived on shared leisure time. But contemporary economic pressures minimize the amount of free time people have and thus jeopardize many friendships.
(B) Once people listened to the radio while pursuing other activities. Now they passively watch television. Therefore, radio was less distracting for most people than television is.
(C) Once sports enthusiasts regularly engaged in sports, but now they watch spectator sports when they could be getting physical exercise. Without physical exercise, health deteriorates. Therefore, the only remedy is to eliminate spectator sports.
(D) Once people were willing to tailor their day to the constraints of a bus or train schedule; now they are spoiled by the private car. The only solution is for government to offer financial incentives to encourage the use of public transportation.
(E) Once people did their shopping in urban retail districts, where they combined their shopping with other errands. Now many people shop in suburban malls, where they concentrate on shopping exclusively. Therefore, shopping has become a leisure time activity.

SN

28. Because of the recent transformation of the market, Quore, Inc., must increase productivity 10 percent over the course of the next two years, or it will certainly go bankrupt. In fact, however, Quore's production structure is such that if a 10 percent productivity increase is possible, then a 20 percent increase is attainable.

If the statements above are true, which one of the following must on the basis of them also be true?

(A) It is only Quore's production structure that makes it possible for Quore to survive the transformation of the market.
(B) Quore will not go bankrupt if it achieves a productivity increase of 20 percent over the next two years.
(C) If the market had not been transformed, Quore would have required no productivity increase in order to avoid bankruptcy.
(D) Because of the transformation of the market, Quore will achieve a productivity increase of 10 percent over the next two years.
(E) If a 20 percent productivity increase is unattainable for Quore, then it must go bankrupt.

29. Terry: If you want to get a decent job, you should go to college.

Mark: That is not true. There are other reasons to go to college than wanting to get a good job.

Mark's response shows that he interpreted Terry's remarks to mean that

(A) college is one of many places to get trained for a job
(B) decent jobs are obtained only by persons who have gone to college
(C) wanting to get a decent job is the only reason for going to college
(D) training for decent jobs is available only at colleges
(E) all people who want decent jobs go to college

30. Nursing schools cannot attract a greater number of able applicants than they currently do unless the problems of low wages and high-stress working conditions in the nursing profession are solved. If the pool of able applicants to nursing school does not increase beyond the current level, either the profession will have to lower its entrance standards, or there will soon be an acute shortage of nurses. It is not certain, however, that lowering entrance standards will avert a shortage. It is clear that with either a shortage of nurses or lowered entrance standards for the profession, the current high quality of health care cannot be maintained.

Which one of the following can be properly inferred from the passage?

(A) If the nursing profession solves the problems of low wages and high-stress working conditions, it will attract able applicants in greater numbers than it currently does.
(B) The nursing profession will have to lower its entrance standards if the pool of able applicants to nursing school does not increase beyond the current level.
(C) If the nursing profession solves the problems of low wages and high-stress working conditions, high quality health care will be maintained.
(D) If the nursing profession fails to solve the problems of low wages and high-stress working conditions, there will soon be an acute shortage of nurses.
(E) The current high quality of health care will not be maintained if the problems of low wages and high-stress working conditions in the nursing profession are not solved.

31. Until he was dismissed amid great controversy, Hastings was considered one of the greatest intelligence agents of all time. It is clear that if his dismissal was justified, then Hastings was either incompetent or else disloyal. Soon after the dismissal, however, it was shown that he had never been incompetent. Thus, one is forced to conclude that Hastings must have been disloyal.

Which one of the following states an assumption upon which the argument depends?

(A) Hastings's dismissal was justified.
(B) Hastings was a high-ranking intelligence officer.
(C) The dismissal of anyone who was disloyal would be justified.
(D) Anyone whose dismissal was justified was disloyal.
(E) If someone was disloyal or incompetent, then his dismissal was justified.

32. Anyone who fails to answer a patient's questions cannot be a competent physician. That is why I feel confident about my physician's competence: she carefully answers every one of my questions, no matter how trivial.

Which one of the following most closely parallels the flawed reasoning in the argument above?

(A) Anyone who grows up in a large family is accustomed to making compromises. Meredith is accustomed to making compromises, so she might have grown up in a large family.
(B) Anyone who is not in favor of this proposal is ill informed on the issue. Leanne opposes the proposal, so she is ill informed on the issue.
(C) No one who likes music misses a performance of the symphony. Paul likes music, yet last week he missed a performance of the symphony.
(D) Anyone who works two or more jobs is unable to find a balance between professional and personal life. Maggie has only one job, so she can find a balance between her professional and personal life.
(E) No one who is hot-tempered and strong-willed will succeed in this business. Jeremy is strong-willed, so he will not succeed in this business.

33. The annual *Journal for Publication*, which often solicits articles, publishes only those articles that are both submitted before March 6 and written by certified psychoanalysts. Stevens, who publishes frequently in psychoanalytic literature, submitted an article to the *Journal* before March 6. This article was accepted for publication in the *Journal*.

Which one of the following conclusions follows logically from the statements above?

(A) Stevens is a psychoanalyst.
(B) The *Journal* frequently accepts Stevens' articles.
(C) Stevens is an authority on a large number of topics in psychoanalysis.
(D) The *Journal* asked Stevens to write an article.
(E) Stevens' recently accepted article will be interesting to *Journal* readers.

34. When the economy is in a recession, overall demand for goods and services is low. If overall demand for goods and services is low, bank interest rates are also low. Therefore, if bank interest rates are not low, the economy is not in a recession.

The reasoning in which one of the following most closely parallels the reasoning in the argument above?

(A) If the restaurant is full, the parking lot will be full, and if the parking lot is full, the restaurant is full, so if the parking lot is not full, the restaurant is not full.
(B) If the fish is ready, it is cooked all the way through, and if it is cooked through it will be white, so if the fish is not white, it is not ready.
(C) If pterodactyls flew by flapping their wings, they must have been warm-blooded, so if they were cold-blooded, they must have flown only by gliding, if they flew at all.
(D) If you want to put in pleats, you will have to double the amount of material for the skirt, and that means you will have none left for the top, so if you put in pleats you will not be able to make the top.
(E) If economic forecasters are right, there will be inflation, and if there is inflation, the governing party will lose the election, so if it does lose the election, the economic forecasters were right.

35. If you climb mountains, you will not live to a ripe old age. But you will be bored unless you climb mountains. Therefore, if you live to a ripe old age, you will have been bored.

Which one of the following most closely parallels the reasoning in the argument above?

(A) If you do not try to swim, you will not learn how to swim. But you will not be safe in boats if you do not learn how to swim. Therefore, you must try to swim.
(B) If you do not play golf, you will not enjoy the weekend. But you will be tired next week unless you relax during the weekend. Therefore, to enjoy the weekend, you will have to relax by playing golf.
(C) If you work for your candidate, you will not improve your guitar playing. But you will neglect your civic duty unless you work for your candidate. Therefore, if you improve your guitar playing, you will have neglected your civic duty.
(D) If you do not train, you will not be a good athlete. But you will become exhausted easily unless you train. Therefore, if you train, you will not have become exhausted easily.
(E) If you spend all of your money, you will not become wealthy. But you will become hungry unless you spend all of your money. Therefore, if you become wealthy, you will not become hungry.

36. Editorial: It is clear that if this country's universities were living up to both their moral and their intellectual responsibilities, the best-selling publications in most university bookstores would not be frivolous ones like *TV Today* and *Gossip Review.* However, in most university bookstores the only publication that sells better than *Gossip Review* is *TV Today.*

If the statements in the editorial are true, which one of the following must also be true on the basis of them?

(A) People who purchase publications that are devoted primarily to gossip or to television programming are intellectually irresponsible.
(B) It is irresponsible for university bookstores to carry publications such as *Gossip Review* and *TV Today.*
(C) Most people who purchase publications at university bookstores purchase either *TV Today* or *Gossip Review.*
(D) Many people who attend this country's universities fail to live up to both their moral and their intellectual responsibilities.
(E) At least some of this country's universities are not meeting their moral responsibilities or their intellectual responsibilities or both.

37. For the writers who first gave feudalism its name, the existence of feudalism presupposed the existence of a noble class. Yet there cannot be a noble class, properly speaking, unless both the titles that indicate superior, noble status and the inheritance of such titles are sanctioned by law. Although feudalism existed in Europe as early as the eighth century, it was not until the twelfth century, when many feudal institutions were in decline, that the hereditary transfer of legally recognized titles of nobility first appeared.

The statements above, if true, most strongly support which one of the following claims?

(A) To say that feudalism by definition requires the existence of a nobility is to employ a definition that distorts history.
(B) Prior to the twelfth century, the institution of European feudalism functioned without the presence of a dominant class.
(C) The fact that a societal group has a distinct legal status is not in itself sufficient to allow that group to be properly considered a social class.
(D) The decline of feudalism in Europe was the only cause of the rise of a European nobility.
(E) The prior existence of feudal institutions is a prerequisite for the emergence of a nobility, as defined in the strictest sense of the term.

38. Advertisement: In today's world, you make a statement about the person you are by the car you own. The message of the SKX Mach-5 is unambiguous: Its owner is Dynamic, Aggressive, and Successful. Shouldn't you own an SKX Mach-5?

If the claims made in the advertisement are true, which one of the following must also be true on the basis of them?

(A) Anyone who is dynamic and aggressive is also successful.
(B) Anyone who is not both dynamic and successful would misrepresent himself or herself by being the owner of an SKX Mach-5.
(C) People who buy the SKX Mach-5 are usually more aggressive than people who buy other cars.
(D) No car other than the SKX Mach-5 announces that its owner is successful.
(E) Almost no one would fail to recognize the kind of person who would choose to own an SKX Mach-5.

39. Elena: While I was at the dog show, every dog that growled at me was a white poodle, and every white poodle I saw growled at me.

Which one of the following can be properly inferred from Elena's statement?

(A) The only white dogs that Elena saw at the dog show were poodles.
(B) There were no gray poodles at the dog show.
(C) At the dog show, no gray dogs growled at Elena.
(D) All the white dogs that Elena saw growled at her.
(E) Elena did not see any gray poodles at the dog show.

40. Only if the electorate is moral and intelligent will a democracy function well.

Which one of the following can be logically inferred from the claim above?

(A) If the electorate is moral and intelligent, then a democracy will function well.
(B) Either a democracy does not function well or else the electorate is not moral or not intelligent.
(C) If the electorate is not moral or not intelligent, then a democracy will not function well.
(D) If a democracy does not function well, then the electorate is not moral or not intelligent.
(E) It cannot, at the same time, be true that the electorate is moral and intelligent and that a democracy will not function well.

41. There is relatively little room for growth in the overall carpet market, which is tied to the size of the population. Most who purchase carpet do so only once or twice, first in their twenties or thirties, and then perhaps again in their fifties or sixties. Thus as the population ages, companies producing carpet will be able to gain market share in the carpet market only through purchasing competitors, and not through more aggressive marketing.

Which one of the following, if true, casts the most doubt on the conclusion above?

(A) Most of the major carpet producers market other floor coverings as well.
(B) Most established carpet producers market several different brand names and varieties, and there is no remaining niche in the market for new brands to fill.
(C) Two of the three mergers in the industry's last ten years led to a decline in profits and revenues for the newly merged companies.
(D) Price reductions, achieved by cost-cutting in production, by some of the dominant firms in the carpet market are causing other producers to leave the market altogether.
(E) The carpet market is unlike most markets in that consumers are becoming increasingly resistant to new patterns and styles.

42. Only an expert in some branch of psychology could understand why Patrick is behaving irrationally. But no expert is certain of being able to solve someone else's problem. Patrick wants to devise a solution to his own behavioral problem.

Which one of the following conclusions can be validly drawn from the passage?

(A) Patrick does not understand why he is behaving in this way.
(B) Patrick is not an expert in psychology.
(C) Patrick is not certain of being able to devise a solution to his own behavioral problem.
(D) Unless Charles is an expert in some branch of psychology, Charles should not offer a solution to Patrick's behavioral problem.
(E) If Charles is certain of being able to solve Patrick's behavioral problem, then Charles does not understand why Patrick is behaving in this way.

43. If the regulation of computer networks is to be modeled on past legislation, then its model must be either legislation regulating a telephone system or else legislation regulating a public broadcasting service. If the telephone model is used, computer networks will be held responsible only for ensuring that messages get transmitted. If the public broadcast model is used, computer networks will additionally be responsible for the content of those messages. Yet a computer network serves both these sorts of functions: it can serve as a private message service or as a publicly accessible information service. Thus neither of these models can be appropriate for computer networks.

The passage is structured to lead to which one of the following conclusions?

(A) Regulation of computer networks is required in order to ensure the privacy of the messages transmitted through such networks.
(B) The regulation of computer networks should not be modeled on any single piece of past legislation.
(C) Computer networks were developed by being modeled on both telephone systems and television networks.
(D) Legislators who do not have extensive experience with computers should not attempt to write legislation regulating computer networks.
(E) A computer network merely duplicates the functions of a telephone systems and a television system.

44. Every adult male woolly monkey is larger than even the largest female woolly monkey. In colonies of woolly monkeys, any adult male will dominate any female.

If the statements above are true, which one of the following must on the basis of them be true of woolly monkeys in colonies?

(A) Size is the primary determinant of relations of dominance among woolly monkeys.
(B) Some large adolescent male woolly monkeys dominate some smaller females of the species.
(C) If a male woolly monkey is larger than a female of the species, that male will dominate that female.
(D) If a female woolly monkey dominates a male of the species, the dominated male monkey is not an adult.
(E) An adult male woolly monkey can dominate a female of the species only if that female is also an adult.

45. Any announcement authorized by the head of the department is important. However, announcements are sometimes issued, without authorization, by people other than the head of the department, so some announcements will inevitably turn out not to be important.

The reasoning is flawed because the argument

(A) does not specify exactly which communications are to be classified as announcements
(B) overlooks the possibility that people other than the head of the department have the authority to authorize announcements
(C) leaves open the possibility that the head of the department never, in fact, authorizes any announcements
(D) assumes without warrant that just because satisfying a given condition is enough to ensure an announcement's importance, satisfying that condition is necessary for its importance
(E) fails to distinguish between the importance of the position someone holds and the importance of what that person may actually be announcing on a particular occasion

46. Emissions from automobiles that burn gasoline and automobiles that burn diesel fuel are threatening the quality of life on our planet, contaminating both urban air and global atmosphere. Therefore, the only effective way to reduce such emissions is to replace the conventional diesel fuel and gasoline used in automobiles with cleaner-burning fuels, such as methanol, that create fewer emissions.

Which one of the following is an assumption on which the argument depends?

(A) Reducing the use of automobiles would not be a more effective means to reduce automobile emissions than the use of methanol.
(B) There is no fuel other than methanol that is cleaner-burning than both diesel fuel and gasoline.
(C) If given a choice of automobile fuels, automobile owners would not select gasoline over methanol.
(D) Automobile emissions constitute the most serious threat to the global environment.
(E) At any given time there is a direct correlation between the level of urban air pollution and the level of contamination present in the global atmosphere.

47. If the majority of the residents of the apartment complex complain that their apartments are infested with ants, then the management of the complex will have to engage the services of an exterminator. But the majority of the residents of the complex indicate that their apartments are virtually free of ants. Therefore, the management of the complex will not have to engage the services of an exterminator.

Which one of the following arguments contains a flawed pattern of reasoning parallel to that contained in the argument above?

(A) A theater will be constructed in the fall if funds collected are at least sufficient to cover its cost. To date, the funds collected exceed the theater's cost, so the theater will be constructed in the fall.
(B) The number of flights operated by the airlines cannot be reduced unless the airlines can collect higher airfares. But people will not pay higher airfares, so it is not the case that the number of flights will be reduced.
(C) In order for the company to start the proposed building project, both the town council and the mayor must approve. Since the mayor has already approved, the building project will be started soon.
(D) Most employees will attend the company picnic if the entertainment committee is successful in getting a certain band to play at the picnic. But that band will be out of the country on the day of the picnic, so it is not true that most employees will attend.
(E) Either the school's principal or two-thirds of the parent council must approve a change in the school dress code in order for the code to be changed. Since the principal will not approve a change in the dress code, the code will not be changed.

48. When people experience throbbing in their teeth or gums, they have serious dental problems, and if a dental problem is serious, it will be a problem either of tooth decay or of gum disease. Therefore, since throbbing in the teeth or gums is a sign of serious dental problems, and neither Sabina's teeth nor her gums are throbbing, Sabina can be suffering from neither tooth decay nor gum disease.

Which one of the following contains an error of reasoning most similar to that made in the argument above?

(A) People who drink a lot of coffee are said to have jittery nerves. Therefore, medical students who drink a lot of coffee should not become neonatologists or surgeons since neither neonatology nor surgery should be practiced by people with jittery nerves.

(B) A legally practicing psychiatrist must have both a medical degree and psychiatric training. Thus, since Emmett has not undergone psychiatric training, if he is practicing as a psychiatrist, he is not doing so legally.

(C) Someone with severe nasal congestion has a sinus infection or else is suffering from an allergy. Therefore, if Barton does not have a sinus infection, Barton probably does not have severe nasal congestion.

(D) If a person is interested in either physics or chemistry, then that person would be wise to consider a career in medicine. Yolanda, however, is interested in neither physics nor chemistry, so it would not be wise for her to consider a career in medicine.

(E) Someone who is neither an ophthalmologist nor an optometrist lacks specialized training for diagnosing defects of the eye. Therefore, Kim must have been trained in ophthalmology or optometry, given that she accurately diagnosed John's eye defect.

49. Unless negotiations begin soon, the cease-fire will be violated by one of the two sides to the dispute. Negotiations will be held only if other countries have pressured the two sides to negotiate; an agreement will emerge only if other countries continue such pressure throughout the negotiations. But no negotiations will be held until international troops enforcing the cease-fire have demonstrated their ability to counter any aggression from either side, thus suppressing a major incentive for the two sides to resume fighting.

If the statements above are true, and if negotiations between the two sides do begin soon, at the time those negotiations begin each of the following must also be true EXCEPT:

(A) The cease-fire has not been violated by either of the two sides.

(B) International troops enforcing the cease-fire have demonstrated that they can counter aggression from either of the two sides.

(C) A major incentive for the two sides to resume hostilities has been suppressed.

(D) Other countries have exerted pressure on the two sides to the dispute.

(E) The negotiations' reaching an agreement depends in part on the actions of other countries.

50. If Blankenship Enterprises has to switch suppliers in the middle of a large production run, the company will not show a profit for the year. Therefore, if Blankenship Enterprises in fact turns out to show no profit for the year, it will also turn out to be true that the company had to switch suppliers during a large production run.

The reasoning in the argument is most vulnerable to criticism on which one of the following grounds?

(A) The argument is a circular argument made up of an opening claim followed by a conclusion that merely paraphrases that claim.

(B) The argument fails to establish that a condition under which a phenomenon is said to occur is the only condition under which that phenomenon occurs.

(C) The argument involves an equivocation, in that the word "profit" is allowed to shift its meaning during the course of the argument.

(D) The argument erroneously uses an exceptional, isolated case to support a universal conclusion.

(E) The argument explains one event as being caused by another event, even though both events must actually have been caused by some third, unidentified event.

51. A certain species of bird has two basic varieties, crested and noncrested. The birds, which generally live in flocks that contain only crested or only noncrested birds, tend to select mates of the same variety as themselves. However, if a bird that is raised in a flock in which all other members are crested is later moved to a mixed flock, then that bird whether crested or noncrested—is likely to select a crested mate. This fact indicates that the birds' preference for crested or noncrested mates is learned rather than genetically determined.

Which one of the following, if true, provides the most support for the argument?

(A) Birds of other species also tend to show preferences for mates that have one or another specific physical feature.
(B) In general there are few behavioral differences between the crested and noncrested birds of the species.
(C) Both the crested and noncrested birds of the species tend to select mates that are similar to themselves in size and age.
(D) If a crested bird of the species is raised in captivity apart from other birds and is later moved to a mixed flock, that bird is likely to select a crested mate.
(E) If a bird of the species is raised in a flock that contains both crested and noncrested birds, that bird shows no preference for one variety or the other in its selection of a mate.

52. Since anyone who supports the new tax plan has no chance of being elected, and anyone who truly understands economics would not support the tax plan, only someone who truly understands economics would have any chance of being elected.

The reasoning in the argument is flawed because the argument ignores the possibility that some people who

(A) truly understand economics do not support the tax plan
(B) truly understand economics have no chance of being elected
(C) do not support the tax plan have no chance of being elected
(D) do not support the tax plan do not truly understand economics
(E) have no chance of being elected do not truly understand economics

53. Everyone who is a gourmet cook enjoys a wide variety of foods and spices. Since no one who enjoys a wide variety of foods and spices prefers bland foods to all other foods, it follows that anyone who prefers bland foods to all other foods is not a gourmet cook.

The pattern of reasoning displayed in the argument above is most similar to that displayed in which one of the following?

(A) All of the paintings in the Huang Collection will be put up for auction next week. Since the paintings to be auctioned next week are by a wide variety of artists, it follows that the paintings in the Huang Collection are by a wide variety of artists.
(B) All of the paintings in the Huang Collection are abstract. Since no abstract painting will be included in next week's art auction, nothing to be included in next week's art auction is a painting in the Huang Collection.
(C) All of the paintings in the Huang Collection are superb works of art. Since none of the paintings in the Huang Collection is by Roue, it stands to reason that no painting by Roue is a superb work of art.
(D) Every postimpressionist painting from the Huang Collection will be auctioned off next week. No pop art paintings from the Huang Collection will be auctioned off next week. Hence none of the pop art paintings to be auctioned off next week will be from the Huang Collection.
(E) Every painting from the Huang Collection that is to be auctioned off next week is a major work of art. No price can adequately reflect the true value of a major work of art. Hence the prices that will be paid at next week's auction will not adequately reflect the true value of the paintings sold.

SN

54. Reptiles are air-breathing vertebrates with completely ossified skeletons; so alligators must be air-breathing vertebrates with completely ossified skeletons.

In terms of its logical features, the argument above most resembles which one of the following?

(A) Green plants take in carbon dioxide and release oxygen back into the air; so it follows that grass takes in carbon dioxide and releases oxygen into the air.

(B) Some red butterflies are poisonous to birds that prey on them; so this particular red butterfly is poisonous to birds that prey on it.

(C) Knowledge about the empirical world can be gained from books; so Virginia Woolf's book *A Room of One's Own* must provide knowledge about the empirical world.

(D) Dierdre has seen every film directed by Rainer Werner Fassbinder; so Dierdre must have seen *Ali: Fear Eats the Soul*, a film directed by Fassbinder.

(E) Skiers run a high risk of bone fracture; so it is likely that Lindsey, who has been an avid skier for many years, has suffered a broken bone at some point.

55. Politician: Now that we are finally cleaning up the industrial pollution in the bay, we must start making the bay more accessible to the public for recreational purposes.

Reporter: But if we increase public access to the bay, it will soon become polluted again.

Politician: Not true. The public did not have access to the bay, and it got polluted. Therefore, if and when the public is given access to the bay, it will not get polluted.

Which one of the following most closely parallels the flawed pattern of reasoning in the politician's reply to the reporter?

(A) If there had been a full moon last night, the tide would be higher than usual today. Since the tide is no higher than usual, there must not have been a full moon last night.

(B) The detective said that whoever stole the money would be spending it conspicuously by now. Jones is spending money conspicuously, so he must be the thief.

(C) When prisoners convicted of especially violent crimes were kept in solitary confinement, violence in the prisons increased. Therefore, violence in the prisons will not increase if such prisoners are allowed to mix with fellow prisoners.

(D) To get a driver's license, one must pass a written test. Smith passed the written test, so she must have gotten a driver's license.

(E) In order to like abstract art, you have to understand it. Therefore, in order to understand abstract art, you have to like it.

56. Reasonable people adapt themselves to the world; unreasonable people persist in trying to adapt the world to themselves. Therefore, all progress depends on unreasonable people.

If all of the statements in the passage above are true, which one of the following statements must also be true?

(A) Reasonable people and unreasonable people are incompatible.

(B) If there are only reasonable people, there cannot be progress.

(C) If there are unreasonable people, there will be progress.

(D) Some unreasonable people are unable to bring about progress.

(E) Unreasonable people are more persistent than reasonable people.

57. There are just two ways a moon could have been formed from the planet around which it travels: either part of the planet's outer shell spun off into orbit around the planet or else a large object, such as a comet or meteoroid, struck the planet so violently that it dislodged a mass of material from inside the planet. Earth's moon consists primarily of materials different from those of the Earth's outer shell.

If the statements above are true, which one of the following, if also true, would most help to justify drawing the conclusion that Earth's moon was not formed from a piece of the Earth?

(A) The moons of some planets in Earth's solar system were not formed primarily from the planets' outer shells.
(B) Earth's moon consists primarily of elements that differ from those inside the Earth.
(C) Earth's gravity cannot have trapped a meteoroid and pulled it into its orbit as the Moon.
(D) The craters on the surface of Earth's moon show that it has been struck by many thousands of large meteoroids.
(E) Comets and large meteoroids normally move at very high speeds.

58. Scientific research will be properly channeled whenever those who decide which research to fund give due weight to the scientific merits of all proposed research. But when government agencies control these funding decisions, political considerations play a major role in determining which research will be funded, and whenever political considerations play such a role, the inevitable result is that scientific research is not properly channeled.

Which one of the following can be properly inferred from the statements above?

(A) There is no proper role for political considerations to play in determining who will decide which scientific research to fund.
(B) It is inevitable that considerations of scientific merit will be neglected in decisions regarding the funding of scientific research.
(C) Giving political considerations a major role in determining which scientific research to fund is incompatible with giving proper weight to the scientific merits of proposed research.
(D) When scientific research is not properly channeled, governments tend to step in and take control of the process of choosing which research to fund.
(E) If a government does not control investment in basic scientific research, political consideration will inevitably be neglected in deciding which research to fund.

SN

59. Further evidence bearing on Jamison's activities must have come to light. On the basis of previously available evidence alone, it would have been impossible to prove that Jamison was a party to the fraud, and Jamison's active involvement in the fraud has now been definitively established.

The pattern of reasoning exhibited in the argument above most closely parallels that exhibited in which one of the following?

(A) Smith must not have purchased his house within the last year. He is listed as the owner of that house on the old list of property owners, and anyone on the old list could not have purchased his or her property within the last year.

(B) Turner must not have taken her usual train to Nantes today. Had she done so, she could not have been in Nantes until this afternoon, but she was seen having coffee in Nantes at 11 o'clock this morning.

(C) Norris must have lied when she said that she had not authorized the investigation. There is no doubt that she did authorize it, and authorizing an investigation is not something anyone is likely to have forgotten.

(D) Waugh must have known that last night's class was canceled. Waugh was in the library yesterday, and it would have been impossible for anyone in the library not to have seen the cancellation notices.

(E) LaForte must have deeply resented being passed over for promotion. He maintains otherwise, but only someone who felt badly treated would have made the kind of remark LaForte made at yesterday's meeting.

60. P: Because an elected official needs the support of a political party to be effective, the independent candidate for the legislature cannot possibly be an effective legislator if she wins.

Q: I disagree. By your reasoning, our current legislator, who has the support of a political party, ought to have been effective, but he has not been.

Which one of the following is the best criticism of Q's statement?

(A) It simply contradicts P's claim without offering evidence against it.

(B) It does not consider the possibility that a political party might decide to support an elected legislator even though he or she ran as an independent.

(C) It fails to provide a precise definition for a key term—the word "effective."

(D) It presupposes what is to be proved—that a legislator must have the support of a political party in order to be "effective."

(E) It mistakenly interprets P to be claiming that a factor assures, rather than is necessary for, a legislator's effectiveness.

61. A cat will not be affectionate toward people unless it is handled when it is a kitten. Since the cat that Paula plans to give to her friend was handled when it was a kitten, that cat will be affectionate toward people.

The flawed reasoning in the argument above most closely parallels that in which one of the following?

(A) Tulip bulbs will not produce flowers unless they are chilled for two months. Since the tulip bulbs in the clay pot were not chilled for two months, these bulbs will not produce flowers.

(B) Beets do not grow well unless the soil in which they are grown contains trace amounts of boron. Since the beets in this plot are growing well, the soil in the plot must contain trace amounts of boron.

(C) Fruit trees will not produce much fruit unless they are pruned properly. That the fruit trees at the local orchard produce a large amount of fruit proves that they have been pruned properly.

(D) Cranberries will not thrive unless they are grown in bogs. Since the cranberries in this area are not grown in bogs, these cranberries will not thrive.

(E) Grass seeds will not germinate well unless they are pressed firmly into the ground. The grass seeds sown in this yard were pressed firmly into the ground, so they will germinate well.

SN

62. Congenial guests and a plentiful supply of good things to eat and drink will ensure a successful dinner party. Since Sylvia has prepared more than enough to eat and drink and her guests are all congenial people, her dinner party is certain to be a success.

The pattern of flawed reasoning exhibited by the argument above is most similar to that exhibited by which one of the following?

(A) The right ingredients, properly combined and baked in a reliable oven will always produce a well-baked cake. Since Emily has properly combined the right ingredients, her cake is certain to come out well if she bakes it in a reliable oven.

(B) If corn is baked with its husks on, the resulting dish will always be moist and sweet. Since George wishes to ensure that the corn he plans to serve is moist, he will be certain both to bake it and to leave its husks on.

(C) Making pie dough using ice water and thoroughly chilling the dough before rolling it out will ensure a flaky crust. Andrew thoroughly chilled his pie dough before rolling it out, so, since he used ice water in making it, his pie is certain to have a flaky crust.

(D) If soup is made with a well-seasoned meat stock and fresh ingredients, it will always be welcome at dinner. Since to his meat stock Arnold added only very fresh ingredients, the resulting soup is certain to be welcome at dinner.

(E) Fresh greens, carefully washed and served with a light dressing, always produce a refreshing salad. Since Tisha has developed an exceptionally light dressing but never washes her fresh greens, no salad she serves will be a refreshing one.

63. Whenever a company loses a major product-liability lawsuit, the value of the company's stocks falls significantly within hours after the announcement. Cotoy has long been involved in a major product-liability lawsuit, and its stocks fell significantly in value today. Therefore, we can be sure that an unfavorable judgment against Cotoy in that lawsuit was announced earlier today.

Which one of the following contains flawed reasoning that most closely parallels that in the argument above?

(A) Whenever a business treats its customers discourteously, its customers begin to shop elsewhere. Shopwell wants to keep all of its customers; therefore, its employees will never treat customers discourteously.

(B) Whenever the large airlines decrease fares, the financial stability of smaller competing airlines is adversely affected. Therefore, the smaller competing airlines' financial stability must be seriously threatened when the large airlines announce a large price decrease.

(C) Whenever a country shows a lack of leadership on international issues, respect for the country's policies begins to decline. Therefore, to gain respect for its policies, a country should show leadership on international issues.

(D) Whenever an entering student at Cashman College wins the Performance Fellowship, he or she receives $10,000. Therefore, Eula, a student who has enrolled at Cashman, must have won the Performance Fellowship, because she just received $10,000 from the college.

(E) Whenever a company advertises its products effectively, the company's sales increase. Oroco's sales have not increased; therefore, it is likely that the company did not advertise its products effectively.

64. The symptoms of mental disorders are behavioral, cognitive, or emotional problems. Some patients with mental disorders can be effectively treated with psychotherapy. But it is now known that in some patients mental disorders result from chemical imbalances affecting the brain. Thus these patients can be effectively treated only with medication that will reduce or correct the imbalance.

The argument depends on assuming which one of the following?

(A) Treatment by psychotherapy can produce no effective reduction in or correction of chemical imbalances that cause mental disorders.
(B) Treatment with medication always shows faster results for patients with mental disorders than does treatment with psychotherapy.
(C) Most mental disorders are not the result of chemical imbalances affecting the brain.
(D) Medication is always more effective in treating patients with mental disorders than is psychotherapy.
(E) Treatment with psychotherapy has no effect on mental disorders other than a reduction of the symptoms.

65. Rhonda will see the movie tomorrow afternoon only if Paul goes to the concert in the afternoon. Paul will not go to the concert unless Ted agrees to go to the concert. However, Ted refuses to go to the concert. So Rhonda will not see the movie tomorrow afternoon.

The pattern of reasoning displayed above is most closely paralleled in which one of the following?

(A) If Janice comes to visit, Mary will not pay the bills tomorrow. Janice will not come to visit unless she locates a babysitter. However, Janice has located a babysitter, so she will visit Mary.
(B) Gary will do his laundry tomorrow only if Peter has to go to work. Unless Cathy is ill, Peter will not have to go to work. Since Cathy is not ill, Gary will not do his laundry tomorrow.
(C) Kelly will barbecue fish tonight if it does not rain and the market has fresh trout. Although the forecast does not call for rain, the market does not have fresh trout. So Kelly will not barbecue fish tonight.
(D) Lisa will attend the family reunion next week only if one of her brothers, Jared or Karl, also attends. Karl will not attend the reunion, but Jared will. So Lisa will attend the reunion.
(E) George will not go to the museum tomorrow unless Mark agrees to go. Mark will go to the museum only if he can postpone most of his appointments. Mark has postponed some of his appointments, so he will go to the museum.

SN

Chapter Seventeen: Cause and Effect Questions

1. A recent study found that snoring, though not common in either group, is more common among smokers than among nonsmokers. On the basis of this evidence, the author hypothesized that smoking by itself can induce snoring.

Which one of the following, if true, casts the most doubt on the author's hypothesis?

(A) Stress induces both snoring and smoking in certain individuals.
(B) Obesity induces many individuals to smoke.
(C) Most snorers do not smoke.
(D) Most smokers do not snore.
(E) Both smoking and snoring cause throat problems.

2. Studies of brain lateralization in animals have purported to show that, whereas most human beings are right-handed, about half of any given group of animals will be left-handed (i.e., showing a preference for their left limbs) and half will be right-handed. This finding is suspect, however; it has long been noted that dogs will almost always shake hands with the right paw.

Which one of the following, if true, is the strongest defense against the counterexample of dogs that shake hands?

(A) Dogs are observed to scratch themselves with the left leg as well as with the right leg.
(B) People who observe dogs shaking hands are observing a behavior that dogs perform only with a front paw.
(C) Left-handed people sometimes feel inconvenienced or even stigmatized in a right-handed world, but dogs face no analogous difficulties.
(D) Dogs that have lost a limb are able to compensate for the loss, regardless of whether the limb was lost from the right or left side.
(E) In learning to perform tricks, dogs are influenced by the behavior of their trainers.

3. Learning how to build a nest plays an important part in the breeding success of birds. For example, Dr. Snow has recorded the success of a number of blackbirds in several successive years. He finds that birds nesting for the first time are less successful in breeding than are older birds, and also less successful than they themselves are a year later. This cannot be a mere matter of size and strength, since blackbirds, like the great majority of birds, are fully grown when they leave the nest. It is difficult to avoid the conclusion that they benefit by their nesting experience.

Which one of the following, if true, would most weaken the argument?

(A) Blackbirds build better nests than other birds.
(B) The capacity of blackbirds to lay viable eggs increases with each successive trial during the first few years of reproduction.
(C) The breeding success of birds nesting for the second time is greater than that of birds nesting for the first time.
(D) Smaller and weaker blackbirds breed just as successfully as bigger and stronger blackbirds.
(E) Up to 25 percent of all birds are killed by predators before they start to nest.

Questions 4-5

Despite improvements in treatment for asthma, the death rate from this disease has doubled during the past decade from its previous rate. Two possible explanations for this increase have been offered. First, the recording of deaths due to asthma has become more widespread and accurate in the past decade than it had been previously. Second, there has been an increase in urban pollution. However, since the rate of deaths due to asthma has increased dramatically even in cities with long-standing, comprehensive medical records and with little or no urban pollution, one must instead conclude that the cause of increased deaths is the use of bronchial inhalers by asthma sufferers to relieve their symptoms.

4. Each of the following, if true, provides support to the argument EXCEPT:

(A) Urban populations have doubled in the past decade.
(B) Records of asthma deaths are as accurate for the past twenty years as for the past ten years.
(C) Evidence suggests that bronchial inhalers make the lungs more sensitive to irritation by airborne pollen.
(D) By temporarily relieving the symptoms of asthma, inhalers encourage sufferers to avoid more beneficial measures.
(E) Ten years ago bronchial inhalers were not available as an asthma treatment.

5. Which one of the following is an assumption on which the argument depends?

(A) Urban pollution has not doubled in the past decade.
(B) Doctors and patients generally ignore the role of allergies in asthma.
(C) Bronchial inhalers are unsafe, even when used according to the recommended instructions.
(D) The use of bronchial inhalers aggravates other diseases that frequently occur among asthma sufferers and that often lead to fatal outcomes even when the asthma itself does not.
(E) Increased urban pollution, improved recording of asthma deaths, and the use of bronchial inhalers are the only possible explanations of the increased death rate due to asthma.

6. Although nondairy coffee lighteners made with coconut oil contain 2 grams of saturated fat per tablespoon, or 7 times more than does whole milk, those lighteners usually contain no cholesterol. Yet one tablespoon of such lighteners causes the consumer's blood cholesterol to rise to a higher level than does an identical amount of whole milk, which contains 2 milligrams of cholesterol per tablespoon.

Manufacturers of coffee lighteners based on coconut oil claim that their products usually cause the typical consumer's blood cholesterol to rise to a lower level than does the use of whole milk as a lightener. Which one of the following, if true, provides the most support for the manufacturers' claim?

(A) Consumers of lighteners made with coconut oil who avoid other high-cholesterol foods and exercise more than average tend to have lower-than-average blood cholesterol levels.
(B) Coffee is frequently consumed with pastries and other rich desserts that themselves result in high blood cholesterol levels.
(C) One popular nondairy coffee lightener that is not based on coconut oil has reduced its fat content by 20 percent while keeping its cholesterol content at zero.
(D) Consumers typically add to their coffee substantially smaller quantities of coconut-oil-based lighteners than of whole milk.
(E) Most consumers are convinced that whole dairy products increase blood cholesterol and that nondairy coffee lighteners do not.

7. When a group of children who have been watching television programs that include acts of violence is sent to play with a group of children who have been watching programs that do not include acts of violence, the children who have been watching violent programs commit a much greater number of violent acts in their play than do the children who have been watching nonviolent programs. Therefore, children at play can be prevented from committing violent acts by not being allowed to watch violence on television.

The argument in the passage assumes which one of the following?

(A) Television has a harmful effect on society.
(B) Parents are responsible for the acts of their children.
(C) Violent actions and passive observation of violent actions are not related.
(D) There are no other differences between the two groups of children that might account for the difference in violent behavior.
(E) Children who are treated violently will respond with violence.

8. It is repeatedly claimed that the dumping of nuclear waste poses no threat to people living nearby. If this claim could be made with certainty, there would be no reason for not locating sites in areas of dense population. But the policy of dumping nuclear waste only in the more sparsely populated regions indicates, at the very least, some misgiving about safety on the part of those responsible for policy.

Which one of the following, if true, would most seriously weaken the argument?

(A) Evacuation plans in the event of an accident could not be guaranteed to work perfectly except where the population is small.

(B) In the event of an accident, it is certain that fewer people would be harmed in a sparsely populated than in a densely populated area.

(C) Dumping of nuclear waste poses fewer economic and bureaucratic problems in sparsely populated than in densely populated areas.

(D) There are dangers associated with chemical waste, and it, too, is dumped away from areas of dense population.

(E) Until there is no shred of doubt that nuclear dumps are safe, it makes sense to situate them where they pose the least threat to the public.

9. If the city council maintains spending at the same level as this year's, it can be expected to levy a sales tax of 2 percent next year. Thus, if the council levies a higher tax, it will be because the council is increasing its expenditures.

Which one of the following exhibits a pattern of reasoning most closely similar to that of the argument above?

(A) If house-building costs are not now rising, builders cannot be expected to increase the prices of houses. Thus, if they decrease the prices of houses, it will be because that action will enable them to sell a greater number of houses.

(B) If shops wish to reduce shoplifting, they should employ more store detectives. Thus, if shops do not, they will suffer reduced profits because of their losses from stolen goods.

(C) If the companies in the state do not increase their workers' wages this year, the prices they charge for their goods can be expected to be much the same as they were last year. Thus, if the companies do increase prices, it will be because they have increased wages.

(D) If airlines wish to make profits this year that are similar to last year's, they should not increase their prices this year. Thus, if they charge more, they should be expected to improve their services.

(E) If newspaper publishers wish to publish good papers, they should employ good journalists. Thus, if they employ poor journalists, it will not be surprising if their circulation falls as a result.

10. The rise in the prosperity of England subsequent to 1840 can be attributed to the adoption of the policy of free trade, since economic conditions improved only when that policy had been implemented.

The reasoning in the above argument most closely parallels that in which one of the following?

(A) An exhaustive search of the marshes last year revealed no sign of marsh hawks, so it can be assumed that a similar search this year would reveal equally little sign of that kind of bird.

(B) Building a circular bypass road around Plainfield probably helped the flow of local traffic in the town center, since a circular bypass road generally cuts a city's through traffic markedly.

(C) Before the banks raised their interest rates, people on average incomes could almost afford a mortgage for an amount twice their salary, hence the rate increase has now put mortgages beyond their reach.

(D) Since the improvement in the company's profitability began to occur after the vice president's new morale-building program was put in place, that program can be credited with the improved result.

(E) The extinction of the dinosaurs was brought about by an asteroid colliding with Earth, so their extinction could not have come before the collision.

11. The brains of identical twins are genetically identical. When only one of a pair of identical twins is a schizophrenic, certain areas of the affected twin's brain are smaller than corresponding areas in the brain of the unaffected twin. No such differences are found when neither twin is schizophrenic. Therefore, this discovery provides definitive evidence that schizophrenia is caused by damage to the physical structure of the brain.

Which one of the following is an assumption required by the argument?

(A) The brain of a person suffering from schizophrenia is smaller than the brain of anyone not suffering from schizophrenia.

(B) The relative smallness of certain parts of the brains of schizophrenics is not the result of schizophrenia or of medications used in its treatment.

(C) The brain of a person with an identical twin is no smaller, on average, than the brain of a person who is not a twin.

(D) When a pair of identical twins both suffer from schizophrenia, their brains are the same size.

(E) People who have an identical twin are no more likely to suffer from schizophrenia than those who do not.

12. Recently, highly skilled workers in Eastern Europe have left jobs in record numbers to emigrate to the West. It is therefore likely that skilled workers who remain in Eastern Europe are in high demand in their home countries.

Which one of the following, if true, most seriously weakens the argument?

(A) Eastern European factories prefer to hire workers from their home countries rather than to import workers from abroad.

(B) Major changes in Eastern European economic structures have led to the elimination of many positions previously held by the highly skilled emigrants.

(C) Many Eastern European emigrants need to acquire new skills after finding work in the West.

(D) Eastern European countries plan to train many new workers to replace the highly skilled workers who have emigrated.

(E) Because of the departure of skilled workers from Eastern European countries, many positions are now unfilled.

13. That the policy of nuclear deterrence has worked thus far is unquestionable. Since the end of the Second World War, the very fact that there were nuclear armaments in existence has kept major powers from using nuclear weapons, for fear of starting a worldwide nuclear exchange that would make the land of the power initiating it uninhabitable. The proof is that a third world war between superpowers has not happened.

Which one of the following, if true, indicates a flaw in the argument?

(A) Maintaining a high level of nuclear armaments represents a significant drain on a country's economy.
(B) From what has happened in the past, it is impossible to infer with certainty what will happen in the future, so an accident could still trigger a third world war between superpowers.
(C) Continuing to produce nuclear weapons beyond the minimum needed for deterrence increases the likelihood of a nuclear accident.
(D) The major powers have engaged in many smaller-scale military operations since the end of the Second World War, while refraining from a nuclear confrontation.
(E) It cannot be known whether it was nuclear deterrence that worked, or some other factor, such as a recognition of the economic value of remaining at peace.

14. Sedimentary rock hardens within the earth's crust as layers of matter accumulate and the pressure of the layers above converts the layers below into rock. One particular layer of sedimentary rock that contains an unusual amount of the element iridium has been presented as support for a theory that a meteorite collided with the earth some sixty million years ago. Meteorites are rich in iridium compared to the earth's crust, and geologists theorize that a meteorite's collision with the earth raised a huge cloud of iridium-laden dust. The dust, they say, eventually settled to earth where it combined with other matter, and as new layers accumulated above it, it formed a layer of iridium-rich rock.

Which one of the following, if true, would counter the claim that the iridium-rich layer described in the passage is evidence for the meteorite collision theory?

(A) The huge dust cloud described in the passage would have blocked the transmission of sunlight and lowered the earth's temperature.
(B) A layer of sedimentary rock takes millions of years to harden.
(C) Layers of sedimentary rock are used to determine the dates of prehistoric events whether or not they contain iridium.
(D) Sixty million years ago there was a surge in volcanic activity in which the matter spewed from the volcanoes formed huge iridium-rich dust clouds.
(E) The iridium deposit occurred at about the same time that many animal species became extinct and some scientists have theorized that mass dinosaur extinctions were caused by a meteorite collision.

15. Several studies have shown that hospitals are not all equally successful: patients are much more likely to die in some of them than in others. Since the hospitals in the studies had approximately equal per-patient funding, differences in the quality of care provided by hospital staff are probably responsible for the differences in mortality rates.

Which one of the following, if true, casts the most doubt on the conclusion drawn above?

(A) The staff in some of the hospitals studied had earned more advanced degrees, on average, than the staff in the other hospitals.
(B) Patient populations vary substantially in average severity of illness from hospital to hospital.
(C) The average number of years that staff members stay on at a given job varies considerably from one hospital to another.
(D) Approximately the same surgical procedures were performed in each of the hospitals covered in the studies.
(E) Mortality rates for hospital patients do not vary considerably from one region of the country to anther.

16. Physiological research has uncovered disturbing evidence linking a number of structural disorders to jogging. Among the ailments seemingly connected with this now-popular sport are spinal disk displacements, stress fractures of the feet and ankles, knee and hip joint deterioration, and tendinitis. Furthermore, these injuries do not occur exclusively among beginning runners—veteran joggers suffer an equal percentage of injuries. What the accumulating data suggest is that the human anatomy is not able to withstand the stresses of jogging.

Which one of the following is an assumption of the argument?

(A) The link between jogging and certain structural disorders appears to be a causal one.
(B) Jogging causes more serious disorders than other sports.
(C) The jogger's level of experience is a factor determining the likelihood of a jogging injury.
(D) Some sports are safer for the human body than jogging.
(E) The human species is not very durable.

Questions 17-18

High-technology medicine is driving up the nation's health care costs. Recent advances in cataract surgery illustrate why this is occurring. Cataracts are a major cause of blindness, especially in elderly people. Ten years ago, cataract surgery was painful and not always effective. Thanks to the new technology used in cataract surgery, the operation now restores vision dramatically and is less expensive. These two factors have caused the number of cataract operations performed to increase greatly, which has, in turn, driven up the total amount spent on cataract surgery.

17. Which one of the following can be inferred from the passage?

(A) Ten years ago, few people had successful cataract surgery.
(B) In the long run, the advantages of advanced medical technology are likely to be outweighed by the disadvantages.
(C) The total amount spent on cataract surgery has increased because the increased number of people electing to have the surgery more than offsets the decrease in cost per operation.
(D) Huge increases in the nation's health care costs are due primarily to increased demand for surgery for older people.
(E) Ten years ago, cataract surgery was affordable for more people than it was last year.

18. Each of the following, if true, would support a challenge to the author's explanation of the increase in the number of cataract operations EXCEPT:

(A) The overall population of the nation has increased from what it was ten years ago.
(B) Any one individual's chance of developing cataracts is greater than it was ten years ago.
(C) The number of older people has increased during the last ten years.
(D) Today, health insurance covers cataract surgery for more people than it did ten years ago.
(E) People who have had unsuccessful cataract surgery are left with more seriously impaired vision than they had before the surgery.

19. An ancient Pavonian text describes how an army of one million enemies of Pavonia stopped to drink at a certain lake and drank the lake dry. Recently, archaeologists discovered that water-based life was suddenly absent just after the event was alleged by the text to have occurred. On the basis of reading the text and an account of the archaeological evidence, some students concluded that the events described really took place.

Which one of the following is a questionable technique used by the students to reach their conclusion?

(A) making a generalization about historical events on the basis of a single instance of that type of event
(B) ignoring available, potentially useful counterevidence
(C) rejecting a hypothesis because it is seemingly self-contradictory
(D) considering people and locations whose existence cannot be substantiated by modern historians
(E) taking evidence that a text has correctly described an effect to show that the text has correctly described the cause

20. Anthony: It has been established that over 80 percent of those who use heroin have a history of having used marijuana. Such evidence would seem to prove that smoking marijuana definitely leads to heroin use.

Judith: Maybe smoking marijuana does lead to heroin use, but it is absurd to think that citing those statistics proves that it does. After all, 100 percent of the people who take up heroin had a previous history of drinking water.

Judith's reply to Anthony's argument relies on which one of the following argumentative strategies?

(A) offering evidence suggesting that the statistics Anthony cites in support of his conclusion are inaccurate
(B) undermining the credibility of his conclusion by showing that it is a statement from which absurd consequences can be derived
(C) providing an example to show that not everything that promotes heroin use is unsafe
(D) demonstrating that Anthony's line of reasoning is flawed by showing that such reasoning can lead to clearly false conclusions
(E) calling into question the possibility of ever establishing causal connections solely on the basis of statistical evidence

21. Eight years ago hunting was banned in Greenfield County on the grounds that hunting endangers public safety. Now the deer population in the county is six times what it was before the ban. Deer are invading residential areas, damaging property and causing motor vehicle accidents that result in serious injury to motorists. Since there were never any hunting-related injuries in the county, clearly the ban was not only unnecessary but has created a danger to public safety that would not otherwise exist.

Which one of the following, if true, provides the strongest additional support for the conclusion above?

(A) In surrounding counties, where hunting is permitted, the size of the deer population has not increased in the last eight years.
(B) Motor vehicle accidents involving deer often result in damage to the vehicle, injury to the motorist, or both.
(C) When deer populations increase beyond optimal size, disease and malnutrition become more widespread among the deer herds.
(D) In residential areas in the county, many residents provide food and salt for deer.
(E) Deer can cause extensive damage to ornamental shrubs and trees by chewing on twigs and saplings.

22. Defendants who can afford expensive private defense lawyers have a lower conviction rate than those who rely on court-appointed public defenders. This explains why criminals who commit lucrative crimes like embezzlement or insider trading are more successful at avoiding conviction than are street criminals.

The explanation offered above would be more persuasive if which one of the following were true?

(A) Many street crimes, such as drug dealing, are extremely lucrative and those committing them can afford expensive private lawyers.
(B) Most prosecutors are not competent to handle cases involving highly technical financial evidence and have more success in prosecuting cases of robbery or simple assault.
(C) The number of criminals convicted of street crimes is far greater than the number of criminals convicted of embezzlement or insider trading.
(D) The percentage of defendants who actually committed the crimes of which they are accused is no greater for publicly defended than for privately defended defendants.
(E) Juries, out of sympathy for the victims of crimes, are much more likely to convict defendants accused of violent crimes than they are to convict defendants accused of "victimless" crimes or crimes against property.

23. Police statistics have shown that automobile antitheft devices reduce the risk of car theft, but a statistical study of automobile theft by the automobile insurance industry claims that cars equipped with antitheft devices are, paradoxically, more likely to be stolen than cars that are not so equipped.

Which one of the following, if true, does the most to resolve the apparent paradox?

(A) Owners of stolen cars almost invariably report the theft immediately to the police but tend to delay notifying their insurance company, in the hope that the vehicle will be recovered.
(B) Most cars that are stolen are not equipped with antitheft devices, and most cars that are equipped with antitheft devices are not stolen.
(C) The most common automobile antitheft devices are audible alarms, which typically produce ten false alarms for every actual attempted theft.
(D) Automobile owners who have particularly theft-prone cars and live in areas of greatest incidence of car theft are those who are most likely to have antitheft devices installed.
(E) Most automobile thefts are the work of professional thieves against whose efforts antitheft devices offer scant protection.

24. In 1974 the speed limit on highways in the United States was reduced to 55 miles per hour in order to save fuel. In the first 12 months after the change, the rate of highway fatalities dropped 15 percent, the sharpest one-year drop in history. Over the next 10 years, the fatality rate declined by another 25 percent. It follows that the 1974 reduction in the speed limit saved many lives.

Which one of the following, if true, most strengthens the argument?

(A) The 1974 fuel shortage cut driving sharply for more than a year.

(B) There was no decline in the rate of highway fatalities during the twelfth year following the reduction in the speed limit.

(C) Since 1974 automobile manufacturers have been required by law to install lifesaving equipment, such as seat belts, in all new cars.

(D) The fatality rate in highway accidents involving motorists driving faster than 55 miles per hour is much higher than in highway accidents that do not involve motorists driving at such speeds.

(E) Motorists are more likely to avoid accidents by matching their speed to that of the surrounding highway traffic than by driving at faster or slower speeds.

25. The great medieval universities had no administrators, yet they endured for centuries. Our university has a huge administrative staff, and we are in serious financial difficulties. Therefore, we should abolish the positions and salaries of the administrators to ensure the longevity of the university.

Which one of the following arguments contains flawed reasoning that most closely parallels the flawed reasoning in the argument above?

(A) No airplane had jet engines before 1940, yet airplanes had been flying since 1903. Therefore, jet engines are not necessary for the operation of airplanes.

(B) The novelist's stories began to be accepted for publication soon after she started using a computer to write them. You have been having trouble getting your stories accepted for publication, and you do not use a computer. To make sure your stories are accepted for publication, then, you should write them with the aid of a computer.

(C) After doctors began using antibiotics, the number of infections among patients dropped drastically. Now, however, resistant strains of bacteria cannot be controlled by standard antibiotics. Therefore, new methods of control are needed.

(D) A bicycle should not be ridden without a helmet. Since a good helmet can save the rider's life, a helmet should be considered the most important piece of bicycling equipment.

(E) The great cities of the ancient world were mostly built along waterways. Archaeologists searching for the remains of such cities should therefore try to determine where major rivers used to run.

CAUSAL

26. The cafeteria at Acme Company can offer only four main dishes at lunchtime, and the same four choices have been offered for years. Recently mushroom casserole was offered in place of one of the other main dishes for two days, during which more people chose mushroom casserole than any other main dish. Clearly, if the cafeteria wants to please its customers, mushroom casserole should replace one of the regular dishes as a permanent part of the menu.

The argument is most vulnerable to criticism on the grounds that it fails to consider

(A) the proportion of Acme Company employees who regularly eat lunch in the company cafeteria
(B) whether any of the ingredients used in the cafeteria's recipe for mushroom casserole are included in any of the regular main dishes
(C) a desire for variety as a reason for people's choice of mushroom casserole during the days it was offered
(D) what foods other than main dishes are regularly offered at lunchtime by the cafeteria
(E) whether other meals besides lunch are served in the Acme Company cafeteria

27. The director of a secondary school where many students were having severe academic problems impaneled a committee to study the matter. The committee reported that these students were having academic problems because they spent large amounts of time on school sports and too little time studying. The director then prohibited all students who were having academic problems from taking part in sports in which they were active. He stated that this would ensure that such students would do well academically.

The reasoning on which the director bases his statement is not sound because he fails to establish that

(A) some students who spend time on sports do not have academic problems
(B) all students who do well academically do so because of time saved by not participating in sports
(C) at least some of the time the students will save by not participating in sports will be spent on solving their academic problems
(D) no students who do well academically spend time on sports
(E) the quality of the school's sports program would not suffer as a result of the ban

28. Despite a steady decrease in the average number of hours worked per person per week, the share of the population that reads a daily newspaper has declined greatly in the past 20 years. But the percentage of the population that watches television daily has shown a similarly dramatic increase over the same period. Clearly, increased television viewing has caused a simultaneous decline in newspaper reading.

Which one of the following, if true, would be most damaging to the explanation given above for the decline in newspaper reading?

(A) There has been a dramatic increase over the past 20 years in the percentage of people who tell polltakers that television is their primary source of information about current events.
(B) Of those members of the population who do not watch television, the percentage who read a newspaper every day has also shown a dramatic decrease.
(C) The time people spend with the books and newspapers they read has increased, on average, from 1 to 3 hours per week in the past 20 years.
(D) People who spend large amounts of time each day watching television are less able to process and remember printed information than are those who do not watch television.
(E) A typical television set is on 6 hours a day, down from an average of 6 1/2 hours a day 5 years ago.

29. Tall children can generally reach high shelves easily. Short children can generally reach high shelves only with difficulty. It is known that short children are more likely than are tall children to become short adults. Therefore, if short children are taught to reach high shelves easily, the proportion of them who become short adults will decrease.

A reasoning error in the argument is that the argument

(A) attributes a characteristic of an individual member of a group to the group as a whole
(B) presupposes that which is to be proved
(C) refutes a generalization by means of an exceptional case
(D) assumes a causal relationship where only a correlation has been indicated
(E) takes lack of evidence for the existence of a state of affairs as evidence that there can be no such state of affairs

30. Data from satellite photographs of the tropical rain forest in Melonia show that last year the deforestation rate of this environmentally sensitive zone was significantly lower than in previous years. The Melonian government, which spent millions of dollars last year to enforce laws against burning and cutting of the forest, is claiming that the satellite data indicate that its increased efforts to halt the destruction are proving effective.

Which one of the following, if true, most seriously undermines the government's claim?

(A) Landowner opposition to the government's antideforestation efforts grew more violent last year in response to the increased enforcement.
(B) Rainfall during the usually dry 6-month annual burning season was abnormally heavy last year.
(C) Government agents had to issue fines totaling over $9 million to 3,500 violators of burning-and-cutting regulations.
(D) The inaccessibility of much of the rain forest has made it impossible to confirm the satellite data by direct observation from the field.
(E) Much of the money that was designated last year for forest preservation has been spent on research and not on enforcement.

31. Advertisement: Northwoods Maple Syrup, made the old-fashioned way, is simply tops for taste. And here is the proof: in a recent market survey, 7 out of every 10 shoppers who expressed a preference said that Northwoods was the only maple syrup for them, no ifs, ands, or buts.

Of the following, which one is the strongest reason why the advertisement is potentially misleading?

(A) The proportion of shoppers expressing no preference might have been very small.
(B) Other brands of maple syrup might also be made the old-fashioned way.
(C) No market survey covers more than a sizable minority of the total population of consumers.
(D) The preference for the Northwoods brand might be based on such a factor as an exceptionally low price.
(E) Shoppers who buy syrup might buy only maple syrup.

32. When girls are educated in single-sex secondary schools, they tend to do better academically than girls who attend mixed-sex schools. Since Alice achieved higher grades than any other woman in her first year at the university, she was probably educated at a single-sex school.

Which one of the following most closely parallels the flawed reasoning used in the argument above?

(A) When students have individual tutoring in math, they usually get good grades on their final exams. Celia had individual tutoring in math so she will probably get a good grade.
(B) When babies are taught to swim, they have more than the average number of ear infections as they grow up. Janice has more ear infections than any other person at the local swimming club, so she probably was taught to swim when she was a baby.
(C) When children study music at an early age, they later tend to appreciate a wide variety of music, so the talent of future musicians is best fostered at an early age.
(D) When children practice their piano scales for half an hour each day, they usually pass their piano exams. Sally practices scales for less than half an hour each day, so she will probably fail her piano exam.
(E) When children have parents who help them with their homework, they usually do well in school. Therefore, having help with homework is probably the cause of high academic achievement.

33. Sea turtles nest only at their own birthplaces. After hatching on the beach, the turtles enter the water to begin their far-ranging migration, only returning to their birthplaces to nest some 15 to 30 years later. It has been hypothesized that newborn sea turtles learn the smell of their birth environment, and it is this smell that stimulates the turtles to return to nest.

Which one of the following, if true, would cast the most serious doubt on the hypothesis in the passage?

(A) Beaches on which sea turtles nest tend to be in secluded locations such as on islands.
(B) Sea turtles exposed to a variety of environments under experimental conditions preferred the environment that contained sand from their own birthplaces.
(C) Electronic tags attached to sea turtles did not alter their nesting patterns.
(D) Unlike other types of turtles, sea turtles have a well-developed sense of smell.
(E) Sea turtles that had their sense of smell destroyed by exposure to petroleum products returned to nest at their own

CAUSAL

birthplaces.

34. A survey of a group of people between the ages of 75 and 80 found that those who regularly played the card game bridge tended to have better short-term memory than those who did not play bridge. It was originally concluded from this that playing bridge can help older people to retain and develop their memory. However, it may well be that bridge is simply a more enjoyable game for people who already have good short-term memory and who are thus more inclined to play.

In countering the original conclusion the reasoning above uses which one of the following techniques?

(A) challenging the representativeness of the sample surveyed
(B) conceding the suggested relationship between playing bridge and short-term memory, but questioning whether any conclusion about appropriate therapy can be drawn
(C) arguing that the original conclusion relied on an inaccurate understanding of the motives that the people surveyed have for playing bridge
(D) providing an alternative hypothesis to explain the data on which the original conclusion was based
(E) describing a flaw in the reasoning on which the original conclusion was based

35. The use of automobile safety seats by children aged 4 and under has nearly doubled in the past 8 years. It is clear that this increase has prevented child fatalities that otherwise would have occurred, because although the number of children aged 4 and under who were killed while riding in cars involved in accidents rose 10 percent over the past 8 years, the total number of serious automobile accidents rose by 20 percent during that period.

Which one of the following, if true, most strengthens the argument?

(A) Some of the automobile safety seats purchased for children under 4 continue to be used after the child reaches the age of 5.
(B) The proportion of serious automobile accidents involving child passengers has remained constant over the past 8 years.
(C) Children are taking more trips in cars today than they were 8 years ago, but the average total time they spend in cars has remained constant.
(D) The sharpest increase in the use of automobile safety seats over the past 8 years has been for children over the age of 2.
(E) The number of fatalities among adults involved in automobile accidents rose by 10 percent over the past 8 years.

36. DataCom, a company that filed many patents last year, was financially more successful last year than were its competitors, none of which filed many patents. It is therefore likely that DataCom owed its greater financial success to the fact that it filed many patents last year.

The argument is most vulnerable to criticism on the grounds that it

(A) presupposes what it sets out to demonstrate about the relationship between the financial success of DataCom's competitors and the number of patents they filed
(B) confuses a company's financial success with its technological innovativeness
(C) fails to establish whether any one of DataCom's competitors was financially more successful last year than was any other
(D) gives no reason to exclude the possibility that other differences between DataCom and its competitors accounted for its comparative financial success
(E) applies a generalization to an exceptional case

37. Pretzels can cause cavities. Interestingly, the longer that a pretzel remains in contact with the teeth when it is being eaten, the greater the likelihood that a cavity will result. What is true of pretzels in this regard is also true of caramels. Therefore, since caramels dissolve more quickly in the mouth than pretzels do, eating a caramel is less likely to result in a cavity than eating a pretzel is.

The reasoning in the argument is vulnerable to criticism on the grounds that the argument

(A) treats a correlation that holds within individual categories as thereby holding across categories as well
(B) relies on the ambiguous use of a key term
(C) makes a general claim based on particular examples that do not adequately represent the respective classes that they are each intended to represent
(D) mistakes the cause of a particular phenomenon for the effect of that phenomenon
(E) is based on premises that cannot all be true

38. Humans began to spread across North America around 12,000 years ago, as the climate became warmer. During the same period the large mammals that were once abundant in North America, such as the mastodon, the woolly mammoth, and the saber-toothed tiger, became extinct. Thus, contrary to the myth that humans formerly lived in harmony with the rest of nature, it is clear that even 12,000 years ago human activity was causing the extinction of animal species.

The argument is most vulnerable to the criticism that

(A) it adopts without question a view of the world in which humans are seen as not included in nature
(B) in calling the idea that humans once lived in harmony with nature a myth the argument presupposes what it attempts to prove
(C) for early inhabitants of North America the destruction of mastodons, woolly mammoths, and saber-toothed tigers might have had very different significance than the extinction of mammal species does for modern humans
(D) there might have been many other species of animals, besides mastodons, woolly mammoths, and saber-toothed tigers, that became extinct as the result of the spread of humans across North America
(E) the evidence it cites is consistent with the alternative hypothesis that the large mammals' extinction was a direct result of the same change in climate that allowed humans to spread across North America

39. Between 1951 and 1963, it was illegal in the country of Geronia to manufacture, sell, or transport any alcoholic beverages. Despite this prohibition, however, the death rate from diseases related to excessive alcohol consumption was higher during the first five years of the period than it was during the five years prior to 1951. Therefore, the attempt to prevent alcohol use merely made people want and use alcohol more than they would have if it had not been forbidden.

Each of the following, if true, weakens the argument EXCEPT:

(A) Death from an alcohol-related disease generally does not occur until five to ten years after the onset of excessive alcohol consumption.
(B) The diseases that can be caused by excessive alcohol consumption can also be caused by other kinds of behavior that increased between 1951 and 1963.
(C) The death rate resulting from alcohol-related diseases increased just as sharply during the ten years before and the ten years after the prohibition of alcohol as it did during the years of prohibition.
(D) Many who died of alcohol-related diseases between 1951 and 1963 consumed illegally imported alcoholic beverages produced by the same methods as those used within Geronia.
(E) Between 1951 and 1963, among the people with preexisting alcohol-related diseases, the percentage who obtained lifesaving medical attention declined because of a social stigma attached to excessive alcohol consumption.

40. The years 1917, 1937, 1956, 1968, 1979, and 1990 are all notable for the occurrence of both popular uprisings and near-maximum sunspot activity. During heavy sunspot activity, there is a sharp rise in positively charged ions in the air people breathe, and positively charged ions are known to make people anxious and irritable. Therefore, it is likely that sunspot activity has actually been a factor in triggering popular uprisings.

Which one of the following exhibits a pattern of reasoning most similar to that in the passage?

(A) The ancient Greeks sometimes attempted to predict the outcome of future events by watching the flight patterns of birds. Since the events themselves often matched the predictions, the birds were probably responding to some factor that also influenced the events.
(B) Martha, Sidney, and Hilary are the city's three most powerful politicians, and all three graduated from Ridgeview High School. Although Ridgeview never had a reputation for excellence, it must have been a good school to have produced three such successful graduates.
(C) Unusually cold weather last December coincided with a rise in fuel prices. When it is cold, people use more fuel to keep warm; and when more fuel is used, prices rise. Therefore if prices are high next winter, it will be the result of cold weather.
(D) The thirty healthiest people in a long-term medical study turned out to be the same thirty whose regular diets included the most vegetables. Since specific substances in vegetables are known to help the body fight disease, vegetables should be part of everyone's diet.
(E) Acme's most productive managers are consistently those who occupy the corner offices, which have more windows than other offices at Acme. Since people are more alert when they are exposed to abundant natural light, the greater productivity of these managers is probably at least in part a result of their working in the corner offices.

Questions 41-42

Monroe, despite his generally poor appetite, thoroughly enjoyed the three meals he ate at the Tip-Top Restaurant, but, unfortunately, after each meal he became ill. The first time he ate an extra-large sausage pizza with a side order of hot peppers; the second time he took full advantage of the all-you-can-eat fried shrimp and hot peppers special; and the third time he had two of Tip-Top's giant meatball sandwiches with hot peppers. Since the only food all three meals had in common was the hot peppers, Monroe concludes that it is solely due to Tip-Top's hot peppers that he became ill.

41. Monroe's reasoning is most vulnerable to which one of the following criticisms?

(A) He draws his conclusion on the basis of too few meals that were consumed at Tip-Top and that included hot peppers.
(B) He posits a causal relationship without ascertaining that the presumed cause preceded the presumed effect.
(C) He allows his desire to continue dining at Tip-Top to bias his conclusion.
(D) He fails to establish that everyone who ate Tip-Top's hot peppers became ill.
(E) He overlooks the fact that at all three meals he consumed what was, for him, an unusually large quantity of food.

42. If both Monroe's conclusion and the evidence on which he bases it are correct, they would provide the strongest support for which one of the following?

(A) Monroe can eat any of Tip-Top's daily all-you-can-eat specials without becoming ill as long as the special does not include the hot peppers.
(B) If, at his third meal at Tip-Top, Monroe had chosen to eat the baked chicken with hot peppers, he would have become ill after that meal.
(C) If the next time Monroe eats one of Tip-Top's extra-large sausage pizzas he does not have a side order of hot peppers, he will not become ill after his meal.
(D) Before eating Tip-Top's fried shrimp with hot peppers special, Monroe had eaten fried shrimp without suffering any ill effects.
(E) The only place Monroe has eaten hot peppers has been at Tip-Top.

43. A certain strain of bacteria was found in the stomachs of ulcer patients. A medical researcher with no history of ulcers inadvertently ingested some of the bacteria and within weeks developed an ulcer. Therefore, it is highly likely that the bacteria strain induces ulcers.

Which one of the following, if true, most supports the argument above?

(A) People who have the bacteria strain in their stomachs have been found to have no greater incidence of kidney disease than do people who lack the bacteria strain.
(B) The researcher did not develop any other serious health problems within a year after ingesting the bacteria strain.
(C) There is no evidence that the bacteria strain induces ulcers in laboratory animals.
(D) The researcher is a recognized expert in the treatment of diseases of the stomach.
(E) A study of 2,000 people who do not have ulcers found that none of these people had the bacteria strain in their stomachs.

44. A recent study monitored the blood pressure of people petting domestic animals in the laboratory. The blood pressure of some of these people lowered while petting the animals. Therefore, for any one of the people so affected, owning a pet would result in that person having a lower average blood pressure.

The flawed pattern of reasoning in the argument above is most similar to that in which one of the following?

(A) Because a single dose of a drug acts as a remedy for a particular ailment, a healthy person can ward off that ailment by taking single doses regularly.
(B) Because buying an automobile is very expensive, people should hold on to an automobile, once bought, for as long as it can be maintained in running condition.
(C) Since pruning houseplants is enjoyable for some people, those people should get rid of houseplants that do not require frequent pruning.
(D) Since riding in a boat for a few minutes is relaxing for some people, those people would be more relaxed generally if those people owned boats.
(E) Since giving a fence one coat of white paint makes the fence white, giving it two coats of white paint would make it even whiter.

45. Chronic fatigue syndrome, a condition that afflicts thousands of people, is invariably associated with lower-than-normal concentrations of magnesium in the blood. Further, malabsorption of magnesium from the digestive tract to the blood is also often associated with some types of fatigue. These facts in themselves demonstrate that treatments that raise the concentration of magnesium in the blood would provide an effective cure for the fatigue involved in the syndrome.

The argument is most vulnerable to which one of the following criticisms?

(A) It fails to establish that lower-than-normal concentrations of magnesium in the blood are invariably due to malabsorption of magnesium.
(B) It offers no evidence that fatigue itself does not induce lowered concentrations of magnesium in the blood.
(C) It ignores the possibility that, even in people who are not afflicted with chronic fatigue syndrome, concentration of magnesium in the blood fluctuates.
(D) It neglects to state the exact concentration of magnesium in the blood which is considered the normal concentration.
(E) It does not specify what methods would be most effective in raising the concentration of magnesium in the blood.

CAUSAL

46. Dr. Godfrey: Now that high school students are allowed to work more than 15 hours per week at part-time jobs, those who actually do so show less interest in school and get lower grades than those who do not work as many hours at part-time jobs. Obviously, working long hours at part-time jobs during the school year contributes to the academic problems that many of our high school students experience.

Dr. Nash: That's not so. Many of our high school students set out to earn as much money as they can simply to compensate for their lack of academic success.

Dr. Nash responds to Dr. Godfrey's argument by doing which one of the following?

(A) attempting to downplay the seriousness of the problems facing academically troubled high school students
(B) offering an alternative interpretation of the evidence cited by Dr. Godfrey
(C) questioning the accuracy of the evidence on which Dr. Godfrey bases his conclusion
(D) proposing that the schools are not at fault for the academic problems facing many high school students
(E) raising the possibility that there is no relationship between academic problems among high school students and part-time employment

47. The population of songbirds throughout England has decreased in recent years. Many people explain this decrease as the result of an increase during the same period in the population of magpies, which eat the eggs and chicks of songbirds.

Which one of the following, if true, argues most strongly against the explanation reported in the passage?

(A) Official records of the population of birds in England have been kept for only the past 30 years.
(B) The number of eggs laid yearly by a female songbird varies widely according to the songbird's species.
(C) Although the overall population of magpies has increased, in most areas of England in which the songbird population has decreased, the number of magpies has remained stable.
(D) The population of magpies has increased because farmers no longer shoot or trap magpies to any great extent, though farmers still consider magpies to be pests.
(E) Although magpies eat the eggs and chicks of songbirds, magpies' diets consist of a wide variety of other foods as well.

48. Several years ago, as a measure to reduce the population of gypsy moths, which depend on oak leaves for food, entomologists introduced into many oak forests a species of fungus that is poisonous to gypsy moth caterpillars. Since then, the population of both caterpillars and adult moths has significantly declined in those areas. Entomologists have concluded that the decline is attributable to the presence of the poisonous fungus.

Which one of the following, if true, most strongly supports the conclusion drawn by the entomologists?

(A) A strain of gypsy moth whose caterpillars are unaffected by the fungus has increased its share of the total gypsy moth population.
(B) The fungus that was introduced to control the gypsy moth population is poisonous to few insect species other than the gypsy moth.
(C) An increase in numbers of both gypsy moth caterpillars and gypsy moth adults followed a drop in the number of some of the species that prey on the moths.
(D) In the past several years, air pollution and acid rain have been responsible for a substantial decline in oak tree populations.
(E) The current decline in the gypsy moth population in forests where the fungus was introduced is no greater than a decline that occurred concurrently in other forests.

49. One year ago a local government initiated an antismoking advertising campaign in local newspapers, which it financed by imposing a tax on cigarettes of 20 cents per pack. One year later, the number of people in the locality who smoke cigarettes had declined by 3 percent. Clearly, what was said in the advertisements had an effect, although a small one, on the number of people in the locality who smoke cigarettes.

Which one of the following, if true, most helps to strengthen the argument?

(A) Residents of the locality have not increased their use of other tobacco products such as snuff and chewing tobacco since the campaign went into effect.
(B) A substantial number of cigarette smokers in the locality who did not quit smoking during the campaign now smoke less than they did before it began.
(C) Admissions to the local hospital for chronic respiratory ailments were down by 15 percent one year after the campaign began.
(D) Merchants in the locality responded to the local tax by reducing the price at which they sold cigarettes by 20 cents per pack.
(E) Smokers in the locality had incomes that on average were 25 percent lower than those of nonsmokers.

50. Parent 1: Ten years ago, children in communities like ours did not date until they were thirteen to fifteen years old. Now our nine to eleven year olds are dating. Obviously, children in communities like ours are becoming romantically interested in members of the opposite sex at an earlier age today than they did ten years ago.

Parent 2: I disagree. Our nine to eleven year olds do not want to date, but they feel intense peer pressure to act grown up by dating.

Parent 2, in responding to Parent 1, does which one of the following?

(A) draws a conclusion about a new phenomenon by comparing it to a phenomenon that is known and understood
(B) refutes a generalization about nine- to eleven-year-old children by means of an exceptional case overlooked by Parent 1
(C) assumes that nine- to eleven-year-old children are as interested in dating as thirteen- to fifteen-year-old children
(D) provides an alternative explanation for the changes in children's dating described by Parent 1
(E) criticizes Parent 1 as a proponent of a claim rather than criticizing the claim itself

51. A study was designed to establish what effect, if any, the long-term operation of offshore oil rigs had on animal life on the bottom of the sea. The study compared the sea-bottom communities near rigs with those located in control sites several miles from any rig and found no significant differences. The researchers concluded that oil rigs had no adverse effect on sea-bottom animals.

Which one of the following, if true, most seriously weakens the researchers' conclusion?

(A) Commercially important fish depend on sea-bottom animals for much of their food, so a drop in catches of those fish would be evidence of damage to sea-bottom communities.
(B) The discharge of oil from offshore oil rigs typically occurs at the surface of the water, and currents often carry the oil considerable distances before it settles on the ocean floor.
(C) Contamination of the ocean floor from sewage and industrial effluent does not result in the destruction of all sea-bottom animals but instead reduces species diversity as well as density of animal life.
(D) Only part of any oil discharged into the ocean reaches the ocean floor: some oil evaporates, and some remains in the water as suspended drops.
(E) Where the ocean floor consists of soft sediment, contaminating oil persists much longer than where the ocean floor is rocky.

52. Brain scans of people exposed to certain neurotoxins reveal brain damage identical to that found in people suffering from Parkinson's disease. This fact shows not only that these neurotoxins cause this type of brain damage, but also that the brain damage itself causes Parkinson's disease. Thus brain scans can be used to determine who is likely to develop Parkinson's disease.

The argument contains which one of the following reasoning errors?

(A) It fails to establish that other methods that can be used to diagnose Parkinson's disease are less accurate than brain scans.
(B) It overestimates the importance of early diagnosis in determining appropriate treatments for people suffering from Parkinson's disease.
(C) It mistakes a correlation between the type of brain damage described and Parkinson's disease for a causal relation between the two.
(D) It assumes that people would want to know as early as possible whether they were likely to develop Parkinson's disease.
(E) It neglects to specify how the information provided by brain scans could be used either in treating Parkinson's disease or in monitoring the progression of the disease.

<u>Questions 53-54</u>

Doctors in Britain have long suspected that patients who wear tinted eyeglasses are abnormally prone to depression and hypochondria. Psychological tests given there to hospital patients admitted for physical complaints like heart pain and digestive distress confirmed such a relationship. Perhaps people whose relationship to the world is psychologically painful choose such glasses to reduce visual stimulation, which is perceived as irritating. At any rate, it can be concluded that when such glasses are worn, it is because the wearer has a tendency to be depressed or hypochondriacal.

53. The argument assumes which one of the following?

(A) Depression is not caused in some cases by an organic condition of the body.
(B) Wearers do not think of the tinted glasses as a means of distancing themselves from other people.
(C) Depression can have many causes, including actual conditions about which it is reasonable for anyone to be depressed.
(D) For hypochondriacs wearing tinted glasses, the glasses serve as a visual signal to others that the wearer's health is delicate.
(E) The tinting does not dim light to the eye enough to depress the wearer's mood substantially.

54. Each of the following, if true, weakens the argument EXCEPT:

(A) Some people wear tinted glasses not because they choose to do so but because a medical condition of their eyes forces them to do so.
(B) Even a depressed or hypochondriacal person can have valid medical complaints, so a doctor should perform all the usual objective tests in diagnosing such persons.
(C) The confirmatory tests were not done for places such as western North America where the usual quality of light differs from that prevailing in Britain.
(D) Fashions with respect to wearing tinted glasses differ in different parts of the world.
(E) At the hospitals where the tests were given, patients who were admitted for conditions less ambiguous than heart pain or digestive distress did not show the relationship between tinted glasses and depression or hypochondria.

55. Legislator: Your agency is responsible for regulating an industry shaken by severe scandals. You were given funds to hire 500 investigators to examine the scandals, but you hired no more than 400. I am forced to conclude that you purposely limited hiring in an attempt to prevent the full extent of the scandals from being revealed.

Regulator: We tried to hire the 500 investigators but the starting salaries for these positions had been frozen so low by the legislature that it was impossible to attract enough qualified applicants.

The regulator responds to the legislator's criticism by

(A) shifting the blame for the scandals to the legislature
(B) providing information that challenges the conclusion drawn by the legislator
(C) claiming that compliance with the legislature's mandate would have been an insufficient response
(D) rephrasing the legislator's conclusion in terms more favorable to the regulator
(E) showing that the legislator's statements are self-contradictory

56. Medieval Arabs had manuscripts of many ancient Greek texts, which were translated into Arabic when there was a demand for them. Medieval Arab philosophers were very interested in Aristotle's Poetics, an interest that evidently was not shared by medieval Arab poets, because a poet interested in the Poetics would certainly have wanted to read Homer, to whose epics Aristotle frequently refers. But Homer was not translated into Arabic until modern times.

Which one of the following, if true, most strongly supports the argument above?

(A) A number of medieval Arab translators possessed manuscripts of the Homeric epics in their original Greek.
(B) Medieval Arabic story cycles, such as the Arabian Nights, are in some ways similar to parts of the Homeric epics.
(C) In addition to translating from Greek, medieval Arab translators produced Arabic editions of many works originally written in Indian languages and in Persian.
(D) Aristotle's Poetics has frequently been cited and commented on by modern Arab poets.
(E) Aristotle's Poetics is largely concerned with drama, and dramatic works were written and performed by medieval Arabs.

57. Videocassette recorders (VCRs) enable people to watch movies at home on videotape. People who own VCRs go to movie theaters more often than do people who do not own VCRs. Contrary to popular belief, therefore, owning a VCR actually stimulates people to go to movie theaters more often than they otherwise would.

The argument is most vulnerable to criticism on the grounds that it

(A) concludes that a claim must be false because of the mere absence of evidence in its favor
(B) cites, in support of the conclusion, evidence that is inconsistent with other information that is provided
(C) fails to establish that the phenomena interpreted as cause and effect are not both direct effects of some other factor
(D) takes a condition that by itself guarantees the occurrence of a certain phenomenon to be a condition that therefore must be met for that phenomenon to occur
(E) bases a broad claim about the behavior of people in general on a comparison between two groups of people that together include only a small proportion of people overall

58. Measurements of the motion of the planet Uranus seem to show Uranus being tugged by a force pulling it away from the Sun and the inner planets. Neptune and Pluto, the two known planets whose orbits are farther from the Sun than is the orbit of Uranus, do not have enough mass to exert the force that the measurements indicate. Therefore, in addition to the known planets, there must be at least one planet in our solar system that we have yet to discover.

Which one of the following, if true, most seriously weakens the argument?

(A) Pluto was not discovered until 1930.
(B) There is a belt of comets beyond the orbit of Pluto with powerful gravitational pull.
(C) Neither Neptune nor Pluto is as massive as Uranus.
(D) The force the Sun exerts on Uranus is weaker than the force it exerts on the inner planets.
(E) Uranus' orbit is closer to Neptune's orbit than it is to Pluto's.

59. Grow-Again ointment is a proven treatment for reversing male hereditary baldness. Five drops daily is the recommended dose, and exceeding this quantity does not increase the product's effectiveness. Therefore, offering a manufacturer's rebate on the purchase price of Grow-Again will not increase sales and consequently would be unprofitable for the manufacturer.

Which one of the following, if true, would most strengthen the argument?

(A) When using an ointment, people tend to believe that applying it in greater quantities can make it more effective.
(B) Grow-Again is more effective on some of the men who use it than it is on others.
(C) The rebate, if offered, would not attract purchasers who otherwise might not use Grow-Again.
(D) Baldness in men can be caused by a variety of factors, only one of which is heredity.
(E) Grow-Again is a product whose per-unit manufacturing cost does not fall significantly when the product is produced in large quantities.

60. That wall is supported by several joists. The only thing that can have caused the bulge that the wall now has is a broken joist. Therefore, at least one of the joists is broken.

Which one of the following arguments is most similar in its logical features to the argument above?

(A) At least one of the players in the orchestra must have made a mistake, since nothing else would have made the conductor grimace in the way she just did.
(B) The first piece must have been the easiest, since it was the only piece in the entire concert in which the orchestra did not make many mistakes.
(C) The players play well only when they like the music, since they tend to make mistakes when they play something they do not like.
(D) One of the orchestra's players must be able to play the harp, since in one of the pieces they are playing at next week's concert the composer specified that a harp should be played.
(E) The emotion of the music is the only thing that can have caused the conductor to look so angry just then, since the orchestra was playing perfectly.

61. An ingredient in marijuana known as THC has been found to inactivate herpesviruses in experiments. In previous experiments researchers found that inactivated herpesviruses can convert healthy cells into cancer cells. It can be concluded that the use of marijuana can cause cancer.

Which one of the following, if true, most seriously weakens the argument?

(A) Several teams of scientists performed the various experiments and all of the teams had similar results.
(B) The carcinogenic effect of THC could be neutralized by the other ingredients found in marijuana.
(C) When THC kills herpesviruses it weakens the immune system, and it might thus diminish the body's ability to fight other viruses, including viruses linked to cancers.
(D) If chemists modify the structure of THC, THC can be safely incorporated into medications to prevent herpes.
(E) To lessen the undesirable side effects of chemotherapy, the use of marijuana has been recommended for cancer patients who are free of the herpesvirus.

62. Premiums for automobile accident insurance are often higher for red cars than for cars of other colors. To justify these higher charges, insurance companies claim that, overall, a greater percentage of red cars are involved in accidents than are cars of any other color. If this claim is true, then lives could undoubtedly be saved by banning red cars from the roads altogether.

The reasoning in the argument is flawed because the argument

(A) accepts without question that insurance companies have the right to charge higher premiums for higher-risk clients
(B) fails to consider whether red cars cost the same to repair as cars of other colors
(C) ignores the possibility that drivers who drive recklessly have a preference for red cars
(D) does not specify precisely what percentage of red cars are involved in accidents
(E) makes an unsupported assumption that every automobile accident results in some loss of life

63. It is probably not true that colic in infants is caused by the inability of those infants to tolerate certain antibodies found in cow's milk, since it is often the case that symptoms of colic are shown by infants that are fed breast milk exclusively.

Which one of the following, if true, most seriously weakens the argument?

(A) A study involving 500 sets of twins has found that if one infant has colic, its twin will probably also have colic.
(B) Symptoms of colic generally disappear as infants grow older, whether the infants have been fed breast milk exclusively or have been fed infant formula containing cow's milk.
(C) In a study of 5,000 infants who were fed only infant formula containing cow's milk, over 4,000 of the infants never displayed any symptoms of colic.
(D) When mothers of infants that are fed only breast milk eliminate cow's milk and all products made from cow's milk from their own diets, any colic symptoms that their infants have manifested quickly disappear.
(E) Infants that are fed breast milk develop mature digestive systems at an earlier age than do those that are fed infant formulas, and infants with mature digestive systems are better able to tolerate certain proteins and antibodies found in cow's milk.

64. Advertisement: A leading economist has determined that among people who used computers at their place of employment last year, those who also owned portable ("laptop") computers earned 25 percent more on average than those who did not. It s obvious from this that owning a laptop computer led to a higher-paying job.

Which one of the following identifies a reasoning error in the argument?

(A) It attempts to support a sweeping generalization on the basis of information about only a small number of individuals.
(B) Its conclusion merely restates a claim made earlier in the argument.
(C) It concludes that one thing was caused by another although the evidence given is consistent with the first thing's having caused the second.
(D) It offers information as support for a conclusion when that information actually shows that the conclusion is false.
(E) It uncritically projects currently existing trends indefinitely into the future.

65. Garbage dumps do not harm wildlife. Evidence is furnished by the Masai-Mara reserve in Kenya, where baboons that use the garbage dumps on the reserve as a food source mature faster and have more offspring than do baboons on the reserve that do not scavenge on garbage.

Each of the following statements, if true, casts doubt on the argument EXCEPT:

(A) The baboons that feed on the garbage dump are of a different species from those that do not.
(B) The life expectancy of baboons that eat garbage is significantly lower than that of baboons that do not eat garbage.
(C) The cholesterol level of garbage-eating baboons is dangerously higher than that of baboons that do not eat garbage.
(D) The population of hyenas that live near unregulated garbage landfills north of the reserve has doubled in the last two years.
(E) The rate of birth defects for the baboon population on the reserve has doubled since the first landfills were opened.

CAUSAL

18

Chapter Eighteen: Numbers and Percentages Questions

1. Water vapor evaporated from the ocean contains a greater proportion of oxygen-16 and a smaller proportion of the heavier oxygen-18 than does seawater. Normally, this phenomenon has no effect on the overall composition of the ocean, because evaporated seawater returns to the ocean through precipitation. During an ice age, however, a large amount of precipitation falls on ice caps, where it is trapped as ice.

Which one of the following conclusions about a typical ice age is most strongly supported by the statements above?

(A) The proportions of oxygen-16 and oxygen-18 are the same in vapor from seawater as in the seawater itself.
(B) The concentration of oxygen-18 in seawater is increased.
(C) Rain and snow contain relatively more oxygen-16 than they do in interglacial periods.
(D) During the ice age, more of the Earth's precipitation falls over land than falls over the ocean.
(E) The composition of seawater changes more slowly than it does in interglacial periods.

2. A medical journal used a questionnaire survey to determine whether a particular change in its format would increase its readership. Sixty-two percent of those who returned the questionnaire supported that change. On the basis of this outcome, the decision was made to introduce the new format.

Which one of the following, if it were determined to be true, would provide the best evidence that the journal's decision will have the desired effect?

(A) Of the readers who received questionnaires, 90 percent returned them.
(B) Other journals have based format changes on survey results.
(C) The percentage of surveyed readers who like the format change was almost the same as the percentage of the entire potential readership who would like format change.
(D) It was determined that the new format would be less costly than the old format.
(E) Ninety percent of the readers who were dissatisfied with the old format and only 50 percent of the readers who like the old format returned their questionnaires.

3. The advanced technology of ski boots and bindings has brought a dramatic drop in the incidence of injuries that occur on the slopes of ski resorts: from 9 injuries per 1,000 skiers in 1950 to 3 in 1980. As a result, the remainder of ski-related injuries, which includes all injuries occurring on the premises of a ski resort but not on the slopes, rose from 10 percent of all ski-related injuries in 1950 to 25 percent in 1980. The incidence of these injuries, including accidents such as falling down steps, increases with the amount of alcohol consumed per skier.

Which one of the following can be properly inferred from the passage?

(A) As the number of ski injuries that occur on the slopes decreases, the number of injuries that occur on the premises of ski resorts increases.
(B) The amount of alcohol consumed per skier increased between 1950 and 1980.
(C) The technology of ski boots and bindings affects the incidence of each type of ski-related injury.
(D) If the technology of ski boots and bindings continues to advance, the incidence of ski-related injuries will continue to decline.
(E) Injuries that occurred on the slopes of ski resorts made up a smaller percentage of ski-related injuries in 1980 than in 1950.

#%

4. The more television children watch, the less competent they are in mathematical knowledge. More than a third of children in the United States watch television for more than five hours a day; in South Korea the figure is only 7 percent. But whereas less than 15 percent of children in the United States understand advanced measurement and geometric concepts, 40 percent of South Korean children are competent in these areas. Therefore, if United States children are to do well in mathematics, they must watch less television.

   Which one of the following is an assumption upon which the argument depends?

   (A) Children in the United States are less interested in advanced measurement and geometric concepts than are South Korean children.
   (B) South Korean children are more disciplined about doing schoolwork than are children in the United States.
   (C) Children who want to do well in advanced measurement and geometry will watch less television.
   (D) A child's ability in advanced measurement and geometry increases if he or she watches less than one hour of television a day.
   (E) The instruction in advanced measurement and geometric concepts available to children in the United States is not substantially worse than that available to South Korean children.

5. Court records from medieval France show that in the years 1300 to 1400 the number of people arrested in the French realm for "violent interpersonal crimes" (not committed in wars) increased by 30 percent over the number of people arrested for such crimes in the years 1200 to 1300. If the increase was not the result of false arrests, therefore, medieval France had a higher level of documented interpersonal violence in the years 1300 to 1400 than in the years 1200 to 1300.

   Which one of the following statements, if true, most seriously weakens the argument?

   (A) In the years 1300 to 1400 the French government's category of violent crimes included an increasing variety of interpersonal crimes that are actually nonviolent.
   (B) Historical accounts by monastic chroniclers in the years 1300 to 1400 are filled with descriptions of violent attacks committed by people living in the French realm.
   (C) The number of individual agreements between two people in which they swore oaths not to attack each other increased substantially after 1300.
   (D) When English armies tried to conquer parts of France in the mid- to late 1300s, violence in the northern province of Normandy and the southwestern province of Gascony increased.
   (E) The population of medieval France increased substantially during the first five decades of the 1300s, until the deadly bubonic plague decimated the population of France after 1348.

6. When 100 people who have not used cocaine are tested for cocaine use, on average only 5 will test positive. By contrast, of every 100 people who have used cocaine 99 will test positive. Thus, when a randomly chosen group of people is tested for cocaine use, the vast majority of those who test positive will be people who have used cocaine.

   A reasoning error in the argument is that the argument

   (A) attempts to infer a value judgment from purely factual premises
   (B) attributes to every member of the population the properties of the average member of the population
   (C) fails to take into account what proportion of the population have used cocaine
   (D) ignores the fact that some cocaine users do not test positive
   (E) advocates testing people for cocaine use when there is no reason to suspect that they have used cocaine

#%

7. Lourdes: Dietary fiber is an important part of a healthful diet. Experts recommend that adults consume 20 to 35 grams of fiber a day.

Kyra: But a daily intake of fiber that is significantly above that recommended level interferes with mineral absorption, especially the absorption of calcium. The public should be told to cut back on fiber intake.

Which one of the following, if true, most undermines Kyra's recommendation?

(A) Among adults, the average consumption of dietary fiber is at present approximately 10 grams a day.
(B) The more a food is processed, the more the fiber is broken down and the lower the fiber content.
(C) Many foodstuffs that are excellent sources of fiber are economical and readily available.
(D) Adequate calcium intake helps prevent the decrease in bone mass known as osteoporosis.
(E) Many foodstuffs that are excellent sources of fiber are popular with consumers.

8. A survey of alumni of the class of 1960 at Aurora University yielded puzzling results. When asked to indicate their academic rank, half of the respondents reported that they were in the top quarter of the graduating class in 1960.

Which one of the following most helps account for the apparent contradiction above?

(A) A disproportionately large number of high-ranking alumni responded to the survey.
(B) Few, if any, respondents were mistaken about their class rank.
(C) Not all the alumni who were actually in the top quarter responded to the survey.
(D) Almost all of the alumni who graduated in 1960 responded to the survey.
(E) Academic rank at Aurora University was based on a number of considerations in addition to average grades.

9. The number of North American children who are obese—that is, who have more body fat than do 85 percent of North American children their age—is steadily increasing, according to four major studies conducted over the past 15 years.

If the finding reported above is correct, it can be properly concluded that

(A) when four major studies all produce similar results, those studies must be accurate
(B) North American children have been progressively less physically active over the past 15 years
(C) the number of North American children who are not obese increased over the past 15 years
(D) over the past 15 years, the number of North American children who are underweight has declined
(E) the incidence of obesity in North American children tends to increase as the children grow older

10. All students at Pitcombe College were asked to label themselves conservative, liberal, or middle-of-the-road politically. Of the students, 25 percent labeled themselves conservative, 24 percent labeled themselves liberal, and 51 percent labeled themselves middle-of-the-road. When asked about a particular set of issues, however, 77 percent of the students endorsed what is generally regarded as a liberal position.

If all of the statements above are true, which one of the following must also be true?

(A) All students who labeled themselves liberal endorsed what is generally regarded as a liberal position on that set of issues.
(B) More students who labeled themselves middle-of-the-road than students who labeled themselves liberal opposed what is generally regarded as a liberal position on that set of issues.
(C) The majority of students who labeled themselves middle-of-the-road opposed what is generally regarded as a liberal position on that set of issues.
(D) Some students who labeled themselves conservative endorsed what is generally regarded as a liberal position on that set of issues.
(E) Some students who labeled themselves liberal endorsed what is generally regarded as a conservative position on that set of issues.

11. The trustees of the Avonbridge summer drama workshop have decided to offer scholarships to the top 10 percent of local applicants and the top 10 percent of nonlocal applicants as judged on the basis of a qualifying audition. They are doing this to ensure that only the applicants with the most highly evaluated auditions are offered scholarships to the program.

Which one of the following points out why the trustees' plan might not be effective in achieving its goal?

(A) The best actors can also apply for admission to another program and then not enroll in the Avonbridge program.
(B) Audition materials that produce good results for one actor may disadvantage another, resulting in inaccurate assessment.
(C) The top 10 percent of local and nonlocal applicants might not need scholarships to the Avonbridge program.
(D) Some of the applicants who are offered scholarships could have less highly evaluated auditions than some of the applicants who are not offered scholarships.
(E) Dividing applicants into local and nonlocal groups is unfair because it favors nonlocal applicants.

12. Rumored declines in automobile-industry revenues are exaggerated. It is true that automobile manufacturers' share of the industry's revenues fell from 65 percent two years ago to 50 percent today, but over the same period suppliers of automobile parts had their share increase from 15 percent to 20 percent and service companies (for example, distributors, dealers, and repairers) had their share increase from 20 percent to 30 percent.

Which one of the following best indicates why the statistics given above provide by themselves no evidence for the conclusion they are intended to support?

(A) The possibility is left open that the statistics for manufacturers' share of revenues come from a different source than the other statistics.
(B) No matter what changes the automobile industry's overall revenues undergo, the total of all shares of these revenues must be 100 percent.
(C) No explanation is given for why the revenue shares of different sectors of the industry changed.
(D) Manufacturers and parts companies depend for their revenue on dealers' success in selling cars.
(E) Revenues are an important factor but are not the only factor in determining profits.

13. Nutritionists have recommended that people eat more fiber. Advertisements for a new fiber-supplement pill state only that it contains "44 percent fiber."

The advertising claim is misleading in its selection of information on which to focus if which one of the following is true?

(A) There are other products on the market that are advertised as providing fiber as a dietary supplement.
(B) Nutritionists base their recommendation on medical findings that dietary fiber protects against some kinds of cancer.
(C) It is possible to become addicted to some kinds of advertised pills, such as sleeping pills and painkillers.
(D) The label of the advertised product recommends taking 3 pills every day.
(E) The recommended daily intake of fiber is 20 to 30 grams, and the pill contains one-third gram.

14. In 1990 major engine repairs were performed on 10 percent of the cars that had been built by the National Motor Company in the 1970s and that were still registered. However, the corresponding figure for the cars that the National Motor Company had manufactured in the 1960s was only five percent.

Which one of the following, if true, most helps to explain the discrepancy?

(A) Government motor vehicle regulations generally require all cars, whether old or new, to be inspected for emission levels prior to registration.
(B) Owners of new cars tend to drive their cars more carefully than do owners of old cars.
(C) The older a car is, the more likely it is to be discarded for scrap rather than repaired when major engine work is needed to keep the car in operation.
(D) The cars that the National Motor Company built in the 1970s incorporated simplified engine designs that made the engines less complicated than those of earlier models.
(E) Many of the repairs that were performed on the cars that the National Motor Company built in the 1960s could have been avoided if periodic routine maintenance had been performed.

15. Comets do not give off their own light but reflect light from other sources, such as the Sun. Scientists estimate the mass of comets by their brightness: the greater a comet's mass, the more light that comet will reflect. A satellite probe, however, has revealed that the material of which Halley's comet is composed reflects 60 times less light per unit of mass than had been previously thought.

The statements above, if true, give the most support to which one of the following?

(A) Some comets are composed of material that reflects 60 times more light per unit of mass than the material of which Halley's comet is composed.
(B) Previous estimates of the mass of Halley's comet which were based on its brightness were too low.
(C) The total amount of light reflected from Halley's comet is less than scientists had previously thought.
(D) The reflective properties of the material of which comets are composed vary considerably from comet to comet.
(E) Scientists need more information before they can make a good estimate of the mass of Halley's comet.

16. The National Association of Fire Fighters says that 45 percent of homes now have smoke detectors, whereas only 30 percent of homes had them 10 years ago. This makes early detection of house fires no more likely, however, because over half of the domestic smoke detectors are either without batteries or else inoperative for some other reason.

In order for the conclusion above to be properly drawn, which one of the following assumptions would have to be made?

(A) Fifteen percent of domestic smoke detectors were installed less than 10 years ago.
(B) The number of fires per year in homes with smoke detectors has increased.
(C) Not all of the smoke detectors in homes are battery operated.
(D) The proportion of domestic smoke detectors that are inoperative has increased in the past ten years.
(E) Unlike automatic water sprinklers, a properly functioning smoke detector cannot by itself increase fire safety in a home.

17. Five years ago, during the first North American outbreak of the cattle disease CXC, the death rate from the disease was 5 percent of all reported cases, whereas today the corresponding figure is over 18 percent. It is clear, therefore, that during these past 5 years, CXC has increased in virulence.

Which one of the following, if true, most substantially weakens the argument?

(A) Many recent cattle deaths that have actually been caused by CXC have been mistakenly attributed to another disease that mimics the symptoms of CXC.
(B) During the first North American outbreak of the disease, many of the deaths reported to have been caused by CXC were actually due to other causes.
(C) An inoculation program against CXC was recently begun after controlled studies showed inoculation to be 70 percent effective in preventing serious cases of the illness.
(D) Since the first outbreak, farmers have learned to treat mild cases of CXC and no longer report them to veterinarians or authorities.
(E) Cattle that have contracted and survived CXC rarely contract the disease a second time.

18. Waste management companies, which collect waste for disposal in landfills and incineration plants, report that disposable plastics make up an ever-increasing percentage of the waste they handle. It is clear that attempts to decrease the amount of plastic that people throw away in the garbage are failing.

Which one of the following, if true, most seriously weakens the argument?

(A) Because plastics create harmful pollutants when burned, an increasing percentage of the plastics handled by waste management companies are being disposed of in landfills.
(B) Although many plastics are recyclable, most of the plastics disposed of by waste management companies are not.
(C) People are more likely to save and reuse plastic containers than containers made of heavier materials like glass or metal.
(D) An increasing proportion of the paper, glass, and metal cans that waste management companies used to handle is now being recycled.
(E) While the percentage of products using plastic packaging is increasing, the total amount of plastic being manufactured has remained unchanged.

19. Politician: From the time our party took office almost four years ago the number of people unemployed city-wide increased by less than 20 percent. The opposition party controlled city government during the four preceding years, and the number of unemployed city residents rose by over 20 percent. Thus, due to our leadership, fewer people now find themselves among the ranks of the unemployed, whatever the opposition may claim.

The reasoning in the politician's argument is most vulnerable to the criticism that

(A) the claims made by the opposition are simply dismissed without being specified
(B) no evidence has been offered to show that any decline in unemployment over the past four years was uniform throughout all areas of the city
(C) the issue of how much unemployment in the city is affected by seasonal fluctuations is ignored
(D) the evidence cited in support of the conclusion actually provides more support for the denial of the conclusion
(E) the possibility has not been addressed that any increase in the number of people employed is due to programs supported by the opposition party

20. At Happywell, Inc., last year the average annual salary for dieticians was $50,000, while the average annual salary for physical therapists was $42,000. The average annual salary for all Happywell employees last year was $40,000.

If the information above is correct, which one of the following conclusions can properly be drawn on the basis of it?

(A) There were more physical therapists than dieticians at Happywell last year.
(B) There was no dietician at Happy well last year who earned less than the average for a physical therapist.
(C) At least one Happywell employee earned less than the average for a physical therapist last year.
(D) At least one physical therapist earned less than the lowest-paid Happywell dietician last year.
(E) At least one dietician earned more than the highest-paid Happywell physical therapist last year.

21. At the end of the year, Wilson's Department Store awards free merchandise to its top salespeople. When presented with the fact that the number of salespeople receiving these awards has declined markedly over the past fifteen years, the newly appointed president of the company responded, "In that case, since our award criterion at present is membership in the top third of our sales force, we can also say that the number of salespeople passed over for these awards has similarly declined."

Which one of the following is an assumption that would allow the company president's conclusion to be properly drawn?

(A) Policies at Wilson's with regard to hiring salespeople have not become more lax over the past fifteen years.
(B) The number of salespeople at Wilson's has increased over the past fifteen years.
(C) The criterion used by Wilson's for selecting its award recipients has remained the same for the past fifteen years.
(D) The average total sales figures for Wilson's salespeople have been declining for fifteen years.
(E) Wilson's calculates its salespeople's sales figures in the same way as it did fifteen years ago.

22. The average literate person today spends significantly less time reading than the average literate person did 50 years ago, yet many more books are sold per year now than were sold 50 years ago.

Each of the following, if true, helps resolve the apparent discrepancy above EXCEPT:

(A) The population of literate people is significantly larger today than it was 50 years ago.
(B) People who read books 50 years ago were more likely to read books borrowed from libraries than are people who read books today.
(C) The average scholar or other person who uses books professionally today owns and consults many more different books than did the average scholar or similar professional 50 years ago.
(D) People of 50 years ago were more likely than people are today to display large collections of books as a sign of education and good taste.
(E) Books sold now tend to be shorter and easier to read than were books sold 50 years ago.

23. A letter submitted to the editor of a national newsmagazine was written and signed by a Dr. Shirley Martin who, in the text of the letter, mentions being a professor at a major North American medical school. Knowing that fewer than 5 percent of the professors at such schools are women, the editor reasons that the chances are better than 19 to 1 that the letter was written by a man.

Which one of the following involves flawed reasoning most like that used by the editor?

(A) Since 19 out of 20 home computers are purchased primarily for use with computer games, and the first computer sold today was purchased solely for word processing, the next 19 computers sold will almost certainly be used primarily for computer games.
(B) Fewer than 1 in 20 of the manuscripts submitted to Argon Publishing Co. are accepted for publication. Since only 15 manuscripts were submitted last week, there is almost no chance that any of them will be accepted for publication.
(C) Fewer than 5 percent of last year's graduating class took Latin in secondary school. Howard took Latin in secondary school, so if he had graduated last year, it is likely that one of the other Latin scholars would not have graduated.
(D) More than 95 percent of the planes built by UBC last year met government standards for large airliners. Since small planes account for just under 5 percent of UBC's output last year, it is almost certain that all their large planes met government standards.
(E) Since more than 19 out of every 20 animals in the wildlife preserve are mammals and fewer than 1 out of 20 are birds, there is a greater than 95 percent chance that the animal Emily saw flying between two trees in the wildlife refuge yesterday morning was a mammal.

24. The city's center for disease control reports that the rabies epidemic is more serious now than it was two years ago: two years ago less than 25 percent of the local raccoon population was infected, whereas today the infection has spread to more than 50 percent of the raccoon population. However, the newspaper reports that whereas two years ago 32 cases of rabid raccoons were confirmed during a 12-month period, in the past 12 months only 18 cases of rabid raccoons were confirmed.

Which one of the following, if true, most helps to resolve the apparent discrepancy between the two reports?

(A) The number of cases of rabies in wild animals other than raccoons has increased in the past 12 months.
(B) A significant proportion of the raccoon population succumbed to rabies in the year before last.
(C) The symptoms of distemper, another disease to which raccoons are susceptible, are virtually identical to those of rabies.
(D) Since the outbreak of the epidemic, raccoons, which are normally nocturnal, have increasingly been seen during daylight hours.
(E) The number of confirmed cases of rabid raccoons in neighboring cities has also decreased over the past year.

25. From 1973 to 1989 total energy use in this country increased less than 10 percent. However, the use of electrical energy in this country during this same period grew by more than 50 percent, as did the gross national product—the total value of all goods and services produced in the nation.

If the statements above are true, then which one of the following must also be true?

(A) Most of the energy used in this country in 1989 was electrical energy.
(B) From 1973 to 1989 there was a decline in the use of energy other than electrical energy in this country.
(C) From 1973 to 1989 there was an increase in the proportion of energy use in this country that consisted of electrical energy use.
(D) In 1989 electrical energy constituted a larger proportion of the energy used to produce the gross national product than did any other form of energy.
(E) In 1973 the electrical energy that was produced constituted a smaller proportion of the gross national product than did all other forms of energy combined.

26. In 1980, Country A had a per capita gross domestic product (GDP) that was $5,000 higher than that of the European Economic Community. By 1990, the difference, when adjusted for inflation, had increased to $6,000. Since a rising per capita GDP indicates a rising average standard of living, the average standard of living in Country A must have risen between 1980 and 1990.

Which one of the following is an assumption on which the argument depends?

(A) Between 1980 and 1990, Country A and the European Economic Community experienced the same percentage increase in population.
(B) Between 1980 and 1990, the average standard of living in the European Economic Community fell.
(C) Some member countries of the European Economic Community had, during the 1980s, a higher average standard of living than Country A.
(D) The per capita GDP of the European Economic Community was not lower by more than $1,000 in 1990 than it had been in 1980.
(E) In 1990, no member country of the European Economic Community had a per capita GDP higher than that of Country A.

27. Researchers in South Australia estimate changes in shark populations inhabiting local waters by monitoring what is termed the "catch per unit effort" (CPUE). The CPUE for any species of shark is the number of those sharks that commercial shark-fishing boats catch per hour for each kilometer of gill net set out in the water. Since 1973 the CPUE for a particular species of shark has remained fairly constant. Therefore, the population of that species in the waters around South Australia must be at approximately its 1973 level.

Which one of the following, if true, most seriously weakens the argument?

(A) The waters around South Australia are the only area in the world where that particular species of shark is found.
(B) The sharks that are the most profitable to catch are those that tend to remain in the same area of ocean year after year and not migrate far from where they were born.
(C) A significant threat to shark populations, in addition to commercial shark fishing, is "incidental mortality" that results from catching sharks in nets intended for other fish.
(D) Most of the quotas designed to protect shark populations limit the tonnage of sharks that can be taken and not the number of individual sharks.
(E) Since 1980 commercial shark-fishing boats have used sophisticated electronic equipment that enables them to locate sharks with greater accuracy.

28. Students from outside the province of Markland, who in any given academic year pay twice as much tuition each as do students from Markland, had traditionally accounted for at least two-thirds of the enrollment at Central Markland College. Over the past 10 years academic standards at the college have risen, and the proportion of students who are not Marklanders has dropped to around 40 percent.

Which one of the following can be properly inferred from the statements above?

(A) If it had not been for the high tuition paid by students from outside Markland, the college could not have improved its academic standards over the past 10 years.
(B) If academic standards had not risen over the past 10 years, students who are not Marklanders would still account for at least two-thirds of the college's enrollment.
(C) Over the past 10 years, the number of students from Markland increased and the number of students from outside Markland decreased.
(D) Over the past 10 years, academic standards at Central Markland College have risen by more than academic standards at any other college in Markland.
(E) If the college's per capita revenue from tuition has remained the same, tuition fees have increased over the past 10 years.

29. John: In 80 percent of car accidents, the driver at fault was within five miles of home, so people evidently drive less safely near home than they do on long trips.

Judy: But people do 80 percent of their driving within five miles of home.

How is Judy's response related to John's argument?

(A) It shows that the evidence that John presents, by itself, is not enough to prove his claim.
(B) It restates the evidence that John presents in different terms.
(C) It gives additional evidence that is needed by John to support his conclusion.
(D) It calls into question John's assumption that whenever people drive more than five miles from home they are going on a long trip.
(E) It suggests that John's conclusion is merely a restatement of his argument's premise.

30. Between 1977 and 1987, the country of Ravonia lost about 12,000 jobs in logging and wood processing, representing a 15 percent decrease in employment in the country's timber industry. Paradoxically, this loss of jobs occurred even as the amount of wood taken from the forests of Ravonia increased by 10 percent.

Which one of the following, if true, most helps to resolve the apparent paradox?

(A) Not since the 1950s has the timber industry been Ravonia's most important industry economically.
(B) Between 1977 and 1987, the total number of acres of timberland in Ravonia fell, while the demand for wood products increased.
(C) Since 1977, a growing proportion of the timber that has been cut in Ravonia has been exported as raw, unprocessed wood.
(D) Since 1977, domestic sales of wood and wood products have increased by more than export sales have increased.
(E) In 1977, overall unemployment in Ravonia was approximately 10 percent; in 1987, Ravonia's unemployment rate was 15 percent.

31. Ditrama is a federation made up of three autonomous regions: Korva, Mitro, and Guadar. Under the federal revenue-sharing plan, each region receives a share of federal revenues equal to the share of the total population of Ditrama residing in that region, as shown by a yearly population survey. Last year, the percentage of federal revenues Korva received for its share decreased somewhat even though the population survey on which the revenue-sharing was based showed that Korva's population had increased.

If the statements above are true, which one of the following must also have been shown by the population survey on which last year's revenue-sharing in Ditrama was based?

(A) Of the three regions, Korva had the smallest number of residents.
(B) The population of Korva grew by a smaller percentage than it did in previous years.
(C) The populations of Mitro and Guadar each increased by a percentage that exceeded the percentage by which the population of Korva increased.
(D) Of the three regions, Korva's numerical increase in population was the smallest.
(E) Korva's population grew by a smaller percentage than did the population of at least one of the other two autonomous regions.

32. In 1980 there was growing concern that the protective ozone layer over the Antarctic might be decreasing and thereby allowing so much harmful ultraviolet radiation to reach the Earth that polar marine life would be damaged. Some government officials dismissed these concerns, since statistics indicated that global atmospheric ozone levels remained constant.

The relevance of the evidence cited by the government officials in support of their position would be most seriously undermined if it were true that

(A) most species of plant and animal life flourish in warm climates rather than in the polar regions
(B) decreases in the amount of atmospheric ozone over the Antarctic ice cap tend to be seasonal rather than constant
(C) decreases in the amount of atmospheric ozone were of little concern before 1980
(D) quantities of atmospheric ozone shifted away from the polar caps, correspondingly increasing ozone levels in other regions
(E) even where the amount of atmospheric ozone is normal, some ultraviolet light reaches the Earth's surface

33. A commonly accepted myth is that left-handed people are more prone to cause accidents than are right-handed people. But this is, in fact, just a myth, as is indicated by the fact that more household accidents are caused by right-handed people than are caused by left-handed people.

The reasoning is flawed because the argument

(A) makes a distinction where there is no real difference between the things distinguished
(B) takes no account of the relative frequency of left-handed people in the population as a whole
(C) uses the word "accidents" in two different senses
(D) ignores the possibility that some household accidents are caused by more than one person
(E) gives wholly irrelevant evidence and simply disparages an opposing position by calling it a "myth"

34. Five thousand of the 50,000 books published in country Z in 1991 were novels. Exactly 25 of the films released in country Z in 1992 were based on those novels. Since 100 films were released in country Z in 1992, no more than one-quarter of them were based on books published in country Z in 1991.

Which one of the following, if assumed, allows the conclusion above to be properly drawn?

(A) None of the scripts used in films released in 1992 were written by professional novelists.
(B) None of the films released in country Z in 1992 were based on books other than novels.
(C) None of the books that were published in country Z in 1992 were based on plots of films released in 1991.
(D) Some of the films released in country Z in 1992 were based on older films that had been released for the first time many years earlier.
(E) Some of the films released in 1991 in country Z were based on novels that were published in 1991.

35. Each December 31 in Country Q, a tally is made of the country's total available coal supplies—that is, the total amount of coal that has been mined throughout the country but not consumed. In 1991 that amount was considerably lower than it had been in 1990. Furthermore, Country Q has not imported or exported coal since 1970.

If the statements above are true, which one of the following must also be true on the basis of them?

(A) In Country Q, more coal was mined in 1990 than was mined in 1991.
(B) In Country Q, the amount of coal consumed in 1991 was greater than the amount of coal mined in 1991.
(C) In Country Q, the amount of coal consumed in 1990 was greater than the amount of coal consumed in 1991.
(D) In Country Q, the amount of coal consumed in 1991 was greater than the amount of coal consumed in 1990.
(E) Country Q, more coal was consumed during the first half of 1991 than was consumed during the first half of 1990.

Chapter Nineteen: Formal Logic Questions

1. Some people are Montagues and some people are Capulets.
No Montague can be crossed in love.
All Capulets can be crossed in love.
Therefore, Capulets are not Montagues.
Anyone who is not a Montague is intemperate.

Assume that all of the statements in the passage are true. If it is also true that no Montague is intemperate, then which one of the following must be true?

(A) The only people who can be crossed in love are intemperate Capulets.
(B) Anyone who is not a Capulet is a Montague.
(C) All intemperate people can be crossed in love.
(D) All intemperate people are Capulets.
(E) All Capulets are intemperate.

2. Although all contemporary advertising tries to persuade, only a small portion of contemporary advertising can be considered morally reprehensible. It nevertheless follows that some attempts at persuasion can be regarded as morally reprehensible.

Which one of the following, in its logical features, most closely parallels the reasoning used in the passage?

(A) None of the chemicals used for cleaning the Sistine Chapel will affect the original dyes. Hence, the colors used by Michelangelo will be fully restored.
(B) Not all operational tracking studies are conducted to illustrate exact corporate returns on investment. Hence, some of these studies are not reliable.
(C) A good manager always makes important decisions on the basis of adequate data, although of course some managers fail to do this. It follows that some managers are not good managers.
(D) There is a direct correlation between the number of times you repeat something and the degree to which you retain it. Therefore, repetition is always a critical factor in remembering.
(E) Some short poems are thematically pluralistic, since some sonnets are characterized by such pluralism, and all sonnets are short poems.

3. All savings accounts are interest bearing accounts. The interest from some interest bearing accounts is tax free, so there must be some savings accounts that have tax free interest.

Which one of the following arguments is flawed in a way most similar to the way in which the passage is flawed?

(A) All artists are intellectuals. Some great photographers are artists. Therefore, some great photographers must be intellectuals.
(B) All great photographers are artists. All artists are intellectuals. Therefore, some great photographers must be intellectuals.
(C) All great photographers are artists. Some artists are intellectuals. Therefore, some great photographers are intellectuals.
(D) All great photographers are artists. Some great photographers are intellectuals. Therefore, some artists must be intellectuals.
(E) All great photographers are artists. No artists are intellectuals. Therefore, some great photographers must not be intellectuals.

4. There is little point in looking to artists for insights into political issues. Most of them hold political views that are less insightful than those of any reasonably well-educated person who is not an artist. Indeed, when taken as a whole, the statements made by artists, including those considered to be great, indicate that artistic talent and political insight are rarely found together.

Which one of the following can be inferred from the passage?

(A) There are no artists who have insights into political issues.
(B) A thorough education in art makes a person reasonably well-educated.
(C) Every reasonably well-educated person who is not an artist has more insight into political issues than any artist.
(D) Politicians rarely have any artistic talent.
(E) Some artists are no less politically insightful than some reasonably well-educated persons who are not artists.

5. Those who participate in local politics include people who are genuinely interested in public service and people who are selfish opportunists. Everyone who participates in local politics has an influence on the community's values.

If the statements above are true, which one of the following must also be true?

(A) Some selfish opportunists have an influence on the community's values.
(B) Some persons who are interested in public service do not have an influence on the community's values.
(C) All those who have an influence on the community's values participate in local politics.
(D) Some of those who influence the community's values neither are interested in public service nor are selfish opportunists.
(E) All those who have an influence on the community's values are either interested in public service or are selfish opportunists.

6. Most parents who are generous are good parents, but some self-centered parents are also good parents. Yet all good parents share one characteristic: they are good listeners.

If all of the statements in the passage are true, which one of the following must also be true?

(A) All parents who are good listeners are good parents.
(B) Some parents who are good listeners are not good parents.
(C) Most parents who are good listeners are generous.
(D) Some parents who are good listeners are self centered.
(E) Fewer self centered parents than generous parents are good listeners.

7. Roses always provide a stunning display of color, but only those flowers that smell sweet are worth growing in a garden. Some roses have no scent.

Which one of the following conclusions can be properly drawn from the passage?

(A) Some flowers which provide a stunning display of color are not worth growing in a garden.
(B) All flowers with no scent provide a stunning display of color.
(C) Some flowers which are worth growing in a garden have no scent.
(D) Some roses which smell sweet are not worth growing in a garden.
(E) No sweet smelling flower is worth growing in a garden unless it provides a stunning display of color.

8. No mathematician today would flatly refuse to accept the results of an enormous computation as an adequate demonstration of the truth of a theorem. In 1976, however, this was not the case. Some mathematicians at that time refused to accept the results of a complex computer demonstration of a very simple mapping theorem. Although some mathematicians still hold a strong belief that a simple theorem ought to have a short, simple proof, in fact, some simple theorems have required enormous proofs.

If all of the statements in the passage are true, which one of the following must also be true?

(A) Today, some mathematicians who believe that a simple theorem ought to have a simple proof would consider accepting the results of an enormous computation as a demonstration of the truth of a theorem.
(B) Some individuals who believe that a simple theorem ought to have a simple proof are not mathematicians.
(C) Today, some individuals who refuse to accept the results of an enormous computation as a demonstration of the truth of a theorem believe that a simple theorem ought to have a simple proof.
(D) Some individuals who do not believe that a simple theorem ought to have a simple proof would not be willing to accept the results of an enormous computation as proof of a complex theorem.
(E) Some nonmathematicians do not believe that a simple theorem ought to have a simple proof.

9. Although all birds have feathers and all birds have wings, some birds do not fly. For example, penguins and ostriches use their wings to move in a different way from other birds. Penguins use their wings only to swim under water at high speeds. Ostriches use their wings only to run with the wind by lifting them as if they were sails.

Which one of the following is most parallel in its reasoning to the argument above?

(A) Ancient philosophers tried to explain not how the world functions but why it functions. In contrast, most contemporary biologists seek comprehensive theories of how organisms function, but many refuse to speculate about purpose.

(B) Some chairs are used only as decorations, and other chairs are used only to tame lions. Therefore, not all chairs are used for sitting in despite the fact that all chairs have a seat and some support such as legs.

(C) Some musicians in a symphony orchestra play the violin, and others play the viola, but these are both in the same category of musical instruments, namely string instruments.

(D) All cars have similar drive mechanisms, but some cars derive their power from solar energy, whereas others burn gasoline. Thus, solar-powered cars are less efficient than gasoline-powered ones.

(E) Sailing ships move in a different way from steamships. Both sailing ships and steamships navigate over water, but only sailing ships use sails to move over the surface.

10. It is clear that none of the volleyball players at yesterday's office beach party came to work today since everyone who played volleyball at that party got badly sunburned and no one at work today is even slightly sunburned.

Which one of the following exhibits a pattern of reasoning that most closely parallels that in the argument above?

(A) Since everyone employed by TRF who was given the opportunity to purchase dental insurance did so and everyone who purchased dental insurance saw a dentist, it is clear that no one who failed to see a dentist is employed by TRF.

(B) Since no one who was promoted during the past year failed to attend the awards banquet, evidently none of the office managers attended the banquet this year since they were all denied promotion.

(C) Since the Donnely report was not finished on time, no one in John's group could have been assigned to contribute to that report since everyone in John's group has a reputation for getting assignments in on time.

(D) Everyone with an office on the second floor works directly for the president and, as a result, no one with a second floor office will take a July vacation because no one who works for the president will be able to take time off during July.

(E) Since all of the people who are now on the MXM Corporation payroll have been employed in the same job for the past five years, it is clear that no one who frequently changes jobs is likely to be hired by MXM.

11. The dean of computing must be respected by the academic staff and be competent to oversee the use of computers on campus. The only deans whom academics respect are those who hold doctoral degrees, and only someone who really knows about computers can competently oversee the use of computers on campus. Furthermore, the board of trustees has decided that the dean of computing must be selected from among this university's staff. Therefore, the dean of computing must be a professor from this university's computer science department.

Which one of the following statements, if true, would weaken the argument?

(A) There are members of this university's staff who hold doctoral degrees and who are not professors but who really know about computers.
(B) There are members of this university's philosophy department who do not hold doctoral degrees but who really know about computers.
(C) Computer science professors who hold doctoral degrees but who are not members of this university's staff have applied for the position of dean of computing.
(D) Several members of the board of trustees of this university do not hold doctoral degrees.
(E) Some members of the computer science department at this university are not respected by academics in other departments.

12. In the Centerville Botanical Gardens, all tulip trees are older than any maples. A majority, but not all, of the garden's sycamores are older than any of its maples. All the garden's maples are older than any of its dogwoods.

If the statements above are true, which one of the following must also be true of trees in the Centerville Botanical Gardens?

(A) Some dogwoods are as old as the youngest tulip trees.
(B) Some dogwoods are as old as the youngest sycamores.
(C) Some sycamores are not as old as the oldest dogwoods.
(D) Some tulip trees are not as old as the oldest sycamores.
(E) Some sycamores are not as old as the youngest tulip trees.

13. Paulsville and Longtown cannot both be included in the candidate's itinerary of campaign stops. The candidate will make a stop in Paulsville unless Salisbury is made part of the itinerary. Unfortunately, a stop in Salisbury is out of the question. Clearly, then, a stop in Longtown can be ruled out.

The reasoning in the argument above most closely parallels that in which one of the following arguments?

(A) The chef never has both fresh radishes and fresh green peppers available for the chef's salad at the same time. If she uses fresh radishes, she also uses spinach. But currently there is no spinach to be had. It can be inferred, then, that she will not be using fresh green peppers.
(B) Tom will definitely support Parker if Mendoza does not apply; and Tom will not support both Parker and Chung. Since, as it turns out, Mendoza will not apply, it follows that Chung will not get Tom's support.
(C) The program committee never selects two plays by Shaw for a single season. But when they select a play by Coward, they do not select any play by Shaw at all. For this season, the committee has just selected a play by Shaw, so they will not select any play by Coward.
(D) In agricultural pest control, either pesticides or the introduction of natural enemies of the pest, but not both, will work. Of course, neither will be needed if pest-resistant crops are planted. So if pesticides are in fact needed, it must be that there are no natural enemies of the pest.
(E) The city cannot afford to build both a new stadium and the new road that would be needed to get there. But neither of the two projects is worth doing without the other. Since the city will not undertake any but worthwhile projects, the new stadium will not be constructed at this time.

14. All actors are exuberant people and all exuberant people are extroverts, but nevertheless it is true that some shy people are actors.

If the statements above are true, each of the following must also be true EXCEPT:

(A) Some shy people are extroverts.
(B) Some shy extroverts are not actors.
(C) Some exuberant people who are actors are shy.
(D) All people who are not extroverts are not actors.
(E) Some extroverts are shy.

15. Planetary bodies differ from one another in their composition, but most of those in the Solar System have solid surfaces. Unless the core of such a planetary body generates enough heat to cause volcanic action, the surface of the body will not be renewed for millions of years. Any planetary body with a solid surface whose surface is not renewed for millions of years becomes heavily pockmarked by meteorite craters, just like the Earth's moon. Some old planetary bodies in the Solar System, such as Europa, a very cold moon belonging to Jupiter, have solid icy surfaces with very few meteorite craters.

If the claims above are true, which one of the following must, on the basis of them, be true?

(A) The Earth's moon does not have an icy surface.
(B) If a planetary body does not have a heavily pockmarked surface, its core does not generate enough heat to cause volcanic action.
(C) Some planetary bodies whose cores generate enough heat to cause volcanic action do not have solid icy surfaces.
(D) Some of Jupiter's moons are heavily pockmarked by meteorite craters.
(E) Some very cold planetary bodies have cores that generate enough heat to cause volcanic action.

16. Some of the world's most beautiful cats are Persian cats. However, it must be acknowledged that all Persian cats are pompous, and pompous cats are invariably irritating.

If the statements above are true, each of the following must also be true on the basis of them EXCEPT:

(A) Some of the world's most beautiful cats are irritating.
(B) Some irritating cats are among the world's most beautiful cats.
(C) Any cat that is not irritating is not a Persian cat.
(D) Some pompous cats are among the world's most beautiful cats.
(E) Some irritating and beautiful cats are not Persian cats.

17. In yesterday's council election a majority of voters supported conservative candidates, and a majority of voters supported candidates who voted in favor of the antipollution act. Therefore, it must be that a majority of voters in yesterday's council election supported conservative candidates who voted in favor of the antipollution act.

Which one of the following is an argument that contains flawed reasoning most similar to the flawed reasoning in the argument above?

(A) Bill claims that soil can be damaged if it is tilled when it is too wet, and Sue claims that seeds planted in wet soil can rot. Therefore, if both claims are true, gardeners who till and plant their gardens when the soil is wet damage both their soil and their seeds.
(B) According to Sara, most children like pies. According to Robert, most children like blueberries. So if Sara and Robert are both right, it must be that most children like pies that contain blueberries.
(C) Mark will go on a picnic today only if it does not rain. Susan will go on a picnic today only if Mark goes too. Since it is not going to rain today, both Mark and Susan will go on a picnic.
(D) The majority of customers who regularly eat at this restaurant always order both fish and stuffed mushrooms. Thus, fish and stuffed mushrooms must be the restaurant's most frequently ordered dishes.
(E) Most people living at Gina's house cook well. Since most people at Gina's house enjoy eating well-cooked meals, most meals served at Gina's house are cooked well.

18. No projects that involve historical restorations were granted building permits this month. Since some of the current projects of the firm of Stein and Sapin are historical restorations, at least some of Stein and Sapin's projects were not granted building permits this month.

The pattern of reasoning in the argument above is most similar to that in which one of the following?

(A) None of the doctors working at City Hospital were trained abroad. So, although some hospitals require doctors trained abroad to pass an extra qualifying exam, until now, at least, this has not been an issue for City Hospital.
(B) None of the news reports from the economic summit meeting have been encouraging. Since some other recent economic reports have showed positive trends, however, at least some of the economic news is encouraging at this time.
(C) None of the new members of the orchestra have completed their paperwork. Since only those people who have completed their paperwork can be paid this week, at least some of the new members of the orchestra are likely to be paid late.
(D) Several films directed by Hannah Barker were released this season, but none of the films released this season were enthusiastically reviewed. Therefore, at least some of Hannah Barker's films have not received enthusiastic reviews.
(E) Some of the city's most beautiful parks are not larger than a few acres, and some of the parks only a few acres in size are among the city's oldest. Therefore, some of the city's most beautiful parks are also its oldest parks.

19. Many artists claim that art critics find it is easier to write about art that they dislike than to write about art that they like. Whether or not this hypothesis is correct, most art criticism is devoted to art works that fail to satisfy the critic. Hence it follows that most art criticism is devoted to works other than the greatest works of art.

The conclusion above is properly drawn if which one of the following is assumed?

(A) No art critic enjoys writing about art works that he or she dislikes intensely.
(B) All art critics find it difficult to discover art works that truly satisfy them.
(C) A work of art that receives extensive critical attention can thereby become more widely known than it otherwise would have been.
(D) The greatest works of art are never recognized as such until long after the time of their creation.
(E) The greatest works of art are works that inevitably satisfy all critics.

20. All cattle ranchers dislike long winters.
All ski resort owners like long winters because long winters mean increased profits.
Some lawyers are cattle ranchers.

Which one of the following statements, if true and added to those above, most supports the conclusion that no ski resort owners are lawyers?

(A) Some cattle ranchers are lawyers.
(B) Some people who dislike long winters are not cattle ranchers.
(C) All lawyers are cattle ranchers.
(D) All people who dislike long winters are cattle ranchers.
(E) All people with increasing profits own ski resorts.

21. Not all tenured faculty are full professors. Therefore, although every faculty member in the linguistics department has tenure, it must be the case that not all of the faculty members in the linguistics department are full professors.

The flawed pattern of reasoning exhibited by the argument above is most similar to that exhibited by which one of the following?

(A) Although all modern office towers are climate-controlled buildings, not all office buildings are climate-controlled. Therefore, it must be the case that not all office buildings are modern office towers.
(B) All municipal hospital buildings are massive, but not all municipal hospital buildings are forbidding in appearance. Therefore, massive buildings need not present a forbidding appearance.
(C) Although some buildings designed by famous architects are not well proportioned, all government buildings are designed by famous architects. Therefore, some government buildings are not well proportioned.
(D) Not all public buildings are well designed, but some poorly designed public buildings were originally intended for private use. Therefore, the poorly designed public buildings were all originally designed for private use.
(E) Although some cathedrals are not built of stone, every cathedral is impressive. Therefore, buildings can be impressive even though they are not built of stone.

22. Nearly all mail that is correctly addressed arrives at its destination within two business days of being sent. In fact, correctly addressed mail takes longer than this only when it is damaged in transit. Overall, however, most mail arrives three business days or more after being sent.

If the statements above are true, which one of the following must be true?

(A) A large proportion of the mail that is correctly addressed is damaged in transit.
(B) No incorrectly addressed mail arrives within two business days of being sent.
(C) Most mail that arrives within two business days of being sent is correctly addressed.
(D) A large proportion of mail is incorrectly addressed.
(E) More mail arrives within two business days of being sent than arrives between two and three business days after being sent.

For a detailed answer key which includes the source of each question, by test date and section, as well as a convenient reverse look-up feature, please visit www.powerscore.com/lsatbibles.

ANSWER KEY

Chapter 2: Must Be True Questions

1. E	11. E	21. E	31. B	41. D	51. E	61. D	71. A	81. B	91. B	101. C
2. D	12. D	22. A	32. E	42. E	52. C	62. A	72. B	82. B	92. B	102. B
3. A	13. C	23. D	33. B	43. B	53. E	63. A	73. D	83. D	93. D	103. D
4. C	14. C	24. D	34. E	44. D	54. C	64. C	74. D	84. E	94. A	104. E
5. E	15. D	25. B	35. D	45. B	55. A	65. D	75. D	85. D	95. D	105. E
6. A	16. C	26. B	36. E	46. D	56. D	66. E	76. B	86. D	96. A	106. C
7. D	17. E	27. E	37. A	47. D	57. E	67. E	77. E	87. D	97. D	107. C
8. C	18. D	28. A	38. D	48. A	58. C	68. A	78. E	88. D	98. D	108. A
9. B	19. D	29. D	39. B	49. E	59. C	69. E	79. C	89. B	99. A	
10. E	20. A	30. E	40. A	50. E	60. A	70. A	80. C	90. B	100. C	

Chapter 3: Main Point Questions

1. C	11. E	21. E	31. A
2. A	12. B	22. A	32. B
3. B	13. C	23. E	33. C
4. D	14. C	24. B	34. E
5. C	15. C	25. A	
6. A	16. D	26. A	
7. E	17. E	27. D	
8. C	18. A	28. A	
9. E	19. D	29. E	
10. C	20. C	30. E	

Chapter 4: Weaken Questions

1. C	11. C	21. B	31. A	41. D	51. B	61. A	71. D	81. A
2. A	12. C	22. B	32. C	42. A	52. B	62. A	72. B	82. D
3. C	13. C	23. B	33. E	43. B	53. A	63. C	73. A	83. A
4. A	14. E	24. C	34. C	44. A	54. D	64. A	74. B	84. B
5. C	15. E	25. C	35. B	45. B	55. D	65. A	75. E	85. E
6. B	16. E	26. B	36. C	46. E	56. A	66. B	76. A	86. D
7. C	17. D	27. E	37. A	47. C	57. C	67. D	77. A	
8. E	18. D	28. B	38. E	48. B	58. B	68. A	78. C	
9. B	19. B	29. B	39. E	49. E	59. D	69. D	79. D	
10. C	20. A	30. E	40. E	50. D	60. D	70. C	80. D	

For a detailed answer key which includes the source of each question, by test date and section, as well as a convenient reverse look-up feature, please visit www.powerscore.com/lsatbibles.

Chapter 5: Strengthen Questions

1. B	11. A	21. A	31. E
2. C	12. D	22. D	32. A
3. C	13. B	23. B	33. C
4. C	14. A	24. A	34. E
5. D	15. A	25. D	35. E
6. D	16. B	26. D	36. D
7. E	17. B	27. D	37. C
8. A	18. D	28. B	38. E
9. C	19. B	29. A	39. C
10. B	20. A	30. B	40. D

Chapter 6: Justify the Conclusion Questions

1. B	11. B	21. C
2. A	12. A	22. E
3. A	13. C	
4. D	14. A	
5. D	15. A	
6. A	16. B	
7. D	17. C	
8. B	18. C	
9. C	19. A	
10. C	20. C	

Chapter 7: Assumption Questions

1. C	11. D	21. E	31. E	41. A	51. A	61. E	71. D	81. C	91. C	101. B	111. D
2. D	12. B	22. A	32. A	42. D	52. A	62. C	72. C	82. E	92. D	102. A	112. D
3. C	13. D	23. B	33. C	43. D	53. D	63. B	73. C	83. C	93. A	103. B	113. D
4. C	14. C	24. A	34. D	44. A	54. C	64. D	74. D	84. D	94. E	104. B	
5. C	15. D	25. C	35. A	45. C	55. E	65. E	75. B	85. B	95. A	105. E	
6. D	16. E	26. C	36. C	46. B	56. E	66. B	76. C	86. A	96. E	106. B	
7. B	17. C	27. D	37. E	47. A	57. D	67. C	77. A	87. E	97. A	107. B	
8. E	18. D	28. A	38. C	48. D	58. A	68. D	78. B	88. A	98. B	108. D	
9. D	19. B	29. B	39. E	49. B	59. C	69. D	79. E	89. C	99. D	109. A	
10. D	20. B	30. C	40. D	50. E	60. A	70. E	80. B	90. C	100. C	110. C	

For a detailed answer key which includes the source of each question, by test date and section, as well as a convenient reverse look-up feature, please visit www.powerscore.com/lsatbibles.

Chapter 8: Resolve the Paradox Questions

1. A	11. B	21. D	31. A	41. C	51. E	61. D
2. E	12. D	22. A	32. D	42. D	52. E	62. C
3. B	13. B	23. D	33. B	43. B	53. A	63. D
4. D	14. A	24. C	34. B	44. C	54. A	64. C
5. B	15. E	25. D	35. D	45. B	55. D	65. B
6. E	16. E	26. C	36. A	46. E	56. B	
7. C	17. E	27. E	37. C	47. C	57. B	
8. E	18. D	28. E	38. C	48. A	58. B	
9. E	19. A	29. E	39. E	49. C	59. A	
10. C	20. D	30. D	40. C	50. B	60. A	

Chapter 9: Method of Reasoning Questions

AP		Method							
1. C	10. C	1. B	10. E	20. E	30. B	40. E	50. A	60. D	70. A
2. C	11. B	2. D	11. D	21. C	31. B	41. D	51. A	61. C	71. A
3. A	12. B	3. E	12. B	22. E	32. D	42. A	52. B	62. D	72. C
4. C		4. A	13. C	23. A	33. B	43. C	53. D	63. D	73. B
5. B		5. E	14. E	24. A	34. C	44. A	54. D	64. B	74. B
6. A		6. D	15. E	25. C	35. C	45. A	55. C	65. D	75. A
7. E		7. C	16. E	26. A	36. B	46. B	56. E	66. E	76. D
8. C		8. D	17. C	27. E	37. E	47. B	57. D	67. C	77. A
9. B		9. B	18. E	28. A	38. D	48. A	58. D	68. B	78. A
			19. C	29. E	39. A	49. C	59. D	69. B	

Chapter 10: Flaw in the Reasoning Questions

1. B	11. E	21. E	31. A	41. B	51. E	61. C	71. D	81. E	91. A	101. D
2. D	12. A	22. D	32. D	42. E	52. E	62. B	72. D	82. B	92. A	102. E
3. E	13. C	23. D	33. A	43. E	53. B	63. B	73. D	83. A	93. E	103. C
4. C	14. E	24. A	34. D	44. B	54. A	64. E	74. A	84. E	94. D	104. C
5. A	15. A	25. C	35. E	45. B	55. B	65. C	75. A	85. B	95. D	105. E
6. B	16. D	26. A	36. B	46. B	56. A	66. E	76. E	86. A	96. A	106. C
7. B	17. C	27. B	37. C	47. B	57. D	67. B	77. C	87. E	97. E	107. A
8. E	18. C	28. B	38. C	48. A	58. A	68. D	78. A	88. D	98. A	
9. E	19. C	29. B	39. E	49. E	59. A	69. A	79. E	89. B	99. C	
10. E	20. B	30. C	40. A	50. D	60. B	70. C	80. E	90. D	100. E	

For a detailed answer key which includes the source of each question, by test date and section, as well as a convenient reverse look-up feature, please visit www.powerscore.com/lsatbibles.

Chapter 11: Parallel Reasoning Questions

1. C	11. B	21. D	31. C	41. A
2. D	12. D	22. E	32. E	42. B
3. B	13. E	23. E	33. D	43. D
4. B	14. D	24. C	34. C	44. E
5. A	15. A	25. C	35. A	
6. B	16. D	26. D	36. C	
7. C	17. D	27. C	37. A	
8. E	18. D	28. A	38. E	
9. B	19. D	29. B	39. C	
10. C	20. E	30. C	40. C	

Chapter 12: Evaluate the Argument Questions

1. A	11. D
2. E	12. E
3. E	
4. B	
5. C	
6. C	
7. D	
8. D	
9. E	
10. C	

Chapter 13: Cannot Be True Questions

1. B	11. B
2. D	12. A
3. C	13. C
4. D	14. E
5. A	15. E
6. D	16. E
7. C	17. B
8. A	18. E
9. B	19. E
10. A	

For a detailed answer key which includes the source of each question, by test date and section, as well as a convenient reverse look-up feature, please visit www.powerscore.com/lsatbibles.

Chapter 14: Point at Issue Questions

		POA
1. A	11. C	1.E
2. B	12. D	
3. E	13. E	
4. A	14. D	
5. A	15. C	
6. B	16. E	
7. C	17. C	
8. A	18. C	
9. E	19. D	
10. A	20. D	

Chapter 15: Principle Questions

1. E	11. E	21. D	31. E	41. A
2. C	12. C	22. E	32. C	42. A
3. A	13. C	23. D	33. D	43. C
4. E	14. E	24. D	34. A	44. B
5. C	15. B	25. B	35. E	45. C
6. D	16. A	26. E	36. E	46. B
7. D	17. E	27. D	37. E	47. E
8. E	18. C	28. B	38. B	48. B
9. A	19. D	29. D	39. D	49. B
10. B	20. E	30. C	40. C	

Chapter 16: Conditional Reasoning Questions

1. B	11. D	21. D	31. A	41. D	51. E	61. E
2. A	12. E	22. E	32. D	42. E	52. D	62. D
3. E	13. D	23. E	33. A	43. B	53. B	63. D
4. A	14. C	24. D	34. B	44. D	54. A	64. A
5. D	15. B	25. B	35. C	45. D	55. C	65. B
6. E	16. A	26. B	36. E	46. A	56. B	
7. B	17. A	27. C	37. A	47. D	57. B	
8. B	18. B	28. E	38. B	48. D	58. C	
9. C	19. C	29. C	39. C	49. A	59. B	
10. A	20. B	30. E	40. C	50. B	60. E	

For a detailed answer key which includes the source of each question, by test date and section, as well as a convenient reverse look-up feature, please visit www.powerscore.com/lsatbibles.

Chapter 17: Cause and Effect Questions

1. A	11. B	21. A	31. D	41. E	51. B	61. B
2. E	12. B	22. D	32. B	42. B	52. C	62. C
3. B	13. E	23. D	33. E	43. E	53. E	63. D
4. A	14. D	24. D	34. D	44. D	54. B	64. C
5. E	15. B	25. B	35. B	45. B	55. B	65. D
6. D	16. A	26. C	36. D	46. B	56. A	
7. D	17. C	27. C	37. A	47. C	57. C	
8. C	18. E	28. B	38. E	48. A	58. B	
9. C	19. E	29. D	39. D	49. D	59. C	
10. D	20. D	30. B	40. E	50. D	60. A	

Chapter 18: Numbers and Percentages Questions

1. B	11. D	21. C	31. E
2. C	12. B	22. D	32. D
3. E	13. E	23. E	33. B
4. E	14. C	24. B	34. B
5. A	15. B	25. C	35. B
6. C	16. D	26. D	
7. A	17. D	27. E	
8. A	18. D	28. E	
9. C	19. D	29. A	
10. D	20. C	30. C	

Chapter 19: Formal Logic Questions

1. E	11. A	21. C
2. E	12. E	22. D
3. C	13. B	
4. E	14. B	
5. A	15. E	
6. D	16. E	
7. A	17. B	
8. A	18. D	
9. B	19. E	
10. D	20. C